Panda Books
Son of Heaven

Ling Li, a native of Yudu County, Jiangxi Province, was born in 1942. Upon graduation from the Xi'an Institute of Military Telecommunications Engineering, she was assigned a job in a factory. She started her literary career in 1968 and in 1978 was transferred to the Research Institute of Qing-dynasty History of the People's University of China in Beijing. Her works include historical novels *The Everlasting Grass*, *The Fall of a Dynasty*, and *Evening Drum and Morning Bell*.

Ling Li

Son of Heaven

Translated by David Kwan

Panda Books

Panda Books
First Edition 1995

ISBN 7-5071-0288-2
ISBN 0-8351-3147-5

Published by CHINESE LITERATURE PRESS
Beijing 100037, China
Distributed by China International Book Trading Corporation
35 Chegongzhuang Xilu, Beijing 100044, China
P.O. Box 399, Beijing, China
Printed in the People's Republic of China

CONTENTS

Preface 11

Prologue 15

Part 1 24

Part 2 98

Part 3 133

Part 4 232

Part 5 314

Part 6 398

Part 7 496

Part 8 590

Emperor Shunzhi and His Family

Emperor Shunzhi: Named Fulin, of the Aisin Gioro clan, the first emperor of the Qing Dynasty following the Manchu conquest and the toppling of the Ming Dynasty.

Nurhachi: Fulin's grandfather, chief of the Jianzhou clan of Nüzhen, who gradually gained control of all Nüzhen territory, declaring himself Great Khan in 1616.

Abahai: Fulin's father who, in 1636, took the title emperor and named his regime Great Qing, reign name Taizong. From that time on the Jianzhou clan of Nüzhen was known as Manchu.

The Empress Dowager: Fulin's mother.

Prince Daishan: Abahai's older brother who helped Fulin's mother to secure the throne for her son.

Prince Jirgalang: As brother of Abahai, he was Fulin's uncle and one of the two co-regents appointed to rule until Fulin came of age by his late father.

Prince Dorgon: Abahai's brother and the second co-regent.

Prince Duoni: Named Duke Xin, the younger brother of Dorgon.

Duke An: Named Yuele, a Manchu prince.

Prince Jian: Named Jidu, the son of Jirgalang.

Prince Xiang: Named Bomubogur, the eleventh son of Abahai, born of Lady Yijing, Fulin's half brother.

Xuanye: Fulin's third son who succeeded to the throne upon the death of Shunzhi, becoming Emperor Kangxi.

Empress: Fulin's niece whom he married after he deposed his first empress.

Lady Shuhui: The Empress' sister and Fulin's concubine.

Lady Jing: The first Empress to Fulin, whom he deposed.

Lady Dongeh: Named Black Pearl, born of a Han/Manchu union, wife to Bomubogur before becoming principal lady of Chengqian Palace. She received the title Precious Concubine and was posthumously awarded the title of empress.

Lady Kang: Formerly Lady Tong, principal lady of Jingren Palace who received the title Lady Kang following the birth of the third imperial son.

Lady Duan: Principal lady of Yonghe Palace.

Lady Gong: Principal lady of Jingyang Palace.

Lady Ke: Principal lady of Yongshou Palace.

Preface

Dai Yi

Ling Li's novel, *Son of Heaven*, depicts the life of the first monarch of the Qing Dynasty, Aisin Gioro Fulin (reign name Shunzhi). His political career and his love for the imperial concubine Lady Dongeh reflected the myriad conflicts both historical and personal that beset his life. This popular and critically acclaimed novel won the Mao Dun Prize for Literature in 1991.

In her work Ling Li has striven to combine historic fact with artistic lyricism. Whether she was writing about a peasant revolt in the 19th century, the fall of the Ming Dynasty and the rise of the Qing, or as in her latest work, the youth of Emperor Kangxi, Ling Li is able to bring a bygone era vividly to life.

Any writer of historical novels is first of all confronted with the question of presentation. Since the subject is grounded in history, fact should have right of place. However, presenting fact as a novel takes it beyond being a recitation of dates and events. A novel is by definition a work of art, not scholarship. Furthermore art not only permits but demands imagination, fabrication, and exaggeration. A creative artist must have the freedom of a broad canvas where thoughts and inspiration may wander unfettered. For an historical novel to stick to proven fact alone would be to deny it the very essence of creative writing. On the other hand to stray too far from reality would be to divorce the work from the context that gave it life. Therefore the more a writer delves into the subject matter, the deeper the understanding of the era they possess, the more freedom they have in recreating it. Ling Li's strength as a writer is her comprehensive grasp of history, and her ability to burnish the truth with her art.

Ling Li not only spends long periods of time in libraries and archives researching her subject, she also delves into every conceivable corner of society, ferreting out remains of the past, rediscovering events that took place hundreds of years ago. For *Son of Heaven* she immersed herself completely in the 17th century, to absorb images, to experience vicariously the events of daily life for the nobility and ordinary people alike, to ponder her own plot with regard to historical fact and to re-create it all as a work of art. As a result her work is vibrant, the plot is full of unexpected twists, and is populated by flesh-and-blood characters. It is not only an artistic *tour de force* but she has accurately fingered the pulse of the times she is writing about and measured its conflicts.

Shunzhi came to the throne at the age of six and died at the age of twenty-four. The outstanding achievement of the early part of his reign was the unification of China. *Son of Heaven* develops around this core. When the Manchu swept into the central plains of China they numbered no more than a few hundred thousand. For such a small number to rule the much larger Han population was a monumental task. The Manchu had military superiority, and an uncanny ability to organize. However, they were a nomadic people, and preserved many of their barbarian traditions and practices. In particular, the oppressive practices of land appropriation, the persecution of runaway slaves and the order of shaving the front of the head caused long lasting racial enmity. In order to consolidate their power and unite the realm the Manchu could not rely on military might alone. They had to establish a correct set of policies, and change some of their traditional habits and prejudices, thus easing the oppression of the conquered masses. Emperor Shunzhi was outstanding in recognizing the needs of his time and striving to exemplify change. The latter half of his reign was marked by reforms and attempts at progress that propelled the Qing Dynasty toward unprecedented heights. Following upon his heels came Emperors Kangxi, Yongzheng and Qianlong, a period of one hundred and fifty years during which the economy thrived, cultural activities flourished, and the empire reached its zenith. With the wisdom of hindsight, we might well say that it was Shunzhi who laid the foundations for the achievements of these future monarchs by his insistence on reform, by assimilating the learning of the conquered Han, and the scientific knowledge of Western nations. By employing able ministers, prosecuting corruption, he succeeded to a large extent in steering the nation in a new direction. He contrived to overcome opposition to his ideas and and managed to abolish certain traditions to lessen interracial tensions, without sacrificing the support he needed. The land appropriation, the fate of runaway slaves, the corruption at the imperial examinations, the employment of Han officials, and the palace intrigues described in *Son of Heaven* are all authentic. The writer has grasped the direction and the characteristics of those tumultuous times and presented them with honesty and insight.

Shunzhi remains an enigma: compassionate but changeable; quick-tempered with a sadistic streak; responsible yet juvenile; weak and inexperienced; clever and eager to learn; chivalrous with a primal barbarity and simplicity lurking close to the surface. While his public life was a success, his personal life was a failure. The author has portrayed all this in a series of dramatic tableaux that throb with life

Most of the events and characters in this book are real. The character of the German Jesuit Adam Schall von Bell, known by his adopted Chinese name as Tang Jo-Wang, and his connection with the imperial court are based on his autobiography. The imperial concubine Lady Dongeh was in fact the wife of Shunzhi's younger brother Prince Bomubogur. His humiliation, and subsequent suicide that paved the way for the Emperor to seize the woman he desired are historic fact. The main events of the plot such as the corruption at the imperial examinations, Shunzhi's devotion to Buddhism and his desire to become a monk, the palace intrigues of the manipulative Empress Dowager, and Lady

Dongeh's elaborate funeral rites are also taken from recorded history.

Not all historical novels contain so many characters and events. In fact such detail is sometimes impossible to achieve. *Son of Heaven* is able to cleave close to the legend and the facts of its central character because this dramatic era, populated by larger than life characters, is well-documented, and the author with her deep sensibility to history, had the courage and vision to retain or discard according to the needs of her art.

Son of Heaven is an important milestone in Ling Li's career.

Dai Yi was born in Changshu, Jiangsu Province in 1926. A graduate of the History Department of Peking University, he is currently Director of the Research Institute of Qing-dynasty History at the People's University. He is also Director of the Chinese History Association, Academic Critic of the State Council, and a delegate to the National People's Congress, in addition to being author of many books on the subject of the Qing Dynasty and recent Chinese history.

Prologue

A broad plain stretching east to west, criss-crossed by mighty mountain ranges and the rivers, Luan, Bai, and Qinglong, separates Shanhaiguan from the capital. The Great Wall meanders across the mountain chain known as Yanshan. Where the mountains and the rivers meet lies the prefecture of Yongping. In this tenth year of the reign of Shunzhi, the Manchu had conquered eighty percent of all under Heaven. However, the adherents of the fallen Ming Dynasty still clung to a corner of the southwest and Zheng Chenggong's* forces continued their desperate struggle on the high seas to the southeast. But to Yongping Prefecture in the far north, war and the chaos it engendered were but remote rumblings. The harvest was in, and the first frost covered the ground. It was a time of rejoicing; a time of the temple fair. Worshippers and fun-seekers alike swarmed from all around to the famous Dongyue Temple in Hongqiao Town.

Soon after daybreak pedlars began setting up their stalls outside Dongyue Temple and at the crossroads leading to the wide countryside. Their customers were not the devout, but idlers and curiosity seekers. For the temple fair was a great melting pot of peoples. Hans, in their cross-cut or stiff-collared gowns popular in the Ming Dynasty, felt hats and shoes, whom Manchus considered "barbarian", mingled with Manchus and Mongolians. In their turn, the Hans referred to

---

*After the fall of the Ming regime, Zheng Chenggong began his anti-Qing activities in 1646 and attacked the coastal areas of Zhenjiang and the lower Yangtze River. In 1661, he sailed across the sea to Taiwan when he expelled the Dutch colonialists and set up regime.

the others in their distinctive waistcoats over long robes, fur hats and leather boots, as "Tartars". On that day old enmities and caste distinctions were laid aside. Peasants and scholars rubbed shoulders to eat, drink and ogle one another, and go home happily clutching some souvenir.

By midmorning the town was bursting at the seams.

"They're coming! They're coming!" A shout went up to the north of the town. The crowd surged along the main road in that direction, craning their necks as they went. Sure enough, the processions from two villages had gathered at the crossroads, their banners forming a multi-coloured forest that moved at a stately pace toward the town, drums thudding and gongs resounding.

At the head of the procession, surrounded by fifes and drums, was a red banner, twenty feet long and three feet wide on which was written "Pilgrims of Zhuanghu Village". Other banners in yellow, orange, red, green, black, white, blue, purple, jade, and pink followed. The banners were richly embroidered in patterns of ocean waves, birds and flowers around names of deities in huge black Han characters. Some of the carrying poles were topped with lotus blossoms, others with tassles, others still with long ribbons.

Images of the deities preceded their banners. Singers and dancers in colourful costumes followed in a long line, their bodies weaving and turning this way and that. The crowd along the route cheered and clapped. But the heartiest applause went to the standard-bearer at the very front of the procession who balanced a flag pole, the thickness of a rice bowl, first on his shoulder, then on his head and belly. Every time the pole teetered the crowd cried out in alarm. But the carrier always righted it in the nick of time.

"Northerners are a rough lot," said a scholar in a wine-red cloak of fine wool. He spoke in a loud voice so as to be heard above the hubbub. His companion shot him a quick glance, and smiled without comment.

Once more the sound of flutes and fifes split the air. Another procession was approaching. Across the black banner leading the procession, were white characters which read: "Pilgrims of Malan Village". A roar of anticipation went up and the crowd pressed forward. Some devout old women fell to their knees and touched their foreheads to the ground. Behind the first banner came another embroidered with green sprigs of bamboo and red characters on a field of white which read "The Goddess of Mercy". On a float under the banner stood the Goddess impersonated by a living person. Her hair piled high on the top of her head was covered by a white veil. Two strands flowed downward to her breasts. Her eyes were hooded, lips slightly pursed. Her cheeks were flushed and a blood-red mole glowed between the graceful arches of her brows. She held a Bottle of Blessings in one hand, and in the other a willow branch. The crowd followed the living Goddess, bowing with hands held in front of them, and as she passed, touched their foreheads to the ground. The cheers of the crowd drowned out the efforts of the musicians. The scholar in the red cloak shouted his approval. His companion looked on thoughtfully stroking his beard.

"Such tranquillity tames the breast of a wild beast," he mused, eyeing the living Goddess. "Perhaps such a one is worth knowing."

The man in red laughed.

"I'll wager he is no more than a third-rate actor. Are you interested, my friend?"

"You are new to the north," the other countered, "and not aware of the depths of depravity to which our theatre has sunk. This lad with his sactimonious good looks might put them all to shame, if he comes to anything...."

As the two spoke, floats, stilt-walkers, and dancing lions passed. The crowd surged after them towards the town. Suddenly a young girl in a red jacket appeared in the crowd. Darting this way and that, she made her way through the throng like a small red fish swimming against the current. Her small pale face was almost entirely taken up by enormous black eyes brimming with fear. As she reached the head of the procession, she muttered something and wailed, and flung herself at a burly man impersonating a boatman in a dance. The crowd was stunned into silence. They all heard her and were stunned by what she said and wanted to return to their village. The big fellow snatched the straw hat off his head and bunched it up in one angry fist. The Goddess of Mercy leaped off the float shouting, "I quit! We're going back to the village!"

That cry was instantly taken up by the crowd. The banners, the floats, the stilts, the sacred images, the two gold and black lions were all abandoned. The crowd turned as a body and, sweeping the girl in red before it, rushed from the town.

"What is going on? Aren't they going to the fair?"

"Something must have happened in their village...."

"Perhaps there's a fire." Rumours flew in all directions. Out of the throng, someone cried out:

"There's a raid! They're expropriating the land!"

An ominous silence fell on the crowd, which then erupted in an anguished roar. A few years earlier the Manchu custom of expropriating land around the capital had caused widespread panic. Now it was happening in Malan Village. Who could say it would not spread to Yongping Prefecture as well! The temple fair was abandoned. Pilgrims, fun-seekers, and pedlars alike wanted only one thing: to get back to their homes as quickly as possible. Adults roared, children wailed. The dust stirred up by countless frantic feet blotted out the sky. In the crush many were trampled.

When the dust settled Hongqiao Town was a disaster area. The happy, vibrant market place of the morning had turned into a nightmare. The ground was littered with abandoned shoes, and bits of torn clothing. Broken baskets lay here and there. Eggs, fruit and other foods were mashed into the earth. Only a few beggars remained to scavenge for edibles.

Outside Malan Village the banners and sacred images were left abandoned by the road side. The villagers still in their festive costumes had scattered to stand like chess pieces guarding their bits of land south of the village.

Under an old poplar tree a troop of cavalry armed with little blue flags fixed to tall stakes stood in smart formation, while the people swarmed around the commander clamouring to be heard.

The commander, who was at his wits' end, lashed out at the crowd with his whip, beating them back. "Stakes!" he cried. The cavalry leaped forward with a blood-curdling yell and galloped through the fields, planting little blue flags as they went.

A villager threw himself on the ground shrieking, "My land! My land! Don't take my land!" The young boy who had impersonated the Goddess of Mercy threw himself on one of the horsemen and knocked him out of the saddle. Two housemen rushed the lad, lances at the ready.

The boy took to his heels. The riders thundered after him, the shadow of their lances pointed straight at the boy's back. With a cry, the boy dived on the ground, rolling himself into a ball. Sunlight glinted off the tip of a lance as it flew past grazing the boy's arm. The boy staggered to his feet, gripping his arm, blood oozing between his fingers. He stood his ground, his chest thrust defiantly at his tormentors and their weapons.

"Stop!" a loud voice shouted in Manchu. A sword flashed, lopping off the heads of two lances pointed at the boy. The startled horses reared. An old Manchu stood, as sturdy as a fortress between the boy and his pursuers. The interference of the old warrior took the soldiers, who were Hans, by surprise. For though the old warrior's battle robe was threadbare he wore the red sash, a symbol of connection with the imperial family.

The old man shook his sword at the soldiers and shouted in Manchu, "What heroes you are! Bullying a mere child!"

The soldiers did not understand the words or the stream of obscenities that followed, but the old warrior's tone was unmistakable. There was one word they did understand.

"Go!"

They turned their horses, bowing and scraping as they left. The old man sheathed his sword and strode back to the village without another word.

The girl in red rushed to the boy, her eyes full of fear and sympathy.

"Brother Tongchun, you're hurt." She held his injured arm tenderly, and repeated "You're hurt..." in a tiny voice, tears coursing down her face. The boy reddened.

"It's nothing," he tried to make light of it. "It's only a scratch."

Villagers gathered round them, grumbling to one another. A boy of about seven or eight years of age, dressed in the Manchu fashion in robe and vest, riding boots, and fur cap, stood to one side with his hands tucked in his sleeves. The bearded scholar hailed him in Manchu.

The boy ran to him, chirping happily in fluent Chinese, "Oh, you speak our tongue!"

"Tell me, boy, what is happening?"

"Staking the land. Some farmer put himself under the protection of Duke An and offered his land as tribute. Then he decided to put himself under the protection of the father of Lady Tong an imperial concubine, with the same land. But he also included the land of his enemy, saying it was his...." The boy spoke animatedly.

"Oh, Duke An...." The scholar mused, and asked again, "Who was the man with the red sash?"

"That's my grandfather," the boy said proudly.

"To which banner* do you belong? How do you come to live here?" the scholar pursued. The boy's face clouded.

"I won't tell you," he cried and stalked away. The two

*The banner system was a form of social organization of the Qing Dynasty and a division of the Manchu army. Those who belonged to the eight banners were called bannermen.

scholars exchanged puzzled looks.

"This is a strange place, with too many strange people and strange happenings," said the man in the red cloak after a pause. "I used to think there was no justice in the south, but expropriating land...." He let the rest trail off. The one with the beard searched his companion's pale ascetic face, and shuddered at the cold glint in the depths of his eyes.

"Tomorrow I'll go to Duke An about this," the bearded man muttered. The other averted his eyes.

"I shall wait on you in the capital," he murmured presently.

"Done!"

They bowed and went their separate ways.

They are two gentlemen from the south. The one with the beard is Lu Zhiyue, familiarly known as Xiaotian and nicknamed Smiley, who hails from Qiantang. About forty-three years of age, he sports a beard that reaches the middle of his chest. A likable fellow, he has an air of amiability about him, and a glint of a smile in the depths of his eyes. The other, Loo Jian, familiarly known as Wenkang, was from the town of Renhe. Scion of an aristocratic family, he is handsome and clean shaven. Though well past the first bloom of youth, he still cuts a dashing figure. It is only on closer examination that one notices the coldness in his eyes which is disguised by an air of magnanimity and leisureliness. Coming as they do from the vicinity of Hangzhou, the two men have known each other a long time and have been good friends. When the Ming Dynasty collapsed Lu Zhiyue's reputation as a scholar caused him to be hired as tutor in the household of a Manchu general. On the other hand Loo Jian had been falsely accused of subversive activities and implicated in the treason trials involving ten of the most prominent families of the south. The trials dragged on for years, starting and stopping, never coming to any conclusion. Owing to the wealth of his family, and a certain amount of bribery, Loo Jian managed to avoid imprisonment. He had come to the capital mainly to try and clear his name, and met his old friend by chance. It happened that upon his arrival in the capital with his employer, Lu Zhiyue attracted the attention of Duke An who favoured the south. As a result Lu became the Prince's resident scholar. Thus he volunteered to make representation to the Duke on his friend's behalf. However, the Duke had been commanded to garrison a border town and the plan fell through.

On the eighth day of the new year, a throng gathered under West Changan Gate of the capital to read a new decree. The decree stated that petitions against the expropriation of land in exchange for patronage were so numerous that they would henceforth cease to be accepted. From now on grievances would have to be settled by county and district courts.

The small courtyard at West Changan Gate contained the Hall of Proclamations. In one corner is a two-storied structure in which a drum is hung, called Drum of Appeals. During the Ming Dynasty, anyone with a grievance which the courts would not hear, could gain a hearing by striking the drum, and presenting a petition. When the Qing Dynasty came to power, this tradition was maintained. The job of supervision was rotated between two clerks: one a Han, and the other a Manchu. However, on that day the gate of the courtyard remained shut.

The crowd did not disperse after reading the decree. Instead the people stood about aimlessly, blowing on their hands and stamping their feet to ward off the bone-crushing cold. They glanced at each other, speechless. As soon as the soldiers opened the gate, people rushed forward. A young man burst through the crowd, took an axe hidden in the folds of his robe and attacked the drum. With one stroke, the face of the drum was split open, leaving a gaping black hole. The crowd was stunned. The soldiers seized the young man and dragged him into the hall. Outside the people stood numb with fear.

Though the people outside could not hear what was said inside the hall, they could see the young man being spread eagled on the ground and beaten with staves. The sound of the beating thudded against their hearts. They counted thirty strokes, yet not a murmur escaped the young man. After the beating the guards hauled him out of the hall and threw him out the gate.

A burly fellow pushed through the on-lookers to his aid. A clerk emerged from the hall and spoke to the assemblage in a loud voice.

"His Excellency has taken into account the man's youth, and has decided a sound beating will fit the crime. He is free to go. However, the Drum of Appeals has been destroyed. As a result this office is unable to function. Hence the gate will be shut as of now. His Excellency has not decided when it will reopen. Now go!"

Hearing this announcement the young man turned shakily to the other and murmured, "Brother Zinian, it's up to you now...." The big fellow blinked, and whispered, "If ... I don't ... make it back...."

"Don't worry, Brother Zinian," hissed the young man. "There are many men of honour in Malan Village".

An hour later the man was seen outside Dongan Gate. Over his old padded robe, he now wore the black jacket of a slave. He watched until two courtiers appeared and quickly stepped into the ranks of their retinue. In this way he quickly passed through Dongan Gate, and Donghua Gate, then followed the crimson walls of the Forbidden City through Quezuo Gate. When they reached the archway under the tall imposing Meridian Gate he separated himself from the others. In the distance he could see a troop of imperial guards coming towards him. He took a deep breath and cried out, "Injustice!"

For a moment the guards were struck dumb by the sight of the big man racing towards them, screaming at the top of his lungs. When he was five to seven yards in front of them, he stopped. A knife flashed briefly in his hand before the blade was plunged into his breast. The man staggered a few paces more, then fell backwards onto the flagstones of the Imperial Way, his eyes fixed upward on the sky, or the yellow tiles and crimson walls of Wufeng Tower. But no one could tell which.

PART I

The tolling of the great bell in Wufeng Tower floated across the rooftops of the old city of Beijing warning the populace of a royal progress.

The sharp report of the Whips of Silence cracked in the streets, driving the people indoors. Doors were bolted and windows kept shuttered. No one dared so much as peep through the chinks, lest they be found out by the ever vigilant street patrols and hauled before the courts. Barriers had been set across the entrances of hutongs and alley-ways. The few people who had not been able to retreat in time prostrated themselves face down on the ground, not daring to lift their heads.

A long procession made its stately way through the deserted streets. At its head were imperial guards carrying red and black lacquer staves traced with gold. Then came a band of musicians, composed of a hundred and fifty fifes, drums, large and small horns, whose triumphal music glorified the Manchu ancestors, while the thud of the great copper drums shook the earth. Three hundred odd imperial guards clad in red, bearing decorative umbrellas of yellow, red, white, blue, and black, marched in the wake of the musicians. Some of the umbrellas were round, others square, decorated with dragons, or flowers. Next came guardsmen holding high great fans of bright red or gold, decorated with a single dragon rampant, or two dragons entwined. Some of these fans were round, others were square or shaped like the wings of a bird in flight. All manner of multi-coloured silk streamers, pennants, and standards fluttered and snapped in the wind. Lances, battle axes, halberds, spears, maces and a dazzling array of small arms with red handles and gold blades surrounded the imperial sedan chair. The sedan chair which was made of gold and covered with yellow silk drapery moved at a swift, even pace borne on the shoulders of sixteen guardsmen, resplendent in leopard fur caps and long heavily embroidered red robes. Close on the heels of the sedan chair came a canopy embroidered with a rampant gold dragon. Imperial guards armed with spears and cross-bows flanked the sedan chair and the canopy. Eunuchs carrying boxes of incense, censers, spittoons, jars, basins, an arm chair, and small table and other paraphenalia all made of gold, followed. A troop of three hundred crack cavalry brought up the rear. The glittering cavalcade moved in cadence with the solemn music, wending southward like a many splendoured river. This was an imperial progress of the third degree, used when the Emperor left the Forbidden City on a private visit.

North of Xuanwu Gate is a wide street that runs east and west, usually a busy thoroughfare, where the Hans who lived in the southern quarter of the city and the Manchus in the north came together to trade. On this day the street had been cleared at dawn. Not a soul stirred out of doors. The snow had been swept off the road, and fine wet sand scatterd over, so that the cavalcade would not stir up dust as it passed.

To the south of Xuanwu Gate was a large Catholic church whose three round domes rose more than ten yards higher than the houses around it. From the top of the central dome rose a great cross that seemed to reach for the sky. Over the doorway, surrounded by rays of sacred light were the Latin letters IHS. The church was six years old. The day it was consecrated Hans and Manchus alike came to marvel at this example of Western Baroque architecture that had no equal in the ancient city.

The imperial procession stopped at the foot of a flight of steps leading to the church. Thus in the midst of solemn music, the ancient trappings of the East and the new architecture of the West came together.

On the steps of the church, the German Jesuit Adam Schall

von Bell, known by his Chinese name as Tang Jo-Wang, Chief Minister of the Imperial Ministry of Astronomy, personally dubbed "Master of all Learning" by the Emperor, waited on his knees, surrounded by other priests. The German had long since abandoned his priestly garb for a costume more in keeping with his rank. On this occasion he was dressed in a court jacket embroidered with peacocks, topped by a court hat decorated with a solitary saphire. A necklace of pale green turquois and a gold crucifix hung from his neck.

The Whip of Silence cracked thrice. At the Master of Protocol's shouted command "*Xing*!" the cavalry leaped off their mounts and stood at attention.

"*Bai!*" the Master of Protocol shouted the next command. The musicians struck up *Hail Son of Heaven* whereupon the entire red-clad assemblage prostrated themselves, scarcely breathing. The curtains of the sedan chair parted, and a young man in a marten fur cap, a bright yellow robe embroidered with coiled dragons, and tall blue satin boots, alighted.

"*Chao*!" A thousand voices were raised in unison, in a great cheer.

"Long live the Emperor! Long live! Long live!"

The first emperor after the Manchu conquest, Shunzhi, named Fulin, stood, tall and proud, glittering as though cast of gold amidst a sea of red and blue.

When the cheering subsided, Fulin strode toward the church, his eyes twinkling with pleasure at the sight of Tang Jo-Wang's blond bearded face. A smile tugged at his lips. His steps quickened in spite of himself. Then a cloud crossed his face, and the look of excitement left his features. He covered the remaining distance at a measured pace. After all he was the Son of Heaven.

At the age of sixteen Fulin's round, fair-skinned face had not quite lost its boyishness. He had inherited the high, slender nose, and the arched eyebrows of the Aisin-Gioro clan. Otherwise his eyes were bright, and tiny flames danced in their depths when he was happy or when he was angered. The full lips were sensuous, red, and moist. A hint of down surrounded the mouth that was not yet a beard. He walked with a slight swagger which probably came from his fondness for riding and the hunt. The natural exuberance of youth was held in check by the strict protocol of his position, like a stream confined in a narrow channel crowded with rocks.

Thus the young Emperor approached Tang Jo-Wang.

"I did not know Your Majesty was coming, else I should have come to meet you. Forgive me." The priest enunciated the formal words of greeting in fluent Chinese.

"Mafa," the Emperor addressed the Jesuit with the Manchu word for grandfather. "Mafa, haven't we forbidden you to kneel to us?" chided the younger man. "I had hoped to go directly to your house without ceremony."

Tang Jo-Wang rose to his feet. There was a twinkle in his eyes when he replied, "Your retinue of eight hundred would have given away Your Majesty's approach even to a foolish old man such as I."

Fulin strode quickly up the steps. Tang Jo-Wang followed close behind. Three hundred imperial guards and eunuchs formed a long line behind them. Only the cavalry stood guard outside.

The Emperor very seldom visited the homes of his subjects. Since Fulin took the reins of government, he had visited Prince Jirgalang, his uncle, and one of the two co-regents appointed by his late father, only once. However this was the fifth time that he had visited Tang Jo-Wang.

Inside the gate of the church was a large cobblestoned space capable of accommodating this dazzling retinue. Fulin stopped, and in a clear voice commanded, "You will wait here. I wish to be alone."

"*Ja*! *Ja*!" responded the retinue. Though they were all noblemen and older than the Emperor, they obediently fell to their knees.

A slender, handsome young eunuch in a red robe stepped forward and falling to his knees enquired, "Majesty, may I please wait upon you?"

Fulin waved him aside, and strode across the open space without a backward glance, accompanied only by Tang Jo-Wang. They passed through a three-arched pylon of white marble and were out of sight.

How did an emperor of Qing come to acquire a German Mafa?

It came about during the year Fulin first took the reins of government. In the third month of that year Fulin and the court left the city to hunt. However, the Empress Dowager commanded Prince Jirgalang and Prince Xun to remain behind in the Emperor's absence.

One day Tang Jo-Wang was visited by three noble Manchu ladies, from Prince Jirgalang's household. They claimed that a noble young lady was ill, and their mistress did not trust the court physician. Would the wise and learned Tang Jo-Wang consent to attend her? Tang Jo-Wang questioned the ladies at length, and was convinced nothing more serious than a cold ailed her. A common occurrance during that time of year. He gave the ladies a gold crucifix.

"Have the young lady wear this round her neck and she will be better in a few days," he said.

Five days later the ladies returned with a gift of five hundred ounces of silver and five bolts of brocade woven with gold thread. The young lady had recovered just as the priest had said she would. Another five days passed and the ladies came again with another gift of money. Tang Jo-Wang became suspicious and refused to accept, whereupon the ladies donated the money to the mission.

Soon afterwards a Mongolian lady visited Tang Jo-Wang, with a large donation. Tang Jo-Wang would not accept, saying that he would not accept donations without knowing whence they came. Thus the lady was forced to spill the truth. Her mistress was none other than the Empress Dowager Zhuang. The girl who had been ill was the Empress Dowager's niece, a Mongolian young lady soon to be the Emperor's bride.

The lady went on to express the Empress Dowager's gratitude, and that henceforth she would hold him in the same esteem as her own father, and would welcome his counsel.

Tang Jo-Wang quickly seized the opportunity to proselytise, and begged the lady to carry a message back to the Empress Dowager. Do not place her trust in the superstitions of monks and lamas, he counselled. For the Mother of a Nation must be above reproach.

The Empress Dowager was quick to respond to the counsel of her wise, new spiritual father. She could not dismiss the monks and lamas all at once, she replied. However, it will be done gradually, by attrition. In any case, she vowed that the monks and lamas would not be permitted to interfere with matters of state.

The mutual respect and understanding between the Jesuit and the imperial lady directly affected the Emperor Shunzhi. Ten years earlier, Grand Academician Fan Wencheng had given his personal endorsement to Tang Jo-Wang during the chaos following the Manchu conquest, and recommended him to the court as a wise and learned astronomer and mathematician. Later he introduced the blond and blue-eyed prelate to the young Emperor. From their first meeting, Fulin was capitivated by the charm of Tang Jo-Wang's personality, the depths of his learning, and the wit of his conversation. He was pleased with his mother and Grand Academician Fan's choice of a personal counsellor for himself.

In the ninth month of the same year the Emperor married. Tang Jo-Wang joined the nobles of the court in the day-long celebrations. At that time he was already in his sixties. The Empress Dowager and her son were both deeply moved by his devotion during the long, weary festivities. Fulin visited Tang Jo-Wang for the first time soon after his wedding. From that day on he addressed the priest as Mafa, the Manchu word for grandfather. After the wedding, Tang Jo-Wang came to court again to celebrate his spiritual daughter's acquisition of a title of honour as a result of her son's marriage. This act cemented the friendship between the Jesuit and the Imperial mother and son.

In the two years that followed a close friendship grew between the priest and the Emperor, which continued uninterrupted even after the Imperial marriage was annulled. The Emperor's pleasure at visiting his Mafa was evidence that Tang Jo-Wang continued to enjoy the esteem of both the monarch and his mother.

Fulin strode quickly along the covered marble corridor, passing from one room to another, stopping now and then, waiting for Tang Jo-Wang to catch up.

"Mafa, I do not wish to sit in the parlour. It's too formal. Let us go to your cell."

"All right."

Tang Jo-Wang's cell was a large room lined with bookcases from floor to ceiling, crammed with manuscripts in Latin, Spanish, Dutch, Portugese and German. There were also books in Chinese and Manchurian. Burners, beakers and other scientific apparatus were ranged in neat rows on the large desk. The large brass bedstead covered with snow-white coverlets seemed curiously out of place in the spartan room. There were only two items that were ornamental. One was a natural crystal, two feet tall and fitted with a round ebony stand. On it was carved the handiwork of famous court calligraphers. The other was a finely rendered model of a two-masted ship.

"Mafa, I've always wanted to try this bed," remarked Fulin sitting on it, crosslegged in the Manchurian fashion. "It looks so big, and soft, and warm too." He reached around as he spoke and took two large, soft pillows and propped them under his arm. He smiled boyishly.

Tang Jo-Wang was silent for a moment before he spoke in a solemn tone. "A priest should not sleep in a bed like that. But one grows lax with age. It is unforgivable."

"But you've earned it, Mafa!" Fulin arched his brows. "A man your age deserves his comfort."

"Well, after Your Majesty has sat on the bed, this old man will have to find another bed to sleep on."

Tang Jo-Wang's gesture included all the chairs and stools in the room covered in yellow cloth and sealed. All had been used by the Emperor at one time or another, and were now sealed, never again to be used. In fact ordinary folk, and even courtiers, had to kneel and touch their heads to the ground in the presence of these pieces of furniture. Like a thoughtless child Fulin had condemned the bed to the same fate.

"I shall have to be strapped to the ceiling to read and sleep from now on," Tang Jo-Wang teased. Fulin laughed. "Mafa, forget all that nonsense. You sit wherever you like." His attention was quickly captured by the model ship.

"What a wonderful craft it is!" he exclaimed. Tang Jo-Wang watched Fulin turn the vessel this way and that, delighting in every detail.

"If it pleases Your Majesty, I will make you a present of it."

"Would you?"

"Yes. Not this one, but one that is a hundred times larger. A real schooner of the Rhine River." Fulin glowed with pleasure.

"You're too kind, Mafa. I will take it and sail the three oceans and catch fish. Oh, that would be such fun!" Tang Jo-Wang responded with a gentle smile, and lapsing into his native German, murmured, "... His hair is black as a winter's night; his brow as fair as summer snow; his cheeks glow as the rising sun...."

"Mafa, what are you muttering?" Tang Jo-Wang translated for Fulin.

"Am I really like that?" beamed Fulin. "But how can there be snow in summer?"

Tang Jo-Wang described the Alps to the south of his

homeland, where snowclad peaks glowed under a bright blue sky from year end to year end. Fulin's eyes widened with wonder. But he controlled himself. Smiling solemnly he said, "Mafa, I have good news."

Tang Jo-Wang nodded. He sensed the Emperor's excitement as soon as he passed under the pylon.

"Cao Zhipan, the bandit of Raozhou, has surrendered. Likewise Xu Kejin the great rebel from south of the Yangtze. Zhu Yuan also. Two armies of Zheng Chenggong have also laid down their arms!" Fulin talked with his hands, biting off one word at a time for emphasis.

"Thank God!" Tang Jo-Wang lifted his face to the heavens and crossed himself. "The greatest virtue of a monarch is mercy."

"From the fifth month of last year till today, is only a matter of half a year, yet we have made so much progress! This proves a caring government wins men's hearts. Only when one captures men's hearts can one rule all under Heaven!" In that moment Fulin became a wise, ambitious young monarch. "Mafa, you and Grand Academician Fan have contributed greatly to society," he concluded.

The Manchu conquest was achieved by force of arms, and wholesale slaughter. However, the more they fought the more they had to fight. Rebellion followed one after another, north and south of the Yangtze, and up and down the length of the Yellow River. Because of endless wars, and the cost of maintaining large armies, by the eighth year of Shunzhi, the imperial coffers were almost empty. The Empire was on the brink of ruin. But Fulin, who had just taken the reins of government was as eager for a fight as his nobles, believing that peace could be achieved only by force. He continued the policy of military conquest. In the ninth year of his reign, Guilin was lost, and Prince Dingnan (Kong Youde) was killed in battle. Prince Jingjin (Nikan), who headed an expeditionary force to capture the provinces of Xiang (today's Hunan) and Qian (today's Guizhou) was routed, and his army annihilated. The loss of these princes was a severe blow.

For days the young monarch pondered his loss in sorrow and confusion. It occurred to him then that he must put to practise all the things he had learned from the books of wise men instead of merely paying them lip service. He must adopt the ways of wise predecessors and rule with justice and mercy. Once his mind was made up, he was eager to put his ideas to the test. In this he had the support of the Empress Dowager, who urged him to follow the wise counsel of Fan Wencheng and Tang Jo-Wang. An armestice was declared and rebels were invited to lay down their arms. At last peace was within reach.

From the fifth month of the tenth year of Shunzhi onward, the Emperor issued a number of decrees and proclamations calling on Zheng Chenggong, and adherents of the fallen Ming Dynasty who called themselves "Southern Ming" and clung to a corner of the southwest, and all rebel forces to end hostilities. The language of these proclamations was sincere and the conditions generous. Within nine months great progress was made. No wonder Fulin was beside himself with joy.

Tang Jo-Wang understood Fulin's happiness.

"This is a sign from God," he told the young monarch, "that He will always bless the just, and the merciful. Your Majesty will become a great emperor."

"I will do my best to be worthy, Mafa." Fulin's eyes glittered. Energy coursed through his body, as if he would sprout wings and take to the sky.

"Mafa, can I be a better emperor than any other in the world?"

"Why not?" Tang Jo-Wang answered quickly. He moved to the map of the world which was tacked to the bookcase and pointed to France. "France is ruled by the Bourbons," he began. "Now, France is an important part of Europe, but it isn't anywhere near the size of China. Their king, Louis XIV, is the same age as Your Majesty. As a matter of fact, he also came to the throne at the age of six. However, he has not yet ruled in his own right. This is because both he and his father had able prime ministers, who helped them build a strong nation. Today France holds her own against Portugal, Spain and Holland in the Americas and the Indies. Their two great ministers were both Princes of the Church, Cardinals Richelieu and Mazarin." Fulin smiled. "But are they as learned as my Mafa?" Tang Jo-Wang was caught off guard. The young Emperor's sharpness was sometimes disconcerting. He gathered his wits about him, and replied, "They come from a long line of Churchmen. Whereas, your Mafa is an outsider.... Perhaps one day you will cross paths with Louis XIV. Your Majesty is brave and wise...."

"No," Fulin shook his head. "China is a large, civilized country that has no aggressive intentions.... Mafa, I shall follow the teachings of my ancestors, and the Heavens shall bless us. Is that not so? Come. Let us go to your study." Tang Jo-Wang hesitated.

"We have acquired a new portrait of the Blessed Virgin for her altar. Would Your Majesty care to see it?"

"First the study, then the chapel," Fulin's eyes glittered with curiosity but he would not be diverted. "You have never shown me your study."

"All right," Tang Jo-Wang acquiesed.

As soon as the door was unlocked, Fulin pushed it open. A choking cloud of smoke struck him in the face. Two Manchu officials from the Imperial Ministry of Astronomy were caught puffing on their opium pipes on a couch. The men scrambled off and fell to their knees, unable to summon a greeting.

Fulin recognized both noblemen. One was the cousin of Sukesaha, Palace Grand Minister, the other was the nephew of Duerma, Grand Minister of the Deliberative Council of Nobles.

"What is the meaning of this?" Fulin demanded. Sukesaha's cousin mumbled, "If it pleases Your Majesty ... we were summoned here by Tang Jo-Wang ... saying we were dismissed.... But we are Your Majesty's servants.... He has no right...."

"Mafa, is this true?" Fulin turned to Tang Jo-Wang and was confounded by the stern look on the old prelate's face.

"It is," Tang Jo-Wang met the Emperor's eyes. He chose his words carefully.

"They are unfit for their posts. They are ignorant, lazy, arrogant and crude. They are ruining the work of the Ministry which I will not permit. I summoned them here to warn them that I intend petitioning Your Majesty for their removal. However, Your Majesty arrived before I could speak to them. Therefore I kept them here for the time being." Fulin laughed outloud and dismissed the two men with a wave of the hand. Then he spoke quietly, "Were you not afraid of offending me?" Tang Jo-Wang's eyes crinkled with gentle mirth as he replied, "Your Majesty would not tolerate stupidity. Only birds of a feather flock together." Fulin sighed, nodding. "Now I understand why you prefer Hans who are like a flock of ducks in your church, and are reluctant to admit Manchus." Tang Jo-Wang shook his head.

"That's not so. God has told me our ducks are really swans."

"But Manchus are not swans?"

"No. They're vultures."

"What did you say?" Fulin's countenance clouded, black brows gathered into a heavy frown. Tang Jo-Wang continued without fear:

"Because of long years of war and pillage, adult Manchus have developed habits which make them unable to accept Christ at this moment."

"But the Hans are ready?" Fulin shrilled.

"The civilization and the moral fibre of the Han are indeed superior," averred Tang Jo-Wang. Fulin's face flushed. His eyes narrowed and he sucked in his lips until they almost disappeared. A storm was about to break.

"How dare you side with the Han!" Tang Jo-Wang fixed the Emperor with his gaze, and spoke calmly: "Your late grandfather and father learned a great deal from the Han. From the art of government to the making of a plough. Today, ninety-nine out of every hundred population is a Han. How can you afford not to understand them? The Manchu's bloodthirsty habits must be restrained and modified by the example of the Emperor, lest they fall into Hell...."

The truth of his words and the sincerity of those blue eyes doused the flames of wrath in the young Emperor. In fact wasn't he learning Chinese as quickly as he could? Did he not admire their ancient culture and study their history? However, as Emperor he could not back down. He quickly seized upon a way of saving face. With the arrogance of a conqueror he attacked the Emperor of the last dynasty. "Mafa, you are so blind to the faults of the Han. Did the Emperor Chongzhen not lose his Empire because of jealousy, greed, and cruelty, and ended by hanging himself on Coal Hill?"

Tang Jo-Wang did not agree. He had held an official post in the Imperial Ministry of Astronomy of the Ming Dynasty as well and knew their fall was due to the attack of peasant insurgents led by Li Zicheng. The Manchus merely seized the Empire he captured. There was a folk ditty, a satire on the Manchu conquest that was making the rounds:

"The Zhus' wheat was milled by the Lis,
And made into a great big bun
as a gift for the Zhaos*...."

"Emperor Chongzhen was learned and full of compassion for his people. But he was over confidant and stubborn...." Tang Jo-Wang started to explain.

"Mafa," Fulin cut him off hotly, "In the last year of Wanli

---

*Zhu, Li and Zhao refer to the Ming Dynasty, the insurgent leader Li Zicheng and the Manchu conqueror respectively.

(1619) the annual tax collected to pay the army was twenty-eight hundred thousand. During Chongzhen's reign new taxes were added left and right, so that the people were burdened with ten times as much. People could not exist under those conditions! The first thing we did after the Conquest was return taxes to the same level as the first year of Wanli (1573). Mafa, tell me who cares more about the people?" Tang Jo-Wang chuckled. "That was the present regime's first wise move. I have lost the argument."

Having regained his good humour, Fulin moved about the workroom with great interest, examining papers, charts, and apparatus strewn across the work benches. He asked many questions. How much time was spent at devotions each day? Where did the formulae for the medicines the Jesuit made for the Empress Dowager come from? Was it from this book or that? Alas they were all in European languages which he could not decipher.

At first Tang Jo-Wang tried to answer each question as it came. Then he passed them off with a smile. The all-powerful Emperor of the world's largest empire was, in fact, no different from any other adolescent. Curious and energetic, he explored every corner of the room.

It was the astronomical instruments that fascinated the young Emperor the most, and Tang Jo-Wang, seeing this, took pains to explain their constructions and their function.

Fulin pointed at the stacks of paper on the desk covered with spidery writing and calculations.

"Is this your reformed calendar?" he asked. "What do your calculations tell you?"

"This year, in the fifth month, the planet Venus will be visible during the day. In the ninth month there will be an eclipse of the moon," Tang Jo-Wang informed the Emperor.

"Mafa, if the passage of stars across the sky can be calculated in advance then it must follow that their path is unalterable," Fulin's eyes flashed with intelligence. "If that is so then the good or evil they foretell is equally unavoidable.

What can your God do about it? Also, do the stars foretell the same things to Zhu Youlang and Zheng Chenggong as they do to myself?" Both Zhu Youlang (Emperor Yongli of Southern Ming) and Zheng Chenggong were still fighting against the Qing regime.

The learned man was dumbfounded. But he quickly composed himself and, taking another tack, suggested they go into the church where he would be better able to explain the problem.

The Jesuit was a devout man of the cloth. To convert the Emperor and bring salvation to the largest empire in the world was his most fervent prayer, and his greatest tribute to God. It would also be the greatest achievement of his life. He recognized Fulin's innate compassion. But he was also of a passionate nature, who could be easily roused into dangerous rages by trivia. These rages could undo everything good his mentor had tried to instill. Therefore, he drew upon the experiences of his predecessor the Italian Jesuit Matteo Ricci, and strove to combine Christian teaching with natural religion, and morality, and the philosophies of Confucius and Buddha. In this way he hoped to guide the young monarch towards salvation, and lead him to God in spite of himself.

Aside from his natural curiosity and his real respect for Tang Jo-Wang, the young Emperor's visit was not entirely prompted by whim. Weightier matters were on his mind.

At the moment the greatest threat to his peace of mind was the activities of Zhu Youlang, Emperor of the Southern Ming regime. Moreover Zhu Youlang, his mother, wife and son, and most of his courtiers and eunuchs were Christians. Tang Jo-Wang had a certain standing within the church, and considerable influence. Therefore, by honouring Tang Jo-Wang the Emperor thought, Zhu Youlang could be persuaded to lay down his arms. Furthermore, if Tang Jo-Wang could be persuaded to intercede on his behalf matters could be much smoother. However, he could not be sure of Tang Jo-Wang's reaction to such a plan. If the Jesuit refused to meddle in politics, there would be a serious loss of face.

The church was vast and deep. Brilliant frescos covered the dome, depicting God in heaven surrounded by a host of angels. The bas-reliefs lining the walls stood in a stark contrast of light and shade. Shafts of light streaming down from the skylights lent an air of mysterious solemnity to five high and beautifully carved altars. Thick carpets deadened their footsteps. Tang Jo-Wang led Fulin to the high altar where a statue of Jesus stood surrounded by banks of flowers and a myriad candles. Jesus was depicted in a long robe, a halo round his head. In one hand he held the globe of the world, while the other was raised in benediction. Little angels and the devout clustered around his feet in prayer.

"Praise God!" Tang Jo-Wang intoned devoutly. "God, the all powerful and all knowing, commands the natural rhythms of the universe to reflect his intentions. This is his way of inspiring mankind, especially monarchs. Therefore, the monarch should believe and honour him. Especially, Your Majesty."

The reasoning that enraged him in the workroom became readily acceptable in this hallowed place. But the priest's last remark pricked his curiosity.

"Why, especially me?"

"Because you are the greatest ruler in the world. You call yourself son of Heaven. Therefore, God has a special regard for you."

"If I mend my ways, will I avoid disasters?"

"Correct. In Europe there is a saying: philosophers guide the stars."

"Mafa, teach me to avoid wrong-doing."

Tang Jo-Wang spoke to him as a kindly teacher, stroking his flowing beard as he spoke:

"The Emperor must constantly keep in mind the duties and obligations that accrue to his position. He must be compassionate towards his people and his ministers. He must serve God alone, eschewing other deities and demons. He must take to heart

Confucius's precept, 'Do unto others as you would others do unto you...' and be guided in all his actions by the Ten Commandments."

Fulin listened carefully. All of it sounded reasonable. Still he bit his lip with doubt.

"Do the Commandments of God apply equally to the people and the Emperor?" "Yes, even more to the Emperor. For the Emperor must set an example for the rest." They fell silent. Fulin's eyes drifted to the great pillars of the church, and the nude figures of winged cherubs with smiling faces. "Why does God forbid a man to have more than one wife?" he asked. Tang Jo-Wang ignored the fires flickering deep in the young Emperor's eyes.

"This is so that children will be properly cared for, and there will be peace in the home. That is God's intention."

"Does that commandment apply to monarchs?"

Tang Jo-Wang realized this was the biggest obstacle to Fulin embracing the church. But he was a devout man, and was unwilling to compromise his beliefs no matter how large the gain. Nevertheless it was with a touch of firmness that he answered, "It does." Fulin fell silent. Tang Jo-Wang led the way to the altar of the Blessed Virgin. The picture on the altar was a copy of one in the Church of Santa Maria de Majore in Rome, and was the work of the painter Schnee. Fulin gazed fixedly at the picture.

"Tell me, Mafa," Fulin said in a whisper, "what manner of empress would the Blessed Mother choose for me?" Tang Jo-Wang realized with a start this was one of the reasons Fulin had come to speak to him.

"She would choose one you love; one who will help you keep the Commandments."

"One whom I love?"

"God took a rib from Adam and created Eve. You too must find a wife whom you will love as you love yourself."

A shadow crossed Fulin's face and he was silent until they

had left the church. Outside an enchanting fountain played in a garden full of flowering fruit trees and fine statues. Fulin was oblivious of all that, even of the eunuchs and guards who swarmed after him.

The warmth of the sunlight, and the soft breath of spring breezes, with a chill edge in it, wafted against his face. Underfoot the grass was turning green. Above the sky was crystal blue and dappled with clouds. The solemnity of the church, the sanctity of God, the mellifluous sound of Mafa's voice had taken him out of himself into another sphere. For a while he was pure spirit, rising skyward. But it was cold in that lofty place, and he longed for the pleasures and pains of the world.

Fulin sat down on a stone bench under a grape arbour, shut his eyes to the sunlight and filled his lungs with spring air. He breathed deep, and said with a smile, "Mafa, I've been here all this time and you haven't offered me food or drink."

"Forgive me. Without your instructions I did not know what to offer."

"I would like a glass of the wine you make."

Red wine was offered in a crystal goblet together with cakes baked in the European style. Fulin downed the wine.

"Mafa, when your grapes are ripe, keep some that I might come and pick them myself." As they parted, Fulin asked, "Mafa, what can I give you?"

"Thank you, Your Majesty. I have all I need."

"That won't do. There must be something!"

"I am grateful for Your Majesty's generosity." Fulin frowned, deep in thought, then brightening he cried, "Mafa, I know what we will do. We will have the guards bring eighteen elephants, and race them in the square in front of the church!"

"Oh, Your Majesty..." Tang Jo-Wang tried to stop the Emperor, but it was too late.

"Mafa, you must keep out of the way, lest the elephants trample you...." Fulin laughed.

The elephants were corralled in the place not far from the

church. In a trice eighteen huge beasts were driven through the streets toward the church. The very houses that lined the street shook as the beasts passed. Soon the spectacle of an elephant race would take place in the streets of the capital of Great Qing.

2

Fulin returned to the palace, rested and then went to visit his mother at Cining Palace. The yellow tiles, the crimson walls, the steps and balustrades of white marble sparkled in the warm westerly sun of late afternoon. From the terrace high above Longzong Gate one could see faintly the blue smudge of the Western Hills etched against the glowing sky. Barely a year after renovations, the luxurious Cining Palace glittered resplendantly. Work continued in the gardens beyond, where gnarled pines and shrubs breathed life into the ancient palace.

Fulin strode through the heavy gates of Cining Palace and up the white marble steps guarded by a pair of bronze unicorns, past prostrating eunuchs and Maids of Honour, into the main hall of the Palace.

"You have returned, my royal son." His mother's rounded well-loved voice greeted him in familiar Manchu.

Fulin returned the salutation, solicitously enquiring into every detail of his mother's life. His manner was that of a filial son, a responsible adult, and a dignified monarch. Fulin had learned the delicate balance of the three parts of his public persona very well. Four imperial concubines, chief ladies of the East and West Palaces followed him into the hall. The ladies greeted the Dowager on their knees. Their glittering brocade gowns, elaborate coiffure topped by gold and silver headdresses studded with precious gems stood in sharp contrast to the blue cloth robes and plain coiffure of the Maids of Honour.

The Empress Dowager was Mongolian, the daughter of Zaisang, a Beileh* of Horqin Mongol. She, as well as her sister and aunt, all married the Emperor Taizong, named Abahai. Be-

*Beileh was a Manchu title bestowed on sons of imperial princes.

cause of this bond of marriage, the Horqins became the strongest allies in Abahai's conquest of all under Heaven. In the process they also became the most powerful of the forty-nine Mongolian banners (army and administration divisions). In her youth, the Empress Dowager had been a famous beauty of the steppes. But she was even more renowned for her kindness and wisdom. She was the youngest daughter of Zaisang, and an exceptionally clever child. She was well spoken, fluent in Mongolian, read history and philosophy. It was said that at the age of seven, she had gone with her brothers to inspect the herds. A lama, skilled in fortune telling, came upon the child and was amazed that such grace should be found in so desolate a place. Her retainers brushed the man's amazement aside, for the child was the daughter of a Beileh. What else would she be? The lama went on to say that she was more than a Beileh's daughter. For she was destined to be wife of a great emperor and Mother of a Nation. The herdsmen were not impressed; for the Beileh had al ways befriended Beileh Yehe, the most powerful of the four clans in the area. Therefore an advantageous marriage was a matter of course, nothing to marvel at. The lama insisted that greater things were in store for the girl. She would wed the emperor himself and be the Mother of a Nation. The herdsmen scoffed at this. Whoever heard of an emperor marrying a barbarian! The lama went his way, insisting on the verity of what he had foreseen ... though he had no idea how it would come about....

People chuckled at the story at the time. However, twenty-five years later, the emperor died, and his son Fulin ascended the throne. That year the armies of Qing swept south and occupied the central plains. Fulin became the first emperor after the Manchu conquest and his mother assumed the title of the Empress Dowager. Thus the lama's prophesy was accomplished.

The legend left out the privations, the suffering and the sacrifices the Empress Dowager endured to secure the throne for her son.

At the age of forty-two she had lost none of her feminine allure. Jet black brows arched gracefully over long, narrow eyes in whose depths shone flecks of warmth. The nose was slender. The firm mouth was finely chiselled. The high cheek-bones and broad jaws bespoke Mongolian lineage. In middle age, a pleasant plumpness smoothed out the angles and planes of her face. She carried herself with an air of serenity and grace, so that anyone coming into her presence was instantly struck by the force of her person as well as her stature.

She smiled at the kneeling women, and beckoned them to rise.

"From now on, Lady Tong need not kneel," she said in even tones. "A curtsy will suffice."

Lady Tong blushed gratefully. Fulin glanced at her with laughter in his eyes. Lady Tong shot him a quick glance full of love, and let her eyes drop. The other ladies snickered, envy in their hearts.

The Empress Dowager turned to Fulin.

"My royal son is in good spirits today," she observed.

"Your son has been talking with Mafa Tang, and then went riding on the plains. Yes, I'm happy." Indeed he cut a dashing figure with his flaming cheeks and eyes.

The Dowager nodded.

"Your spiritual father is a wise and learned man, who would give good counsel. Did you send him our greetings?"

"Indeed we have. Mafa sent you two crucifixes which have been blessed on the altar of the Blessed Mother." He handed the Empress Dowager two gold crosses fastened to gold chains. "Mafa says to wear them under your garments and they will protect you against illness and harm."

The Empress Dowager examined the gold chains and the crosses, then calmly slipped them over her head to join the necklaces and the Buddhist prayer beads strung around her neck. The ladies of the court were aghast at the Empress Dowager's actions. Whereas the foreigner had advised wearing the crosses under her garments for the sake of protocol, the Empress Dowager had no such scruples.

The Empress Dowager challenged the assemblage with her eyes. None dared meet her gaze.

"Why did Mafa Tang send these crosses," she asked in a casual tone. Fulin averted his eyes when he replied.

"One is meant for the Empress."

The four concubines present bowed their heads at his words. Lady Tong dabbed at the corners of her mouth with a whisp of handkerchief, to hide a tremulous smile. The two sisters from the Boerjijite clan, their eyes meeting unconsciously, averted them quickly as if scorched.

The Empress Dowager steered the conversation in another direction.

"My royal son studies too hard. It is good that you have a wise mentor to talk to and to amuse you. It is not good to work night and day, as you did last autumn, until you spat blood."

Fulin chuckled.

"I shall try to do as my Imperial Mother commands. Lately I have been studying the root causes for the fall of the Yuan and Ming dynasties. I have concluded as Emperor of China, I must be fluent in Chinese. If I am to make something of myself I must also master the art of warfare."

The Empress Dowager chuckled at his seriousness.

"That's good. Our dynasty was founded on military skills. That certainly must not be overlooked. However, hunting should be curbed. Too much hunting is injurious to the health. It would be a great pity if it should interfere with the proper running of the Empire."

"Mother, this year I haven't hunted at all," protested Fulin, boyish again for the moment. Then deftly turning the conversation away from himself he added, "However, you have been cooped indoors too long. In a few days the gardens will be ready. Then we shall enjoy them together."

The restoration of Cining Garden was entirely Fulin's idea.

The Empress Dowager had forbidden the expenditure time and again because the Empire was not yet stable and the imperial coffers were almost empty. However, Fulin saw himself as a filial son, insisted on the restoration and would brook no objection. To appease the Dowager he agreed to limit the restoration and to keep expenditure as low as possible.

"I have been told the calligraphy on Azure Cloud Pavilion is the finest in the country," remarked the Empress Dowager.

"Yes, indeed. It is said to be the work of Dong Qichang,* wonderfully bold, dashing brush strokes! As a matter of fact, I am trying to imitate him. The Academicians of the Palace Academies are reasonably impressed with my attempts...."

The Empress Dowager chatted for a while longer, then dismissed the assemblage.

The ladies of the harem formed a line, curtsied, took a few backward steps then quickly left the hall, their shoes with soles thick and high in the middle part making clicking sounds even on carpeted floor. The ladies walked with rigid bodies held ramrod straight and tightly corsetted, for protocol forbade the body to sway. This custom also applied to the only concubine who was a Han. Although Lady Shi of Yongshou Palace was permitted the traditional tunic and skirt of the Han, she was expected to affect the stiff-backed gait in spite of her bound feet.

Fulin frowned, watching the ladies go. He had no intention of leaving just then.

"My royal son, go and rest," the Empress Dowager commanded. Fulin shook his head.

"I will not!"

The Empress Dowager shot him a questioning look.

"Mother, can't you see I'm hungry!" cried Fulin.

The Empress Dowager ordered food and wine, then dismissed

---

*President of the Ming-dynasty Ministry of Rites and well-versed in calligraphy and painting, he also wrote several books on the theories of art and his unique style of calligraphy had great influence on later articles.

the Maids of Honour. It was an informal meal, served in the Empress Dowager's chambers. There were no menus to approve or eunuchs presenting and removing dishes, nor going through the ritual of tasting and testing the foods with silver to see if they were poisoned. Without these interruptions the meal was pleasant and relaxed.

The mother's conversation naturally drifted on to the thorny question of selecting a new empress.

"I shall abide by my Mother's directions," Fulin said after a moment's thought.

"You're grown up now. Perhaps you will not want to listen to your mother," the Dowager's gentle irony was unmistakable. It was the first time she had expressed her displeasure, even obliquely, since the Empress was put aside.

Fulin bowed his head and waited.

The former empress had been the Empress Dowager's niece, daughter of her brother Wukeshan, a Beileh of Horqin Mongol. The Regent Dorgon had proposed the match. It was because of Dorgon that Fulin objected to the marriage regardless of the bride's beauty and virtue. Fulin believed that Dorgon had designs to betray him. A few months before the wedding the regent died, and Fulin wanted to cancel the wedding. However, the Empress Dowager would not consent. Besides Wukeshan had already delivered his daughter to the capital. For political and family reasons the wedding could not be delayed. After the wedding the Emperor and his Empress were soon at loggerheads. In less than two years, Fulin made up his mind to have the marriage annulled. The Dowager opposed him, until she realized that her son would not be swayed, and the failed marriage was beginning to take its toll on his health. So reluctantly she bowed to the inevitable. Nevertheless this created a crisis. Many of the courtiers, especially the Hans, seized upon old traditions and counselled the Emperor to reconsider. As a compromise, the Manchu nobles proposed that the Empress should remain at the Central

Palace while giving similar titles to the Principle Ladies of the East and West Palaces. Fulin would not agree. His wrath was particularly directed at the Han nobles for creating the crisis. In the end these nobles were forced to withdraw their petition and sue for forgiveness. When the assistant regent Prince Jirgalang expressed his support for the Emperor, the die was cast. The marriage was annulled and the hapless Empress relegated to living in a minor palace the rest of her life. The court had glimpsed the young Emperor's obstinacy for the first time.

The Empress Dowager's feelings about the incident were far more complex and far-reaching than the court realized. However, the past is the past. She shook her head as if to dismiss disturbing thoughts and asked, "Whom do you have in mind?"

Fulin hesitated. "I haven't decided.... Since I am Emperor of China ... of the Han as well as the Manchu ... couldn't the choice of empress...." He allowed the sentence to trail off.

The Empress Dowager arched her brows.

"You already have one concubine who is Han, and four of the Han generals who threw down their arms have been named Princes of Kong, Wu, Geng and Shang. Surely that is enough to cement relations between our two races. The empress is the mate of the Son of Heaven and Mother of a Nation. As such she must be from a noble origin."

"As they say, a mother glories in her son. Thus if Lady Tong bears a son...." The Dowager shook her head. She chose her words carefully when she spoke.

"The choice of empress has to be made with the good of the Empire in mind. Last year when the Empress was put aside, do you think the forty-nine banners of Mongolia were not incensed? When the Empire is still unstable, any false move could mean cutting your own throat."

Fulin was silenced. The idea of having a Han as empress was a frivolous thought that family traditions would not countenance. If he were to choose for himself, Mafa Tang's idea suited him the best. He would seek an empress that he truly loved. He craved new experience; new emotions. However, none of the ladies who would qualify pleased him. Only Lady Tong came close to his heart's desire. After all said and done, he realized, he had to bow to his mother's wishes for the sake of Empire.

When he emerged from Cining Palace, Fulin once more assumed the demeanor of the benevolent but dignified monarch. Nothing had come of the discussion with his mother. The eunuchs helped him onto his sedan chair. The gathering mist of twilight, tinged with indigo shadows, shrouded the turrets and gables of the palace with mystery. Even the figures of the guardian beasts at the ridge corners of buildings seemed to take on other-worldly qualities. The silence along the footpaths and terraces echoed the nameless melancholy yearning in the young Emperor's heart. What was he seeking, he asked himself. Was it heroic ambitions, or was it the thought of having to choose another empress that oppressed him. It was probably a little of all those things, Fulin sighed.

His personal eunuch, the handsome Wu Liangfu leaned close and enquired which lady should be summoned for the night. Lost in thought, Fulin did not answer.

"Perhaps Your Majesty would like to make the rounds among the palaces," the eunuch suggested.

At the age of sixteen, Fulin was more sophisticated than his peers. The old tradition of keeping a harem had encouraged the youthful lasciviousness in his passionate nature. The end of the Ming Dynasty was marked by decadance. Eunuchs left over from the previous reign such as Wu Liangfu were schooled in debauchery. Indeed, it was his ability to anticipate his master's needs that helped Wu Liangfu to win and keep the youthful Emperor's favour. Fulin was excited by the perverse pleasures the eunuch could provide. This was Wu Liangfu's hold on his master. Fortunately, Fulin was intelligent, and his mother was a strict disciplinarian. These two factors kept him more or less on the straight and narrow. Even so, the eunuch was amazed that his master, who needed the services of one of the ladies every night, had shaken his head.

A first star appeared in the sky, reminding Fulin of the coquettish lights that flickered in the depths of Lady Tong's eyes.

"I would like to visit Lady Tong. However, the Empress Dowager might not approve if she found out."

"Your Majesty is master of all under Heaven," the eunuch was quick to interject. "We are all your slaves. Lady Tong would be honoured indeed...."

Fulin was pleased. The sedan chair was signalled to turn through Qianqing Gate and head for Jingren Palace. A eunuch was sent ahead to announce the Emperor, so that Lady Tong, surrounded by other concubines, Maids of Honour and serving wenches knelt at the gate of Jingren Palace to receive him.

Fulin leaped from the sedan chair.

"The Empress Dowager has forbidden you to kneel to her," he chided as he raised Lady Tong to her feet, "therefore let us have no more ceremony."

After formal greetings were exchanged, the Emperor went straight to Lady Tong's chamber. The other ladies retired to theirs.

"I don't suppose you're riding anymore," Fulin smiled tenderly, his cheeks glowing. Lady Tong ducked her head, and replied formally: "I have been blessed by Heaven, and shall be most careful with my precious burden." This respectful but formal reply sent a chill through Fulin. How could she be so unfeeling? Had she forgotten how it had been?

A year ago when the quarrels between Fulin and his empress were reaching a crescendo, he often went riding to take his mind off his troubles. It was spring and the crabapple trees in the West Gardens near Mingxiu Pavilion were in bloom. Fulin had gone there one morning to practice archery, and mesmerised by the profusion of blossoms, lingered in the garden. Suddenly voices and laughter drifted from the pavilion nearby. A group of ladies of the palace, accompanied by eunuchs had come there to see the flowers. The eunuchs had also brought along a tame white horse. The ladies had been boasting about their horsemanship to one another. However, confronted with a horse, none would be the first to show her skill. Lady Tong, the youngest and a new-comer to the palace, stepped forward.

"Our ancestors were horsemen. They have conquered the country on horseback. We ought to be good riders. I'll give it a try." The other ladies clapped their hands with glee.

"Lady Tong is young, but she has a long memory," one of the ladies jeered. "The Empress Dowager will take special notice of her when she hears of this."

One of the others picked two crabapple blossoms growing on the same stem and stuck it in Lady Tong's coiffure.

"This is an omen," she giggled. "Tonight the Emperor will summon you."

Lady Tong blushed and pretended not to notice. She took the reins from the eunuch, stepped into the stirrup and swung into the saddle. A figured emerged from the clump of flowering trees and the assemblage fell to their knees. Lady Tong slid from the saddle and knelt. Shunzhi strode to where she knelt, a smile hovering round his lips. Then turning swiftly, he left.

That evening, when the eunuch presented the green cards of the concubines on a jade platter, as was the custom, Fulin looked for the card of the lady equestrian. On it was written: "Lady Tong of Jingren Palace. Age: thirteen. Daughter of Tong Tulai, from the Blue Banner of the Han army."

Fulin turned that card over.

That night Lady Tong was brought to the royal bed chamber for the first time.

Afterwards, she was frequently summoned to his bed in spite of the Empress' jealous outbursts. He liked her. He liked her childishness, her daintiness, and her tenderness. The poignance of her timidity at her deflowering and her awakening sexuality filled Fulin with an unspeakable sweetness reminiscent of the erotic poems of Tang and Song which he loved. Yet when he recited them to her, Lady Tong was unmoved in her innocence. After he had put aside the Empress, a subtle change came over her. She had become formal, correct in every detail. The touching tenderness which first attracted him had disappeared.

The maids held mirrors while Lady Tong arranged her coiffure for the night. In the mirror, her cheeks were full and fair as peach blossoms. Large round eyes were moist and lustrous, full of romance. Fulin recited a poem for her.

When he finished she turned to him, wide-eyed, her face blank, uncomprehending. Fulin was dismayed by the prim haughtiness that replaced her natural vivaciousness. Does she think she is empress already, he mused.

Fulin's face clouded. In a loud voice he ordered Wu Liangfu to bring the petitions received that day. He would read them now.

Lady Tong quietly went about tidying his desk as though nothing unusual had happened. Fulin stole a glance at her, hoping to catch some indication of discontent in her attitude, but there was none. None at all.

Wu Liangfu got another eunuch to carry in a box of petitions. The first to be opened was one penned by Fu Yijian, Academician of the Palace Secretariat Academy.

"... We do not have a court of law, or any institution for meting out justice. Thus, ten days ago an unknown male killed himself at the gate of the palace in protest of an injustice. I was shocked by this incident. However, the Ministry of Justice glossed over the incident without taking any action. Hence, a further incident occurred at the same place a few days later. When two suicides occur within days of each other a great wrong must surely exist. For no man, however humble, would willingly end his life unless he was driven by despair. At this time, draughts and floods have caused great hardships among the people. Your Majesty must read the will of Heaven, and right these wrongs that all may live in peace...."

Fulin threw down the petition in anger.

"I will get to the bottom of this!" he roared, breathing hard. "Why did they wait until a second death took place before they reported? And the report was not from the Ministry of Justice either!" He saw himself as being a just ruler and these deaths were a personal reproach, an intolerable attack on his pride.

Lady Tong fell to her knees in fright at this violent outburst.

"Get up!" Fulin shouted. "This has nothing to do with you." Then turning to Wu Liangfu, he ordered Lord Aobai be summoned into the presence at once.

He glanced at Lady Tong as he spoke, and noticed a flicker of disappointment in her eyes. However, it was too late. With resolution he returned to his own palace.

3

The burly Mongolian giant grunted as he lifted the imperial guardsman Shang Zhixin off his feet and sent him sprawling on the carpeted floor. The guardsman rolled to his feet, growling with fury, ready to leap at his opponent again.

"Shang Zhixin!" cried the Commander of the Guards, Fei Yanggu.

His Commander's voice cleared Shang's befuddled brain, reminding him where he was. This was Baohe Hall, and he was in the Presence. The Mongolian stood, rooted like an ancient pine, fists at the ready, a shake of the head signalled he would not go another round with his defeated opponent.

Including Shang Zhixin, the son of Prince Pingnan named Shang Kexi, the big Mongolian had defeated three of the bravest among the imperial guards.

The air crackled with excitement.

The guests at the royal banquet exchanged looks fraught with anger. They were good wrestlers themselves. But their status prohibited them to take the giant on. Fulin's eyes narrowed and the muscles on his cheeks twitched. Sitting on his left Regent Jirgalang was worried lest the young Emperor should lose his composure before the guests. All smiles, the Ambassador of Khalkha Mongol filled a goblet, and left his seat to the right of the Emperor to offer it to the giant wrestler. Win two more rounds and he would be the undisputed victor.

Khalkha Mongol ruled northern Mongolia. Like the other forty-nine banners of the south, it also descended from the Yuan Dynasty. But unlike the former it had not submitted to Qing-dynasty rule. However, each year it presented a gift of eight white horses and one white camel to the emperor. In his turn, the Qing emperor responded with gifts of gold, silver, silks, tea, tobacco and salt as tokens of friendship. As in previous years, Emperor Shunzhi gave a banquet in Baohe Hall for the Ambassador. During the banquet the Ambassador had raised the question of the Emperor's annulled marriage and the fate of the former Empress who was Mongolian. This topic of conversation displeased the Emperor. Thus when the Ambassador proposed a wrestling match between his guards and members of the imperial guard as a diversion, Shunzhi was quick to accept the challenge. However, he did not foresee the outcome. Already his guards had lost three rounds. It would be a terrible disgrace if they suffered total defeat.

Fei Yanggu approached the Emperor and whispered something in his ear. A look of elation flashed across the Emperor's face and he nodded.

"Let it be done," Fulin murmured.

At a signal from the Commander a fourth guardsman stepped from the ranks and prostrated himself to the Emperor. A gasp swept the hall as the new contender faced the hulking Mongolian.

The challenger was of medium build, but small compared to

the Mongolian, like a child pitted against a grown man. He did not remove his yellow waist-coated uniform, and his fur-trimmed cap was clamped low across his brow. Even so it was evident he was not a young man. On yet closer inspection, one sensed an inner strength, like a tightly coiled spring, black with the stench of battle. A high-bridged nose and eyes keen as a vulture's were set in a long, square face fringed with scraggly whiskers. The man was a diamond in the rough; a shining sword in a rusty scabbard.

The victorious Mongol was quick to recognize the strength of his new adversary. The two men faced each other like tiger and leopard. They circled each other, arms outstretched, fists half clenched, following each move with their eyes, waiting for an opening. A breathless hush descended upon the great hall.

The Mongol weighing about three hundred pounds let out a low growl and leaped for the dark guardsman, taking advantage of his great bulk. However, the much smaller guardsman was swift. He nimbly side stepped the onslaught, and in a swirl of yellow too fast for the eye to follow sent the giant crashing to the floor where he lay senseless.

Everything happened so fast that the assemblage was left speechless.

"Bravo!" shouted Fulin.

Applause thundered through the hall as the guardsman and the court prostrated themselves to congratulate the Emperor on his victory. The Ambassador and his entourage were stunned by the unexpected turn of events, but quickly gathered their wits about them and joined the others in their felicitations.

The downed giant staggered to his feet and raised a thumb at his conqueror and cried out in Mongolian, "You are a brave man!"

Fulin signalled for the prizes to be brought forth. A gold goblet weighing ten ounces went to the Mongol and the dark guardsman. Fifteen bolts of fine silk went to the other contestants. The musicians struck up a merry tune and the banquet continued in this happy mood.

When the banquet ended and all the guests were gone, the dark guardsman prostrated himself before the Emperor once more.

"You have saved the honour of Great Qing in the nick of time," the Emperor enthused.

"Your slave had just arrived from Yongping Prefecture when Fei Yanggu acquainted me with what was happening. I am honoured to have been permitted to take part in the guise of a guardsman."

"I have seen the despatch you sent. You did well. This is a grave matter and the Princes and Grand Ministers of the Deliberative Council of Nobles and the Chief Ministers and officials of the various ministries have been instructed to discuss the matter thoroughly. You will present your report to the Council tomorrow."

"As Your Majesty commands."

As he left the hall, Lord Aobai wondered why the Emperor wanted all the court officials to discuss the land-seizing at Yongping Prefecture, and what this would lead to.

It was some distance to the palace gate. Shouts of "Attention!" rang along the pathways where he passed. It was the custom of the Imperial guards to stand at attention for the Grand Ministers of the Deliberative Council of Nobles. But today their shouts rang out louder for Lord Aobai. Being one of the last living warriors who fought for the overthrow of the Ming, he was already a hero in the minds of the Manchu. Today's feat added lustre to his reputation. Now he had no peers. Lord Aobai, who tended to be sombre, accepted the salutation with a brief nod of the head. He seldom smiled. At the moment he was absorbed with the thorny issue that would be laid before the Council in the morning.

The Council met in a small hall to the east of Taihe Hall. A small throne had been set at the centre. Behind it stood a screen on which was a painted landscape. Tall fans of coloured plumes with gold handles stood on either side. Incensers, placed before the throne, filled the room with lazy spirals of scented smoke. Two rows of cushions fanned out from the throne. Those closer to the throne were higher and more ornate; the two closest being elaborately decorated with dragon and phoenix motifs.

Prince Jirgalang was seated on the small throne in the centre. At the time Shunzhi was proclaimed emperor, he and Prince Dorgon had been appointed joint regents. As Dorgon was ambitious and anxious to seize power for himself, Jirgalang soon found himself being edged out of the corridors of power. Although he was perceived as ineffectual, he was unswerving in his devotion to Shunzhi. Even when Dorgon confiscated his lands and heaped humiliation upon him, he did not murmur. Thus, when Dorgon's ambitions became dangerous to the young Emperor, he was able to work behind the scenes to protect him. Upon the death of Dorgon, the banner leaders became restive. Rebellion was in the air. The situation was critical. With the help of the Empress Dowager, Jirgalang rallied the Yellow, White and Yellow-bordered banners around the Emperor, thus safeguarding the throne. The leader of the conspiracy, Prince Ajige, was commanded to take his own life, and the eight banners were neutralized from the interior. Shunzhi respected Jirgalang's integrity and relied upon his judgement. In the three years since he assumed the reins of government, Jirgalang has risen to be the most powerful figure at court next to the Emperor himself.

In his fifty-sixth year Jirgalang's hair and beard were completely white. Long years of campaigning and being wounded several times had taken their toll. The Prince seemed older than his years.

Seated next to Jirgalang was Prince Chengze (Shuosai), Shunzhi's older half-brother. Of the late emperor's eleven sons, eight survived. However, only two, Prince Su (Haoge) and Shuosai took part in the wars of conquest. Haoge was a gallant soldier. In the fifth year of Shunzhi, Regent Dorgon imprisoned

Haoge on trumped-up charges, and removed his title. The Prince then killed himself in prison. Shuosai had the title of Prince as his birth-right, being son of one emperor and brother of another. Though his contribution to the conquest was less noteworthy than Haoge, at the age of twenty-six he was commander-in-chief of the army. The first seat on the other side of Jirgalang was left empty for Duke An (Yuele). Because he was implicated in the matter under discussion, he was excluded from the meeting.

The other Grand Ministers present were Jidu, Prince Jirgalang's son, Duke Xin (Duoni), and Beileh Shangshan. Aside from these nobles the noted bannermen Fan Wencheng, Xifu, Yitu, Duerma, Suoni, Fei Yanggu, Aobai, Ebilong, were also present.

Aobai rose to address the Council:

"The incident took place in Malan Village, which was under the jurisdiction of Yongping Prefecture. One Wang Yongxiu had been renting thirty mu of land he owned to a tenant farmer Qiao Zinian for years. Wang decided to seek the protection of Duke An, and pledged his land to his overlord for that privilege. However, he continued to exact rent from Qiao. Then Wang became enamoured of Qiao's wife. His relentless pursuit of the woman finally drove her to suicide. This earned the man the Duke's wrath and he was flogged. Disgruntled, Wang then pledged his land to Tong Tulai under a banner of the Han army. This time he not only pledged his own land but that of several families toward whom he bore a grudge, claiming them as his. Qiao Zinian attempted to seek justice for them all, but was refused a hearing. At his wits' end, he stole to the Forbidden City and committed suicide in front of Meridian Gate."

None of the Council commented after Aobai's recital except Prince Jirgalang.

"Although Tong Tulai is the husband of my niece I will not protect him," Jirgalang was quick to respond. "In the eighth year of Shunzhi, it was decreed that land expropriated from the populace must be returned. Since Lord Aobai has already investigated the case thoroughly, I move that the land be restored to the rightful owners at once."

"But Tong Tulai was tricked," smiled Shuosai. "Under those circumstances he should not be penalized."

Everyone nodded agreement.

Fan Wencheng coughed, and all eyes turned to him. Fan Wencheng, Grand Academician and principal advisor of the late Emperor, was one of the best known courtiers of early Qing Dynasty, one of a handful of Hans who were instrumental in the Manchu conquest. A heavy-set man from Liaodong, at the age of fifty-seven he was quick-witted and decisive. When Dorgon was regent, Fan recognized the man's ambition and distanced himself. Nor was he persuaded to join Haoge's faction after the regent's death. Nevertheless, in later discussions of Dorgon's misdeeds Fan Wencheng also came under fire and was forced to retire for a time. At the instigation of the Empress Dowager, Shunzhi made amends for this great wrong. Fan Wencheng was brought back to court, given an official title and made a Grand Minister of the Deliberative Council of Nobles. He quickly became the Emperor's trusted advisor. His way of cutting straight to the heart of a problem soon won him the grudging respect of the Deliberative Council of Nobles. Now he was about to make another unpalatable pronouncement.

"To my mind," Fan Wencheng began, choosing his words, "Lord Aobai's report referred not only to the expropriation of Qiao's land. Other people's was also involved. Thus, the disputed land between Duke An and Tong is more than a matter of thirty mu. If the land is to be returned at all, then it must include all the expropriated land."

Although Duke An had gone to the border wars when Wang Yongxiu gave his land to Lord Tong, the Duke's retainers reappropriated it immediately. Whereupon Lord Tong's clan, not to be outdone, returned the favour. Thus the two clans fought over the land until finally all the farmland of Malan Village had been seized between them. Still the feud raged on.

Duke Xin, Duoni, a youth the same age as the Emperor and a great admirer of Duke An, spoke next: "Land originally given Duke An need not be returned."

Jirgalang's tall, husky son, Jidu spoke in a loud commanding tone: "Wang Yongxiu, who offered allegiance to one overlord then another, deserves to be punished."

Aobai's eyes were trained to the ground when he retorted, saying, "The Tongs have flaunted the Emperor's decree, and should be put to the sword."

Earlier he had mentioned that when the retainers of the Tong clan went to seize the land, the people had protested on the grounds that such activities were now outlawed by imperial decree. However, the man in charge retorted, "The Emperor is only a child. What does he know about decrees!" The assemblage had apparently missed this detail in Aobai's report. Having it brought to their attention in this way was a shock.

Suoni who was honest and thoughtful agreed.

Jirgalang paled. When his son Jidu leaped to his feet ready to rebut, the father motioned him to be quiet.

Fan Wencheng observed all these and, calmly weighing the pros and cons, spoke in a flat, calm voice: "The retainers of the Tong clan can be disciplined by their banner. However, all the land that the two clans expropriated must be restored to their original owners. The question is how to deal with Wang Yongxiu? Since he has caused the loss of two lives, I maintain his own is forfeit."

There was a moment of silence. Then the council chamber erupted into shouts. Nearly all the Council members, including Aobai, were was opposed to that proposal.

As the commotion died down, Jirgalang spoke with knitted brows. "Wang Yongxiu cannot be held responsible for the suicides of Qiao Zinian and his wife. Since Qiao continued to work the land that Wang had put under the banner of Duke An, he became the slave of a slave. As such his death is not worth considering."

Jidu, who had just sat down, leaped to his feet.

"Whose household has not suffered the death of eight or ten slaves a year?" he demanded hotly. "Even animals die! If the lives of slaves have to be taken into account we would all end up in gaol!" Everyone agreed.

Ebilong was one of the most influential councilmen present. His father, Eyidu, was one of the five nobles honoured by the late Emperor for the part he played in the conquest, and his mother was Princess Heshuo, the daughter of Nurhachi. Furthermore, he enjoyed a close relationship with the imperial family through marriage. Five of his sisters-in-law were royal princesses, and one of his sisters had been the late Emperor's chief concubine. Though quite young, Ebilong was deferred to because of his connection with the imperial family. Ordinarily he didn't have much to say, seeming to have no strong opinions about anything. However, on this occasion he was voluble.

"We Manchus have come east, and carved out a corner of the earth for ourselves by the sweat of our brow," he said in a soft voice. "That accounts for a residence, a bit of land, a few animals and slaves. Those who throw themselves upon us for protection and offer up their land for the privilege are a bonus. To kill these people is like killing our livestock. It's robbery! You say the Emperor is thinking of the good of his people. Then return the land. We can always get it back. But killing the people who come to us with their land is like killing the goose that lays the golden egg. Who would dare pledge themselves to us then? Wang Yongxiu pledged himself to two men. Well, punish the one who accepted him. But it must end there, otherwise what did we fight for?"

Ebilong's candid remarks reflected the consensus of those assembled. Even Fan Wencheng had to back down and agree.

As usual the meeting of the nine Chief Ministers, Supervising Secretaries of Offices of Scrutiny and Circuits, and Investigating Censors took place near Quezuo Gate. As each post was manned by one Manchu official to one Han, about a hundred courtiers attended the meeting. It had been a stormy session. Many were still arguing and gesticulating as they dispersed to their various offices. The Han officials kept their heads down, walking in twos and threes, whispering together.

Usually the opinions of the Manchus were deferred to at these meetings. The Han officials were merely rubber stamps, who approved everything as a matter of course. For some reason that day twenty-nine Han officials raised an objection to a Manchu proposal. The Manchus had proposed that Duke An and Lord Tong be required to return the land they appropriated, and that Wang Yongxiu be disciplined by his master. The twenty-nine disagreed, insisting on the death penalty for Wang Yongxiu, and a full inquiry into the activities of the officials who out of fear had refused to hear Qiao Zinian's complaint which ulimately led to the man's suicide.

Academician Fu Yijian of the Palace Secretariat Academy, who had been ordered to attend the meeting by Imperial decree, accepted the petition of the twenty-nine Han officials.

"Gentlemen, I admire your courage," he addressed himself to their leader. "But haven't you gone too far?"

Chen Mingxia, Minister of Personnel laughed out loud.

"How so? We are merely demanding that the letter of the law be followed. the Emperor will understand."

"Are you not concerned you would be looked upon as a clique?" Fu Yijian pursued.

"I wonder where that clique comes from!" Chen Mingxia gave his sleeve a contemptuous shake and took his leave. Fu Yijian sighed as he watched him leave.

"Pride comes before a fall," he murmured ominously. Chen Mingxia met two other officials outside, and the three chatted as they headed for their offices. Just then Fan Wencheng and Ning Wanwo came out of the Inner Palace.

The five men exchanged greetings. As they were all Hans, they conversed in Chinese. All five were renowned Grand Academicians. Fan and Ning were from Liaodong and had gone over to the Manchus as soon as invasions began. As a result both became bannermen; Fan under the yellow-bordered banner of the imperial house and Ning under the red banner of the Han army. Later both became powerful Grand Ministers of the Deliberative Council of Nobles. Chen Mingxia and the other two were equally learned, yet they were only ministers.

Chen Mingxia brought up the deliberations of the Council again. "Wang Yongxiu must be executed to appease the populace, and the county and provincial officials have to be disciplined as a warning to others of like mind," he opined. "The Empire is still unstable. There is a shortage of manpower everywhere; the land is wasted, the coffers are empty and the people poor. If the court fails to secure men's hearts, the dynasty will not endure."

Fan Wencheng listened without comment. When the other had finished his discourse, he joined both hands and raised them high in a gesture of farewell. "I must go now, for other matters are pressing. Forgive me." And with that he went off in another direction.

Ning Wanwo shot a disparaging glance at Chen Mingxia. "By the sounds of it you have the safety of the dynasty under control," he sneered.

"Of course," Chen Mingxia replied. "Follow me on two matters and there will be peace on earth!"

"And what might they be?" Ning Wanwo fixed Chen with his gaze. Chen Mingxia pushed his red-tasseled headdress backward, revealing an expanse of shaven forehead.

"To have peace on earth, let the hair grow and resume the old habits of dress."

Ning Wanwo paled. Though he despised Chen Mingxia, he did not think the man would dare utter such treason. Chen Zilin and Jin Zijun were horrified at what they heard.

Chen Mingxia laughed at their consternation. "I said as

much to the Emperor himself," he chortled. Days before when the Emperor visited his ministry, Chen had brought up the subject, using Prince Yu's campaign south of the Yangtze as an allegory. Wherever he went, the Prince endeavoured to persuade the Ming officials to lay down their arms in exchange for amnesty. A high official of the Ming Dynasty, Li Qiaoyu went further. Not only did he side with the Manchu, he shaved his head as they did. This obvious attempt at currying favour roused the wrath of the Prince to such a degree that Li was publicly humiliated as a warning to others. The people of the south were peace-loving and prosperous. Had they been treated with consideration they would have come over to the Qing willingly. However, the Prince Regent's policy of shaving the head alienated the entire region south of the Yangtze. Henceforth one rebellion followed another. There was never a day of peace. "It goes to show, the hearts of the people have to be won," Chen Mingxia concluded. He also nodded, "The Emperor acquiesed."

Ning Wangwo excused himself and turned away nervously. Chen Mingxia grunted his disdain.

Jin Zijun, always a diffident soul, cautioned, "He is one of the founding ministers of the nation. It does not bode well to offend him." Chen Mingxia brushed his remark aside. "He's nothing but a monkey in an official's cap. Why, he didn't even pass the imperial examinations during the previous regime! A few days ago he mocked me for going over to the Manchu. Just like the pot calling the kettle black. I gave it back to him in good measure. He is but a official left over from the Ming, not a Manchu of good family. I don't see what he has to swagger about."

"Still it's best to be careful," Jin Zijun warned.

"Don't you understand, Brother Zijun?" Chen Mingxia smiled. "The Manchu have conquered all under Heaven, but they govern according to the laws of Ming. They need men like us, the remnants of Ming to show them how. Why, the Court can't function without us. Also, the young Emperor is uncommonly wise and is bent on a policy of benevolence. He has often repeated the slogan 'Hans and Manchus unite.' That surely is a good omen for us."

They continued talking, their voices fading into the distance as they were dwarfed by the towers and the walls that reared against the sky.

The next day Fulin sat in the east side chamber of the Yangxin Hall (Hall of Mental Cultivation) reading documents. The more he read the less he liked what was presented to him. In exasperation he ordered Grand Academician Jin Zijun and Academicians Fu Yijian and Wang Xi to attend him at once.

The three hurried into the Presence and prostrated themselves before the Emperor, holding their breath. The Emperor threw a petition at them.

Jin Zijun was shocked by the petition from the Imperial Superintendant of Instruction Li Chengxiang suggesting the removal of all Manchu officials from the Ministries and Academies, replacing them with Hans. It is true that the illiterate and ignorant Manchus held positions of power for which they were often unqualified, while intelligent Han officials served as window dressing. As a result there were many costly mistakes. However, there was nothing to be done; members of the imperial family controlled all six ministries of government. Li Chengxiang was a fool to have presented such a petition.

Fulin's eyes flashed fire.

"Li Chengxiang's petition is rubbish!" he cried in a loud voice. "We have never made distinctions between Hans and Manchus in our appointments. Still you Han officials are discontent. Would we not be within our rights to favour the Manchus? Where would you be today, had we not come east?"

The three Han officials removed their hats and pressed their foreheads to the ground.

Fulin threw another petition on the ground. This one was

signed by twenty-nine Han officials the day before. Fulin's voice shook with anger as he spoke, "This is the work of a clique, a taboo of all dynasties. I hate to see a clique in mine. It is clear these Hans are bent on disrupting government by raising objections to the recommendations of Manchu officials. This will not be tolerated."

Jin Zijun prostrated himself, scarcely breathing.

A third petition fluttered to the ground. Jin Zijun glanced at it and great beads of sweat popped out all over his brow. In it Ning Wanwo charged Chen Mingxia of heading a subversive clique. It went on to say that Chen despised the Manchu habit of shaving the head and their style of dress, and that he had publicly called for a return to the former habit of wearing the hair long and reintroducing the former style of dress as a means of achieving universal peace...."

"Investigate this with extreme care and give severe punishments," Fulin's voice was grim.

The three officials pressed their foreheads to the ground once more, backed out of the Presence and hurried away.

Fulin was caught between the devil and the deep blue sea. On the one hand the Manchu nobles and even the Empress Dowager privately chided him for favouring the Hans. On the other hand, the ungrateful Hans were taking a yard for every inch they were given. They even dared to challenge him like this! He was the grandson of Nurhachi, and the son of Abahai, the Emperor of Great Qing, and not to be trifled with.

Fulin paced the terrace outside Yangxin Hall in his agitation. The wind of February had a cold cutting edge, and he shivered in spite of himself. Wu Liangfu bustled over with a coat for his master.

Fulin ignored the kneeling eunuch and quickened his step.

"Your Majesty, please put on a coat, lest you take a chill," Wu Liangfu begged in a solicitous voice.

"Don't bother me!" Fulin shouted. Anyone else would have retreated, but Wu Liangfu was the Emperor's confidant.

"Majesty, please put on a coat. Your slave will be to blame if Your Majesty falls ill...." He broke into an obsequious smile.

Fulin snatched the whip that was tucked in Wu Liangfu's sash and beat the kneeling eunuch. Wu Liangfu knelt there like a rock, not moving. Not a whimper or groan escaped his lips. He kept his obsequious stance until Fulin wearied and threw down his whip.

"Get out of my sight!" he shouted, and went back into the hall.

When the Emperor was gone several young eunuchs came to Wu Liangfu's aid. A few welts had risen on the eunuch's handsome face, and the others feigned solicitude.

Wu Liangfu touched the welts on his face gingerly.

"The Emperor is a real dragon, the Son of Heaven," he said with a wry smile. "This is a manifestation of the dragon's nature. Let it be a lesson."

The others, who had often been whipped by Fulin, made a face as though they understood.

4

Morning audience was over.

As was his custom, Fulin went first to Cining Palace to pay his respects to his mother.

A small retinue accompanied the Emperor. Four imperial guards armed with spears led the way. Guardsmen armed with short swords flanked the Emperor's sedan chair, shaded by feathered fans and a sun-shade of gauzy yellow silk carried by eunuchs. A coterie of young eunuchs responsible for the Emperor's comfort brought up the rear.

Fulin left the audience deeply troubled. He had not been prepared for the sensation caused by the case of Chen Mingxia. The entire court was agog. Both the Manchus and the Hans had their eyes on his every move. The pressure was unbearable.

Ning Wanwo had brought a total of eight charges against

Chen Mingxia. Both Chen and his father were accused of corruption, abuse of their official positions, and conspiring to further their personal ambitions. In addition, Chen was also accused of tampering with imperial edicts. These activities, which were contrary to the common weal, caused father and son to be hated by the masses. The most damaging charge was Chen's advocacy of a return to old Ming ways of dress and grooming. Of all the charges levelled against him, Chen Mingxia admitted his guilt only to the last. Otherwise he insisted upon his innocence. However Ning Wanwo had the corroboration of Academician Liu Zhengzong of the Palace Secretariat Academy. The joint verdict of the Ministries of Personnel, Rites, and Justice, was heard at the morning audience. The mood of the court was clear when the death penalty was demanded. The Princes and the Manchu nobles were pleased. Although most of the Hans remained close-mouthed, their attitude left no doubt that they were crying crocodile tears. The only voice raised in defence of Chen Mingxia was that of a foreigner, Tang Jo-Wang.

The sound of clap-boards, drums, fifes and singing voices greeted the Emperor as he entered Cining Palace. In the east hall a small stage had been erected where the Empress Dowager, accompanied by Grand Concubine Yijing, Lady Kanghui, both concubines of his late father's harem, and Great Grand Concubine Shoukang, of Nurhachi's harem, were watching a puppet show presented by the eunuchs. A morality play called the *Fish Buddha* was reaching its exciting climax. The quarter-life-size puppets were so expertly manipulated that movement, speech and song were completely life-like. At the Emperor's entrance, the Maids of Honour and wives of officials quickly withdrew to the back of the hall where they prostrated themselves.

Fulin greeted his mother and the other ladies each according to her rank. Lady Shoukang was honoured as a great grandmother. Next the Empress Dowager, and finally the Ladies Kanghui and Yijing. After courtly pleasantries had been exchanged, the ladies rose to leave, but the Empress Dowager pressed them to stay. "It's a good play and the performance is excellent. Stay to the end. Today we have fresh pine and gingko nuts from the north to go with our tea."

The white-haired Lady Shoukang was quick to accept, smiling as she resumed her seat. The Ladies Yijing and Kanghui followed suit. The Empress Dowager made her apologies to the ladies and smiling, led Fulin toward the main hall of the palace. At the door she stopped, beckoned to one of the serving wenches and sent her to fetch Madam Tong from the chamber she had just left.

A lavishly gowned lady approached and prostrated herself to the Emperor.

"This is your mother-in-law," the Empress Dowager said to Fulin with a twinkle. "Such ceremony is uncalled for."

It was the custom at court that when a lady of importance was about to give birth, her mother was allowed to be present to assist.

"How fares Lady Tong?" Fulin asked. Lady Tong's mother replied that her term was due within the month.

"This is the first royal birth of a major concubine in the palace," the Empress Dowager smiled at Madam Tong. "Take good care of her...." Madam Tong bowed and backed out of the hall.

Fulin was annoyed. He suspected the introduction of Madam Tong at this time was his mother's subtle way of showing that the family of Tong Tulai was held in high esteem. More pressure was brought to bear on himself.

No sooner had mother and son taken their seats when an eunuch entered to announce the arrival of Prince Jirgalang. The Empress Dowager shot an enquiring look at her son.

"No doubt the Imperial Uncle has come on account of the Chen Mingxia affair," Fulin remarked dryly. The Empress Dowager raised her eyebrows but did not comment.

"I brought the documents of the trial. Perhaps you might want to see them." As Fulin spoke, the eunuch Wu Liangfu sidled forward to present the document case, which the Empress Dowager's personal maid Sumalagu took from him, opened and laid it on the table beside the Empress Dowager. The Empress Dowager ordered the Prince to be admitted, then turning to the Emperor said, "My royal son, I think you had better tell me everything starting with the dispute between Duke An and the imperial kinsman Tong over the appropriation of peasant land. What is the consensus at court?"

On many occasions Fulin discovered that his mother knew the details of major events at court before he mentioned them. No doubt the swarm of ladies and serving women around her were her eyes and ears. Nevertheless, her forthright question still startled him.

"Mother, you know everything already." The Empress Dowager ignored her son's remark.

"Tell me," she insisted.

And so the Emperor related the whole story in great detail from the suicide at Meridian Gate to the trial of Chen Mingxia. The Empress Dowager listened without comment until the tale was told. Then she turned to the documents without uttering a word.

Prince Jirgalang was admitted. As he was about to prostrate himself, the Empress Dowager stopped him, and directed him to be seated on a yellow brocaded cushion to her right. The Prince sat cross-legged, his breath coming in short harsh gasps. He had turned quite pale. The Empress Dowager ordered tea for the Prince. When it was brought, she said in her amiable way, "My Prince Brother must take better care of himself. A man grows old. In future come on horseback instead of on foot. We are family, and there's no need for ceremony."

To be permitted to ride in the Forbidden City was a great honour. Once more the Prince was about to prostrate himself to thank the Empress Dowager, and again he was stopped from doing so. The Prince downed the steaming cup of milk tea. His pulse and breathing gradually became normal.

"Does Your Majesty intend to pardon Chen Mingxia?" the Prince enquired.

Fulin did not reply at once.

"I beg Your Majesties to weigh the case carefully. Chen Mingxia cannot go free. I am aware that Your Majesty values learned men, but the Empire is broad. There is no dearth of brilliant men. On the other hand this man is treacherous, as Your Majesty already knows...." He let the rest trail off.

Prince Jirgalang was hinting at an incident which took place two years earlier. Censor Zhang Xuan had presented a petition in which he accused Chen Mingxia of subversive activities, and nepotism. When the Deliberative Council investigated the complaint, Grand Minister Tan Tai testified on behalf of Chen Mingxia. A counter suit of making false and libellous charges was brought against Zhang Xuan. As a result Zhang Xuan was sentenced to death. Shortly afterwards, Tan Tai was implicated in the misdeeds of the late Regent Dorgon and put to death. Shunzhi then ordered the case against Chen Mingxia reopened. Chen Mingxia did his best to defend himself at his new trial. When all else failed, he threw himself on the Emperor's mercy, pleading for clemency in recognition of his surrender as a Ming official in the early days of the Qing conquest. At that time, Fulin had said to the Grand Ministers of the Council of Nobles, "This is a crafty fellow who does not deserve mercy. However, we have pardoned all those who were connected with the Tan Tai affair. If this man is singled out for punishment, then we would have broken faith with the people." As a result Chen Mingxia was dismissed from his post but his life was spared. However, Fulin admired the man for his learning, and later restored him to favour. Barely a year afterward and he was again embroiled in controversy.

Fulin was displeased with Prince Jirgalang for raking up the past.

He spoke in defence of his actions, saying, "We have taken the example of wise emperors in the past in dealing with this man, weighing his virtues against his faults. Just as there is no gold without impurities, so there is no man without fault."

In fact he had spared Chen Mingxia not so much to keep his word, as on account of the man's abilities.

Jirgalang was no match for Shunzhi when it came to debating historic precedent, for he was barely literate, and still had difficulties with the Han language. However, he also had grave responsibilities to the Empire.

"Your Majesty is correct," the Prince conceded. "However, this time Chen Mingxia's greatest offence is subversion. He is the instigator of the twenty-nine Han officials who banded together in opposition of the proceedings of the Court. Chen Mingxia is the bad apple that will spoil the whole barrel. He must be stopped!"

Fulin hesitated. "Perhaps he could be relieved of his post and banished...."

The Prince sighed.

"Your Majesty is merciful. But a jackal can't be tamed. His continued presence makes me tremble for the safety of the throne. Your Majesty has been kind to him in the past, yet how has he repaid you?" He shot a quick glance at the Empress Dowager, but if the Prince's rhetoric affected her at all, she gave no indication. Jirgalang decided it was time to take the bull by the horns.

"When Prince Dorgon was regent, and Your Majesty was young, did Chen Mingxia not secretly urge him to usurp the throne?"

Fulin gritted his teeth as the Prince continued:

"Dorgon refused, citing family code which outsiders are privy to. However, Chen Mingxia's position at Court rose quickly. He became very influential. But the gods are not blind to the wicked. Dorgon died ... otherwise...." Jirgalang bowed his weary old head without finishing his discourse.

Fulin also bowed his head, lost in thought. Watching him Jirgalang knew his words had found their mark. As far as men were concerned, the slightest connection with Dorgon earned

Fulin's distrust and even hatred. On the other hand, anyone who had suffered at Dorgon's hand earned his unquestioning goodwill. Such was the case with men such as Suoni, Xifu, Aobai and Ebilong, who rose to prominence after Dorgon's death.

The Prince rose to his feet, bowed deeply to the Empress Dowager and the Emperor. He loved his sixteen-year-old nephew and it hurt him to have to stir up painful memories. Yet it was because of that love that he could not remain silent.

"Your Majesty do not distress yourself unduly.... I beg to withdraw...."

After the Prince was gone, the Empress Dowager glanced at her pensive son and said in a quiet voice, "He is a good and loyal courtier. What does my imperial son think now?"

"Chen Mingxia does not deserve to die. Today Mafa Tang petitioned me on his behalf, reminding me that a monarch must be compassionate. I have tried to be wise and merciful in all my undertakings. What right have I to take a man's life!" the Empress Dowager smiled.

"Mafa Tang is a virtuous old man. But a foreigner does not understand our people, the rise and fall of dynasties, or the art of government." Fulin fixed his mother with his fathomless eyes, fighting the rebellion that roiled in his breast. The Empress Dowager, sensing this, continued unperturbed,

"It is not impossible to pardon Chen Mingxia. But if you do, how will you deal with Li Chengxiang? After all he is less important and holds a lesser position than Chen Mingxia. Let us say you pardon them both. What are you going to do about the twenty-nine Han officials? They are less important than Chen and Li put together. Supposing you throw out all three cases, would the Grand Ministers of the Deliberative Council of Nobles agree? Will the Manchu nobles and the generals of the eight banners agree? My imperial son, consider ... who stands behind your throne?"

Fulin shuddered. His long eyelashes quivered against his tightly shut lids.

"Can you trust the Hans?" the Empress Dowager drove her argument home. "My imperial son, time and again I have exorted you to think. You are riding a chariot drawn by six untried horses. One false move and the empire your Grandfather and Father fought so hard for could be dashed to pieces. My son, take care...."

Cold shivers rippled up and down Fulin's spine. Sweat beaded his brow.

"I only thought Chen Mingxia need not die..." he muttered.

The Empress Dowager's smile was kindly when she spoke.

"There is no further need to wrestle with guilt or innocence." She sighed. "Tampering with imperial edicts and conspiracy is enough to put him to death without bringing in the business about returning to the old Ming ways."

Fulin had to admire his mother's sagacity. By putting it the way she had, the whole affair saved his imperial honour. His former acquiescence of letting the hair grow and resuming the old habit of dress needed not be brought up at all. Even the Hans, nobles and people alike could not fault him for passing the death sentence on Chen Mingxia.

Madam Tong passed through Jingren Gate, skirted the intricately carved marble screen in the front courtyard and turned west into a rear courtyard where she found her daughter seated in a pool of sunlight on the verandah of her bed chamber. Serving wenches were feeding birds kept in several fine gold filigreed cages hanging from the beams. Lady Tong's mouth puckered with concentration as she lifted her face to the green parrot with a yellow apron and red beak.

"Oh, my goodness! Just look at you!" her mother exclaimed as soon as she gained the verandah, without bothering with the niceties of protocol.

"Is something wrong?" Lady Tong's eyes widened.

"Your dear uncle has gone to ask the Empress Dowager to

speak to the Emperor about that Chen person, that barbarian from the south. If the Emperor is determined to pardon him, I daren't imagine what might happen!"

Lady Tong was no more than a child when she came to the palace, who missed her mother and cried all the time. Then she stopped crying. Now at fourteen she was pregnant but still tied to her mother's apron strings. In her heart there was only room for the Emperor, the Empress Dowager and her unborn child. She had no interest in anything else. Especially not politics. Since her mother came to the palace she had been instructed in many things but all of it was way over her head. "Oh, what do a few Han officials more or less matter to us?"

"Oh, my precious bane!" fumed the Mother. "It's like talking to a brick wall! How many times have I told Your Ladyship, this southern barbarian by the name of Chen has got together a gang of Han officials to make trouble for us!"

"It's still about the expropriated land, isn't it? Well, the Emperor said it had to be returned, and that's that." There was no doubt that Lady Tong supported the Emperor.

"A hundred odd mu of land is nothing compared to what this barbarian is demanding. He wants the one who offered the land put to death, and the county officials punished. It's quite clear his real target is the likes of us. If he succeeds we bannermen won't have a pot to piss in...."

Lady Tong's childish unconcern goaded her mother into a fresh outburst. "My little sweetheart, this concerns you!"

"Me?" Lady Tong arched her brows in amazement.

"Who else!" The mother helped her daughter into the bed chamber, and saw to it that she was comfortable on her thick, soft bed. Then she dismissed the serving women, and drawing a divan close to the bed sat down. When she spoke, she kept her voice low. "Now, tell me you don't want to be empress?"

The mother's question struck a nerve. Lady Tong blushed to the roots of her hair. Although she was very young, and childish in many ways, she was aware of her position in the palace. Since the Empress was removed she had been waking in the dead of night and praying the gods would see fit to make her the successor. Instinctively she kept this secret and fervent wish of her heart to herself, fearing that if it were known she would lose the love of the Emperor and his kindly but imperious mother. More than anything she feared the fate of the former Empress would be hers if she ever fell from grace. To be banished to some remote corner of the palace, forgotten among the multitude of concubines was unthinkable. Yet her mother had discovered her secret and what is more, put it into words. She was on the point of tears.

"There's nothing to blush about!" Nothing escaped Madam Tong's knowing gaze. "Although the Emperor already has one son and two daughters, their mothers are nobodies. You are the first lady of rank to conceive. By the shape of your belly, I would swear it's a boy! Mothers bask in the reflected glory of sons. Thus it has been for millenia, and so it will be now."

Lady Tong frowned, and gently stroked her belly in which a little devil was turning somersaults. Actually her mother's remarks were superfluous. She had thought the same thing a million times or more. "Your becoming the next empress is almost an accomplished fact but for this barbarian. If the Emperor pardons him, I'll tell you what it means to us. It means your dream of being empress is over!"

Lady Tong was shocked. She had never thought that far ahead. "Can you blame me for being nervous while you go on as though nothing's afoot? You'll have to bend the Emperor's ear a little, lest he gets hoodwinked by that barbarian." Lady Tong pulled the coverlets over her face, and spoke in a voice that was barely audible.

"There are rules in the palace about pregnancies. The Emperor hasn't been here in half a month. Besides, concubines are forbidden to interfere with politics...." Madam Tong fell silent for a moment, then with a deep sigh she resumed, "If this beautiful thing goes sour because of the barbarian, I swear I won't die in peace! The thing is I can't figure out the hold he has on so many people! What is the spell that makes them forget their ancestors and their traditions? If you ask me, Duke An is in cahoots with them...."

"Do be quiet! Anyone hearing you would think we are ignorant people!" Lady Tong's sharp tone brought the older woman up short. Taking another tack, she bowed and in accordance with protocol begged her daughter's forgiveness. A serving woman came in to say that Madam Tong's serving maid had come for her. Madam Tong half rose, then sat down again, whispering to her daughter, "It must be word from your uncle." Lady Tong pushed herself up.

"Bring the woman in!" she ordered.

The serving woman who was admitted first prostrated herself to Lady Tong, then to her own mistress.

"Well, what's the news?" Madam Tong demanded. The serving woman's eyes went from mother to daughter, and their agitation infected her. She became tongue-tied, and with great effort stammered, "Mindful that he was first to swear allegiance to the Emperor ... and of his many years' of service...." The serving woman stopped, gasping for breath. Mother and daughter blanched. Madam Tong raised a hand to strike the servant, who gathered her wits and blundered on, "... His Majesty has ordered Chang Mingxia to be hanged ... instead of beheaded...." In the silence that followed, colour seeped back into Lady Tong's cheeks. She shut her eyes, smiling, as she sank back into her pillows. Madam Tong slapped her thigh with glee.

"That's our good Emperor!" she chortled. "A true grandson of Nurhachi!"

For a split second she had reverted to the wild exuberence of the tribeswoman that she was. Then turning again to the serving woman she demanded in a severe tone, "Is there anything more?"

The serving woman thought for a moment.

"Censor Li Chengxiang has been banished. The twenty-nine Han officials have been either dismissed, demoted or fined...."

Madam Tong could barely contain her joy.

"Go home at once and fetch me some fresh clothes," she ordered the servant, shoving her out the room. "But I want you back in the palace tonight."

The servant scampered away in search of the eunuch in charge of identification for re-entering the palace.

With no one else in the room, Madam Tong gave full rein to her pent-up emotions.

"Now your father will be the Imperial Father-in-law. I suppose that makes me the Imperial Mother-in-law. And your brothers will be proper Imperial Uncles. I don't expect us to be given any fancy titles, like Prince, and so forth. A dukedom would do nicely! All that land at Yongping Prefecture will be undisputably ours!" She took her daughter's hand between both of hers, and continued tenderly, "You were born to greatness, my dear. Several Daoist monks predicted it. One old buddhist even came right out and said you were born to be Empress. We knew but we kept it quiet. However, we've prayed for this day ever since you came to court...."

"Your Majesty, food is served!"

The eunuch in charge of food service prostrated himself. Fulin, who had been moodily gazing at a potted peony, wandered into the East Chamber. Two serving eunuchs stood on either side of a table on which an array of food had been temptingly laid out. Four other eunuchs from Yangxin Hall stood at attention before the table as he took his seat. The servers quickly lifted the lids of the covered dishes, presenting the food for Fulin's inspection, watching for the least flicker of interest. However, Fulin showed no interest in any of the food.

Wu Liangfu sidled forward and signalled the others to stand back with a glance.

"Your Majesty has been working hard for hours," he began

with an obsequious smile. "Do have a little food ... just a taste."

He pointed out the dish of shredded swallow's nest cooked with slivers of chicken, ham and black fungus; a sizzling pot of swallow's nest cooked in a broth of chicken and bamboo shoots; a plate of roasted deer meat next to fried chicken and sun-dried mutton, a famous northern delicacy. Then there was a bowl of venison cooked with garlic sprouts, a tribute from the ancestral temple. Tiny steamed buns, soft and spongy; skimmed milk and yogurt....

Wu Liangfu's recital, like an over-anxious waiter of a restaurant, finally wrung a reluctant smile from Fulin.

"You greedy good-for-nothing!" Fulin scolded with mock anger. Wu Liangfu quickly prostrated himself.

"I wouldn't dare. If only Your Majesty would take a little food, your slave would gladly go without for three days!"

"Spare me the fancy talk!" Fulin was half annoyed but flattered nevertheless. He took a few mouthfuls from the proffered dishes and laid down his chopsticks.

"Send these dishes to the ladies of the harem," he ordered with a frown. "Lady Tong will get two extra dishes." The eunuchs quickly packed the food containers in padded warmers and carried them to the ladies of the East and West Palaces.

Anticipating his master's thoughts, Wu Liangfu remarked, "Lady Tong is due any day now. It would be a great blessing for great Qing if she bears a son...."

Why must she have a son, thought Fulin? Perhaps Lady Tong sees herself as the future Empress.... What right has she?

Other things weighed on his mind.

That morning, after visiting the Empress Dowager, Fulin quickly wrote the decree condemning Chen Mingxia to death, and settling the punishment to be meted out to the twenty-nine Han officials. When the decree left his hand and the whole affair was finally behind him, he felt a rush of relief. Still his thoughts kept wandering back to Chen Mingxia inspite of himself, though other matters occupied him. He realized with a pang, the ablest of his courtiers, the only man with whom he could discuss poetry and history, the dashing man who stood head and shoulders above all others, would be no more. That thought filled him with rage and anguish at his own impotence. He did not blame his mother for she meant well. But he couldn't stand his Uncle Jirgalang who had tried to compel him by bringing up Dorgon and using his hatred for Dorgon. On the surface Jirgalang acted for the good of the Empire. In fact he was motivated by self interest. He attacked Chen Mingxia only to protect Tong Tulai, the husband of his niece. And by protecting Tong Tulai, he was paving the way for Lady Tong to become the next empress....

All these things that lurked in the nether regions of Fulin's mind were brought into focus by Wu Liangfu's casual remark.

Fulin faced the bookcases hidden behind a blue silk curtain which contained histories of past dynasties; records of the rise and fall of emperors, generals and ministers; power-mongering, bartered pride, and the folly of emperors who allowed themselves to be manipulated like puppets on a string. But he was made of sterner stuff. He would not be used by anyone! He returned to his desk with a purposeful step, hands clasped behind his back. He found the two documents, picked up his vermillion brush and began to write.

When Madam Tong's serving woman returned to Jingren Palace it was after dark. Meanwhile the Emperor's gift of food had only added to the euphoric mood of mother and daughter. There was a dish of swallow's nest cooked with shredded chicken, ham and black fungus in an enamal bowl decorated with the character *fu*, symbol of happiness and prosperity. A duck stewed with yams was served in a red bowl. A yellow platter with purple dragons contained dainty pastries. A milkcake was served on a five-inch plate decorated with yellow dragons. Finally there were four little silver plates of appetizers. Lady Tong dutifully tasted every dish. At nightfall the lavish tableware was still spread on the table waiting to be cleared by the eunuch from the imperial kitchens.

Lady Tong was complacent. Her mother was exhilarated. Surveying the fine tableware she babbled, oblivious of who might hear her.

"Think of it! In the morning he sentenced the barbarian to be hanged, and at noon he sent all this food! Don't you see what's in his heart?" Her voice grew loud, throwing caution to the wind. "Look at this tableware! Using this yellow dragon plate, and that purple dragon platter must mean something! And it isn't trifling either! Oh! What are you doing here?" She wheeled on the servant standing in the doorway, and beckoned her to enter.

"Well, is everybody happy at home? Your Master isn't pulling a long face anymore, I warrant. And it's all reflected glory from her ladyship.... Well, say something." The servant prostrated herself and stammered, "My lady ... my lady...."

"Tell me, whatever it is."

Nothing could spoil Madam Tong's happy mood.

"My lady, an imperial edict has been sent to the Master. All expropriated land has to be returned. All county and district officials who failed to investigate the people's complaint are to be dismissed and will be investigated. The Master's income has been confiscated for three months, and he will be demoted by two grades...."

Madam Tong struck the serving woman across the face with the flat of her hand.

"You cheap liar!" she shrieked stamping her feet. "I'll flog you to death!" The servant grovelled on the floor, sobbing, "Your slave wouldn't dare mis-represent an imperial edict...." Lady Tong took a sharp intake of air, biting her nails, as tears spilled down her face. The mother's brain was in a whirl. She left the servant to comfort her daughter.

"Never mind. Don't cry," the mother cooed. "You mustn't upset yourself. It might injure the baby. We mustn't believe everything an ignorant serving woman says...."

"How are you, Sister Tong?" A clear voice tinkling with laughter called from the courtyard outside. In a moment Lady Duan of Yonghe Palace and her sister, Lady Gong of Jingyang Palace, appeared in the doorway. The two daughters of Horqin Mongol, dressed in pink and dark blue silk robes in the Mongolian style, seldom visited Jingren Palace. Since Lady Tong became pregnant these two ladies became even less friendly. However, because of the Empress Dowager's strict adherence to family code, neither dared to be openly hostile. What is their errand, Lady Tong wondered. Lady Tong shifted her ungainly body to a more comfortable position, and invited the visitors to be seated on the short kang under the south-facing window. The ladies exchanged pleasantries while servants quickly plumped the orange-coloured cushions and backrests. When the ladies were comfortably seated, buttered tea was served.

Lady Duan's quick glance took in the dishes on the table.

"My dear Sister Tong, the eunuchs of the imperial kitchens cleared my table ages ago!" she remarked with a meaningful glance at the remnants of the meal.

"Mine too. The dishes His Majesty sent today were quite delicious," Lady Gong chimed in with a smirk. Lady Tong glanced at her mother in spite of herself. The mother glared at the visitors, seething with anger. The two visitors exchanged knowing glances. It was Lady Duan who brought the conversation round.

"My sister and I have something important to tell you...."

Lady Kong cut her off, "Don't blurt it out. Let Sister Tong guess what it is...." Lady Tong forced a smile and shook her head, "I'm afraid I can't..." she murmured in a childish voice. Lady Duan's smile broadened. "We are going to have a new empress. Guess who it's going to be?" The two ladies fixed Lady Tong with their eyes. Lady Tong shuddered at their smiles. Her cheeks turned chalky; her heart hammered against her ribs, and her palms were damp with perspiration.

"I don't know," she stammered in a strange croaking voice.

Lady Duan's eyes glittered with malice as she continued, still smiling. "It's another young lady from Korqin Mongol like us, our Empress Dowager's own grand niece, and Lady Jing's niece."

"The imperial edict was issued just this afternoon," added Lady Gong.

There was a roaring in Lady Tong's ears, and cold sweat trickled down her back. The rest of the conversation washed over her. She forced herself to smile, struggling to keep up appearances until the two ladies took their leave. Their laughing words carried back to the room. "Huh, she thought she could climb to the top because she's got a bun in the oven!"

"Well, she's got her come uppance now!"

Lady Tong was assailed by a wave of nausea which left her dazed and swooning.

That night the Imperial Physician was summoned. The eunuch on night watch and the Imperial Pharmacist were also roused. Lady Tong's groans had turned to piercing screams. A Manchu witch doctor with a strange-looking cap on her head and bells attached to her sash, dipped and whirled to the rhythm of a drum, chanting all the while in a high reedy voice. As the thud of the drums and the jangling of the bells became faster the dance and the chanting became more frenzied. The witch danced through Jingren Gate, across the courtyard, and onto the terrace outside the bed chamber. The din could not drown out Lady Tong's cries or the mother's tearful words of comfort.

In the hour before dawn, said to be the darkest of the night, an infant's cry ripped the air. It was a vehement cry, full of rage and protest. But clear too, as though the newborn was sucking all the sweetness and the pain of the world into its tiny being as it began its journey through life. Though in time he would perform great deeds and be immortalized in history, yet this paean to life was no different from that of lesser beings.

The Morning Star rose above the Forbidden City and the eighteenth day of the third month in the eleventh year of Shunzhi dawned.

5

On the sixteenth day of the sixth month of that same year Fulin celebrated his second wedding with great pomp and circumstance. Although the continuous war with the last Ming adherents Zheng Chenggong and Zhu Youlang had dangerously depleted the imperial coffers, the luxury and extravagance of this second wedding rivalled the first.

An Imperial Edict of Joy had gone out not only to the people of the capital but to the whole realm. This was designated a day of rejoicing. Everyone was commanded to wear red and green, the colours of happiness, and houses were festooned with lanterns and streamers as an expression of universal felicity. Thirteen new yamen or government offices were created and bailiffs led by eunuchs went into the poorer districts distributing wedding pastries. This caused a great disturbance in which many people were injured. The cries of the injured mixed with the tumultuous merry-making created an unprecedented din.

A festive air enveloped the Forbidden City. All the footpaths were covered with thick red carpets. Fresh images of Door Gods and couplets expressing wedded bliss were painted and glued to every door. All the gates and towers inside Meridian Gate were hung with great red lanterns. Colourful bunting, on which the double happiness symbol was repeated over and over, fluttered from the Gate of Supreme Harmony, and the hall which bore the same name. The Palace of Heavenly Purity and the Palace of Earthly Tranquility were also a riot of coloured banners and streamers.

From the Hall of Supreme Harmony extending to Tiananmen (Gate of Heavenly Peace) was a mass of colour as banners, flags, fans, and sun-shades rioted with the golden flash of sword, battle ax, halberd, spear and lance. Large and small chariots with yokes of wood or jade stood beside the elephants and horses used to draw them. Flanking the Meridian Gate were four huge elephants which would lead the cavalcade and four elephants carrying jars decorated with gold and precious gems and pearls. The fierce aspect of these gigantic creatures were enough to frighten any timid soul. A band of musicians was stationed on two sides of the front terrace of the Hall of Supreme Harmony. Another group was placed just inside the Gate, while a third band of fifes and drums was set near the elephants south of Meridian Gate. At the start of the wedding ceremony the musicians would play in unison, blanketing the entire Forbidden City with a happy din.

Outside Cining Palace a retinue of several hundred waited on the Empress Dowager. Inside, gathered the principal ladies of the various palaces and the ladies of the late Emperor's harem. Ranged on either side of the Empress Dowager according to rank, they waited in silence for the ringing of the great bell signalling the commencement of the ceremony.

The Empress Dowager was seated on a tall throne, in full regalia. On her head was a crown encrusted with three tiers of precious stones. In the centre was a large ruby nestled in pearls. Nine gold phoenixes, set with pearls, decorated the sides of the crown, their beaks held five strands of pearls which fell level to the forehead at the front, while at the back they trailed shoulder level. A pale blue waistcoat embroidered with patterns of mountains, ocean, sun and moon, dragon and phoenix, and a matching cape were worn over the court robe of dark purple with sleeves in the shape of horse hoofs. The Empress Dowager was dignified but not intimidating. In spite of the pomp of the occasion she still exuded a natural warmth.

The bell on top of Meridian Gate sounded. Spritely music of fifes preceded the mace bearers out of Longzong Gate. Behind them followed the Minister of Rites, leading the splendidly dressed Emperor toward the Empress Dowager's palace. While the musicians and the retinue remained outside Cining Gate, the Emperor entered the palace. The concubines, Maids of Honour of various grades, eunuchs and serving wenches prostrated themselves. The Empress Dowager, flanked by the Ladies Yijing and Kanghui, concubines of his late father, received the Emperor's formal greeting.

Mother and son faced each other smiling. In the Dowager's smile there was a hint of compassion and encouragement. In the son's there was an answer of understanding and resignation.

The Empress Dowager remarked: "This girl has a warm, loving nature. She knows her place. Now that there is a suitable empress, I trust you two will live in harmony. I too can rest in peace."

Fulin bowed to the waist and replied with the proscribed speech of acceptance full of poetic platitudes. But he ended his speech with words of his own: "As my Imperial Mother has commanded, so it shall be done." Fulin bowed once more and withdrew. The musicians struck up another spritely air, but Fulin's last words lingered in the Empress Dowager's ears. Ripples of disquietude and foreboding spread through her. She shut her eyes for a moment to quiet the fluttering of her heart.

The white-haired Prince Jirgalang and Prince Chengze (Shuosai) were led in by the mace bearer to escort the Empress Dowager to the Hall of Preserving Harmony where she would formally receive the new Empress' mother and the princesses and courtladies. Afterwards, the Empress Dowager would receive the Emperor and the Court and hold a banquet for the Empress' mother.

The Empress Dowager rose from her throne and, followed by the ladies in order of their rank, proceeded toward the Hall of Preserving Harmony where the wedding ceremony would be held. As she left the room, she suddenly stopped to look back at Lady Tong. She looked thin and haggard, and terribly out of place beside the other ladies.

Smiling she said in a quiet voice, "Lady Kang, you have not recovered since your confinement. It is our wish that you return to your quarters and rest. I will order the feast to be brought to you later."

Lady Tong had been given the title Lady Kang after the birth of her son. Her eyes brimmed at the Empress Dowager's concern. On a festive occasion tears were not permitted. Still there was a suggestion of tears in her voice when she thanked the Empress Dowager for her kindness.

Outside Cining Palace music rose to a crescendo. Lady Tong knew that the Empress Dowager had entered her sedan chair. She waited a few moments longer till the Empress Dowager was out of sight, then helped by two of her serving women, she staggered from Cining Palace. On this day she was forbidden to cut across the centre of the Forbidden City to her own quarters. Today the centre was the exclusive domain of the Dowager, the Emperor and the Empress. Lady Kang was merely a concubine of the third degree. Between her and the Empress there were two more hurdles, the positions of Precious Concubine and Imperial Concubine. Both those positions had been left vacant by the Emperor. Her ambitious dreams had come to nought.

She trudged on in a northerly direction, along narrow passages between high walls topped by yellow tiles, flanked by high towers on whose protruding eaves nine mythic beasts clawed at the sky. A sliver of blue sky showed between the top of the high walls and buildings looming beyond. Their footsteps crept eerily up and down the walls. They had gone to the northernmost corner of the Forbidden City without encountering another living soul. Had it not been a bright sunny day, this would have been a grim and frightful place.

By the time they reached the Imperial Garden Lady Tong was exhausted by the heat of the day and the heaviness of her garments. The garden, shaded by ancient pines and cedars, was a cool oasis. A breeze sent a shiver through her fragile frame.

On one side of the garden was the Pavilion of a Thousand Autumns. On the opposite end was the Pavilion of Ten Thousand Springs. When she first caught the Emperor's fancy this used to be their trysting place. She had taken the names of these two pavilions as good omens. However, a year later all was changed. In spite of the birth of a son, she was out of favour.

Fulin had taken another empress. Nothing could change her fate now. Perhaps soon he would take a Precious Concubine and Imperial Concubine, and many other ladies of lower rank. All of them could give him sons and daughters. It was the hope and indeed the requirement of the imperial family to have numerous children and grandchildren. Why else were the two gates to the Garden named Gate of a Hundred Sons, and Gate of a Thousand Infants?

The bell and drum atop Meridian Gate were struck in unison proclaiming the arrival of the new Empress. The sound shattered Lady Tong's reverie. The happiest, sweetest year of her life, and all her dreams and ambition were dashed to pieces, vanished as a waking dream, gone forever like the water in the moat. All that remained was a three-month-old infant. In all the vastness of the Forbidden City, this tiny being was her only comfort....

She did not dare to blame anyone for her troubles, or even grumble at capricious fate. Resentment was an unforgivable sin in a royal concubine. Not to be envious or complaining were virtues to be cultivated. At that moment Lady Tong longed only to see her son, who, according to the time and date of his birth, was the third son of Emperor Shunzhi.

As soon as he was born, the infant had been given into the care of a wet nurse. It was the custom of the Qing Court that Princes and Princesses could not be brought up by their natural mother; though some concubines were permitted to mother children of other ladies of the court, or children of members of the Imperial family as a special favour.

In this the Qing had taken the warning of an ancient adage to heart: "A son is ennobled by the reflected glory of the mother, and vice versa." These inhuman measures were taken purely to forestall nepotism and conspiracies against the regime.

Thereafter Lady Tong had seen the child only once, when he was a full month old, and taken by the wet nurse to meet his grandmother.

This was an opportunity to visit her child while the court was otherwise engaged.

She tucked a few loose strands of hair into her elaborate chignon, shook the dust which only existed in her imagination from her robes, and walked unaided toward East Qiongyuan Gate.

Lady Tong turned a corner and headed east without a backward glance. Her Maids of Honour exchanged looks of consternation and hurried after their mistress wondering if she was taking a roundabout route to her quarters.

At the Gate of a Thousand Infants, Lady Tong stopped for a moment then turned abruptly northward. The Maids of Honour cried out in alarm when they realized where she was headed. They prostrated themselves before her. "My Lady!" they cried in remonstration. Lady Tong cocked an eyebrow at them, and her almond-shaped eyes flashed fire.

"Out of my way, or I'll have you flogged!" The Maids of Honour fell back. Lady Tong went through a gate, and instinct led her to her destination. There, on the verandah a nurse dandled a fair, fat infant on her lap. In honour of the imperial wedding, the child was dressed in a tiny yellow satin robe with a dragon embroidered on it. Tufts of soft black down covered its head. "My child! My child!" Lady Tong cried inwardly as her heart filled of bitter tears.

The child looked around and, fixing Lady Tong with its gleaming black eyes, stretched out its tiny dimpled hands to her. Something snapped in Lady Tong. She snatched the child from the nurse and clasped it to her breast, showering it with kisses, laughing and weeping at the same time.

Being little more than a child herself, Lady Tong was not much moved when the child was taken from her at birth. It meant no more to her than the loss of a favourite toy or an ornament, so obsessed was she with her own precarious fortunes. At this moment the dormant mothering instinct emerged. This little bundle of soft living flesh was part of her. The touch of its cheek against hers, the feel of its hand and the incomprehensible noises it made sent ripples of happiness and sweetness through her. Tears flooded her cheeks as she examined every feature. In the shape of its face and nose, and in the arch of its brow she saw him. She also saw herself in the shape of the child's eyes and mouth.

The startled nurse and the two wet nurses present prostrated themselves before Lady Tong not knowing what to do. The two Maids of Honour made frantic signals at the nurse. It took the woman a moment to grasp the situation. When she did she banged her head to the ground several times and beat a fast retreat. Soon the eunuch on duty appeared with the staff of forty responsible for the care of the infant Prince. The whole assemblage of eight nurses, eight wet nurses, four each of seamstresses, laundresses, servants in charge of lights, cooks, and eunuchs who were gate keepers, and even scavengers prostrated themselves.

The eunuch on duty said in an unctuous voice, "The Third Lord has been happy and healthy. My Lady can rest assured." Lady Tong took no notice of him, stroking the child's black downy hair.

"My Lady, please leave. If the overlords hear of this, your slave will be in trouble." Lady Tong looked through the man, oblivious to his pleading as he banged his head against the ground. "My Lady have mercy!" The forty men and women responsible for the Prince's comfort wailed and banged their heads on the ground, trembling for the livelihood which they were in danger of losing.

A Maid of Honour pleaded, "My Lady, let us leave before others hear of this...." She tried to take the child from Lady Tong, however, the little Prince who had never known a mother's touch, perversely clung to his mother's neck, pressing his body against her breast. Lady Tong trembled violently, and she could not bear to give up the child.

The music floating from the front hall of the palace indicated that the wedding banquet would soon be over.

"Hurry, My Lady," pleaded the Maid of Honour. "We mustn't tarry. Once the other ladies return, we'll be lost!"

"My Lady, have mercy!" cried the assembled servants on their knees. One of the Maids of Honour motioned the chief wet nurse to come forward. The woman unbuttoned her blouse as she approached, exposing a round full breast. The child was at last lured away. Cradled in the arms of the wet nurse, it suckled noisily, but its eyes were fixed on its mother.

Lady Tong could not bear to stay any longer. As she stepped across the threshold the child let out a piercing wail. Lady Tong stumbled and almost fell. A Maid of Honour caught her. Lady Tong gritted her teeth and stumbled away with her head bowed, putting as much distance as she could between herself and the child. But the wailing seemed to pursue her down the narrow alleys and across her own threshold, where she crumpled to the floor. Still the child's keening wail sounded in her ears.

The banquet was over. After the Emperor had taken leave of the Empress Dowager, and she had departed, he headed for the Palace of Earthly Tranquility attended by eunuchs carrying the imperial mace and red lanterns.

Fulin walked at a leisurely pace. He was mulling over the banquet. He had tried in vain to spot some depression from Prince Jirgalang during the festivities. The Prince's enthusiasm for the wedding surprised him. Indeed Prince Jirgalang had drunk a little too freely so that the red glow of liquor made him appear years younger. Fulin had beckoned him to approach the throne, and remarked,

"Uncle, you seem to be enjoying yourself."

"Indeed, Your Majesty," replied the Prince. "To tell the truth, I had my doubts about this match in view of Your Majesty's unhappy marriage. But the Empress Dowager's wisdom saved the day. Horqin Mongol has historic ties with Great Qing by marriage. This marriage will safeguard the northern frontiers as well as our ancestral tombs. The Empress Dowager is indeed a great blessing to Great Qing!"

Though drink loosened the tongue of the usually taciturn Prince he remained as lucid as ever.

The year before, Duke An had been ordered to the border town of Guihua to ward off a possible rebellion by Khalkha Mongol. It was only because Horqin Mongol, the most renowned of the forty-nine Mongolian banners, was loyal to Great Qing, Khalkha Mongol was convinced to back down and present tribute as usual. This happy turn of events freed Duke An to return to the capital. The defense against Ming adherents in the south would not have been possible without a stable north. Jirgalang smiled complacently as he stressed.

"Your Majesty has acted for the common weal." The Prince's ruddy cheeks framed by silvery hair glowed with undeniable loyalty. Fulin was convinced he had not been scheming to raise Lady Tong to be empress. Regretting his suspicions, Fulin called for his own gold goblet to be filled and offered it to the aging Prince.

Fulin then summoned Tang Jo-Wang.

"Mafa ... I'm married again...." He had to force the last words out. Both recalled their conversation about a new empress that day in the church. The Jesuit nodded, his eyes full of understanding and compassion for the troubled young Emperor. "I don't know her, Mafa. I have no choice."

"Majesty, it is your duty. Love the lady as much as you can.... I wish you joy...." Tang Jo-Wang bowed and withdrew. Though the interview was brief Fulin sensed his unspoken regret and sympathy.

As Fulin approached his wedding chamber the voices of the two old courtiers sounded in his ears. A melancholy descended upon him. He heaved a sigh as he crossed the threshold of the Palace of Earthly Tranquility.

Fulin surveyed the bridal chamber from the doorway. Under the south-facing window was a wide kang on which were placed two thrones finely carved of sandalwood separated by a table on which were laid jade talisman and vases of porcelain and enamel. The symbols of double happiness were repeated across the crimson walls, on lanterns and lamps. The east end of the north wall was occupied by a simple arrangement of chairs. The wedding bed hung with colourful drapery was placed at the west end. The red mattress of fine satin was decorated with dragon and phoenix and a symbol of double happiness at one end of which was placed a folded up rich coverlet of bright yellow and deep red. A jar containing jewels, gold, silver, and grains of rice sat on the coverlet. The bride dressed from head to toe in red sat demurely at the edge of the bed with bowed head. The red of her costume blended with the red of the chamber in an oppressive sameness that reminded him of his first wedding night. The oppressive atmosphere made him gasp for breath. Even the new bride seemed to have come from the past. He had married another complete stranger whom he had never met before. Furthermore, she was the niece of the former Empress.

Would she be as haughty and shrewish as the other, with whom he had spent three stormy years, he wondered. He doubted whether this one would be better. She was just as big boned.

He started to leave. The eunuchs hurried to cluster round him, falling on their knees. "Your Majesty mustn't..." they chorused.

Fulin frowned, then broke into a wistful smile. "What's the matter with you? It's hot and I need a breath of air. That's all. Don't follow me like a shadow!"

Fulin strolled along the verandah of the Palace of Earthly Tranquility. The red and gold of the twilight sky touched the roofs and turrets of the Forbidden City glittering against an indigo sky. A flock of pigeons wheeled overhead, their tinkling bells echoing across the sky as they melted into the molten mass of the setting sun. The sight of them gave his spirits a momentary lift which made the emptiness in his heart all the more poignant.

An errant breeze caressed his cheeks, laden with the scent of jasmine and tuberose. Fulin drew a deep breath, and murmured to himself, "Where does the scent of flowers come from?"

A voice, deep and sweet as a flute, answered out of the scented air. "How can I forget the south." The voice went on to recite an erotic Tang-dynasty poem in Chinese. "It has always been in my thoughts."

In the palace, from the Empress Dowager down to the lowliest eunuch and serving wench, everyone spoke Manchu. Fulin was immersed in the Manchu language from dawn to dusk, thus the sound of Chinese was like a breath of fresh air, or a ray of moonlight in a pitch-dark room. He was deeply moved, and leaned against a thick red-lacquered pillar to listen, hiding from the speaker.

"Oh, one doesn't crave anything else when one has tasted of the melons of Wuxi or the loquats of Lake Tai, you would not crave anything else...."

Fulin recognized the mellifluous voice of Lady Liu Sanxiu, wife of Prince Yu, whom the Manchu nicknamed the Barbarian Lady, for she was from south of the Yangtze. When Prince Yu led his army south, Liu Sanxiu was a pretty young widow who had been abducted by the army. Her beauty, cleverness, and worldliness brought her to the Prince's attention. The Prince married her and she bore him a son, became the head of his household, and was given a title. From then on she became a frequent guest of the Empress Dowager. Now she was one of four ladies who were attendants at the wedding feast.

"It's time His Majesty came in...." The other voice was youthful, soft and appealing.

"When His Majesty comes, be careful not to speak Chinese, lest you offend," the Barbarian Lady cautioned.

"But right now, we're quite alone, aren't we?" There was laughter in the youthful retort.

Although Fulin had recognized the wife of Prince Yu at once, her lavishly costumed companion who stood with her against the railings of the terrace was a complete stranger. For a moment the young woman's fragile beauty was caught in a shaft of light from the westering sun. As Fulin stepped from his hiding place their eyes met and locked. Fulin's heart lurched against his ribs so that he could hardly breathe. His pulse raced; his cheeks blazed. It was an effort to gather his wits. It seems his very soul had momentarily left his body, for she was the most beautiful creature he had ever seen. Her beauty was not merely physical. It extended beyond a complexion as delicate as a peach blossom, or the pearly whiteness of her teeth, or the fine chiselled nose, the coral pink mouth, the vivacious eyes. Her beauty was in her bearing, her intelligence, her sensitivity and sincerity. She was peerless among the Manchu ladies of the court.

Lady Liu Sanxiu, fearing they had been overheard conversing in Chinese, prostrated herself. Her companion hastily followed suit.

"Majesty, it's late. Time to go inside." The voice seemed to come from a great distance. Fulin was enthralled.

Fulin entered the wedding chamber in spite of himself. Everything from that moment on became a blur. Later he would recall sitting on the wedding bed and eating the little pastries that symbolize many offspring only because the unknown lady had offered him the chopsticks. He would recall watching her dressing the Empress' hair. He would recall the wedding supper when he and the Empress faced each other across a table laden with food. Though he would have no impression of what he ate, he would recall the auspicious names of the contents of each dish that was presented, because she announced them in her inimitable fashion. He was oblivious of everything else. The beauty of the tableware, the incessant music provided by two guardsmen and their wives from the terrace outside did not touch him. His whole being was immersed in the beautiful stranger.

Fulin forgot time, and place, the three other ladies serving him, even the Empress, his bride, and that this was his wedding night. He was aware only of her. It was the dignity of his position that shielded him from the eyes of the others in the room.

The nuptial meal, the final ritual of the wedding, was over. The Emperor of Great Qing had a new Empress.

The four ladies prostrated themselves in preparation to leave.

"Must you go?" Fulin stammered.

Those vivacious eyes flashed with amusement, and a faint smile tugged at her lips. Fulin blushed. The Barbarian Lady saved the day by decorously reminding the Emperor it was his wedding night.

The ladies quickly retired. Left alone Fulin realized the awful irony of his position. On his wedding night, he had no thought of his bride. Instead his heart had been captured by a woman he had just met. The stranger had taken a part of him with her, leaving an empty space within his breast.

He glanced at the bride who sat beside him, her head bowed demurely. The more he thought about it the more she resembled her aunt. Her body encased in ceremonial robes was shaped like a barrel. The chalky face was like an adobe wall smeared with white-wash. Suddenly he felt as though he had swallowed something disagreeable. A wave of nausea assailed him. He rose and went outside. The light had gone from the sky, and a myriad stars gleamed in the firmament, some bright, others dim; some glowed with a blue flame, others with yellow; too many to count. In the east a full moon rose, silvery, cold as ice, its light obscuring the stars.

She was like the moon, obscuring everything before her, lighting such a blaze in his heart that his soul trembled. Malicious Fate had dealt him another blow for the bride waiting in the bed chamber should have been her.

Fulin sighed in the moonlight.

"Your Majesty, go to bed," Wu Liangfu whispered as he prostrated himself.

"You're still here?" Seeing Wu was like having a friend near. The Emperor helped the young eunuch to his feet, and asked, "Who were the four ladies who served supper?" Wu Liangfu rolled his eyes. "I think Your Majesty means the youngest one. Has Your Majesty forgotten? Last year when Your Majesty was selecting beauties for the harem she was one whom the Empress took exception to."

Fulin remembered it as if it were yesterday. Two hundred girls ranging in age from thirteen to seventeen had been brought before the Emperor and Empress in groups of five. The choice had to be unanimous. At fourteen, and being the youngest of her group, she stood out among the older girls. The Empress was quick to seize upon his interest, and set about to thwart him. This group was too old, she said. Their posture and the way they walked swaying their hips was contrary to protocol. Furthermore, they were barbarian to the core, and therefore, unsuitable. Fulin was swift to rebut her. A quarrel ensued. The eunuch in charge quickly dismissed the girls before the quarrel went out of control.

No wonder she seemed familiar. She would be fifteen, now; a year younger than himself, Fulin thought.

"She is now..." Fulin started to say. Wu Liangfu cut in before he could finish.

"Begging Your Majesty's pardon, the Empress Dowager has given her to Your Majesty's eleventh brother."

"You lie!" cried Fulin seizing Wu Liangfu and shaking him till his teeth rattled.

"Forgive me," whimpered the eunuch, "but it is the truth. She is Your Majesty's eleventh brother's wife."

Fulin released the trembling eunuch. It was as though ice water had been dashed in his face.

Why should Abahai's fourteen-year-old eleventh son, Bomubogur, born of the Grand Concubine Lady Yijing, be so blessed?

Why was Fate toying with him?

Fulin's mouth filled with bile. The only woman who had ever kindled the flame of love within him belonged to another. Though he had three thousand beauties in his harem, and all the honours and riches befitting the Son of Heaven, he was destitute.

Part II

In the green dappled shadows of the maple grove, Liu Tongchun took out the silk purse that Menggu had made for him. He traced the patterns of water, lotus pods, lotus blossoms on intertwined stems and a pair of affectionate mandarin duck and drake, and his heart fluttered with anticipation.

He was an orphan brought up by Master Liu who lived in Malan Village of Yongping Prefecture. From Master Liu he learned the art of acting. He also toiled in the fields.

He grew up with Menggu. They loved each other. Menggu never teased him for being a "Little Actor". When he had been wounded during the land expropriation, it was Menggu, her mother and sister who nursed him back to health. Afterwards, families who lost their acreage were unable to live. So Master Liu apprenticed his two disciples-cum-adopted sons, Tongchun and Tongqiu to the Qingle Opera Troupe. With the money he received Master Liu was able to help the needy through those hard times. After Qiao Zinian committed suicide at Meridian Gate and the scandal caused the appropriated land to be returned, life in Malan Village became easier. The villagers did their best to help Mrs Qiao and her daughters, Menggu and Ronggu, to plough and plant the fields. Much of this was due to two bumper crops. Meanwhile, Tongchun had made a name for himself in the capital, and was as popular as the renowned Liu Yinguan and Chen Yuguan. With fame came wealth. His adoptive father who was ailing decided it was time to arrange a marriage for Tongchun. The natural choice was Menggu with whom Tongchun had grown up. That spring, Tongchun asked for leave and returned to the village during the Qingming

Festival intent on finalizing the wedding arrangements. He could not foresee any obstacles in his way. However, he had not reckoned with Mrs Qiao, who used the excuse that Menggu was still young and insisted on putting off any discussion of marriage for another two years. Tongchun was disappointed but also suspicious of the mother's motives. Finally it was Menggu's younger sister, Ronggu, who let the cat out of the bag in her childish way.

"My mother doesn't object to you personally. It's just that you are on the stage!"

Tongchun was furious. He earned his living by his art; not by robbing or stealing or selling his integrity. He was as good as the next man.

"What does your sister think?" he wanted to know.

Ronggu frowned. "My sister cried till her eyes turned red. Anyway, she told me to give this to you...." She handed Tongchun a small parcel. In it were a pair of plain cloth shoes, a red stomach warmer and a silk purse. In his turn Tongchun handed his wedding gift of a pair of jade bracelets to the girl and bade her take them to her sister. Then he hurried back to the capital.

Tongchun could not get Menggu out of his mind. Time and again he would fondle the purse she made for him and the distance between them seemed to shorten. He vowed he would never forsake Menggu.

"Tongchun, Tongchun, Master Zhang is waiting!" someone was calling.

The voice shattered Tongchun's reveries and brought the realities of life into sharp focus.

That day was Lu Zhiyue's forty-fifth birthday. A feast was arranged at an elegant restaurant outside Zhengyang Gate. The brothers Tongchun and Tongqiu together with several other popular young actors had been engaged as paid companions.

The host entered the room with a new arrival and the assemblage rose to its feet, each one clasping a fist in the other hand before his face in a gesture of welcome.

Since his protector General Ershuo recommended him to Duke An, Lu Zhiyue was held in even higher esteem. An affable, unobstrusive, and versatile man, he could discuss poetry with a poet, music with a musician, or history and chess with anyone who cared to. He loved to travel alone and was wont to accost a peasant, a woodsman or shepherd and happily engage them in conversation.

He was a southerner from Hangzhou. After a sojourn of several years in the north his wife wrote him, time and again, urging him to return. Each time his protector persuaded him to stay. Soon after he joined the household of Duke An another letter from his wife arrived. He wrote a poem which he presented to Duke An in which he compared the humbleness of his home to the luxury which surrounded him, ending: "For whom do I linger at the ends of the earth?"

Duke An was delighted with the poem which convinced him all the more of Lu's superb scholarship. Above all the Duke was convinced he must keep this witty and congenial companion at his side. The request to return home was denied.

On the occasion of his forty-fifth birthday, Lu's wife sent him a landscape painting of his home by her own hand, with a question appended to it:

"When will you return?"

The story soon made the rounds. Would the Duke relent and allow him to leave?

The new arrival was a tall, big-boned, broad-shouldered man about forty years of age, as plainly dressed as his host. The fearless directness of his gaze, and the sense of strength he exuded made Lu seem weak and very scholarly beside him.

None of the guests knew the tall man. And Lu's usual casual manner did not belie the man's status. The man greeted the assemblage in a loud voice, "I'm sorry to have disturbed your enjoyment. Please forgive me."

The assemblage returned his greetings. In a lull the stranger asked to see the handiwork of Lu's wife.

Lu smiled his consent, saying that the painting had just been mounted on a scroll and now hung in the adjoining room. A few servants all clad in black started to follow them as the two men left the banqueting hall, but the tall stranger stopped them at the door.

"Wait outside," he commanded.

The small room was decorated in the southern style. On a long, low table were two pots of spring orchids. Beside it stood a screen on which was painted a misty landscape of the south. Southern decor was repeated in the finely wrought cornices and window frames of the room, and in the high-backed chairs inlaid with marble and the dainty side tables. The scroll which depicted the West Lake was stretched across the back wall. The stranger examined it, his hands folded pensively behind his back, murmuring a poem of praise under his breath.

Lu smiled his appreciation.

The visitor steered the conversation around to Lu's calligraphy. Expressing his admiration for Lu's art he asked for a memento Lu was happy to oblige and called for Tongchun to bring writing tools. When they were set before the master, Lu asked what he should write.

"Would you like a Tang poem?" suggested Lu.

"No. I will dictate, and you will write..." said the other. "We will call it *Ode to the Snow*...." Thus the one recited while the other wrote. At the end of the first two lines Lu laid down his brush with a chuckle, "I didn't think you would remember." For the poem was about the tragedy of land seizures the year before.

The other laughed out loud.

"How could I forget! While others petitioned on their knees or with tears, you created a new form. Petition by poetry!"

"His Majesty was enraged, and I was afraid that many lives would be taken. I was afraid to speak out, yet I could not keep silent. It was a coward's way out of a quandary...."

"Speak no more," the other dismissed further discussion with a wave of the hand. "I regretted it afterwards for I was at fault. It was my stupidity to accept the land offered to me for my protection. The Emperor's decision of returning the appropriated land to the villagers was entirely correct for the sake of Empire and society, and for the foundation of Great Qing. I have no complaint." He paused. "Am I a righteous man?"

"You are indeed," Lu responded without hesitation. The two men smiled into each other's eyes.

Tongchun was fascinated by the stranger whose heroic bearing surpassed that of any Han he had ever encountered. The dashing, romantic air about him also out-shone the Manchus. He had neither the arrogance of a princeling, nor did he exhibit the cringing humility of the courtier. Who was he, Tongchun wondered.

Tongchun arranged the go game. The two men took their seats opposite each other. Tongchun scrutinized the stranger's hands. They were thick and broad. Veins stood out on their backs, but the skin was translucent and smooth. The nails were carefully pared, and on the right thumb he wore a large jade ring. The hands did not reveal anything of the man.

The chess pieces made a pleasant sound as they were placed on the board. The stranger spoke as he played: "Since you insist on returning home, we will not force you to stay. However there is one favour you must grant us. The dynasty is young. The Court needs men of wisdom, and looks to you for recommendations. However, the calibre of men we seek is not to be found in the cities. Most of them have retreated to the remote corners of the countryside. Since you are fond of travelling, we ask that you keep a weather eye open for likely candidates."

"And if I agree?"

"Then we shall return you to the south with honours."

"It's agreed."

Tongchun reached for Lu Zhiyue's sleeve as he was about to make his move and pointed to the southeast corner of the board. If he made the move he intended, the whole lower corner of the board would be lost. Lu hastily changed his strategy and the situation was saved. The stranger fixed Tongchun with a searching gaze that made the lad quake inwardly.

"This bit of fluff is loyal to his master, and quick-witted to boot," remarked the stranger.

"He is pure," Lu Zhiyue said drily, "when one in his profession can't afford to be. He will have a tough row to hoe one day."

"So he is one of the three stars of the theatre." The stranger fixed Tongchun with his gaze and nodded imperceptibly. Afterwards, Lu Zhiyue accompanied the stranger to the gate before bidding him farewell.

Tongchun was waiting at the door when Lu Zhiyue returned. Falling on his knees he cried, "I can't go on with this life! Buy my freedom and let me go back to the land!" Lu Zhiyue nodded with a sigh.

"I know you have come to the end of your tether. You are beautiful but you have a manly and heroic spirit. You will not tolerate the life of playing female roles on the stage. Nevertheless, you are a star. Your freedom will cost at least a thousand ounces of gold. Where would an old man in a strange land raise that kind of money? Let us say you win your freedom, do you think you are fit for farming? I think not. You will end up being a page boy or a bond servant. Why exchange one form of slavery for another?"

"Master Lu, I vow never to set foot on the stage again," cried Tongchun.

"Maybe it is just as well, if your mind is made up..." murmured Lu Zhiyue. He glanced back at the gate of the house whence the stranger had gone. "If he spoke for you things would be a lot easier."

"Who?"

"The guest who played go with me," chuckled Lu Zhiyue.

"He is a fine gentleman. Who is he?"

Lu Zhiyue answered casually, "He is Duke An." That name sent a shiver down Tongchun's spine.

2

Lu Zhiyue was able to prevail upon Duke An to buy Tongchun from the Qingle Troupe. Because it was the Duke who demanded Tongchun's services, the owner did not dare ask an exorbitant price. Instead they merely added thirty-three percent to the price they paid for him, and rounded it off at four hundred ounces of silver. The Duke paid the price, and set Tongchun free. Hearing that Lu Zhiyue was leaving the capital, Tongchun eagerly offered to be his guide as far as Malan Village. He left the city bubbling over with high spirits.

They stopped by a brook, and as Tongchun dropped his pail into the water, extolling its purity, a sheet of paper floated by. He quickly fished it out, and saw it was a page torn from a book. As the men examined it, wondering whence it had come, another page drifted by. This they also intercepted. Its contents indicated it had come from the same source.

"This being Duanwu Festival, it must follow that someone is commemorating the great poet Qu Yuan who drowned himself in a river in protest to the King of Chu who did not fight against the State of Qin's invasion," suggested Lu Zhiyue.

"Perhaps wise men live in this wilderness," responded Zhang Han, a young man whom Lu had recently taken as a disciple. Tongchun suggested they follow the brook upstream. By so doing, they would surely come upon the person who had floated the pages down. Lu Zhiyue was quick to accept the suggestion. The three men followed the stream which wound its way through the forest among strange and wonderful boulders. As they climbed steadily upward, chanting voices drifted down to them from somewhere near the mid-level of the mountain where a pavilion stood. For the moment the owner of the voice was hidden from view by trees. They crept stealthily toward a pavilion.

Three men were in the pavilion. One in a long blue robe stood with his hands folded behind his back. It was hard to tell by his abstracted air whether he was admiring the scenery or listening to a man in a white monk's habit and hat, reading from a book. As Lu and his companions watched, they noticed the reader would tear off each page as he was done, and drop it into the stream. A page boy in a brown doublet stood behind him, watching without much interest.

In a while the poem was read and the last page of the manuscript had floated away. The white-robed monk suddenly burst into vociferous tears, and sobbed out a self-pitying poem on the trials and tribulations of a wandering scholar.

The man in the blue chided him in a cold, clear voice, saying that the life of a monk was meant to be ascetic, therefore such a display of emotion was unseemly.

Listening, Lu Zhiyue thought he recognized the voice of his old friend Loo Jian.

Tongchun was delighted. For he recognized the man in white to be the very same monk who had passed through his village in the spring. A man versed in medicine and geomancy.

"A true Daoist," he proclaimed

Zhang Han who mistrusted all monks excused himself and went on ahead.

The men in the pavilion noticed the others approaching. Lu Zhiyue advanced bowing in salutation and enquiring in a gentle manner whether the two men and their page had come up the mountain to perform the customary rituals of the festival.

The monk's glance quickly swept over Lu Zhiyue, "Obviously our paths were destined to cross," he observed.

Loo Jian's heart skipped a beat for he thought he recognized Lu Zhiyue's voice. When he turned and discovered it was indeed Lu Zhiyue, his face clouded. Tongchun recognized Loo Jian too, and was about to cry out in delight, but a flick of Loo's sleeve warned him to keep silent. Tongchun had been in the theatre long enough to understand these subtleties and did not let on. Loo calmed down when Lu Zhiyue also pretended not to know him. The two men greeted each other coldly as strangers, and sat round the stone table to talk.

"I was much moved by the poem my Brother Monk read," remarked Lu Zhiyue. "It seems you were much troubled." The monk dismissed the remark with a smile, saying it was merely a poet's conceit.

"Then my Brother Monk must have been a scholar at one time," Lu continued to probe. "Brilliance unrecognized is a great pity." However, the monk would not be drawn out.

"The past is the past. It does no good to dwell upon it."

With his long flowing beard, the monk cut a dashing, almost supernatural figure. A peculiar light gleamed in the depths of his eyes like that of a falcon's, wild and untameable. One could tell this was not a man that would lightly bow to defeat. Lu Zhiyue made a mental note of this to himself.

Loo Jian took up the conversation as it petered out. "Speaking of Fate," he began, "there is a legend which I will relate. In the final year of Ming, the Emperor Chongzhen was worn out by cares of state, and the rapid advance of bandits. One day he sent a trusted eunuch into the streets to bring him news of his people. On the way the eunuch encountered a fortune teller who claimed to foretell the future from a given word. The eunuch gave him the word *you* meaning friend.

"The fortune teller asked in what context he wanted to know the future. When he was told it was about the fate of the Empire, the fortune teller said all was lost."

The three men fell silent at the end of the tale. Were they still mourning the overthrown of the Ming? The only sound was the wind humming through the trees and the rustling of leaves. Presently Loo Jian rose to his feet, and bowing to his companions said, "To everything there is a season. As one falls another rises. Thus is the will of heaven!"

The monk rose too and bowed. "If what you say is true then

all ambition comes to nought." He bowed once again to the others. "Heaven bids me live, and heaven bids me die. Why then should I rebel?" And with that he took his leave with his page boy scampering after him. When they had disappeared into the trees, and his voice faded in the distance, he was still repeating those lines. Loo Jian and Lu Zhiyue clasped hands as old friends.

They were happy and sad all at once. Tongchun hurried forward to thank Loo for his help during the land seizure years ago. It was only then that Lu Zhiyue discovered the whole truth about the incident at Yongping Prefecture.

"How have you been these last two years? And your troubles in the south..." his question trailed off.

"I'm still a fugitive ... hiding in the mountains."

"I am sorry I could not get you a pardon, my friend...."

"It was beyond your ability to help. I fear the case of the ten families will never be resolved. Too many people were implicated. In a way it was their fault. They were wicked during the Ming Dynasty, abusing their power and rousing the hatred of the people. They reap what they sowed when the dynasty fell."

Loo Jian told his friend it was because he had been charitable that when his troubles of being falsely accused of subversive activities started, those whom he had helped rallied to his aid. With their help he was able to elude capture. Fortunately the warrant for his arrest was only circulated south of the Yangtze, so that it was relatively safe for him in the north.

"But you can't end your days as a fugitive! You have too much to offer!" exclaimed Lu Zhiyue.

"What does a tired rabbit hiding from the hounds as I have to offer?" scoffed Loo Jian.

"Isn't there someone at Court who will vouch for you? You have helped so many people in your time...." Loo Jian's brows knit, deep in thought. Then he shook his head. "People have short memories."

"There must be someone," Lu Zhiyue insisted. Loo Jian

searched his old friend's face to be sure that he could be trusted. Then he answered, "There is Fu Yijian."

"Now, that's a name to conjure with! In the eighth month last year Fu Yijian became Grand Academician! Do you know him well?"

"That depends..." Loo Jian hesitated. As Loo Jian did not wish to discuss the matter any further, Lu Zhiyue did not press him.

"I will do what I can for you, but I am only a nobleman's honoured guest. You had best write a letter to Fu Yijian and have this youngster take it to the capital post haste. Believe me, there is hope."

Loo Jian agreed. Tongchun prepared paper and brush, and Loo Jian quickly wrote a letter. When the letter was sealed, there was a moment of hesitation before he handed it to Tongchun.

"Be sure this letter is delivered only to Lady Wang and no one else in Grand Academician Fu's household," he cautioned Tongchun. "Say it's greetings from her family."

"I will do as you say," Tongchun replied.

"Have you known that monk a long time?" asked Lu Zhiyue, steering the conversation in a new direction.

"We only just met. He seemed quite learned, but arrogant. I sensed something in his conversation. He is after something...."

"Money?"

"No. I had the feeling he was sounding out my talent. Hoping to rope me in. As a matter of fact I don't think you're here for the scenery either. Why, I think you have designs on both of us." Lu Zhiyue chuckled. "I dare say you haven't changed. At least you've kept your wits. But, I beg you listen to an old friend...."

Lu talked about the changes that had taken place since the Emperor took the reins of government. He lauded the Emperor for attempting to rule with justice and mercy, and turning from force of arms to the power of the quill. As a result the Ming adherents were laying down their arms. Though there was sporadic resistence in the southeast, the people were weary of war and longed for order. In this time of transition bandits roamed the countryside.

"Be careful of whom you ally yourself with," Lu Zhiyue warned, "lest you fall into an abyss from which you cannot extricate yourself."

Loo Jian grinned wryly. "Rest assured. I have never been enamoured of officialdom. Besides I have had enough of the hurly-burly in these ten years."

"You must leave this place. I don't trust that monk."

So saying, Lu Zhiyue counted fifty ounces of silver from his travelling money, and gave them to Loo Jian. Then they parted, Lu Zhiyue to continue up the mountain, while his friend accompanied by Tongchun took the way down.

3

The door burst open. Nine-year-old Ronggu rushed into the room chirping merrily, "Sister! Brother Tongchun is coming home and he's given up being an actor!"

Menggu stopped her spinning wheel. Her eyes went wide with excitement.

"Where did you hear that?"

"Everybody in the village knows," the girl replied. "Tongchun said so in a letter that a Daoist monk brought to Master Liu. Everyone is saying he did it for you."

"Don't talk nonsense!" Menggu scolded, blushing to the roots of her hair. In two summers and autumns, the little girl in the red jacket had turned into a comely young woman. Her small oval face was dominated by brows that rose like twin peaks. The round eyes had lengthened. The dainty mouth was finely moulded and red as the petals of a flower, giving her a kind and loving expression.

The younger girl was not so easily silenced.

"I'm not talking nonsense," she cried rolling her eyes. "Everybody knows you want to marry Brother Tongchun...."

"You little vixen," Menggu covered her burning face with her palms, feigning anger. "I'll whip you for that!"

The girl skipped out of the room chanting, "My sister wants Tongchun ... Tongchun...."

Left alone, Menggu pondered what she had just heard. Tongchun was famous in the capital. He dressed well, ate well, lived well. His friends were famous artistes. Yet he was giving up a life of luxury for her.... Tears of joy spilled down her cheeks.

She wondered whether her mother had heard the news and how she would react to it. Her mother had been befriended by Abbess Yuan of the Huanxiu Nunnery. She had gone to the nunnery early that morning. Perhaps she had already heard the news.

Because Duke An returned the expropriated land, the Qiao family now had thirty mu of land to work. As the Duke did not claim part of the crop or levy taxes over and above the rent, the family was better off than before. As a result Mother Qiao's expectations for her daughter also rose. Would she approve of Menggu's choice?

The news made Menggu so restless that she could not settle down to work. So, leaving Ronggu alone in the house, she went to the nunnery in search of her mother.

The white-robed monk had gone straight to Huanxiu Nunnery. The Abbess was not averse to putting him up, and immediately vacated four rooms that flanked the main hall for him, while she and two disciples moved to the back of the nunnery. Since their family and the Abbess were good friends, Menggu went straight to the nun's cell.

The courtyard was strewn with pine needles and the air was alive with the chirping of crickets. It was a place of tranquility and meditation. Menggu trod softly. Even her breathing had become light, for fear of disturbing the serenity of the place. The silence was broken by someone sobbing softly in one of the cells, and the murmur of a comforting voice held low. "There's nothing to cry about. Great ladies of the past have been nuns. One needs only think of Yang Yuhuan, the favourite concubine of Emperor Xuanzong and ... Empress Wu Zetian. Both of the Tang Dynasty and they both had taken vows at one time...."

Menggu was mystified by what she overheard. She found it odd that the nuns should discuss such worldly things! But she had things on her mind and went quickly to the Abbess' cell. Lifting the curtain hanging at the door, she softly called, "Auntie...."

The room was empty. However, incense was lit on the altar which probably meant the Abbess could not be far. She waited. When no one returned, she peeped into the adjacent room to the west. That room was also deserted. The paraphernalia of worship, all made of brass, were neatly stacked. Bedclothes and robes were neatly folded. Everything was in its right place except an old cupboard that seemed to have been moved from its place against the north wall, and left there. When she went to push it back into place, she discovered a secret door behind it.

The door looked quite new. With a pounding heart Menggu pushed it open a crack, and found herself looking into one of the front rooms of the nunnery. The room was brightly lit. A meal was set on a table in the centre of the room. On it were dishes of fowl and fish. The imposing looking monk's servant was setting wine cups on the table. The other person in the room was an elderly gentleman in black with flowing white hair and beard. He and the monk in white were engaged in a lively conversation. Menggu wondered how a religious man could so easily set aside his vow of abstinence to meat.

Another door opened with a creak. The new arrival startled Menggu, for she recognized the young acolyte who always followed and watched her whenever she came to pray. The fiery gleam in his eyes frightened Menggu for he seemed ready to eat her alive. But today he was different. He was pale. His thick brows were knit in a deep frown. He seemed so dejected that her heart went out to him involuntarily. Had he come to confess some transgression or be punished, she wondered.

To Menggu's astonishment the two men rose hastily to their feet and stood in a straight line together with the servant. Then they prostrated themselves before the young man. The young acolyte took the seat of honour at the table, and with a wave of his hand he invited the others to sit on either side of him.

Menggu's head swam. Was the scene she had just witnessed real or was it something conjured up by a feverish imagination. She curled herself into a ball afraid of being discovered.

The young acolyte broke the silence in a croaking voice:

"I have gone from province to province, but there is nowhere to rest. Now I hear Li Dingguo has lost Guangdong, and Prince of Le'an has been defeated. All is lost, my friends. You have followed me faithfully, hoping to help me reclaim my heritage. But that is not to be. What shall we do?"

The servant in brown fell to his knees and said, "The assistant regent Prince Jirgalang has died, and all the commanders of the conquest are dead, leaving an inexperienced young emperor in a vacuum. Meanwhile Zheng Chenggong has taken Zhoushan and his influence is increasing. Go to him and all will be well."

However, the white-robed monk did not agree. Zheng Chenggong was not a true adherent of Ming, he said, but one who wanted independence and power. Besides Zhoushan was too small to be of any real significance. Though the Tartar Emperor was young he had a good head. He had also the wise counsel of his mother and the court. Thus he would not be easily removed.

"A better plan would be to gain the support of Yongli of Southern Ming in the south and Zheng Chenggong in the east and move slowly...."

The man in black took out a roll of paper secreted in his sleeve and laid it before the young acolyte.

"I have studied the situation for six years and this is the only area where we could set up a state," he said. "Several former generals of Ming wrote to me recently saying that they had been secretly training their forces and storing grain for an uprising. In my opinion the three mountains must first be taken. With them as base and My Lord at its head, the army will be invincible...." He lowered his voice so that the rest could not be heard.

Although Menggu did not understand the full import of what she overheard, she realized the young acolyte was more than he appeared. He was a fugitive in disguise like one of the heroes of romantic adventures that blind story-tellers told. Her sympathy for the hapless young man increased as fear and loathing disappeared.

After a few rounds of wine, the young acolyte leaned over the table and whispered something at his companions. Their reluctance roused the young man's anger.

"You profess to follow me, yet you deny me..." he thundered.

The monk smiled sourly, "My Lord, we urge you to think about the future. At present...."

"At the present I have no heir," the younger man cut him off. "What good is the future without an heir?"

"Forgive us, My Lord," the monk explained. "We had in mind the tragic consequences of your brother Emperor Hongguang's folly in our counsel. However, we have conveyed your wishes to the Abbess."

The young acolyte brightened.

"There doesn't seem to be any impediment. Except the woman demands proof," concluded the monk.

"That's easy," the young acolyte chortled. "Summon her to us."

The servant in brown left the room and returned with two women. The one in front was the Abbess, but the woman behind she couldn't see clearly. Menggu crept forward and looked again, then shrank in horror, for it was her mother.

When the Abbess and her mother prostrated themselves before the young acolyte Menggu's heart began a fearful hammering. She was a timid soul, complacent and obedient. Though she did not understand all that she witnessed, these mysterious goings-on were more frightening than any tale or opera in the story-teller's repertoire. She crept home trembling uncontrollably.

Menggu laid her feverish cheek on the low kang table, lost in thought. All she had to go on were stories and operas. Nothing she had ever heard related to, or shed any light on what she had seen. She reached into a hollow in the kang wall and found a small cloth packet. She carefully unwrapped the two jade bracelets, and rubbed them against her cheek. Their touch conjured up the dear image of Tongchun.

A knock on the door sent her scurrying to hide her treasure before she lazily answered the door.

"What do you want?" Menggu was surprised to find the young acolyte on her doorstep. The young man fixed her with his burning eyes, and the tip of his tongue flicked deliberately across his cracked lips.

"You," he said.

"My mother's out and no one is allowed in," Menggu started to shut the door, desperately controlling the tremor in her voice. But the young acolyte had wedged himself in the doorway.

"I know. Your mother just gave me this." He lifted his left hand and showed her a ring of tiny pearls set in gold he wore on the fourth finger. Menggu recognized her mother's ring at once. It was the only piece of jewellery her mother had, an engagement present. Its mate had been buried with her father years ago.

The young acolyte pushed past her into the house, and quickly latched the door. Menggu started to scream, but the man smothered her cries with a hand over her mouth and commanded her to be still. No one had ever spoken to her in such a tone before. The young acolyte half pushed and half dragged her into the inner room.

"Your mother gave me this ring as dowry. You belong to me." Menggu tried to back away from him, but she could not struggle free. All she could do was scream inwardly, "No, no, no...."

Madam Qiao stayed with Abbess Yuan a long time, and came home content with all that had transpired that day.

In the few months that he had been in Malan Village the man in white had cured many ailments and saved a few lives. His reputation as a miracle worker had spread like wild fire. People hung on his every word. The Abbess herself was impressed, and she was no fool. The Abbess was right when she said the present regime was not to be trusted. It was true they were more compassionate than the previous dynasty, but they were barbarians. Mercy and compassion were mere tools to win men's hearts. Madam Qiao was the wife of a *gong-sheng* (tribute student) of the previous dynasty, and a woman with a little learning to whom ideas such as faithfulness and integrity meant something. The man in white himself had praised her for those traits. How sweetly his words had fallen upon her ears! Still she was not about to accept the young acolyte as a prince of the previous dynasty without some proof. In fact she had insisted and was not satisfied until a gold seal was produced which identified him as Prince of the Imperial Household of Ming. There could be no mistake then. The more she listened to the discourse of the man in white and the man in black, the more was she convinced that the present reign would not last. Rebellion was everywhere. Within a few years great Ming would rise again, and Menggu would be Empress!

Madam Qiao did not believe it possible that such good fortune could fall upon her family. It was only today, when she got a good close look at him that she realized the young acolyte did have the look and bearings of a prince. Thus convinced, she had gladly agreed to a secret marriage between the young acolyte and her daughter. On the surface nothing would be changed. When she arrived home, she found the door latched from inside.

Knocking loudly, she called for Menggu to open the door.

Hurried footsteps approached from within and the bolt was withdrawn. The young acolyte stood before her, sweaty and his clothes in disarray.

"You..." Madam Qiao gulped.

"Yes, dear mother-in-law," chuckled the young acolyte, "I have just taken your daughter to wife." He nodded and left.

Madam Qiao slumped against the door jamb, her brain in a whirl. The sound of her daughter weeping sent her rushing to the inner room. One look at her daughter, half-naked and dishevelled, frantically knotting a sash around a beam brought everything into focus.

"Stupid girl!" she cried, throwing her arms around her daughter.

"I'm so ashamed," sobbed Menggu, "I want to die!" The mother held her tenderly, murmuring words of comfort.

"...My good daughter.... He is a prince.... I have given you to him.... He is your husband...."

Menggu sobbed hysterically, cursing the Prince, the husband that deserved a thousand deaths.

Madam Qiao rocked the girl in her arms till she was calm. Then she dressed her and combed her hair. Then she explained about the wedding.

"But Brother Tongchun is quitting the theatre and coming home..." sighed Menggu sorrowfully.

The mother trembled and her eyes misted. She had gone to the Abbess with the idea of discussing marrying Menggu to Tongchun. She had taken the ring with her to show the Abbess to ask if it would suffice as dowry. But once she saw the Abbess everything changed.

"Child," she said to Menggu in a soft voice, "in a woman's life there can only be one man. You are his, so make up you mind to follow him the rest of your days. Forget Tongchun."

The seriousness of this day's events finally penetrated Menggu's foggy brain. Up till now she had lived in a fantasy world woven out of a young girl's dreams, and ideals of love. But they were merely dreams; hers and Tongchun's, dreams that had been dashed to pieces. Everything went black and she swooned.

"Menggu! Menggu!" the woman shook the girl. Finally Menggu opened her eyes.

Just then a loud voice was heard outside the front door shouting,

"Is anyone home?" With a start Madam Qiao realized she had left the front door open. She rushed out the room to be confronted by a tall bearded stranger whose ruddy face somehow seemed familiar.

"Mother! Don't you recognize me?" The stranger fell to his knees. "I am your first born, Bainian."

"Good heavens!" Madam Qiao tottered over to him. Her knees gave way and she slumped to the ground. She reached for him, feeling his head, shoulders and arms. "It's really you ...." she murmured full of wonderment. "And all this time I thought all the men of this family were dead! But you're so big ... and strong ... and alive!"

Bainian dabbed his eyes and answered in a husky voice, "I've hoped for this day for ten years...." Madam Qiao could not take her eyes off her son.

"You remembered the way and came straight to the door. My, you gave me a turn!"

"I really didn't recognize the house any more. It was a young fellow I met on the way who pointed it out to me." Madam Qiao gave a start.

"Who was it?" she asked.

"A handsome young fellow called Liu Tongchun. Perhaps you know him, Mother." Madam Qiao did not answer. She took her son's big strong hands in hers and wept. The sound of weeping also issued from the inner room. Not the hysterical sobs of a moment ago, but the soft unending tears of despair.

4

"Madam, a lady wishes to see you."

Gu Meisheng frowned as she laid down the book of poetry she had been reading.

"Well, its stupid not to announce who is calling," she scolded.

The old servant bowed obsequiously. "Madam, she would only say she is an old friend. She has come in a splendid sedan chair with a huge retinue...."

Gu Meisheng mulled that over. "Invite her into the inner parlour. Serve tea. I shall be there shortly."

The old servant hurried down the stairs. Gu Meisheng lifted a cup of tea to her lips, took a mouthful and rinsed her mouth. A maid hurried over with a small spittoon. Gu Meisheng spat into it and the servant quickly took it away. Gu Meisheng was in no hurry to receive her mysterious guest. She moved in a leisurely fashion across the room to an oval-shaped window framed by finely carved cranes and clouds and covered with a pale green gossamer. From this vantage point she had a clear view of the front gate, the inner gate and the forecourt without being seen.

Her old servant led in two pretty serving wenches, followed by a great lady leaning on the arm of another serving wench. Two more serving girls followed behind. The lady wore a long cloak of pale blue woven through with threads of gold and silver. Her face was hidden behind a veil. Gu Meisheng was not pleased. I don't care who you are, don't put on airs with me, she thought angrily.

Nevertheless, she quickly went down the stairs. When she entered the inner parlour she was beaming with affected pleasure. The visitor had removed her veil and cloak and stood turned away from her admiring a painting by the Song-dynasty artist Xu Hancheng. The lady wore a pale green blouse cut in the

Han style over a white satin skirt. Her hair was piled high on top of her head and fixed with a gold hair-pin studded with pearls. Although her face was hidden for the moment, the slender beauty of her figure was breathtaking.

At the sound of footsteps, the lady turned and, with a smile that dimpled her cheeks, said, "I have heard so much about you Madam Gu, that I was compelled to come and pay my respects. I hope I have not been presumptuous.... "

She smiled showing a row of neat white teeth.

"I am honoured...."

Gu Meisheng responded with a smile and invited the stranger to be seated and offered tea.

The visitor fascinated her. She seemed familiar yet she could not place her. By the way she spoke Gu Meisheng surmised she might be the wife of some official from the south.

"Madam Gu, do you not recognize me?"

Still smiling, Gu Meisheng's eyes quickly swept the visitor, taking in every detail without giving offence. She shook her head almost imperceptibly.

The visitor's smile vanished.

"Sister Mei, have you really forgotten?" The visitor's tone turned grave. "Fifteen years ago when the lotus blossoms were in bloom we became sisters in spirit at Xi Shi's Well on Tiger Hill, near Suzhou...."

She switched to the vernacular of the south. Gu Meisheng remembered her instantly, and quickly reached for the visitor's hands.

"Suyuan, my little sister!" she cried excitedly, the airs and graces of a great lady were tossed to the winds. "I never thought we would meet again! Where have you been all this time? How did you survive the troubled times? And why haven't you been to see me sooner?" Excited tears tumbled down Gu Meisheng's cheeks.

Suyuan gently caressed Meisheng's hand. "The troubles have been over for twelve years now," she comforted. "You and I are both alive and well. I came to renew an old friendship."

Gu Meisheng gradually calmed down. The way the other had subtlely emphasized the words "old friendship" had not gone unnoticed. She understood.

"We can't talk here," she said to Suyuan. "Let us go upstairs to my chamber." And leading the way, they went across the courtyard and up the stairs. On the way she had a chance to study her visitor.

"Sister Suyuan, you are exquisite," she exclaimed. "You must be about thirty yet you seem not a day older than twenty. Just look at you! With all your servants! You must be the wife of a very rich man. Who is he?"

Suyuan smiled without answering directly.

"You haven't changed either. Still as vivacious as ever. When we became spiritual sisters you were older in years, but youngest at heart...."

"To think that you still remember such trivia!" exclaimed Gu Meisheng.

Fifteen years ago they had both been famous courtesans of Suzhou. Both were about sixteen years of age. The twenty-second day of the sixth month is a festival which the people of Suzhou call the Birthday of the Lotus. They had chosen that day and a place known as Xi Shi's Well to become sisters in spirit because of its poetic and historic significance. Both girls were educated, skilled in poetry, calligraphy, painting and chess. Also, the lotus was a symbol of purity, rising untouched by the filth in which it grew. The legendary beauty Xi Shi, who was also a courtesan, had risen to dizzying heights in spite of her lowly origins. She was their inspiration.

Years ago, when Gong Dingzi was an important minister, the court had honoured him by bestowing a title upon his wife. However, the title was intended for his legal wife. Therefore Gong Dingzi sent to his native city of Hefei and bestowed the title on his first wife. The lady would not accept the honour, saying that she had already been honoured twice by the previous dynasty, and suggested this time it should go to Madam Gu. So she was addressed Madam Gu ever since. Gu Meisheng happily accepted that though it still fell short of being referred to as Lady Gong, yet it gave her the respectability that being a second wife or concubine lacked, and which she disliked. That happened eight years ago. In the meantime, Gong was dismissed from his post and had lived in obscurity ever since.

"Sister, you must've been in the capital all this time. Why didn't you come sooner?"

"Of course I heard of you," Suyuan smiled. "Earlier on I could not come. Later I dared not. I hope you understand."

"I'm afraid I don't."

Suyuan smiled, glancing meaningfully at the servants going back and forth, laying food on the table. Gu Meisheng knew that she was deliberately keeping her waiting for the explanation, but she still waited until everything was in place before she dismissed them.

Left by themselves, she turned to her visitor.

"We can talk freely now."

"In the beginning, your husband was an important man, and mine was a nobody. It was not fitting for us to socialize. These days although Hans and Manchus have the same titles at Court, they do not enjoy the same status. One always has to be careful lest one is accused of forming cliques and conspiracies...."

"Then how was it that you dared come today?" demanded Gu Meisheng testily. Still smiling sweetly, Suyuan explained, "My husband is away with the Emperor on an Imperial Progress, and I had time on my hands."

"Imperial Progress!" Gu Meisheng was startled. "Who is your husband?" Suyuan laid a hand on Gu Meisheng's shoulder and whispered, "He's from Liaocheng City in Shandong.... His name is Fu Yijian...."

"Oh! An academician of the Palace Secretariat Academy?"

Suyuan leaned her head on Gu Meisheng's shoulder almost as shyly as a young girl half her age.

"Oh! You're a great lady!" Gu Meisheng pushed her aside and half rose as if she were about to fall to her knees. Suyuan quickly stopped her.

"Sister, don't be ridiculous!" she chuckled.

Gu Meisheng threw back her head and laughed out loud. When she was young, her unrestrained laughter had been celebrated among the dandies of the south. Indeed her unbridled merriment had not changed with the years, nor did it detract from the persona of a respectable lady she had cultivated. She was pleased. She felt this meeting could not harm her husband's future prospects.

She patted Suyuan's dainty hand.

"When we became spiritual sisters you were the youngest. You wanted a simple life. What do you say now?"

Suyuan smiled, and drawing Gu Meisheng close to her, enquired about the fate of the other sisters, saying she had no news of them in years.

"Those of us who have no official position are more socially active. Zhilu is fond of entertaining so we get to hear about everybody."

Gu Meisheng prattled on about the other girls in the group, counting them off on her fingers. Liu Rushi, the oldest of the group, married Qian Qianyi, an official of the Museum of the History of Ming, who now lived in retirement and devoted himself to writing. They led a quiet, happy life. The second was herself. The third, Chen Yuanyuan became a concubine of Prince of Pingxi. When they lived in the capital, she and Gu Meisheng saw each other frequently. Later, when her husband's army was ordered elsewhere, Gu Meisheng had accompanied her a distance out of the city when she left the capital to join her husband. The youngest Dong Xiaowan married Mao Bijiang, scion of a prominent southern family. Unfortunately, she died three years ago.

"Only common people like me are left bobbing about in this sea of misery," Gu Meisheng sighed as she picked at a few choice morsels of dried fruit from a plate in front of her.

"My dear sister! You must stop eating these fattening foods. It will be difficult to have children when you're fat."

"Vixen! Your tongue's as sharp as ever."

"Sister, you hear about everything. Have you heard about the case of the ten southern families accused of plotting rebellion? Were any of our sisters implicated?" Suyuan adroitly brought the conversation round to the reason for her visit, making the question sound conversational.

"Yes, of course. But that was a long time ago. Heaven knows how many people died or lost everything they owned. If my husband had been in the judiciary at the time he would certainly have petitioned the court. As for our sisters, the only ones that might have been implicated were the Maos and the Qians. But I don't know for sure."

"I was thinking of Loo Jian's family," Suyuan brought up the name that was foremost on her mind, still sounding casual, as if in passing.

"That's right. It was very sad. Their vast estate was turned into a dormitory and everything in it was confiscated."

"Did any of the family survived?"

"Some are lanquishing in prison. Others have been killed. I can't remember the details.... Did you know the Loos?"

"Not really. A relative was a schoolmate of Loo Jian's."

Suyuan nibbled pensively on a piece of lotus root and sighed. The seed of thought that she had sown took root. For Gu Meisheng immediately launched into a recitation of the case. What she related was gleaned from the gossip of scholars, proteges of Gong Dingzi, and far more intriguing than transcripts of court documents. It seemed this Second Sister knew little about Suyuan's life after she left Suzhou, or if she did, she had forgotten.

Suyuan picked at the food and sipped tea absent-mindedly, absorbing every word yet seeming not to pay any attention at what was being said. It was only when Gu Meisheng changed the subject that she rose from her seat, to pace about the room, taking in every detail of her sister's boudoir. When she stopped in front of the window and looked out she was surprised to see her old servant chatting with a handsome page boy. The very same one she had been seeking everywhere. And here he was.

"Sister, does that young fellow belong to your household?"

Gu Meisheng went over to the window and looked.

"Why, that's my husband's disciple, Zhang Han's page. A pathetic creature really. He used to be a popular actor, but he quit the stage, bought his freedom intending to go home to the land. But when he got back his father had died, and his betrothed had thrown him over. He had nowhere to go, so he came back to the capital. He admired Zhang Han's character and learning, and applied to be his page. Mind you, he wouldn't sell himself into bondage. He is just an ordinary servant. Zhang Han doesn't seem to mind. Actually, they make a fine-looking pair, master and servant...." Gu Meisheng covered her mouth and giggled. It was the lewd chuckle of a middle-aged woman contemplating a handsome young man.

"Sister, let's go downstairs. I want to talk to him."

"My dear little sister, won't your great scholar be jealous!" exclaimed Gu Meisheng, her merriment had become malicious.

"Sister, I've not been looking for him because of his good looks. It's because a month ago he brought a letter from my mother. I didn't have a chance to talk to him or thank him at the time. He disappeared so quickly. I didn't know where to find him. And here he is! There are some things I have to ask him...."

When Suyuan returned home, she found the servant who had accompanied Fu Yijian on the Imperial Progress had returned reporting that his master was well and would arrive home in the afternoon.

The news gave Suyuan a brilliant idea. She tottered to her

bed, complaining of headache and nausea. The midday meal was foregone. Soon the entire household knew she was suffering from heat prostration.

Silence enveloped the courtyard, and especially Suyuan's vast bed chamber. A silence so deep that one could almost hear the clouds of scented smoke rising from the incenser. Serving maids stood holding their breath by the door and beside the bed, while behind the pale green gossamer drapery of the bed Suyuan lay, suppine, unmoving. However, her mind was in a turmoil. The passage of fourteen years lifted like a heavy curtain, and with the clarity of hindsight Suyuan surveyed the past with the detachment of a bystander and not as a participant.

Loo Jian of Zhejiang was the handsome, dashing scion of a prominent family. Like most young men of his caste, he had a roving eye for songstresses and courtesans. During a spring visit to Suzhou he made the acquaintance of the sixteen-year-old courtesan Suyuan. He was enchanted by her, and for three thousand ounces of silver bought her as a concubine. Suyuan's beauty and accomplishments outshone the other women of the household. Thus she became the favourite.

One day a student from Shandong came to the door and asked to see the master. The gatekeeper would not admit him, since he was a stranger. However, the dusty young man was exceedingly stubborn. He refused to leave and, seating himself on the doorstep, was content to wait until Loo Jian came out. Loo Jian was forced to receive him. The young man, who called himself Fu Yijian, skirted the social niceties and came to the point of his visit immediately. He had heard that Loo Jian owned a serving woman called Suyuan who was a peerless beauty, and he had come expressly to beg a glimpse of her.

Loo Jian was astonished at the other's candour, and hesitated.

"Sir, you have journeyed far," he said in an effort to gain time. "Have some tea and we will talk."

Fu responded with some emotion.

"I have come a thousand miles on foot. If you will grant my request, sir, I will gladly stay. Otherwise, do not keep me."

Loo Jian had to consent. Then Fu took his seat. It being close to nightfall, Loo Jian ordered food and wine for his guest. After several rounds of wine had been served, lamps were lit, and surrounded by lavishly gowned serving maids, Suyuan appeared before them. Fu rose to his feet, gazing at her long and hard. Finally he sighed, "She is exactly as they said: a flawless beauty. I have not come in vain." And with that he took his leave of Loo Jian. Loo Jian insisted that he stay a few days. "I have seen the beauty of beauties," Fu chuckled. "That is all I asked and that wish has been granted. I did not come seeking hospitality." He bowed and left.

After his visitor was gone, Loo Jian was restless. It was as though something had gone from his life. Suddenly he slammed his palm on the table and cried out, "Loo Jian! Loo Jian! How can you lose an esteemed scholar over the love of a woman!" He ordered a horse to be saddled at once and rode northward as fast as he could. He finally caught up with Fu Yijian thirty miles away and induced him to return home with him. Fu Yijian was treated as an honoured guest. The next night, Loo Jian invited Fu Yijian into a bed chamber lit with red candles and furnished with the finest silk draperies and luxurious bedding. He clasped his hands before him and said to Fu, "Though you came here without any designs, yet Fate seems to have a hand in these events. Hence I give you Suyuan. And this will be your wedding chamber and your wedding night."

Fu Yijian refused to accept, saying it would be unchivalrous to steal another man's love. However, Loo Jian brush his objections aside.

"Nonsense, sir! There is a tradition from antiquity of making a gift of a courtesan. I recognize your circumstances do not permit you the luxury of a pretty woman, while I have many. This one will not be missed. I do this because I respect you as a man among men. Therefore, why imitate the demure scholar?''

As he finished speaking a serving maid brought in Suyuan. Fu Yijian accepted this gift without further reservations.

Fu Yijian and his new wife stayed in Loo Jian's house for a month. Then with a dowry contained in ten trunks, and a thousand ounces of gold, Loo Jian sent them back to Liaocheng City. Through Loo Jian's largesse Fu Yijian became wealthy and he was able to concentrate on his studies in preparation for a career.

Later, the turmoils of the conquest of the Qing severed all contact between the Loos and the Fus for a period of twelve years.

Suyuan turned over on the bed. Immediately a serving maid was beside her with a dainty little teapot. Suyuan took a sip of tea and lay down again, and once more the past engulfed her.

From beginning to end, the two men in her life had behaved chivalrously toward each other, weaving a tale that would go down in history. Yet neither had considered Suyuan's feelings, nor consulted her in any way as to whom she preferred, in spite of the fact that she had cost three thousand ounces of silver and was reputed to be the most beautiful woman of Suzhou. It was only in the afternoon before her wedding night that Loo Jian apprised her of his intention to give her to Fu Yijian.

This came as a severe blow. Suyuan was humiliated. To be truthful, on first meeting him, Suyuan had been impressed by Fu Yijian. His high forehead, his wide mouth, sparkling eyes and his manliness told her this was no ordinary man. There was greatness in him. Yet it was the dashing Loo Jian whom she loved and considered her master. She wept.

Her tears seemed to have moved Loo Jian, for he said to her gently, "So he's too poor for you? And I thought you were above all that. But I was wrong. Think for a moment. Even if you stayed with me ten or twenty years you will still be what you are: a courtesan. But you will be his wife. He is the salt of the earth, and with him, you will one day be a great lady."

Suyuan stamped her foot angrily and cried, " I love you with all my heart. But you treat me like an object you can give away to whomever you please."

Loo Jian did not speak again for a long while. He stared out the window, brooding, his back turned to her. When he finally did speak again, the sadness of his tone and the wistfulness of his expression would stay with her always.

"Suyuan, though I'm only two or three years older than you, real emotions between man and woman have been buried long ago. Life is but a heady whirl of wine and song. Why take it seriously? You are no more to me than that. There is nothing worthy of regret. It is true, that in giving you away, I treated you as less than human. Therefore, I will treat you like a sister from now on, if you like. There is nothing unbecoming for a brother to marry off a sister...."

He was true to his word, for her dowry was the same as his sister's. After she had gone to Shandong with Fu Yijian, he wrote to them as an older brother would, addressing them as sister and brother-in-law....

How did he manage all these years? By the way the page described their meeting in Panshan, she surmised that his circumstances were quite desperate. After fourteen years he must have aged considerably.

She had spent fourteen loving years with Fu Yijian who was indeed an unusual man. He was not put off by her humble origins, nor did he question her about her life as a courtesan in Loo's house. She was simply his legal wife. After she gave him a son and a daughter, he would not consider taking a concubine.

In the third year of Shunzhi, he was placed first in the imperial examinations. As the foremost scholar of the realm, he was appointed scribe to the Palace Academy for the Advancement of Literature. Unlike the other successful candidates of the imperial examination he did not seek self aggrandizement by taking a concubine as soon as he arrived in the capital. When Suyuan asked him about this, he replied with a smile, "Though there be a stream before me, I crave to drink from only one dipper. In the midst of a swarm of beauties, there is none to equal my wife."

Fu Yijian was a cautious official, particularly after he was promoted to the rank of Grand Academician. He had to mingle with the nobles of the Deliberative Council on the one hand and the Manchu officials and members of the Imperial family on the other, always mindful not to give offence to either. The conspiracy case involving ten prominent families of the south which began in the early days of Shunzhi's reign had dragged on to this day. Because the ten families involved were rich and powerful in the Ming Dynasty, and had produced many scholars, in the eyes of the Manchu they were guilty beyond a shadow of a doubt.

It was felt that unless they were suppressed, the south would never be subdued. Would Fu Yijian dare to touch the case? One false move could cost him not only his position but his life. The condemnation of Chen Mingxia was a terrifying example.

But a man must have a conscience. Suyuan racked her brains for some way of convincing her husband to help.

"My Lady, what ails you?" Fu Yijian enquired anxiously as soon as he entered the bed chamber. He had been told of Suyuan's illness as soon as he arrived home, and he went straight to her shedding his court robes and hat as he went. He crossed the bed chamber in a few strides, and the serving maids quickly lifted the drapes and fastened them to silver hooks.

Suyuan turned slowly to face him. She lifted her eyes to her husband's face. In the last ten years, his greatest change was that he had grown a moustache and beard which partially hid his wide mouth. His shaven head made his forehead broader than it used to be. However the high-bridged nose and the sparkling eyes had not changed. He was a reliable man. She felt a rush of relief.

"You seem thinner. Was the journey tiring?" she enquired with a smile.

"I am fine. But what happened to you? How did you get

heat prostration?''

"I was in the garden, in the sunlight too long."

"Why didn't the maids hold a parasol over you?'' he turned angrily to the maids. Suyuan quickly dismissed them with a wave of the hand.

"Don't blame them. I was careless."

"How do you feel now?''

"I am better. Only ... I am worried, and cannot seem to put it out of my mind.'' Fu Yijian took a few sips from the teapot close at hand, and comforted her saying, "What can be so terrible? Let me help.''

"I've been plagued by strange dreams. Each night I dream the God of Judgements in the temple chiding me, saying a woman must not forget her parents who provided for her. And this has happened three nights in a row. I am deeply troubled. However, I left my home so long ago, and in these times of turmoil, I have no idea where my family is.''

Fu Yijian thought about it for a moment and suggested, "Has my dear wife forgotten the house of Loo? By rights they should be your family.'' Suyuan brightened, then nodded pensively. "You are right. But I wonder what has happened to Loo Jian?''

Fu Yijian sighed and replied in a whisper, "I heard that in the first years of Shunzhi, the Loo family was implicated in the conspiracy of the ten southern families. Last year, in my official capacity, I secretly sent to Renhe for news. The report I received was that the entire family was dead. I did not tell you, because I did not want you to be distressed.''

Suyuan contemplated Fu Yijian for a moment and said, "My Lord was once a poor scholar. That you were enabled to devote yourself to your studies and to achieve your present station in life was due to Loo Jian's generosity. That My Lord and I have shared these fourteen years of happiness is also due to his gallantry. I trust My Lord has not forgotten these favours.''

"These things are engraved upon my heart,'' replied Fu

Yijian solemnly.

"If Loo Jian were alive, how would you repay him?" pursued Suyuan, fixing him with an unswerving gaze. Fu Yijian was astonished to see that his wife seemed completely recovered. "If that were so," he said without hesitation, "I shall do all within my power, even to laying down my life."

"Do you mean that?"

"Heaven is my witness!"

Suyuan quickly showed him Loo Jian's letter.

Fu Yijian blanched. With trembling fingers he unsealed the letter and read it through. It was the usual letter addressed to sister and brother-in-law enquiring after their health and welfare. At the end there was a sentence that gave him pause. It read: "I have been falsely accused of conspiracy, and have been forced to live as a fugitive for the last few years, with no means of clearing my name."

"A page boy had delivered the letter while you were away. But he didn't know where Loo Jian was at present."

Fu Yijian returned the letter to its envelope. His demeanor had become grave.

Seeing his hesitation, Suyuan leaped out of bed, and taking a pair of scissors from under her pillow, hacked viciously at her hair. Fu Yijian tried to stop her, but she had already cut off a two-foot length. Holding the severed hair in both hands Suyuan cried out to the heavens, "In life, faithfulness is the paramount virtue. If one is unable to repay a debt of gratitude, then one is no better than a dog. What good then is fame and riches!"

Fu Yijian snatched the scissors from her and spoke angrily:

"You are an impatient woman! What sort of man would I be if I reneged on a debt of gratitude? You are not ignorant of matters of the Court. Power is in the hands of the Manchu; and Han officials are mere window dressing. In spite of my position all I can do is carry out the wishes of the Emperor and the nobles of the Deliberative Council. I have no say in anything. Especially not in a case of conspiracy which is the preserve of the

Manchus. A Han official cannot interfere...."

"In that case, repaying a debt of gratitude to Loo Jian is only empty words."

"I think the only hope is the Emperor himself; if he can somehow be persuaded to declare an amnesty. But it will take time. I shall find learned men, and jointly petition the Emperor at the proper time. However, this cannot be done within ten days or half a month."

Suyuan accepted that. Nevertheless she had to ask one more question.

"Did I have to remind you to pursue a solution to the injustice in the south?"

"Nonsense. These days making false charges has become a fad. Every Han official is quaking in his boots. If a stop is not put to this, what will become of the Court and the world?" Suyuan heaved a sigh and lay down again.

"I only hope the Emperor will investigate this case and correct this injustice so that the south can be as prosperous as before."

Part 3

Winter melted into spring. It was the eighth day of the second month in the thirteenth year of Shunzhi; sacred birthday of the Empress Dowager. Like the Emperor's birthday, this was an occasion for universal celebration.

At dawn the Emperor led the princes, the nobles, and all the officials of court, both civil and military, to Cining Palace to pay their birthday homage. No sooner had they retired, when the Empress followed by the imperial concubines of the six palaces, the princesses, and the titled ladies came to pay their respects. Finally, a third group made up of sons of Shunzhi led by eunuchs were brought into the Presence to prostrate themselves. The ceremonies accompanying these three groups took up most of the morning. Then followed the birthday banquet. Cining Palace was festooned with lanterns and streamers. According to tradition, the banquet was held in the main hall of the palace. The Empress Dowager's throne was placed facing south. The Empress and the imperial concubines served tea and wine. To the south of the hall a stage had been constructed on which opera, dance and various other entertainments would be performed. This was the Empress Dowager's forty-fifth year. The last year had been prosperous. The Empire was stabilizing at last, and the Empress Dowager was gratified. Her Majesty was determined to make this a family celebration, and commanded the presence of the ladies of all princely households, as well as the Emperor's half brothers and their children. In a break with the tradition of seating men and women separately, she also commanded husbands and wives to be seated together. Concubines who had children were also permitted to sit with their offspring. In this way the banquet became a truly family occasion. The Empress Dowager, being the great and revered matriarch of this noble family, took infinite pride and pleasure in these celebrations.

A eunuch's high, reedy cry, "The Lord of Ten Thousand Years has arrived" sounded from outside the gate of Cining Palace. All the people under the verandah of the palace prostrated themselves. Fulin crossed the threshold in a few quick strides. Stopping inside the gate, hands folded gravely behind his back, he surveyed the prostrated figures one by one, and a vague uneasiness passed over his features.

"Rise," he commanded and walked briskly toward the inner hall, where the Empress Dowager waited surrounded by still more noblewomen and titled ladies.

As he appeared in the doorway, the ladies of the court prostrated themselves. Fulin greeted his mother formally, then softly commanded the ladies to rise. They stood before him, stock still, as beautiful as spring flowers. His gaze swept over them, his visage clouded and his eyes fell with disappointment.

Noticing that look, the Empress Dowager said in a teasing manner, "I should not have let you come. In your presence everyone will go away hungry." Fulin laughed.

"What nonsense, Mother! How could I be perceived as a virtuous ruler if I were absent from my Imperial Mother's birthday celebration? I should then be the sinner of all time! As for the guests, I fear they will not be able to carry themselves out of Cining Gate."

"Why is that?"

"It's your fault for training the cooks of Cining Palace to excel one another."

The quick-witted Fulin knew how to humour his mother. The Empress Dowager chuckled happily.

"Empress Mother, what do you think of my idea of a family banquet at Cining Palace? The imperial family is bound by too many rules and restrictions. Wouldn't it be wonderful if we could be like ordinary folk when we celebrate the first month of new-borns, hold wedding feasts and mingle with one another!"

"There must be rules, but I do agree family gatherings can be more relaxed and enjoyable." The Empress Dowager spoke gently, however, in her heart she laughed at her son's clumsy attempt of hiding his mind. She steeled herself for what she was sure would come within the next five words. This passionate and impatient son of hers was bound to blurt out what was really in his heart. She was not surprised when Fulin asked, "Why isn't Prince Xiang here?"

A year ago, at the Empress Dowager's birthday celebration, Fulin had sought out his younger brother Bomubogur and his wife and enjoyed their conversation. A few days later he sent a gift of books, scrolls and curios by a eunuch. On the twenty-second day of the second month, Bomubogur who was not quite fourteen years of age was named Prince Xiang by the Emperor. From then on the Emperor showed a special interest in his younger brother. This attention caused many tongues to wag at court. With his new title, Bomubogur was required to attend the daily audience as well as many functions that he had hitherto been barred from. This new title also made it convenient for the Emperor to command his presence and that of his wife at many banquets within the palace. At the Mid-Autumn Festival, the Double-Ninth Festival, and at the Commencement of Winter, when family banquets were held, the Emperor had shown particular favour to Prince Xiang and his wife. Before long the gossip reached the ear of the Empress Dowager. However, the most disturbing tale was that the Emperor had several private meetings with the Prince's wife in the Imperial Garden. During these meetings, it was said, the two always spoke Chinese. As a result the Empress Dowager's informants were unable to report what was said.

Aside from a few trusted eunuchs, the Empress Dowager's informers included maids of honour and their mistresses. These reports were usually received without comment. However, if they smacked of vitriol, the tale-bearer would be roundly rebuked for lack of breeding. Furthermore, speaking ill of the

Emperor was strictly forbidden. These matters fell within the realm of palace ethics, which called for the guilty ones to be punished by flogging or caning. However, the kind-hearted Empress Dowager never resorted to those measures. Because he was the supreme master of all under heaven, the Empress Dowager supported her son in all things. She understood him, knew his mind and heart. However, nothing escaped her benign eyes.

From the day after his wedding, the Empress Dowager surmised that Fulin was not pleased with the new Empress. When he proposed a title for Bomubogur the Empress Dowager more or less guessed what was at the back of his mind. However, she was not an ordinary woman, nor an ordinary mother. She was keenly conscious of her position as the Empress Dowager and knew how to deal with her son, the supreme autocrat. She decided to compromise. So long as the situation did not get out of hand she would turn a blind eye. In fact this was the only way of dealing with her exceptionally clever, but mercurial and headstrong son. She had learned a great deal from her late husband Abahai. Consequently, as a schemer, she was more than equal to any man.

Hearing her son's question and taking note of his expression, everything was as clear as a piece of charcoal on the snow. Though she understood perfectly she did not let on. Instead she replied placidly, "They have gone to Shoukang Palace to fetch Yijing and Kanghui."

Yijing, the Grand Concubine, was Bomubogur's natural mother. She and Kanghui were both direct descendants of the Yuan Dynasty and wives of Lindan Khan of Qahar Mongol. In the eighth years of his reign, Abahai invaded Qahar and wiped out the last remnants of Genghis Khan's blood line. Abahai then took the women of Lindan Khan for his own. In the first year of Chongde, Abahai changed the dynasty name to Qing, and called himself the Good, Wise and Magnanimous Emperor. The Empress of Qingning Palace was the aunt of the present Empress Dowager who was then the concubine of the West Yongfu

Palace. At that time Yijing and Kanghui were Abahai's concubines too. Earlier, Yijing had given Lindan Khan two heirs, Erzhe and Abunai. When the forty-nine banners of the Mongol submitted, Abahai did not wish to kill them. Instead Erzhe was named Chief of the Qahar Banner with the title of Prince Heshuo. Abahai also married his second daughter, Princess Makerda, to him. In the second year of Shunzhi, Erzhe died and his younger brother Abunai married his brother's widow and inherited his title as Chief of the Banner. Bomubogur was born in the sixth year of Chongde and thus shared a mother with Erzhe and Abunai but had Abahai as father.

The Empress Dowager had always been kind to the women of her late husband. After Bomubogur and his wife had paid their respects earlier, the Empress Dowager sent them to fetch the Grand Concubine Yijing and Lady Kanghui. Fulin had always admired his mother's generosity. Satisfied that Prince Xiang and his wife would return, he allowed the conversation to drift onto the programme of entertainments that would be presented at the banquet.

Musicians stationed in the east and west verandah struck up a solemn air. Accompanied by the music the Empress Dowager ascended the throne placed in the centre of the main hall of Cining Palace. Led by the Emperor and the Empress, all the imperial harem, princes, nobles and their wives knelt in neat rows before the throne. When the Empress Dowager was seated and the music stopped, the eunuch in charge of ceremonies led the assemblage in a great chorus:

"Long live the Empress Dowager! Long live! Long live!"

A multitude of voices, mostly female, rose in unison, producing a curious melodic sound that was followed by echoes throughout the great hall.

The smiling Empress Dowager announced brightly, "This birthday banquet is a family gathering. We are family, therefore, eat and drink to your heart's content and speak without ceremony. This old woman wishes to enjoy her sons and grandsons."

Laughter rippled through the great hall. The atmosphere was much more relaxed than usual as these celebrations tended to be dreary and solemn. Nevertheless Fulin was determined not to treat the occasion too lightly, and insisted on performing the formal offering of tea and wine to the Empress Dowager. The musicians ranged under the threshold of Cining Gate struck up *Hail Son of Heaven* and Fulin led his five brothers toward the throne, arranged according to their respective ages. This was a departure from normal practice. Because of the difference in rank, the five princes could not be present at the same time. Furthermore, Bomubogur had only recently been given a title. Therefore, his inclusion was a sore subject among his older brothers. However, this was a family banquet in which distinction of rank was set aside in favour of age and generation, with the exception of the Emperor and Empress. The princes' ire was assuaged by placing Bomubogur at the end of the procession, as befitting the youngest in the group. Still they had to take care not to express their pleasure in this arrangement.

Bomubogur, however, did not bother to mask his displeasure at what he considered a slight. He expected a certain amount of respect and defference to accrue to his title. Therefore he was pleasantly surprised when Fulin stopped, looked back at him, and beckoned him forward with a smile. Bomubogur hurried to his side. Fulin took his arm, and shoulder to shoulder, carrying the gold goblet between them, they approached the Empress Dowager's throne. A gasp of amazement and shocked whispers swept the hall. All eyes were fixed on the faces of Fulin and Bomubogur. Bomubogur was in his element. His other brothers had to follow step for step behind the Emperor and himself. A respectful smile wreathed Fulin's face. He was everything he was expected to be. There was a warmth in his breast, for somewhere in that throng were a pair of black, shining eyes gazing at him full of amazement, dismay and even fear. Yet also full of praise and affection. It was enough. Aside from her a thousand pairs of beautiful eyes meant nothing to him. They simply did not exist. His footsteps became firm and purposeful; his figure more dashing; the smile that lit his handsome face never left his lips or the corners of his eyes.

The Empress Dowager accepted the goblet from her sons and drained it in one draught. Then she offered them wine in return. In that moment, Fulin's eyes quickly swept the ranks of concubines and other ladies ranged around his mother. His heart skipped a beat. Where was she? His eyes searched the assemblage again, and still those incomparable bright eyes were missing. Suddenly, Fulin felt as though he was covered in cobwebs. He was suffocating. A shadow passed over his visage. If she was not there, and had not seen or heard what he had done, then it was all for nought. Fulin seated himself on the throne to the left of the Empress Dowager. He was so preoccupied that even the glitter of gold utensils laid out before him lost their lustre.

Hail Son of Heaven was played again and again. A chorus accompanied by the musicians sang verses celebrating the birthday and drinking songs in voices that shook the rafters. Led by the Empress, the concubines of the six palaces, the princesses and wifes of princes offered tea and wine to the Empress Dowager. There was a burst of riotous colour in the middle of the hall, like a dazzling bouquet or a flock of gaily coloured song birds. Fulin watched them dully.

Suddenly she appeared at the end of the third row. She was the last of the princes' wives. Fulin watched her with joy and amazement. Evidently she had been hidden from view by a group of big-boned, clumsy, though colourfully attired Manchu and Mongol ladies. By contrast she seemed all the more dainty, graceful, refined and elegant. She seemed as though made of glass, glittering in the light. "Ah! The clouds have parted and the moon is out!" Fulin thought. His chest seemed to expand. Everything around him glowed. The hall was vast and high; the throne glittered; the tea, the wine and the food more delicious. The song of the chorus became unbearably sweet. Fulin seemed to have strayed into fairyland. His heart was light and bubbling with joy. When the Empress Dowager laughingly offered him wine, he took advantage of the moment and laughed out loud, like a child whose happiness knew no bounds. Though the startled Empress seated opposite him made frantic eye signals at him, he was beyond caring. Happiness flowed like a sweet, impatient torrent, engulfing his heart and, indeed, his entire being.

An orchestra of stringed instruments struck up a spritely tune, *The Golden Hall Is Filled with Joy* signalling the official start of the birthday banquet. The maids of honour serving tea and wine had changed their plain blue cloth robes for brightly coloured silks. Their black glossy braids were decorated with bright silk flowers at the end and at the nape of the neck. Their faces lightly dusted with rouge and powder, they darted back and forth between the guests like brightly coloured butterflies.

The Emperor and Empress left their seats to kneel before the Empress Dowager. Fulin smilingly said, "On the occasion of Your Majesty's birthday, your son presents the following gifts: ten thousand ounces of silver; one hundred bolts of superior quality satin and gossamer; six hundred strings of pearls; and six hundred strings of coral beads. I pray my Imperial Mother will accept the above with joy." This was an annual tribute which was expected. On behalf of the Empress Dowager, Sumalagu happily accepted the list of birthday gifts written on red paper. The musicians repeated *The Golden Hall Is filled with Joy* with gusto.

Next the principal concubines of the various palaces presented their gifts. Because the magnificent gifts of the Emperor and Empress already represented all the lower echelons, these gifts were mostly symbolic. Lady Duan of Yonghe Palace presented a string of prayer beads. Lady Gong of Jingyang Palace presented a gold statue of Buddha. Lady Ke of Yongshou Palace, the only Han concubine in the harem, presented a pair of yellow satin shoes cleverly embroidered with the traditional pattern of the phoenix worshipping the sun done in gold and silver thread.

This unusual gift won the grudging admiration of all the assembled ladies.

Lady Kang of Jingren Palace was the only principal concubine who had a son. Being permitted to attend the banquet with her child was a great joy. She approached the Empress Dowager, gratefully clutching her child to her breast. As she knelt, her not quite two-year-old child, third son of Shunzhi, lifted a tiny hand-warmer woven of gold and silver thread clutched in his chubby hands and cried out in his childish voice, "Granny, warm your hands!"

In the midst of ponderous court etiquette, the childish voice was a breath of fresh air in the vast and solemn hall. This little prince was exceptionally clever and vivacious, neither awed by his surroundings nor intimidated by the throng of strangers. His boldness pleased the Empress Dowager. She left her seat and approached the child to receive his gift.

"I appreciate it," she said to Lady Kang. She hadn't finished what she was going to say when another unexpected occurrance happened. The healthy child, with his rosy cheeks and bright, shiny eyes, suddenly thrust his arms out and demanded in a loud voice, "Granny, carry me!"

The whole assembly was aghast. Even the Empress Dowager was at a loss as to how to respond.

Because it was a birthday banquet, the guests were not required to wear court dresses. Therefore, Lady Kang's coiffure was suitable for a formal occasion, but she did not wear her gold coronet. She wore a robe of satin trimmed with marten fur. This made carrying a child easier. However, the Empress Dowager was the "birthday star" and wore her full regalia. This included a crown studded with jewels and pearls, court robe and jacket, necklaces and cloak. This heavy, glittering attire made it difficult to bend the arms in order to carry a child. Furthermore, a child might damage the jewels she was wearing. Most of all carrying a child was beneath her dignity.

Lady Kang patted the child and bid it be quiet.

Nevertheless, the Empress Dowager took the little prince in her arms. Even a child knows instinctively whether it is genuinely loved; whether affection is a mere pretence, a mask for real dislike. This instinct exists in children before they learn to speak. The young prince burrowed into the Empress Dowager's ample bosom, his tiny arms wrapped tight around her neck, his tender little face pressed against his grandmother's cheek.

The little bundle of warmth; this tiny body held tight in her arms; the tender little arms around her neck; a tiny cheek, smelling of milk, pressed against hers, full of trust and love — all these were something the Empress Dowager had not experienced for years. Her arms tightened around the child in spite of herself. As she pressed her lips against a plump little cheek, her throat tightened with warmth, and her eyes brimmed with moisture.

The whole assemblage gazed on in speechless amazement. The Empress Dowager broke the silence with a chuckle. "The Third Imperial Son is an interesting child. Last year at his first birthday, he seized everything on the birthday platter. That shows he will have a long, blessed life, with great ability in both civic and military matters...."

According to Imperial Family custom, a jade platter was presented to a royal child on his first birthday. On it were placed two jade ornaments, two jade pendants designed to be attached to fans, one gold spoon, one silver box, a bell and rod of rhinoceros bone, a bow and arrow, and writing implements known as the "four treasures of the study". Last year the little prince grabbed everything on the platter. The delighted grandmother, taking this as a good omen, presented the child with many toys, and bolts of silk and satin. Even now she recalled the incident with pleasure.

Now that the Empress Dowager had introduced the topic, the aunts and uncles of the child chimed in, outdoing each other with flattery. The little prince's eldest brother had died young. So he had now one older brother, two older sisters, and two young sisters. However, their mothers were ladies of low rank, and were not included in the royal banquet. Nevertheless, their mothers joined in the general merriment though there was a sourness in their hearts.

Taking the child back from his grandmother was another hurdle. The child clung to his grandmother like glue, and it was all Lady Kang and the nurse could do to pry him loose. In the end they had to resort to the old ruse of using the wet nurse to calm his wailing.

The Empress Dowager relinquished the child with a deep sense of regret. For a short while the child's affection filled her with an indescribable warmth and comfort.

Fulin was wreathed in smiles as he watched. He was happy because his mother was happy. When his oldest son had died in the ninth years of his reign he was not much moved. The child was very young, barely three months old, thin and sickly, born of a very low-ranking concubine. Also Fulin was very young himself, just fourteen years of age. It was only in the last two years that he became more aware of the importance of heirs. His second son was only eight months older than the third, but was nowhere as clever or healthy. Furthermore, the latter's mother was a high-ranking lady, and Fulin was fond of the child. However, today his mind was not on the child. He was anxious to witness his brothers present their birthday offerings.

Yebushu, Gaosai, Changshu, Taosai, and their wives stepped forward presenting their gifts: a Buddha, prayer beads, a white jade pagoda, and a gold incenser. Since each was given a principality, their annual gifts were formal, rich but safe, nothing unexpected or contrary to protocol. Sumalagu accepted the gifts formally, and the Empress Dowager nodded and smiled her approval.

The fifteen-year-old Prince Xiang and his seventeen-year-old wife, a glittering couple, approached the throne together. Each carried a *ruyi*, an S-shaped symbol of good fortune carved from coral. They knelt and presented their gifts. The Empress Dowager took the gifts from Sumalagu's hand, gently stroking their smooth surface. The two *ruyis* were an exact match in shape, size and colour. The sparkling white tassels attached to them brought out the warm inner glow of the coral.

Just as she was about to speak, Prince Xiang and his wife knelt again, each holding up a jade platter. On the platter the Prince held up was a tea-pot whose base was shaped like a lily root, its body like a lily blossom, with a lily pod for its lid. Beside it was a matching cup shaped like a lily leaf. So realistically were they crafted that they seemed almost alive. Prince Xiang's wife presented a platter on which was a bright red-lacquered food box.

"Will Your Majesty kindly examine these new things?" they chorused.

Sumalagu knew her mistress well. First she took the pot and from it filled the cup with a pale green tea, whose fragrance quickly spread around them. Then she lifted the lid of the box which was divided into nine compartments like the segments of an orange. Each compartment contained some fresh or dried fruit.

The Empress Dowager quaffed a mouthful of tea, savouring its sweet fragrance which seemed to penetrate the core of her being. From the box she took a peanut, called the "fruit of longevity", and crunched it between her teeth, delighted with its delicious crispness.

"How was this tea brewed?" asked the Empress Dowager. "It is so fragrant and refreshing."

Prince Xiang stammered, "Something ... was added ... to the tea...."

"What was it?"

"I'm not sure." He nodded at his wife in a childish gesture and added, "Ask her...."

"May it please Your Majesty," Prince Xiang's wife, Lady Dongeh spoke quietly, flashing a row of pearly teeth in a smile. "The water was from snow swept off pine needles and bamboo leaves last winter and kept in jars. At the time of brewing, pine seeds, a finger-shaped citron known as 'Buddha's hand' and plum blossoms were added. Finally, the water had to be brought to a boil thrice."

"No wonder!" The Empress Dowager smiled her approval. "We shall call it the tea of three purities! There is something special about this box too, is there not?"

"Yes, indeed," replied Lady Dongeh. "It is called the Box of 'Nine Times Nine'. Each of its compartments contains nine morsels of fruit, and each has an auspicious meaning. Your slave has written their names on cards which have been placed at the bottom of each compartment."

"Ah. Why don't you read them for me? My royal son, you and your wife draw near that you may better see and hear." The Empress Dowager was in high spirits and quite taken with her youngest daughter-in-law.

Fulin was hoping for this invitation, and quickly approached the Empress Dowager. Prince Xiang's wife stood close to the Empress Dowager, and showed each item in turn.

"Longan, represents pearls of the southern sea. Chestnut, for perfect beauty. Lily seeds are drops in a jade pool. Grapes, for sweetness surpassing fairy nectar. Litchi, a fairy's gift in a silk pouch. Gingko nuts, silver fruit of a magic tree. White dates, a treasure of tranquil times. Pine seeds are seeds of jade from the fairy mountain. Peanut, the fruit of longevity."

"Wonderful!" chortled the Empress Dowager. "How well you recite. I see your education has certainly not been neglected."

"Your slave accompanied her father when he was posted to Hangzhou. My father had tutors in both Manchu and Han to teach me."

"No wonder you have the bearing of a cultivated young lady of the south, so unlike our Manchu girls." The Empress Dowager chose a pine seed and savoured it. Lady Dongeh was not sure whether the last remark was censure or praise. "I thank Your Majesty," she said shyly. As she lifted her face to steal a glance at the Empress Dowager, she encountered Fulin's fiery gaze. Averting her eyes, she quickly retired to her seat.

Seated between Fulin and the Empress Dowager, but slightly behind them, was the Grand Concubine Lady Yijing. The Empress Dowager turning remarked over her shoulder, "My royal sister, Bomubogur has matured considerably since his marriage."

The Grand Concubine started to smile but changed her mind, and frowned instead.

"At this rate he will soon become a southern barbarian."

"How is that? Do you find this daughter-in-law...?" the Empress Dowager deliberately left the sentence dangling.

"Not at all," the Grand Concubinc continued. "The Empress Dowager's choice has always been good. I am merely saying our eight banners of Manchu and Mongol are a war-like race. Whereas Bomubogur shows none of those traits."

Food was brought on. The Empress Dowager who was in a happy mood said no more. The guests saluted the Empress Dowager and began to partake. Outside on the stage, an ancient dance commenced, accompanied by fast-tempo music. Eight dancers, dressed in armour and brandishing bow and arrow as horsemen of the eight banners, pranced about the stage, battling grotesque monsters with elephant's trunks. Inside the hall, revellers with cup in hand wandered from table to table as they would in an informal gathering of family and friends.

Fulin went to the table of Prince Xiang and his wife and seated himself between them. The two of them did not know what to do, and started to rise to prostrate themselves. But Fulin stopped them.

"The Empress Dowager has made this a family banquet. Therefore we shall be family and not monarch and subject."

Bomubogur quickly filled a goblet of wine and offered it to Fulin. He drained it in one draught, then handing the gold goblet to Prince Xiang's wife said, "It's your turn, my brother's wife."

Lady Dongeh darted a quick glance at Prince Xiang, who immediately responded saying, "Quick! Re-fill the Emperor's cup!" She lowered her eyes, smiling, and topped the goblet. Fulin drained it again.

"The Emperor holds his wine well," remarked Lady Dongeh. Fulin smiled as he replied, "Alas, there is no good wine." Prince Xiang was astonished. "Is not the palace's Jade Spring wine the best in the world?" Fulin shook his head and smiled as he regarded his younger brother and his wife.

"One can drink this wine from dawn to dusk and not be drunk. It is most uninteresting. I hear there is a wine in the south called 'Pear Blossoms of Spring' with a fine bouquet, sweet, and full-bodied. A thimbleful and one is drunk! I wonder if I shall ever taste it!"

Prince Xiang was quick to respond. "What is a jar of wine? Tell them to send some as tribute." Fulin sighed, "The mountains are high and the rivers deep. Who knows whether I will ever have that happiness.... Yet it seems today I catch a whiff of 'Pear Blossoms of Spring' in the very air I breathe. As they say, 'it's not wine that makes a man tipsy, but man is tipsy already....' My brother's wife must think I am a drunkard...' Lady Dongeh did not reply directly, but tried to steer the conversation elsewhere.

"'Pear Blossoms of Spring' is indeed a fine wine. Its colour is the pale green of bamboo leaves, full-bodied and its aroma fills the room...."

"How do you know?" asked Prince Xiang.

"When I lived in Hangzhou, my tutor once received a jar of the wine. It lasted him a whole month. He had one cup a day. Invariably it put him to sleep for the rest of the day. Whenever the jar was opened, those of us who did not drink became dizzy from the aroma. Even the servants in the courtyard were swallowing saliva. One day, the aroma of the wine brought my father. The two old people drank together that day, becoming so tipsy that it was all the servants could do to carry them back to their rooms. And all the way they kept muttering, 'Excellent wine, excellent wine!'"

Bomubogur and Fulin laughed.

"Your tutor was fond of his drink?" Fulin asked. Lady Dongeh quickly replied, "Not at all. He did not hold his wine well, but having a cup in hand is a fad among the literati of the south. He was a learned and articulate man whose wits became sharper the more he had to drink." She went on to relate how once while their tutor dozed off in a drunken haze she and her brother puzzled over how to complete a rhyming couplet. The tutor provided them with the solution and went soundly back to sleep and later did not even remember the incident.

Fulin chuckled.

"Did he quote from the Tang-dynasty poet Li Bai? Would you please recite it in Chinese?"

She did as she was asked. When she had finished, Fulin said in Chinese, "These poems have to be read in Chinese in order to savour the rhyme and the beauty of the language."

Lady Dongeh replied also in Chinese. "I agree. Actually I intended to write a few birthday verses for the Empress Dowager. But read in Manchu it would be meaningless. So I desisted."

They continued to converse in Chinese. Although he did not understand, Bomubogur did not dare to interrupt or give any indication of his displeasure. Fulin said, "Why not let me read it?" Lady Dongeh demured, saying, "My poor efforts would be an insult to Your Majesty. However, I have learned the lute, and will play for the Empress on her birthday." Fulin was displeased, so he said instead:

"This tutor who drank, made poetry and played the lute must have been a romantic."

Lady Dongeh smiled to herself and replied obliquely:

"At one time, my tutor was in Yangzhou. There he met a man selling cranes. Though he was poor, he spent every last penny and acquired a pair to take home. For this foolish gesture he became the laughingstock among his friends and acquaintances. His explanation was that he and his wife were old and lonely. As they had no children, having the cranes and being able to watch them dance and hear them sing would give them joy. And on that theme he composed ten poems which became quite popular. It was on the strength of those poems that my father hired him, at considerable expense, to teach his children."

"Ah, and what was your tutor's name? And will he not come to us?"

Lady Dongeh spoke solemnly:

"My tutor's name is Lu Zhiyue, with the scholastic name of Xiaotian. He has said the Emperor of Qing is a righteous man. However, he is a man of Ming, fed on the rice of Ming. Therefore he cannot serve two masters and disgrace his descendants. His only hope is that the new dynasty will be benevolent, aware of the needs of the people."

"He is a man of lofty principles. Where is he now?" Fulin asked.

"Some time ago my mother said he was an honoured guest in the household of Duke An. But he has since returned to the south."

"Retired?"

"No. It is said that there is much injustice in the south. Many people have been implicated in the case of the ten families accused of plotting against the throne. However there are many contradictions in the evidence and the case remains unresolved after more than ten years. My tutor has gone south to find some solution."

Fulin did not comment. On one hand he admired the tutor's righteousness and his courage. On the other he was annoyed by his meddling. Before the conquest, a number of wealthy families around Yangzhou and Jiangyin, south of the Yangtze, had considerable influence on the economics and the politics of the region. Their influence was such that the new Qing Dynasty saw them as a threat. In the second year of Shunzhi, one of these powerful clans was accused of fomenting sedition. The court seized upon this as an excuse in mass arrests. Actually more than ten clans were implicated. Cries of injustice spread throughout the south.

"Your Majesty," Lady Dongeh had adopted a more formal tone, "The southerner is gentle, unwarlike. The south is a place of riches and learning. At present, when the rebel Southern Ming regime of Yongli, and Zheng Chenggong have not yet been subdued, it is important to win men's hearts and establish peace in the south. Your Majesty is no doubt aware of this need."

Fulin looked at her in amazement. The smooth and beautiful face, the eyes that flashed like the morning star, lit now by a flame of fervour, moved him deeply.

"Tell me your name," he demanded impulsively. In a barely audible voice she breathed, "Your Majesty..." Prince Xiang's wife blushed and ducked her head, pretending to rearrange the cups and dishes of food on the table.

A eunuch approached and fell to his knees.

"Your Majesty, the Empress Dowager invites you to examine a tribute from the Siam." Fulin reluctantly rose to his feet, as he turned to leave, he asked again, "Do you refuse to tell me?" Prince Xiang's wife shot him a quick glance, and bowed her head again. Then in a tiny voice she said, "Black Pearl...."

"Black Pearl...." Fulin's heart lurched within his breast. The name whirled about madly in his brain. It was an apt description of those brilliant eyes. Those beautiful eyes! Why weren't you a Mongol born on the steppes? Ah, but if you had been, you would not be so clever and full of scholastic airs or have the fragile beauty of the marshlands of the south....

2

To the west of Qianqing Palace or the Palace of Heavenly Purity is Hongde Hall or the Hall of Enhanced Virtue. Like the East Chamber of the Yangxin Hall or the Hall of Mental Cultivation, this hall was also used for imperial audiences. However, being summoned to meet with the monarch in the Hall of Enhanced Virtue was considered more important.

Tang Jo-Wang was quick to prostrate himself. His face, flushed with excitement, made his hair and beard seemed whiter and his eyes bluer than ever.

Fulin chuckled. "Mafa, why are you prostrating yourself? So Holland has sent us a gift. Is that worth so much excitement? Come, sit and talk with us."

According to custom Tang Jo-Wang seated himself cross-legged on cushions placed beneath the dias. He spoke more rapidly and louder than usual. "Your Majesty does not understand. Your servant has been away from his homeland for several decades. To meet someone of his own race thousands of miles from home is exciting indeed."

"But Mafa, aren't you from the city of Cologne in Germany? Holland is a different country!"

"Your Majesty, though we come from different countries, we are from the same race. When I was studying in Cologne many of my schoolmates were Dutch and I learned their language in my youth. Since your old servant has the honour of Your Majesty's friendship, I have to do something for these compatriots who have journeyed so far. I beg Your Majesty's indulgence, to accord the highest honour to these ambassadors, for my poor sake." Fulin smiled when he replied, "Mafa, how can I refuse you, seeing your happiness? Have you any idea whether these these ambassadors have any other mission?" Tang Jo-Wang's excitement cooled.

"They come as representatives of the King of Holland, to pay their respects," he replied. "I have seen the list of gifts they bring, and assure Your Majesty it is very sumptuous indeed! The gifts to Your Majesty, Empress Dowager and the Empress can be considered national treasures. There are also an assortment of finely crafted astronomical instruments, and clocks. Ah! In the four decades I've been away there have been huge advances in metal work."

Tang Jo-Wang grew animated as he spoke. Fulin listened with amusement. In the last few years Tang Jo-Wang had counselled him to be mindful of his dignity in word and gesture; to be discreet in the presence of courtiers and so forth. Yet today, his kindly mentor showed that under certain circumstances he too could behave like a child.

Fulin responded thus:

"Mafa, we shall be happy to do as you ask. You will receive the Dutch Embassy on our behalf, accompanied by the Minister of Rites. However, Mafa, do not forget your advice to us when the Dalai Lama came."

In the ninth year of Shunzhi, the Dalai Lama who was revered as the Living Buddha, sent word that he wished to visit the capital. He was accompanied by a retinue of three thousand lamas and thirty-thousand Mongolians for protection. At first Fulin planned to journey to the frontier to greet the holy man personally. Many courtiers objected. Tang Jo-Wang was one of the most vociferous. Aside from composing a long petition, he also counselled the Emperor in person against such a move, saying it would be beneath his dignity. Tang Jo-Wang's advice was accepted. Instead, the Emperor sent Prince Jirgalang to greet the Dalai Lama some distance outside the city while the Emperor went hunting at Nanyuan. It was there that he waited upon the holy man. When the Dalai Lama was brought into the Presence, the Emperor stood and extended his hand in a gesture of friendship, then he showed him to the first seat among the princes who were ranged to the right of the throne.

Later it was learned that the main purpose of the Dalai Lama's visit was his desire to convert the Emperor and make him a lama. When Tang Jo-Wang got wind of this, he again counselled the Emperor, saying the Dalai Lama's intention was not compatible to his position as monarch. The Emperor and the Lama each had duties and functions to which they must devote themselves. In the end, though the Dalai Lama was accorded every courtesy, his greatest wish was not granted. Nevertheless, the following year the Emperor bestowed the title of Buddha of Unfettered Benevolence of the Western Heavens upon the Dalai Lama together with the right to proselytize Buddhism.

The reference to the past gave Tang Jo-Wang pause.

"Your Majesty need have no fear. Your old servant knows what he is doing. I will go at once to the embassy. Someone among them might be acquainted with some of my old friends in Amsterdam and other places in Holland."

Tang Jo-Wang was so excited that Fulin did not have the heart to throw cold water on the old man again. Fulin dismissed him. However Tang Jo-Wang had sat so long with his legs crossed that they had gone numb and he was unable to rise. Fulin helped him to his feet, and held him up until the guards came to his aid. Fulin raised his hand and four imperial guardsmen quickly approached and fell to their knees.

"You will escort Mafa to the ambassador's residence," he ordered. "See to it that nothing startles the horse on the way, and that no harm comes to Mafa."

Fulin stood, watching the guards escort the white-haired Jesuit from the hall.

The four Grand Academicians who witnessed this interview were moved by the Emperor's concern for the old man. Each had personal reasons for being grateful to the monarch.

Tuhai, styled Linzhou, surnamed Majia, was a Manchu of the Yellow Banner clan. When Fulin first took the reins of government he was merely a Secretariat Drafter in charge of the imperial seal. It was his duty to carry the imperial seal whenever the Emperor went out of the city. A serene, methodical, and unobstrusive fellow, Fulin thought him quite out of the ordinary, and considered advancing his career. However, he was concerned that other courtiers might object. Therefore, in his youthful way, he thought of a simple ruse. At a formal audience when the nobles of the Deliberative Council and all the Grand Academicians were present, Fulin announced without warning, "Secretariat Drafter Tuhai's behaviour is unacceptable. Let him be beheaded."

The assembled lords were aghast, and immediately pleaded Tuhai's innocence. Lord Aobai went as far as to state the wanton killing of the innocent would brand the monarch as venal and unjust. When the debate reached fever pitch, Fulin said with a straight face, "If we do not kill him, then we must reward him according to his potential so that he would not do anything untoward."

From that moment Tuhai became an academician of one of the three palace academies. Before long he was advanced to Grand Academician of the Palace Academy for the Advancement of Literature and Grand Minister of the Deliberative Council. Other honours followed and he became the fastest rising courtier.

Jin Zhijun, styled Qifan, was a native of Wujiang south of the Yangtze. He had passed the imperial examination in the forty-seventh year of Wanli in the Ming Dynasty, and was appointed as Vice Minister of War. In the first year of Shunzhi when the armies of Qing seized the capital, all members of the Grand Secretariat and officials of various ministries were ordered to remain at their posts, but to work side by side with Manchu officials. Jin Zhijun continued in his post and became renowned for his handling of land taxes, declaring an amnesty for those who submitted to the new regime, and regulating the use of the canals. For this he won the trust of the court. When Fulin took the reins of government, Jin Zhijun also secretly petitioned the Emperor suggesting that all bannermen be prohibited from engaging in commerce, princes be forbidden to leave the capital without permission, and eunuchs who left the palace without permission be sentenced to death. All these proposals met with the Emperor's approval. As a result Jin Zhijun's career rapidly advanced until he was Grand Academician of the Palace Historiographic Academy. Though he was one of the twenty-nine officials who had opposed the Emperor in the execution of Chen

Mingxia his career did not suffer. For that he could not help but feel some remorse. At the time when the plight of Chen Mingxia and Kong Dingzi were being satirized in the popular play *The Journey South*, a ditty about Jin's climb up the ladder of officialdom was also making the rounds:

"From Ming to rebel and then to Qing,

He has truly made a success in all three regimes."

So distressed was he by the satire that Jin Zhijun fell ill, and petitioned the Emperor to allow his retirement. The Emperor not only forbade it but commissioned the imperial painter to make a portrait of Jin Zhijun to be hung in his private chamber as a reminder of his absence.

At the beginning of this year Jin Zhijun, having recovered from his illness, returned to court. Fulin was glad of his return, and spoke thus to the assembled lords: "The relationship between monarch and subject is precious and must be maintained. Last year when Zhijun was seriously ill, we commissioned his portrait because he is aged, and we fear that we might not see him again.... All those whom we employ we wish to keep at our side, always. My Lords must henceforth dismiss all thoughts of retirement...."

The assemblage was greatly moved. Jin Zhijun was especially affected, and tearfully banged his forehead on the floor, swearing eternal fealty to the Emperor.

Cheng Kegong, Grand Academician of the Palace Historiographic Academy, shared Jin Zhijun's sentiments. Cheng's father had been a Grand Academician in the Ming Dynasty. He himself had passed the imperial examinations in the sixteenth year of Chongzhen. During the first tumultuous years of the new dynasty he lived a retired life. After the new dynasty was established in Beijing he was recommended for a post in the Palace Historiographic Academy. After Shunzhi took the reins of government and established the policy of employing able officials of the previous regime, Cheng came to the monarch's notice because of his family connections with the Ming Dynasty and his knowledge of its workings. He was often consulted on matters of government, and his career advanced. Now he was Senior Guardian of the Heir-Apparent. With his background, how could he not be grateful for the Emperor's favour?

Fu Yijian, however, was different from the others. He had been a student in the previous dynasty and only sat for the imperial examinations under the present regime. During the ten springs and autumns that separate the third and the twelfth year of Shunzhi, he had risen steadily through the ranks to the post of Grand Academician of the Palace Secretariat Academy and of the Palace Historiographic Academy and Senior Guardian of the Heir-Apparent. As the Qing Dynasty treated him far better than its predecessor, it naturally had his loyalty. Fu Yijian found there was some truth in the ancient precepts "Respect those who respect oneself", and "A gentleman would lay down his life for a friend".

Fulin turned away from the four Grand Academicians, satisfied with their obvious loyalty. When he had resumed his seat, he turned to them and in a conversational tone commented that he had studied historical books on the art of government and the history of Ming, and asked which of the emperors of Han, Tang, Song, and Ming did they consider the greatest.

Jin Zhijun said, "Taizong of Tang was the greatest."

"I think not," objected Fulin. "I consider Taizu of Ming the greatest, for he established wise laws which will stand the test of time. None of the others could equal that feat." Cheng Kegong quickly interjected, "Your Majesty has great vision. In the sixth month of last year you decreed iron-clad rules of ethics for thirteen government offices, and also forbade palace officials from accepting bribes and interfering with government policy. Subsequently, in the eleventh month, the official Gu Ren was executed for corruption. These two events were widely publicized throughout the land, showing all and sundry that the letter of the law is being enforced. Such is the way of a wise and able ruler...."

Fulin scowled as he spoke, "Have you forgotten that last

year we also acknowledged that in these ten odd years of our reign, we have failed in many things? For instance the frontiers have not yet stabilized.. The floods, draught and earthquakes that have plagued our land are retribution for our failings in the eyes of the gods. Yet in your petitions you persist in addressing us with words such as 'almighty' which only adds to our transgressions. Kegong, are you not aware of this?"

Cheng Kegong fell to his knees, quickly dofted his cap and pressed his forehead to the floor, begging forgiveness.

Fulin said, "There is no need for that. In future such words must not appear in petitions..." He paused, and continued more gently: "In all the thousand matters that we must attend in the space of one day, there are bound to be things that offend the gods, and are contrary to the wishes of man. You must bring these matters to our attention. Your good counsel will be suitably recognized. Truth cannot offend."

The suddenness of the Emperor's pronouncement threw the Grand Academicians into confusion. They did not know how they should respond. Fu Yijian was about to speak, but a warning look from the elderly Jin Zhijun caused him to curb his tongue. The execution of Chen Mingxia still weighed heavily on all Han officials. They were struck down the first time they had spoken their minds, encouraged by the Emperor's friendly and compassionate attitude. Thereafter they had kept silent for two whole years. Now the young Emperor was encouraging them to speak out again.

"A monarch's wisdom wins the hearts of his people," Fulin continued, "and maintains order by exercising his right to punish. Law and punishment must be applied with justice. The charge of treason levelled against ten prominent families in the south has dragged on for ten years, and implicated many people. If the charges are true, let the Ministry of Justicc present its evidence. If false, the accusers must bear the consequences. We cannot allow the case to remain unresolved."

The incumbent Minister of Justice, Tuhai, hastily delivered a statement: "The treason of ten prominent families was placed on file for investigation in the second year of Shunzhi. At first it was in the jurisdiction of the Commander of the Forces in the south. The handling of the case was only transferred to the Ministry of Justice after they were already condemned. Though doubts were raised, there was no conclusive supporting evidence. After the eighth year of Shunzhi when Duke Shuncheng took charge of the Ministry of Justice, everything had to be referred to him. Being a man with immense responsibilities which constantly require his attention, the Duke did not have time to devote to the case. Nor did the Minister and Vice-Minister of Justice have the courage to protest."

Fulin's face clouded. "You are now the Minister of Justice. Why have you not settled the case?"

Tuhai hesitated. Fulin's eyes flashed daggers that pointed straight at his heart. However Fulin controlled his anger, and in anequable voice continued: "Where law prevails there is peace. Preferences must not be allowed to overule common sense. As Minister of Justice it is your duty to speak fearlessly in our Presence."

Tuhai fell to his knees, whipped off his cap and pressed his forehead to the floor. "Begging Your Majesty's pardon, it is a question of caste that prevents your servant from speaking. The case was under the personal jurisdiction of Duke Shuncheng until his death in the ninth year of Shunzhi. His young son who inherited all his titles and responsibilities did not see fit to investigate the case. It is known the Duke often arrives at his conclusions and submits his judgement on complex cases before all the evidence has been collected and examined by the Minister and Vice Minister. Who would dare object? Your Majesty, forgive me for speaking plainly. In your slave's humble opinion princes and dukes can be warriors, or imperial counsellors but should not be heads of the six ministries of government."

Tuhai's words trailed off. Though he had not said everything on his mind, he had said all he needed to.

Fulin was calm though his eyes flashed fire. He had taken Tuhai's words to heart and an unaccustomed excitement engulfed him.

"If such is the case with the Ministry of Justice," he said, "I can imagine the condition of the other five ministries. No wonder this case drags on. Yijian, what is your opinion?"

Fu Yijian approached the throne and said, "In the third month of last year, Your Majesty issued a proclamation, declaring that education and Confucian virtues are the means of achieving universal peace. Your Majesty encouraged all courtiers to improve their minds and to promote the talents of the wise and able. These bold and sage innovations will be the foundation of an empire known for both its military prowess and a high degree of culture. The south is noted for its learning. Moreover, the ten families have been known and respected for generations as erudite men. This is the time to settle the case once and for all."

Fulin nodded, his jet black eyes flashed with impatience.

"Zhijun, you are the eldest and the wisest. What do you say?"

Jin Zhijun bowed before replying.

"Last year when Your Majesty decreed that all levels of society had the right to petition the court, a number of petitions from the south related to the case, pleading for justice, were presented to Your Majesty. At present, making false charges to settle petty grudges has become a common practice. Furthermore, the law requiring the punishment of escaped slaves has been used as a weapon against the people. By settling this case we can also hope to put an end to these abuses."

Fulin levelled his gaze on Jin Zhijun, but did not speak.

After the custom of land expropriation was stopped, escaping slaves became a serious social problem. Through long years of war, bannermen of all castes acquired a large number of slaves. Because of cruel treatment slaves escaped whenever they could. To stem the flood the court promulgated harsh laws. An escaped slave was given a hundred lashes, branded and returned to his master. He would be hanged if he was captured after a third attempt at escape.

Furthermore, whoever harboured a runaway slave was immediately put to death, his family exiled and his property confiscated. The reason people dared to harbour escaped slaves was because they were either parents, children or siblings who had been abducted by the Manchu bannermen years ago. Therefore, the Hans saw the law against escaped slaves as a terrible means for genocide. In the early years of Shunzhi when the dynasty was at war, slaves followed their masters into battle, and escape was not a serious problem. Recently more and more slaves were escaping as the war zone shrank to the borderlands, while peace came to the central plains and the north. Consequently, in the eleventh year of Shunzhi the Deliberative Council of the Nobles proposed not only to punish those who give succour to escaped slaves, but ten neighbouring families as well. All their property would be confiscated. Every member of their families would be given forty lashes and banished to a far-off place. The local officials in whose jurisdiction these incidents occurred would be demoted. If a captured slave attempted to escape again while being returned to his master, the guards in charge of transportation would also be banished. The emperor considered the punishment excessive and ordered the nobles to reconsider. However, after deliberation the law was re-submitted unchanged. Fulin was forced to acquiesce. These measures, coupled with human greed and deception, caused great consternation among the people.

Encouraged by Fulin's silence, Jin Zhijun continued:

"It is the duty of a courtier to bring abuses to light. Besides, Your Majesty has decreed that the people should voice their concerns without fear of reprisal. I beg Your Majesty's indulgence for speaking out. The lack of outspoken men is detrimental to the court."

In the first month of the previous year, after the Emperor's proclamation of free speech had gone out there had been an outcry against the laws relating to escaping slaves. Li Yin, Supervising Secretary of the Office of War, produced a petition in which he listed seven tragic effects that could result from the enforcement of the law.

Li's petition remained on the Emperor's desk for more than ten days. The more he studied it the more alarmed he became. Finally, he sent it down to the Council of Nobles for their deliberation. He was surprised that all the nobles in the council were unanimous in their condemnation of the document. In their rage, they declared it to be revolting, even slanderous, and demanded its author be executed. The Emperor flew into a rage, and vetoed their motion, demanding they reassess the issue. The council softened. Their demand of the death penalty was reduced to eighty lashes of the cane and banishment. Seeing that the nobles had backed down, the Emperor also had to compromise. Although Shunzhi disallowed the caning, Li Yin was exiled to a frontier post.

The four academicians were aware of these events. Although their remonstration was addressed to the Emperor, its actual target was the Council of Nobles. The council was above the three palace academies. Being the actual governing body of the empire, it not only placed the academies in a subserviant position, it also robbed the Emperor of some of his authority.

Fulin's fingers beat a nervous tattoo on the finely sculpted dragon's head on the arm-rest of his throne. His brows were knitted in a deep frown. He was silent for a moment then spoke slowly:

"The Manchus, nobles and commoners alike, have fought hard to help us establish the dynasty. They have acquired the slaves in wars they fought with unstinting efforts and sacrifice. Owning slaves to the Manchu is what owning land and houses is to the Hans. Who could have foreseen that within a decade, more and more slaves would be running away, and those who harbour them increasing at an alarming rate. If this is allowed to continue the Manchus will suffer tremendous loss. We have, therefore, promulgated harsh laws to put an end to this. It is not our desire that many should suffer for the acts of a few, but circumstances have forced it upon us...."

The academicians were taken aback by the Emperor's candour. They exchanged glances and decided to let the matter drop.

Fulin smiled faintly. The fire in his eyes went out, and he dismissed the academicians saying, "We will give these matters careful thought before we make a decision."

As the four turned to leave, Fulin spoke again, "Yijian, stay a moment."

Fu Yijian was an important official of the regime and, therefore, trusted by Fulin. When he stood beside the throne again, Fu Yijian noticed the fires were flickering once more in the Emperor's eyes, a sure sign that some serious matters were simmering close to the surface. Fulin fixed Fu Yijian with his gaze.

"It seems to me you haven't said everything that's on your mind," he observed.

Fu Yijian's brain worked with lightning speed. Fulin's mercurial personality and his circumstances made Fu Yijian apprehensive of this youthful and highly volatile Son of Heaven. When he needed the support of the Manchu nobles, Fulin shunned the Han officials. On the other hand, when he felt a need to control the Manchu nobles, he would play up to the Hans. He was unbelievably arrogant at all times. Once a courtier proposed that Prince Dorgon's reputation should be rehabilitated since his contributions to the Empire surpassed his wrongdoing, he was banished for his pains. On another occasion, an official reported a rumour that eunuchs had gone to the city of Yangzhou to buy women for the palace. This report so angered the Emperor that the official was banished to a far-off place. Because of these precedents Fu Yijian chose his words with care when he addressed the throne.

"Your Majesty has the mandate of the gods to rule all under Heaven," he began. "Thus Your Majesty must think of all the people in the country and not only of the nobles or the eight banners of Manchu." He paused. When he resumed, he seemed to have strayed onto something unrelated. "Of all the dynasties since the beginning of history, the Yuan was one that most lacked rules and regulations. They conquered all under Heaven on horseback, so they ruled from horseback without thought of laws that would ensure permanency and peace. They controlled the populace through force of arms. That was why within a hundred years factions rose against one another, and their empire collapsed. After the collapse of Yuan, the wise and heroic monarch, Taizu of Ming studied the strengths and weaknesses of previous dynasties and devised a code of law to rival that of Han and Tang. But to succeed, Taizu also had to be decisive, and autocratic. He could not be controlled, or manipulated. A man of his word, he valued results. The law was paramount and carried out to the letter. If his successors had not been foolish men who submitted their power to other men, Ming would not have perished after only two hundred and seventy years."

Fulin averted his face and, with his eyes fixed to the lavishly carved ceiling of the hall, retorted:

"However, at the beginning of his reign, Taizu of Ming slaughtered his meritorious courtiers. Was that not a blot on his reputation?"

Fu Yijian retreated, bowing with his hands clasped before his face. Then he replied, "The Han Dynasty had Han Xin a brilliant strategist. The Ming had Lan Yu, also a brave warrior. Both had many military feats and were appointed generals at the beginning of the dynasties. Han Xin was later killed for fear that he might usurp the throne. Lan Yu was killed for his unlawful deeds. For the good of a newly founded nation, some restraints must be put on veteran military men. For left uncurbed, their prowess on the field of battle becomes a weapon, which the arrogant will not hesitate to turn upon the populace. A regime that allows its people to suffer cannot last. Both Gaozu of Han and Taizu of Ming slaughtered their generals for that very reason.

Though they may be censured for breaking faith with their followers, it was a wise move. Otherwise Han and Ming would not have stabilized their empire as swiftly as they did."

Fulin nodded, his blazing eyes fixed upon Fu Yijian. The expression in those orbs was a complex mixture of astonishment, pleasure, fear, anger, pride and suspicion. Fu Yijian forced himself to be calm. He knew full well that the slightest sign of nervousness and what he just said would be misconstrued as an attempt at subverting the monarch. These simple truths could cost him and his family their lives.

The youthful Fulin broke the silence with a laugh.

"Yijian is indeed learned, with an unerring grasp of history and its meaning."

Fu Yijian breathed easier as the Emperor steered the conversation toward a discussion of history. Fulin ordered tea for Fu Yijian, signalling an end to their private conversation. Both men knew that they had reached a point in their candour with each that had been pushed to its limit.

After Fu Yijian left him, Fulin was restless.

He had only intended to resolve the charge of treason against the ten families at that morning's audience. It did not occur to him that the custom of appointing princes and dukes as the heads of the various ministries would be touched upon. Even the traditional Deliberative Council of Nobles had been subtly brought to the fore. These matters had stuck in his craw for a long time. Yet having them brought out into the open was still a shock.

Being aware of the hardships his forebears had endured to secure his empire, Fulin had to bow to tradition and protect the interests of the eight banners of the Manchu. However, he was also emperor; a young, hot-blooded man with a fierce determination to do the right thing. Therefore, he had to strike a balance between the welfare of his people and that of the Manchus. That delicate balance was extremely hard to achieve. Fulin strode out of the hall and turned toward the Palace of Heavenly Purity.

The eunuch Wu Liangfu, thinking that his master was returning to his residence, hastily ordered the young eunuchs to make preparations. Fulin waved him aside. "I'm going for a walk."

"Shall I order a sedan chair to follow?"

"No." Fulin turned south from the Gate of the Palace of Heavenly Purity and headed for an alley paved with slabs of white marble.

"Which of the ladies will Your Majesty visit?" Wu Liangfu enquired discreetly.

"None," Fulin replied curtly, continuing in a southerly direction. The tone of his voice warned Wu Liangfu to keep silent. Since the sixth month of last year when Fulin had an iron placard forged, stating rules forbidding eunuchs to interfere with affairs of state, the eunuchs had been going about like beaten puppies with their tails between their legs. In fact the Emperor had changed greatly in the space of a year. From giving himself up to sensuality, he had become ascetic. He had never been a frequenter of Kunning Palace, the residence of the Empress. Now he avoided it completely. He seldom summoned the principal concubines, while the lesser concubines never saw the Emperor at all. The Emperor lived in seclusion in the Palace of Heavenly Purity, studying the classics when he was not occupied with official business. At times he would be found staring vacantly at the flickering flame of a lamp, lost in thought. Everyone who saw him thus was puzzled. Wu Liangfu guessed the cause of his master's pensiveness, but like the others, did not dare put his thoughts into words.

Fulin strolled southward from the Gate of Heavenly Purity, his thoughts in a turmoil. Appointing princes and dukes as heads of ministries was done when Fulin first took the reins of government. The idea had originated from the regent Prince Jirgalang, and was meant as a reward for those who had rallied to Fulin's cause at the death of Prince Dorgon. Though these princes and dukes made a great show of their loyalty, in fact they did as they pleased, making Fulin feel restrained at every turn. As for the Council of Nobles, their deliberations constantly went against him. What is to be done? He could not act as Taizu of Ming, for he was not the founder of the dynasty, and did not have the power to carry it off. On the other hand he was not willing to be a puppet emperor.

Fulin's mind was entirely focused on what he should do.

The year he took charge of government, the princes and dukes who were appointed as heads of the six ministries were his cousins and men who had acquitted themselves well on the battlefields, and men of renown, and therefore unimpeachable. However, all except Yuele who was Minister of Works, all the others had since died and been replaced by their sons.

What did he fear from them? Though the Council of Nobles was protected by tradition and could not be touched, that did not apply to the six ministries. Fulin quickly made up his mind. That was where he would begin! He smiled complacently: The unresolved case of treason would furnish an excuse to begin with the Ministry of Justice and end by terminating the practice of patronage appointments...This momentous decision would have wide repercussions. No doubt there would be more jousting with the Council of Nobles.... Should he discuss the matter with his mother?

Fulin stopped and looked about. To his amazement he found himself under Youyi Gate. The ten or dozen eunuchs, who trailed behind him like a tail, huddled together uncertainly, afraid to speak. He chuckled to himself at their discomfiture. Cining Palace was behind him. At the end of winter, the needles of the pine and cedar peeping over the wall of Cining Garden were inky green. Between them he could see the tender green of gingko trees and phoenix trees, harbingers of spring.

Why not take a stroll round Cining Garden while he pondered the means of winning over the Empress Dowager. Then he would go straight to Cining Palace, which would be closer.

Inside the south gate of the garden, grey rocks fanned outward from the foot of the walls, some lying flat on the ground, others rearing upward, forming a small knoll. The stones were grey, their shape and size in perfect harmony; their strata arranged in pleasing symmetrical patterns of vertical and horizontal lines, giving the knoll a feeling of strength and depth. From the top of the knoll he could see the glazed roofs and ridges of Cining Palace that reminded Fulin of the Empress Dowager's birthday celebration half a month earlier.

The guests had all gone, and mother and son were left alone in the hall, reminiscing on the past. The Empress Dowager was recalling how Fulin's grandfather Nurhachi defeated Qahar Mongol's Lindan Khan. She told the story in great detail, paying special attention to how Abahai made Lindan Khan's son Erzhe the banner chief of Qahar Mongol, and thus won the hearts of all the Mongol banners. The Empress Dowager chuckled as she went on:

"Of the forty-nine banners, Qahar Mongol was the last to submit and their strength was only slightly less than that of Horqin. Therefore, their submission was important. Their loyalty has been unquestioned ever since. With the north stabilized, we were able to turn our full attention to the south. Actually, Lindon Khan's sons Erzhe, Abunai and your brother Bomubogur are half brothers, and therefore related to you. You have taken a special interest in Bomubogur and that pleases Abunai. Hence the Qahar Banner would also be grateful to you. And that pleases me."

Fulin smiled and nodded. But both mother and son understood what the conversation was about, and who it was about. Both were thinking of the same person, though that person was not mentioned by name.

The passionate feelings roiling in Fulin's breast did not cool because of the Empress Dowager's disapproval. On the contrary the forbidden fruit became all the more desirable. The beauty of her face and figure had taken root in Fulin's heart. It was she who had brought the injustice suffered by the ten southern families to his attention. And that had led to thoughts of breaking the power of the governing clique. She might not have meant this to happen, but he took her as a confidante from that moment on. He loved her to distraction. However, he could not summon her at will. He could only wait with an impatient heart for festivals, hoping to encounter her when she went to pay her respects to the Empress Dowager. Though they may not speak, a fleeting glimpse would satisfy him.

There were many things Fulin longed to tell her.

Who would dare spill their heart to the Emperor? Fu Yijian was afraid, and Tang Jo-Wang could not. Even his mother was unwilling. They had either been afraid or concerned, worrying about prestige. Hadn't he been unable to speak his mind too? He had to maintain the dignity befitting the Son of Heaven; to be inscrutable. Yet, how he longed to speak candidly, and how he longed to be understood and appreciated. The Empress was kind, virtuous but guileless. As for the concubines, they only hoped for his favour. Aside from bearing him sons and thus improving their lot in life, they had no other concerns. She was like a spring of fresh water in a desert, or the sound of a playful flute in the wilderness. How could he not be moved by her? It seemed that from the moment of their first meeting, nothing could be held back. On this of all days he longed desperately to see her. Her bright and clever eyes, her tender smile would give him the courage and the strength he needed.

Fulin skirted the flowerbeds in a few quick strides, and continued down the cobbled path south of the pavilion that stood beside the stream. Ancient gingko trees covered with tender green leaves stood on either side. The peonies in the flowerbeds had not sprouted yet. All around the branches of pine and cedar intertwined, so that all one could see was masses of green foliage blotting out the path beyond.

A flapping of wings disturbed the still air. Two red-crowned cranes with white feathers and black tails took to the sky, circling lazily over the tree tops. As Fulin stopped to gaze at them, a tinkle of laughter came from beyond the trees. A woman's voice full of laughter said, "How shall we call you in the future: Lady? Or Princess?" A voice sweet and low that Fulin would have recognised anywhere answered, "Call me Princess in the palace, and Lady in public. Will that be all right?" Fulin quickened his step to a sprint. The eunuchs hurried after him wondering what was the matter with the Emperor, but they could not keep up. Fulin rounded the pavilion and stood before Prince Xiang's wife. The startled ladies quickly fell to their knees.

Fulin took no notice of the others. His full attention was riveted upon her. He blurted out the name Black Pearl, a name he whispered to himself countless times in the gardens under the moonlight. Yet when he spoke it out loud, it sounded strange. What was wrong with his voice?

Black Pearl knelt and touched her forehead to the ground in greeting. Then she rose smiling. "If it pleases Your Majesty, the Empress Dowager summoned me to her today and took me as her adoptive daughter."

"Oh!" Fulin gazed into her vivacious eyes and a chill ran through him. Inwardly he cried out, "Mother, mother, all this is useless. It's too late to stop me now!" Aloud he said pleasantly, "That's wonderful! From now on I shall call you Imperial Sister." Black Pearl blushed, and continued in a low voice, "The Empress Dowager has also asked me to teach her to speak Chinese and to read Chinese poetry.... " "Really?" Fulin arched his heavy black brows in amazement and delight.

"Yes. Her Majesty was delighted with our gift of the fruit box, and all the sweets it contained. She was particularly pleased with the poetic symbolism, and thought how nice it would be to be able to repeat them in their original language, which is bound to sound more pleasing."

"Ah ... you...." He reached out and seized her by the wrist. "I have something important to discuss with you," he said. "Let us sit a while in the pavilion." Black Pearl was embarrassed, and protested feebly, "Your Majesty...." It was only then that Fulin noticed that other ladies were present. In his eyes they did not exist, so he did not let go of Black Pearl, but half dragged her into the pavilion. He did not let go of her wrist until they were seated on the stone drums on opposite sides of the stone table.

While the eunuchs and the maids arranged seat cushions, Fulin composed himself and then spilled out all his thoughts about the treason case, the practice of appointing princes and dukes as heads of the six ministries, and the machinations of the Council of Nobles.

At first Black Pearl was embarrassed and afraid, her eyes darting fearfully at the serving maids standing outside the pavilion. However, her attention was soon captured by what Fulin had to say. Then her eyes never left his face. Nothing else mattered. Although she was silent, her wide expressive eyes mirrored her heart. In their warmth, Fulin felt the understanding and support he craved, giving him the courage and the stimulus that mere words could not.

Finally, Fulin fell silent. She seemed to sense something in his gaze and blushed. But she quickly collected herself, and reached up to tuck in a lock of hair that a breath of spring breeze had worked loose from her coiffure. She no longer tried to avoid Fulin's blazing eyes, and spoke in a calm, decisive tone. "Your Majesty is ruler of all under Heaven, and not merely chief of Manchu tribes. The Empress Dowager will help you...."

"Black Pearl!" Fulin breathed her name shakily. He wanted to shout the name out loud.

Two pairs of eyes grappled with one another. Two youthful hearts trembled with feelings. The silence, charged with deep emotion, held back the floodtide of passion. Fulin struggled within himself. When he spoke again it was in his normal voice. He spoke of the things that he desperately wanted to share with Black Pearl. "Imperial Sister, I have been studying the history of Ming and learned some valuable lessons. I have concluded the fall of Ming was due first to the impotence of its law, then to the mediocrity of its officials. In general, the monarch was foolish and muddleheaded, and the officials abused their positions. In the end, it led to national bankruptcy and the empire was toppled from forces within and without."

From the beginning of the Qing Dynasty, Nurhachi and Abahai had probed the reasons for the demise of Ming. Some attributed it to the indiscriminate trust in eunuchs, others insisted it was due to civil officials abusing their power, still others thought it was due to rampant corruption and low morale among the people. None of them had probed the heart of the matter as Fulin had. Black Pearl's eyes glistened like morning dew, her face was lit with a smile of admiration. Fulin was encouraged to speak more freely.

"I believe that although Ming collapsed with the death of Chongzhen, the seeds of destruction were sown in the reign of Zhengde and Jiajing (1506-1566). By the timc Wanli came to the throne (1573) it was beyond help. After that it went from bad to worse. That is why Chongzhen's dying words, 'I am not the destroyer of my empire,' revealed him as a stupid, unrepentant man."

"I agree," Black Pearl replied solemnly. "Just as the fall of a dynasty is not the fault of one generation, so the rise of another is not the achievement of a single generation either."

"You're right!" Fulin exclaimed. "I will use the fall of Ming as a reminder and model myself after sages of the past to direct my descendants along new pathways.... However," he paused and shook his head doubtfully, "now the Empire is just becoming stable. There are many wounds that have to be healed. I fear I may never see the days of peace and prosperity...."

"Howevcr, the pioneers of an empire will go down in history and be revered for generations to come."

"In your mind, am I a pioneer of an empire, or am I merely

its keeper?"

"Setting the boundaries of Great Qing and establishing laws are the work of a pioneer, are they not? And the two matters Your Majesty spoke of, are they not innovative?" Black Pearl fixed Fulin with a gaze full of confidence.

"You're right," Fulin quickly grasped her meaning. "A pioneer must endure some pain and difficulties...."

"Is Your Majesty afraid?" Black Pearl spoke as to a friend, her encouragement not unmixed with concern.

"Me?" Fulin looked deep into Black Pearl's eyes. Ambition and tenderness coursed through his veins like a warm, happy torrent.

He dropped his voice so that only she could hear. "I will talk to the Empress Dowager.... I need your help. I'm not afraid."

3

The third month of the year was full of sunshine and flowers. In Cining Garden purple and white magnolias were in bloom. The waxy blossoms poised like delicate goblets of white and purple jade, filled with the intoxicating wine of spring. A heady perfume wafted through the tranquil courtyard to steal unseen along the verandah into the elegant room.

Under a window facing south on a long kang covered with a woolen blanket, a bright yellow satin mattress had been spread on which the Empress Dowager reclined, propped up by bright yellow cushions and arm rests decorated with phoenixes. A young serving maid gently pommelled her legs with a pair of massaging pounders. On either side of her, seated on intricately carved ebony chairs were her two adoptive daughters. Prince Xiang's wife, the Lady Dongeh whom those close to the Empress Dowager called Princess Black Pearl, and the daughter of Prince Dingnan, Princess Sizhen. Sizhen was a pretty fifteen year old. However, the arch of her brows suggested a touch of haughtiness which made her seem hard but with less strength of character compared to Black Pearl. Yet there was still an appealing childishness about her. She was relating the fall of Guilin and her father's death.

"... I recall my princely father saying to my mother, 'I have been a soldier from my youth and spent my days between Mount Tie and the Yalu River, hoping to distinguish myself and earn a title and a place in history. When General Mao, though the most loyal of men, was executed, I decided to submit to the present dynasty. From then on my fortunes changed. I was given a title and a duchy. Great Qing has been kind to me, and I shall serve it with my life. You must plan for yourself.' My mother, indicating my brother and I, replied, 'My Lord need have no fear that I will not die. However, the younger generation are innocent. Why should they share our fate?' As my father hesitated, my mother called a nursemaid and commanded her to escape with my brother and me. My mother followed us weeping to the gate. The last thing she said to the nursemaid was, 'If this boy survives, let him be a monk, instead of following in his father's hectic footsteps, only to end in disaster!' By the time we reached the city gate, my father's mansion was on fire. It burned and burned. My brother and I got separated. I never saw him again...."

Sizhen broke into tears, and Black Pearl hurried to comfort her. The Empress Dowager spoke with a sigh: "Prince Dingnan was a man of the wilderness and a man of fierce loyalty who died for his Emperor. Did you know, Black Pearl, that Sizhen's mother and several lesser ladies of the house hanged themselves? It was the Prince himself who set fire to the mansion, after paying his last homage by kneeling thrice and touching his forehead to the floor nine times, facing north. Then he killed himself with his sword. The household of a hundred and twenty souls perished. Their sacrifice makes one tremble with horror and admiration...."

Lady Dongeh quickly interjected, "The Prince was mourned by

the entire court. The year before last when Sister Sizhen brought the Prince's remains back to the capital, a retinue of thousands met her outside the city. Several hundred officials above the third grade held vigil over the body day and night. The Prince was buried with full honours with a tomb and stone tablet erected in his memory. Then Your Majesty took Sizhen as adoptive daughter. The Prince in the nether world can rest in peace."

The Empress Dowager sighed again. "Prince Dingnan was the first among the four Han princes to submit. He had won great honours on the field of battle under Great Qing. He died too early...." She let her words trail off, for had the Prince lived, Wu Sangui would not be in such lustrious position. His present power was a thorn in her side.

Smiling, she steered the conversation into another direction.

"Sizhen has lived in the palace from a tender age, but she isn't spoilt and helpless. I believe you're quite a good equestrian."

"My father encouraged my brother and I to learn martial arts, constantly emphasizing the importance of being able to ride and shoot, for the Empire was not yet stable. We became good archers though we spent less time on book learning. Sister Black Pearl is a lady of learning."

The Empress Dowager chuckled. "You two compliment each other. You are both outstanding women. Black Pearl, do you ride and shoot? Black Pearl...."

Black Pearl had been gazing out the window, lost in thought. She turned to the Empress Dowager's smiling face with a start. Sizhen giggled.

"Sister, where are you? Our Mother Empress was asking about your skill with horses and the bow and arrow."

Black Pearl fell to her knees and begged forgiveness for being inattentive, then she replied that she could ride but she was unskilled in martial arts.

The Empress Dowager said with a smile, "My dear, nobody blames you. However, you do seem distracted?" Black Pearl bowed her head and replied, "I slept poorly last night, and am not quite myself. Please forgive me."

The Empress Dowager murmured her understanding. She scrutinized the girl but said no more.

Sizhen, who was fluent in the Manchu language, prattled on in a high clear voice about the beauty of Guilin whose mountains were like monoliths of pure jade, and whose rivers were ribbons of green satin. Black Pearl forced a smile and tried to be attentive, but her mind wandered. Ever since last evening she had been uneasy. For today the question of the ten southern families, and the matter of not appointing princes to head the six ministries would be on the agenda of the Council of Nobles. These were the most important matters that Fulin had tackled since he took the reins of government. Would he succeed? No wonder she was at sixes and sevens.

The Empress Dowager had been listening to Sizhen, when she suddenly raised her hand, shifted her body slightly, and commanded the girl to be quiet. The serving maid who had been pommelling her legs stopped. The maids of honour and the eunuchs both indoors and out held their breath, wondering what was the matter. Something had attracted the Empress Dowager's attention.

Silence descended upon the room. A breeze worried the magnolia tree outside, and the blossoms falling on the cobblestones made a sound like raindrops.

"It's only blossoms falling, Imperial Mother," whispered Black Pearl.

"Of course," the Empress Dowager chuckled and settled back into her cushions. "I thought it was your Imperial Brother. The morning audience should be over...." She scowled as though something was on her mind.

Sizhen complained coquettishly, "Here I am talking about this and that, trying to be amusing and nobody listens! Both Imperial Mother and Imperial Sister are preoccupied!" She darted a glance at Black Pearl and pouted. The Empress Dowager giggled in spite of herself.

Black Pearl quickly put her arms around the younger woman's shoulders and cajoled her softly!

"My sweet sister, everyone knows how much our Imperial Mother loves you. But there are important things going on at court, so naturally her thoughts are with the Emperor."

Sizhen giggled. "I was only teasing. What kind of fool would I be, if I didn't understand that!"

The Empress Dowager turned to Black Pearl, and after a moment of silence said, "I didn't sleep well either. I kept tossing and turning all night. Can you two guess what was bothering me?"

Sizhen quickly answered happily: "I know! I know! You want another ten or twenty fat, healthy grandsons!"

The Empress Dowager laughed out loud, "Listen to this slip of a girl!" she exclaimed. Just then the voice of the Chief Eunuch was heard announcing the Emperor's arrival.

A whip cracked somewhere outside. A moment later Fulin entered the room in quick strides. The Empress Dowager had seated herself properly and the two ladies knelt to receive him. Fulin's eyes lit up and a smile tugged at his lips when he saw that Black Pearl was present. None of that escaped the Empress Dowager, but she let it pass, pretending she had not noticed, and exchanged the ritual greetings with her son. She could tell by his footsteps and his manner that things had not gone badly. Still she needed reassurance.

Fulin could barely contain himself until the formal greetings had been exchanged, before he told his mother what had happened.

"Imperial Mother, I never dreamed things would go so smoothly," he began.

As planned, Tuhai brought up the miscarriage of justice in the case of treason against the ten families in the south. Princes and Grand Ministers defended the conduct of the case till they were red in the face. Lerjin insisted that his father's judgement was correct. Whereas Tuhai was able to present evidence to the contrary and confessions of persons who had given false evidence, Lerjin had nothing to bolster his case. In the end he had to admit defeat.

"Mother, I thought dismissing the princes and dukes from their posts as heads of ministeries would meet with stiff opposition. As it turned out quite the opposite happened...."

To Fulin's surprise, Prince An was the first to offer his resignation, saying this would be a wise move that would benefit the nation. Prince Kang followed suit. Lord Aobai was of the same mind. Although old Lord Suoni had nothing to say, he did not oppose the motion, and it was unanimously passed.

The Empress Dowager nodded her approval.

"My Imperial Son, among the princes and dukes of your generation, the most respected after Prince An will be Prince Jidu. Since he is fighting in the south, the others look to Prince An for leadership. As for the council, Suoni is the eldest and Aobai the most meritorious general. It is good these two are loyal to our Imperial Son."

Fulin paced the floor, rubbing his hands together, as excited as a child. His eyes, filled with laughter, rested briefly upon Black Pearl, then skipped over Sizhen to the Empress Dowager.

"Mother, there is nothing to worry about."

"Don't be too sure. There might still be trouble," the Empress Dowager replied with a smile.

The smiles disappeared almost simultaneously from Fulin and Black Pearl's faces.

"How? Why?" he demanded. The Empress Dowager adopted a comforting tone saying, "Be calm. There is a saying: 'When a soldier comes against us, send a general to fight him. When a flood threatens, build a dyke.' Take things as they come. Oh, Black Pearl and Sizhen, did you understand what we were talking about?"

Lady Sizhen shook her head. It was obvious she did not comprehend.

Black Pearl's expression matched that of Fulin's so exactly that it proved the Empress Dowager's suspicions. Black Pearl hesitated, then spoke with her usual candour, "It was a wise move of the Emperor that will have far-reaching results."

"You seem to have known ahead of time," the Empress Dowager remarked.

Black Pearl blushed. Fulin bit his lips and willed her to look at him, but she kept her eyes averted when she replied:

"Your Majesty, I met my Imperial Brother here the other day, and he mentioned it."

"And did you say what you had just said then?" the Empress Dowager persisted.

"Yes."

The Empress Dowager frowned. Her mind was in turmoil. This brilliant girl whom the Emperor loved should have been his. She regretted allowing the Grand Concubine to persuade her into giving Black Pearl to Bomubogur instead. In doing so the talents of the girl who could have been the Emperor's help-mate might be wasted.

The Empress Dowager was fond of Black Pearl, but she had to weigh personal feelings against the good of the monarchy and the feelings of other members of the Imperial Household. Therefore she had had to devise barriers to keep Fulin and Black Pearl apart. However, she had failed. She was a woman of experience. She had only to look into their eyes to understand what was happening. It was the love of an eighteen-year-old man for a seventeen-year-old woman, beautiful, pure, and urgent.

As the Empress Dowager pondered this problem, the chief eunuch of Kunning Palace presented himself saying the Empress requested the presence of Black Pearl to recite poetry and to paint. Would the Empress Dowager permit it?

The Empress Dowager chuckled. "Black Pearl, you will soon be the distinguished scholar of this family!" Black Pearl bowed, "I wouldn't dare aspire to such an honour." The Empress Dowager chuckled again.

"Since your sister-in-law has asked for you, go. It's good for you to spend time together. Perhaps you will pass on some of your spirit and cleverness as well as your learning." Black Pearl fell to her knees. "Your daughter will return home directly from Kunning Palace. I will bid Your Majesty farewell. Your daughter will return to pay her respects in a few days." The Empress Dowager replied, "We will send for you when we miss you. The next time you must stay longer."

Black Pearl left Cining Palace in the sedan chair carried by four eunuchs sent from Kunning Palace. A stiff wind was blowing as they wended their way along the Imperial pathways, and the chief eunuch solicitously dropped the silk curtain. The sedan chair swayed gently. Black Pearl shut her eyes and imagined herself adrift on a small boat. Once again the image of Fulin came to mind, not as he was now but as he had been four years ago, when she saw him for the first time. She had just arrived in the capital and he was the fourteen-year-old Son of Heaven... .

The daughters of the eight banners could aspire to being selected for the imperial harem, and even of becoming highly respected imperial concubines. Therefore they were guarded like precious jewels. At home they were doted upon by parents, deferred to by siblings, and feared by slaves.

Before the conquest, Manchu women did not have the same rigid controls and restrictions put upon them as their Chinese counterparts. They had freedoms that Han women did not dare to dream of. Their feet were not bound; they were not kept in isolation; they could receive guests or go out into the streets whenever they chose. They were good equestrians and archers. Although they were taught the womanly virtues of obedience to fathers and husbands during the reign of Nurhachi and Abahai, these new notions were not deep-rooted, nor were age-old customs easily supplanted. Black Pearl was typical of her caste. She was well loved, unrestrained, open, and free. Her mother was a "barbarian", a southern woman of culture. She had a famous scholar for a tutor too who honed into brilliance the gift of cleverness she received from her mother. The south where she grew up imbued her with its warm, tender romanticism. The mingling of these influences created a rare being, an indomitable spirit cloaked in tender beauty that combined the best qualities of the Manchu and the Han. She was thoughtful and quick-witted, but inobstrusive.

At the age of twelve, her parents and tutor discovered to their astonishment that the awkward fledgling was turning into a peacock before their eyes. The family, though startled and pleased, was not a little dismayed. For they realized they could not keep her for long. They saw a special destiny before her. From then on her tutor became more exacting. The girl herself became more reserved, her smile more beautiful but pensive.

At the age of thirteen, the time of being selected for the imperial harem drew near.

On midsummer's eve, she faced her mirror in the quiet of her boudoir, smiling at the image in it. She whispered to that mirrored self she admired, "You have the face of spring blossoms, and eyes like ponds in autumn. Pretty on the outside, clever on the inside, you are perfection. Who would not love you to death! But you mustn't allow yourself to be mediocre. You must fight for a mate worthy of you, with whom you will enjoy conjugal felicity." Her cheeks reddened, and her fathomless eyes glittered....

She wondered what sort of man the Emperor was, and whether she would find in him a worthy mate. She had heard he was young and handsome, that he was kind and studious, that he was wise and strongminded. But was it true? Such thoughts sometimes kept her tossing and turning till late at night.

The selection of harem beauties was an important national event. Black Pearl was confident she would be chosen. But what if he were not worthy of her? She knew what to do. The choice was based on figure, bearing, and the beauty of her face. Black Pearl knew she could alter any of these things without difficulty.

"I must see him before the selection," she confided to the self in the mirror. If he could use a grand ceremonial occasion to choose her, then she also had the right to choose him. If he did not live up to her expectations, she would not enter the palace; she would forego a life of pampered luxury to seek her ideal mate elsewhere.

Finally an opportunity presented itself. There was to be a hunt at which the Emperor and all the princes and nobles would be present. The hunt was arranged on the plains north of the capital near the county town of Yanqing. Her father, General Ershuo, had to be present. At the head of a squad made up of household officers and guardsmen, he cut an obscure figure in a retinue ten thousand strong. When the long horns shrilled in the distance, the marchers swiftly fell into formation along both sides of the road as the imperial cavalcade thundered past. The Emperor was mounted on a fiery chestnut horse, surrounded by princes and dukes, beilehs and beizis and members of the imperial family. Lord Ershuo and his men fell to their knees, eyes trained to the ground. However, someone to his left had dared to lift his head and gaze upon His Majesty. Lord Ershuo wheeled upon the offender angrily. The handsome guardsman flashed him a smile that was half shy, yet impish, and the quick surge of anger dissipated in him. In a guardsman's waistcoat and robe, his daughter made a very comely youth, though she seemed diminitive beside her burly companions. He understood and forgave her recklessness.

Before daybreak, the signal guns were fired thrice. Then the standards were unfurled. Ten thousand beaters let out a mighty roar. Flags fluttered in the air as the shriek of horns and the thud of drums shook the earth. The beaters had been stationed in a circle several miles in radius. As the circle gradually closed, deer, foxes, rabbits and mountain goats broke from the underbrush, darting this way and that. The Emperor, standing on a watch tower, gave the order for the hunt to begin. The hunters lifted their bows with a joyous cry. Horsemen galloped past, their sabres flashing in the sunlight, hot on the heels of the frightened prey, kicking up a cloud of yellow dust that hovered between earth and sky. The wild, exultant cries of the hunters, the thunder of hoofs, the terrified cry of the quarry mingled with the sound of horn and drum rose in a deafening cacophony.

Ershuo kept Black Pearl close to him. Suddenly a red fox flashed past, rousing his keenness for the hunt. He pressed his mount into a gallop and gave chase. He had not gone far when his daughter's cry made him turn. A wounded leopard was about to leap at Black Pearl. A cold shiver rippled down his spine. With a wild cry, he wheeled around as Black Pearl turned her mount and fled. The leopard gave chase, snarling with fury. All this happened so fast that everyone was taken by surprise.

Before the beater had begun, the Emperor had ordered his shooters to kill all the savage beasts that were driven out of the bush. However, the leopard was only wounded. A wounded beast is especially dangerous. Ershuo raised his bow, but the animal was already out of his range and rapidly gaining on Black Pearl. The other hunters were afraid to shoot for fear of harming the rider. Black Pearl's horse was heading straight for a ditch two yards wide and one yard deep that marked the perimetre of the hunting ground. A cry of terror went up. Ershuo let out a howl of despair. If Black Pearl were not killed by the leopard, she would surely fall to her death.

Black Pearl tightened the rein and suddenly let it go. At the same time she brought her whip down hard on her horse's flank.

"Charge!" she commanded. The horse leaped high into the air, its four legs stretched almost in a straight line. A great shout rose as horse and rider cleared the ditch. The by-standers cheered the rider's courage.

The leopard stopped at the rim of the ditch. Snarling angrily it crouched down till its belly touched the ground. Its haunches and tail rose as it prepared to leap across the ditch. The hunters aimed their arrows.

As the leopard leaped, a shaft whistled through the air and struck the animal in the throat and sent it plummeting into the ditch.

"Long live His Majesty! Long live!" A cheer sounded from all sides. A group of riders in yellow waistcoats approached from the far side of the ditch, the Emperor on his chestnut horse in their midst. He had shot the lethal arrow.

Black Pearl wheeled her horse around and came back in a wide circle. By this time Ershuo and his followers had reached the Emperor. He quickly led Black Pearl to His Majesty, and pushed her down on her knees to thank the Emperor for saving her life. Black Pearl trembled like a leaf. Colour had drained from her face and she was speechless with fright.

Ershuo quickly spoke on her behalf.

"This is a youngster from my household, Your Majesty. Ignorant and timid. On his behalf I thank Your Majesty for saving his life." Fulin chuckled. "He is only a child! Were you frightened, boy? By the way you handled your horse, I'd say you were not."

Black Pearl slowly raised her head and darted a quick glance at the Emperor who was looking at her casually. Quickly she bowed her head, her heart beating a wild tattoo. The Emperor seemed surprised. By the way he arched his brow, she thought he was about to speak. Ershuo's palms were moist with fear. Just then a messenger arrived saying that Prince Jirgalang had driven out a flock of deer, and the Emperor was invited to hunt.

Fulin's youthful face flushed with excitement. He glanced across the ditch at the hunting grounds where many animals still darted hither and yon. "Open one end of the hunting ground and let them escape, that we may hunt another day," he ordered. With that he motioned the messenger to lead the way. From a short distance away he looked back as though he had suddenly remembered something. But there were too many followers in the way, and he was riding at a gallop so that he could not see Black Pearl clearly. Nor could she see him. He and his followers quickly disappeared like a brilliant yellow cloud.

More than the fact that he had saved her life, Black Pearl was captivated by the Emperor's handsomeness, his dashing personality, and his compassion. When she left the hunting grounds, Fulin had already taken possession of her heart. She was head over heels in love. Secretly she prayed for the day of selection that she might once more see the man of her dreams.

What happened thereafter was a complete reversal. She had been given instead to the Emperor's younger brother. Bomubogur was an ignorant boy. She was heart-broken. She hated the jealous Empress; hated the capriciousness of fate; she even hated Fulin. However, she was a daughter of a bannerman. They did not abide by the same puritanic mores as the Han. Therefore, in her disappointment at being forced into a marriage between a phoenix and a crow she did not turn to thoughts of suicide. On the surface she was a tender lady of the Imperial Household, but in the depths of her heart she nurtured a secret love. She was glad, in a way, that she was able to marry his younger brother. For her position would always afford her opportunities of seeing the Emperor again.

Her emotions were in a turmoil until Fulin finally discovered her. By then she had matured into a beautiful, vibrant young woman, longing to love and be loved, but leading an empty life as a prince's wife. Fulin's interest in her filled her with joy and amazement, and not a little fear. Brother wedding a sister-in-law or uncle taking a nephew's wife were not uncommon practices among the Manchu. In years gone by the Empress Dowager and her husband's brother Prince Dorgon had such a relationship too. With those precedents in mind she would never think of rejecting him.

The sedan chair stopped, and the eunuch lifted the curtain. Black Pearl steadied herself with a hand on the eunuch's shoulder and alighted. She had been so wrapped up in her secret thoughts that for a moment she did not know where she was. All the palace gates were more or less the same, set in crimson walls topped by green tiles, and decorated with nine times nine rows of brass studs. Outside, on the wall opposite the gate was carved a rampant dragon. Inside was ascreen wall made of glazed tiles set in a floral pattern. Black Pearl did not recognize her surroundings at once, nor was she interested in the intricacies of the bas-reliefs. She had been summoned by the Empress. Court etiquette and the strictures of family code warned her to be on her guard.

Peonies were in bloom, filling the garden with a riot of colours. The fragrance attracted swarms of bees and butterflies who danced in the air. Black Pearl picked her way through the narrow path that meandered between the potted plants, stopping here and there to read the gold and silver labels attached to the plants. There were countless varieties of peony. A crimson flower was called "Coral in the Sun"; "Hibiscus Tent" was a pink bloom; "Moon Reflected in a Cold Pond" was white; "Smoke Engulfing a Jade Dish" for deep purple, and so on. Black Pearl was so dazzled by the famous flower of Luoyang that she did not know which way to turn.

However she had not lost sight of the purpose of her visit, and did not dare tarry. Only when she had gone up a flight of steps and reached the verandah did she look up to read the name of the hall written in gold Chinese characters and Manchu script on a blue shingle under the eave. It read: "Yangxin Hall" (Hall of Mental Cultivation).

Black Pearl hesitated. Then she understood and her cheeks flamed like the flowers in the garden. Two eunuchs had come out of the hall to greet her. In her confusion, Black Pearl looked back across the garden, but the sedan chair from Kunning Palace had gone. Silence enveloped the Hall of Mental Cultivation. Her heartbeat pounded in her ears, mingled with the buzzing of the bees and the fluttering of butterflies

Black Pearl lingered a moment longer and her mouth stretched into a thin determined line. The moment she had longed for had finally arrived, yet she was afraid. She shut her eyes and laid a hand on her breast to calm her wildly beating heart. When her breathing became normal again, she slowly undid the collar of her cloak. The eunuch hastened to take it from her as she stepped over the threshold into the hall. She prostrated herself before the throne in the centre of the hall, then she raised her head and looked about the place where he worked and studied.

The gold wall hangings, the mirrors fitted into the lofty ceilings, the incensers from which clouds of scented smoke billowed and all the other glittering decorations that surrounded the throne, she glanced at only fleetingly. It was the huge sandalwood bookcases lining three walls of the room that drew her like a magnet. She lifted the blue silk drapery in front of them with a deep sense of awe. So many books! Mountains and oceans of books! She sighed with wonder and envy, also contentment.

The situation in which she found herself reminded Black Pearl of a play. Choosing to tryst with her lover, Lady Xiumei who was placed in the same predicament spoke the following lines: "The timid part of me clings to virtue; but the daring part of me wants other things. Therefore each must go its own way." Was she daring enough to go her own way? Black Pearl searched the section of the bookcase marked plays of the Ming Dynasty and found a volume by the Buddhist devotee, Hu Yuan. Ah, there it was! *The Jade Palace of Xiumei*. The book fell open at the page where an ivory book marker had been inserted. Someone had annotated the line of dialogue she remembered; for written in the margin in bold red characters were these words: "Only the bold can utter such words."

Who would dare to annotate a book belonging to the imperial library except he! That their thoughts should dovetail so neatly deeply moved her and her eyes misted.

"Black Pearl!" Fulin called her from the threshold. Black Pearl trembled as she turned to him. He came towards her, his footsteps becoming slower and lighter. As the distance between them shortened his face was drained of colour, his brows becoming blacker, and the banked-up fires within blazed in his eyes. Black Pearl did not shrink from him. Her eyes were fixed upon him, welcoming him not as a monarch but as a man ablaze with undeniable desire, whom she loved and from whom she could deny nothing.

"Black Pearl...." Fulin's eyes were fixed upon her unblinking. His voice pitched scarcely above a whisper.

"Your Majesty...." Black Pearl started to kneel but Fulin caught her. The last barrier between them fell away. Fulin drew her into his arms, and Black Pearl melted against him. They stood clasped tight in each other's arms, not moving. Blood pounded through their tightly twined fingers. Their hearts beat fiercely in their breasts. Moments passed. Then Fulin swept Black Pearl's tiny frame off her feet, and carried her into the inner chamber.

The dappled sunlight of noon, and the heady perfume of the flowers filled every corner of the Hall of Mental Cultivation.

4

No sooner had the Empress Dowager returned from Cining Garden when Duke Lerjin begged an audience with his Great Grand Aunt.

Lerjin was barely twenty years of age. His effete mannerisms, pale complexion, willowy figure were evidence that he had been raised among women. However, he had inherited the bold, straight brows of his great grandfather, and there was a faint echo of his grandfather's hauteur in the high, straight bridge of his nose. Otherwise the eyes, mouth, colouring, and especially the dainty hands were weak and effeminate.

Upon the death of Nurhachi, Abahai's older brother, Prince Li (Daishan), had refused the succession in favour of his younger but more able brother. For this wise act he was much admired. When Abahai died, the various banners squabbled among themselves for the right of succession. Matters reached such a pitch that blood-letting was almost inevitable. The Empress Dowager, with Prince Daishan's help and support, secured the throne for Fulin. The dispute was finally settled when the Princes Dorgon and Jirgalang were appointed joint regents. Half a year later the Manchu conquest of the central plains was completed, and the capital was established at Beijing. For his enormous contributions to the Empire, three of the eight hereditary titles created in the early years of the dynasty went to Daishan's clan. Moreover, Daishan's third son Sahalin was given the title of Prince Ying. His son took the title of Duke Shuncheng. That title eventually passed onto to his son Lerjin. This placed him two generations behind Fulin. Thus Lerjin was the Empress Dowager's great grand nephew. Being young and immature, Lerjin played up to his venerable great aunt.

"Great Grand Aunt!" he cried, approaching on his knees, and addressing the Empress Dowager in familiar Manchu. "Mafa doesn't trust us! We've been dismissed from the six ministries! His own flesh and blood! He prefers the wily barbarians from the south!"

The Empress Dowager forced a smile.

"Stop snivelling!" she chided. "You ought to be ashamed! A man of the eight banners behaving thus! You are all members of the imperial family, with high positions and lives of luxury and ease. The court has not treated you shabbily. There is no reason to mistrust one's own family. However, the work of the six ministries is complex and must be conducted to the letter of the law. The princes are fighting men who may not have a good grasp of matters of state. Therefore, why not take steps to avoid serious mistakes before they occur? Believe me, His Majesty has acted for the good of the princes as well. I see no cause for complaint."

Lerjin gulped and dabbed at his moist eyes. "Having the six ministries taken away is only secondary. There's something else that sticks in the craw. Emperors Nurhachi and Abahai both admonished the princes to discuss policy with the Emperor. Now that we have no say at all in the six ministries, isn't that going against the wishes of our ancestors?''

The Empress Dowager surmised that Lerjin was not speaking for himself. He was too lazy and lacked learning to think of these things. By the way he spoke, she could tell he had learned his speech by rote. The other princes must have put him up to it, thinking because of his youth, he was not likely to anger the Emperor. Also, he was more likely to get a sympathetic hearing from the Empress Dowager. In her heart the Empress Dowager was relieved that within two or three years of her son's taking the reins of government, all the princes of power and prestige had died one after the other. Otherwise it would not be this non-entity Lerjin demanding to be heard.

She responded solemnly: "The Emperor has always respected the laws of Heaven and the family code. That the princes should head the six ministries of government was not a part of that code. Besides, during Nurhachi's lifetime many laws and regulations were amended. This is only a minor matter.... I suppose all these tears are because you can't bear to relinquish control of the Ministry of Justice. Let me examine you a little. Can you recite some laws, or cite a few precedent setting cases?''

Lerjin bowed his head, not daring to reply.

"In that case you must sit in court everyday from now on and learn. And you will give up riding and hunting. What do you say to that?''

"That won't do,'' wailed Lerjin, "Great Grand Aunt, I don't speak Chinese and I don't read their language. Besides we're the cream of the crop. I won't rub shoulders with riff-raff!''

"Then what do you propose to do?'' demanded the Empress Dowager with a sigh. "Your grandfather Sahalin was broad-minded and possessed of a sharp wit. He was fluent in Manchu, Han and Mongolian. He made great contributions to the establishment of law in the Empire. If you had his wisdom and abilities you would be much more than the head of just one ministry."

Lerjin blinked dry-eyed. He dared not look at the Empress Dowager. As far as the Empress Dowager was concerned everything that needed to be said had been said. At the beginning of the conquest, the clan of Aisin Gioro had produced some outstanding men of letters as well as warriors. These were the men who rallied round Nurhachi and Abahai. It was the finest hour of the monarchy. A few decades later those men either retired or died. How would the Emperor Shunzhi govern the Empire he inherited? He needed able men not only for conquest but to govern.

As soon as Lerjin left, Suoni entered Cining Palace. After he had paid his formal homage to the Empress Dowager, he remained prostrate, not saying a word.

The Empress Dowager guessed he too had come on behalf of the Deliberative Council of Nobles. Didn't they say he had not opposed the Emperor?

The Empress Dowager spoke in a friendly tone, "Suoni, you were a ranking officer in Nurhachi's court, and you have served three generations of monarchs well. Therefore, there shouldn't be any reticence between us."

When Abahai died, Suoni was the first to favour the ascension of the Emperor's son to the throne, rather than his brother, and was instrumental in forcing the Princes Dorgon and Duoduo to agree to proclaiming Fulin. Later, during the regency, Suoni did not blindly follow Dorgon's policy. In order to protect the young monarch, he incurred the regent's enmity. As a consequence he was dismissed twice. In fact he almost lost his life. It was not until Shunzhi took the reins of government that Suoni was rehabilitated. Finally his star rose. Now he was the Lord Chamberlain. Like his father Shuose and his elder brother Xifu, who had been renowned civic officials of Nurhachi's court, Suoni was fluent in Chinese, Manchu and Mongolian. Theirs was an unusually learned Manchu family. Above all, Suoni was a man of integrity, though sometimes obstinate. His loyalty to

Nurhachi, Abahai and their heir Shunzhi was unquestionable, and selfless. Now he prostrated himself once more before the Empress Dowager, saying, "Your Majesty, in all his life, your slave has devoted himself to the Emperor, and has never questioned the Emperor's way of management...." His thick brows were tight-knit and quivering with emotion. His heart was so heavy that he could not continue and words failed him.

The Empress Dowager gently bade him rise, "Now tell us slowly."

"No! No! Though what I have to say is for the good of the Emperor, the Empire and society, yet in speaking I fear I will most certainly offend. Therefore, your slave must remain on his knees...." The Empress Dowager came to the point at once.

"You did not raise any objections in this morning's audience."

"No! No! I would never go against the Emperor's wishes. Your slave begs Your Majesty's indulgence, to advise the Emperor to go no further. He must not continue along the same lines...."

"Then you think the Emperor was wrong?"

"No! No! The Emperor is not wrong! It is just that ... the ancestors of the princes were followers of Nurhachi and Abahai who fought for the dynasty, renowned for their loyalty and contribution to the Empire. They may be alienated. All under Heaven is not yet stable. Many generals of the eight banners are still fighting in the field. Might not the Emperor's act affect morale?"

"You think it's as serious as that?" the Empress Dowager asked innocently.

Suoni hurriedly banged his head on the floor. He was about to reply when a maid of honour entered to announce the Grand Concubine, Lady Yijing. The Empress Dowager reflected a moment, and quickly decided to admit her. Why not let her hear what Suoni had to say, and get a second opinion? After Suoni had made his obeisance, and the Grand Concubine had been seated, he was asked to repeat everything he had just said.

"In that case, Suoni," the Empress Dowager chose her words carefully when he finished, "in your opinion the charges of treason against the ten families should not be delved into, and the princes should retain their posts?"

"No! I wouldn't dare! A monarch's word must stand for all time, and cannot be changed. Your slave merely petitions that firstly, these matters must not be taken further along. And secondly, that restrictions must be placed on Han officials, so that they will not be tempted to take a yard when they are given an inch. Thus the generals of the eight banners will be appeased, just as the execution of Chen Mingxia and the punishment of twenty-nine Han officials two years ago served to preserve the peace both at court and among the populace."

The Empress Dowager pondered the courtier's words.

The Grand Concubine grasped Suoni's intentions immediately, and interjected, "Imperial Sister, Suoni is a courtier of three generations of monarchs, and he speaks the truth. Our ancestors had bound the Manchus and the Mongols to one another in marriage, and those bonds were further strengthened by Nurhachi and Abahai. The Mongols played an important role in the conquest, and are still guarding the northern frontiers, and our ancestral tombs. The forty-nine banners of the Mongols will bow to the eight banners of the Manchu, but will not permit themselves to be superseded by the barbarians of the south. The Hans are a cunning race. They can be used but not trusted. I am sure my Imperial Sister has considered that."

The Empress Dowager smiled as she spoke:

"I hear that during the council meeting Duke An was the first to offer his resignation as head of Minister of Works. Duke Kang, Aobai and Tuhai also supported the motion."

Suoni's heart hammered sickeningly. On his knees, he gestured with his hands. "Don't even mention it! Tuhai and the others who head the six ministries chafe under the control of the princes. Naturally, they would not object. Aobai never goes against the Emperor's wishes. As for Duke An and Kang...." Suoni swallowed hard, reminding himself that they were related to the royalty. "Your Majesty, Their Highnesses are among the new generation of Manchu who have learned Chinese and adopted Chinese customs. They have become closer to the Han and drifted away from the ancient ways of our forefathers...."

The Grand Concubine quickly interposed, "Imperial Sister, this new wave exists not only among our family, but is everywhere in the palace. Even among the women. If the Emperor takes up with this so-called new wave, and adopts Chinese ways, it will be a case of changing the content without changing the form for Great Qing."

Suoni quickly knocked his forehead against the floor, crying out, "Exactly so! That is exactly your slave's concern.... His Majesty is too fond of learning, art and poetry. Sooner or later he will be drawn to the poets and learned men of the Han whose works are truly formidable. It is an instantly addictive drug. Your slave is keenly aware of the danger. I do not blame His Majesty.... I merely pray he will consider the larger picture, and bear in mind the welfare of Great Qing...."

The Empress Dowager responded solemnly: "The Emperor is ruler of millions. Ninety-nine out of a hundred are Hans. How can he rule them without being fluent in their language and familiar with their writings? So long as he is not too immersed in it and it does not interfere with his ability to govern, all is well." Suoni had to agree. After he had humbly accepted tea which was proffered, he withdrew. The Empress Dowager studied the Grand Concubine quietly, then spoke pleasantly, "Just now my Imperial Sister spoke of the 'new wave' among the women. Whom did she have in mind?"

The Grand Concubine had retained the forthright, out-spoken manner of Manchu women in spite of her years in the palace. She envied the Empress Dowager for her gentility which she could never emulate. Like all women she was quick to find fault with a daughter-in-law.

"Who else is there!" she began hotly. "I regret persuading you to give her to Bomubogur! She doesn't resemble our Manchu or Mongol women in the least. Bind her feet, put her hair up in a chignon, and dress her in a tunic and she'd be a barbarian. The way she sways when she walks is something I can't abide! And my Imperial Sister has taken her as an adoptive daughter to boot! What a waste of affection! What worries me most, dear Sister, is that there is a bit of the temptress in her, don't you think? I'm afraid she might get her claws into the Emperor...."

The Empress Dowager sighed.

"It has occurred to me too. In these thirteen years since the conquest, we can't be as unrestrained as we used to be. The Emperor has to abide by rules, and a code of honour, lest the southerners think us uncouth."

The Grand Concubine was silent for a moment.

"I realize this puts my dear Sister in a predicament. However, the Emperor is almighty. I was thinking out of the fourteen daughters of his late Majesty, twelve are older than the Emperor. Aside from the five who have gone to our ancestors, five married Mongols. My Imperial Sister's Princess Yongmuchang and Princess Shuhuichang are blood sisters of the Emperor who doted on him as a child. Why not summon them back to court so that brother and sisters may be reunited. The princesses can help guide the Emperor on the right path. Besides Princess Yongmuchang is also the Empress' mother."

The Empress Dowager nodded her agreement. She was convinced the Grand Concubine had spoken only out of concern for the good of the imperial family. Her daughter Princess Duanshunchang had been married to a Mongol prince, but died in the seventh year of Shunzhi. The court then gave Prince Daishan's daughter to the bereaved prince as a second wife. Although the Grand Concubine had taken the girl as an adoptive daughter, the proposed reunion would not affect her in any way.

The Empress Dowager spoke thus:

"You have thought of everything! My Imperial Son is capricious and stubborn. He seems to have a special regard for the Lady Dongeh, because he is unhappy in his marriage. I feel repressing him is not a solution. Now Duke Dingnan's daughter Sizhen is elegant and pretty, and descended from a loyal courtier. If she could be raised to the stature of a Guifei, an imperial concubine of the third rank, she might be a suitable distraction."

The Grand Concubine concurred:

"The Empress Dowager is wise and far-seeing. This is indeed an admirable solution. Not only will Sizhen be a distraction for the Emperor, by making her an imperial concubine, Prince Dingnan's followers will be eternally bound to the royal house. Both Prince Dingnan and Prince Pingxi are Han noblemen. With Dingnan's daughter an imperial concubine, and Pingxi's son wedded to an imperial princess, all the barbarians under heaven will submit."

The Empress Dowager's smile vanished. The Grand Concubine had struck a nerve. She steered the conversation in another direction.

"My Imperial Sister's idea of a family reunion is a good plan. Now if the princesses were to bring with them the young princesses of the forty-nine banners to fill the harem, it would be even better.... I shall give it serious thought...."

The Grand Concubine understood the interview was over, and rose to take her leave. Before quitting the chamber she turned and whispered, "My dear Sister, our Bomubogur is still young and doesn't take the relation between men and women to heart. But he is extremely thin-skinned, and mustn't be hurt...."

The Empress Dowager reassured her with a smile.

"Don't worry."

Sumalagu helped the Empress Dowager to her feet, and walked with her slowly to the bed chamber. Usually the Empress Dowager would exchange a few pleasantries with the serving woman who had been at her side since childhood. But today she was not in the mood for banter.

Sumalagu searched the Empress Dowager's face and was troubled.

"Majesty, shall I order some ginseng soup?" she enquired. The Empress Dowager nodded.

Seated on the wide bed in the bed chamber, the Empress Dowager laid the bowl upon the low table beside her. She had just quaffed a mouthful of ginseng soup. Now she looked at Sumalagu thoughtfully and asked, "Do you think the Empress knows?"

"Why not ask her?" Sumalagu answered sensibly.

The Empress Dowager considered that remark for a moment before sending for the Empress.

The Empress came as she was bidden. After offering her obeisance, she stood to one side, waiting to be spoken to. The Empress was tall and sturdy, with a plain, honest face that reflected a kind and gentle nature. Her father was the son of the Empress Dowager's older brother Wukeshan. Her mother was the Empress Dowager's own daughter Princess Yongmuchang. Thus, she was not only the Empress Dowager's great niece, she was also her granddaughter. Now she was her daughter-in-law as well. It was as they say, "relationship upon relationship". However, there had been an error in the arrangement of generations, and Fulin was in fact her uncle. As one of a lesser generation, the Empress could not stand on her own. She was often intimidated. In spite of herself, the Empress Dowager who admired women of ability, was disappointed in this great niece who was unable to take charge of the women of the six palaces as she was expected.

The Empress Dowager did not observe the niceties, but came to the point at once.

"Is the wife of Prince Xiang still in your palace?" The Empress was startled and did not know how to reply. The Empress Dowager glanced at her coldly. She guessed there was more than what met the eye, and pressed her advantage.

"Didn't you summon her to Kunning Palace this forenoon?"

"Yes ...." The Empress hung her head and finally blurted out, "It was the Emperor.... He ordered me to summon her."

"Where was she taken?"

"To the Hall of Mental Cultivation...."

"And you did as you were told?" The Empress, blushing helplessly, murmured, "I did...."

"You were brought into the palace in a sedan chair to be Empress. And you are a daughter of the Boerjijite clan," the Empress Dowager spoke ponderously, her heavy black brows raised like the wings of an eagle in flight. The Empress fell to her knees holding back her tears.

"Mother Empress..." she murmured.

The Empress Dowager glared at her in silence, then said with a sigh, "You were too ... kind...." She had seized upon a word whose deeper meaning conveyed what was in her heart: weak and helpless. "I am going to the Hall of Mental Cultivation right now. You will come with me."

The Empress bowed her head even lower so that her face was completely hidden. In an almost inaudible voice she murmured, "Forgive me, Mother Empress, I really cannot go...."

The Empress Dowager approached the Hall of Mental Cultivation with a heavy heart. This daughter-in-law was a disappointment even to her. Therefore, how could she expect her son not to be displeased? To have a good marriage there must be equality of social status, appearance, ability and personality. It was clear this marriage was another failure. The Empress Dowager sighed for her son. But there is no help for it, she thought. This is the predicament of an emperor.

Fulin stood at the entrance to the hall, bowing to the waist as the Empress Dowager made her way through the flowering peony bushes. The Empress Dowager's appreciative glances travelled from the flowers to her son's face. Fulin's fair-skinned face, tinged with brown, was aglow. The eyes were moist and filled with blissful weariness. An irrepressible smile tugged at the corners of the full, sensitive red lips. There was even a touch of langour about the usually vigorous brows. A chill wrapped itself around the Empress Dowager's heart. Too late! She was too late!

The Empress Dowager stepped into the East Chamber, and asked casually, "Why were you not studying in the West Chamber?" She had seen the cup of hot tea and an open book on the small table on the kang under the south-facing window. The West Chamber was the usual place where the Emperor studied and perused documents of state.

Fulin replied uneasily, "I wanted a change."

The Empress Dowager picked up the book. Though she was not fluent in Chinese, she knew enough to read its title, *Amid the Flowers*. She flipped through its pages, and suddenly lifting her eyes to her son's asked bluntly, "Was Lady Dongeh here?"

Fulin blushed to the roots of his hair, he averted his eyes from his mother's riveting gaze to the delicately carved screen, unable to speak.

"When did she leave?"

"Just now." Though Fulin's voice was held low there was no trepidation.

"There are limits to youthful indiscretions. Never forget who you are!" Fulin was silent for a moment. Then he faced his mother with determination.

"Mother, this is not youthful foolishness. Lady Dongeh is my ideal mate. She has the ability to control the six palaces and the learning and wisdom to be empress. Does my Mother not see that?"

The Empress Dowager shook her head. The sternness of her countenance softened slightly when she spoke.

"Imperial Son, don't you understand? As the Hans would say, you are not destined for one another."

"Mother!" Fulin turned deathly pale. Rage swept across his face, and angry words spilled out willy-nilly. "I've been saddled with two mediocrities of the Boerjijite clan! Is it not enough?"

"You forget yourself!" The Empress Dowager raised her voice.

There was instant silence in the hall. Mother and son glowered at one another. Their fair skin and heavy brows were strikingly alike. Gradually, the anger left the Empress Dowager's face, and her calm was restored. In a tone hard as steel and cold as ice she announced, "Let it be known that I have decreed from this day forward none of the wives or ladies of the imperial family are permitted in the palace without my permission. Those who disobey this ban will be severely dealt with."

None of the eunuchs or maids of honour had ever heard the Empress Dowager speak so harshly before. The entire assemblage prostrated themselves, not daring to lift their heads.

Fulin also fell to his knees and bowed his head as the Empress Dowager left the hall. He was too numb to protest. As she passed, the Empress Dowager darted a quick glance at her son. His heavy brows were tightly knit, and his lips were clamped in a stubborn line. The Empress Dowager left with a measured gait, without a backward glance. Her son had dealt her pride in the Boerjijite clan a severe blow. One she would not easily forgive.

Dusk enveloped the Forbidden City. Halls and towers were silhouetted against the evening mist. A nameless melancholy permeated the palace that even the warmth of early summer could not dispel. From the Hall of Mental Cultivation came the sound of a flute whose soft, plaintive notes floating on the wings of song added to the tender melancholy of the night.

I have never been lovelorn, yet now I am, I have to be.
I float like a cloud, my thoughts scattered,
My breath coming in gasps.
You are gone, leaving a lingering scent.
Where is the one I long for?

When will you come again?
Perhaps before the lamps burn out
Or when the moon is low.

The sweet and elegant tune coupled with simple words found an echo in Fulin's heart. He laid down his flute before the end of the verse and lay down on the royal bed. Wild thoughts chased each other through his brain. When the flute stopped, the young eunuchs who accompanied him on fife, lute and clappers, and the singer also stopped, eyeing the Emperor uneasily. Fulin bade them continue.

"I will listen," he said with an abstracted air.

One of the young eunuchs took up a bamboo flute and the music began again:

Longing is a debt that demands payment.
A load of heartache gets very little back,
When will she pay her debt?

Fulin listened with his eyes shut. His thoughts had fled the Hall of Mental Cultivation, had, indeed, fled the palace in search of one he longed for.

After the Empress Dowager's visit, six days passed during which Fulin shut himself away in the hall, going nowhere and seeing no one. He was a lost soul, unable to eat or sleep. Even the daily protocol of paying his respects to the Empress Dowager was omitted. The Empress and the concubines who came to enquire after his health were barred from entering the Hall of Mental Cultivation. Finally, on the seventh day the Emperor, remembering his duties, attended the morning audience. He dealt with matters of state that had accumulated over the last days and returned early to the hall. The Chief Eunuch Wu Liangfu, fearing that the Emperor might do himself injury with prolonged melancholy, summoned musicians, singers and eunuchs to play for the Emperor. Fulin was fond of music and especially loved the flute. However, even music had lost its charm.

Fulin suddenly said to Wu Liangfu, "Go and find out if Sukesaha is on duty today. If he is, send him to us."

Wu Liangfu quickly despatched one of the eunuchs.

Wu Liangfu and Sukesaha were old acquaintances. Sukesaha had been campaigning in the field ever since he reported Prince Dorgon's plot to overthrow the Emperor through Wu Liangfu. That was years ago. Why was he being recalled?

Sukesaha was soon brought into the Presence. As commander of the palace guards, Sukesaha was one of the officials close to the Emperor, and therefore, less bound by protocol.

Sukesaha was portly and fair, tall, broad-shouldered, and carried himself with the air of a nobleman. His features were regular: a flat brow, a straight nose and mouth. He looked honest but was actually crafty. His mother had been the sixth daughter of Nurhachi, and from childhood he was familiar with the imperial family. Later, as Prince Dorgon's confidant, he became familiar with the nobles, the relations between the chiefs of the eight banners, and the royal house. When Dorgon died, he waited for the right moment and with the corroboration of Dorgon's guards revealed Dorgon's treason. This coincided with the needs of Shunzhi and Prince Jirgalang. Prince Dorgon's titles were all removed and the power of his clique quickly disintegrated. As a result Sukesaha became Grand Minister of the Deliberative Council of Nobles. However, he was not a complacent man. He realized he would be despised for gaining power through the downfall of others. Therefore in the tenth year of Shunzhi he volunteered to join the campaign to recapture the province of Hunan. In three years of warfare, he had won major victories at Yuezhou and Wuchang. As a result he was raised to the rank of reginal Commander and Commander of the Palace Guard and given the title of Senior Guardian of the Heir-Apparent. Yet today he seemed despondent.

Sukesaha had been on duty at that morning's audience. He had stood beside Fulin the whole time. Noticing that he was unwell, Sukesaha had urged the Emperor to retire early. His solicitude reminded Shunzhi that Sukesaha was from the clan of the white banner, just as Lady Dongeh. Sukesaha who had probably heard the rumours already, casually mentioned his close friendship with General Ershuo and his family. Then he let slip that his wife and Lady Dongeh were bosom friends. The Emperor was delighted. He immediately wrote a letter and asked Sukesaha to deliver it. A reply must be brought back in the evening. Now Sukesaha prostrated himself before the Emperor. After he had performed his obeisance, **he** handed the Emperor a light blue envelope.

Fulin tore open the envelope impatiently. There were only two lines of dainty calligraphy.

"Your Majesty must rule all under Heaven by placing filial piety first. The Empress Dowager's command must be obeyed. There is no hope in this life. We can only hope for the next."

Fulin slumped against the back rest of his chair. He expected Lady Dongeh to come to him. Instead this was her heartbreaking response.

Sukesaha watched the Emperor stealthily, and said, "Black Pearl is an outstanding beauty of the white banner, and learned too. All of her relatives thought she was destined to marry the Emperor. Who would have thought...."

"Was her mother truly a learned woman of the south?" Fulin asked weakly.

"It is true," Sukesaha replied.

Black Pearl's mother had come from a prominent family in Suzhou. She had gone to Jinan to visit relatives when the armies of Qing pressed south. She was captured by the men under Ershuo and given to him. Ershuo accepted her as an ordinary hostage and was about to take her by force. However she would not submit. She scrawled a poem on the wall and hanged herself. Ershuo was like Duke An, one of the new breed who admired the barbarians, and loved to associate with their scholars, drinking together and making poetry. When he saw the poem on the wall, he realized that he had been hasty. Fortunately the attempted suicide was discovered in time by servants. The lady did not die. Thereafter, Ershuo treated her like a Buddha. As time went by, the woman was moved by Ershuo's love, and married him. A few years later, Ershuo's wife died. Taking advantage of the court's decree allowing marriages between Manchus and Hans, the woman became Ershuo's wife. Thus, her daughter was a proper young lady of an influential Manchurian household. Who knows what magic the woman possessed for all her children were beautiful.

"Do you know that poem of farewell?" Fulin asked.

"I do indeed." He recited it in heavily accented Chinese.

Fulin listened, his head bowed. At the end he sighed.

Tracing the Emperor's thoughts, Sukesaha put into words the things roiling in Fulin's heart.

"Like mother like daughter, Black Pearl started writing poetry when she was ten years of age. There was one particular poem that all the Manchu young ladies used for learning Chinese. Mind you it only consisted of twenty characters, but it still created quite a sensation at the time."

Sukesaha glanced at the Emperor's face which looked pasty in the lamp light. Suddenly he said, "Majesty, why trouble yourself? We aren't Hans, not bound by their social codes. Didn't the late Emperor give Degelei's wife to her husband's brother after her husband died? Also, when the late Emperor's elder brother died, didn't his late Majesty give the Prince's wives and concubines to Prince Xiao and Duke Keqin? Aunts marrying nephews no less!"

Fulin motioned him to be still. Black Pearl's letter had been quite plain. She wished him to be a filial ruler. They were no longer in the wilderness. The rules had changed.

After Sukesaha had gone, Wu Liangfu, in order to distract the Emperor, slipped into a costume and performed a short play. Resplendent in a loose-fitting robe and tall headdress he impersonated a man of great learning, a know-all well versed in all religions and every school of thought. In short, a very arrogant man.

In lampooning doctrines and classics he finally coaxed a laugh from Fulin. Seeing the Emperor laugh, Wu Liangfu leaped off the stage and prostrated himself.

"Liangfu, you haven't been on stage for a long time," said Fulin. "How shall we reward you?" Wu Liangfu replied, "Your Majesty's laughter is reward enough." Fulin was moved by the eunuch's concern. When he appeared again in his own clothes, Fulin drew him aside and said, "I've been hard on you of late." Wu Liangfu fell to his knees. "Your Majesty cannot remain locked in solitude forever. Your slave's poor efforts only lifted Your Majesty's melancholy for a moment and nothing more."

Fulin sighed staring up at the star-spangled night sky.

"Your Majesty, please forgive your slave speaking bluntly. Your Majesty must not quarrel with the Empress Dowager over this attachment. Not only will the eight banners and the royal house not stand for it, the people too will oppose it. Besides, Your Majesty is emperor and the six palaces abound with beauties. Why must this one alone take your fancy?"

Fulin's mind was in a turmoil. Absently he quoted a line of poetry:

"No water's attractive for one who's seen the ocean,
No clouds beautiful besides those on Mount Wushan."

"That maybe so, but why look for trouble? An emperor should not be pining away! That is a great folly."

Fulin was brought up with a start. Half laughing, he turned to Wu Liangfu and chided, "We have decreed that household staff may not interfere with affairs of state. Dare you petition?" Wu Liangfu tremblingly replied, "Your slave does not presume to interfere, but merely suggests that Your Majesty should not belabour himself over matters of morality which are, after all, too abstract. Only wine and women are real. They can dispel unhappiness. Although this is a banter, it nevertheless has some truth in it. To be immersed and not drown, to be enchanted but not lost, must surely be ... bliss...."

Fulin stood gazing up at the night sky, his hands folded behind his back. No one could tell whether Wu Liangfu's words had made an impression. For the moment his eyes were dazzled by the stars.

Less than three days later the Emperor changed again. He became completely debauched. His desires knew no bounds. He was completely dominated by his sensuality, and sought every opportunity of appeasing his boundless passion and energy. The Empress, concubines, ladies and maids of honour were all afraid of him. The imperial pharmacist was ordered to prepare daily doses of aphrodisiacs. When an official of the imperial pharmacy counselled prudence, Fulin angrily dismissed him. He had resumed his custom of paying daily respects to his mother. During these visits he did not trouble to disguise his lust for the Empress and the concubines. He even took a fancy to the Empress Dowager's serving women. Soon afterwards a rumour began to make the rounds. The wife of an official had entered the palace to serve the Empress, and returned home an altered person. Though the official did not dare to complain the word got around. Before long it reached the Empress Dowager's ears, and she decreed that the wives of officials were henceforth not to be admitted to serve the imperial household.

Scandals involving the Emperor were regularly reported to the Empress Dowager in Cining Palace. However, she adopted a wait-and-see attitude because Fulin was carrying out his duties as Emperor and thus far had not made any terrible mistakes. However, at the end of the sixth month, he fell ill. Then the Empress Dowager became alarmed.

5

Armed with the Empress Dowager's decree, Sumalagu hurried to the church at Xuanwu Men to summon the Jesuit Tang Jo-Wang. However, the gatekeeper prevented her from entering.

"Someone's dangerously ill," the woman cried. "I have come to beg the Lord Tang to save his life!"

The gatekeeper turned obsequious at the sound of the woman's halting Chinese and heavy Mongolian accent.

"It isn't that I won't let you in," he explained, "but Lord Tang is preaching at the moment. At such times he cannot be disturbed. Once I admitted a messenger from the house of a prince, I got a fierce tongue-lashing. As a matter of fact, he almost sent me packing."

"I thought Lord Tang was a kindly old man with no temper at all." Sumalagu was surprised.

"Who said he isn't kind? He's as soft as water with the poor, the sick and the children. But if you get in the way of his preaching, it's like putting a lighted match to a bunch of straw. When he goes up in flames it's a sight to behold! Fortunately he always feels badly afterwards, and he's never vindictive."

"Oh! A man in his sixties shouldn't upset himself!"

"He isn't like an old man. He's busy from morning to night, preaching, giving baptism, saying Mass, and visiting his congregation. Besides he also works at the Imperial Ministry of Astronomy. He's even busy at home, writing, calculating, mixing medicines, building machines. And he finds time to play the piano. Do you know the weight of the stone tablet commemorating the deeds of Prince Dorgon? Why, he built a machine that could lift it up in the air! Aya! It was wonderful!" When it came to singing the praises of Tang Jo-Wang, the gatekeeper could go on and on, as if he were counting family jewels. It was obvious that this was only the preamble to recounting how Tang Jo-Wang built the church, cast cannons and designed fortifications. Sumalagu adroitly forestalled him. "I don't have to see him at once. Can I go inside and listen to his sermon?"

"Of course!" The gatekeeper was more than pleased to admit her. "Go in quickly. After you've heard him you'll want to be a Christian too. Lord Tang's sermons are so moving that they would wring tears out of a statue." Tang Jo-Wang's voice filled the great domed church. Sumalagu joined the shadowy rows of the faithful who were hanging on his every word, with their eyes opened wide.

"The world is full of sin. Mankind is full of sin. This is Original Sin, a legacy from the first man, Adam. An unavoidable sin that all his descendants are born with. It is the sin that will cause him to be condemned to Hell. In order to save those who believe in him, God sacrificed his own son, to atone for our sins! Our Lord Jesus gave us his body and his blood in the form of bread and wine.... Believers, he did this for you and me, to save our souls!"

Tang Jo-Wang spoke with such passion that not only the women of the congregation were murmuring the name of Jesus, even Sumalagu was moved by the white-haired old man who lifted his arms piously to heaven.

"Believers, the end of the world will arrive one day. Then our Lord Jesus will sit in final judgement of all mankind. The children of God will be lifted up to Heaven, while the wicked, the sinners, and the unbelievers will be cast to the eternal misery of Hell. My dear Believers, I pray that you will constantly remind yourself of this, and strengthen your faith in God...."

After the sermon the faithful clustered round Tang Jo-Wang asking questions, begging advice and blessings. Sumalagu stood apart watching, knowing it was impossible to approach him just then. She retreated to wait in the beautiful marbled verandah outside. Gradually the congregation dispersed until only a few sacristans were left to clean the church. But Tang Jo-Wang had also disappeared. The gatekeeper spotted Sumalagu and came up to her asking, "Haven't you seen Lord Tang yet? To see him you have to be alert. He's gone to the gardens at the back to pick grapes. You'll find him there if you hurry."

The garden was blanketed in green. The air was filled with the scent of roses. There were many fruit trees. Pink and white peaches hung from the branches, and shining purple clusters of grapes dangled from the vines. Someone standing on a ladder was picking fruit, but the branches and leaves hid his face, and for a moment she could not find Tang Jo-Wang.

A loud voice speaking a strange gibberish came from somewhere beneath a tree. Peering in the direction whence it came, Sumalagu was just in time to see the owner of the voice remove a wide-brimmed hat decorated with an ostrich feather, making a graceful bow at someone on the ladder. The person on the ladder responded in the same gibberish. Though she did not understand a word they said, it sounded like a friendly conversation. Moreover she was sure she had recognized the familiar voice of Tang Jo-Wang. But who was the other person? She slid behind a tree to watch.

Tang Jo-Wang came down the ladder carrying a small basket full of peaches. The two blue-eyed foreigners seated themselves at a small stone table under the trees while servants placed plates of cakes, wine, roast chicken and meat before them. The two men slapped each other on the back and laughed together like brothers. Then they lifted their glasses, and Tang Jo-Wang recited a few lines of a poem in Dutch, that tripped off the tongue like a song:

Roses dazzle the earth;
Buds suck the breath of spring
Blessed are the lovers of wine
Blessed are they indeed!

The other foreigner lifted his goblet with one hand, and gesturing expansively with the other, responded with a verse of his own, his face tilted to the sky:

Lift the cup of wine on high
For in this world of freedom
The lover of wine and the saint are one,
The farmer is not lesser than the king!

The two men clicked their goblets and drank heartily.

Tang Jo-Wang ordered the servant to load all the grapes and the peaches that had been gathered and all the wine in the cellar onto a cart and send them to the ambassador's residence. When the servant hesitated, Tang Jo-Wang rebuked him with his eyes, and added, "Hurry! Everything must go!" The servant, still doubtful, left them. Tang Jo-Wang turned to his guest and said, "These people have no idea of the hardships of being far from home." His guest made a helpless gesture with his hands and shrugged. Tang Jo-Wang smacked himself on the forehead and laughed out loud. For he had lapsed into Chinese with his guest who did not understand the language.

Before taking his leave, the visitor embraced Tang Jo-Wang warmly, and murmured something. Tang Jo-Wang nodded. The visitor bowed with a great flourish and left with a spritely gait.

"Mafa Tang!" Sumalagu rushed forward to greet the Jesuit.

Tang Jo-Wang had known her since his first meeting with the Empress Dowager which she had arranged. Nevertheless, he was surprised to see her. He quickly rose to his feet.

"Sumalagu, what are you doing here? Is the Empress Dowager unwell?"

"Her Majesty is in good health. However, there is a matter which she wishes to discuss.... Perhaps this is not a convenient place?..."

Tang Jo-Wang led her to his small study. There Sumalagu repeated what the Empress Dowager had instructed her to say, about Fulin's changed behaviour and his illness, and begged him for a cure, and also to counsel Fulin about his licentiousness.

Tang Jo-Wang's visage darkened. Aside from his missionary interest in his host country's ruler, he was genuinely fond of this clever, studious but capricious young man. Then too, Fulin's respect and love for him roused in the Jesuit a paternal concern for the Emperor. In the last month he had been so preoccupied with entertaining the ambassador from Holland that he was unaware of the emotional quagmire that Fulin was embroiled in, and that weighed upon his mind. He immediately replied, "Please tell the Empress Dowager I will do my utmost. That is my duty."

"Her Majesty is worried. Can you come in the next few days?" pressed Sumalagu. Tang Jo-Wang rose to his feet. "I mean to go at once. I have an important matter to report to His Majesty." Sumalagu rose to her feet, relieved at the outcome of her errand. As she took her leave, she mentioned as an afterthought, "The hat of the foreign gentleman who just left was most attractive."

"So you noticed," Tang Jo-Wang answered. "Dutchmen are great sailors who have been all over the world. As a result their clothing is also unique."

"Oh, so he is a Dutchman."

"Yes. He is assistant to the ambassador from Amsterdam, and the younger brother of an old schoolmate. To meet someone from one's hometown so far away is one of the joys of life!"

"This time their tribute was really extravagant. The Empress Dowager was impressed."

"That is true," Tang Jo-Wang smiled. "I figure the gifts must have cost Holland about twenty thousand ounces of silver." There were gifts not only for the Empress Dowager, the Emperor and the Empress, but also every prince and grand minister of the Council of Nobles.

"Why did they spend all that money?" Sumalagu probed.

"They want a trade treaty and the right to settle in Macao.... Well ... they want to open up China...."

"They were indeed fortunate to have met you, Mafa. You are not only of the same race, but from the same place, and an old friend to boot. Besides, you're kind and enthusiastic." Tang Jo-Wang chuckled, Sumalagu laughed also.

"That's exactly what the ambassador's assistant..." he quickly caught himself before he said too much.

"If I were you, Mafa, I would do my best for him," remarked Sumalagu. Tang Jo-Wang fixed her with his blue eyes and said, "The decision rests with the Empress Dowager and the Emperor."

"I'm sure it will be all right," countered Sumalagu with conviction. "Mafa, they brought precious gifts and great friendship. Their Majesties are well aware of that." Tang Jo-Wang smiled and nodded but said no more. Sumalagu hurriedly took her leave.

Tang Jo-Wang thought a moment, then he wrote a petition, using very stern language, and ordered a sedan chair to take him to the palace. He was immediately admitted and directed to the Hall of Mental Cultivation.

Bare-headed and dressed in an informal yellow silk robe stitched with a pattern of dragons, Fulin was reading, leaning against a low table set on the kang. Tang Jo-Wang breathed a sigh of relief, for at first glance he did not seem ill. Fulin laid aside his book, and prevented the Jesuit from dropping to his knees.

"Mafa, I haven't seen you for some time!" Fulin's smile was unnatural, even pathetic. At close range Tang Jo-Wang was dismayed by the Emperor's appearance. The cheeks were sunken and dark circles rimmed the eyes. The lips and cheeks were flushed and feverish. He seemed listless. According to a plan formulated on the way to the palace, Tang Jo-Wang spoke first of the Dutch trade proposals.

"Mafa, we have studied this matter," Fulin replied wearily. "The Palace Academies and Court of Colonial Affairs will discuss it. We can see no objection to the treaty so long as both sides benefit."

"Not so. Trade is only an excuse masking certain evil intentions. Your old courtier has petitioned Your Majesty repeatedly to proceed with caution, because of this."

"You mean to say...." Fulin gazed at the Jesuit in confusion.

"Your Majesty, Holland is becoming a great power. For decades she has been building her armed forces. Now her navy is at the peak of its strength. Soon she will surpass Spain as the world's leading colonial power. China is large, rich in natural resources, with a huge population. No wonder Holland drools for her. Beware. Once the gate is open, it will not be easily shut again."

Fulin nodded his agreement. "Our island of Taiwan, isolated in the oceans, is now the bone of contention between Spain and Holland."

Tang Jo-Wang quickly interposed, "That is why it is best to leave Macao to Portugal and deny the Dutch the right to live there." Fulin chuckled. "Is it Mafa's intention to have the three of them at each other's throat?"

"Exactly. Your Majesty still has to deal with Zheng Chenggong in the south and Yongli of Southern Ming. Having them fight among themselves is to Your Majesty's advantage." Fulin was deeply moved.

"The Dutch are of your race and you have been generous to them, and concerned for their welfare. Naturally, I expected you to speak on their behalf. But such is not the case! We are grateful for Mafa's loyalty. There has never been a foreigner in our midst to equal that." Tang Jo-Wang blushed as he replied, "Does Your Majesty doubt the sincerity of your old courtier? Though the Dutch are of my race and my delight in seeing them is heartfelt, I am equally sincere in my concern for the Empire, knowing their intentions. Your Majesty must bear in mind I am a man of God."

Fulin fixed Tang Jo-Wang with his gaze, momentarily unsure

of the older man's purpose.

Regardless of his honoured position at court, his work at the Imperial Ministry of Astronomy, and how the Manchus revered him for his erudition, Tang Jo-Wang was first and foremost a missionary. All his activities, his incessant learning, his travelling, his physical labour was all done in the name of his God. His prime purpose was to see that belief in his God should take root and flourish in China; that her millions would swear allegiance to the Holy See of Rome; and that the souls of the suffering millions would finally be wafted to Paradise. His delight in receiving the Dutch envoys was marred by the fact that they were Calvinists, a Christian sect opposed to the church of Rome. Tang Jo-Wang would never permit Calvinism a foothold in China. Therefore, while he was delighted in their company and used his influence to ensure they were accorded the highest courtesies, he was also assiduously working to defeat their purpose.

Tang Jo-Wang explained how the Calvinists would interfere with his missionary work, adding, "Your old courtier deemed it the only way to satisfy a personal friendship without jeopardizing the general situation."

"In Mafa's mind," smiled Fulin, "how should we answer the ambassadors?"

"Some recognition is necessary since they have come a long way with lavish gifts."

Fulin wrote on a sheet of paper: "Let Tribute be made every eight years. A small amount of trade may be carried out at the same time."

Tang Jo-Wang had won. Now his thoughts turned to the Empress Dowager's concerns.

"Mafa, tell me something amusing," Fulin leaned back into his cushions, wan and haggard.

Tang Jo-Wang chose his words carefully when he spoke.

"What I have to say, may be said only when there are two pairs of eyes present." It was a signal between them, begun when Fulin first took the reins of government. This was Tang Jo-Wang's ploy when he wished to counsel the Emperor on a delicate matter, being mindful of the latter's fragile pride. Fulin understood and dismissed the eunuchs and the guards. Then Tang Jo-Wang presented his petition without further hesitation.

Fulin unsealed the document, languidly scanned the opening lines, and threw it down on the table.

"What do you take us for!" he shouted, flushed with shame and rage. He stalked from the room, his hands folded behind his back.

Tang Jo-Wang stood alone in the room trembling. What would the capricious young Emperor do now? Jail him or behead him? The hall was silent. No one could tell what might transpire. He was known for his frankness in his petitions. Would the Emperor execute an honest courtier, and in so doing heap dishonour upon himself? Tang Jo-Wang thought not. He shook out his sleeve, and calmly smoothed his whiskers. He left the hall, walking in an unhurried gait down the steps of the terrace and across the courtyard toward the Gate of Mental Cultivation.

"Tang Jo-Wang. Stop!" cried the chief eunuch of the Hall of Mental Cultivation. Tang Jo-Wang turned back with a wildly beating heart.

Fulin was seated on thc informal kang in the East Chamber. Tang Jo-Wang was motioned to a chair. Tea was brought.

"Mafa, which is the greater sin," Fulin spoke in a serene voice, "miserliness or debauchery?"

"Debauchery. Particularly in great men. For their example can cause great harm." Fulin listened calmly and nodded assent. He asked again, "What if the debauchery was not for pleasure but to dispel depression?"

Tang Jo-Wang spoke solemnly: "Debauchery is a disgrace. So is incest. It is improper to substitute one disgraceful act for another."

"Oh, Mafa..." cried Fulin, "I can't endure it any

longer ....'' He shot to his feet as though he was about to say something. But he blanched, and tottered. A eunuch rushed forward to hold him up. In his weakened state, he was overcome by the emotional exchange.

Fulin was carried into the bed chamber between Tang Jo-Wang and two ennuchs, and laid on the bed. A light quilt was laid over him. Tang Jo-Wang was about to leave, but Fulin clung to him like a child, commanding him to sit beside him, and dismissing the others. When they were alone, he sighed and said sadly, "Mafa, I'm like the lark in your foreign poems. Only they won't let me into the rose garden....'' His voice dwindled into a barely audible whisper. The words were like the soft murmur of a brook on which floated the scattered petals of fallen blossoms. Tang Jo-Wang had to bend over the bed to catch every word, mulling them over in his mind.

It was as Sumalagu had told him, yet hearing it this way, he found in it beauty, sadness and despair.... In spite of the tears there was a sweetness not unmixed with the sharp bitterness of old wine.

When Tang Jo-Wang left the Hall of Mental Cultivation the sun was sinking in the west. His heart was heavy, and his feet dragged. Fulin's depression infected him. This is only the beginning, he thought. The Emperor's condition could worsen.... Should the Empress Dowager be told?

After Fulin had spilled out all his woes he felt better: as though he had just been bathed, he was weary but at ease. After he had taken the medicine sent round by the imperial pharmacy he fell into a deep sleep.

The Empress Dowager was alarmed by Tang Jo-Wang's report. The dignity of her situation gave way to a mother's anxiety. Attended only by Sumalagu, she immediately went to the Hall of Mental Cultivation to see for herself. As Fulin was sound asleep, she did not have the heart to wake him. It had been a long time since she had seen her son at such close range, and she could not tear herself away. She lifted the flimsy drapes of the bed and fastened them with a gold hook then, taking up the duster lying beside the bed, kept the errant flies at bay.

The steamy air outside did not penetrate the cool bed chamber. The scent of orchids and benzoin hung in the air. All was silence. Sumalagu stood guard outside the door. Inside, the Empress Dowager scrutinized her son's haggard features. Short down surrounded the mouth. The eyebrows seemed more black and heavy against the pale skin of his face. Her heart was filled with love and regret. Her eyes blurred as she sought a small, red, down-covered face in her son's handsome, manly features — the infant's face of her only son, in which the eyes barely opened.

She married when she was a young girl of twelve and Abahai was twenty-one years older. Because she was pretty, clever, and broad-minded she became a favourite. When she showed an ability to understand affairs of state, she became Abahai's confidante. Whenever he could not make up his mind he consulted her. She learned from her husband the art of using men and deploying generals to the optimum of their ability. She learned the art of government as well. However, she was less fortunate in her conjugal duties. At the ages of 16, 19 and 20 she produced three daughters. The year she turned twenty-two, her older sister was brought into the palace. The following year, the first year of Chongde, Abahai took the title of Emperor and formally changed his dynastic name to Great Qing. She was given the title of Lady Zhuang, Concubine of the West Yongfu Palace, while her sister was named Lady Chen, Concubine of the East Guanju Palace, and the new favourite had the Emperor's undivided love. In the seventh month of the second year of Chongde she bore him a son. The Emperor planned to make this eighth son his heir, and marked his birthday with a general amnesty. If this child had lived, Abahai's ninth son, Fulin, would never have aspired to the throne. However, on the twenty-eighth day of the first month in the third year of Chongde, he died, just two days before Fulin's birth. The Emperor's grief was as deep as Lady Chen's, and unrelieved by the birth of a ninth son. Lady Chen fell ill in the sixth year of Chongde. At the time Abahai was in the midst of a campaign at Songshan and Ningyuan against the adherents of Ming. Nevertheless, he left his generals and hastened back to the capital. Lady Chen died shortly afterwards. Overcome by grief, the Emperor swooned several times. Thereafter he aged visibly, and wasted away. A year later he was dead. Left with the five-year-old Fulin, Lady Zhuang fought hammer and tongs to set her son on the throne, to make him the Emperor Shunzhi.

Would he too waste away over a woman, and lose everything she had fought for?

Fulin tossed restlessly in his sleep, muttering, "Royal Mother ... you were young once and in love.... Why are you so set against me?"

The Empress Dowager gave a start. With a thumping heart she scrutinized her son. Fulin was sound asleep. She realized he was talking in his sleep. And Sumalagu remained standing as still as a statue at the door. Reassured, she breathed easier. She sat down again but her tranquillity had flown.

Youth and love, she reflected, began when her husband's affections turned from her to her older sister. The Emperor's handsome and dashing younger brother, Prince Dorgon, was the same age as she, and a man of many parts. They fell in love, passionately and obsessively. After Abahai died, Prince Dorgon was the most qualified successor. But he was willing to step aside as Regent in favour of the five-year-old Fulin. This was prompted by many reasons. Chief of which was one he had reiterated hundreds of times. He had done it for her! Her feelings for Dorgon was an open secret. She was grateful, and she loved him for the days and nights of sweetness they shared.

If later, he had not imprisoned and killed Prince Haoge and married his wife, and had he not secretly gone to Lianshan and there married two Korean princesses, she would not have agreed to posthumously condemn him for treason.

What would happen now? The past was gone like a torrent flowing to the sea. But memories of youth still fire the blood. She is still swept along on a flood of emotion fraught with pain.

A long while later, the Empress Dowager dashed the tears from her eyes and softly, wordlessly left the hall.

When Fulin woke the sun was half hidden behind the Western Hills. A thin veil of green cut off the golden shafts of sunlight. The blood-red glow of the setting sun turned the evening mist into pale purple swirls. Staring in the direction of the setting sun which was swallowed slowly by the craggy mountains Fulin was gradually enveloped by a dismal hush. Happiness and ease seeped away. A sad emptiness took hold of him once more. He dreaded the loneliness of dusk which sharpened his longing for the one he loved. And that longing became despair which in turn became an endless melancholy.

The days and nights of debauchery were merely a despairing struggle to shake off a hopeless love. The madness had not only robbed him of his health, but deepened the loneliness that plagued him. None of the women understood his needs. They were intent on securing his favour, and thus, position, power and riches. They flattered him, complied to his every whim, and feared him, but none loved him. Of that he was certain, for now there was a powerful contrast in his heart. Therefore, afterwards, he was disgusted. He hated the women, but he hated himself more. He suffered great pain and must try to extricate himself from it. He could only assuage by repeating the cycle until it became a compulsion.

Finally illness put an end to his mad cycle and confined him to the palace to contemplate his sins. Tang Jo-Wang's petition struck fear in his heart. No, there would never be a repeat of that madness. But he could not forget that day when the peonies were in full bloom. A thousand women could not give him what she brought to him in one moment, for it was the blending of heart and soul. It was not the thousands of stars in the firmament he craved but one immaculate moon. He did not want to be surrounded by a thousand blooms, but only one perfect peony. Heaven! Why will you not grant this one fervent wish?

He looked up at the smudge of red fading fast in the dwindling light. There seemed to be a spark of life in it from which he derived a flicker of warmth. He lingered, unwilling to return to the bed chamber. Dusk deepened. The greenish glow of fireflies flitted among the shrubs. The sound of bell and drum rolled from the Meridian Gate, shaking the encompassing silence. He sighed and muttered the lines of an ancient poem full of the poignance of approaching night and loneliness. Centuries had passed, yet nothing had changed between then and now.

"Your Majesty, the Empress Dowager has sent Sumalagu with a gift of food," the young eunuch spoke softly.

Fulin nodded. Sumalagu approached followed by a maid of honour carrying a food container. The women made their obeisance and Sumalagu offered the Empress Dowager's greetings. Fulin gave his formal reply. Then Sumalagu bade the maid of honour take the food indoors, and a young eunuch quickly led her away.

"Her Majesty needs me, so I beg to withdraw," said Sumalagu. "When the maid of honour has served the food, she will return to Cining Palace."

Then she quickly retreated.

It had grown dark and Fulin could not clearly see the expression on Sumalagu's face. Still he was surprised. Before he fell ill this had happened quite frequently. Under the present circumstance, would he be interested in this maid of honour? He stood unhappily under the terrace, not wanting to go indoors. But the maid of honour dawdled. He thought he had better send her away himself. She was from the Empress Dowager's palace. He had better not cold-shoulder her.

The maid of honour, dressed in a plain blue cloth robe, had her back to him arranging the food on the table as Fulin entered the bed chamber. A glossy black braid hung down her back, qivering slightly as she moved. It was pretty but Fulin was not interested.

"It's late. I'll have someone see you back to Cining Palace," he said.

The maid of honour trembled violently at his voice. She turned slowly and fell to her knees with a tearful cry, "Your Majesty...."

"Black Pearl!" Fulin was barely able to croak her name. He rushed blindly to help her to her feet, knocking over furniture and smashing a few jade ornaments in his haste.

They fell into each other's arms weeping like two children, mingling their tears.

Later, with Black Pearl's tears still damp upon the pillows, his shoulders and his chest, she exclaimed between sobs, "How thin you have become...."

And Fulin, caressing the one he loved, forced a smile. "Your waist is smaller than before..." he whispered with tears in his voice.

Black Pearl had to be back at Cining Palace before daybreak. Fulin held on to her.

"As long as there is heaven and earth, nothing must separate us," he said gazing tenderly into her ink-black eyes. "Always remember this day!" Black Pearl's eyes shone like the Morning Star. Fulin ran across the room and taking paper and brush quickly penned a poem of the Tang Dynasty:

Last night in the winds of love,
I remembered a beauty from the banks of River Xiang
And in the space of seconds, upon my pillow
I traversed a thousand li to the south.

A gift for Black Pearl
Thirtieth day of the sixth month in the thirteenth year of Shunzhi.

Fulin handed the sheet of paper to Black Pearl and said, "Let this be a pledge that you will always be in my mind. Do you remember ... the first time we met ... this was the poem."

"I remember," Black Pearl's eyes were soulful. "It was two years ago ... but I actually met you four years ago...."

"Oh, when?"

"I won't tell you!" Black Pearl teased him with her smile. He took her in his arms again, and pleaded with her, "It's not light yet. I'll send someone with you.."

"No. Sumalagu will fetch me...."

Two days later Fulin summoned Bomubogur to the West Chamber of the Hall of Mental Cultivation. He had been thinking of a way to settle matters once and for all with his younger brother. However, he hesitated, afraid of being branded an adulterer. Something unexpected brought matters swiftly to a head.

Fulin forced himself to control his anger which threatened to sweep away the last vestiges of guilt and shame as he accepted the homage of Prince Xiang.

Bomubogur was always a little intimidated by his brother the Emperor. After his formal obeisance to the Emperor, and the usual greetings to a brother, he stood to one side waiting to be spoken to, unaware of what was going to happen.

Fulin could contain himself no longer and angrily came to the point. "How dare you lock up Lady Black Pearl and deny her food and water?"

Bomubogur never dreamed the Emperor knew and would summon him about it. "She ... she...." He darted a nervous glance at the Emperor's stern face and blurted out, "I ... I want to divorce her...." He stuttered in confusion.

Delight and shock warred in Fulin when he asked, "Why?"

Just fifteen Bomubogur was only answerable to the Emperor, the Empress Dowager and the Grand Concubine. He spoke without fear determined to make his position clear.

"For a long time, she has refused to let me touch her. Isn't she my woman? It was because she had another love!" He paused, blushing. It was a shameful thing for a man to admit that his wife was an adulteress. It was something one didn't speak of, yet to his consternation he found the Emperor was as red-faced as he. Moved by his brother's apparent empathy, Bomubogur resolved to tell everything.

"The other day ... while she slept ... I wanted to .... but in her undergarments I found a slip of flowered paper. Your Majesty, isn't this poem the purest filth! The man must be a southern barbarian! A shameless libertine! A scoundrel!"

Fulin recognized the slip of paper at once. Never in his life had he been so mortified.

"Stop!" he shouted in uncontrollable anger. He bounded from his chair, and struck his younger brother hard across the face.

Bomubogur fell to his knees. The gold edged slip of paper fluttered to the floor. The eighteen-year-old Emperor faced his fifteen-year-old brother, both breathing hard. One was bewildered by the sudden assault, while the other trembled with things he could not put into words.

A moment passed. Fulin gathered his wits and with an arrogant, almost callous air said, "I gave her that poem."

Bomubogur was thunderstruck. What the Emperor said next was so clear and simple that it made his head spin.

"I want to marry her."

Bomubogur's face had turned to chalk, his vacant eyes fixed straight ahead, swaying as if he were about to fall had the Emperor not held him up.

"Go now. I will want your answer in three days," he said glaring into his younger brother's glazed eyes.

The next day, the third day of the seventh month, Bomubogur's death was announced from the residence of Prince Xiang.

When the news reached the palace, the Grand Concubine swooned. The Empress Dowager and even the Emperor shed tears. A few days later, the Grand Concubine tearfully told the

Empress Dowager that Abahai's eleventh son, Prince Xiang, Bomubogur, had hanged himself.

In the middle of the same month, the Ministry of Rites, acting on the Empress Dowager's decree to keep the Lady Dongeh in the palace, petitioned the Emperor to take the lady for himself, naming her the Concubine Xian. The suggested date of the ceremony was the end of the same month. However, in view of Prince Xiang's recent death, the Emperor commanded a delay to some auspicious day in the following month.

6

It was the ninth of the ninth month, or the Double Ninth Festival. The autumn air was brisk and clear. White clouds scudded across the blue sky.

A hexagonal thatched pavilion had been built on top of the hill by the special command of Duke An, named Yuele. Four pillars supported a thatched roof under which were a stone table and benches. Surrounded by a railing, the pavilion was built for use during the festival when it was the custom to climb a hill as a pious deed, and also for the convenience of travellers.

Lu Zhiyue drained his cup of wine and said to his companion Yuele:

> "*I drink the wine you offer upon alighting from my mount,*
> *To ask whence you are bound?*"

Yuele laughed out loud, and returned the toast, saying, "This is only a diversion on a festival day. If this bit of food and wine was meant as a welcome then people would blame me for denying you your due, and for being a miser to boot. Now for the rest of that poem:

> '*You say disappointment leads you*
> *To desire to rest at the southern slopes.*'

That has nothing to do with me at all."

The two men put down their cups and stepped out of the pavilion to admire the view. Both were tipsy.

On a clear day such as this, one could see for miles around. To the north were mountains, criss-crossed by deep gorges. To the south were rolling plains through which a river meandered. Wafted by the brisk wind of autumn, and being thus placed between heaven and earth, one felt the heartbeat and breath of the universe. Man became an insignificant speck, and life as short as a flicker of an eyelash. In such a moment one became broad-minded and unprejudiced. The nobleman forsook the dignity of his caste; the commoner his habitual arrogance. They became natural, human, vibrant with life.

"Don't for a moment think that being dismissed from controlling one of the six ministries has disgruntled me," Yuele said, gazing at the mountains in the distance. "I am glad to be relieved of the burden of government. Though the Emperor might overlook errors, one's reputation is always in peril. Now there is time for poetry, wine, feasting and hunting. Life is sweet. I am content with my present post in the Court of the Imperial Clan. It is only assigned to people connected to the imperial family. At least I know what I'm doing."

Lu Zhiyue responded by saying, "I heard that the plan to remove the Princes as heads of the six ministries caused a great controversy. I am amazed that My Lord takes the matter so lightly."

"It was not always thus." Though Yuele was fond of Han civilization, he retained the blunt honesty of the Manchu. "When the imperial decree first came down I was not pleased. But when I reflected upon it I had to admit that we Manchus won all under Heaven through our skill on the battlefield. Few of us are literate, and even fewer have any knowledge of governing. Though I know the Han language, I am often bewildered by the intricacies of government. The younger princes are not only ill-educated but unwilling to learn. In their ignorance, many errors were made. The six ministries are the heart and soul of the Empire, and this kind of sloppiness cannot be allowed to continue. I am the oldest and the most learned among the princes. If I stepped aside of my own free will, the others would have to follow."

Lu Zhiyue thought to himself, if only there had been more noblemen like this, the wars would not have lasted so long. He folded his hands in front of him in a formal gesture and said aloud, "To serve the dynasty and the Emperor with such faith, My Lord, you have achieved true nirvana, where material wealth does not bring joy, nor lack of recognition bring dismay."

"I suppose you know that the policy of removing the princes from heading the six ministries and the treason charges against the ten southern families are linked?"

"Is that true?" Lu Zhiyue was amazed.

"Absolutely. You have just come from the south. What did you hear?"

"Ah, that is something to write about! The day the prisoned members of these families were released, the streets to the governor's office were jammed with people waiting to welcome their loved ones. Some were crying, others were laughing. Everybody was shouting. It was bedlam! Everybody rejoiced when it was announced that those who gave false testimony would be gaoled. One of the scholars who was freed turned to face the north and shouted in a loud voice 'Long live the Emperor'. Then everybody started shouting 'Long live the Emperor!' The sound shook the sky...."

Yuele beamed with satisfaction.

"This can never be achieved through force or torture." The remark of Lu Zhiyue smacked of a penetrating sharpness.

Yuele's cheek twitched. He darted a glance at Lu Zhiyue, a glance full of menace and a deep-rooted cruelty. Lu Zhiyue brushed the look aside as though he hadn't noticed.

"A wise and compassionate ruler will keep his empire. A cruel one may win his empire quickly and just as quickly lose it. That is because one wins people's hearts and the other does not. The Emperor was wise in his disposition of the treason charges. It was an act that comforted the people. The people had been suffering terribly by the end of Ming and were turned against the ruler. If the Emperor shows compassion he will win them over, for who would not abandon the bitter for the sweet?"

Yuele nodded and resumed his pleasant demeanor.

Lu Zhiyue steered the conversation in another direction and asked, "On my way northward, everywhere local governments were preparing to open up wasteland according to imperial decree. What is that about?"

Yuele flashed a smile full of mischief that was fitting to neither his age nor rank. "Never mind. There is something more important that you might not have heard. Your pupil has gone into the palace."

"If you mean Ershuo's daughter Black Pearl, I knew she became Prince Xiang's wife three years ago. Before I left the capital I also heard the Empress Dowager had taken her as adoptive daughter."

"No! No! She is now the chief lady of Chengqian Palace. Last month she was given the title of Concubine Xian, this month she has become the Precious Concubine (Huangguifei). The formal ceremony will take place before the end of the year."

Lu Zhiyue was stunned by this announcement. "How can that be?" he asked.

Yuele chuckled. "Would I lie? Don't forget I head the Court of Imperial Clan."

"As far as beauty and learning go, Black Pearl is worthy of the Emperor. But ... but ... what about Prince Xiang?"

"Prince Xiang died on the third day of the seventh month."

"Taking a younger brother's woman to wife would not be permitted among ordinary folk, not to mention the Emperor. Marriage between kin folk is not allowed. The barbaric customs of sharing spouses cannot exist in today's society."

Seeing Lu Zhiyue's indignation, Yuele rubbed his hands together with glee. "This is the decadence of the Hans," he chortled. "Gaozong of Tang took his father's woman, and Minghuang of Tang took his son's wife, and you celebrated those aberrations in poetry and song. It goes to show Hans do not practise what they preach. You are hypocrites! On the other hand, these two are not blood kin. The Emperor is merely performing his younger brother's duties. A common custom among Manchus." And he roared with laughter.

Yuele continued more solemnly: "Your pupil is indeed the Emperor's good helpmate. Since she has been in the palace, the Emperor has been in good health and in good temper. Furthermore, the Emperor and the Empress Dowager have increased the allowances of the nobles, and that pleased the eight banners. In recent months, the Emperor has issued three decrees. All provincial governors are required to cultivate wasteland; backlogged court cases are to be cleared, and corrupt officials punished. Although these measures have been decreed before, now reward and punishment have become definite. In future officials will be advanced according to the amount of wasteland they brought under cultivation. Officials of the judiciary who allow cases to lag over one year are dismissed. Officials who accept more than ten ounces of silver in bribes are caned, and dismissed, and barred for life from holding office. The Emperor is clearly mindful of his people and his government. I venture to guess it is due in no small measure to the influence of the Precious Concubine...."

Lu Zhiyue asked, "And what of the southwest and the eastern sea?"

"Zheng Chenggong has been defeated, and his general Huang Wu surrendered. Zhoushan is now in our hands. Li Dingguo, Sun Kewang, supporting Zhu Youlang, have retreated to Yunnan. Hong Jinglue, Wu Pingxi, Shang Pingnan, Geng Jingnan and Kong Dingnan hold Sichuan, Guangdong, Guangxi, and Guizhou between them. As for Zheng and Zhu, the Emperor has called upon them to lay down their arms and serve the Emperor. For the time being, all is peaceful...."

Lu Zhiyue raised his hands to heaven with brimming eyes and murmured, "Gods in heaven! You have finally given the people peace!"

"What is the matter?" Duke An asked in confusion. Lu Zhiyue shook his head in embarrassment. "It's nothing. I am getting old and mellow."

Lu Zhiyue smilingly brushed his companion aside and began picking the wild flowers that grew around the pavilion — yellow ones, blue ones and red ones, selecting the brightest to decorate his robe and cap.

Duke An chuckled. "It is the custom to wear branches of cornel during this festival but you wear flowers. You are a true romantic!"

"Poets say if the old are not ashamed to wear flowers, then flowers should be ashamed of decorating an old one's head."

Yuele said, "The Empire will soon be at peace, and wise men are needed...."

"Yes, yes. And I almost forgot.... While I travelled north I met three men whom I would recommend. Xiong Cilu of Xiaogan in Hubei. Xu Yuanwen of Kunshan in Jiangsu, and Loo Jian of Renhe in Zhejiang."

"Slowly! Let me take this down!" They went back to the pavilion and their attendants brought paper and brushes. Yuele carefully wrote down the names and places of origin of the three men. Lu Zhiyue continued, "Xiong Cilu is a brilliant philosopher. In these times when there is a need to secure peace, remove abuses, and pacify the people a Confucian philosopher is required. Xu Yuanwen is young with the talent and ability for administration; a young man with a future. Loo Jian was freed in the recent amnesty. He is a learned man well known in the south. All three are scholars of high repute. My Lord should look in to them."

"Where are these men?"

"Xiong and Xu might be in the capital. Loo Jian has been a fugitive for years. Since his pardon, he might have gone home.

He might not want an official position...."

"Perhaps our sincerity might move the wise man to reconsider. However, there is one other you have left out of your list."

"Who?"

"Yourself."

"Me?" smiled Lu Zhiyue, shaking his head. "How can one gauge one's own wisdom or lack of it? Besides, I can be a pleasant companion and a guest, but I will never do as a servant."

Yuele's face darkened. Anger simmered close to the surface, but he controlled himself. Yet to let those remarks pass was unthinkable. The man was as brilliant as he was arrogant. He was on the point of exploding when a strange sound broke into his thoughts. They paused to listen then, following their attendants, they searched the hillside whence the sound had come. The sound came from a wooden box hidden in the underbrush. It was evidently the wailing of a child, vehemently giving vent to anger and discomfort.

When the box was opened it revealed a pair of twin girls, about six months old, wailing and gasping for breath. Lu Zhiyue joyfully took them in his arms and wrapped them in the folds of his robe. The infants were naked except for red bibs embroidered with lotus leaves and blossoms, and silver bracelets with minute silver bells attached.

Lu Zhiyue ordered the servants to lay some cushions on the stone table and laid the infants on them. There they lay side by side, gazing up at him with their wide black eyes. Somehow the old man had stopped their wailing, and they examined him with interest. And this old man who never had children of his own was filled with love and confusion, not knowing what to do.

Yuele followed him to the pavilion.

"A fine pair of infants. Yet their parents chose to abandon them. However, by the number of air holes punched through the box, I would venture they wanted them to live."

The Duke's remark reminded Lu Zhiyue of something. He

quickly examined the infants and found a scribbled note pinned to the under side of one of their bibs. Someone had written in a very cramped hand: "May the heavens have mercy on these innocent babes, that they may be found and saved from the jaws of wild beasts."

Lu Zhiyue handed the note to Yuele and exclaimed, "Heaven has given two daughters to one who has no children. They must be from a family with many daughters. But the parents didn't have the heart to drown them, so they abandoned them. I will thank heaven and earth and their parents for this gift."

Standing over the infants he joined his hands and made obeisance to heaven and the earth around him.

Yuele was also thrilled by this unexpected turn of events.

"This is indeed a blessing. When you take these twins home to the south, your wife will be overjoyed."

Lu Zhiyue chuckled: "She will be beside herself." He picked up the babes and said, "My Lord, we should return. The babes need food."

"You've only just become a father and already you're a worry wart," Yuele teased. "That is a blessing for the little ones, I suppose."

The attendants, carrying the infants, followed the two men down the hill. On the way Yuele leaned over and in a low voice whispered, "You take the infants with you now. After you get to the capital would you quietly send one to me?" Lu Zhiyue was shocked by the strange request. Although he had the infants for no more than half an hour, he had grown attached to them.

"Why?" he asked. Yuele was embarrassed when he spoke again, "Everyone has a secret prayer. I will not be ungrateful."

"Well," Lu Zhiyue groaned.

"In that case, would you do it for the sake of friendship?"

Lu Zhiyue nodded in spite of himself, but he was dismayed. Yuele spoke cheerily in his usual voice, "In the middle of this month a princess who married a foreign prince is returning to court. Naturally the Court of Imperial Clan and Court of Colonial Affairs will be very busy. We should return to the capital tomorrow."

"Maybe that's the best," Lu Zhiyue concurred without enthusiasm.

"Also about finding Loo Jian, I shall need your help...."

A curious procession wended its way down the hill. The attendants went ahead, loudly shouting at the locals to make way. Yet no one could tell who the two men in plain clothes were, whose conversation was accompanied by the cries of infants.

A few days later, Lu Zhiyue secretly sent one of the infants to Duke An. Later the two men met in secret and drafted a simple agreement. Yuele demanded that Lu Zhiyue must never reveal what really happened, and that the infant he kept must never come to the capital. Lu Zhiyue also had demands. He specified that the bibs and the bracelets the infants were found with be kept as proof when they should find their natural mother in the future. They ruminated a long while before settling on names for the infants. Because both were fairskinned, one was called Bingyue or Icy Moon, and the other Yingchuan, or Gleaming Stream. Soon afterwards, Lu Zhiyue took the child Yingchuan and went back to his home in the south.

Yuele took pains to trace Loo Jian who seemed to have vanished. And so he sent a special emisary to Zhejiang to await his return. Actually Loo Jian had not left Zhili. Liu Tongchun, whom the wife of the Grand Academician Fu had sent to find him, soon returned with a letter. Loo Jian expressed his regrets at refusing the invitation to return to the capital. He wrote: "...My one kind deed has been repaid. Hereafter, you will be an important official of the court and I will be a hermit among mountains. Both have no regrets. We shall not meet again...."

Fu Yijian and his wife were dismayed. They spoke of it for days. The letter filled Fu Yijian with a nameless melancholy, and his wife, Suyun, with a deep sense of loss that stayed with her a long time, and from which she could find no peace.

PART 4

Once again hill and dale turned green in the breezes of spring. It was Qingming, a festival at which the Chinese worship at the graves of loved ones gone.

The gnarled old apricot tree that stood on top of a knoll was naked and forlorn, stripped of the pink blossoms that enveloped it like a small cloud only a short time ago. Fallen petals blanketed two simple graves at the foot of the hillock, where a young woman knelt in the dappled shade of a few young willows. Like the fallen petals around her, she was pale and wan.

In the two intervening years Menggu had changed. No one would recognize her now as the young girl who used to be regarded as a "great beauty". Nor would anyone comprehend the circumstances that led her to these graves.

When Menggu could no longer conceal her pregnancy, the Young Acolyte abandoned the religious life and married her. Her older brother was enraged. He cursed her for disgracing the family name. Throwing her a handful of silver he ordered her from the house. It was only because of their mother's tearful pleading that the brother relented, and the money was used to build an additional room at the back of the house for the young couple.

From the start Menggu was afraid of her husband's baleful gaze and sinister silence. Most of all she was terrified of his insatiable lust. To him she was less than a prostitute. She was a mere object; a bundle of clothes. After she became pregnant he stopped beating her. Menggu realized this was for the sake of the unborn child and had nothing to do with her. That was also what the White-robed Monk had in mind when he insisted the Young Acolyte abandon the celibate life. They were anxious for an heir for the Zhu family. Menggu also hoped for a son, so that her life might be made easier.

To everyone's disappointment she produced twin girls. The Young Acolyte rushed into the room when he was told and fixed Menggu with hate in his eyes. He approached her deliberately, then pounced. Seizing her by the hair, he twisted her face toward his and struck her again and again till blood oozed from the corners of her mouth. Only when Madam Qiao begged on her knees did he desist. From then on he seemed to derive a perverse pleasure from maltreating her. The frustration of personal ambitions, the despair at reviving the lost dynasty, the failure in fathering a son and his hatred of the new regime were all centred upon Menggu. Scarcely a day passed without a beating. Only when he saw pain in her face and heard her cries did he break into a sadistic, self-satisfied smile.

In her loneliness, Menggu turned to her mother for comfort. The mother commiserated with her, but dared not complain. Often she would say, "When the dynasty is restored, Menggu will be empress. To be the superior being one must first wade through fire."

As though Fate had not punished Menggu enough, further trials were in store for her.

Half a year earlier, the White-robed Monk had gathered together a band of men, intending to attack the county town during the Double Ninth Festival. It was a desperate undertaking. If it did not succeed they would have to abandon everything and become outlaws in the mountains. The Young Acolyte actually smiled with pleasure at the thought of this adventure, sure that success was within his grasp. However, they were betrayed. The news reduced the Young Acolyte to a mass of blubbering flesh. Though the White-robed Monk begged him on his knees to show some manliness in the crisis it was to no avail. Just then their servant spotted a troop of Manchu soldiers approaching the village, and rushed back to break the news. Believing they were surrounded and in danger of losing their lives, the Young Acolyte finally forced a few words through his quivering lips.

"All the women must die!" he commanded. Thus the three men could escape without entanglement. Their women would not be captured and insulted. It would also eliminate witnesses.

The Young Acolyte had briefly considered following Emperor Chongzhen's example and killing his children with his own hand. But he lacked his forebear's fortitude. Instead he ordered the servant to dispose of his twin daughters, then turned to Madam Qiao, her daughter and the Abbess Yuan and demanded they take their own lives. The women wept and protested, refusing to die. In a frenzy, the White-robed Monk drew his sword and was about to despatch them when Qiao Bainian, calling for his mother to go home for a meal, stayed his hand. However, it was only a brief reprieve. The White-robed Monk let the woman join her son, but held the other women hostage. When Madam Qiao returned a while later the crisis was over. What the soldiers spotted approaching the village turned out to be the vanguard of a troop protecting a duke on a festive outing. The White-robed Monk heaved a sigh of relief at the news, while the Young Acolyte swooned. Later it was learned that their allies in the south had escaped. One of their two leaders who had made contacts with them had committed suicide by leaping off a cliff, and the other had been killed by an arrow. Thus their secret was kept.

Menggu had only one thought in mind: to save her babes. Though the servant came back to say they had been thrown into a ravine, Menggu rushed up the mountain determined to find them. When she came upon the broken wooden box in which the babes had been carried away she despaired. Her mind snapped and she never smiled again.

On Qingming Festival Menggu built two small graves in a corner of her family plot, in which she buried the tiny clothes, hats and shoes belonging to her daughters. She burned paper offerings and prayed as though their tiny bodies were really interred there. She prayed fervently that her babes would visit her in dreams and relieve the bitter loneliness in her heart.

A breeze blew a branch of the willow tree across the top of her head. Startled, Menggu looked up at the willow tree — the very same tree that Tongchun planted the first time he came home from the capital. At that time, he had softly asked her, "Do you know why I planted a willow in your family plot?"

Menggu understood its significance. Tongchun's family name was Liu, which stands for willow. Planting it in her family plot meant he wanted to live and die with her. Menggu was so overcome with joy and shyness that she had to avert her face.... All that seemed far away now.... Perhaps it had happened many years ago, or even before she was born ... or it might have happened to someone else.... Menggu leaned against the sapling, staring at the white clouds scudding across the sky and mumbled to herself, "Where are you, Brother Tongchun? Will I ever see you again?"

Tears trickled down her face.

"Sister, might I ask some information?"

The light, gentle sound of a woman's voice startled her. Menggu turned to face a young woman standing by the roadside. She was dressed in travelling garb, with a bundle strapped to her back. A kerchief, tied low across her forehead, did not quite hide a young, pretty face. Two other women waited further up the road, their heads bowed even lower.

"Is there a monk who dresses in white in your village?"

The question startled Menggu. She looked at the stranger more carefully. The stranger was plainly dressed in a long blue cloth robe over a pale yellow skirt of rough silk and fastened by a green sash about the waist. She seemed sincere, and her smile was deferential as one might expect from a stranger seeking help. Her attitude allayed Menggu's suspicions.

"Do you want to see him?"

The woman became even more deferential.

"His fame has spread hundreds of miles around. We have come expressly to beg a cure."

Menggu was relieved. Pointing at the monastery nearby, she

told the woman the man she sought was there every afternoon to see patients and distribute medicines.

The woman bowed gratefully, but raised one more question. "The White-robed Monk has a disciple called Yueming. Is he here too?" Menggu bit her lip in confusion. Yueming was the name her husband took when he was an acolyte preparing for the religious life.

"I am not sure..." she muttered.

The three women hastened toward the monastery. Menggu watched them until they were out of sight then slowly gathered the remains of her offerings. She dawdled, putting off going home. The mere thought of her husband's lopsided grin sent shivers down her spine. She lived in constant fear, not knowing when he might turn violent.

Menggu stumbled along the deserted road. The landless villagers of Malan were overjoyed when the edict calling for the cultivation of wasteland was handed down at Yongping Prefecture. The law promised the pioneers six years free of taxation; a great boon to the poor. In accordance with the law, they applied for loans to acquire an ox as beast of burden, and seeds, and proceeded to cultivate wasteland. Others returned to Henan and Shandong whence they had come. It was spring and the time for planting. Everyone was working in the fields. During the day hardly a sound could be heard in the village except dogs barking and the occasional cackle of chickens.

Menggu's brother was pacing the courtyard, reading aloud from a book when he saw her pass. She quickly bowed and offered her greetings. Qiao Bainian turned his back to her. He had treated her thus since her marriage, and Menggu had become used to his insolence and no longer felt the pain. She hung her head and slowly went around the corner to her own courtyard. She trembled uncontrollably as she crossed the threshold as though she had a touch of the ague. The Young Acolyte sat cross-legged, practising calligraphy on the low kang table. This was a regimen that the White-robed Monk insisted upon. When

Menggu came into the room he did not bother to glance at her. But after he had written several lines, he yelled at her to fetch tea.

Menggu trembled within as she brought the tea. She approached him one step at a time. He greeted her with a menacing grin as she looked up. She drew back instinctively. As the Young Acolyte brought his hand down heavily on the tabletop, Menggu trembled.

A loud knocking and the voice of the White-robed Monk demanding to be admitted intervened in the nick of time. Menggu laid down the tea cup and flew to answer the door. The Young Acolyte arranged his robes and waited.

As soon as the gate opened a few hysterical women rushed in and fell to their knees around the Young Acolyte. The White-robed Monk followed grim faced. Madam Qiao was wiping away tears, and Abbess Yuan hovered in the background full of dismay. Madam Qiao latched the gate and threw her arms around her bewildered daughter cowering by the gate and broke down.

Menggu was surprised and not a little troubled when she recognized the three women who had asked the way earlier. Without their kerchiefs, they were pretty young women. Prettier in fact than the Abbess' two disciples who were also present. Without their nun's habit, they were fresh and youthfully alluring. Menggu stole a glance at her husband. The last vestiges of embarrassment had vanished. He stood feet planted wide, smiling coolly. "What brought all of you here at once? And what's the commotion about?"

The woman who had asked the way broke into loud sobs. The others followed suit. The Young Acolyte shouted angrily, "Stop the wailing! I'm not dead yet!"

The women's sobbing subsided into whimpers, coughs, and blowing of noses. The woman who had asked the way spoke in a tearful voice: "My Lord has been gone three years! The Lady Mengjiang of ancient myth who journeyed ten thousand miles in search of her husband inspired me. Nothing daunted me. Finally I came to Yongping Prefecture pretending to seek a cure from the White-robed Monk, only to discover these others are also yours...." She covered her face and burst into tears again.

"My Lord! My Lord!" cried one of the young nuns. "When you possessed my sister and I you never mentioned there were other women...."

Madam Qiao spoke sternly in a loud voice, "Quiet, the lot of you! My daughter was properly married to him. None of you can supersede her."

Instantly the women began to squabble, each trying to prove she was the rightful wife. One saying that My Lord had given his personal word, and the other countered by claiming she was the first to wed him, and therefore she was the legal wife. Yet another claimed that the one he lived with the longest took precedence. The dispute rose to a feverish pitch. Fisticuffs would break out any moment. Menggu alone leaned against the jamb of the gate, quietly dabbed at her eyes, while the Young Acolyte looked on with malicious glee.

"Stop shouting!" the White-robed Monk warned. "Are you looking for trouble?"

The women quieted down and bowed their heads shamed into silence. The White-robed Monk approached the Young Acolyte. Bowing deeply he spoke in a solemn tone. "I came across My Lord in exile many years ago. Since then my aim has been to aid My Lord in the restoration of his dynasty. To succeed, My Lord must overcome all difficulties, learn and work hard. Instead he wallows in debauchery. He has forgotten the Empire, more bent on failure than success. Thus I wash my hands of him and take my leave."

As the White-robed Monk raised his hands in farewell, the Young Acolyte took fright. He quickly blocked the man's retreat. Smiling sheepishly, he pleaded: "It's my fault! Blame it on ... youth and ... thoughtlessness...."

"You are young, but the man who sits on your throne is

younger!" replied the White-robed Monk coldly. "He is rewarding those who break new ground; he is punishing the corrupt; he is meting out justice. He is laying claim to the loyalty of all under Heaven. What hope have you against such odds?"

"My Lord, calm yourself," the Young Acolyte continued to plead. "Surely the people have not forgotten that in the three hundred years of my dynasty we have done much good. Though the incumbent is a clever man, he is merely a barbarian chieftain, not the rightful monarch of China. In all under Heaven, ninety-nine out of a hundred are Han. Would they bow to such a ruler? I know I have erred. However, according to protocol, the Son of Heaven is allowed seventy-two concubines, and eighty-one other women.... Yet none of these women have given me a son. Of the three acts against filial piety, the lack of heirs is paramount. Naturally, I am anxious."

"Such things are frivolous when one is a fugitive with a price on his head...." "Of course, of course," the Young Acolyte endeavoured to smooth the other's ruffled feathers.

Both men were in earnest. But there was also a certain familiarity about the incident. It had happened before, and was likely to happen again. Both men understood that they were bound to each other, two grasshoppers tied to the same thread. Neither could exist without the other. The Young Acolyte needed the White-robed Monk to regain the paradise he had lost, while the White-robed Monk needed the Young Acolyte as a rallying point to succeed in his personal ambitions. Therefore, when conflict between them reached a fragile point, one or the other invariably backed down for the sake of the alliance. However, the women were all at sea. Vying to be Empress, they forgot the seventy-two concubines or the man they were fighting over. Instead they were filled with anticipation as they knelt before him. When the Young Acolyte spoke of them as hens that did not lay, some of them actually wept with shame.

The White-robed Monk spoke in a more conciliatory tone, "Henceforth it is hoped that My Lord will keep the restoration of Ming constantly in mind...."

"Stop!"

A figure leaped off the wall. The women shrieked in fear as the Young Acolyte beat a fast retreat into the house. The White-robed Monk unsheathed his short sword and lunged at the stranger. But the intruder side-stepped the thrust, seized the man's sword handle and wrenched the weapon from him. With his free arm he held the White-robed Monk by the neck in a vice. The man was none other than Qiao Bainian. Without turning a hair he faced the assemblage as implacable as a steel tower.

"Who are you?" he demanded in a low voice. Madam Qiao tried to placate him, "My son, please don't be hasty...."

"Mother," Qiao Bainian turned on his mother, "this man could lose his head for what he said. We have to be careful." The White-robed Monk stood his ground proudly. He had no fear of the short sword. "You are right. We talk treason. If you go to the authorities, remember your mother and sister are implicated. In fact your whole family face execution."

Qiao Bainian laughed contemptuously.

"I'm not stupid! I'll kill you and destroy the evidence. So many have died these twenty years that two more won't make a difference."

Madam Qiao threw herself on her knees and cried, "Take pity for your mother and sister's sake!"

The White-robed Monk broke into peals of hysterical laughter tinged with tragedy.

"What's so funny?" shouted Qiao Bainian.

"I laugh at myself. I considered myself clever, but I couldn't even tell a dung heap from a pearl. Because you were the son of a tribute student of the previous dynasty, brought up on the writings of sages, I took you to be a man among men. However, you are a person who doesn't know your sovereign, doesn't remember your father, and a man with no loyalty. There is no common language between us. Kill me now! I am but a useless blind man." He attempted to throw himself upon Qiao Bainian's sword. But Qiao Bainian was too quick for him and drew back in the nick of time.

"Spill everything," he said coldly. "I'm sure you are in no hurry to die."

The White-robed Monk surveyed his interrogator, calmly smoothed his rumpled robes and hair and spoke in a measured tone:

"Fourteen years ago, on the eighteenth day of the third month in the seventeenth year of Chongzhen, traitors opened Zhangyi Gate to the rebels who flooded into the capital. Our heroic Emperor watched the city burn from the vantage point of Coal Hill and wept for his people."

The placid face of the White-robed Monk became flushed, and his voice shook with agitation as he continued: "Then the Emperor returned to Palace of Heavenly Purity, despatched the crown prince together with Prince Yong and Prince Ding to the homes of his noble relatives Zhou Kui and Tian Hongyu. He slew his daughter with his own hand and ordered his empress to kill herself. Before daybreak he went up Coal Hill again, and there hung himself with a sash...." The White-robed Monk burst into tears. Qiao Bainian gritted his teeth to fight down his own emotions.

The White-robed Monk darted a quick glance at his captor and, swallowing his tears, continued: "The crown prince was betrayed by Zhou Kui and put to death by the Manchu. Prince Yong was also killed." He drew a deep breath, gathered all his flagging strength and finished distinctly, "Only the youngest prince survived."

"What!" Qiao Bainian exclaimed. "Where is he now?" The White-robed Monk scrutinized Qiao Bainian before continuing:

"He met a courtier of his late father, and the two travelled together disguised as a Daoist priest and his disciple. In recent times, he married into the Qiao family. The mother of the house understood his importance, however the son...." He let the rest trail off.

"You're talking about my sister's husband!" roared Qiao Bainian. The White-robed Monk nodded, stroking his beard, fighting to disguise the look of triumph.

"Prove it!"

The White-robed Monk calmly took a small object wrapped in silk from his pocket and, placing it on the ground, prostrated himself thrice before it. Then he removed the wrapping, revealing three precious items. They were a piece of jade which was embedded in a gold chain worn round the young prince's neck; a gold seal which belonged in the prince's palace; and a poem written in the hand of the Emperor Chongzhen, with a dedication to his third son.

Qiao Bainian blanched in the presence of this indisputable evidence. He threw himself on the ground and wept. The women also fell to their knees in tears. Though the tears and lamentations were real enough, whether it was prompted by joy or sorrow, regret or fear, only the individuals knew.

Qiao Bainian dashed away his tears and, joining his hands, bowed to the White-robed Monk, speaking with great emotion, "I, Qiao Bainian, am an educated man. I chafe under the yoke of barbarians who destroyed my country, my home, and desecrated the shrines of my ancestors. As they say, the killing of a wife may be left unavenged but not the wrongs suffered by father or emperor. I vow that I will not rest till the barbarians are driven from our land."

The White-robed Monk cocked a thumb at him, chuckling his approval. "A hero indeed! Then what you said just now...."

Qiao Bainian chuckled also. "Never pray until you face the Buddha, is what I always say. I suspected you were not an ordinary man. This was a chance to find out once and for all, and to test your courage. I suppose you didn't notice that I did not hold the blade of my knife to your neck!"

The White-robed Monk laughed. "Of course I knew. Otherwise I wouldn't have spoken so freely!"

The two men examined each other, then burst into laughter. Qiao Bainian threw his knife on the ground, point first, sinking it almost to the hilt. The White-robed Monk gave a start, then chortled, "Such strength! Such skill!"

From his pocket Qiao Bainian took a small object wrapped in red silk which he quickly opened, revealing a seal cast in silver and a slip of paper bearing its imprint.

"Kindly examine this," said he.

The White-robed Monk examined it carefully and took a similar seal from his pocket wrapped in yellow silk. The imprints of the two seals were laid side by side. One read: "Qiao, Regional Commander of the forces of Yongli Reign of Great Ming", and the other read "Zhu, Regional Commander of the forces of Yongli Reign of Great Ming". The two men smiled in recognition of one another before they put away their seals. Qiao Bainian joined his hands and saluted the White-robed Monk saying, "You, sir, must be related to the royal house?"

"Indeed. My forebear was Marquis Xianning."

"Why did you not report that the third prince survives to the Court?"

The White-robed Monk's face darkened. His brows knit, and his eyes glazed. "My dear brother must recall the case of the impostor in the Hongguang reign. Most likely he was not a hoax. Nevertheless, Emperor Hongguang had him imprisoned. When the barbarians pressed south, the so-called impostor mysteriously died. With that example fresh in our minds, and our military strength inferior to that of Prince Gui in the southwest, such an announcement would be premature. However, while the third prince lives, restoration is not impossible."

Indeed the third prince was a rallying point for raising an army and calling for the submission of other rebels including the adherents of Prince Gui of Yongli and Zheng Chenggong. That was the undeniable advantage of legitimacy. As his supporter, Qiao Bainian would one day be the imperial brother-in-law, and one of the first nobles of the realm. Wouldn't that be a more prestigious and desirable outcome than following the Yongli reign?

Having the authority and financial support of the Yongli reign but secretly working to restore the third prince was an act of betrayal. However, the third prince was the legitimate claimant of the throne. That sheds a different light even on treason. Legitimacy turns black into white.

Qiao Bainian straightened his rumpled clothing and led the others into the house to be presented to the prince. However, the Young Acolyte was nowhere to be seen. They looked at each other in dismay and the women began to whimper. Then they noticed a strange sound coming from a trunk in the corner. The White-robed Monk lifted the lid and the Young Acolyte curled up inside let out a piercing scream. Seeing that it was only the White-robed Monk, he calmed himself. The others came and helped him from his hiding place.

Qiao Bainian dropped to his knees and begged the Young Acolyte's forgiveness for past slights.

The Young Acolyte had always been intimidated by Qiao Bainian. In fact he was still a little afraid, so he quickly helped the other to his feet.

Then Qiao Bainian also knelt to his sister, addressing her as imperial concubine, begging her forgiveness for his ignorance.

Madam Qiao was delighted; and Menggu found a little relief for her suffering.

Qiao Bainian then proposed expanding the courtyard by building a central, east and west chambers to accommodate all the ladies.

"Of course, my dear sister will occupy the central chamber," he concluded.

The women were delighted with the proposal. The Young Acolyte was grateful, and Menggu's position was secured.

The White-robed Monk observed Qiao Bainian's assignment

of living quarters and the distribution of furniture and money with a watchful eye. He calmly stroked his beard and kept his own counsel amid the hubbub. The man is able, he concluded, but a potentially dangerous adversary. Thus it was behoven him to keep Qiao Bainian on his side and make him a useful ally in the meantime.

Abbess Yuan, who had remained silent all this while, spoke up. "For the present all ceremony must be put aside. If it is noised abroad, all our lives are forfeit!" The White-robed Monk readily agreed.

"Henceforth we will address one another as ordinary relatives and friends." Qiao Bainian then commanded his mother to entertain the ladies, while he and the two men retired to his study.

Three ordinary men, though a prince and two officials of the former Ming Dynasty, left Menggu's small courtyard and went around the corner to the new residence that Qiao Bainian recently built for himself to continue their deliberations.

2

The day in mid-summer when the elephants of the imperial menagerie were bathed was a festival for the people in the capital. It took place at the Xiangshui Sluice-gate near Xuanwu Gate.

Every year on that day, noblemen and officials, scholars and intellectuals, merchants and ordinary folk, vagabonds and slaves gather along the banks of the moat to watch the spectacle. Sometimes the crowds grow to tens of thousands. Those with money rent a room in one of the houses along the moat. Because supply never equalled demand, rents increased to an astounding twenty ounces of silver a day. Money conscious landlords set out chairs along the canal, renting them at two or three thousand coppers a day. In this way, some enterprising souls became wealthy enough to finance a small business on the proceeds. That day, after breakfast Qiao Bainian made his leisurely way northward from his lodgings. He had paid an unconscionable price for a seat at the water's edge.

How would Qiao Bainian dare show his face in the capital? After he and the White-robed Monk had revealed their true identities to one another, they decided to work together. Before this each had gone his separate way, trying to prepare for a rebellion that never materialized. Able men were lukewarm to their schemes, unwilling to take the dubious honour of being the restorer of the former monarch. The populace with whom they came into daily contact were weary of a decade of turmoil. They longed only for peace and a full belly. Besides the new dynasty's policy of repealing three taxes and ending the draft, together with the new decree encouraging the cultivation of wasteland, gave them a broader livelihood. Unlike the intelligentsia, the populace was not bound to the former dynasty by notions of loyalty to the dead.

Qiao Bainian and the White-robed Monk divided the task between them. The White-robed Monk, his disciple and servant, together with Abbess Yuan, were responsible for manpower, enlisting men of courage wherever they could be found, particularly among those who had been forced into outlawry. Qiao Bainian had originally been ordered by Emperor Yongli to infiltrate the present government for the purpose of creating disturbance from within when the time was ripe. However, to penetrate the government required not only a great deal of money but the right background. While the Southern Ming was more than generous with cash, the only legitimate way of overcoming the lack of background open to a son of a tribute student was through the imperial examinations. This year the examinations would be held at Shuntian. Qiao Bainian had come to the capital, intent upon kicking down the doors of officialdom with money and intelligence.

By the time Qiao Bainian reached Xuanwu Gate, he was soaked with sweat. A huge throng gathered around Xiangshui Sluice-gate. The street was clogged with carriages and sedan chairs.

There was a terrific din. To his dismay, he found there wasn't space to stick a pin. Though he was young and vigorous, he still found himself pitched in one direction then another. His breath came in harsh gasps and sweat ran down his back. With all his might he pushed through the crowd, forcing his way to the seat he had rented in front of a small house by the moat.

The shrilling of horns and fifes from inside Xuanwu City Gate flooded across the noise of the crowd.

"They're coming! They're coming!" The throng squirmed, pushed and shoved with excitement. Qiao Bainian angrily folded his arms across his chest and using his heavily muscled shoulders and elbows propelled himself forward.

"Brother Qiao!" A cry from the crowd arrested his footsteps.

"Aren't you Tongchun?" Because Tongchun was the first person he encountered when Qiao Bainian returned to his village, and also because of the broken engagement with his sister, Qiao Bainian remembered the young man very clearly.

"Fancy finding you in the capital!" He grasped Tongchun's hand and shook it vigorously. "You've grown. What are you doing these days?"

In his delight at seeing a familiar face in a strange place, Tongchun forgot old grudges and shook the other's hand with equal enthusiasm.

"When did you arrive in the capital?" he cried. "Is everyone at home well?" What with the heat of the day and the heaving crowd, Tongchun's face was red and hot. Runnels of sweat trickled down his cheeks, but his eyes glowed with genuine pleasure.

Qiao Bainian happily responded, "Everybody's fine. My mother is slowing down. It's age. And my sister is maturing. They often speak of you and about the time when they tried to expropriate the land...."

Tongchun's eyes dimmed, his smile faded, and a muscle twitched in his cheek. He loosened his grip on the other's hand. With a great roar, the crowd suddenly rushed toward the bridge that straddled the moat around the city. The elephants had emerged from the city gate, and the throng rushed toward them with deafening cries. A torrent of humanity separated the two men, propelling them in opposite directions.

"Where do you live?" Qiao Bainian waved and shouted. Liu Tongchun waved back and shouted something. However, the din of the crowd, inflamed by the sight of the huge elephants, drowned out Tongchun's reply.

Qiao Bainian fought his way to the house, produced a slip of paper the landlord had given him and was shown to a seat in front of a window on the second floor. Qiao Bainian mopped the sweat from his brow and gazed out over the heads of the crowd. Twenty-four elephants were lined up along the moat like a grey wall. The thud of drums was like distant thunder in a sudden squall at sea. The thousands thronging the banks of the moat fell silent. Ah! The elephants were moving on legs as thick as pillars, striding into the water, splashing the crowd, which retreated laughing. The cool water of the moat must have pleased the giant animals. They frolicked, raising their heads and fanning their great ears, spraying themselves with water sucked up in their trunks, and squealing with delight. Each of the elephants carried an attendant on its back. Stripped to a loin cloth, the attendant was submerged as the elephant soaked itself, so deep at times that only the man's hair bound on top of his head could be seen.

"A wonderful sight indeed!" sighed Qiao Bainian. His three thousand coins were well spent. Someone behind him laughed and interjected, "It's not only the elephants that are wonderful, it's the people who come out to see them." Qiao Bainian turned. A handsome young man dressed like a scholar was standing behind his chair smiling complacently.

The three-thousand-coin seats in front of the windows were full. However there was also standing room which sold for only two thousand coins. These places were sold to the patrons of the tea shop on the second floor. Although the buyer was not entitled to a seat he got a good view of the elephants, and saved money.

In fact standing room was harder to get than a decent seat. Of course this was a trick that only locals knew. Not being a local, Qiao Bainian was not privy to these tricks. Having a seat marked him as a country bumpkin with more money than sense.

"What's so wonderful about people?" Qiao Bainian wanted to know. The scholar smiled instead of a reply and jutted his chin at the crowd outside.

"Ah!" exclaimed Qiao Bainian. "There's a lot of them!"

The stretch of moat in which the bathing of the elephants took place was lined with Chinese scholartrees. People covered the entire mud slope from the water edge up, not only in the greenish shade of the trees but in their branches as well which drooped dangerously.

The scholar's voice sounded once again: "Me thinks the road is paved with heads and faces. Do you agree, honoured brother?" Qiao Bainian assumed the remark was addressed to himself and replied, "To me they seem more like sunflowers when the seeds are ripe." The scholar laughed, "Very apt indeed."

After the elephants had been in the water a while, the sound of drums and gongs from the shore signalled the attendants to drive their charges back to shore. With cries and smacks of the cane, the lumbering beasts were coaxed out of the water. The crowd edged backward to make way, and once more there was a tumult.

"It's over so quickly!" Qiao Bainain exclaimed in disappointment. "Bathing must not be too long," the scholar explained languidly. "Elephants, if left too long in the water, will want to mate and go wild. Onlookers could be injured."

To the sound of drums and horns, the elephants fell in line and, following the banners of the imperial guards, moved with ponderous, earth-shaking steps through Xuanwu Gate. There was another commotion along the banks of Xiangshui Sluicegate as thousands who gathered there dispersed.

The waters of the moat became still once more. A cool breeze drifted upward from the green shadows of the Chinese scholartrees. The curiosity seekers were mostly wilting from the heat, exhausted by the noise and excitement. According to custom, cups of tea and small dishes of delicacies were served.

An excellent selection of dumplings, pastries and meats were placed on Qiao Bainian's table. He invited the handsome young scholar to dine with him. The young man did not decline.

Qiao Bainian introduced himself, saying he had come to the capital to take part in the imperial examinations.

In turn, the young man introduced himself as Zhang Han, a student of the Directorate of Education, from Jiaxing.

They exchanged formal greetings. As they raised their cups, they were interrupted by a sudden burst of merriment from a neighbouring table. The offenders were five or six young men engaged in a boisterous discussion.

"...Do you remember Xu Juyuan, the wag who wrote a play satirizing Chen Mingxia and Gong Dingzi for submitting to the new regime? Well, he is on the list of candidates for the exams!"

"There's nothing strange about that. Aside from a dozen or so real men of learning, many are sitting the exams. I wrote a little ditty about it...." And he commenced recitation of a limerick jabbing fun at scholars of the old regime, who dusted off their scholarly cap and gown and submitted hoary essays to try for posts with the new regime now that the hope of restoration had dimmed.

They roared with laughter. Qiao Bainian and Zhang Han exchanged knowing smiles without comment. An old Confucian scholar, stroking his beard, calmly intoned, "That's nothing to laugh about. A man should be ambitious."

In the midst of laughter, a handsome, beardless young man stood up and motioned his companions to be quiet. When silence was restored he proceeded solemnly to tell a tale in a different vein. "Once upon a time a man went down to Hell. Confronted by the Lord of the Netherworld with the prospect of reincarnation, the man said, 'If I am to return to the land of the living, it must be according to my demands.' The Lord of the Netherworld asked what his demands were. The man said, 'Let my father be a minister and my son be a great scholar. Let my house be surrounded with a thousand fertile acres, that orchards, gardens and fish pond be constantly full. Let me have wives and concubines who are beautiful and virtuous. Let my storerooms be filled with jewels, and grain, bolts of silk, and silver coins. And let me be a courtier of the first degree to live in ease and luxury a hundred years.' The Lord of the Netherworld laughed saying, 'Under those circumstances I would go myself instead of sending you.'"

All the guests of the teahouse were amused by the witty exchanges of the group.

Liu Tongchun ran up the stairs. When he saw Zhang Han, he cried out, "You've taken me on a merry chase, Sir! Why didn't you tell me you were going to the teahouse?"

"Tongchun!" Qiao Bainian got up in surprise, "Is this gentleman your master?" Liu Tongchun glanced at Qiao Bainian, and his smile turned into blushing confusion. "Tongchun!" Zhang Han was intrigued. "Do you know Master Qiao?"

"Yes. We come from the same place," Tongchun answered truthfully. Then he added, "How did you two gentlemen meet?"

Qiao Bainian laughed out loud: "Truth is stranger than fiction!"

Zhang Han added with a smile, "Fate moves in mysterious ways."

The two men were happy in one another's company. Drinking and eating, all constraints fell away, and they exchanged light-hearted anecdotes. Qiao Bainian was new to the capital and needed company. For the sake of his career and future Zhang Han was seeking rich men who had come to sit the examinations. Standing behind the two, Tongchun had his own concerns. If these two struck it off, he thought, he would be able to hear news of Menggu.

Zhang Han's smile faltered and the hand that was delivering a dumpling into his wide-opened mouth was arrested in mid-air. He shot a glance at Qiao Bainian and inclined his head ever so slightly in the direction of the boisterous Confucians. They were discussing the imperial examinations. Someone had just put forth the idea that considering the relative numbers of commoners and aristocrats taking the examinations, the successful candidates on a provincial scale were bound to be dominated by tribute students.

Several persons demanded how that conclusion had been drawn.

"They are the cream of the cream! Either their fathers or brothers are important officials, or they are scions of wealthy families. They have wide connections with notable people who can further their careers. Though they might think they could shake the earth with their theses, everyone knows the importance of connections. And who is not striving for an entree? Ordinary students are not their match."

"Exactly! It will be extremely hard to succeed this year. The adjudicators are either corrupt bribe-takers or panderers to the rich and powerful. Heaven knows how many places were sold by Li Zhenye alone! I tell you there is no fair play in these exams."

"Ah, these are only the fifth examinations since the new dynasty came to power, and corruption becomes more serious all the time. Yet the court turns a blind eye."

"It's simple. All the adjudicators are Hans, since few Manchus are familiar with the classics. The Manchus are straightforward, upright men who have no notion of connections and so forth. Young adjudicators like Li Zhenye would run rings around the semi-literate Manchus." Qiao Bainian softly asked Zhang Han, "Brother, who is this Li Zhenye?"

That question struck a chord. Zhang Han sighed and smiled

complacently as he replied, "If it were someone else, I might or might not be able to say. But you could not ask anyone more knowledgeable about Master Zhenye than my humble self." By the way he spoke, one would think that the subject of his discourse was not a corrupt official, but someone who had made huge contributions to society. Since the end of the Ming Dynasty, he who is adept at making connections is the most prized.

Qiao Bainian's brows arched in amazement. "Are you acquainted then with this adjudicator?"

"Indeed!" Zhang Han was as content as if he had just swallowed a cooling draught on a hot summer's day.

"I beg your pardon.... Do I perceive a family connection?" Qiao Bainian felt his way gingerly.

"He is a teacher, a friend and a distant relative. You might say we are family friends."

"Ah, that is indeed fortuitous!" Qiao Bainaian turned to Tongchun and asked, "I suppose you too have met the great man?"

When Tongchun nodded, Qiao Bainian inwardly congratulated himself on his amazing good fortune. He addressed Zhang Han in a flattering tone, "My dear brother, what uncommon luck to have such connections! May one assume that Master Li has already been assigned his area as an adjudicator?"

"Exactly! He was appointed adjudicator of the northern region in the fifth month."

"Then you will pass without the slightest doubt!" Qiao Bainian smiled ingratiatingly and gave Zhang Han a playful tap on the shoulder. Zhang Han narrowed his eyes without a word, caressing a cheek with the pointed tip of a finger. Qiao Bainian drew closer and whispered, "Would you give a brother candidate a helping hand?" Zhang Han turned his laughing, self-absorbed eyes on Qiao Bainian and murmured, "That's not difficult. But it depends largely on you...."

"Really?" Qiao Bainian pursued, laughing softly. Zhang Han's reply was softer still. "Believe it or not...."

Their voices were pitched lower and lower so that even Tongchun could not hear what they said. However, their hands became more and more animated.

"Master Zhang! Here you are at last!" a middle-aged man in a short tunic cried as he came into the room. "Your lady wants you home at once. It seems that something urgent has come up."

Zhang Han rose to his feet and gave Qiao Bainian's hand a squeeze. "I'm so glad we met."

Qiao Bainian responded with a smile, "I depend on you."

"Are you worried?'

"A man's word, once given, cannot be taken back."

Zhang Han's smile became even more mysterious. "Very well. I'll concede to you. We will meet tomorrow at Yousheng Nunnery."

"It's agreed. First we feast then I'll pay you. I pray you will not be late."

The two bowed to each other and parted, full of happy expectations. Each thought he had attained what he wanted. Nevertheless, Qiao Bainian wondered about the middle-aged man who had come to summon Zhang Han. What was the meaning behind his sly smile when Zhang Han's back was turned? It seemed to presage disaster.

At the end of a narrow lane, behind a double-panelled gate hidden by trailing green branches of two willow trees, was a small house. A gigantic Chinese scholartree shaded a courtyard consisting of three south-facing rooms and several smaller rooms on the west side. On the gate was an ancient inscription:

Prosperous business links the four seas;
Wealth springs from the three rivers.

At one time this might have been the residence of a wealthy trader. Now it was Zhang Han's home.

The gate was tightly shut. Deep shadows dappled the cool and quiet courtyard. Because the trees deadened sound, this was a world apart in the middle of a bustling city. The curtains in the windows were tightly drawn, and the door discreetly shut. Only the cicadas whirred tirelessly.

As buzzing of the cicadas suddenly ceased, a woman's voice held very coquettishly low was heard whispering, "If My Lord really loves me, he wouldn't refuse such a small request. Do it for my sake...."

The speaker was Zhang Han's new bride who was familiarly called Pinky. At that moment she was clad only in a bright-red stomacher, fastened round her neck with a silver chain. Her two smooth white arms were twined around Li Zhenye's neck so tightly that the romantic scholar was in danger of losing his senses.

What was going on?

When Zhang Han first became acquainted with Li Zhenye, he realized this was a man who would surely be chosen as an adjucator of the imperial examinations that autumn. So he attached himself to Li, hoping for a hand up the ladder of success. Li Zhenye also thought of taking advantage of Zhang's wide circle of friends to grasp a large sum of money through the imperial examinations that autumn. The two became fast friends. As Zhang Han was poor, he became a house guest of Li's. Thereafter, they were inseparable, day and night.

Pinky had once been a courtesan in a house in the southern quarter of the town. Two years ago Li had bought her as a concubine. When his wife sent word this spring, that she intended to come to the capital at the Duanwu Festival and establish a home there, Li's situation became untenable. He had always been in awe of his wife. Now he thought it expedient to give Pinky to someone else. However, he could not find a suitable person. One day in a casual conversation, Li Zhenye brought up the subject of being alone and far from home, and asked why Zhang Han did not find himself a woman to amuse himself.

Zhang Han dismissed the suggestion, saying it was beyond the realms of possibility, unless he stumbled across hidden treasure. Li Zhenye, however, would not let the subject drop. "My wife will soon arrive in the capital. I have a concubine whom I would gladly give you," he said expansively. "Of course I will also provide the house and furnishings as well."

This generosity was more than Zhang Han could conjure up in his wildest dreams. He thanked his friend effusively, comparing Li to the great men of chivalry in ages past. Pinky was instantly taken with Zhang Han's good looks and courtly manners, and so they were married.

The couple's new home and all its furnishings came with Pinky. Most of it was used furniture from Li's house. Li Zhenye was a resourceful man. His wife's presence in the capital did not dampen his interest in Zhang Han or Pinky. Soon Pinky began to live a double life. She was Zhang's wife by night, but Li's mistress by day. Only Li's wife was kept in the dark.

What about Zhang Han?

Three days earlier when Li Zhenye had trysted with Pinky, she had complained coquettishly in the midst of his ardour, "My Lord has cast me off, yet he comes to me still. If you had any pity, you would have given me to a rich man, instead of a poor nobody. Am I to gulp the northwest wind the rest of my life?"

Li Zhenye comforted her saying, "Have no fear. In memory of our love, I have plans that will ensure you a comfortable life. I will soon be adjudicating the imperial examination. You must quietly urge your husband to find some candidates who wish to pay for their success. Demand six thousand from each, plus twenty percent for expenses. Turn over the larger sum to me, and you pocket the expense money. In that way you will have more than enough to live on without lifting a finger."

Pinky was overjoyed. That very night she broached the subject to Zhang Han. Zhang Han was wild with excitement, thanking his pretty wife, hugging and biting her in his exuberance, and she had to fend him off as best she could, squealing and laughing. When he quieted down, Zhang Han considered the scheme more carefully.

"Instead of finding candidates for the exams, why don't I sit myself? I will give half price. The other half will be a present from him to us. When I pass the examinations, you will be a respectable lady. That would be more useful than three thousand. Tell him that. He can't object!"

That day, Li Zhenye again visited Pinky. Again she played the coquette, intent on making him accede to the new plan.

Li Zhenye frowned.

"What's the use of wasting a position on Zhang Han? He has neither power nor riches. He isn't even a famous scholar! Being an adjudicator is not a simple matter. Right now there are more candidates than there are positions. Who in his right mind wouldn't try to make an extra buck?"

"But you said if we found three candidates you would get eighteen thousand and we'd get three thousand six hundred. Say we skipped the twenty percent and asked for an extra eight hundred to a thousand from each, you wouldn't be losing much!" Pinky reeled off the figures on her finger tips. Li Zhenye had to agree there was indeed not much difference. His objections faded. Seeing that Li Zhenye was beginning to come round, Pinky played the game to the bitter end.

"You won't even help in little ways!" she cried, her slender body writhing. "You don't care about Pinky, so why are you here! Go back to your wife!" She slid off the bed, and tossed his discarded clothes at him. "Get out! Get out! It's my rotten luck! I'll go apologize to your wife, then I'll kill myself! What's there to live for?" Li Zhenye softened.

"What's the matter! We can talk it over! But I think there's only room for Zhang Han in your little heart!"

Pinky turned on him with her little fists, hammering hard against his chest. Li Zhenye threw his arms around her, pinning her down. "All right! I give in!"

Gradually Pinky stopped crying. She turned to Li Zhenye, flashed a coquettish smile and threw herself into his arms, purring like a little cat. Li Zhenye chuckled.

"One more thing. Tell Zhang Han that when I go to the examinations he must lend me his page Tongchun for the duration. It would be delightful having a clever and pretty boy at one's beck and call."

When Zhang Han crossed his own threshold, he was filled with foreboding. The courtyard was silent. He hesitated a moment before he gently tried the bedchamber door with two fingers of his right hand. It was latched from within. He bit his lip in confusion.

Seeing this Tongchun interjected, "The mistress must be inside. Let me knock."

"Wait!" Zhang Han blocked him with his arm.

He blushed to the root of his hair. He could not meet Tongchun's eyes, afraid of revealing too much of himself. He was overcome by shame; shame that would devastate any man.... But he had to think of his future, his ambitions. A shudder rippled down his back which was soaked in cold sweat. He gritted his teeth till the shock of pain and mortification subsided. Still avoiding Tongchun's curious gaze, he paced back and forth under the willow tree, desperately trying to compose himself. Tongchun watched him in amazement. On a day such as this, what was the sense in dawdling in the heat when one was hot, thirsty and in need of a change of clothes?

"Didn't the mistress send for you?" Tongchun grumbled. "Let me knock. If she's displeased, blame me."

Zhang Han finally got a grip on himself. Though he smiled awkwardly without a word, Tongchun understood and knocked the door. "Who is it?" Pinky demanded, trailing the words to show her annoyance.

"Mistress, the Master's home," Tongchun answered in a loud voice.

"Wait!" Pinky sounded angry, but there was also a snicker in her voice.

In the time it took to smoke a pipe of tobacco, the door was unlatched. Li Zhenye emerged. Tongchun was speechless with surprise. Zhang Han blushed as red as a fresh-cooked shrimp. Li Zhenye's usually sallow cheeks had taken on a pinkish glow as though he were wearing a light rouge. Although he was embarrassed he had the *sangfroid* to weather the awkward situation he found himself in. He patted Zhang Han gently on the shoulder and said in a friendly tone, "Something good awaits you inside." Before Zhang Han could reply, he turned, bowed, said his farewell and swaggered out of the courtyard.

Zhang Han calmed himself. At any rate he was able to control the violent surge of jealousy and rage that welled within him. Carefully avoiding Tongchun's grim expression, and forcing himself to appear natural and, smiling, he lifted the curtain and went into the main chamber. Pinky greeted him happily. Dressed in a pink silk tunic over a pair of rosy wide-legged pants, Pinky approached him languidly swaying her hips. Over her shoulder he could see the rumpled bed in the inner room. Though he reddened again, his expression of open admiration never faltered. It was the look that pleased her most.

"He agreed!" Pinky chirped.

"Really?" Zhang Han almost leaped with excitement. He reached for Pinky's tiny hands, swallowing hard before he asked, "Did he agree to everything?"

"What are you worried about? Your hands are trembling. Oh, and he gave you this note. He said to destroy it after you've read it. Is it what they call a 'connection'?"

Zhang Han took the slip of paper from her with trembling hands. When he had read it he fell to his knees in front of Pinky and cried, "Dear wife, I will never forget this deed! I swear I will make you a great lady!" Pinky blushed with pleasure for the slip of paper contained Li's instruction for the examinations. Nevertheless, she put on a stern face and said, "What are you going on about! He wants to borrow Tongchun!"

"All right! All right!" Zhang Han got to his feet, read the note several times more to fix its contents in his mind, then he tore it, rolled it into a ball and tossed aside with a triumphant laugh.

"Ha! Now I see the light at the end of the tunnel!"

Pinky arched her brows at him and chided, "Aren't you counting your chickens before they're hatched?"

"You're right." Zhang Han quickly controlled himself. ."One can't be too cautious."

Pinky had reminded him of rumours that had been circulating the last few days. When he spoke again it was not without a sense of worry.

"If he had only sold the positions to a few people, I have nothing to fear. But they say there have been many buyers. In which case success will go to whoever pays the most. In that case where would Zhang Han be, who pays only half the going price?" Pinky frowned, and shaking her dishevelled head said, "Don't worry. when he comes again in a day or two I'll tell him you must succeed."

Zhang Han was startled by this revelation. He was about to cry out, "Why is he coming again in a day or two?" Instead he said, "I leave the matter in your capable hands.

When Pinky left the room to prepare food and wine, Zhang Han quickly retrieved the ball of paper, smoothed out the shards and slipped them into his pocket.

Tongchun went straight to the hot and stuffy servant's quarters he occupied. Sprawled on the bed, staring up at the smoke-blackened ceiling, the rise and fall of voices and laughter grated upon him. He could imagine what was going on in Zhang Han's chamber. Everything was so sordid and obscene. Isn't there a shred of decency left anywhere, he wondered? In spite of himself his thoughts fixed upon the blanket of wild flowers at Malan Village, the tender green grass of the graveyard, the young willow tree he planted. He recalled a pair of bright eyes, pure and full of love. He thought of a silk purse embroidered with a pair of madarin duck and drake nestling under lotus blossoms joined at the roots.... What a beautiful and innocent time it had been! As pure as the moonlight, as sparkling as spring water! Compared to this it was heaven.

The feast at Yousheng Nunnery had reached its climax. Although there were only a handful of guests all were wealthy. Zhang Han had invited them only to mingle with the rich in order to gain fame and wealth. His guests had responded by placing him in the seat of honour, content to be the moths dancing round his flame. At this moment Zhang Han was well pleased with himself.

"...Brother Li succeeded in the highest imperial examination at a tender age. His appointment as adjudicator shows his erudition and his prospects are limitless. It's my good fortune to have such a friend and mentor for so many years."

Once started, flattery came thick and fast.

"...That I was admitted to study at the Directorate of Education was entirely due to Brother Li's recommendation. However, as far as the examinations are concerned...."

Zhang Han almost wished everyone would be quiet, so that he might shut his eyes and soak up words that were music to his ears. However, his attention was distracted by the clatter of a horse's hooves outside the gate. He peered through the gate that stood ajar and, slamming his palm on the table top, he sprang to his feet.

"Speaking of the devil," he cried happily, "Brother Zhenye is dismounting in front of the gate! I must go and greet him and introduce you."

Zhang Han was so proud and delighted that he babbled. The unexpected appearance of Li Zhenye, no matter what his errand, was an opportunity to make an impression. Hoisting up his robes, Zhang Han hurried down the stairs. Half way down he tripped and might have fallen if Qiao Bainian had not caught him in time. He laughed and the others laughed with him. To meet such an important personage at this crucial moment was the dream of everyone who came to the examinations. They could not be more impressed with Zhang Han if he were a god. As Qiao Bainian stopped his fall, others sprang forward to beat dust from his robes that wasn't there. Everyone was clamorous with solicitude.

"Did you hurt yourself?"

"You must be more careful!"

"Take my arm."

Zhang Han and his guests met Li Zhenye on the front steps. Zhang Han joined his hands and, bowing deeply, greeted his friend, "Brother Li, have you come looking for me?" Sweating profusely, Li replied testily, "Who else would I be seeking?" Zhang Han was taken aback by the other's tone of voice. Before he could gather his wits, Li Zhenye had struck him across the face several times with the flat of his hand.

"Ungrateful swine!" Li Zhenye cried in a loud voice. "I gave you my friendship yet you spread calumny behind my back, destroying my good name...."

The assemblage was aghast at the scene they were witnessing. Qiao Bainian was the first to recover and leap between the two. The others rushed forward to try to meddle on Zhang Han's behalf. However, Li Zhenye had already spoken his mind and vented his spleen with his fist. He strode out of the nunnery, leaped on his horse and galloped off. Earlier Li Zhenye had again trysted with Pinky. According to plan, Pinky had revealed Zhang Han's concerns about securing a place when rumour suggested there were so many buyers thinking to settle matters. However, she did not think that Li Zhenye would assume the gossip had originated with Zhang Han. He rode out in a rage to confront Zhang Han and committed this comedy of errors.

It took a while for Zhang Han to gain control of himself. When he did he leaped to his feet ranting, "Li Zhenye, you are the ingrate! Gentlemen, I swear I will not take this insult lying down. This very day I shall confront him in his own lair!"

The others tried to pacify him. Though they mouthed all the right platitudes, they could not hide the contempt in their hearts. Soon they began to leave, pleading pressing business elsewhere. Finally only Qiao Bainian was left. Fighting down disappointment he waited while his host continued to rail against Li Zhenye.

Zhang Han suddenly stopped his raging and, eyeing Qiao Bainian craftily, asked, "Have you decided on what we discussed yesterday?"

Qiao Bainian smiled mirthlessly but did not reply. He was thinking the fellow was a shameless charlatan and a thug.

"What happened just now must have been a misunderstanding. My honoured brother must not let it blind you to opportunity," said Zhang Han. In spite of himself Qian Bainian added, "If the adjudicator treats you thus, what influence can you wield?" Zhang Han stroked his bruised face with a languid finger tip and replied, "There are things you don't know; things in my grasp that will force him to come to heel." Qiao Bainian shook his head in disbelief. Li Zhenye's actions were not those of a man who felt threatened.

Zhang Han hesitated only a moment to make up his mind, and in a whisper related Pinky's history and how Li Zhenye came to borrow Tongchun. He fixed Qiao Bainian with his eyes and concluded, "So you see, there are secrets within and secrets without. He has to be careful."

Qiao Bainian was revolted by what he heard. It took a supreme effort to prevent himself from striking the shameless fellow himself. He turned his back on his host and stared out of the shadow-dappled garden.

"The business with Pinky is something the three of you agreed to. Let it lie. But I don't believe Tongchun is that kind."

Zhang Han chuckled. "You should know. Tongchun comes from your village. I don't suppose he is that sort either. Otherwise he would not have bought himself out of the theatre. Let us say, 'The falling blossom has intentions but the running stream is pitiless.' He was bait, and Li Zhenye snapped it up. Besides, I've the important document...."

"Oh...?" Qiao Bainian turned to face him.

Zhang Han observed Qiao Bainian out of the corner of his eye and burst out laughing. "Dear friend, you are cautious! Since you don't trust me ... pay half now ... and leave the rest till everything is accomplished."

"What if things don't turn out?"

Zhang Han's face was distorted with rage. He spoke in a low voice between gritted teeth, "If things don't turn out; if I am ruined, there'll be hell to pay!"

He lifted his eyes to Qiao Bainian's astonished gaze and, quickly controlling himself, smiled obsequiously and continued, "I'll make you a promisory note. If you don't succeed, I'll refund this payment in full."

Qiao Bainian gazed at Zhang Han in silence. To achieve his goal, he must seize every opportunity, grasp the slightest thread of hope. Reluctantly he handed Zhang Han a note for four thousand ounces of silver.

A wave of nausea overcame Qiao Bainian when he regained his lodgings. Leaning against the table he retched till he was emptied of all the rich foods he had consumed at the feast at Yousheng Nunnery.

3

The results of the autumn examinations which were announced during the ninth month of that year caused a scandal. Many of those who failed accused the adjudicators of corruption and bribery. Zhang Han was one of the first to shave his head in protest. He also wrote to all departments of government concerned, charging Li Zhenye with corruption. At the same time, Jiang

Wenzhuo, a scholar from Jiashan, circulated a satirical pamphlet on corruption in the imperial examinations that stood the capital on its ears. The matter did not end there. A scholar from Hangzhou named Zhang Xiuhu seized upon these accusations to extort the sum of one thousand and two hundred ounces of silver from Li Zhenye and his colleagues. The news infuriated the populace. Corruption in high places became the main topic of conversation. The people waited as one scandal followed the other. They knew the best was yet to come.

The household of Grand Academician Fu Yijian was not impervious to gossip. Though he had given strict orders for his servants to refrain from discussing national affairs, two page boys and two serving boys, loitering in the little courtyard outside the study, were engaged in an animated discussion with their master's valet Deshou.

"The human body is a sacred legacy from one's parents. It is a sin to injure it in any way. Therefore, in cutting off his hair as a gesture of protest, the candidate Zhang must really have a case."

"Huh! Adjudicators have always taken bribes!" Deshou said in a condescending tone, showing off his worldliness. He continued his harangue: "I tell you the adjudicator by the name of Zhang Wopu has been taking bribes a long time. Three months before the examinations he hung a cage with a yellow bird in it under his verandah. When visitors came seeking a favour, he would invariably be seen fussing over his bird, loudly ordering his servants to feed and water it. When the visitor asked what bird commanded so much attention, he would reply, 'This bird comes from a forbidden place and communes with the gods themselves. If a successful candidate's topknot on his official cap is worth two or three hundred ounces of silver, mine must be worth twenty or thirty times more.' That remark was not lost on the visitor, and silver rolled in."

"What if the visitor did not bring silver."

"If there is no money there has to be connections. Have you

noticed how the sons of officials above the third grade have all passed?"

"Only the poor but brilliant ones fall by the wayside."

"That is exactly so!" Deshou wagged his head importantly.

As they say, a prime minister's servant is the equivalent of an official of the seventh grade. Deshou, being the close body servant of a grand academician, was full of the airs and graces of a minor official. The other servants also minded their p's and q's.

Clearing his throat, Deshou continued in a ringing tone, "The successful candidate Wang passed because of his uncle's influence; and that fellow Zhao somebody got by because of his rich wife. A gold hairpin and a pair of pearl circlets were worth ten thousand pieces of gold...."

"Really!" cried an innocent young serving boy.

"Haven't you heard the story of the three scholars playing a drinking game? The first said, 'In the capital there was a man. The man had a brilliant uncle. Would he not be satisfied?!' The second said, 'The beauty wore gold in her hair. The successful candidate wore silver. How many people have gold and silver in this world?' The third said, 'When one has no almighty uncle, nor a wife with riches and wealth, what will become of him?'"

Deshou's droll expressions and strange falsetto voice drove the four youngsters into peals of laughter.

"Shut up!" Grand Academician Fu Yijian strode angrily onto the verandah, his bulk obliterated half of the red door. His official robes embroidered with coiling dragons, his waist-coat decorated with cranes, his necklace of precious stones, and his cap crowned with a topknot of red coral added to his imposing presence. The servants hurriedly fell to their knees. Their master had returned earlier from the morning audience than they expected.

"Brazen fools!" Fu Yijian thundered. "How dare you discuss affairs of state? Have you forgotten my orders, Deshou? Do you know the penalty?" Deshou shrivelled into a quivering lump.

"Master ... forgive your slave ... this ... once...."

Fu Yijian turned away grimly. "That's not possible. To kill one is to deter a hundred. It is the only way to maintain discipline."

"Master..." wailed Deshou, and the others also banged their heads against the ground. They were interrupted by a servant bearing a tray with a calling card.

"Master, Master Ren Kepu of the Ministry of Justice begs an interview."

Fu Yijian glanced at the card and turned away angrily, "I will tend to your hides later.... Show Master Ren into the front parlour. Serve tea." The servants did not dare budge until their master's footsteps had faded in the distance. Deshou was beside himself with fear. The grand academician seldom punished his servants. However, when he was disobeyed he was unrelenting. One of the pageboys suggested that Deshou should seek their mistress' aid. Deshou slapped himself on the forehead. That was the way out, and he scurried away to the inner courtyard.

The elegant reception room of the inner courtyard was filled with the scent of perfume. Suyun was entertaining her bosom friend, Gong Dingzi's wife Gu Meisheng. At the moment Suyun was reclining on a couch, while Gu Meisheng occupied the bamboo couch next to it. Beside each was a small round table spread with tea and a collation of dainty dishes.

Neither was inclined to partake of food. Both were languidly reminiscing on their lives, from twenty years ago to the present; from friends and relatives to children and husbands. Gu Meisheng was hoping through Suyun and therefore Fu Yijian's influence to get her husband reinstated to his official position. On the other hand, through her husband Suyun was already aware of the Emperor's admiration of Gong Dingzi's erudition and his position among the literati. There was also her enduring friendship for Gu Meisheng. However, they were in the midst of discussing another matter of great mutual interest, but so delicate in nature that both were loathed to speak openly.

"Suyun," Gu Meisheng lowered her voice. "I hear the Precious Concubine has given birth to a son."

"Oh, according to my husband, the Emperor has put on weight and seems in a happy frame of mind. That is probably the cause. However ... the Court of the Imperial Clan has not made an anouncement."

"I heard the prince was born on the seventh day of the fourth month," Gu Meisheng whispered.

"Is that so?" Suyun exclaimed. It was impossible to tell whether she had already heard the news from another source. Both were titled ladies who participated in important court celebrations. At times they knew more about what went on in the palace than their husbands.

"When did the Precious Concubine enter the palace?"

"Toward the end of the eighth month last year, on the thirtieth." Suyun remembered the exact date.

"The ninth month ... tenth ... up to the seventh day of the fourth month this year.... "Gu Meisheng counted the months off on her finger tips. "That's only seven months. The prince must have been premature!" She covered her mouth with a wisp of pink handkerchief and giggled. Suyun glanced at her out of the corner of her eyes and giggled too. The more they tried to control themselves the less they could. Finally they were laughing out loud, shaking like a pair of blossoms caught in a breeze. They laughed till they were breathless before they stopped. Gu Meisheng put the subject of their laughter neatly into a nutshell.

"If the highest of the high can behave thus, why should I be ashamed of my romantic past?"

"My dear sister, be careful of what you say.... They are a different race with different customs.... Do you want to bet as soon as this birth is announced he will be made crown prince?"

Gu Meisheng snapped her handkerchief at her companion.

"Devil! Who's going to bet on a sure thing!" The maid

came in with fresh plates of sweetmeats and tea. She carefully examined her mistress' expression before saying that Deshou begged an interview. "Oh, what's the matter?" Both ladies sat up straight. "He offended the Master and begs Your Ladyship to intercede on his behalf." Suyun patted a few loose curls into place and ordered the man brought in. The frivolity a moment before disappeared. She was now the kindly but prim wife of a prime minister.

Deshou knelt outside the door, banging his forehead against the ground, not daring to look up.

After she had heard his tale of woe, Suyun said in an even voice, "Go to the market, buy a large fish, and have them prepare it for the midday meal. Go, now."

Though Deshou did not fully comprehend the significance of the order, he hurried to carry it out.

When the two friends were left alone once more, Gu Meisheng asked, "What trick are you playing? I swear I'm all at sea."

Suyun did not answer. Instead she pressed her friend to try the little cakes that were just placed before them.

"These are our cook's specialty," she said. Gu Meisheng nibbled a small cake glistening with oil which fairly melted in her mouth. Yet she was not sufficiently distracted to abandon the problem that Deshou had just related.

"I suppose your man must have heard about the corruption in the imperial examinations at Shuntian. The people are up in arms." Suyun smiled as she sipped plum juice from a small jade goblet. "How can the secretaries and censors not be concerned?" Gu Meisheng pursued.

In reply Suyun teased her companion about her interest in affairs outside the home and pressed another delicacy upon her. Gu Meisheng was forced to accept the proffered silver plate, muttering half complaining and half in admiration, "You are indeed the wife of a prime minister."

Fu Yijian came to the midday meal lost in thought. His brows were tightly knit and he showed scant interest in the food spread before him. As always, Suyun gently and solicitously placed each dish before him. The maid was ordered to pour a goblet of a rich red wine.

"Whatever troubles you surely can be put aside while you eat. Have you forgotten the sage Qiu's precepts for a healthy life?"

When the famous Daoist sage from Jiangxi came to the capital he was immediately lionized by the aristocracy. At a feast given in his honour, Fu Yijian questioned the sage about the art of prolonging life. The sage replied, "My Lord is clothed in satin and served the finest foods. Therefore, My Lord has achieved the life of the divine." He pointed at the roast pig that was laid on the table and added, "Eating a roast pig is one of the finest ways of prolonging life. What more can you hope for!" Fu Yijian was overcome with admiration for the sage. To Suyun he averred, "Such a notion can only come from a truly learned Daoist."

Suyun had deliberately brought up the sage Qiu as a diversion. Fu Yijian put aside the wine goblet and shaking his head said, "The nation is up in arms over the scandal of the examinations at Shuntian. You may recall Master Cao Benrong who assisted me in annotating the *Book of Changes* at the beginning of the year? He was the chief adjudicator. I cannot understand what caused him to allow his subordinates to make such a mockery of the examinations. It's obvious we are not among moralists."

"My Lord, you are the Grand Academician of the Palace Historiographic Academy. Your responsibility is for the compilation of books and histories. The examinations are outside your mandate. Why interfere?"

"The examinations at Shuntian were scandalous. All the adjudicators had proteges. Though pseudonyms were used on the papers, they had secret codes so that the papers could be easily singled out. Papers were also switched. It was utter bedlam.

When the results were announced and there was widespread criticism you would have thought the adjudicators would try to cover their tracks. Instead the younger ones such as Li Zhenye went about blowing their own horn, telling everyone how so-and-so succeeded because of him. Another person should have failed but was given a second-class passing grade. As for so-and-so, he had done his best, but interference from this one and that one caused him to fail. There were dozens such cases. Do you wonder people are bitter?''

"My Lord was not a part of the examination process. How do you know so much?''

"Just now, Ren Kepu of the Ministry of Justice was here and spoke of these things.''

"Does he intend to pursue the matter?''

"Yes. According to him Vice Consor-in-Chief Wei Yijie is of the same mind.'' Suyun was shocked at the news. Deftly she probed her husband's feelings on the subject.

"Master Ren must have come to sound you out. What is your position?''

Fu Yijian lifted a sliver of bamboo shoot into his mouth and spoke as he chewed,

"Corruption in the imperial examination was common in the previous dynasty and has continued to this day because people are used to it. But our dynasty is young and greatly in need of able men. Besides this occurred in the capital. All eyes are upon us. Therefore, it cannot be overlooked. The scandal has reached such proportions that even slaves and servants....'' That reminded him of Deshou and anger flared. Fu Yijian briefly related the incident involving Deshou to his wife and concluded severely, "When servants start discussing affairs of state, that's outrageous! Where is Deshou? Have him brought here at once. He will not get away with it!''

Suyun quickly ordered the maid to serve the fish.

An oval-shaped platter was brought in, on which lay a foot-long carp, braised to a turn and covered in a rich red sauce. A mouth-watering aroma drifted across the table. Fu Yijian was partial to fish. For the moment Deshou was brushed aside. He pierced the fish's belly with the tips of his chopsticks, tore off a large chunk and masticated it appreciatively, chasing it down with red wine, draining his goblet in one draught. Taking the silk handkerchief tucked into his sleeve, he passed it over his whiskers with a satisfied sigh.

"Wonderful! Where did such a delicious fish come from?"

Suyun smiled faintly and, catching her husband's eye, spoke carefully, biting off each word, "It comes from generosity."

Fu Yijian stopped to mull over his wife's remark. Then he looked up at Suyun and burst into delighted laughter. "They say anger can be soothed by gentle words. I had no idea my lady was familiar with that saying. You are indeed a wise woman of the boudoir. For your sake, Deshou is forgiven."

Suyun smiled faintly as she spoke:

"I was not only thinking of Deshou." She became serious as she continued: "My Lord, they say 'A horse can gallop across a minister's wide head, and a boat can sail in a nobleman's big heart'. They also say, 'One can only live to be an old man when one is deaf and dumb'. All that aside, since its beginning, the new dynasty has held annual examinations, and all those who have succeeded have been Hans. That must be a thorn in the side of the Manchu nobles. If the abuses are publicized wouldn't it be playing into their hands? It would certainly give them an excuse to blow the incident out of all proportion. You have managed to maintain a delicate balance between the two races. Why place yourself in the position of being the first to expose the corruption among the Hans?"

Fu Yijian could not give his wife a sensible argument.

Gu Meisheng left Suyun's home in a sedan chair and went straight to a jeweller's shop at the First Langfang Lane near Qianmen, where she collected a pearl circlet she had ordered. Then she purchased bottles of four select wines. Satisfied with her goods she returned home in a leisurely fashion. Before she alighted from the sedan chair, she peeped through the curtain in time to see her husband bidding farewell to a visitor at their front door. As the visitor rode off, she saw her husband Gong Dingzi joining hands and bowing in a final salutation.

"Ah, My Lady has returned!" Gong Dingzi exclaimed, stroking his salt-and-pepper beard and glowing with delight as his wife emerged from the sedan chair. The two strolled toward the inner courtyard of the house side by side with Gong Dingzi enquiring solicitously whether she was tired, hungry or thirsty, as though she were a child — a common occurrence of an old man with a much younger wife.

"Freshen up and rest a while," he said. "I have ordered your favourite roast duck!" Gu Meisheng gave him a sidelong glance.

"And only roast duck?"

Gong Dingzi chuckled. "I wouldn't forget the deep-fried bones. They have to be served piping hot to be crisp and tasty. So I've ordered them to have everything ready. When you give the word, they'll start frying."

He sighed when he saw the happy glow in Gu Meisheng's lustrous eyes. Gu Meisheng was especially fond of deep-fried duck bones as hors d'oeuvres. She derived great pleasure from crunching the bones between her teeth.

Gu Meisheng was not ready to rest. She was anxious to try on her new jewellery. Seated before her mirror she put them on. At the age of thirty-five, she had retained her youth. Her eyes were liquid, flashing as brilliantly as her jewels. Watching her, Gong Dingzi leaned close to her ear and whispered, "You are divine! To what do I owe such a blessing!"

Gu Meisheng darted a contented glance at her husband. Shaking off her languor, she leaped to her feet.

"Wait here," she said.

Swaying her hips, she slipped into a tiny dressing room that adjoined the boudoir. Gong Dingzi smiled to himself. Having such an enchantress at his side, he would die content. He let his eye-lids droop.

"Hey! Look at me!" Conceit rang in Gu Meisheng's voice. Gong Dingzi blinked owlishly at the apparition before him. He was dazzled. Her hair was piled high on the top of her head and fixed with gold pins. A cluster of crystals fastened to a gold headdress cascaded in glistening droplets across her brow, past her ears and down to her shoulders shining like stars in an ink-black sky. Tiny sparks of blue and green, shimmering against a setting of silver and pearls, captured the raven black beauty of her hair, and set off the tender beauty of her face. Over a short silk tunic the colour of moonlight, she wore a short cape of lake water blue decorated with pictures of trees, rocks and pavilions. A large red stone fastened her collar. A satin skirt of green, fastened high on the waist, swept gracefully to the floor. The long sash was fastened by a jade buckle of nine entwined dragons and a milk white jade pendant. A flimsy shawl thrown over her shoulders trailed down her back, further accentuating the slenderness of her body.

"Wonderful! Wonderful!" crowed Gong Dingzi. "It is like turning time back twenty years. Time is pitiless to everyone, except you...." He stopped himself abruptly, and his heart lurched painfully within his breast. It was the popular costume during the waning years of the previous dynasty that he was applauding.

Gu Meisheng was too self-absorbed to notice the subtle change in her husband's mood. She vanished once more into her dressing room using the dainty gait that she had learned years ago when she was on the stage. When she reappeared the tall, elaborate headdress was gone. Now the shiny lacquered hair was combed straight back and divided into a short swallow's tail at the nape of the neck. The broad headdress was edged with gold and studded with jade. On each end was a large red satin flower. In her ears she wore three ear-rings with three pendants. Her voluminous robe fell to the tops of her shoes. The robe was trimmed with an embroidered white satin border and framed with ribbons. On its silvery red background eight bunches of greenish-yellow chrysanthemums were embroidered. Around her neck she wore a pale blue scarf that fell to the hem of her robe, under which a pair of thick-soled shoes heavily embroidered in gold thread could be seen. In her right hand she held a long-stemmed pipe carved of ebony and topped with a brass bowl. Fastened to the pipe was a tobacco pouch decorated with a red tassel. In her left hand she held a gold ornament. This was the attire of a fashionable Manchu lady of quality when she went into society.

Gong Dingzi was completely captivated.

"Wonderful! Dashing and graceful!" he finally mumbled,

Gu Meisheng giggled with delight. The ornament she held in her hand, studded with jade and pearls, was fastened now to her hair. She lifted her head proudly to her husband. "How do I look? The jeweller assured me it's the latest thing in court circles."

Gong Dingzi forced a smile as he replied, "It is certainly eye-catching. However, the addition of the gold ornament on your hair is overdone. It should be worn with ceremonial court dress..." His words trailed off, and his eyes became fixed and vacant.

Gu Meisheng spun around on her heels, striking poses and tossing questions over her shoulder.

"Do you like me better in Han or Manchu costume?" When her husband failed to answer, she wheeled upon him. The sight of him depressed her. Lately he often had spells like this. She was sure it was the first signs of senility, and rage flared in her. Her face fell. Imperceptibly she switched to her native Suzhou vernacular and scolded, "Silly goose! Have you swallowed arsenic? Give me a reason for this dumb act!"

Gong Dingzi drew a chair, sat down heavily and mused dully, "Who would have dreamed that the arrogant Xu Juyuan would pass the exams."

Gu Meisheng fell silent. Since the examination results were announced she had heard her husband repeat the same remark over and over, at times with regret, at others in anger, but never tinged with sorrow as now. When she stopped to think about it, she understood. While she was trying to amuse him with her changes of costume, she had inadvertantly stirred memories of his being humiliated at the theatre. What could she say? Hadn't she wept bitter tears at the time? Hadn't she been bathed in a cold sweat of fear? But she was a woman. Time passes, and time heals all wounds. Never did she dream that her husband, who was over fifty years of age, still harboured such bitter thoughts. Her anger quickly subsided, and she spoke in a sweet, conciliatory tone:

"The adjudicators were bribed. His getting through is no proof of his worth.... " "Quite right!" Gong replied vehemently slapping his thigh. "Just now Ren Kepu said exactly the same thing. He means to press charges."

"Marvellous! It's time you got your own back. You must encourage him!" Gu Meisheng cried.

"We can't. This thing is too big to take on casually."

"At least the successful candidate's title should be removed from him!" cried Gu Meisheng.

"Ah, the pros and cons must be carefully weighed...."

Gu Meisheng stared at her husband in disbelief. Her husband's tearful vow to avenge himself on the man who had insulted him in public still rang in her ears. She was about to question him further, when the maid outside the door announced that the deep-fried bones were ready.

"Let us dine," Gong Dingzi said hurriedly.

Two serving girls laid a table in the middle of the boudoir. Dishes of food cooked in southern style were laid out. At the centre was a plate of crisp fried duck bones, crackling with heat. Gu Meisheng was delighted. She called for goblets to be filled. Each would be served with four goblets.

Before Gong Dingzi could control his astonishment, the

serving wenches had served the wine his wife bought. The intoxicating perfume of the wine filled the room. The goblets were a sight to behold. Red as ruby; golden as amber; clear as crystal and green as jade. Gong Dingzi opened his eyes wide feigning amazement. Gu Meisheng laughed at his drollness and, giving him a playful push, said, "Don't pretend you don't know what this is! You who entertain so often." Then she named each wine, tripping the poetic names lightly off the tongue.

Gong Dingzi responded with a lavish if somewhat comical bow, saying, "My Lady is fond of colour. I am truly lucky to have such a collection of fine wine on one table." Gu Meisheng smacked her husband lightly on the cheek, "Who in all the world is more fond of 'colour' (a euphemism for 'women') than my husband?"

Gong Dingzi laughed out loud. Husband and wife toasted each other merrily. Taking up the conversation again, Gong Dingzi declared, "I am romantic, but not promiscuous. There are many promiscuous men around us, but none the equal of Li Zhenye and Zhang Han!"

"Oh, but aren't they both your students?"

"That is why I know their stories. They are fond of both sexes. You are familiar with their dalliances with Pinky, but the other...." Gu Meisheng became serious.

"Did you discuss this with Ren Kepu? Did you not see this as your opportunity to make a comeback."

Gong Dingzi's eyes flashed fire. The flame quickly died but not before Gu Meisheng had noticed. She rose to her feet angrily and, keeping her voice low, scolded, "You know things but you won't speak up. Very well, I'll say it for you. The Han and the Manchu are oil and water. You can't make them mix. The Emperor has always admired your learning. The only thing missing is the approval of the Manchu aristocracy. If you denounce the corruption of the examinations, you will gain the support of the Manchu. Then you will not end your days in obscurity."

Gong Dingzi's eyes filled with contradictions – sadness and glee; laughter and tears; sighs and wonder; shame and regret. He rose and left the room without another word.

4

On a balmy Indian Summer day in the tenth month of the year, a large hunting party gathered on the endless grasslands of Nanyuan or South Park. Dragon banners snapped in the breeze. Hunting horns shrilled. Handsome steeds pranced to the merry jangling of copper bells. A festive air flooded the plains.

Nanyuan was one of the forbidden preserves of the imperial family. A wall a hundred and twenty *li* long surrounded the great square-shaped expanse, approached through nine gates. Within the grounds were many small lakes fed by streams that crisscrossed the deep forests and plains of tall grass. This park had been the private domain of emperors since the Yuan Dynasty, when the monarch used to practise falconry and archery here. It was during the Ming Dynasty that the park was expanded to its present size. With the coming of the Qing Dynasty and its effort to keep old traditions alive, a thousand and six hundred peasants were brought in, each given twenty-four mu of land to cultivate, and whose task was also to care for the animals. Nowadays the park was used not only for hunting but also for military manoeuvers. Several imperial villas dotted the grounds where the emperor stayed and conducted the affairs of state from time to time. In the heat of summer, the Empress Dowager and some of the ladies of the harem used the park as a resort. Today the visitor was Emperor Shunzhi who had come to Nanyuan directly after the midday meal, served after the morning audience.

Fulin was dressed for hunting. With a black velvet cloak draped over his shoulders, he cut a handsome figure mounted on his favourite horse. Even without formal court robes and crown his appearance was unmistakably regal. Aside from his imperious bearing, and his fine steed, two things marked him for who he was. On his head he wore a red cap with a matching top-knot that no one else would dare to wear, and he sat on a lavishly decorated saddle. The saddle was trimmed with silver thread plaited with gold and studded with two thousand large pearls and thirty thousand seed pearls, two hundred and fifty pea-sized coral beads, and more than ten thousand tiny coral beads. Three eastern pearls the size of quail's eggs adorned the prominently raised rounded guard at the front. It is perhaps not difficult to imagine the value of such a saddle. However, because it was for the Emperor's personal use, it was deemed priceless.

The young Son of Heaven, mounted on his priceless saddle, turned his face into the autumn wind. A seamless canopy of sky spread over his head. He drew a long, contented breath. At this moment he was a boy again, about to throw up his arms and shout for the sheer joy of being alive. Instead he reined in his horse, and his followers did likewise. A cavalcade, bright with pinks, reds, and greens, and chirping as merrily as a flock of birds, appeared in the distance. They were the ladies of the harem. Fulin enjoyed watching pretty young women on horseback, and these ladies made every effort to please him. However, Fulin's gaze was trained exclusively on the rider of the chestnut-coloured mare who was in the lead.

The last rays of the setting sun caught the face of the rider, making it glow like the first peach of summer. She was in a form-fitting pink riding habit, topped by a rose-coloured silk cape. She rode as though she had descended from heaven like the evening mist. When this apparition stopped before Fulin, the rider prepared to dismount and prostrate herself, but he prevented her with a swift gesture of the hand.

"There's no need for ceremony! You came very quickly. You have not been in a saddle for two years, and been confined to the palace for another. It is good to take advantage of the fine autumn weather for a little recreation."

"I thank Your Majesty for his concern," Lady Dongeh, the Precious Concubine, smiled her gratitude. They rode shoulder to shoulder, the one sitting handsome and tall in the saddle; the other daintily pretty. They were a perfect match. Their followers quickly re-arranged themselves. The ladies in waiting and the maids of honour, who accompanied the imperial concubine, quickly surrounded the royal pair while the emperor's retinue of servants and guards fell back.

Fulin leaned over from the waist and whispered in Black Pearl's ear, "Come, sit on my saddle." Black Pearl blushed prettily, and started to protest.

"I only meant well." It was Fulin's turn to protest. "It's been just six months since your confinement. I do not want you to become weary. See, how pale you are! You have never been robust!" Black Pearl laughingly reminded the Emperor that the first time they met she had also been on horseback.

Fulin's eyes brimmed with love. Sweetness filled his being. His breath came in short gasps. A fierce surge of joy filled his breast so that his heart seemed to leap from its casing of bone and tissue. Nor would he try to keep it confined. He threw back his head and laughed out loud. Raising the crop with a jade handle inlaid with gold, he brought it down sharply on the horse's flank. Simultaneously he loosened the silken reins. The horse let out a joyous whinny and shot across the plain in a southerly direction, its hooves devouring the green and yellow dappled plain, streaking away in a white blur. Concerned, Black Pearl whipped her horse into a gallop and followed. But she could not keep up with the white streak that arched away toward the east. Black Pearl reigned in her mount, turned it around to face the east, and once more urged it into a gallop. She would take a straight line to cut Fulin off. The chestnut mare seemed to understand its mistress' purpose and moved at a steady pace. Within two miles, Black Pearl had headed Fulin off by several tens of yards. Seeing one of its own kind, Fulin's horse slackened its speed to a canter to match the mare's slower pace.

Fulin chuckled with delight. "That was a neat trick! You are indeed clever to cut me off thus!" Black Pearl smiled and spoke between quick intakes of breath, "It was luck." Fulin reached over and gently dabbed the drops of perspiration from her brow. "So beautiful and clever! How can I not love you to death! An angel has come among us Manchus!"

"You mustn't say things like that! It's embarrassing," Black Pearl made a face. "The gods do not favour a particular race. One must not forget my mother is an outstanding southern intellectual!"

"Quite so! Had there not been war clouds on the horizon, a southern beauty would not have produced so remarkable a concubine for me!" As he spoke, the horse stepped on some wet grass and stumbled, nearly throwing its rider. Black Pearl cried out, and attempted to catch Fulin, who was out of her reach anyway, and almost fell herself. However, with a quick tug on the reins, horse and rider recovered their balance. Fulin laughed delightedly. "Hah! What do you think of our horsemanship? What's the matter? Did I give you a fright?"

Black Pearl dabbed the cold sweat that beaded her brow. "Though Your Majesty has mastered horsemanship an animal cannot be trusted implicitly. I am concerned for Your Majesty's safety and the great legacy of your ancestors."

"My dear lady, you make it sound as serious as a petition," Fulin dismissed her words flippantly.

"Your Majesty rides like the wind.... It frightens me. Your Majesty ought to think of me ... the Empress Dowager ... and your son...." Fulin was deeply moved, he smiled as he replied, "I am so very happy today. The fine autumn weather and a swift horse made me forget all my troubles."

"What troubles?" Black Pearl turned to examine Fulin's mobile face.

"Oh! You have no idea. I cannot fathom what those old

men of the council have in mind...." Then he told Black Pearl about something that had rankled for a long time.

In the spring General Jidu's forces drove Zheng Chenggong onto the islands off the shore of Fujian Province and returned to the capital in triumph. Thereafter Fulin's full attention was fixed upon the southwest which was still held by Zhu Youlang of the Southern Ming. Full powers were given to Hong Chengchou to pursue the war. However, since Hong's appointment was announced the Manchu aristocrats had been filling Fulin's ears with complaints against him. Particularly during the last two years, when Hong had been holed up in Hunan Province, refusing to deploy his troops. Though petitions against him came in thick and fast, Fulin trusted Hong, knowing he was doing his best to his utmost to carry out the Emperor's policy of using force as a last resort. However, this only caused the Council of the Nobles to bring up other grievances. Southern Ming had able generals such as Li Dingguo and Sun Kewang, they said. Both were invincible. Faced with such opponents in inhospitable terrain, the council saw no hope of victory. Instead they proposed to quit the provinces of Yunnan and Guizhou altogether and adopt some form of peaceful co-existence. Fulin who fancied himself a conqueror was really angered.

When he spoke of this to Lady Dongeh he could barely contain his anger.

"If we are to conquer all under Heaven, we cannot tolerate leaving out one small piece. We have been in power only fourteen years, and already these men are old, scared and useless. Where is the dedication of the early days! I would dearly love to punish the most incompetent of the lot."

Black Pearl replied serenely, "In my humble opinion, the lords have the welfare of the Empire at heart. Though they may have blundered, they were not feathering their own nests at the nation's expense. Therefore, Your Majesty need not be angry. Rather, bring them over to your side through gentle persuasion. For if the council is unconvinced of your policy how would it be possible to win the hearts of the people?" Fulin replied with gratitude, "With you beside me, the burden of statecraft is less onerous."

They rode side by side, talking intimately and happily. Before they knew it the imperial villa was within sight. As it was still light, Fulin suggested that Black Pearl should rest, while he rode and hunted a while longer. "I will bring down a few pheasants and rabbits for tomorrow's feast." Black Pearl's brow knotted. "Your Majesty must ride carefully. Keep the Empire in mind."

Fulin shot her a tender smile, waved, and followed by his guards sped away. Fulin lingered till the sun sank beneath the horizon. When he finally returned to the East Villa, he avoided the main hall and went straight to the bed chamber. As soon as he came around the corner of the main hall he saw Black Pearl anxiously waiting at the top of a flight of white marble steps. She had changed into informal attire. Over a light green tunic suitable for fall, she wore a marten fur coat trimmed in white, the collar and the cuffs of which were embroidered with silver thread. A foot of jade green skirt that fell to the floor showed under the coat. Her hair was arranged in a chignon fastened with a single jade pin. Though she hardly wore any jewellery, her appearance was simple and elegant. Fulin found her refreshing, both in the way she dressed and in her wilfulness.

She came down the steps to greet him.

"You're dressed too lightly," she said with great concern. "The air gets chill when the sun goes down. Come inside before you catch your death." As soon as he had taken his seat on the throne specially set for him in the bed chamber, she was at his elbow with a steaming cup of tea like a common serving wench.

"You must be tired after such a long day. A cup of tea will refresh you." Fulin took the cup from her and seized her hand at the same time.

"I'm not at all tired and not cold either. It was a good

hunt. We bagged at least thirty or forty pheasants, so fat they could hardly fly...."

"But your hands are like ice," she complained and, extricating herself, went into the inner chamber returning with a hand warmer made of filigree enamel and insisted he tuck it under his tunic.

Fulin chuckled. "I wish you wouldn't fuss so! Haven't I told you to leave these things to the serving maids and the eunuchs?"

Black Pearl acted as though she hadn't heard and hurried out to order food.

When the meal was spread on the table, Black Pearl stood behind Fulin, serving him food, shelling prawns, boning fish and chicken, ladling soup and gently blowing away the steam and fat floating on the surface, and urging him to eat.

Fulin said, "Sit down. Eat with me." Black Pearl smiled. "I appreciate Your Majesty's generosity. Your Majesty should sit at table more often with his nobles. By honouring them you secure their hearts."

"I've heard that before, and I often eat with them. I also send them gifts of food from time to time. But I want you to share this meal."

"Your Majesty, I am unworthy...."

"Nonsense! Are you not my son's mother?" Fulin scolded laughingly and, slamming down his chopsticks for emphasis, declared, "If you refuse I shall stop eating."

"Your Majesty!"

"Even the humblest of my subjects do not live under such restraints. We have less connubial freedom than they." He grabbed her wrist and forced her to sit beside him on the imperial couch. Black Pearl struggled to her feet.

"Your Majesty we mustn't! Even the Empress is not permitted...."

"The Empress?" snorted Fulin and shook his head. Then he added softly, "We're not in the palace now, so let's do away with protocol and have a few carefree days together. Rongniu, bring a soft chair that your Mistress can have a meal comfortably."

Rongniu was Black Pearl's trusted personal maid. She and a serving wench quickly brought in an upholstered chair and placed it to the right of the imperial couch. Black Pearl was forced to sit down. Only when she had taken up the ivory chopsticks encased with silver did the grim look leave Fulin's face.

When the meal was over, the Empress Dowager's serving woman Sumalagu was announced. She had brought Fulin's wet nurse to see him. Lady Dongeh quickly had them admitted and Fulin rose from the kang on which he was reclining to receive their homage. He enquired after the old woman's journey home, asking why she had stayed away so long, and whether everyone at home was in good health. Then he turned to Sumalagu and inquired after his mother, and what errand had sent her to him so late at night.

Sumalagu replied that her errand was not important. "It's Momo whose business is urgent," she ventured.

The wet nurse was a kind-faced woman with a ruddy complexion. Two years ago she had gone home to her native land to visit relatives and the graves of the departed. She had only returned to the palace that day and demanded to see Fulin at once. However, since she came into the room, her eyes had been fastened upon Black Pearl. Now she broke into a smile saying, "What urgent business do I have? It's just that I haven't seen Your Majesty in two years and I miss you something awful. Thanks to you and the Empress Dowager, these two years my family have lived quite well. Is Your Majesty well? I do not know this lady. Let your old slave offer her homage." She started to get down on her knees, but Black Pearl stopped her.

"Momo, I'm an ignorant young girl, unworthy of such ceremony."

"Of course she's worthy!" Sumalagu chimed in. "Momo, this is Lady Dongeh who has recently been conferred the title

Precious Concubine. That fat and bouncy baby, the fourth Imperial son you saw in the palace today is her son."

"Aya! Buddha be praised, that he has brought to earth such an angel for Your Majesty. The eyes of this old woman have been blessed indeed."

"Momo," Fulin, pretending to be vexed, interrupted, "I thought you came to visit me, but you've ignored me completely!"

"Aya! I should die!" The nurse slapped herself lightly on the cheek. "As soon as I came into the room I was so taken by My Lady. She is exquisite. Look at them! Aren't they a perfect pair?" The old woman was so delighted she had forgotten etiquette. Indeed, Sumalagu was also taken with the young couple, both in informal garb, standing side by side like a pair of lotus blossoms springing from a common root. However, she was not as spontaneous as the nurse, whom she cut off, saying, "Momo has been so happy today, that she may have had a little more wine than she should...." With both hands she proffered a bundle wrapped in satin. "Her Majesty, the Empress Dowager, ordered me to bring these two marten fur jackets, saying Nanyuan is colder than the palace, and bid Your Majesty and My Lady to take care and not catch a chill."

Black Pearl and Fulin stood to receive the gifts of the Empress Dowager.

"Her Majesty also said not to tarry too long away from the palace. Should Your Majesty wish to hunt a few days longer, My Lady should return ahead of him."

Fulin winked slyly at Black Pearl but she pretended not to notice.

"Her Majesty bade her slave remind Your Majesty that My Lady's confinement is not long passed, and she must avoid over exertion. Any mishap will be Your Majesty's fault. Before her slave left the palace, Her Majesty again reminded me to bid My Lady return to the palace soon." Fulin chuckled and again winked at Black Pearl. "I am Her Majesty's own son, yet she is more concerned about your welfare. I could die of envy!" Everyone understood he was teasing, and they all grinned. The nurse and Sumalagu went back to their quarters which were located in the low buildings behind the villa. In low tones Sumalagu admonished the nurse, "I'm saying this for the sake of our friendship. I must warn you don't get silly in your old age. If anyone from Kunning Palace overheard the nonsense you were spouting, do you think any good would come to you?"

"Oh! I'm really getting to be an old fool! When I saw how beautiful she was I just forgot myself...."

"Oh, this lady is exceptional. She is not only beautiful, but clever, and really kind. She knows how to treat people. No wonder the Empress Dowager adores her. It must have been either in the third or fourth month of this year, when her child was about due that both her father and brother died. She was heart-broken. Cried and cried, she did. When the Empress Dowager and the Emperor came to console her, she vowed not to cry anymore, saying, 'How could I trouble Your Majesties with my personal grief? I wept in gratitude for the love and care my father lavished upon me and for the loss of a sibling. My father and brother were arrogant men, and in their conduct of public affairs, might have been tempted to over-step the boundaries of propriety because of powerful connections. I feared such conduct would reflect badly upon myself, causing the populace to blame Your Majesties for allowing their wantonness for the sake of a worthless woman. Happily they have both died with untarnished reputations. Therefore, I have nothing to grieve."

"That is indeed exceptional!" sighed the nurse.

"She is very learned; plays the lute, and chess; is familiar with literature and art. In short she shares all the things that interest the Empress Dowager. Naturally she is loved for that. The Empress Dowager cannot bear to be without her for a moment. You see, she has only been out of the palace half a day, and already I've been sent to take her back."

"A pity!" the nurse sighed.

"For what?"

"I'm talking nonsense again. If only the Emperor had seen her first, she would be empress now." Sumalagu was silent for a while before she picked up the conversation again.

"Ah, what do us slaves know about such things! The Emperor has already deposed one empress. He can't do it again. Besides, no matter how much the Emperor and the Empress Dowager love this lady, there is no escaping her one defect."

"What may that be?"

"Her mother is a southern barbarian."

The two women had no idea that the daughter of a southern barbarian was discussing them at the same time.

"Your Majesty, was the Momo your very first nurse?"

"That's right. I was fed on her milk. I slept with her till I was eight. She took care of me."

"But Your Majesty was proclaimed at the age of six."

"That's right. I remember on that day, she was the one who carried me out of the palace." Fulin was reclining on a divan, his head pressed against Black Pearl's breast and an arm around her waist. He recalled the day happily.

"It was bitterly cold, and one of the servants brought me a marten fur cloak. I took one look at it, and pushed it aside."

"But why?"

"Don't be impatient. I will tell you. The imperial sedan chair had arrived and Momo wanted to ride with me, but I said, 'This is not for you to ride in.' Momo was surprised but pleased too. She put me in the sedan chair and knelt on the pavement till I left. You see, she does know protocol. When we arrived at the Hall of Supreme Harmony and I was seated on the throne, I could see all the officials, both civic and military, thronged outside. I wasn't a bit frightened. But the sight of all my uncles and brothers waiting in front of the hall made me nervous. I did not know how I should behave, so I whispered to a courtier, 'When my uncles, brothers and other princes come forward to pay homage do I sit still, or do I return the salutation?' The man answered it would not be appropriate to return the salutation. Then the bells and drums were struck, and the court came forward according to their rank to pay homage. I sat perfectly still to receive them."

"The Son of Heaven had the poise of a monarch even as a child," Black Pearl praised, gently laying a cheek against his shiny black head.

"However, I felt awkward having my uncles who were old men kneel to a six-year-old child. When the audience was over I stood and insisted that my uncle Daishan precede me out of the hall. Only then would I step into my sedan chair. I remember my uncle Daishan was moved to tears by this gesture. We succeeded to the throne largely due to his efforts."

"In my mind, it was mainly the effort of the Empress Dowager," Black Pearl said evenly.

"You're right, of course. I was speaking of persons outside the palace." Fulin took Black Pearl's hand and lightly kneaded it.

"But what happened to the marten fur cloak, Your Majesty?"

"Ah, the cloak!" Fulin chuckled. "When the audience was over, and I had returned to the palace, I summoned the servant who had presented it. I said to him, 'Had the cloak been lined in bright yellow silk, I would have accepted it gladly. But it was lined in red which is unsuitable.' The servant knelt to beg forgiveness, but I did not make an issue of it." Black Pearl laughingly replied, "It is most unusual for a child of six to be so conversant with protocol. How would Your Majesty explain inviting your humble concubine to dine just now?" Fulin laughed out loud.

"That was then; this is now. To everything there is a season. I acquiese to what pleases me. As to what displeases me, I'll think of a way out. Otherwise, where is the joy of being emperor?"

Before Black Pearl could think of a rebuttal, the chief eunuch of the Hall of Mental Cultivation was announced, bringing with him petitions received that day. Fulin leafed through the documents perfunctorily and threw them on the desk. He was annoyed that matters of state had intruded upon his moment of warmth and contentment.

Black Pearl eyed the documents uneasily.

"Your Majesty shouldn't leave matters of state unattended."

"There's nothing important. Just routine business that can take care of itself. Let us have a quiet evening together...."

Black Pearl mulled that remark over and counselled, "Can Your Majesty be sure that among those unimportant, routine matters, there isn't some item that requires immediate attention before it becomes a problem? Or some matter that requires further study because of a variety of reasons? Your Majesty has made it his motto to honour heaven and the laws of the ancestors; to govern with diligence and love for the people. Therefore he must be tireless in his endeavours, even in moments of leisure."

Fulin gently stroked Black Pearl's back. "You have become my conscience. Come ... we will read together...." Black Pearl quickly rose to her feet.

"Your humble woman must have no outside interests. Therefore, she cannot interfere with matters of state in any way. However, she will stay by Your Majesty's side while you attend to the documents."

"As you wish," Fulin shrugged and took his seat behind the desk.

Black Pearl ordered two table lamps covered with white silk shades placed on the desk. The four ebony floor lamps were lit as well as the nine lamps that hung from the ceiling. The room was now as bright as day. Black Pearl had the serving maids bring in her embroidery frame and place it to one side of the imperial desk. The serving maids ranged themselves to one side while Fulin studied his documents, and Black Pearl did her embroidery. The silence of the chamber was only broken by the soft popping of lamp wicks as they burned down, and the sizzle of the charcoal burning in the filigree brazier.

Fulin studied one document several times. Each time he took up his brush to write his instructions, he laid it down again.

"Your Majesty," Black Pearl asked, "why are you troubled?"

"In the autumn the courts condemned ten felons to be executed which each requires my signature. I cannot make up my mind."

Black Pearl approached the desk and stared at the documents on which the black rows of characters spelled death. She knit her brows and spoke with sad resignation.

"These cases were not tried by Your Majesty. In this humble woman's view, there is no guarantee that the truth is out even if Your Majesty did try them yourself. Also, there are many foolish and venal men among court officials. One cannot be sure that all the accused were really guilty. Life is precious. Therefore, your humble woman begs Your Majesty to weigh each case on its own merits." Then she added as an afterthought, "Better an error of omission than one of commission."

Fulin nodded in silent agreement. He read the papers one more time and marked several with the words, "To be reviewed", and others he marked "Mitigation".

"Your Majesty, to execute on the spot persons who harbour runaway slaves is perhaps a little too..." Black Pearl interrupted herself, for she noticed Fulin shiver, hunching up his shoulders as though he was cold. She quickly fetched the marten fur coat the Empress Dowager had sent and draped it over his shoulders. Fulin seized her warm little hand, and gazing earnestly into her eyes said, "You must know I think the law is is too harsh. But what can I do? It's not something I relish...."

He let go of her and took up his brush again as though determined to annotate the documents. But he could not ignore the uneasiness that Black Pearl's remarks roused within him. Black

Pearl stood beside him a moment, gently stroking his free hand, then she softly stole away to tend to the two three-feet high bronze braziers. Into each she threw a couple handfuls of incense, and she ordered a serving maid to fetch a foot warmer for Fulin.

When Fulin laid down the last of the documents it was late night. Black Pearl carefully laid down her embroidery and went into the west chamber where rock sugar and tremella, a type of tree fungus, had been simmering over a small brazier for the Emperor. Fulin paced the room with measured steps. He seemed relaxed, but Black Pearl knew him well enough to sense he was wrestling with some problem. As she offered the jade bowl to him, she softly inquired, "Is something wrong?"

Fulin accepted the bowl, stirred its contents with a spoon, and quaffed a mouthful.

"The day before yesterday, Duke An mentioned the corruption surrounding the examinations at Shuntian, and the public outrage it has caused. Many highly qualified candidates refused to attend as a result. Does this mean the integrity of the examinations is suspected? This incident cannot be overlooked by a new regime. I am perturbed that in the month since the results were announced there has not been one single petition about this matter. Is it not strange?"

Black Pearl replied, "Everybody is talking about it in the capital. However, the Manchu officials, who usually pay scant attention to the examinations, probably overlooked it as something unimportant. While the Han officials might see it differently, they are mostly unwilling to take the risk of writing reports. Furthermore, most of those involved were Hans. Therefore, it can be expected that some will act incorrectly to protect one another."

Fulin frowned. "We have never distinguished between Hans and Manchus, and we try to employ both equally. I have been especially keen on cultivating Han intellectuals. Why, then, do Han officials always give us trouble?"

"Your Majesty, if you would put yourself in their shoes, everything will become crystal clear. They say, to win the hearts of the people, first win the hearts of the intelligentsia. The examinations are the most expedient way of winning them over and, therefore, must be treated with utmost seriousness. The relationship between monarch and subject is liken to that between father and son. Why not give your underlings a severe tongue-lashing as a warning against such behaviour in the future?"

"These few days I have been considering issuing a censorious edict, but then I thought it lacked weight. It seems...." He paused, took a few spoonfuls of the rock sugar and fungus, and put the bowl down heavily. The flicker of fire in his eyes showed he had made up his mind.

"Tomorrow I will summon the Han officials and all those involved with the examinations."

"You will do it tomorrow?" There was surprise in Black Pearl's voice, but her smile and the expression in her eyes was proof of her approval and love for the young Emperor. "Shall we return to the palace?"

"No. We're staying here."

The main hall of the imperial travelling lodge at Nanyuan was not as vast as the Hall of Supreme Harmony or the Palace of Heavenly Purity in the Forbidden City, but it was nevertheless an imposing structure. The throne was an exact replica of the one in the Palace of Heavenly Purity and rivaled it for its splendour. On either side of the throne stood two cloisonne elephants known as the elephants of peace. Each figure, encrusted with pieces of glassware, carried a vase on its back. There were also a pair of cranes made of similar materials. Behind the throne stood a large fan embroidered with the sun, moon and stars. To the left and right, in front of the throne were four tables on which stood incensers on tripods containing burning sandal wood filled the hall with fragrance. An air of solemnity enveloped the hall.

At the foot of the dais, where the paving bricks of the floor shone like inky black jade, knelt row upon row of Han officials arranged according to their rank. At the front were the famous grand academicians of the three palace academies: Wang Yongji and Cheng Kegong of the Palace Secretariat Academy; Jin Zhijun and Fu Yijian of the Palace Historiographic Academy; Liu Zhengzhong from the Palace Academy of the Advancement of Literature. Behind them were the nine ministers, followed by the lesser dignitaries of the Six Offices of Scrutiny. However, the largest number were the censors. They were clerks and lesser functionaries of the various departments. Though they seemed relatively unimportant, these men could have a great effect on the court. For theirs was the responsibility of scrutinizing the work of the huge bureaucracy, with the right to report any misdeeds that came to their notice directly to the Emperor. However, the same short-comings of the system hampered them from fully exercising their mandate. An example of this occurred three years earlier. The official censors had focused upon the unfair laws governing runaway slaves and submitted a series of reports. The Council of the Nobles not only rejected these reports and discredited them, but caused four prominent censors to be banished for their zeal.

Aside from the imperial guards and the eunuchs, a handful of Manchus, including the armed commanders of the imperial guards, Lord Aobai and Sukesaha, stood in solemn attendance of their monarch as he faced the prostrate Han officials. Like the Han officials they were also decked out in full regalia, but they did not feel the tension like the Han officials.

Fulin spoke slowly but clearly. His voice sounded strange in that vast hall, hovering in the air, reverberating with a fuzzy echo.

"...Since we have taken the reins of government, our paramount concern has been to honour the memory of our sage ancestors by ruling in peace, bringing prosperity to the people and thus pleasing the gods. However, till now our borders remain unstable and our land plagued by flood and draught. Our officials are corrupt, and the people are exhausted. As we take stock of our misdeeds, so shall officials high and low. We must work together to correct these faults."

So far the Emperor's words were conciliatory. He had not shifted the blame entirely upon the officials. The speech was even friendly.

"We have established departments of government whose responsibility is to supervise, control, and apprehend official wrongdoers. Yet, of late these departments have adopted an attitude of compromise, contrary to our intentions. Only the faults of minor officials have been looked into. Henceforth anyone whose judgement is clouded by personal considerations shall be severely dealt with."

Why had he brought this matter forward when the officials concerned were not present?

"The aim of the imperial examinations is to select outstanding scholars and capable men for the court. Fraternizing between the rank and file and their superiors has created a conduit for bribery. Corruption has become a way of life. Henceforth all officials shall restrict themselves and be mindful of their responsibilities. Transgressors shall be severely dealt with!"

The speech was slowly approaching the heart of the matter. Many of the prostrate officials were desperately controlling the quivering in their limbs, as though they had a fever.

"As for the censors, who are our eyes and ears, we must once more exhort you to speak without fear. Place the nation's good before any other consideration. Henceforth, the censors will not limit their attention to the insignificant, but must concentrate on the misdeeds of the great. Only by a thorough cleansing of the system can we arrive at a new politic."

Fulin ended his speech with a few formal remarks. The assemblage cheered and touched their foreheads to the ground, then stood before the hall according to their rank.

The Master of Protocol was about to announce the end of the audience, when an official stepped out from the ranks of the censors and prostrated himself before the throne. The man was short and thin but agile. He held high a heavy pile of petitions and cried out in a loud voice, "Your Majesty's servant, supervising secretary of the Ministry of Justice, Ren Kepu, begs to present a petition concerning the corruption during the imperial examinations at Shuntian."

The assemblage was shocked, but Shunzhi was pleased. In a moment the petition was spread across the imperial desk.

A deadly silence descended upon the great hall. The assembled Han officials fixed their gaze upon Ren Kepu, but their ears were tuned to sounds coming from the throne. Some were uneasy, others gleeful. Naturally there were those who were completely unmoved. However, none of these emotions were allowed to show on the surface, or the culprit would be punished on the spot for flippancy.

Fulin's face was suffused with anger when he finished reading the petition. He slammed the desk with the palm of his hand, and in a stern voice ordered all those named in the petition to be arrested immediately and jointly tried by the Ministry of Personnel and the Ministry of Justice.

When all the culprits had been apprehended, another decree was issued, naming the Lords Sukesaha and Aobai as the presiding judges. The former was one of the Emperor's most trusted courtiers, and the latter was known for his fair-mindedness and decisiveness. Their appointment showed the importance of the case. Thus the ministers of the two departments, particularly the Hans, were also forced to be extra careful of their words and actions.

5

Wang Yongji, Grand Academician of the palace academies and the Minister of Personnel, alighted from his sedan chair outside the ministry. Once through the gate, he followed a wide flagstoned path to the main hall. Going through a side door brought him to a small courtyard bordered on all sides by trellises covered with wistaria vines. The old vine, twined together like grey serpents, reminded the civil servant of the convoluted intrigues, plots and counter-plots that plagued the service. The name, Wistaria Hall, was displayed on a wide plaque hanging from the eaves. As everyone including Wang knew the wistaria was planted almost three hundred years ago by the Minister of Personnel of the early Ming period named Wu Kuan. Today Wistaria Hall was the office of Kerkun, a Manchu official of the Ministry of Personnel. Wang felt a rush of pride as he crossed the threshold, for he was the only Han official present that day. Later the Lords Sukesaha and Aobai, together with Tuhai, Minister of Justice, would arrive to discuss the second phase of the investigation.

Hot tea was served and the officials took their seats. The proceedings began solemnly.

According to the imperial decree Li Zhenye, Zhang Han and many others had been arrested for questioning. Because of the difference in their status, they were divided into three groups for investigation.

The first phase of the investigation ended in a stalemate. Due to cause of the presence of members of the Council of Nobles and venerable men such as Kerkun and Tuhai as observers, the Han officials had little to say except agree to everything they heard. The Manchu officials, who took a dim view of the examinations in the first place, could not make head or tail of the case. Everything remained murky. How would they report to the Emperor?

Sukesaha flashed a complacent grin at his colleagues. "The preliminary investigation was a sham!" said he, toying with the lid of his tea cup. He was fair and plump and ruddy cheeked. He knew how to please the Emperor, who reciprocated by letting him have his own way in most things. Nevertheless, from time to time his brows would knit and the flash in his eyes was evidence of carefully banked fires within. However he took care that this seldom happened.

Aobai nodded and quaffed a mouthful of tea. His position at

court was beneath that of Sukesaha though he was older and had a more noteworthy military record. He preferred the position of a subordinate. He was a man of few words, and in a case which involved Hans, he felt at a disadvantage. His Chinese was far from fluent, and he was content to keep silent.

Tuhai, who was a solemn man, scratched the shaved side of his head thoughtfully and agreed the investigation had not produced any concrete evidence.

Being more out-spoken, Kerkun blurted, "All that came out of this investigation is connections. Connections! Connections! What are connections?"

The eyes of the four Manchus were now focused on Wang Yongji.

This naivety amused Wang Yongji. In fact his amusement was close to the surface. He had a round laughing face with twinkly eyes. Before he spoke his lips parted in anticipation and his moustaches lifted at the corners. Now he stroked his beard complacently, shifted his position in his seat and, in the tone of an expert, spoke in fluent Manchu.

"As far as the examination are concerned, the term 'connections' means the secret signals arranged between candidates and adjudicators. With the help of these signals the adjudicator can single out the papers of particular candidates from any number of submissions. Naturally, adjudicators sell these favours for power, or money, or some other consideration. The so-called connection takes many forms. For example a candidate may incorporate his name and the name of his hometown into his thesis. Or he might invent a character; quote a line of poetry, or a well-known essay that both sides have agreed upon beforehand. The average 'connection' at the Shuntian exams sold for between about three and ten thousand ounces of silver. If a candidate wishes to ensure success, he has to buy extra connections. That means spending vast sums."

The four Manchu lords finally understood the situation.

"These wily southern barbarians are really hateful!'' exclaimed Kerkun.

"It has been thus since the system began,'' smiled Wang. "No wonder poor grand academicians grind their teeth with chagrin.''

Kerkun scowled, "These wily barbarians have slithered through the preliminary investigation. How should the next phase be conducted?''

In fact the adjudicator Li Zhenye and his colleagues vehemently denied their guilt. Even the witness Ren Kepu mentioned in his petition could only accuse Zhang Han and another candidate on evidence that amounted to hearsay. There was no concrete proof to support the charges. In their turn Zhang Han and Jiang Wenzhuo charged three adjudicators with accepting bribes. Though they divulged the amounts involved, they could not produce proof.

"The reason these Hans have been able to pull the wool over My Lords' eyes,'' Wang Yongji chuckled amiably, "is because they are unfamiliar with the examinations. If My Lords will accept my suggestion, everything will become quite clear.'' When Wang left the room, Tuhai said, "Why not follow his advice?''

Sukesaha and Aobai exchanged a look. Scowling deeply, Aobai said, "If he gets to the bottom of this, won't we look foolish?''

Tuhai laughed mirthlessly. "Let a southern barbarian deal with his own kind. We'll sit back, watch and listen.'' Sukesaha nodded vigorously. Kerkun raised a thumb and chortled, "Good idea!'' Finally Aobai also agreed.

The first session of the second phase of investigation began with accusations and counter-accusations between Li Zhenye and Zhang Han.

Sukesaha and Aobai were seated at the centre of the hall, flanked on the left and right by Kerkun and Tuhai. Slightly in front and to the left was the seat and desk prepared for Wang

Yongji. A secretary was seated beside him. In front of these four men and a little to the right were places reserved for vice ministers of the Ministries of Personnel and Justice. The hall was lined with heavy- and medium- weight canes, finger screws, whips, chains, and other grim paraphernalia of interrogation and torture. Ordinarily instruments of torture were not displayed in the Ministry of Personnel. However, this was a joint investigation with the Ministry of Justice, and Wang Yongji deemed it appropriate to make such a display.

When Li Zhenye and Zhang Han were brought into the room, the arrangement of the room struck fear in their hearts. However, when they came face to face with each other, fear gave way to rage.

"So you have come to this, Li Zhenye!" Zhang Han remarked coldly. Li Zhenye turned and spat in his face. The two would have been at each other's throat had they not been subdued by the guards.

Wang Yongji deliberately asked, "Is this enmity between you new, or something lingering? It seems to me only two people who have known each other well could develop such a hatred." Zhang Han fell to his knees and cried, "My Lord, I have known this man three years. I am acquainted with all his misdeeds. In this year's examinations he dared break the law. Therefore, disregarding any personal feelings, I accused him in the name of all the down-trodden under Heaven that they might receive justice."

"Ah! You seem a righteous fellow!" Wang Yongji's remark sounded almost like praise. Turning to the other he asked, "Li Zhenye, do you know this man?"

"My Lord, he is an ungrateful cur. It is a pity that his venomous nature was not detected sooner." Zhang Han tried to leap to his feet and was again held down by the guards.

"What do you mean by ungrateful?" Wang Yongji feigned astonishment.

"When he arrived in the capital penniless and alone, I took

him in out of an appreciation for his talents. Through my efforts he became a student of the National University. Seeing that he was poor and lonely, I also found him a wife and bought him a house. But the man's ambitions knew no bounds. When I was appointed adjudicator, he insisted on a 'connection'. I, of course, refused, and rebuked him for it publicly at Yousheng Nunnery. From then on he hated me, and this accusation is the result. I beg Your Lordship to ferret out the truth...."

"You lie!" Zhang Han shouted, cutting off Li Zhenye's discourse. As he struggled to his feet, the guards tried again to push him down, but a slight shake of the head from Wang Yongji caused them to desist. Stamping his feet with rage, Zhang Han pointed a finger at Li Zhenye and roared, "Shameless hypocrite! There is nothing lower than this scum!" Shame and anger pushed him over the edge. Disregarding such considerations as face or dignity or that he might well be burning all his bridges, he blurted out all his dirty secrets.

"Taking me in because of his appreciation of talent! Doesn't that have a noble ring! Actually he seduced me into becoming his male whore. As for finding me a wife! Who was that wife? One of his cast-off concubines. After she married me, she still had to service him! I am a man and a scholar!"

Then the whole sordid story tumbled out, willy-nilly. The secretary scribbled as fast as he could with scarcely time to dip his brush in the ink. Wang Yongji smiled broadly, darting glances at the stunned Manchus. Zhang Han spoke with such passion that he was soon bathed in perspiration. His voice was giving out, and the queue he wore, which had been roughly cut short, wagged like a tail attached to the back of his head. Li Zhenye was growing impatient. When he thought of the slip of paper he had given Pinky on which he had written a secret code, its subsequent destruction gave him a little ease. Zhang Han had no proof. As soon as Zhang Han stopped, Li Zhenye leaped in with his rebuttal.

"These are all lies and deliberate calumny! Whether it was male lover or abandoned concubine, it was games people play. Nobody forced him. However, selling 'connections' is completely false."

Wang Yongji interposed a single remark: "Of course, Adjudicator Li. Can you prove it, Student Zhang?" Zhang Han tore at his padded robe like a mad man, until clumps of snow-white cotton spilled out and fluttered in the air. He reached in the tear and pulled out a slip of paper which he presented to Wang with both hands.

Wang Yongji saw that it was six or seven fragments of paper that had been reassembled and glued together on a sheet of stiff paper. The writing on the paper was perfectly legible. Wang chuckled and beckoned to Li Zhenye.

"Come. Is this your handwriting?" Li Zhenye glanced at the sheet of paper and blanched. He fell to his knees and struggled to control his voice before he spoke.

"This never actually happened.... I did not allow Zhang Han to pass...." "What about the others?" yelled Zhang Han, naming names, eyes bulging from their sockets. Facing Zhang Han's burning gaze, Li Zhenye began to tremble. However, he gritted his teeth and through trembling lips muttered, "Who has the proof?" "The people who passed you the five thousand ounces of silver from each candidate!" shouted Zhang Han hysterically. Their names were the fatal blow. Li Zhenye's legs buckled and he fell senseless to the floor.

Wang Yongji smiled contentedly at the outcome and turned to gauge the effect it had upon the Manchus. They nodded their approval. Wang Yongji raised a hand and motioned the guard to remove Zhang Han.

"Li Zhenye, have you anything to say?" Li Zhenye looked about the hall in a daze, unable to speak.

"Your corruption has been proved. However, there is no evidence against your colleagues. Therefore, you must be the sole culprit in this scandal. How many connections did you peddle to create such a furore? Unless you are given the ultimate penalty, the Heavens will not be appeased...."

"No! No!" cried Li Zhenye, clawing the air. "To punish me alone would be a grave injustice! Injustice!"

"Did you have accomplices?" Wang Yongji's question was almost a reminder.

"They each took a thousand ounces...."

"Who are they?"

Li Zhenye quickly gave the names and added, "They had connections of their own as well." Seizing the opportunity as it arose, Wang Yongji moved in for the kill. He ordered the two other defendants brought in. The unassailable barrier of silence began to crumble. The three men attacked each other like mad dogs. Wang Yongji sat back calmly, throwing out questions from time to time, allowing the men to unravel their own secrets.

The investigation was finally over. When the four Manchus returned to Wistaria Hall, Wang was ready to present the transcripts in both Chinese and Manchu script. Aobai accepted the document without a word. Sukesaha smilingly complimented Wang saying, "Master Wang is indeed as astute as I have been made to believe."

Wang Yongji demurred. "I am most unworthy. I owe everything to my Master Gong Dingzi who is ten times more able than I." Wang Yongji considered himself to be a clever man. He had put in a good word for Gong Dingzi, without revealing that his strategy had been originated by Gong. In this way he had repaid Gong's kindness without compromising his own abilities. Tuhai countered saying, "You are too modest."

"Not at all," Wang Yongji chuckled. Kerkun remarked that so long as the guilty had been apprehended and evidence was in hand, the case could be closed and reported to the Emperor accordingly. Wang Yongji shook his head.

"That would be premature. Many more are involved. We must, as they say, trace the vine to the melon, and thus uproot the bad lot."

"Oh?" Aobai's hawk-like eyes shot fire. "There are others?"

"Absolutely," Wang Yongji spread out the transcripts, indicating certain lines. "If My Lord will examine this statement."

Li Zhenye: "When I sent Tongchun to you, what did you do?"

Zhang Wopu: "He never came to me!"

Li Zhenye: "You lie! You sent him back to me!"

During the interrogation the Manchu nobles had been totally absorbed by the confrontation that they had not paid attention to this exchange. Now Kerkun, a little nonplussed, asked, "This was only a bit of jealousy. What connection can it have on the case?"

"Not so," countered Wang Yongji. "This person, Tongchun, played an important role in this affair." Sukesaha spoke slowly, "Do you mean...."

"I propose to question Tongchun at once," replied Wang solemnly. Kerkun rose from his seat. "I will have him brought here at once." Wang Yongji rose also. Wagging a finger for emphasis, he added, "This man must be treated with kid gloves...."

The interrogation of Tongchun took place in a smaller chamber to the east of the room used previously. When Tongchun entered, the Manchus exchanged astonished glances, for this was indeed a beautiful youth. Unfortunately Wang Yongji was not fond of the theatre or he would have recognized the young man as the actor who had been the toast of the capital. Tongchun, as actor and as page boy, was familiar with the houses of the aristocracy and their protocol. However, this was the first time he had been involved in criminal proceedings and he was nervous. Therefore he fell to his knees as soon as he entered the room.

Wang Yongji, seated sedately behind his desk, ordered him to identify himself by name, place of birth and age.

"Your humble servant is Liu Tongchun from Yongping Prefecture, Shuntian. I am eighteen years of age."

"Are you a slave in the household of the student Zhang Han?"

"You humble servant is not a slave, but a free man. I have been employed as page boy for a period of three years."

"How did you also come to serve the adjudicator Li Zhenye?"

"Master Li and my master were close friends. I was loaned to look after him when he became adjudicator."

"Now Zhang Han has accused Li Zhenye of corruption. Can you shed any light on this?"

"Your humble servant knows nothing."

"You served Li Zhenye, how could you not know he was selling connections?"

"My Lord, your humble servant is ignorant...." Wang Yongji smiled. He ordered his chair be moved away to the side of the table. When he resumed his seat he beckoned Liu Tongchun to come closer.

Liu Tongchun approached tearfully, kneeling close to Wang Yongji. Wang Yongji spoke in a kindly voice:

"Listen. You have nothing to fear. You were brought here as a witness. Nothing more. Li Zhenye's corruption has nothing to do with you. You are not related and therefore, cannot be implicated. As long as you tell the truth nothing will happen to you." Tongchun hung his head without a word.

"You see, your master has laid charges against Li Zhenye. Evidence and witnesses are needed to support those charges, or Zhang Han will be guilty of mischief. Will you not help?"

Tongchun was confused. He hated Zhang Han for his obsequiousness. However, how many scholars can remain unimpeachable when fame and fortune are at stake? The slights that Zhang Han endured and his protection for himself roused Tongchun's sympathy. Also, Tongchun had a strong sense of selfworth. Moreover, he was a man of integrity.

Since he was Zhang Han's servant, he owed him loyalty. But what of Li Zhenye? Tongchun loathed the man's unctuous smile and his lascivious intentions. Li's unbridled lust made his stomach churn. However, Li Zhenye was an official....

"I understand that Zhang Han is a learned man. There are many other able men who have fallen by the wayside unable to fulfil their potential. That is a great loss, and most unfair. Now, Li Zhenye steadfastly refuses to confess his infamy though several men are willing to testify against him. It seems unusual that you, being his body servant, saw nothing untoward."

Actually Tongchun held evidence that would send the culprits to the gallows. However, he had hung on to it with another purpose in mind...

One day, while he was reading the exam papers, Li Zhenye handed Tongchun a piece of paper on which were written the names and places of birth of twenty-five candidates. Tongchun's task was to go to his colleague Zhang Wopu and look through his papers for submissions by these men. All the adjudicators had proteges. However, each only read a limited number of papers. Therefore a trusted servant was sent to verify names with fellow adjudicators. Though the candidate's name was covered over with a strip of gummed paper, these could be torn, read and re-sealed. Tongchun knew this was breaking the law, but he could not refuse. He was able to account for half the names listed by Li. Meanwhile, Zhang prepared a list of his own, and also asked Tongchun to verify them on his behalf at Li's place. Again, Tongchun identified a goodly number. Afterwards both Li and Zhang were busy entertaining their proteges and the lists were forgotten.

Tongchun had kept Li's list of names purely for the sake of self-preservation. Li Zhenye had made repeated advances which he managed to fend off. A time would come when Li's demands would become relentless. Then Tongchun would use the name list as a weapon to force him to desist. It never occurred to him to profit from it. As for Zhang's list, he had kept it without any premeditated motive.

Tongchun shot a fearful glance at Wang Yongji and asked in a tiny voice, "If Masters Li and Zhang are found guilty would their lives be forfeit?" Wang Yongji shook his head. "It won't come to that. But they will be dismissed and barred from public office for life."

"It serves them right," thought Tongchun. His mind was made up. He undid his tunic and from the pocket of his undergarment removed the two sheets of incriminating papers. He explained how he came by them and verified they were Li and Zhang's handwriting. This was indisputable evidence.

Wang Yongji was elated. Though the Manchu lords did not speak fluent Chinese, they understood the gist of what was said. Wang Yongji scrutinized the two slips of paper and was gratified that he recognized several names. Suddenly his face darkened. His eyes glazed and his hands shook. Seeing this Tuhai snatched the papers from him, glanced at them and grinned with satisfaction. Then he gestured for Tongchun to be removed. When Tongchun was out of the room he turned to Wang Yongji. "Grand Secretary Wang, what is your connection with the fifth name on this list — Wang Shude from Gaoyou?"

Sukesaha, Aobai and Kerkun, hearing this question, also came forward to examine the slip of paper. Wang Yongji was white as a sheet. He wilted like a blade of grass in the cold blast of winter. Still he struggled to compose himself to answer Tuhai.

"He is my nephew. I did not think he would stoop so low. I beg My Lords' permission to withdraw. I shall present a self criticism on the morrow and await judgement." His tone was full of remorse. Though he did his utmost to maintain a dignified demeanor it was beyond his strength, and he shuffled out of the hall in dejection.

Sukesaha exchanged a look with Aobai, and burst into guffaws. Kerkun spat, "The wily barbarian!" and burst out laughing as well. Tuhai shook his head as he laughed. Even the usually dour Aobai allowed himself a wisp of a smile.

During the three days that Zhang Han and Tongchun were detained, Qiao Bainian changed his place of residence three times. The scandal of the examinations touched many people, prompting him to be cautious. However, he was an adventurer at heart and relished danger. In the end, his curiosity to know the final outcome of the case kept him in the capital.

On the twenty-seventh of the tenth month, he went to visit the ancient Jiufeng Temple. As he strolled toward the pylon that straddled Xidan, he noticed the street was teeming with people, young and old, on foot, on horseback, or riding in sedan chairs, all streaming southward. He was travelling against the crowd.

Qiao Bainian collared a passing youth.

"Hey! What's the matter with you?" The youngster struggled to free himself. "All the best spots will be taken if you're late!" Qiao Bainian chuckled without loosening his grip on the boy. "Where are you going in such a hurry?" The youngster, squirming, shouted angrily, "Going to a be-heading!"

"Whose?" Qiao Bainian loosened his grip and the boy ran off without answering.

Executions usually took place at noon. Now the sun was not yet directly overhead. The boy must really be fond of a spectacle. Qiao Bainian grinned to himself and swaggered on with his hands folded behind his back. He had changed direction and was now heading south along the street inside Xuanwu Gate where the crowds were thickest.

He came upon a tea-house. As it was still early, and he was thirsty, Qiao Bainian stepped inside. Near the entrance several licentiates, dressed in scholarly robes, sat round a table talking and laughing. One of them raised a cup on high and declared in a loud voice, "The adjudicators recognize power but not talent. All they care about is money and many a good man's future come to nought. This is the day of reckoning."

"All those who have suffered will breathe easier," chorused

another raising his cup.

"A toast with tea is as good as wine," a third voice rang out.

"Hear! Hear!" The entire group got to their feet, raised their cups and knocked them together with such force that several shattered, spraying tea in all directions. Laughter shook the tiny tea-house.

Qiao Bainian did not want tea anymore. He walked quickly toward Xuanwu Gate. Could the case have closed? Whenever there was an execution, a notice would be posted at Xuanwu Gate. He walked as though his feet had wings. Soon he had caught up with a few lavishly dressed young Manchu aristocrats on horseback. He slackened his pace, straining to overhear their conversation. Though none of them was more than twenty years of age, all spoke fluent Chinese. As he suspected the young Manchus were discussing the case.

"...Ren Kepu laid his charges on the sixteenth; the Ministry of Personnel and the Ministry of Justice made the arrest on the eighteenth. On the twenty-sixth a verdict came down, and today they execute. It was clean and swift!"

"This time the Emperor is really angry. Word is unless stern measures are taken the loyalty of the intelligentsia will be jeopardized. Therefore the Emperor made his decision as soon as the joint report of the two ministries was submitted."

"These southern barbarians don't know when they're well off. They got their positions through us Manchus and this is how they serve us. They deserve to die."

"There's not an honest man among these Han officials. I say kill the lot of them. That'll make me happy."

"As a matter of fact, my old man has invited some of his cronies for drinks to celebrate."

"That's what mine is doing too."

Qiao Bainian had heard enough. He hurried toward Xuanwu Gate. As he expected, a notice of execution was posted to one side of the massive city gate together with an account of the incident issued jointly by the two ministries. A proclamation issued by the Emperor and stamped with his flaming red seal was also posted. A crowd had already gathered round to read. As soldiers were guarding the proclamation, Qiao Bainian did not try to push his way to the front. Instead he stood back to listen as someone read aloud:

"...Corruption has been prohibited by imperial decree. The examinations are to select talented scholars. The capital, an example for all, tolerates no bribery. Those found guilty of offering and accepting bribes will be severely dealt with as a deterrent to others...." There followed the names of Adjudicators Li Zhenye and Zhang Wopu and three others, and two candidates, who were sentenced to death by beheading. "...Their property will be confiscated and their parents, siblings and children banished to Shangyangpu...."

Qiao Bainian did not wait to hear the rest but headed for the market place at Caishikou. This was an execution he did not want to miss. Deep down an inner voice was chanting gleefully, "They're getting what they deserve for serving the Tartars!"

The sun was now overhead. The clash of gongs, the blast of long horns and the wail of a reed instrument called the *bili* sounded from the inner city. Spectators lined both sides of the street outside Xuanwu Gate all the way to Caishikou. Ten thousand curious souls crammed into the open space in front of the Pharmacy of Pine and Cranes. An excited cry of "They're coming! They're coming" caused the throng to crane their necks toward the north one moment and to fall back in impatient anticipation the next.

The officer-in-charge appeared on horseback surrounded by a simple retinue of four staff bearers, four flag bearers, two fans and a sun-shade. Then came the red-clad executioners, hefting broad swords. Last of all came seven tumbrels surrounded by armed guards. Excitement sped through the throng like wild fire. Everybody was yelling and pointing, trying to identify Li Zhenye and Zhang Wopu and the hapless Loo Yiji.

"Why do people sympathize with Loo Yiji?" Qiao Bainian asked a man near him who seemed to know everything.

"Oh him. Because he hardly got anything out of it. He was only a go-between. But because he knew what was happening and did not report, he was dragged in."

"What happened to Chen Qixian who passed these exams as a provincial graduate?"

"He was clever. He cheated the executioner by committing suicide in his prison cell."

The officer-in-charge had seated himself behind a table on which brush and ink-stone had been laid out together with orders of execution. At a distance of about three yards before him, knelt the seven prisoners in a straight line, separated by an armed guard on either side. Behind each prisoner stood an executioner ready to do his duty. As it was not yet time, the officer sat stiffly alert, waiting for the seconds to slip by.

The sun blazed down on the executioners' bare arms and shoulders. Beads of oily sweat popped out all over their bald pates. The noise of the market place died down. It was customary that if there was a last minute pardon, it would arrive at this very moment. Would there be a pardon? By the arrogant look on Zhang Wopu's face, one might surmise such a thing was possible.

Suddenly there was a stir among the crowd. The excitement was not caused by the arrival of a last minute pardon but by a slender woman dressed from head to toe in white mourning. She swayed on tiny bound feet, weeping softly into a hand cupped over her mouth. Over one arm was slung a bamboo basket covered with a white cloth. Qiao Bainian's mouth fell open with astonishment for he recognized the woman as Zhang Han's wife Pinky. Had she come to beg forgiveness for Zhang Han or was she there for the sake of an old love? See! She was kneeling before Li Zhenye!

Some where at the back of his be-fogged brain Li Zhenye seemed to hear a woman calling him. He opened his eyes wearily and found himself gazing into Pinky's tear-streaked face. His brain cleared. He forced a smile and murmured, "What are you doing here?"

Pinky did not reply. Instead she lifted the white cloth covering her basket and produced rice soaked in wine and water and a few dishes and lit a stick of incense in a small burner. This was an offering to the dying, a ritual that neither the officer-in-charge nor the executioner could deny. Of the seven men to be executed, Li Zhenye was the only one to be honoured in this way. Li Zhenye spoke with great emotion, "I, Li Zhenye, have relatives and friends everywhere, yet only a woman I abandoned comes to bid me adieu.... Heaven! Pinky, do you not hate me?"

"I do! That's why I gave your secrets to Zhang Han. I meant you to suffer a little, but not this.... Do you hate me?" Li Zhenye shook his head.

"What more is there to say? I got what I deserve.... Did you come to witness my shame?"

"No. All the hate and the anguish are cancelled by death. They say, to be man and wife one night is to share a hundred days of love...." She turned away to hide her tears. Li Zhenye lifted his head and sigh, "If only it could be thus! Pour wine."

After Li Zhenye had eaten, Pinky presented a bowl of strong wine in which the rice had been soaked and held it to his lips. He drank deeply, draining the bowl to the last drop. Then smiling, he said, "Pinky, I thank you for sending me to heaven in drunken bliss." Li Zhenye wavered on his feet. He was dead drunk.

The horns blared. The time of execution had come.

Pinky cried out and, hiding her face, fled into the crowd. Zhang Wopu's angry voice rang across the open space.

"Hear me, lords of the court! I have protected you with my life, yet you did not lift a finger on my behalf. Heaven and Earth will not permit such callousness. Vengeance will be mine!"

The guards seized him, struck him in the face and gagged him so that he could not utter another word. Seething with rage and hate he was forced to his knees and the executioner raised his blade.

The day after the executions, the property of the seven men were confiscated and their families arrested and made ready for banishment to Shangyangpu.

In the purge that followed, some fifty odd persons who were involved were arrested. Most were candidates who had attempted to buy favours in the examinations. Soon afterwards their families were also arrested.

The arrests did not end there. Next, all Han officials who had any contact with these candidates were detained for questioning. Last of all, those officials connected with the examinations, who were aware of but failed to report the corruption, were sent to prison. The ripples spread wider and wider. When the court finally ordered a re-examination, candidates had to be rounded up like convicts by district and county authorities and sent to the capital in chains. By this time, government offices were half empty while prisons were bursting at the seams. A curious phenomenon occurred. Teashops and taverns near the bureaus of public security did a roaring trade. While the same two noblemen and two ministers, all Manchus, were in charge, Han officials and scholars regarded their futures with wary caution, wondering when the case would finally be laid to rest.

Part 5

As usual Fulin went to pay his respects to the Empress Dowager after the morning audience. This morning he was particularly impatient to see her. His footsteps quickened as he issued from Longzong Gate and broke into a sprint when Cining Gate came into sight, like an adolescent without a care in the world. The band of servants and eunuchs, that followed him like shadows and laden with all sorts of utensils of precious metals for the Emperor's use, ran pell-mell after him. But they could not keep pace. Before they reached Cining Gate they were out of breath and lagged behind.

From the gate, Fulin caught a glimpse of his mother's tall jade headdress between pots of late blooming chrysanthemums and shouted her name as he flew toward her. The Empress Dowager turned and arched her fine brows in astonishment. The jaws of her ladies and eunuchs dropped in confusion. It was unthinkable that the lord of all under Heaven and the monarch of millions should make such an unseemly entrance.

But a further shock was in store for them. In his haste Fulin tripped over the threshold and fell face down on the ground. It happened so quickly that even the eunuchs guarding the gate were too stunned to help the Emperor to his feet.

Fulin scrambled up, ran down the flight of steps and along the footpath of white marble toward his mother.

"Imperial Mother, I bring good news! Sun Kewang has surrendered!"

"What did you say?" The Dowager's eyes widened in disbelief.

"There was a clash between Sun Kewang and Li Dingguo.

Sun was driven from Yunnan and he surrendered."

"Ah! Buddha be praised!" The Dowager joined her hands and lifted her eyes piously to the heavens.

"Now we will know everything about Zhu Youlang — from the strategic points of Yunnan and Guizhou to the deployment of troops. I shall order Hong Chengchou to attack at once. And I must also appoint a general as pacifier of the frontier to take Yunnan...." He gesticulated wildly as he spoke, pacing back and forth, now lifting his head, now waving his arms. "The heavens have blessed me in my enterprise," he cried in a loud voice, "to unite all under Heaven and to establish a dynasty to last ten thousand years!"

"Imperial Son, you are indeed worthy of your forefathers...."

"Imperial Mother, my ambitions do not end there. I want to surpass the Ming and the Han dynasties, so that I will be known as the greatest Emperor of all times."

"Good!" The Empress Dowager's glance took in her son's shining eyes and his flushed cheeks, and her heart was so choked with pride and joy that all she could say was, "You've ripped your robe. Did you hurt yourself?" Fulin extended his hand toward her. Blood oozed from the scratches on his palm. "Imperial Mother, your palace is kept so clean that my hand isn't even dirty," he said ruefully. The Empress Dowager took his hand and tenderly dabbed the cuts with a white silk handkerchief. In a soft voice she murmured, "So after holding off for four years Hong Chengchou has finally succeeded."

"If your Imperial Son had taken the advice of the lords of the council and removed Hong Chengchou, we would not have this day. I insisted on keeping him because I trusted his judgement. I knew he would not hold back without good reason. During these four years he has made secret contacts with key personages of the Yongli court, until finally he pulled away their pillar. Imperial Mother, would you say that your son is a good judge of men?" The Empress Dowager chuckled. "Do not be hasty, my son. Have you considered who to send for the conquest of Yunnan?"

"Jidu has only returned from the field this spring and should not be sent out again. Therefore, what do you think of sending Yuele?"

The Empress Dowager fingered the delicate petals of a yellow chrysanthemum absently and shook her head. "Yuele is wise and versatile. He will be more helpful at court. Why not send Duoni instead?"

"Duoni?" Fulin trembled inwardly. Duoni was the eldest son of Prince Duoduo who was the younger brother of the hated Dorgon. Fulin could not help having second thoughts about sending him on such a mission. He gazed at the dazzling autumnal blooms before him as he struggled with his thoughts. The Empress Dowager sensed her son's hesitation and added softly, "An emperor should be as magnanimous as the wide broad sea. Duoni is like Yuele, never goes against your wish. Why not trust him?"

"Duoni is a passable horseman and archer. But he does not strike me as particularly intelligent."

"Duoni will go into Yunnan as his Emperor's emissary. Hong Chengchou will be responsible for strategy and the actual fighting will be headed by Wu Sangui, Shang Kexi, and Geng Zhongming. There are also the commanders of the eight banners who can be called upon.... What my son must grasp is that the Han have ruled all under Heaven for a thousand years by fostering the talents of able men. We Manchus are comparatively backward in that regard. Therefore, we must learn. Furthermore, we must subdue the Han by their own kind. That must be our plan."

"The Imperial Mother is a fount of wisdom. I shall follow your advice and appoint Duoni as commander of the Southern Expedition within a few days," Fulin's eyes flashed fire as he spoke. The Empress Dowager was pleased, but she controlled the sudden rush of maternal tenderness and steered the conversation in another direction. "You must come to the east wing with me," she said.

"Ah! You've prepared something delicious to eat!"

"Not to eat; to see."

Mother and son chatted happily until they reached the long corridor leading to the east wing. The Empress Dowager signalled Fulin to be quiet and to tread softly. She herself led the way on tiptoe. Fulin entered into the spirit of the intrigue wondering whom they were approaching so stealthily. Soon they heard Sumalagu speaking slowly in rhythmic Manchu. The Empress Dowager signalled Fulin to stop. Standing outside the gate they could hear Sumalagu quite clearly.

"... The pond on Mount Changbai was as green as the sea, and on its surface floated a juicy red fruit. It was more beautiful than anything the Fairy Koolun had seen in heaven. So she swam to it, took it and ate it. Ten months later, she gave birth to a bouncing baby boy, and he was the ancestor of us Manchus, Bukuliyongshun...."

"I know all that," piped a child's voice. "I can even sing it!" And forthwith he began to sing in a clear, sweet voice, full of childish enthusiasm.

When the song was done, he said, "When my father went on a royal progress the musicians played that song. When I grow up and go out riding I'll have them play it for me too."

Outside the gate, the astonished Fulin asked his mother who the child was.

The Empress Dowager smiled and whispered, "I took it upon myself to bring all three of your sons to Cining Palace to be brought up near me, so that I might enjoy the bliss of being grandmother." Fulin smiled back at her.

"It is as you wish, Imperial Mother."

"Sumalagu spends her days with the Second Imperial Son and Third Imperial Son. She is beside herself with joy...."

"And what about the Fourth Imperial Son?" asked Fulin. The Empress Dowager shot him a sidelong glance and replied,

"We know he is your favourite, so we take special care of him. A separate courtyard has been assigned to him. Rest assured he is well cared for." Fulin was embarrassed by the implied favouritism and quickly countered, "Does my Imperial Mother not love him too?" The Empress Dowager chuckled. "Of course I do. They are all my grandsons. The Fourth Imperial Son is like a jade doll. He has his mother's clever eyes. The Third Imperial Son dotes on him and refuses to go to bed at night without seeing him first. So you can imagine how a grandmother must feel."

"Sumalagu!" A child's voice sounded again. "Tell me the story about the seven stars on the soles of the feet."

"But I've told it ten times or more!"

"I want you to tell it again!"

"Oh, all right! But you must promise to sit properly like a good prince and not climb all over me...." Then she told the story of the old King Ha, as Nurhachi was called, who was said to have had seven red moles on each sole in a pattern like the Big Dipper. The birth mark was considered an omen of kingship, and as a result he was persecuted by the Ming Dynasty. However he escaped their clutches and eventually became emperor.

In the corridor outside the Empress Dowager smilingly whispered to Fulin, "Did you hear? The Third Imperial Son is just as fond of that story as you were." "When the Fourth Imperial Son is older he will too.... Why do we not hear the Second Imperial Son?" Fulin asked as they pushed open the door.

Sumalagu hurried to her feet to greet mother and son, while a child with arms out-stretched rushed to the Empress Dowager shouting, "Imperial Grandmother!" Then he knelt to Fulin and in a grown-up voice said, "The Third Imperial Son greets his Imperial Father."

The small figure not even as tall as a table, yet so grown-up in demeanor made the Empress Dowager laugh in spite of herself. She gathered the child into her arms and planted a kiss on his cheek. "Just now your Imperial Father was asking after the Second Imperial Son," she remarked.

The Third Imperial Son's arms tightened round his grandmother's neck. He pressed his mouth against her ear and whispered, pointing at the ebony couch in the adjoining room. "Big brother is over there ... sleeping," he said. "But you mustn't scold...."

Following the child's fingertip, the Empress Dowager and Fulin saw the Second Imperial Son sprawled on his back on the couch sound asleep. Fulin frowned in spite of himself. The Third Imperial Son prattled on.

"Imperial Grandmother, I also have seven stars on the soles of my feet, like in the story...."

"You do?" The Empress Dowager was both amused and surprised.

"Yes! I'll show you!"

The Third Imperial Son struggled from his grandmother's arms, sat on the carpet and had his boots and socks off in a trice. Then he lifted his bare feet to his grandmother and crowed, "Look at my seven stars!"

To their astonishment, on the soles of the child's chubby feet were seven red moles arranged in the pattern of the Great Dipper. The Empress Dowager and Fulin stooped down together and each took hold of a foot to examine it more closely. It was only when they touched the moles and they smudged that they discovered the hoax.

"So that was what you were doing with my rouge!" scolded Sumalagu.

The Empress Dowager and Fulin did not know whether to laugh or cry. Fulin deliberately frowned and, putting on an angry tone, scolded, "Playing a prank at your age!"

The Third Imperial Son's eyes snapped wide.

"Imperial Father, am I not a prince?" he asked. "Those with seven stars under their feet will be emperor or at least a king. How can I be without them?" He folded his hands behind his back and paced the carpet in his bare feet, head erect, mimicking his father.

"When I grow up, I'll be like my Imperial Father and be master of all under Heaven!"

Fulin gathered the child impulsively into his arms. "Such ambitions already! You are indeed the pride of the Aisin Gioro clan!" However, when he encountered the child's eyes which were so like his mother's, he cooled. He let go of the child and asked in an even tone, "Have the two Imperial Sons learned to speak and read Chinese?" Sumalagu quickly replied that out of forty wet nurses more than half were Hans, so the two princes speak fluent Chinese. However, none were literate, and there was no one to teach them. Fulin pondered this a moment and said, "Imperial Mother must find learned scholars to educate them." The Empress Dowager nodded assent.

"Shall we visit the Fourth Imperial Son?" The Third Imperial Son leaped at the suggestion, clamouring to be allowed to accompany them.

At six months the Fourth Imperial Son was a healthy infant brimming with high spirits. Wrapped in soft white wool clothing, his cheeks were as rosy and fresh as the petals of a flower, his big eyes were black as the night sky shimmering with stars. When the visitors entered he struggled from his wet nurse's arms, reaching for the newcomers, making incoherent sounds and kicking his tiny feet in excitement.

The Third Imperial Son ran into the room and the nurse had to squat down for him to hug the infant.

"Call me big brother," the Third Imperial Son begged earnestly. "Say ... brother...."

The Fourth Inperial Son's eyes flashed with intelligence and, smiling, opened his toothless mouth and laboriously tried to mimick the sounds.

Suddenly a pair of hands snatched the child up. Fulin clasped it tightly to him, pressing his lips against its tender cheeks and neck. Fulin's whiskers made the child wince, and he began to whimper. The Empress Dowager quickly took the child and tenderly comforted him. She darted angry glances at Fulin who smiled without a word.

"Why does the Imperial Father kiss my baby brother and not me?"

The Third Imperial Son's question took Fulin by surprise. Fulin shot a startled glance at his mother to which she responded with a derisive look. Fulin reddened instantly, but he quickly recovered himself and replied, "Fourth Imperial Son is little but you are a man."

"Really?" The Third Imperial Son was pleased and strutted about, his face glowing with pride. "Then I can ride a horse and shoot arrows?"

"Next year you can...." Fulin was quick to promise. A thought occurred to him and catching his mother's eyes asked the child, "If after I have gone into history and your Fourth Brother becomes emperor, what will you do?" The Third Imperial Son answered quickly, "Then I'll be Prince General and help my Fourth Brother...." He paused and added, "I have seven stars under my feet, why can't I be emperor?"

The childish remark for which neither grandmother nor son could find a quick answer stirred uneasy thoughts in both. The Empress Dowager changed the subject.

"My Imperial Son doesn't have many sons. Is it possible that none of the beauties of the harem have the power to attract? This single-minded devotion to one woman may cause jealousy. To have many sons is to prosper and have support in one's enterprises. This is especially so in the Imperial Family."

"Yes," Fulin bowed gravely.

Nevertheless, the lady who was summoned that night to the bed chamber in the Hall of Mental Cultivation was again the mother of the Fourth Imperial Son, the beloved Lady Dongeh.

That evening there were not many documents that required his attention. By the second watch he had finished. As Fulin rose from his desk to stretch the kinks out of his back and limbs, Lady Dongeh emerged from the east chamber with a steaming cup of tea.

Fulin smiled as she entered. "What were you doing that you can time your entrance so precisely?"

Black Pearl responded with a twinkle:

"I was embroidering, and then I was practising calligraphy." Actually both tasks were a camouflage for her attention was entirely centred upon the Emperor.

"Show me what you've been doing." Fulin was full of enthusiasm. With the tea cup in one hand and the other arm draped across Black Pearl's shoulders, they went into the east chamber. Black Pearl's handiwork done on snowy white paper, a tribute from Korea, was spread across a square table. Fulin examined each sheet by turn.

"I had no idea what an expert you've become," he finally pronounced full of admiration. "But today I will test my clever lady's gift for poetry," he added with an air of mischief. His eyes swept past the sumptuous appointments of the room — the Western clock cast in gold, the S-shaped jade ornament symbolizing good luck, the screens inlaid with crytalline precious stones — and finally rested upon a tiny square of gossamer-covered window through which he glimpsed the shadowy eaves of the palace and a crescent moon.

"Your subject will be the new moon." He nodded complacently at Black Pearl.

"Will there be a prize?"

"Of course. If you do well, my matching pair of jade paper weights are yours. However, if you fail...." He gazed into her laughing eyes and leaned closer to whisper in her ear. Black Pearl blushed to the roots of her hair and turned away. She lifted the lid off a cup of tea, gently pushed aside the leaves floating on the surface with the edge of the lid and sipped. Then she opened a food container shaped like a ripe pomegranate, selected a small cake with pine seeds and offered it to Fulin. Fulin did not accept the offering with his hand but opened his mouth instead. When she popped the morsel in his mouth, he caught her fingertip gently between his teeth.

"Oh! Your Majesty is naughty! An emperor and a father too!" Black Pearl complained feigning anger.

"I am monarch to the people; father to my babes, but with you, I am only husband." Fulin laughingly drew her close to him with one arm and with his free hand lifted a sweet to her mouth. "Don't think you can bribe your way out so easily. Compose your poem."

"Your humble servant does not have the ability. Besides Your Majesty is not an imperial examiner."

"Says who? All the scholars under Heaven are my students. Why when the corruption at the Shuntian examinations was discovered are we personally supervising a re-examination? If we are not familiar with the works of the sages how would we dare undertake such a task? However, we surmise that since your confinement, you have become intellectually lazy. Perhaps you really are incapable...."

"Do you really think that?" Black Pearl's brows arched. She faced the window and the crescent moon, and softly intoned:

Through wisps of cloud peeps a crescent moon
Its silvery light dapples a shadowy tower
As a maiden awaits her suitor
Knowing fetters will soon bind her.

"Wonderful!" Fulin applauded. "A poem of great emotion and delicacy. You are indeed a talented woman. I suppose you are the maid waiting for her suitor.... But never mind all that. My jade paper weights are yours!" As Black Pearl reached for her prize, Fulin snatched it back. "Wait! I see another subject for a poem." He pointed at the embroidery frame lying on the table.

It was an embroidery of ink-black bamboo rising straight and tall amid lichen-covered rocks. The space usually reserved for poetry was blank. However, a date had already been stitched in. It was the date of the royal hunt that summer.

Black Pearl said, "Your humble servant has a new poem which she begs Your Majesty to inscribe."

"For you to embroider over? What a charming idea!" Fulin sat down at once, and taking up his brush said, "You may begin."

With her face turned again to the window Black Pearl slowly recited:

Parting now, I pray you return swiftly,
That I might not toil up the mountain to watch for you.
When you see the bamboo groves at the temple by River Xiang
You'd know the dewdrops thereon are my pining tears.

Fulin wrote with swift strokes, choked with emotion. When he was done, he laid his brush on its rack and crossed the room to where Black Pearl stood. "Black Pearl!" He spoke her name huskily as he put his hands on her shoulders. She nestled against him, tilting her head to whisper in his ear, "I made this embroidery so that, one day, when I am gone from you, it will go to the grave with me. Having your calligraphy beside me I will be comforted and rest in peace."

"Black Pearl!" Fulin's voice was choked with emotion as he clutched her to his heart. Suddenly he released her, and rushing back to the table hastily took paper and brush and wrote a pair of scrolls:

"*As the white banners unfurl, the knight performs his sword dance*
And the cute little maid softly sings to my flute."

Then in sure quick strokes he added a footnote:

"The first scroll represents heroism and the second represents love. Thus is life."

Having finished, he threw the brush across the room in a fit of exuberance, speckling the floor with a trail of black spots. He was still filled with excitement when he turned to Black Pearl. "What do you think of that? "

Black Pearl smiled. "They are wonderful, but...."

"But what?"

"But ... for Your Majesty it seems a little shallow." Fulin found her critique most interesting, and putting on a long face demanded an explanation.

"From a heroic point of view, it ought to encompass the universe...."

"And what of the romantic?" Fulin pursued. Black Pearl smiled. "I was afraid Your Majesty places too much importance upon love. I would suggest adding to the footnote...."

"How?"

"You have written: 'The first scroll represents heroism and the second represents love. Thus is life.' I would add: 'Striking a balance between the two is true virtue.' Does Your Majesty approve?"

Fulin laughed.

"With you at my side, I have all I desire. You have freed me to realize my ambitions." He drew Black Pearl inpulsively to him. There was a faraway look in his eyes as though they were already contemplating a glittering future.

"In a few days Duoni will receive the seal of general and march south. When Yunnan and Guizhou are subdued, I will begin the task of building anew. It is my hope that while I live the Empire and its people will prosper, and our achievements will surpass the Han and the Tang...."

His dreams, plans, determinations poured forth in a torrent, exciting, heroic, dazzling. Black Pearl was swept along with it. Her eyes flashing and her cheeks flushed she hung upon his every word. Fulin was overwhelmed by his own dreams.

"Do you think we can do it?" he asked squeezing Black

Pearl's hand.

"I bless the day when Black Pearl met Your Majesty," she breathed. "Your Majesty has been trained since the age of four to accomplish these great tasks. Black Pearl shall be Your Majesty's faithful foot-soldier in your endeavour." A warm current gushed through her body. This day would be etched forever in her mind and heart. Before this she had loved the Emperor more than the man; now she loved the man more than the Emperor.

"You are my soul mate," sighed Fulin. On an impulse she threw her arms around him and planted quick kisses across his face. Fulin was taken by surprise, for Black Pearl had always been soft, gentle and passive, never passionate. He seized her by the waist and twirled her around in circles. His spirit soared like a rainbow arching over the sky after a storm — pure, bright, and shining. He reached for his bamboo flute kept in a glass case with his other treasures.

"Black Pearl ... you and I ... are perfect together...." He pressed the flute to his lips and music, tender and passionate, drifted out of the bed chamber, out of the Hall of Mental Cultivation, up to the star-speckled sky to fall gently upon the six palaces of the harem.

Kunning Palace was ablaze with lights. The Empress, accompanied by the principal concubines, were sipping milk tea and chatting about the old days, recounting the brave deeds of their ancestors, Nurhachi and Abahai, as though they were examining family treasures. The conversation was lively, full of the exuberence of women of the grasslands; for three of the four ladies present, including the Empress, her sister Lady Shuhui and their aunt the Lady Jin who was also a cousin of the deposed first empress, were from the clan of Boerjijite. Since the first empress was deposed Lady Jin had lived in obscurity. The fourth lady present was the principal lady of Jingren Palace, Lady Kang.

As the sound of the flute drifted into the room, the chatter suddenly stopped. The soft light shed by lanterns covered with red gossamer shades cast a soft pink glow upon the ladies. In their jewels and satins they appeared like figures in a fairy-tale. In the sudden silence, the ladies avoided each other's eyes, desperately hiding the pain within.

The music finally stopped, but the grim silence persisted. Lady Kang bowed her head lost in thought. The Empress sipped at her milk tea. Lady Jin's eyes clashed with those of the Empress, and both quickly turned away. No one attempted to break the silence.

Barely seventeen years of age, Lady Shuhui was the youngest among the women. When she accompanied her sister to the palace she had been no more than a child. She was attached to her sister, the present Empress, and distressed by the Emperor's neglect of her. She had been pouting and absently playing with her handkerchief. When the others remained silent, she spoke bitterly. "It's the principal lady of Chengqian Palace again! The Emperor plays his flute for no one else."

The Empress remarked as though she hadn't detected the note of displeasure: "His Majesty plays very well."

Lady Shuhui made a face at Lady Jin. Taking the hint Lady Jin said, "For me it's all over. I'll spend the rest of my life in obscurity, never seeing the Emperor. That's fate. But you are the Empress! Lady Shuhui is young and beautiful, and Lady Kang has borne a son! You are ladies with a position. Are you going to suffer humiliation without a fight?"

Lady Shuhui's mouth, as tender as the petals of a flower, went into a pout.

"Don't forget. She is the Precious Concubine, only lower in rank than the Empress by a hair, but much more important than us!" She glanced at the Empress who looked back with her usual hopelessly placid look.

Lady Kang added softly, "It seems that the Fourth Imperial Son will be named Crown Prince." Her voice faded into a sad, despairing whisper.

Lady Jin's eyebrows rose viciously as she hissed, "Huh! That Fourth Imperial Son! Who knows where he came from!"

The Empress glared at Lady Jin and ordered her to be quiet. From a personal point of view the Empress was Lady Jin's niece, but in terms of rank, Lady Jin was five grades lower. A gulf yawned between them. Lady Jin said no more. The Empress continued in her placid tone, "The Precious Concubine is clever, virtuous, filial and kind. Everyone in the palace adores her. The Empress Dowager treats her as her own daughter. Though she is the Emperor's favourite she has never used that as a lever to interfere with matters of state. One cannot find fault...." She let her voice trail off.

But Lady Shuhui was quick to pick up the conversation. "They say that the Emperor's interest in Han ways, trusting Han officials, and ignoring our traditional customs at will, is all because of her."

"Who has been saying such things?" The Empress demanded of her younger sister.

"The Grand Concubine and the Great Grand Concubine both said it." The Empress shook her head and sighed. "The Grand Concubine is still grieving for the death of her son Prince Xiang, naturally she is not pleased with the Precious Concubine...."

"But she is half a southern barbarian," Lady Jin chimed in spite of herself. She rose to give emphasis to her words.

"It's her southern ways that bewitched the Emperor and the Empress Dowager! She with her harp playing and her painting! Now if the Fourth Imperial Son is named Crown Prince then, my dear, how long do you think you can last as empress?"

Lady Shuhui quickly cut her off. "Stuff and nonsense. He's already deposed one empress; he wouldn't dare do it again. The Empress Dowager won't allow it. She's still one of us."

Lady Jin said angrily, "I can't bear the thought of the Fourth Imperial Son becoming Crown Prince. We Manchus have conquered all under Heaven. How can the blood-line be tainted by allowing the son of half a barbarian to take the throne! There are so many Manchu ladies in the harem who could produce worthy sons, yet our bellies betray us!"

The Empress glanced at Lady Kang who had not joined the conversation and chided the others, "What are you jabbering about!"

Lady Jin quickly laid a comforting hand on Lady Kang's shoulder and said in her straightforward if thoughtless manner, "Don't you worry, my dear. Your family comes from the banner people. I would sooner see your son as Crown Prince."

Lady Kang got to her feet, her face expressionless. In a reverent voice she said, "It grows late. Your Majesty should retire. Lady Jin, we should withdraw."

Lady Shuhui also rose to take her leave. As she left, she whispered urgently to her sister, "You must bear a son! If it happens before the Crown Prince is named, then the Fourth Imperial Son's chances will be dashed, and nobody can take your place as empress."

The Empress replied, "You better leave, and speak no more nonsense."

However, when the ladies in waiting had turned down her bedcovers and drawn the drapes and Kunning Palace sank into a nocturnal silence, the Empress stiffled her sobs with her pillow. She was alone. There was no need to maintain the dignity of empress. At that moment she was a poor, lonely woman fearful of her future....

2

On the fifteenth day of the eleventh month a grand audience took place. The route from Daqing Gate leading to the Hall of Supreme Harmony was lined with sentinels carrying ceremonial clubs. Bands of musicians played before the hall. Bells and drums sounded from the top of Meridian Gate as princes, nobles, the entire court comprising officials both civil and military, together with foreign ambassadors filed in to pay homage to the Emperor. Afterwards, a ceremonial cup of tea was served to the courtiers. Regal music signalled the end of the audience. As a rule these grand audiences were held once a month mainly to show off the power and splendour of the Emperor. Being a hard-working monarch determined to stamp out slothfulness at court, Shunzhi held grand audiences more often. Nor did the young monarch permit this display to interfere with the daily business of government. Instead of retiring after the grand audience, officials of the various ministries would proceed along pathways and corridors guarded by soldiers armed with broad swords to the Hall of Heavenly Purity as they were summoned. Courtiers walked with heads bowed, eyes fixed upon the line between the skirt of the robe and the boots of the man in front.

The fifty-six-year-old Wang Chongjian, academician of the Palace Historiographic Academy, was a portly, jovial fellow, often likened to the Happy Buddha. On this occasion he was out of sorts. He could not keep his eyes on the court boots in front of him, whose movements seemed as jerky and unnatural as those of a marionette. Though he tried to calm himself, he could not control the wild beating of his heart, or his uneven, rasping breath. He racked his brain to remember who had witnessed his indiscretion.

Grand Academician Jin Zhijun obviously overheard. For hadn't he shown his distress also? Even the usually impassive Imperial Astronomer Tang Jo-Wang had sighed and crossed himself. Fu Yijian, who was in Jin Zhijun's company, on the other hand, did not seem to notice. However, it was the three men in front of him that he feared the most: the Lords Sukesaha, Aobai, and Ren Kepu, prosecutors in the corruption case involving the imperial examinations.

He remembered that Lord Sukesaha had scowled at him and turned to Ren Kepu; obviously to ask the latter something. Ren Kepu had turned a reproachful eye at Wang and nodded in spite of himself. Then the two noblemen had turned to him and his son. Aobai's gaze was full of menace, while Sukesaha grinned maliciously, showing a row of sharp teeth. How could I have lost control, he sighed. Am I in danger? In the tense atmosphere after the corruption trial, when every Han official felt vulnerable, he wondered whether his slip had put himself and his son in jeopardy. The more he thought, the more nervous he became. But there was no help for it now. All he could do was brazen it out.

Wang Chongjian followed the others into the Presence and having made his abeisance joined the ranks of the academicians. When his eyes met those of his son Wang Xi, he could sense the latter's disquietude.

The provincial governor of Henan was making a presentation. On his knees, he spoke in a loud voice that echoed through the hall:

"A miraculous herb has been found at Songshan in Henan Province. Its discovery is an omen of great good fortune. I am now presenting it...." He paused and raised an elaborately carved wooden box together with a red envelop high above his head, waiting for a eunuch to take it.

From his throne, Shunzhi pondered the official.

"Good harvests and happy people are the only good omens we recognize. Your duty is to maintain peace and harmony among our people; not to occupy yourself with frivolity. Go!"

The provincial governor hurriedly pressed his forehead to the ground then bowed his way back into the ranks of officials. Only then did he dare dab the sweat that beaded his brow.

The court proceeded with the daily business of government. The atmosphere became less tense and Wang Chongjian exchanged a look of relief with his son.

However when it came time for the Six Offices of Scrutiny to present their petitions, Shunzhi unexpectedly summoned Yin Yingjie. "You will present your report on the imperial examinations in the south now."

Yin Yingjie knelt and read his report out loud:

"Corruption at the imperial examinations in the south exceeds that of Shuntian in both depth and scope. The chief adjudicators Fang You and Qian Kaizong are the principal culprits. One Fang Zhangyue, who was passed as a provincial graduate, is the fifth son of the Imperial Superintendant of Instruction Fang Gongqian who has familial ties with the chief adjudicator Fang You. Bribery and collusion were involved. I pray Your Majesty to order an investigation." Yin Yingjie continued after a pause, "The prosecution of corruption in Shuntian in the north restored the people's trust. Likewise, corruption in the south must not be allowed to persist. When the adjudicators Fang and Qian left for home after the examinations, they were jeered at and stoned. This gives some indication of the indignation of the people. The south is the seat of learning and the intelligentsia must be treated with care...."

Shunzhi was a commanding figure in full regalia. With a slight frown he spoke in an even tone:

"In a unified nation the south should not be different from the north. We have long been aware of the existence of corruption in the south, and we are grateful for your report. As for the adjudicators Fang and Qian, whom we personally admonished to exercise their duties wisely and to discover able men for our court...." His voice rose sharply in anger, "...and this is how they have acquitted themselves!"

He handed Yin's report to a eunuch and turned to the Grand Chamberlain and the palace minister on duty.

"Let Fang You and Qian Kaizong be dismissed from our service, and the provincial graduate Fang Zhangyue be apprehended and brought to the capital for questioning. Furthermore, our governor-general of the south is empowered to conduct a full enquiry into corruption and to arrest all persons implicated."

Although what was said could not be immediately heard by all those present, when the Emperor's decree was read aloud by the Grand Chamberlain moments later, a tremor ran through the hall. The atmosphere became tense once more. The Han officials quaked in their boots, as though a great black cloud had descended upon them.

The scandal of the northern examinations were barely six months old. Now a new scandal threatened to further diminish their position. Everyone was anxiously peering over their shoulder, for nearly half of the Han officials at court were implicated one way or another. The execution of Li Zhenye, Zhang Wopu and the others seemed to have intimidated the intelligentsia. And the reputation of the remaining Han officials had suffered. Already under the thumbs of ignorant and unschooled Manchus, they could expect to be more down-trodden than before. That was obvious from the triumphant looks of the Lords Suoni, Sukesaha, Aobai, not to mention the sneering Prince Jidu and Prince Changahdai. Would all Han officials be dismissed from court?

The Emperor's pronouncement was a heavy blow to Wang Chongjian and his son Wang Xi. The older man turned quite pale and trembled uncontrollably. A year ago, on a visit to the palace academies the Emperor had complimented Wang Xi on his oratory skills. As a mark of his appreciation Shunzhi named Wang Xi academician of the Palace Academy for the Advancement of Literature, "... in recognition of his abilities and integrity". At that time Wang Chongjian was already an academician of the Palace Historiographic Academy. Thus both father and son held important posts in the academies. Why would Han officials personally honoured by the Emperor be fearful, reasoned Wang Chongjian?

After the business of the day had been concluded, just as the assemblage drew a breath of relief there was another upheaval. According to custom the official in charge of protocol, who kept an eagle eye open for any misdemeanor or infractions against the strict rules of protocol at audience was called upon to report whether or not any were found. The Officer of Protocol for the day, Ren Kepu, stepped forward.

"Officer of Protocol Ren Kepu reports that prior to the grand audience this day, in the presence of officials of court and foreign ambassadors filing through Zhendu Gate, Academician Wang Chongjian gave vent to an unseemly display of emotion as the ambassador of Korea passed. I beseech Your Majesty's judgement on this serious breach of protocol." Shunzhi demanded details.

Lord Aobai stepped forward and spoke in an even voice:

"Your slave witnessed this incident. The courtiers had just gone through Zhendu Gate when the ambassadors filed past. The ambassador of Korea was in full regalia including marten fur ear-shields. As he passed, Wang Chongjian pointing at the ambassador said to his son Wang Xi, 'That was the way they dressed at the court of Ming.' He was visibly distressed. His son also appeared to be deeply moved. Your slave believes this incident goes beyond a breach of protocol. It smacks of treason! The Wangs, father and son, have been honoured by Great Qing, yet their hearts belong to Ming."

Wang Chongjian and his son Wang Xi quickly stepped forward and knelt before the Emperor.

Shunzhi faced them angrily. "How do you plead?" he demanded.

Wang Xi spoke quickly: "Your Majesty, your slave is at fault, but my father is innocent. Let Your Majesty's wrath fall upon my head alone."

Lord Suoni intervened: "Your slave observed that others were also involved. Grand Academicians Fu Yijian and Jin Zhijun were present. The former abstained from reporting the incident and the latter expressed similar sentiments. Imperial Astronomer Tang Jo-Wang also showed sympathy. I beseech Your Majesty to deal with these persons as well."

The assembled Han officials were aghast. Suddenly the most renowned and honoured members of the court were being accused of serious crimes. Everyone including the eunuchs and servants trembled. Silence descended upon the Hall of Heavenly Purity, waiting for the storm to break.

Shunzhi's eyes travelled from one end of the great hall to the other, then lifting his hand he said, "Leave me!" He rose to his feet indicating the audience was over. The assemblage fell to their knees as he departed.

Fulin arrived at the Hall of Mental Cultivation at mid morning, tired and hungry after the grand audience and the daily audience. Breakfast was laid before him at once. This morning's meal had been prepared by a famous chef sent to him by Lang Tingzuo, governor-general of the south. Fulin had been looking forward to southern dishes, but he was too hungry. He was also troubled by the problems encountered that morning to do them justice.

Fulin laid down his bowl absently and glanced at a silver dish of milk curd.

Just then the chief eunuch followed by four young eunuchs entered, each carrying a silver platter, which they presented by turn. Fulin wiped his mouth on a white silk napkin, leaned forward and glanced at the proffered trays. His eyes widened imperceptibly at the red cards that filled the platters.

It was the custom that on certain fixed days the Emperor would receive courtiers for private audience or consultation. Those who wished to be received had to submit their cards while the Emperor was having his morning meal. The nobility and those connected to the royal house would use a red card; high-ranking civic and military officials, green cards; high-ranking officials from the provinces, pink cards. On each card would be recorded the bearer's name, place of origin, family background, age, rank, qualifications and any imperial honours.

Fulin examined the cards at random. Aside from a few green ones from members of the council and officials of various departments, the rest were all red. Not a single Han official had submitted his card. His thoughts returned to the morning audience, and he was disturbed.

Manchu officials trooped into the Presence one after the other. The last to be announced was Duke An, named Yuele.

After Yuele prostrated himself, he was offered a seat. Tea was served. Yuele observed the weariness that the young Emperor took pains to hide, and he understood why he had been kept waiting till the last. Although he was connected to the imperial family, Yuele was not close to the Emperor. Yet whenever there was a crisis or a difficult policy decision the two men came together, joined by an unspoken bond. They also shared a love of ancient Chinese culture. But for the constraints of their respective positions imposed they might have been friends. Though their conversation was always strangely impersonal to the bystander, each understood the other perfectly.

"Your Majesty, did they all come?" Yuele smilingly asked.

"Of course!" Yuele's question came as a welcome relief. "It's as though they planned it beforehand. They came to pledge their loyalty and to denounce the southern barbarians. Of course the old ways of Nurhachi and Abahai were recalled and, using that as an excuse, some even begged permission to go into Shandong and the south to appropriate land and also to persecute runaway slaves! It seems the Manchu aristocracy are forming cliques for their private interests!"

Yuele fixed the Emperor with his eyes and spoke solemnly:

"I agree the reference to Your Majesty's illustrious ancestors was an excuse to pursue personal interests. Your grandfather hated the Han and particularly distrusted the intelligentsia. Many were slaughtered. However, your father reversed that thinking. Instead he gave Han officials and generals important posts, and thus succeeded in conquering all under Heaven."

"True. To govern successfully there must be laws that are constantly renewed and changed to suit varying circumstances. Take the practice of land appropriation for instance. In the beginning, there was turmoil. The people abandoned the land to escape the wars, and famine resulted. And the generals who came east had no livelihood. Under those circumstances it was practical to seize land for pasture and the production of food. However, we are now at peace and the people have returned to their land. To seize their land now would cause widespread discontent. These men cannot see beyond the tips of their noses. Concerned only for their own personal gain, they have no conception of the larger picture, of nationhood. They know nothing about government and are unwilling to learn. Governing cannot be left in such hands. On the other hand, the Han officials, though learned, are not necessarily loyal to us.... It is a difficult situation...."

"Your Majesty," Yuele chose his words carefully, "is one who recalls the Ming less loyal than one who does not?" Fulin blinked uncertainly, then responded softly, "Imperial Brother, pray continue."

"Your Majesty, the number of red cards submitted today is an indication that the Manchu nobles scheme to oust Han officials from court. The incident at this morning's audience was an excuse. The corruption of the imperial examinations at Shuntian was another. Your Majesty must keep these things in mind."

Fulin flushed. He said:

"These annual examinations are intended to search out able men for public office. Yet the adjudicators have used them for selfish ends. These activities must be severely dealt with to gain the people's trust."

"Corruption at the imperial examinations is indeed a troublesome matter that must be corrected. However, the search for wise men has never been successfully accomplished with sword and club. There is the human factor that must be considered. Beheading or banishment places the offence on the same footing as treason. Is it not too harsh?"

Fulin's brows arched, on the verge of rebuttal, but he changed his mind. Yuele was well aware of the Emperor's quick temper, yet he continued in the same amiable tone, "Has Your Majesty noticed Han officials attend morning audiences like sheep led to slaughter ever since the corruption at the imperial examinations was exposed. The Manchu nobles have used their investigations as an excuse to implicate so many persons that none dare speak. If the corruption in the south is not handled carefully, the result could be disastrous. Your Majesty must weigh the matter with care...."

"Advise us, Imperial Brother?"

"It would be wise to err on the side of compasssion rather than harshness."

"What!" Fulin struck the table with the palm of his hand as he shot to his feet, his eyes flashing fire. Yuele had touched a nerve.

"Please forgive my bluntness, Your Majesty," Yuele continued unperturbed. "Soon Duke Xin will march on to Yunnan and Guizhou, and the great task of unification will be completed. However, a large part of his support will come from troops under Han generals and Han banners. Before the country is stabilized, it would be wise to show compassion. This is my counsel...."

Fulin bit his lip, and the anger that flared a moment ago died. He would not allow anything to jeopardize unification, the glittering and cherished jewel in his crown that he coveted above all else. For a moment he was lost in thought. When he turned to Yuele a smile creased his lips. Lowering his voice he said, "Imperial Brother, there is something I would want you to do and it must be treated with utmost secrecy...." The two men spoke in hushed voices, then laughed companionably and exchanged looks like two children planning mischief.

Fulin left his palace just before noon. Though it was mid-winter the sun was pleasantly warm. It was his custom to pay his daily respects to his mother at this time, a ritual he enjoyed. In fact the day was not complete without visiting his mother.

Before he reached the gate of the Empress Dowager's Palace, the eunuch Wu Liangfu reported the Empress Dowager had gone to Yanshou Pavilion in her gardens. Why not surprise her by going through Lansheng Gate? Fulin was delighted with the suggestion. The Empress Dowager would never dream the Emperor would arrive through a side entrance. When they had reached the gate, Fulin had ano ther idea. He signalled his attendants to remain quietly outside, while he tiptoed into the garden alone and hid behind some shrubbery.

Fulin peered at his mother through the leafless branches of lilac and crabapple trees.

Seated in an armchair placed on the verandah in front of the pavilion the Empress Dowager basked in the warmth of the sunlight. Her jet-black hair was loose, and Lady Dongeh was combing it with an elephant bone comb, now rising on her feet, now squatting in rhythm with her strokes. The Empress Dowager spoke in her slow measured fashion:

" ...Grouse live in tall grass. A horseman passing would startle it into flight. But it can only fly a short distance before it becomes breathless and has to come down again. Then it burrows in the grass thinking it's invisible because it can't see the humans. That's when they're caught ... alive." "Imperial Mother, when will you show us this wonderful sight? It's perfect weather for a winter hunt, and I promise to catch some juicy grouse for you." Lady Dongeh prattled merrily as she knotted the Empress Dowager's hair into a large chignon at the nape of her neck and fastened it with a crystal hairpin.

"The grouse you sent me last night were delicious. They must have come from a pine wood, for only birds fed on pine and cedar seeds have that special flavour," said the Empress Dowager.

"Imperal Mother is absolutely right. My young brother caught them in the pine forest at Western Hills...." Taking a round European mirror, Lady Dongeh held it up for the Empress Dowager to examine her handiwork. The Empress Dowager smiled her approval, "You can do no wrong."

As the two women chatted, two small boys in robes, leather

boots, and armed with miniature bows and arrows, swords and daggers ran to them, their armament jingling.

"Imperial Grandmother! Imperial Mother! We've been shooting!" they chorused. The Emperor's second and third sons, aged five and four respectively, were active children who revelled in their maleness with an unself-conscious innocence. The two women chuckled. The Empress Dowager stretched out her arms to them. "And how many times did you hit the bull's eye?" she asked.

The Third Imperial Son smiled shyly. The Second Imperial Son piped, "I didn't do so well. I got two out of five shots, but Third Brother got three."

"You both did well," Lady Dongeh exclaimed. "By the time you're ten you'll hit the bull's eye every time. And here's a reward for your marksmanship...." She unfastened two small silk purses embroidered with silver thread that hung from a button on the front of her robe. The two small boys rushed to her with whoops of joy.

"The purses you make are the daintiest in the Palace," observed the Empress Dowager to Lady Dongeh as, with deft fingers, she fastened them one each to a button on the boys' robes. "Too good for children really," she added.

"They are not wasted, Imperial Mother," Lady Dongeh countered with a smile. "Excellence in horsemanship and archery, the traditional skills of our ancestors, must not go unrecognized. Even one as ignorant as I understands that...." Then she called for the nurses, for the children were not wearing outer jackets and might catch a chill.

A nurse appeared at once and kneeling offered the appropriate garments. Lady Dongeh helped the two boys into jackets and caps and, taking a handkerchief pinned to her robe, she gently wiped the sweat from their brow. The Empress Dowager watched this byplay through narrowed eyes, nodding imperceptibly. She took out two small gold ingots shaped like plum blossoms and gave one to each of the boys, saying, "These are to keep in your purses. Now remember what your Imperial Mother said: be worthy of your forefathers."

In his hiding place Fulin's heart swelled with pride, so that when he stepped into view it was as a man, and not as emperor surrounded by ceremony.

Lady Dongeh was about to withdraw with the children, but the Empress Dowager bade her stay. "The nurse can take the children. Our Imperial Son is no stranger to you. He won't bite."

The Empress Dowager seldom cracked jokes, but today she was especially happy. Fulin too was in a happy mood. Lady Dongeh darted him a querulous look and turned away blushing.

As usual Fulin related everything that happened during audience to his Mother and, as usual, she listened without interruption. Only Lady Dongeh standing apart felt out of place.

When Fulin finished, the Empress Dowager remarked, "Our Imperial Son governs wisely and does honour to the ancestors. May the country prosper in peace." Turning to Lady Dongeh she said, "And what do you say?"

Lady Dongeh bowed. "Imperial Mother, your obedient child is unworthy of commenting on matters of state."

The Empress Dowager nodded her approval and addressed Fulin once more, "A wise monarch takes notice of petitions, thus avoiding error..." she paused, then continued carefully, "Duke An, Yuele, has served the nation long and well. Now that the men who helped establish the dynasty have gone to their rest, is it not time to honour Yuele with the title of prince?" Fulin was delighted that in this regard he and his mother were in complete accord. "That has long been my plan," he said.

"That is good," the Empress Dowager smiled, her gaze resting lovingly on her son. "You ought to visit Kunning Palace in the afternoon."

"Imperial Mother," Fulin responded with a mischievous

smile, "I have important matters of state to attend at Yingtai in the afternoon."

"Imperial Mother," Lady Dongeh bowed her head and, reddening, said in a low voice, "His Majesty usually studies, practises calligraphy or archery in the afternoons and does not attend matters of state."

"Who said so?" Fulin retorted, but was smiling when he turned once more to his mother. "I have summoned Wang Chongjian and his son, Fu Yijian and Mafa Tang Jo-Wang." The Empress Dowager searched her son's face suspiciously at first, then broke into a smile.

"You are maturing," she said leaning back in her chair, "and we are pleased. However, go when you have finished your business at Yingtai." And in a softer voice she added, "Never forget that you are Emperor, not an ordinary husband or father...."

"Yes," Fulin quickly responded, "I will obey the Imperial Mother's command."

As Lady Dongeh saw him out of Yanshou Pavilion, Fulin moved closer and whispered, "How dare you sent me away to Kunning Palace to the Empress! Tonight when I come to Chengqian Palace you will pay for it!"

A retort rose to Black Pearl's lips, but before she could utter it Fulin was gone. She was left to ponder the difficulties that beset a wise concubine. Had she turned she would have caught the Empress Dowager's troubled gaze resting upon her. For the older woman was also wrestling with her heart.

When Wang Chongjian and his son received the Emperor's summons the first thing that occurred to them was the incident at the morning audience, and they quaked. However, the eunuch who came for them did not seem hostile. With trembling hearts they seated themselves in their official sedan chairs and were swiftly carried to the West Gate of the Forbidden City. Fu Yijian, Jin Zhijun, Tang Jo-Wang, Li Wei, and Yisangah had already arrived. Aside from Tang Jo-Wang and Yisangah, the others were all Han officials. Of the assemblage only Yisangah was not involved in that morning's controversy. The men acknowledged one another but were in no mood to converse.

Guided by eunuchs, they passed through the West Gate, skirted a small lake on which a first thin layer of ice was forming, to a stone dyke decorated with an elaborately carved stone balustrade. From here the yellow and green tiled roofs of Yingtai could be seen rising from a dark fringe of pine and cedar like an enchanted tower gleaming in the sun. They did not approach the tower but followed a cobblestone path between two pavilions lined with grotesque rockery, overshadowed by pine and cedar. They seemed to have been plunged into a wilderness where the only sounds were the sighing of the wind and their own footsteps.

They came to a narrow green gate set in high walls over the top of which one caught a glimpse of roofs and two tall Tong trees. The gate was so narrow that it would allow only one man of Wang Chongjian's girth to pass at a time. Did this bode good or ill?

The door opened onto a small garden scented with the delicate perfume of winter-plum flowers and surrounded by artificial mountains made from rocks from Lake Tai. Under the eaves of the three rooms to the north was a plaque that read "Tranquil Chamber". A similar plaque under the eave of the room opposite read "Tong-Shaded Library". The eunuchs retreated to stand before the door and under the verandahs. The men glanced at one another uncertainly.

"His Majesty approaches!" In a moment Shunzhi appeared escorted by a handful of young eunuchs. On this occasion he wore a felt cap with a red topknot and a marten fur tunic over a dark green silk robe, fastened at the waist by a yellow sash. His feet were shod in a pair of thick-soled boots. His informal attire and benign demeanour reassured the courtiers that all was well as they fell to their knees.

"We seldom have the opportunity to meet privately with My Lords," Fulin said by way of greeting. "You gentlemen are all distinguished scholars whom we greatly admire. Let this be a meeting of minds. There will be no ceremony."

He led the way into the library. The others, bowing to the waist, followed into a room unlike any other they had ever seen. The walls were lined with shelves neatly stacked with books. Between these were high cupboards in which were displayed a dazzling collection of antiques. Scattered throughout the room were chest-high vases containing scrolls. Fragrant incense spiralled from the hot embers in braziers scattered round the place. Fulin was amused by the men's obvious amazement.

"Let there be no ceremony," he repeated and ordered tea.

The servants presented each guest with a steaming cup.

"This tea is made of pine seeds and a variety of herbs, known as Sanqing tea in the palace. Do you like it?" enquired Fulin. His guests sipped, carefully savouring it. Yisangah was the first to break the silence.

"Your Majesty, it is the most delicious tea I have ever tasted!"

"How does it compare to milk tea?" teased Fulin.

"Each is delicious in its own way," replied Yisangah.

"There is a sweet perfume to this tea, like a fine wine," offered Li Wei.

"I agree," said Fulin. "Among friends a good tea is like a fine wine!"

Everyone laughed. Today the Emperor was in an amiable mood. His naturalness won the hearts of these learned men, and the atmosphere became relaxed and open.

Tang Jo-Wang said, "If it pleases Your Majesty, would you let your old servant have the recipe that I too may prepare it?"

"If I had known you liked it sooner," Fulin countered, "I would have sent you a supply to last thirty years!" Tang Jo-Wang also laughed till his white brows and whiskers shook. "Ah, but your aged servant does not have thirty years to look forward to."

Fulin turned to Jin Zhijun and remarked, "If I recall correctly, My Lord is the same age as Mafa, which makes you sixty-six? Yet you both are so youthful. My Lords must be contented men! "

The old men bowed and responded in unison, "Your Majesty is too kind!"

Fulin pointed to a long table set under the south window and said, "There are some scrolls of calligraphy and paintings dating from Tang, Song and Ming dynasties. My Lords please examine them and give me your assessment of their true worth."

All the men were connoisseurs and needed no further prompting to examine the contents of the table. Fulin stood apart watching the expressions playing across their faces. Tang Jo-Wang stayed aloof. "Why don't you join them, Mafa?" Fulin enquired softly.

"Your Majesty knows I am not versed in Chinese art."

A thought came to Fulin and, winking at the older man mischievously, he led him to the table set in the centre of the room, smoothed out a sheet of paper, selected a brush from its stand, dipped it in ink, and said conspiratorially, "Mafa, I will draw someone for you!"

"Your Majesty, this is wonderful! So alike, yet so unlike! That must be the secret of Chinese art!" Tang Jo-Wang's exclamation brought the others to his side.

Fulin smilingly showed the picture to the others without comment.

"Why it's Academician Wang!" they cried.

Indeed it was a sketch of Wang Xi. The lines of his robes were done in bold strokes but the pose and attitude were exactly right. And the face was finely detailed. The men compared the picture to the man and were full of praise for the Emperor's artistry.

Wang Xi fell to his knees and begged for the picture.

"No," replied Fulin. "I am not skilled at portraiture. Landscapes are more my forte." He took up the brush again, thought a moment and with a few strokes produced a landscape of simple elegance. The assemblage was loud in its praise.

"Your Majesty's picture contains the principles of Song and Yuan painting!" Jin Zhijun opined, stroking his beard.

"Your Majesty is an able soldier but a skilled artist as well. A most astonishing combination of talents!" sighed Fu Yijian. Fulin turned to Wang Chongjian and asked, "Chongjian, you are a connoisseur of painting. What is your judgement?"

Wang Chongjian, bowing deeply, replied, "Your Majesty has succeeded where others fail. Yours is a gift, unlike any other...." Fulin handed the picture to him and said, "Then this little picture is yours, as a memento...." Wang Chongjian was so surprised that it took him a moment to gather his wits and fall on his knees to accept the gift. Fulin then turned to Wang Xi and said, "You are young and will serve us a long time. Therefore the gift goes to the father rather than the son." Wang Xi reddened and falling to his knees thanked the Emperor for his largesse.

"Are the scrolls My Lords examined authentic?" enquired Fulin.

The scholars agreed that the Emperor's collection was completely authentic and priceless. Fulin then ordered several scrolls of calligraphy written in the cursive hand to be unrolled. Jin Zhijun's face darkened when he examined them, while the others were full of praise for the strength and fluidity of the brushstrokes. Only Tang Jo-Wang remained impassive.

Fulin said, "This is art of the highest order ... the handiwork of Emperor Chongzhen...." Silence fell upon the room. Fulin calmly unrolled another scroll himself and, gazing at it intently, sighed, "That a brilliant emperor should come to such a tragic end makes one weep...."

Wang Chongjian felt the blood rush to his head. Jin Zhijun bowed his white head in sorrow.

Fu Yijian spoke, "In taking the Empire the present regime avenged the honour of the Ming Emperor." Yisangah added, "Just so! For Great Qing took the capital not from the Ming Dynasty but from the rebels. Therefore, the reluctance of the remnants of the previous regime to serve Great Qing is most ill advised."

Fulin laughed. "Come, this is not the time for discussing old grievances. Bring lights!"

The servants busied themselves lighting lanterns and candles before inviting those assembled into the Tranquil Chamber. Fulin led the way across the garden. Inside, several tables laden with food and wine had been laid out. Fulin invited his guests to be seated.

"Tonight we drink in these charming surroundings which should inspire memorable poems from each of you. He who fails will have to down three cups of wine!"

The Emperor's remarks were greeted by applause. Tang Jo-Wang bowed and said, "Your aged servant begs to be excused as this is a day of abstinence in my religion."

"Ah, that is too bad," Fulin answered. He asked for a fan personally painted and inscribed with his signature and seal to be brought. Handing it to Tang Jo-Wang as a memento, Fulin allowed the old man to withdraw.

Yisangah laughed saying, "Perhaps Mafa Tang was scared off by having to compose poetry." Li Wei added, "And the priceless fan painted by His Majesty was probably beyond his appreciation."

Fulin nodded and said with a sigh, "Mafa Tang is our loyal servant. Though well versed in astronomy and mathematics, and a fervent believer of his god, he has little understanding of our ways. It's a pity...."

Taking this opportunity Wang Chongjian and his son knelt before the Emperor and said, "We, father and son, breached protocol in this morning's audience, an offence that deserves death. Nevertheless, we beg Your Majesty's mercy."

Fulin's eyes went from the kneeling pair to the others and responded thoughtfully, "An official of Ming who does not recall the former regime with nostalgia could not have been loyal. We understand this."

The Emperor's reaction moved Wang Chongjian and his son to the verge of tears. All the others also fell to their knees.

"My Lords, what are you doing?' exclaimed Fulin.

It was Jin Zhijun who tremblingly responded on all their behalf:

"Your Majesty has moved us with his graciousness; Zhijun will never forget...."

"My Lords, please take your seats!" Fulin once more invited his guests to enter the Tranquil Chamber. However, the plum blossoms in the lamp-light and their intoxicating fragrance caused him to linger among the trees a moment longer. Almost absently he murmured four lines of poetry:

Lamps hung high amid sparse plum branches
Shed light on the banquet table beneath.
Are these the flamed twigs of plum
Or the burnt-out wicks of lamps?

Jin Zhijun loudly applauded the poem and then, catching himself, bowed to apologize for being momentarily carried away by enthusiasm.

Fulin laughed happily. For this was exactly the relaxed atmosphere he strove for. Saying that he had long heard of Wang Xi's skill at poetry, Fulin called on him to improvise.

Wang Xi pondered a moment and began. It was now the Emperor's turn to applaud.

"Come, we must write this down," he cried and led the way indoors. Jin Zhijun's eyes never strayed from the Emperor. To Fu Yijian he whispered, "The Emperor also has the air of a man of culture. All under Heaven will soon forget he is descended from barbarians...."

Fu Yijian glared at him but, nevertheless, nodded in agreement.

3

The snow drifts were high outside the crude bamboo gate to Xiong Cilu's dwelling.

It had been snowing all night but at dawn it stopped. Blowing on his hands for warmth, Xiong Cilu took up his broom to sweep a path from the door of his cottage and out through the gate. The snow glowed pink, with pools of pale blue shadows where the early morning light did not reach. At this time of day the untouched snow seemed especially pure. As Xiong Cilu turned his face to the sun, his friend Xu Yuanwen, muffled in a heavy coat and hat, was coming toward him.

Xiong Cilu and Xu Yuanwen met three years ago at a farewell banquet for Loo Jian. At first meeting neither had impressed the other. Xiong Cilu despised Xu Yuanwen's effete affectations, while Xu Yuanwen was repelled by Xiong's asceticism. This was understandable as the two men's backgrounds and experiences were exact opposites.

Xiong Cilu, styled Jingxiu, was born to an intellectual family of Hubei Province. His father died when he was a child and he was brought up by his mother in genteel poverty. His mother was a hard taskmaster Indeed it was largely due to his mother's persistence that he was able to pursue learning and acquire wisdom. Three years ago, it was again at his mother's urging that he came to the capital to broaden his horizons. Although he was admired and even respected for his learning, many found his stoicism and self-absorption off-putting. Thus he acquired few friends. He found employment in a few schools, and much of what he earned was sent home to support his aging mother. The rest was used to purchase a two-roomed cottage to the south of the capital between Longquan Temple and Taiqing Nunnery. There he lived quietly alone, coming and going as he chose, pursuing his studies, practising calligraphy, composing poetry when the spirit moved him, and gardening. He was content. Those who knew him nicknamed him "the Gentleman in the rough cloth robe".

Xu Yuanwen's antecedents were quite different. He was scion of a wealthy southern family which produced a number of notable scholars over several generations. They tended to inter-marry with families with similar roots. Xu Yuanwen's uncle, his mother's brother, was none other than the famous man of letters, Gu Yanwu.

Xu Yuanwen, styled Gongsu, was one of three brothers, all of whom were known for their brilliance. Xu Yuanwen earned the reputation of child prodigy by attempting the imperial examinations at the age of twelve. As a young man he cut a romantic and dashing figure that was all the rage among the smart young dilettantes.

If it hadn't been for a chance encounter they would not have become friends for they had nothing in common.

One year during the Qingming Festival, Xu Yuanwen and some friends met in Longquan Temple to improvise poetry. It was a jolly gathering. However, on his way home Xu Yuanwen was caught in a sudden downpour. He ran to a cottage nearby and hammered on the gate, asking for shelter. To his surprise the man who answered his knock was Xiong Cilu. The two men recognized one another at once, and Xu was invited in.

The small garden into which he was admitted astonished Xu Yuanwen. Though it was early spring, the air was still cold, and the city and its suburbs were still in the sullen grip of winter; this small garden was full of greenery. The sparsely furnished front room into which he was ushered was scrupulously clean. Though its walls were bare, table, chairs and stove were placed in exactly the right spot. The walls and windows were lined with tubs and porcelain containers of green grass. Xu Yuanwen was dazzled by their beauty and variety. Xiong Cilu had a passion for grass, and Xu Yuanwen's obvious admiration pleased him. And so, he invited the latter into the inner room to view his favourite, a grass called Cuiyun or Jade Cloud. Xu Yuanwen noticed at once that brush, ink and paper were spread out on the desk. But it was an old dilapidated chair with an opened umbrella fastened to it that intrigued him. Obviously, the owner had been writing under the shelter when he was interrupted. Xiong Cilu pointed at the roof casually and remarked, "It leaks."

On the desk was a pot of Cuiyun grass. Beside it were two small bowls one containing white peas and the other black peas. Xu Yuanwen picked up one of the bowls and examined it curiously.

"What does this represent?" He wanted to know.

Xiong Cilu shook his head and explained,

"This was the methods the sages used to discipline their minds. After reading or writing they would meditate. Whenever a good thought came to mind a white pea was dropped into a bowl, and when an unworthy thought occurred a black pea was dropped. At first there were more black peas than white. Gradually there were more white peas than black. Later still the black peas disappeared altogether. When there are no peas at all then perfection has been achieved. I am still far from that stage as you can see." He picked up another bowl to show Xu Yuanwen, who could see for himself that there were as many white peas as black peas.

Xu Yuanwen admired the man's perseverence in spite of himself.

Xu Yuanwen stayed until the rain stopped and the westering sun splashed across the rain-soaked garden where the grass glistened like a jewelled carpet. There was such peace and serenity that he found it difficult to tear himself away.

Days later Xiong Cilu was invited to Xu's home. The large and imposing residence was a far cry from his own humble dwelling. However, the study with its scrolls and pictures was a place of quiet and pleasing elegance. The two talked together over cups of tea. Xiong Cilu was particularly drawn to the inscriptions on an inkstone, tea-pot and even a porcelain pillow, done in various styles by his host. Moreover, each inscription showed Xu Yuanwen's personality in a different light: now serious, now wryly humorous. Xiong Cilu was especially taken with the inscription on the pillow.

Sweetness, drunkeness, tenderness,
All are empty dreams

It struck a chord within him. However, he refrained from any demonstration of enthusiasm for it was not his way. Nevertheless he had to admit the frivolous young dandy had hidden depths.

Xu Yuanwen chuckled knowingly, and Xiong Cilu's usually expressionless countenance softened. The two men had finally discovered some common ground, and a friendship began. However, one was rich and the other poor. The impoverished one was proud and honest, and would not take advantage of the friendship. He would not accept any financial aid and refused many invitations. Xu was not offended and would visit Xiong's cottage from time to time where they would spend the day happily together, drinking and making poetry. Afterwards, each retreated to his separate world. However, the friendship between the two men remained.

They had last met in the ninth month on the Festival of Double Ninth and Xiong was surprised to see him again so soon. Xu Yuanwen came to the point of his visit at once.

"Soon the country will be unified. With peace, the state will need many learned men. Does my brother not have ambitions to make something of himself?"

Xiong Cilu countered, "Does that mean you are contemplating some official post?" Xu Yuanwen laughed out loud, "And why not? As the old adage goes, the rise and fall of empire is everybody's business. Therefore, why not ours? If men of learning such as us can do something to help the people live in peace and prosperity, and in the process earn our page in history, where is the harm? This year the corruption at the imperial examinations at Shuntian resulted in the execution of Li Zhenye and Zhang Wopu. The Emperor is bound to deal harshly with the new scandals surrounding the examinations in the south as well. This is our chance to get ahead!"

Although he was interested, Xiong Cilu would not show it.

"Some friends are coming to my house to discuss this, why not join us?" Xu urged. Xiong Cilu pondered a moment and answered, "I must think about this. Today I really cannot spare the time."

"Oh! Are you busy at the school?"

"No. I am going to pray at Haihui Temple outside the city."

"It's just stopped snowing and it's bitterly cold. Why not put it off?"

"A man's life must follow a certain set path, from which he must not deviate because of weather, be it hot or cold...." Seeing that his friend's asceticism was roused, Xu Yuanwen laughingly retreated, saying,

"Never mind. We will meet another time...."

When Xiong Cilu left Haihui Temple the sun was shining. The snow in the fields glistened, about to melt. The air was crisp. The countryside was a refreshing change from the city. He felt aglow, and alive. Much of his happiness came from praying before the Buddha and having his fortune told. The omens had all been good. Also, his mother's letter telling that a marriage had been contracted for him with the daughter of the Ye family filled him with excitement. So much so that he was compelled to come to the temple and have his fortune read. Even a man of learning looks to the supernatural for guidance when he is faced with the unknown. However, he was conscious of his reputation and, to avoid gossip, chose Haihui Temple which was far out of the city.

Strolling at a leisurely pace southward, he saw a square building in the distance. Even at that distance he could make out the two huge characters painted on the sign: wine and tea. Suddenly he was thirsty, and he quickened his footsteps.

It was a tumbled down building, but placed strategically, with the highway on one side and the bridge across the river on the other. There were windows on all four sides, making the space within bright and cheerful. Wine, tea and food were sold. But the snowstorm had just blown over, and there were few guests. The publican greeted Xiong Cilu effusively. Looking around, a pair of scrolls caught his eye.

Busy for fame, busy for wealth; in the midst of the hurly-burly have a cup of tea.
Toil for clothes, toil for food; in the midst of toiling a pot of wine cheers the heart.

Though they seemed common, there was a touching sadness under the rough humour. Xiong Cilu nodded and followed the host to a seat beside a pillar. A waiter brought tea and a few small dishes which he ate with relish, for he was famished.

Outside there was a clatter of hoofs. Moments later five or six soldiers in cavalry uniform burst into the tavern. The customers peered at the Manchus and bowed their heads over their food and wine; and all conversation died down.

Their leader, an officer, stopped before the pair of scrolls and read them in a low voice. Although he had a Manchu accent, he was fluent. Some of the customers stole glances at him. Only Xiong Cilu sat stiff backed, looking straight ahead.

"Patron, are these scrolls new?" asked the young officer.

"No, no. They were already here when I bought the business."

The young officer smiled, "They are quite apt". He looked about the room. Everyone present avoided his eyes, except Xiong Cilu who drank his tea as though no one else was present. The Manchu noticed Xiong Cilu and, ignoring the publican, sat down facing him.

"You must be a scholar, Sir..." the newcomer began.

"You're too kind.... I'm only a student...." Xiong replied and glanced up at the stranger. Then, in spite of himself he looked up again. There was nothing extraordinary about the man's marten fur cap, old robe, or black boots. But he was strikingly handsome, and the way he carried himself showed he was more than a common soldier. Yet he did not have the suavity of an aristocrat nor the haughtiness of a member of the imperial family. Xiong Cilu wondered who the young man could be. Nor did the stranger seem offended by his chilly scrutiny, but seemed quite content to remain in his seat. The tavern keeper and his helpers quickly spread tea and food before him.

The Manchu officer sat with one hand on the table and the other arm thrown casually across the back of his chair, a pose at once informal and attractive. It was obvious he wished to engage Xiong Cilu in conversation. Meanwhile two of the riders who came in with him had sat down with a monk and began bantering in loud voices, attracting everyone's attention

"I say, Monk, how is it that you are eating steamed buns? Are you not breaking the vow of abstinence from meat?" The speaker was the shorter of the two Manchu soldiers, speaking impeccable Chinese with a Beijing accent.

"Buddha be praised! This humble monk eats buns without fillings," replied the old monk in slow measured tones.

"Oh! Oh! No wonder you eat so many!" The soldier would not let the monk off. His derisive glance swept across several plates of buns. "Look at all this," he quipped, "it's like ... it's like...." As he struggled for the right words he happened to glance out the window, and he finished gleefully, "It's like the grave mounds here outside the city...." The comparison pleased him. He and his companion burst into peals of laughter. However, the soldier also kept a weather eye open for his officer hoping to win his approval as well. The old monk squinted past the soldier at the grave mounds outside. Indeed they resembled the buns. Under his breath he murmured,

Outside the city there are buns of earth.
Inside the city dwell their fillings.

Xiong Cilu was aghast at what he heard. But the old monk seemed unconcerned that his meaning was over the heads of the two soldiers.

"Nonsense! You're deliberately talking rubbish!"

"What's this about buns and fillings! What are you talking about!" they clamoured.

The old monk, with his eyes half shut, murmured, "This old monk seeks enlightenment lest, like you, he ends as stuffings for buns.... Fate is unalterable. Those destined to be bun fillings will be... those who seek nirvana will achieve it...."

"You are confusing me ..." the Manchu soldier complained loudly.

The monk smiled blandly and said, "Let it go. I will tell you a story. There was once a man who was a good fortune teller. One day a man came to consult him and, upon entering his room, sat himself down on the man's bed. Whereupon the bed collapsed. The man immediately offered to pay for the damage, but the fortune teller refused. Picking up one of the broken bamboo legs of the bed he showed it to his visitor. On it was carved in tiny characters: 'On a certain day a fairy will sit on this bed and it will break.' 'You must be that fairy!' cried the fortune teller. The astonished visitor exclaimed, 'Even fairies can't escape destiny!' and vanished." All those within earshot were spellbound by the old monk's tale. Xiong Cilu alone remained unmoved. His companion nudged him stealthily and demanded, "Who is the monk?" Xiong Cilu shook his head. He really did not know.

The monk was pleased with the response to his story. He swept the remaining buns into his satchel and rose to leave. At the door he said to the host, "These scrolls are really too common. Would you accept a new pair from me?" The host simpered, "I shall be honoured. You on the counter, listen carefully and be sure you write it down correctly!" Whereupon the monk shut his eyes and joined his palms for a moment of deep thought, then slowly recited one word at a time:

"All is void; sit together and we are the same.
The road forks; drink a cup and we'll go our separate ways."

And with those words, he went away.

"Stop, Old Monk!" shouted the Manchu officer and rushed out after him. "Old Monk, what is your name and where are you from?" When the old man fixed his eyes lengthily at him, he added in a friendlier tone, "I overheard your discourse, and your verse impressed me with its simplicity of language and its profundity." The old monk levelled his gaze at the other and said, "I am Cong Hanpu from Haihui Temple." The officer said, "Old Monk, you speak glibly about fate, yet you seem to hide your light beneath a bushel." The monk responded with a gentle smile, "It is my fate to meet great ones today." The smile vanished from the officer's face as he surveyed the old monk. The latter bowed and strade off in big strides. The officer, spellbound, followed him out the tavern. The two soldiers seeing this rushed after him. The host cried out and started after them, but when he saw them talking outside he turned his attention to other things.

Xiong Cilu left his money on the table and departed by a side door. The sky was clear. The mountains to the west were etched upon the horizon. He did not want to return to the city just yet, and so he turned his face to the sun and walked along.

When the sun began to sink, a cold wind came up, and Xiong Cilu thought of turning back. He was not afraid of the cold, but he was concerned about the time. For the city gates would close at sunset and he would not be able to go home. For the moment his attention was drawn by a strange sound coming from a hovel at the edge of the field. He was amazed that those broken walls shivering in the wind could be shelter for a human being. As he approached he saw a ragged old man, with limbs dry and gnarled, laboriously splitting firewood.

The pathetic sight roused Xiong Cilu's pity, and he joined his hands and greeted the old man as old uncle. The old man paused to wipe the sweat from his brow with his sleeve. Though he turned toward Xiong Cilu he did not seem to see him. He raised his axe once more.

"Old Uncle, why is a man your age doing such heavy work? Haven't you sons or grandsons to help?" The old man dropped his axe and faced him with surprise.

"My Heaven! Do I hear a Hubei accent?" he cried.

"Indeed, I am a scholar from Hubei. We have the same accent!"

"Oh! We are from the same place!" exclaimed the old man, his native accent hardly changed by the years. He essayed a gummy smile as he dabbed his eyes with his sleeve.

"Old Uncle, you...." Before he could finish the old man lunged at him and threw him to the ground. At the same moment an arrow sped through the air and found its mark in a rabbit at the edge of the field. Actually the arrow passed some distance from the two men. Nevertheless the old man was quivering with fright.

The same Manchu officer that Xiong had encountered earlier galloped by. He dismounted, picked up the rabbit which he fastened to his saddle and, leading his mount by the reins, turned back.

"Aha! So we meet again! Perhaps it is fate," the officer was both delighted and surprised. "I apologize if I frightened you."

"Not to turn a hair in the face of danger is the test of manhood," Xiong Cilu replied in a scholarly manner. The other laughed and indicating the old man asked, "Is he your friend?"

"No. A stranger. Yet it saddens one to think that people live in such abject misery so near the capital."

The officer's curiosity was roused. He scrutinized the old man and then went into the rude hut. When he emerged his in a deep frown and the flippancy of a moment ago had evaporated. Xiong Cilu was puzzled by the change. The old man had been intimidated by the man's military garb at first. Realizing that he meant no harm, he was emboldened to look at him more closely. Finally the officer asked, "Old man, how did you come to such a state?" The old man looked at him dumb with misery. The officer addressed the old man again:

"Have no fear, I am a mere secretary attached to the grand council from one of the banners...." This remark caused Xiong Cilu to look at the speaker more closely. To his surprise the officer reddened and hurriedly added, "I am nobody, but I have an uncle, my mother's brother, who works for the Ministry of Justice. If anyone has wronged you, he will make it right." The old man looked at him suspiciously, afraid to speak. "Old man, you are in such dire straits, perhaps another of my mother's brothers who works for the Ministry of Personnel and in charge of relief funds for the poor can help." This fellow seems to have an uncle for every need, thought Xiong Cilu, and scrutinized him more closely. This time the officer pretended not to notice. The old man, however, finally understood and, falling heavily to his knees, cried out, "My Lord, help me! Help me!"

As it was, the old man's heavy Hubei accent made him difficult to understand. But when he started to pour out his troubles he became completely unintelligible. The officer waved his hands for him to stop. Xiong Cilu interrupted saying he came from the same place as the old man and would interpret for him. Then he bade the old man to tell his story calmly and clearly for the kind-hearted lord.

The old man spoke of his sufferings with tears streaming down his face.

Forty years ago, during a famine in his native place, the man came to the capital to seek a new life. From the humble beginnings of peddling pancakes and fried dough strips, he was finally able to save enough money to buy some land, build a house, marry and beget children. In fact he became almost well-to-do. When the dynasty changed, his good farmland was appropriated. He took his complaint from one ministry to the next, but his pleas fell on deaf ears until an official of the Ministry of Personnel gave him a hearing. As a result he was given a few plots of sandy soil by the river. As the plots were separated from each other, he was forced to live apart from his two sons.

From then on each farmed their own land and managed to scrape a living. In the early years of Shunzhi, his youngest son who had been abducted and sold into slavery escaped from his cruel master. He sought shelter with his second brother. As a result, when the boy was recaptured, the second son was charged with harbouring an escaped slave and executed according to the law. Subsequently, the boy escaped again and was taken in by his oldest brother. Again he was recaptured. This time the oldest son was executed, and the boy was beaten to death. Thus, the old couple were left alone in the world. Life went on, but misfortune continued to dog them. A bannerman took a fancy to the old man's land and demanded it as tribute. When the old man refused he was accused of harbouring runaway slaves. His old wife died of shock, and the old man was forced to give up everything he owned. Left completely destitute, he came to live in this hovel, eking out a meagre living by selling firewood.

As he translated Xiong Cilu's eyes moistened.

The officer's face grew grim as the tale unfolded, and his breathing became audible.

"Why did you not complain to the authorities?" he finally stammered.

Xiong Cilu sighed. "To whom could he turn? Harbouring runaways is a capital crime. No one dares to speak out against it. Even ministers and officials have been dismissed or banished for criticizing it. Therefore, how would a poor peasant dare speak out?" The old man understood what was said and quickly added, "I wouldn't dare complain! I wouldn't dare complain against someone connected to the imperial family!" The officer trembled at those words. "This was done by a member of the imperial family?"

The old man fell to his knees trembling and, banging his head against the ground, said, "I didn't say that! I didn't say that!" he cried. It was only with a great deal of reassurance that the old man was finally persuaded to reveal that the mother-in-law of the man who seized his land was a Mongolian young lady who had married a Manchu. That lady's half sister was now an imperial concubine.

The officer was speechless at this revelation. Xiong Cilu cast a deprecating glance at him. Here was another man with feet of clay. His eyes might have betrayed his thoughts, for glancing up at him, the officer reddened.

"I'll teach you..." he shouted and caught himself.

"My Lord," Xiong Cilu placated, "I said nothing...."

The officer grunted angrily. "You didn't have to. Your eyes said it all."

"My eyes!"

"You ... hate the laws governing land appropriation and run-away slaves."

"Ah, My Lord, those laws have created such hardships for the people, who would not hate them? You have seen the result for yourself." The officer could not rebut that statement.

Xiong Cilu sighed. "When the people are poor the country is weak. When the people are discontented there will be upheaval. Such are the lessons of history." The officer's anger evaporated. "Repeat what you just said."

Xiong Cilu took this opening to speak his mind.

"The sages have said just as a river might float a boat, it can capsize it. The court is full of learned men, yet it ignores simple truths." The officer gazed at Xiong Cilu long and hard.

"Who are you, Sir?" he asked. Xiong Cilu reluctantly introduced himself.

"Ah! So you are Xiong Cilu!" exclaimed the officer. It was Xiong Cilu's turn to be surprised.

"Your reputation precedes you," The officer explained. "I shall call upon you soon. In the meantime, you will want to return to the city."

"You too," Xiong Cilu countered. "But what about this old man?"

"Leave everything to me. I have ways." The officer had recovered his confident air. Bending down he spoke gently to the old man: "You will ride with me to the city. We will deal with the man who wronged you." And turning he winked mischievously at Xiong Cilu.

Xiong Cilu watched them go, the old man mounted on the horse which the officer led on foot. Astonishment, respect, not unmixed with concern, rolled through his mind. The memory of those two moving off into the twilight with the wind whistling across the empty plain would remain in his mind for a very long time.

Xiong Cilu mulled over the events of the day as he trudged home. But more amazing events were to come.

In the middle of the night, Xiong Cilu was wakened from a sound sleep by loud hammering on the door. He had nothing worth stealing and by the noise the intruder made, it did not seem to be someone bent on mischief. In a loud voice he demanded to know who was there.

"Open the door, Sir! It is a matter of urgency!" an unknown voice replied.

Xiong Cilu lit a lamp and dressed carefully before he opened the door. In the uncertain light of the lamp and the starlight he saw that his small garden and even the lane beyond the bamboo gate was filled with shadowy figures. The men clustered round the door were dressed in black livery and fur caps with upturned brims. The dimness of the light made them all the more menacing.

Xiong Cilu was frightened, but he comforted himself with the sage's saying that a superior man fears neither violence nor power, and put on a brave face. With head held high, he asked in a calm voice, "What is your business with this poor scholar?" A man in black livery replied, simpering, "I bring good tidings. Master Luo, one of the wealthiest men in the capital, wishes you to set up a school in his residence." Xiong Cilu was taken aback. He searched his mind but could not recall a wealthy Master Luo among his acquaintances.

"Master Luo has come in person," the man concluded. The others stepped back and stood stiffly erect with heads bowed, opening a path in the middle. Xiong Cilu was at first concerned that his plants might be trampled, but was relieved when he saw that the man had taken care not to.

Master Luo approached with quick steps, wreathed in smiles and greeted Xiong Cilu with joined hands.

"Master Xiong, your reputation is like thunder to the ears! I am honoured to meet you at last!" Scholarly pleasantries tripped off Master Luo's tongue. Xiong Cilu replied in kind, "It is I who am honoured. Please enter my humble abode." Master Luo entered the house without further ado. When both were seated, Xiong Cilu apologized, "My honoured guest has arrived so unexpectedly that Cilu is unable to offer tea or wine." Master Luo brushed aside Xiong's remark, "It is I who must apologize for intruding at such an hour. I enjoy some celebrity within the city, but am unobstrusive by nature. Hence I prefer nocturnal visits. I trust this idiosyncrasy has not offended."

Master Luo was a charismatic personage. His black beard and brows, and particularly his eyes that flashed with intelligence and humour, captivated Xiong Cilu. With the pleasantries out of the way, Master Luo came straight to the point. "Your reputation for virtue and learning was already widespread in your native place. Now that reputation is everywhere in the capital as well. I have two young nephews who are without a tutor. It is my hope that the Master would consent to teach them." Xiong Cilu shook his head. "I fear my reputation is exaggerated. I am only an ordinary scholar from the south, unworthy of such a task. It is true that I have taught these three years. But I am weary of it and plan to return to my native place soon."

Master Luo spoke earnestly,

"My widowed mother's most fervent wish in life is that her sons might become men renowned for their learning. However, my brothers and I were not the studious type, and were a great disappointment to her. Thus she has fastened her hopes on the next generation, that her grandsons might become great men of letters. However, good teachers are hard to find. None have been suitable till now. Having heard the Master's reputation, she set her heart on engaging your services. What is a son to do? Moreover, I too am a great admirer. Therefore I pray the Master will give due consideration to this earnest request...."

Xiong Cilu could not find it within himself to refuse the man's plea, also he was much taken with the other's openness. He finally consented.

"Our family is honoured by the Master's kindness." Master Luo, having expressed his thanks formally, called for servants and horses.

Several servants appeared to ask Xiong for instructions for packing his belongings.

"Would you have me move immediately?" Xiong Cilu was aghast. Master Luo chuckled. "Have no fear. I have a fetish for efficiency. Everything that can be accomplished today must be done today. Therefore, I have come personally to escort the Master." Xiong Cilu could find no rebuttal. Horses were brought, and the two men surrounded by servants bearing lanterns and torches left Xiong Cilu's humble dwelling.

Before long, Xiong Cilu was lost in a maze of twisting, turning streets, till they came to a large mansion blazing with lights. Never had he been in such a splendid place as this. Another of the sage's saying, "Be not dazzled by the possessions of others, and thus bemoan one's own lack," rang through his mind, and he kept his composure as befitted a superior man.

Master Luo conducted him into a small, quiet courtyard and

took his leave. A few handsome pageboys hurried forward to offer tea, turn down the bed and lower the drapes. Presently an old servant presented himself and reported in a respectful tone:

"Master, this is a large place with a large population and strict protocol. The Master will convey all his needs to myself, and I will do all possible to fulfil them. On no account must the Master wander unaccompanied beyond this courtyard, lest the servants be punished...."

Xiong Cilu was beginning to regret his decision. Indeed the environs of the rich and powerful were as fathomless as the sea.

The next day Master Luo brought the two children to meet their teacher together with a gift of a hundred ounces of silver. The gift helped change Xiong's mind about leaving this post. Also, the two little boys were bright and intelligent, a far cry from the dullards he taught during the last three years.

Master Luo cautioned Xiong Cilu saying, "My mother dotes upon the boys and will not permit them to rise too early in the morning. Also, the Master must refrain from any physical punishment. Any misdemeanor must be reported to myself, to be dealt with according to family code."

From then on the two boys came to him every day at noon for their lessons. Xiong Cilu settled down to teaching. He was well paid, and Master Luo visited him from time to time to pass the time of day. Without his mentioning it a stipend was sent home to Hubei, and from time to time a short note from his mother would arrive acknowledging money received and bidding him do his work in peace.

And so Xiong Cilu settled in, sacrificing a part of his freedom for the sake of the gracious treatment he was accorded.

4

The winter of the fourteenth year of Shunzhi was the mildest in living memory. The bone-piercing wind did not howl till quite late in the year. Nor did the icicles hanging down the eaves survive beyond noon. However, the tempests raised by imperial decrees that came close on the heels of one another, which Shunzhi issued from his hunting lodge at Nanyuan, shook the nation. Whether one agreed with them or not all were affected by their forcefulness. The Manchu aristocracy was especially distressed.

The first decree, issued in the twelfth month, reiterated the end to appropriating land and houses. "...Land appropriation has caused untold hardship among the people, depriving many of a livelihood, and thus a will to live. Others have been forced into a life of crime, posing a danger to the peace and security of the nation. By this decree, land appropriation is henceforth forbidden."

The next day another decree followed ordering the Ministry of Personnel to list the officials who had been exiled for petitioning against the harsh laws dealing with runaway slaves.

A third decree was specifically directed at the Manchu nobility reminding them that slaves were allowed them as reward for their efforts on behalf of the dynasty. However, their harsh treatment of slaves resulted in escapes, which caused laws to be proclaimed to stem the tide. However, these laws had been misused to such an extent that innocent people had suffered. In his decree, the Emperor called upon the aristocracy to mend its ways, to treat slaves with compassion and thus win their respect and devotion. Furthermore, he reminded them that he was ruler of all peoples under Heaven, without exception. Henceforth, bannermen would not be exempt from arrest and prosecution for lawlessness.

The latest decree struck like a bolt of lightning. Its impact was felt in every level of society. The aristocracy who had enjoyed the protection of their banners were now open to arrest and prosecution. That was without precedent. Some rushed to spread the news with glee. Others found this food for sombre reflection. Still others were despondent or roused to fury. In a word, Hans and Manchus, aristocrat and ordinary folk — the nation at large — was in an uproar.

Emperor Shunzhi seemed oblivious to the furore sweeping the

nation when he issued a fourth decree instructing the civil service to promote men of true ability to replace deadwood. The Emperor also provided his personal list of names for official posts such as Li Wei, Wang Chongjian, his son Wang Xi and so on. All were Hans except Yisangah who was a Manchu of the Yellow Banner and had passed the metropolitan imperial examination in the ninth year of Shunzhi. It seemed to bode well for scholars.

The chief eunuch Wu Liangfu, accompanied by the young eunuch Wu Lu, rode from Nanyuan to the capital in a blinding blizzard. Wu Liangfu was muffled in a great coat and cap of marten fur, while Wu Lu was clad in a great cloak.

As they entered the busy streets of the capital through Qian Men, Wu Liangfu was drawn to a tavern by the sweet aroma of wine. He dismounted in front of the two-storeyed establishment under the eaves of which hung a plaque of wood on which were painted the name Apricot Blossom Village. Beside it was displayed the names of a dozen fine wines written on smaller plaques hung from strips of red and green silk.

Wu Liangfu handed his reins to the waiter, who rushed out to greet him, and entered the tavern. Wu Lu hesitated, looking stealthily to right and left, barely keeping up with the chief eunuch. The host showed the men into an elegant private room. Food and wine were quickly served. Wu Liangfu set to at once and bid his companion to eat and drink as well.

Wu Lu, a handsome, vivacious youth, not quite eighteen years of age, had entered the palace at the age of ten. It was through the influence of Wu Liangfu that he was educated at Wanshan Hall in the Forbidden City and trained specially to serve the Emperor. These were honours that most young eunuchs dared not dream of. That Wu Liangfu opened doors for this youth was due in part to the fact that they shared the same surname, and also because of the boy's amiability. The relationship between Wu Liangfu and Wu Lu was a complex one. The older man treated the youth as confidant, son or nephew, brother or bosom friend. Wu Liangfu was a man of considerable influence, lionized by the officials at court. To the other young eunuchs he was a fearsome, even sinister figure with whom their relationship was that of cat and mouse. However, with Wu Lu he was different. Wu Lu's presence brought joy. Wu Liangfu nicknamed Wu Lu the "Little One" and craved to pass everything he knew onto the youth as he would a son, as most influential eunuchs were wont to do.

Wu Liangfu downed a couple cups of wine and was beginning to feel their warming effect. He reached over and gently tweaked Wu Lu's ear. "Drink, Little One. It will warm you."

Wu Lu was worried. "Chief, we were ordered by His Majesty to see the Empress. If we delay...."

"Delay!" Wu Liangfu laughed unpleasantly. "I read His Majesty like a book! If it wasn't for family code and etiquette he wouldn't send us in this fool's errand at all." Wu Lu raised his eyebrows quizzically. "But we can't possibly go into Her Majesty's presence drunk."

"No problem. Take a few mouthfuls of vinegar and it will sober you. Anyway, she won't be empress much longer ...." Wu Lu was shocked but he doubtfully lifted the wine cup to his lips.

"Little One, I've been so busy lately that I haven't had a chance to ask what the old monk Hanpu said to His Majesty that day in the country teahouse. Did you hear what was said, and was His Majesty moved?"

Wu Lu recounted everything that happened and the Emperor's reaction with embellishments. Wu Liangfu listened with grave interest.

"The monk claimed to have travelled extensively through the south and recited some poetry with one of the courtiers. His Majesty was delighted and promised to visit him at Haihui Temple."

"That is wonderful!" exclaimed Wu Liangfu clasping his hands before his breast in a womanish gesture that most men would find revolting, but which Wu Lu was accustomed to. Curiosity prompted his next remark.

"Wouldn't it have been simpler to send the monk to His Majesty than beating about the bush?" asked Wu Lu.

"You don't understand," Wu Liangfu replied patiently. "You haven't grasped His Majesty's personality yet. By creating what seems like a chance meeting, His Majesty is intrigued. Whereas, if the same humble monk were presented to him, he would quickly forget the encounter. Also, presenting the monk to His Majesty would cause Tang Jo-Wang to complain, and he can be such a meddler!"

"But everybody says...." Wu Lu hesitated then finally mumbled, "... Well ... they say Tang Jo-Wang is a saint! So why are we...?"

Anger flickered in Wu Liangfu's eyes, but he smothered it with an enigmatic smile. "I'll tell you the truth, my Little One. This effort was to get His Majesty closer to the Buddha and away from that saint. As long as he's around there will be no peace for the likes of us. He thinks of himself as the Emperor's spiritual advisor. Think of it! Who in China subscribes to his god or his holy mother? Are they the equal of our buddhas and gods? And when you consider the man: prim and proper, law abiding, but what does that prove? The fact is he is our stumbling block.... Oh, my Little One, are Chen Zhilin's promissory notes in hand?"

"He will give the money when the deed is done."

"Ha! That devil always has his way...." Wu Liangfu sighed and seizing Wu Lu by the shoulder continued, "What do men like us have to look forward to? Therefore, while we're young and healthy and have the Emperor's trust, we must make hay while the sun shines. Get a little nest egg while we can. Otherwise there will be no one to bury us...." He shook his head sadly, and for a moment his handsome face seemed to age, the crow's feet at the corners of his eyes and mouth deepened.

"But both His Majesty and the Empress Dowager dote upon

Lord Tang, how can we touch him?"

"That is why we must proceed with care. But there is the other side of the coin." Although they were in a private room, Wu Liangfu still peered about suspiciously and, lowering his voice, further continued:

"Why do you suppose Their Majesties call him Mafa? I'll tell you, my dear Little One, it's because of Yongli of Southern Ming...." Wu Lu's eyes and mouth made circles of astonishment.

"You're too young to understand the ins and outs of these things. You see, the entire house of Yongli are Catholic converts. Their chief civic official, Qu Shisi, and chief general, Jiao Lian, are converts as well. Catholicism has been in China for at least eighty years. Missionaries are everywhere, and quite a few have sided with Yongli. Tang Jo-Wang, however, is the most learned and renowned of them all. Is it any wonder that he is respected and trusted at court?"

"Ah! Their Majesties are canny indeed!" sighed Wu Lu.

"It's called the art of government," remarked Wu Liangfu drily. "Since Sun Kewang surrendered, Yongli will fall any day now. Once Southern Ming has succumbed, Tang Jo-Wang's good days will be numbered! Wait and see...." Wu Lu, concerned that the chief eunuch might have had too much to drink, suggested they should be on their way.

"What's the hurry!" Wu Liangfu's face clouded. He was on the verge of losing his temper but again controlled himself. Instead he smiled lovingly at the younger man. "Ah, I remember now! You've acquired a soul sister recently. A young girl from Jingren Palace I believe? No wonder you're in a hurry. Separated for more than half a month, you must simply be dying to see her!" Wu Lu giggled.

"All right! Let's go!" Wu Liangfu lifted the vinegar jar to his lips and took three big swigs, grimacing hideously as the liquid went down. Still he quipped, "Little One, now that you've found your little playmate, don't forget your brother. Jealousy is a terrible thing."

It was snowing more heavily now. The Forbidden City was draped in a thick, swirling white veil lending towers, halls and pavilions an air of mystery and unearthly beauty.

Inside Kunning Palace it was as warm as spring. Charcoal glowed red and bright in the braziers, rivalling the warm glow of gilded filigree lanterns hanging from the ceiling. The east chamber was lit as bright as day. Branches of pink and white plum blossoms stood in a pair of tall, gaily decorated vases. Delicate oval-shaped basins contained white narcissus with yellow centres rising tall and proud amid jade green leaves. The heavy fragrance of the flowers mingled with burning incense filled Kunning Palace with an intoxicating atmosphere of voluptuous pleasure.

Some new furnishings had been brought in to the Empress' residence that day and the ladies who had come to visit and to pass the time of day were unanimous in their admiration. Lady Shuhui, the Empress' younger sister, who was a daily visitor, was less constrained than the others. She had taken a fancy to an ebony dressing table. While she enthused over the elaborate but delicately carved dragons and phoenixes, she admired herself in the round mirror at its centre which had been a gift from Holland.

Lady Duan insisted on showing Lady Gong the mythical animals of white jade set in a screen. In her turn Lady Gong wanted the other to admire a fine tea tray. In the end the two ladies went over to Lady Jing who stood alone by the south corner of the kang gazing intently at something on a square table. The object of her scrutiny was an ancient flower bowl shaped like a banana leaf so delicately cast in bronze that it seemed real. In its centre grew two red herbaceous peonies. They were cultivated specially in the Palace greenhouse.

Lady Jing was the first empress who had been deposed four years earlier. Usually she was not a part of these gatherings. As the Emperor was away she had joined the other ladies visiting

Kunning Palace. Since she was seldom seen in public, Lady Jing neglected her appearance. However, on this occasion she had made an effort. Lavishly gowned and coiffured she was as regal as she had been in happier days. This was because although position and rank was paramount at court, in the Boerjijite clan she belonged to an older generation. She was the present Empress' aunt, and therefore had to maintain a certain dignity. Nevertheless the slings and arrows of fate had left their indelible marks upon her. At the age of twenty-two or three, the deep lines on her forehead and at the corners of her eyes could no longer be hidden by the most diligent applications of rouge and powder. When she smiled she appeared even older.

Lady Jing forced a smile as the two ladies approached.

"Look at this! Isn't it precious!" she exclaimed.

Lady Duan smiled saying, "Lady Shuhui says it's a gift for His Majesty's second wedding. Your Ladyship's wedding gifts must have been...." A look from Lady Gong cut her short. "...That was thoughtless.... I meant no harm..." she ended in confusion.

It was an insult, but Lady Jing was used to it by now. She spoke as though nothing had happened:

"The red peonies bring out the beauty of the bowl. The effect is quite breathtaking."

"Herbaceous peonies are lovely, but they are nothing compared to the tree variety," said Lady Duan.

"They are greenhouse flowers," Lady Gong smiled wickedly, "Otherwise they are out of season now." Lady Jing glanced at them coldly and retorted, "This not being the season, all flowers, however beautiful, must wither."

The two ladies exchanged looks and had to agree.

At the other end of the room, the Empress' younger sister Lady Shuhui was primping and posing before a mirror.

"Sister," she said, addressing the Empress without turning her head, "it seems somebody must have sent invitations. Everybody of our clan is here except Lady Jin." When the Empress did not reply she looked around. The Empress was absent-mindedly gazing at a large round fruit platter decorated with a hundred gambolling infants. Lady Shuhui felt a rush of pity for her older sister, not without a pang for herself. However, she was young and her burden less onerous. Furthermore she had the capacity to shuck off unpleasant thoughts. Laughing, she waved a silk handkerchief in front of her sister's face and suggested, "Send for Lady Jin, then we'll have enough people for a few rounds of mahjong." The Empress lifted her eyes to her sister and sighed without much interest.

"Don't you want to?"

The Empress shook her head.

"Sister," Lady Shuhui whispered. "You're going to make yourself ill. Shall I send for the imperial physician? Or would you like a stroll in the snow?"

"Please don't fuss." The Empress smiled sadly. Lady Shuhui made a face. "Of course I haven't got Lady Jin's sharp tongue. We can't get a laugh out of you without her ... but ... speaking of the devil ... here she is...."

Indeed, Lady Kang and Lady Jin, cloaked in furs, had just entered the room. As they approached to pay their respects to the Empress, quick-witted Lady Shuhui noticed both were preoccupied. Lady Jin was not her usual bubbly self. In fact her eyes were quite red. Something was wrong.

The chief eunuch of Kunning Palace entered to announce that His Majesty had sent chief eunuch Wu Liangfu and young Wu with a message. The ladies in the room fell silent. The Empress' heart skipped a beat. In a shaky voice she bid them enter.

Wu Liangfu and Wu Lu prostrated themselves; then rising to a kneeling position on the carpet before the kang, Wu Liangfu offered his greetings to the ladies.

"Never mind that. What brings you back to the palace?"

"If it pleases Your Majesty, the Emperor wishes to inform Your Majesty that two nights ago the Empress Dowager woke in the middle of the night, complaining of a headache and dizziness. She also had a fever. Yesterday she seemed worse. Today we could not wake her...."

"Has the imperial physician been summoned?"

"The imperial physician and eight other court physicians are in attendance at Nanyuan. His Majesty is deeply concerned and went to pray at the Imperial shrine yesterday, and again today, inspite of the storm. Precious Concubine has been at the Empress Dowager's bedside, day and night...."

Lady Shuhui pouted and turned away saying nothing. Lady Duan and Lady Gong exchanged knowing glances, their faces mirroring their displeasure. However, Lady Jin who was usually most jealous of Lady Dongeh, fixed her eyes on the floor and displayed no emotions whatever.

Wu Liangfu continued with his report,

"If Your Majesty and the ladies would like to go to Nanyuan...."

Seated next to the Empress, Lady Shuhui cut him short.

"If we were needed at Nanyuan we would have been sent for sooner. We are a stupid lot, not clever with flattery, or skilled in poetry and painting and so forth. We'd only be in the way."

Wu Liangfu bowed his head and fell silent.

In the middle of the eleventh month, the Emperor and Precious Concubine had accompanied the Empress Dowager on a royal progress to Nanyuan like a family outing. Although she never breathed a word, the Empress was not pleased at being left out. Neither were the imperial concubines and other ladies. Everyone was grumbling. In spite of everything, so long as the Emperor was in the Forbidden City there was a sliver of hope. It was that intangible hope that kept the inner palace alive. But in this month, the life of the court had shifted to Nanyuan, and the inner palace was desolate. Now that the Empress Dowager was ill, the Emperor remembered them. Whoever wanted to go could suit herself was the thought that ran through the minds of the ladies present, including the Empress. However, no one dared put such sentiments into words except Lady Shuhui.

As the two eunuchs touched their heads to the ground and prepared to withdraw, Lady Shuhui shot a sidelong glance at her sister and shouted, "Wait! One question please!"

"Yes. Yes." The two eunuchs knelt bolt upright.

"How is His Majesty?"

"My Lady, His Majesty has been hunting. He eats well and sleeps well and has put on weight. I am pleased to report he is the picture of health."

"What else?"

"What else?" Wu Liangfu was at a loss to understand the question.

"Brazen fool! Tell us what else His Majesty has been doing that has the capital in an uproar."

"My Lady, indeed His Majesty has done something extraordinary that has not only set the capital on its ears but the entire country. Young Wu was in the Presence when it happened. Young Wu, report to Their Ladyships."

After he had made his salutations, Wu Lu seized this opportunity to demonstrate his facility with words and his talent to amuse. He launched into the tale of how the Emperor went hunting dressed as a commoner and his encounter with the old woodsman. He was really in his element when he came to the part where the Emperor took the old man to confront his tormentor.

When they reached the regimental commander's home, the gatekeeper would not let them near. It was only the Emperor's fluent Manchu speech that made the man change his mind and went inside to report. The commander, however, dismissed the visitors as beneath his dignity to bother with. Instead he sent his wife to deal with them. The tall, obese woman was a harridan whom an old barbarian and a young bannerman did not impress.

"So what if we took your property!" she cried. "That's what happens to barbarians! What can you do about it?" The Emperor was furious.

"How dare you flaunt the law! How will it benefit you if the complaint is taken to court?"

The commander's wife laughed unpleasantly. "Take it to court if you dare!" she cried. "I'll be a dog in the next life if that frightens me!" Then with brows bristling she ordered them to leave. But the Emperor stood his ground. The woman was in a rage now. Seizing a wooden pole leaning against the door she struck out at him.

"I'll kill you, you meddling bastard!" she shrieked.

The Emperor let out an angry roar and parried the blow with his bow, sending the pole flying out of the woman's hand. Instantly the Emperor's guards appeared. Several hundred soldiers surrounded the commander's house. When it dawned upon the commander and his wife that the young bannerman was none other than the Emperor they swooned with fear. The Emperor ordered the commander and his entire household beheaded on the spot as a warning to other wrongdoers.

Before leaving, the Emperor issued an edict giving all the commander's land and goods to the poor old man who was to be honoured as the elder of the town.

The Empress and the ladies were struck dumb by Wu Lu's narrative.

Winding up, Wu Lu concluded, "The story spread like wild fire. Within days everybody knew it, and all agree that His Majesty is a wise and just monarch...."

For some time after Wu Liangfu and Wu Lu had departed, all was silence in the room. No one spoke.

Suddenly Lady Jin broke into loud sobs. The others sensed her tears were a harbinger of disaster. The timid Lady Gong trembled and pressed closer to Lady Duan. Lady Jin, still weeping, fell to her knees before the Empress, her head bowed as though she could never lift it again.

"What is the matter, Lady Jin? Stop crying...." the Empress spoke in her usual calm voice.

"Your Majesty ... he was speaking of my niece!" sobbed

Lady Jin.

"You mean...." The Empress was shocked. "... That woman...." Lady Jin nodded through her tears. Lady Kang who was usually reticent softly explained,

"My mother who came to the palace today also spoke of this incident. The beheaded woman was indeed the daughter of Lady Jin's half-sister...." The Empress mulled this over a moment.

"Lady Jin control yourself," she said at length. "Surely His Majesty did not know it was your relative." Lady Kang's face darkened.

"He knew! My mother made enquiries!" she cried vehemently. All the ladies were shocked by this outburst for Lady Kang was usually reserved. No one suspected she was capable of such passion. As all eyes were upon her, Lady Kang bowed her head and said no more.

"His Majesty has no pity..." sobbed Lady Jin. The Empress spoke patiently:

"Lady Jin, control yourself. That niece of yours was not without fault. She did attack His Majesty, the master of all under Heaven."

"Sister, how can you defend him!" cried Lady Shuhui, not bothering to hide her indignation. "How could Lady Jin's niece know it was the Emperor? The fact is he does not care about us. He is so bewitched by that barbarian woman that he has turned on his own kind."

"Lady Shuhui!" The Empress' voice was severe. "How dare you!"

Lady Shuhui dropped to her knees, and the others followed suit to plead forgiveness on her behalf. Nevertheless, in their hearts, they were glad that Lady Shuhui had voiced sentiments they did not dare to.

When the other ladies withdrew, Lady Shuhui tarried longer as usual. Left alone, the Empress took her sister's dainty hand and asked, "What should I do? Go to Nanyuan personally, or send someone?"

"Don't go!" Lady Shuhui replied angrily. "None of us of the Boerjijite clan should go. The Emperor is so enchanted by a concubine that he is ignoring family code and tradition, and the Empress Dowager lets him. What angers me is the way she dotes on that barbarian woman too! You are the Empress! Are you going to take these insults without protest? If all of us stay away, maybe the Empress Dowager will realize that the daughters of the Boerjijite clan are not to be trifled with."

"However, His Majesty," the Empress protested, "... has always placed great importance on filial piety.... If I don't go...."

"What can he do to you? He can't depose you because he has already done it once. That has never happened before among our ancestors and not even in the annals of the Han is there a record of such an occurrence. He wouldn't dare touch you. Sister, you have to be strong."

The Empress did not go to Nanyuan. Nor did she send a representative.

The Empress Dowager was seriously ill. Wracked with fever for three days and nights, she hovered on the brink of consciousness, troubled by visions of awful demons.

"Dont! Oh ... please ... don't...."

She tried to ward them off, to tear away the bands and dots of coloured light that threatened to smother her. In fact her fingers hardly moved, and her cries were barely audible whispers. Her head ached. Finally she slipped into oblivion.

Somehow she was back on the grasslands again, where the sky was infinitely high, free of dust; where the seamless earth was unending; where the air was fragrant from a riot of wild flowers. She leaped from her horse and threw herself on the grass, and the grassland she loved embraced her like a mother. It was so peaceful!

There was a thunder of hoof beats. A rider was approaching. He was handsome and brave. What a magnificent sight he was on his black horse, his red cloak billowing against the green of the grassland and the blue of the sky. Before she knew it he was upon her, scooping her up from the ground where her horse had thrown her. Now their eyes met. Dorgon ... her Dorgon.... The past claimed her once more.... Her husband preferring her sister neglected her. She buried her loneliness and found solace hunting on the grassland. That time when she was thrown by her mount, Dorgon had come to her aid. Dorgon, the ninth prince, was handsome, young, and gallant. She was moved by him, but did nothing improper, for she was an imperial concubine and his sister-in-law.

But this was not the young Dorgon. It was the regally attired regent, smiling the same mocking smile he had given her when she upbraided him for secretly marrying the wife of Prince Su. He was repeating the same words he had flung at her then.

"I, Dorgon, am a man!" Oh, the shameless, faithless beast! He filled her with rage, even hate, yet she still desired his wide, sensuous mouth and his pale alabaster body.

The face changed. It wrinkled before her eyes, sprouted whiskers. It had turned into the face of Abahai, her husband. She crumpled to her knees, head drooping.

"Are you begging forgiveness, wretched woman?" her husband roared. "You have caused me such pain that I can find no peace even in my grave! I shall never forgive you!" He raised his bow ready to strike.

"Hit me! It's true I wronged you, but not your ancestors of the Aisin Gioro bloodline. After you died, it was I who won the loyalty of Prince Li and Prince Rui and with their help proclaimed our son Emperor, thus putting an end to the struggle for power that was brewing. Otherwise, the eight banners would have gone to war with one another, and the Empire Nurhachi envisioned would have blown away like dust. Yes I wronged you ... but I have done well by your ancestors...." Her husband lowered his weapon.

"You mean to say it was all for the sake of the Empire?

Nothing personal?" She did not know where she found the courage, but she faced him boldly. "Yes, there were personal feelings. But that was your fault. When you took my sister into the palace, you turned your back on our love. I was still your wife, but only in name."

"You lie!" Suddenly, her sister, Abahai's favourite concubine, was jabbing her with an angry finger, shrieking with fury. "You wanted your son to be Crown Prince, that you would one day be Empress Dowager! So you cast a spell on mine and he died!"

"That's not true! When your son died, I was just about to give birth..." she protested weakly. Her sister's eyes pierced the depths of her soul.

"Oh, yes, you're full of sweetness now. But you cursed my son. You wished him dead to make way for yours. Are you satisfied now? Oh, my poor son!"

The distraught woman let out a blood-curdling wail, horrible to hear. The Empress Dowager quivered, for deep in her heart she had wished the prince a short life. It was a secret she never breathed to another living soul. How did her sister find out? Abahai's mournful words rolled over her head like the rumble of distant thunder: "Ah, the sons of kings are unfortunate. How many die of misadventure...."

She was bathed in sweat, yet she was cold, and the violence of her trembling finally woke her. Someone seated in the dimly lit bed chamber was asleep with her head cupped in her hands.

"Water..." moaned the Empress Dowager. The sleeping figure rose quickly, took a small teapot from its padded cozy and, holding the Empress Dowager up in the crook of one arm, placed the spout between her parched lips with a free hand. The Empress Dowager gazed at her through eyes she could barely keep open. "Dongeh ... you ... are still ... here..." she murmured. Lady Dongeh enquired softly, "How are you, Imperial Mother? The doctors say you need rest...." The Empress Dowager shook her head wearily, "I'm finished.... Abahai has sent for me...." Lady Dongeh fell heavily to her knees.

"Imperial Mother, you mustn't say that," she cried. "His Majesty needs you. Let me go in your place...." The Empress Dowager forced a smile. "Silly child.... Are we alone?"

"His Majesty has just left," replied Lady Dongeh. "He has been praying at the imperial shrine for three days. The gods will reward his piety and bless Your Majesty." But the Empress Dowager had already slipped back into unconsciousness.

On the morning of the eighth day, as the first shafts of sunlight crept into the bed chamber and the gold filigreed clock chimed seven, the Empress Dowager woke. Her mind was clear. She was cool and comfortable, but weak. She called at once for Sumalagu.

Although her voice was low, it woke those around her. Instantly word passed from those who stood watch beside the bed to others seated on low stools outside the door and so on down the corridors.

"The Empress Dowager has spoken.... She is calling for people...."

Lady Dongeh quickly lifted the drapes, fighting back tears of joy.

"Oh, Imperial Mother, you are well!" she exclaimed. Sumalagu approaching the bed added, "Your Majesty, Precious Concubine has been at your side seven days and nights!"

"My dear child...." The Empress Dowager reached out and clutched Black Pearl to her breast. Sumalagu tiptoed from the room to send word to the Emperor.

The Emperor who had already heard the glad tidings was just in time to witness this touching scene. He knelt and greeted his mother formally.

"Imperial Mother," he cried. "I have been out of my mind with worry! If you do not get well soon, I think I will die too!"

"What nonsense!" chided the Empress Dowager. "Your prayers ... and your wife's care ... have made me well.... But where is the Empress, and the other ladies?"

Lady Dongeh quickly replied, "There's been a blizzard for days, and messengers could not get through. The ladies have not been informed...."

Fulin's face clouded. He shot an angry glance at Lady Dongeh, but when he saw the dark rings round her eyes and her weary smile, he turned away to gaze out the window.

"They don't know?" repeated the Empress Dowager, frowning. She turned to Sumalagu and added, "Surely they could have enquired...." Sumalagu bowed her head to avoid the disappointment in the Empress Dowager's eyes.

"I haven't heard of ... any messengers...."

Again it was Lady Dongeh who broke the awkward silence. "Imperial Mother, it's the fault of the snow blocking the roads." Forcing herself to sound cheerful she added, "Snow at this time of year is a good omen. There will be a good harvest, the people will live in peace."

"I don't want to hear all that," the Empress Dowager said testily. She shut her eyes. "The courtiers have been forming cliques, now the ladies of the inner palace are doing the same. The daughters of the Boerjijite clan, my own flesh and blood, are banding together to defy me."

"Imperial Mother mustn't be angry. They are young and thoughtless. But in their hearts they are filial and each has her good points. For example, the Empress manages the six palaces and takes a great deal of the burden off my Imperial Mother's shoulders. As for Lady Shuhui, Lady Duan and Lady Gong, they were charming companions for the Imperial Mother on the visit to the hot springs. And how solicitous they were on the way...."

The Empress Dowager cut her off. "You don't have to remind me. Those young ladies are spoilt, selfish and ignorant.... On the other hand, you are wise beyond your years.... What a pity there are so few like you...." Fulin interrupted saying, "Don't I count among the few?" The Empress Dowager sighed wearily, "Including you, there are two...."

Fulin pressed on trying to divert her, "Don't forget Prince An, and Duke Kang." The Empress Dowager shook her head. "Not enough.... There is power in numbers.... It will be ... very difficult...." She shut her eyes again.

Fire flickered deep in Fulin's eyes as the Empress Dowager's words sank in. His mother had never spoken so frankly before. He was confident of himself, his strength and his grasp on power. The obstacles in his path would not deter him. "Mother, I will show you that I am emperor!"

The Empress Dowager did not open her eyes, but sighed softly. "Even the Emperor cannot always do as he wishes.... Black Pearl, come close...." Lady Dongeh approached the bed, and the Empress Dowager grasped her hand and whispered sadly, "My poor child ... this has been very hard on you. But it can't be helped...." Black Pearl could fight the tears no longer, and they trickled down her cheeks. Fulin silently ground his teeth, his nostrils flaring. A patch of red spread gradually across his face, flooded round his eyes to congeal between his tightly knit brows.

Black Pearl gently rearranged the bedclothes for the Empress Dowager, softly comforting her, before she took leave of the Emperor and retired. Her footsteps were light, almost floating as she left the Empress Dowager's bed chamber. The sun newly risen shone in her face. Suddenly she felt faint. "Don't let the Empress Dowager know..." she managed to murmur before she slumped senseless in the arms of her attendants.

5

Between the winter of the fourteenth year of Shunzhi and the following spring a number of large and small events kept the court in a constant state of turmoil. Everyone was on edge wondering what would happen next.

On the twenty-fifth day of the twelfth month the Empress Dowager returned from Nanyuan. Three days later, to celebrate her recovery, the Emperor ordered eighty thousand ounces of silver to be taken from treasury funds, half to be distributed to the soldiers of the eight banners, and the remainder to the needy in the capital.

The next day, the Emperor cancelled all the New Year celebrations in the Inner Palace on the pretext that the Empress Dowager needed rest, and Precious Concubine was ill from over exertion tending her. Thus, the Forbidden City was shrouded in gloom when it should have been ablaze with festivities. Everyone within those vast walls was infected with a vague disquiet. None more than the Empress who was a sensitive, introspective soul.

On the third day of the New Year the Empress and Lady Shuhui were walking in the back gardens. Lady Shuhui was prattling away in her usual irrepressible way.

"My dear sister, you're making yourself unhappy for nothing. The Empress Dowager hasn't said a cross word to us. When we went to beg her forgiveness for not going to Nanyuan, she was all smiles. She even gave us gifts of game meat. Didn't I say, if we stood up to her, she'll back down?" The Empress sighed. "Nevertheless, we failed in our duty as daughters-in-law. I regret it...." She shook her head, her eyes hooded.

They walked along a path of pebbles laid in intricate patterns. In the spring, the flower beds bordering the footpath would be a splash of colour with peonies and roses in bloom. Now the wind whistled through the leafless branches poking out of the frozen earth. However, pine and cedar, still green, lent the gardens an air of regal mystery. Serving women and eunuchs stood along the path, as still as the ancient fossilized trees and eroded rocks that decorated the garden. The only sound was the clicking of the thick-soled ladies' shoes against the cobblestones, underscoring the soft murmur of their voices.

"Nonsense! You've already begged forgiveness, what more can you do?" Lady Shuhui giggled as she adjusted her sister's hood.

"...Precious Concubine is ill.... I should visit her..." muttered the Empress.

"Oh! So now you want to visit her!" Lady Shuhui flared. "If it wasn't for her you wouldn't be in the predicament you're in!"

"She became ill looking after the Empress Dowager...."

"She got what she deserves pandering to the Empress Dowager and the Emperor. There's never been a wilier vixen!" Lady Shuhui made no attempt to hide her hatred. She bristled at the mere mention of Lady Dongeh. The Empress sighed helplessly.

"After all this time, you still haven't grasped jealousy is one of the seven capital sins for an imperial concubine...."

Lady Shuhui covered her ears and stamped her foot before the Empress could finish, reverting to being the Empress' spoilt, wilful younger sister.

"I don't want to hear that!" she cried. "Those are the traditions of the southern barbarians, not ours!"

The Empress stopped, and with her eyes fixed on the grey squirrel skin muff she carried murmured, "The Emperor hasn't been to Kunning Palace since he returned.... Has he summoned you?"

Lady Shuhui flushed. She quickly composed herself and replied in a stiff voice, "Not once! Who cares for such a feelingless man!"

"Sister," the Empress cautioned, "that was not my meaning. I was wondering whether because we neglected the Empress Dowager, His Majesty might...."

"He wouldn't dare! He wants to be known as a wise and compassionate monarch. His reputation is already tarnished by deposing one empress. And an empress is not just some concubine or serving wench. What is at stake is the good reputation of the monarchy!"

In spite of herself, the Empress had to admit Lady Shuhui was correct in her analysis of the situation and she was comforted. Hurried footsteps approaching interrupted their conversation.

The chief eunuch of Kunning Palace prostrated himself before them. It was evident he was distraught and for a moment could not find the proper words to speak. The ladies sensed another disaster was about to occur.

"What is it?" The Empress had recovered her customary calm. Lady Shuhui stepped back a pace behind and to one side of her sister, as befitting her status.

"Your slave begs to report His Majesty issued two decrees today. The first, in honour of the Empress Dowager's recovery, which is a blessing to all under Heaven, an amnesty has been granted. All prisoners, except those convicted of the ten capital crimes, will have their sentences reduced or released...."

The Empress nodded.

"His Majesty is an example of filial piety and compassion. The universal amnesty will be lauded by the people...." She waited to hear the rest, but the chief eunuch bowed his head and seemed to have lost his voice.

With an effort to sound casual she asked, "And the rest?" The chief eunuch banged his forehead against the ground and stammered, "Your Majesty ... forgive your slave.... I dare not speak...." The Empress felt her heart lurch within her, however, with steely resolve she commanded the eunuch to continue.

"His Majesty's decree chides Your Majesty saying that during the Empress Dowager's illness His Majesty prayed at the imperial shrine three times, yet Your Majesty did not send so much as a word of greeting. Nor did Your Majesty send representatives. This was a failure in filial duty. Therefore ... as of this day Your Majesty's right to grant indulgences has been revoked...."

Lady Shuhui cried out in alarm. The Empress paled. The eunuch bowed his head and stammered on, "His Majesty has ordered the Council of Nobles ... to deal with the formalities...."

The Empress' indulgence was a tradition symbolic of her status. On the three main festivals of the year, such as the Emperor's birthday, the first day of the New Year, and winter solstice, or other special occasions, the Empress had the right to petition the Emperor directly. Whatever indulgence she craved would be granted. By revoking this right, the Emperor had removed what little power the Empress enjoyed. Furthermore, by referring the matter to the council suggested that he intended to depose her.

The Empress wavered on her feet. She lifted a hand to her forehead, assailed by dizziness and a wave of nausea. Lady Shuhui screamed and threw herself on her knees. "Your Majesty!" She cried between sobs, "It's my fault. It was my idea.... Let me go to the Emperor.... Let him punish me...." Wordlessly the Empress helped her to her feet. Both women were in tears.

As the news spread, a dark cloud descended upon the inner palace, making it colder, more forbidding. Anxiety among its denizens grew. Those who were sensitive to the prevailing winds were quick to take action. Suddenly visitors to Chengqian Palace to enquire after Precious Concubine's health increased.

When Lady Dongeh first fell ill after her sojourn at Nanyuan only a few ladies of low rank visited her. Now the street leading to Chengqian Palace was a continuous stream of traffic. Aside from the minor concubines, the ladies in waiting, the haughty daughters of the Boerjijite clan — Lady Duan, Lady Gong and even Lady Jing — had visited. However, the imperial physician had ordered a complete rest. Visitors were only permitted to pay their respects and quickly leave.

Fulin was constantly at her side, feeding her medicine, or sharing a meal. Often the two would sit on the bed, talking in hushed voices and giggling. If Lady Dongeh was asleep when he arrived, Fulin would examine the ginseng soup and medicine simmering on a small brazier in a corner and, gently lifting the drapes of the bed, adjust the bed clothes, scrutinize the sleeper to see if there was any improvement. He would sit by the bed, hours at a time, his eyes shut as though asleep. Only the wisp of a smile on the corners of his mouth suggested he was merely lost in sweet memories. An old eunuch, left over from the Ming, remarked to his companions, "I have never seen such love in a monarch before! No wonder they say the people from beyond the border are romantics!"

Lady Dongeh was much loved by her ladies in waiting, the servants and the eunuchs of Chengqian Palace for her generosity. Most of all, she was warm and friendly, never putting on the airs and graces of a great lady. She did not live lavishly. Indeed most of her allowance was used to help servants in difficulties. Furthermore, the special gifts of food from the Emperor or the Empress Dowager's table were also distributed among the ladies living in her palace. From time to time she also recommended certain of her ladies to the Emperor. Thus, the few nights away from her, he spent with women from her entourage. And they were grateful for this honour.

When Lady Dongeh fell ill, the household was shrouded in gloom. People spoke in hushed voices; walked on tiptoes; were even loath to eat their fill. Now that she seemed to be on the mend, the household regained its buoyancy. Everyone had heard the news that the Empress' indulgence had been revoked, but no one expressed their feelings on the subject except in surreptitious winks or smiles which showed their satisfaction at the turn of events and their confidence in the future.

This important piece of news was kept from Precious Concubine. Fulin was not ready to tell her, and her household probably felt the excitement might be detrimental to her recovery.

On the morning Precious Concubine left her bed for the first time, the ladies attending her toilette were especially animated. Dressed and coifed, Lady Dongeh was settled among plumped up pillows on the kang. Her personal maid Rongniu brought in three dainty blue porcelain bowls on a round platter. As usual Lady Dongeh drank the ginseng tea, then the milk tea, and finally the lotus seed gruel, savouring every tiny mouthful.

"My Lady enjoys her food today," remarked the maid happily. Lady Dongeh rewarded her with a smile.

"Indeed, I am much better. Rongniu ... everyone seems happy these days...."

"Your slaves are happy because My Lady is better."

"That's not what I meant. You're hiding something from me." Rongniu tilted her head and grinned impishly, "We weren't supposed to breathe a word...."

"Stop playing the fool. Did you think you can go about making eyes at each other without me noticing? You better spill the beans before I lose my temper!" Although her words were stern, Lady Dongeh smiled in spite of herself. Rongniu sidled close to her mistress and whispered, "Your Ladyship, yesterday His Majesty revoked the Empress' indulgence."

"What did you say?" Lady Dongeh was shocked.

"Your slave wouldn't dare lie." Rongniu was quite full of herself as she added, "There must be an uproar in Kunning Palace right now." Lady Dongeh paled. Her eyes darted nervously from the maid to the garden outside the window and back again. Rongniu sensed her agitation.

"What is the matter, My Lady?" she asked in puzzlement. "... Your slaves are happy because...." Taking Lady Dongeh's startled look as encouragement the maid blurted, "... My Lady will soon be Empress...."

The maid's unadorned word struck Lady Dongeh like a swift blow to the heart. She trembled, cheeks flaming, but her thick lashes held back the tears that brimmed. She sat motionless, fighting for composure. Presently, she sighed and spoke sternly: "What nonsense is this?" Rongniu fell to her knees in confusion.

"Rongniu, have I ever treated you badly?" Rongniu was frightened now. Banging her forehead on the ground, she cried out, "My Lady has been the soul of kindness. This year when both my grandfather and father died, it was Your Ladyship's generosity that enabled me to give them a decent burial. It is a blessing I will never forget!"

"Never mind that. Just between us, as mistress and servant,

how has the news been received? Are people for it or against it?"

"Well ... among the Mongolian ladies ... there are more of them than us...."

"If His Majesty deposes the Empress, do you think people in the palace would be for it, or against it? What about the Council of Nobles, the courtiers and the people? Would they consider an emperor who had deposed two empresses a wise and just ruler?"

Rongniu's eyes bulged from her head. She had no answers for her mistress. Lady Dongeh dismissed her maid with a wave of the hand. Left alone, she slumped against the low kang table, her chin supported by her cupped hands, lost in thought. She was as still as a statue. Though outwardly calm, her thoughts were in a turmoil. It was deeper, more far-ranging than she dared give utterance to.

Rongniu's voice announcing His Majesty's arrival scattered her gloomy thoughts. The next moment she caught the sound of his familiar footsteps. She hurried off the kang, patted a loose curl into place and straightened her robe, intending to meet him outside. But Fulin was already in the room, reaching for her hands.

"You're up and about!" he exclaimed with almost childlike pleasure. "You're better." He released her hands and stepped back the better to see her.

"Let me look at you!" His glance encompassed her from head to toe. "As elegant as a fairy, or a spray of pear blossoms in the morning dew."

Lady Dongeh giggled with delight.

"Your slave does not deserve such praise. In the next life I shall be a flower sprite that can take many forms to please you. How else could I be a plum blossom yesterday, a pear blossom today, and maybe a lotus tomorrow...."

Fulin was reminded how he had compared her to a plum blossom standing in the snow, filling the dew-spangled morn with her fragrance, and laughed out loud.

They talked companionably together, gradually Black Pearl turned the conversation to a discussion of *The Romance of the Three Kingdoms*, one of Fulin's favourite books.

"Some say *The Romance of the Three Kingdoms* is one of six great literary masterpieces, and I heartily agree," Fulin pronounced. "Abahai had it translated into Manchu and commanded all his military men to read it. It was a wise move...."

"Just so!" Black Pearl echoed. "In the book Cao Cao is described as a traitor and an opportunist, but he had great ambition, and he was a brilliant strategist...." Picking up on the topic, Fulin continued with enthusiasm:

"I admire Cao Cao the most, after his defeat of Yuan Shao. Among the papers captured from his enemy were a cache of letters from his own officers offering to surrender. Cao's advisors urged him to take this heaven-sent opportunity to rid himself of traitors from within, but he refused. His reason was simple. Yuan Shao commanded a superior force that swept everything before him, while Cao Cao was seriously outnumbered. Therefore he could not blame his followers for putting their personal safety ahead of his cause. Instead of pursuing the faithless, he ordered the documents destroyed. Without such courage great ambitions come to nothing!"

"Your Majesty, I agree Cao Cao was a man of vision, able to weigh a situation and plot the right course of action. Furthermore, he was a man who knew himself." Fulin and Black Pearl faced each other across the kang table, sipping tea.

"How sayest thou! Thy student craves instruction!" Fulin, quoting a line from a *Kunqu* opera, drew a smile from Black Pearl.

"Three kingdoms stood against one another. Wei was the strongest. To the east of the river, Sun Quan sent a note to Luoyang, inviting Cao Cao to take the throne ... but he refused..." said Black Pearl.

Fulin quickly understood.

"You know everything," he said.

"Yes, Your Majesty. The Empress is kind and loyal, without blame."

"Not true! We regard filial piety as the paramount virtue, and she is found wanting."

"Your Majesty's displeasure is understandable. However, the Empress is related to the Empress Dowager by blood and must surely have been distressed at the time. Her neglect was probably an aberration for which she has already been reprimanded by the Empress Dowager. Surely that's enough...."

Fulin gazed at Black Pearl with a mixture of surprise, suspicion, admiration, and deep love. He was at a loss for words.

"Your Majesty has always acted wisely ... but in this ... your slave is deeply disturbed...." Black Pearl continued firmly, "The Empire has just been secure and the people are uneasy. A wise ruler will win men's hearts and there will be peace. But they will turn against one whose worthiness is in doubt. As ruler of all under Heaven, Your Majesty's every step must be taken with care, taking into account the sentiments of Manchu and Han alike. Deposing one empress is already perceived as a breach of propriety. Therefore it must not be repeated. Moreover, both empresses come from the Boerjijite clan. Has Your Majesty considered how this will affect the loyalty of the Mongolian banners?"

Fulin paced back and forth before the kang. Finally, frowning, he stopped before the window and with his back turned said, "That person is quite useless ... completely unsuited to managing the six palaces...." He whirled about to face Black Pearl, eyes blazing. "Surely you must understand why I am doing this!" Before he could say more, Black Pearl had prostrated herself at his feet.

"If Your Majesty deposes the Empress, then your slave must die!" she cried. "If Your Majesty will permit your slave to go on living and serving him, then you must not depose her!"

Fulin sucked in his breath with surprise. The maids and eunuchs within earshot were so stunned by the scene they had witnessed that they scarcely dared breathe.

Fulin sighed. "Throughout history trouble within the inner palace was always triggered by jealousy and jockeying for position. You are certainly the exception...."

Black Pearl threw her arms round Fulin's legs and pressed her cheek against them like a small child.

"As long as the Empire is safe, and the Manchus, Mongols and the Han live in peace, your slave is content to be concubine for the rest of her life..." she choked out.

Fulin helped her to her feet, stroking her thin shoulders, his eyes lingering lovingly on her haggard but still beautiful face. When he spoke his voice was choked with emotion. "Our wise ... and much loved concubine.... So beautiful ... and wise.... Such a waste...." He was too choked to continue.

Black Pearl buried her face against his chest, feeling the throbbing of his heart. The thought of her fate, and the pain that she must endure at all cost, made her tremble. Gently stroking her back, Fulin strove to comfort her. At length Black Pearl lifted her face to Fulin and, in an almost undiscernable voice, murmured, "Your slave is terribly afraid...."

The news that the Empress' indulgence had been revoked struck Jingren Palace like a bolt of lightning.

To add to the disquiet, at first light the nurses came with news that the Third Imperial Son had been taken ill during the night, and was unconscious. The usually unruffled Lady Kang rushed to see for herself. At dusk she returned in great agitation. A few serving wenches who spoke too loudly were angrily rebuked, and the eunuchs were ordered to slap them across the face twenty times each. Thus, everyone in Jingren Palace was made aware the Third Imperial Son was seriously ill. Since Lady Dongeh became the favourite, everyone here had pinned their hopes on the Third Imperial Son. If anything happened to the boy, what would become of their mistress? Indeed, what future would all of them have?

As lamps were being lit in the Jingren Palace, a messenger arrived with more news. The imperial physician had diagnosed the Third Imperial Son's illness as smallpox, and the Emperor had ordered him removed from the Forbidden City.

Smallpox was a disease the Manchus dreaded. Before the conquest, marauding bands that came south always gave infected areas a wide berth and, on some occasions, withdrew altogether. After they were established in Beijing, many of the imperial family and the aristocrats succumbed to the disease in epidemics which swept the city from time to time. Smallpox was particularly deadly to the Manchus. Nine out of ten did not survive. Thus, during the season when outbreaks were likely, the Emperor would move to Nanyuan or even to the grasslands beyond the Great Wall until the danger was over. Because of the fear of smallpox, a law was enacted early in Shunzhi's reign banishing anyone infected with the disease to a distance of not less than forty miles from the city. As a result, not only those infected with smallpox but those with scabbies or any kind of rash was driven from the capital. When the disease struck, panic seized the city. The afflicted and their families were driven out. Many died of hunger and exposure. Children of the poor were abandoned by the roadside to live or die at the whim of fate. This was one of the injustices of the early Qing Dynasty. It was only through the efforts of Zhao Kaixin, an official from the southern district of the capital, that more humane measures were eventually adopted.

However, the Manchu's fear of smallpox was not diminished, which explained the Emperor's reaction when the Third Imperial Son's illness was diagnosed. To Lady Kang and indeed all those who lived in Jingren Palace this was as heavy a blow as that which had befallen the Empress. It was a wakeful night for everyone. The lights in Lady Jin's chamber was not dimmed till the wee hours, while those in Lady Kang's bed chamber burned throughout the night.

Early next morning Lady Jin, accompanied by three ladies in waiting, went to pay her respects to Lady Kang. As usual, Lady Kang accepted their greetings with reserved graciousness and bade them withdraw. The three ladies in waiting departed, but Lady Jin tarried. A serving maid brought milk tea, and Lady Kang gestured for her visitor to be seated. The two women faced each other, taking occasional sips of tea, gently blowing aside the steam. Neither could think of anything to say. The silence became oppressive.

Lady Jin stole a glance at her hostess and was shocked by the changes wrought by a sleepless night. Lady Kang seemed to have aged overnight. Her face was chalky and the eyes were black stagnant pools.

Lady Kang also shot a few quick glances at her companion, and what she saw made her frown. For Lady Jin's somewhat masculine features were flushed with excitement. The heavy brows which arched over the long narrow eyes quivered ever so slightly, as though she was making an effort to hide the restless gleam in the eyes. What are you excited about, Lady Kang thought to herself.

Both ladies had drained their cups, and still neither had spoken. Finally it was Lady Jin who broke the awkward silence.

"Has My Lady enquired where they've taken the Third Imperial Son?" Lady Kang answered sourly, "They can take him wherever they like. I don't care."

"My Lady...." Lady Jin was shocked by the response.

"The child is the bloodline of the Aisin Gioro clan. If they don't care, why should I?"

"My Lady, if you don't care about the Third Imperial Son, then...." Lady Kang laughed out loud; a barking laugh that filled the hearer with horror.

"It would suit them if both of us were to die..." said Lady Kang between clenched teeth. "We'll see who lasts longer."

The venom in her tone gave Lady Jin the courage she lacked. She shot to her feet excitedly and in a torrent of words blurted out how she had received a sign from their ancestors in a dream. In the dream Nurhachi and Abahai told her they could not rest in peace unless she took matters in her own hands to prevent the Empire they had carved out from falling to the son of a barbarian.

Lady Kang mulled the tale over without a word. Bursting with excitement now, Lady Jin said, "My Lady needs have no fear. I will do everything. No one else will be involved." Lady Kang looked about her fearfully. Lady Jin purposely raised her voice and said, "My Lady wore a beautiful pair of shoes the other day. May I see them again?" The two women rose and went into the inner room of the bed chamber.

A short while later when they emerged again, a subtle change had come over both ladies. Lady Kang was not her usual quiet self, nor was she coldly calculating as she was a while ago. She seemed confused, her movements unco-ordinated. Instinctively she picked a rose from a plant and began pulling off its petals with her long trembling fingers. She bit her lip as she watched the petals flutter to the ground, as silent as though she would never speak again.

By now Lady Jin's excitement had dissipated. She was determined and coldly efficient as she whispered to Lady Kang, "Fire and water cannot exist together. Drastic action must be taken or you offend the ancestors and wrong your descendants."

Lady Kang's voice was pitched so low it was hardly audible. "Nevertheless ... I haven't the heart...."

Again Lady Jin reminded her of her vision and swore she would do anything to prevent the barbarian's son from becoming crown prince. As they spoke the sound of music, played on a lute, floated over the wall that separated them from Chengqian Palace. Mixed with the music they thought they heard a soft ripple of laughter.

Lady Kang shivered, her face twisted in a frightful spasm. She shut her eyes painfully. When she opened them again she had recovered her cold, expressionless demeanor. Dropping the half destroyed flower, she strode out of the bed chamber to stand on the terrace outside.

"Send word to the Empress and the Empress Dowager that I crave permission to leave the Forbidden City to visit my son," she said in a dead voice.

According to protocol, when a prince falls ill with smallpox only his mother may visit him. Thus, Lady Kang, accompanied by a few of her ladies, left the Forbidden City for Fuyou Monastery without any obstruction.

However, a few days later, the playful and charming Fourth Imperial Son also fell ill with smallpox.

Part 6

Winter sunlight, passing through a coin-size puncture in the window paper, threw a round patch of light four or five times larger on the opposite wall. Menggu watched that patch of light shift from the end of the kang to its far corner, then slowly creep up the eastern wall, turning from yellow to gold to crimson. She trembled, dreading her husband's return.

A hubbub of voices and laughter issued from the east wing where some of the women were gambling, while sounds of bickering came from the west wing. Nobody paid the least attention to the so-called "empress" nor did Menggu dare interfere in any way with the "royal concubines".

Since the White-robed Monk had revealed his true identity and that of his pupil to her brother Qiao Bainian and formalized her marriage, Menggu's husband Zhu Cizhao no longer beat her.

However those peaceful days were short-lived. As soon as Qiao Bainian left for the capital to take part in the imperial examinations, Zhu Cizhao's sadistic streak reasserted itself. Furthermore, the women of the east and west wings also banded together to make her life miserable. As the saying goes, when the tiger leaves the mountain, the monkeys come out to play. Since Menggu had neither the courage nor the temperament to assert herself the others took advantage of her, heaping her with scorn and ridicule. Only the former nun of Huanxiu Nunnery was civil towards her.

With her brother out of the way, Zhu Cizhao immediately excluded Madame Qiao from the inner courtyard of his house. However, he permitted Ronggu to visit her older sister from time to time. Ronggu was twelve years of age, and innocent. One day while Menggu was bathing, Ronggu entered unexpectedly and saw the purplish bruises that covered her body. Menggu did her best to calm the horrified young girl. Afterwards she forbade Ronggu to visit her. Thus the only human contact she had was severed. Mired in a hellish predicament, Menggu led a life that was such a burden that she lost the will to live.

As the year wore on to its end, she began to wonder what had befallen her brother and why he had not returned.

The patch of light on the east wall had turned deep red and inched upward. Watching it Menggu trembled like a leaf. Three days earlier Zhu Cizhao had left with the White-robed Monk saying he would return three days later. Those three days were a respite, almost like a festival recalled from her childhood. And like festival days they passed all too quickly. She sensed that soon she would be plunged into darkness again where pain and misery lurked in wait of her.

The outline of the patch of light blurred. Its redness deepened till it became a patch of blood; blood from her wounds. Menggu stared at it with terror. Perhaps that hateful patch of moving light was dragging her into the abyss. She must stop it! She leaped for the cupboard, rummaged in it till she found a hammer and nails. She would nail the patch of light to the wall so it couldn't move. Then time would have to stand still. She hammered the nails into the wall with feverish urgency. But nothing could stop the patch of light from moving relentlessly upwards.

Menggu threw down the hammer in despair, tore a strip from her blouse and held it against the hole in the window paper with both hands. Now she would never see the blood-red patch of light again!

Outside, the gate creaked. Menggu dropped the piece of cloth and shrivelled up into a tiny ball as heavy footsteps slowly moved towards her chamber. Zhu Cizhao required all his women to greet him on their knees in the courtyard. Menggu wondered who was there.

A hand lifted the curtain in the doorway, and her husband, the lord and master of all of them, stood before her. He wavered like a dilapidated straw hut about to fall down. His arrogance and sadistic cunning were gone. His bloated cheeks and the corners of his eyes drooped. Though his terrified, bloodless visage was turned to Menggu, he was scarcely aware of her.

Menggu was afraid to look at him. She scurried about setting a table with food, wine and tea, then according to custom, rushed to summon the other ladies to serve him. But he stopped her with a loud cry.

"Don't summon them! None of them can be trusted!"

As Menggu backed away, she stumbled against the kang. Zhu Cizhao leaped at her and came crashing to his knees. He clutched her about the legs and pleaded, "Don't leave me! Don't leave me alone! I beg you! I'm finished! Finished!"

Zhu Cizhao knocked his head against the ground, breaking into loud sobs.

Menggu's heart fluttered like a caged bird. She was too frightened to move. Yet in spite of the fear and loathing, she felt a shred of pity for the man grovelling before her. It was all she could do to tug timidly at his sleeve, urging him softly to rise and sit.

Zhu Cizhao was like a beaten child. Seated on the kang, he wiped away his tears. Between sobs, he spilled his troubles to Menggu whom he had never respected before.

Three days ago Zhu Cizhao had gone to Dushan with the White-robed Monk to meet with a band of outlaws. The band, believed to be five thousand strong, had agreed to support Yongli of Southern Ming, to repel the Manchu and re-establish Han supremacy. Assuming the title of prince, Zhu Cizhao had gone to bestow titles and seals of office upon his new followers. This was his first public act in his new status, and he was puffed up with pride and excitement. It was as though the empire was already in his grasp. However, there were only eight hundred men to meet him, and the band of gallant fighting men he expected was nothing more than a ragtag bunch of brigands with tired horses and rusty weapons. Furthermore, the unruly, blood-thirsty men frightened him. However, the leaders had prepared a feast of sorts to welcome them ceremoniously the first day. Their lack of numbers was said to be due to the Qing government 's granting tax exemptions to pioneers who settled hitherto uncultivated land. Though four thousand men and horses had been lured away, the leaders assured him that those who remained were the best; men who would help him regain the throne of Ming.

The next day, when Zhu Cizhao, as prince, distributed honours and seals of office, the atmosphere changed. Although the heroes paid their homage, they clamoured for gold. Zhu's tiny cache was a mere drop in the bucket. It not only failed to placate but turned the men against him. The leaders' attitude was no longer friendly. That night the White-robed Monk and Zhu Cizhao were relegated to a hovel far from the camp. Nor were servants provided to see to their comfort. At dawn, Zhu Cizhao and the White-robed Monk hurried to the camp to try and salvage the situation, but it had been razed to the ground. Men and horses had disappeared. In a panic they left the encampment as fast as they could. Only when they had put some distance between themselves and the camp did they discover from other wayfarers that the outlaws had surrendered to the Qing government in exchange for amnesty. That Zhu Cizhao and the White-robed Monk had not been turned over for bounty was the only sign of the brigands' regard for the Ming Dynasty.

Zhu Cizhao became quite hoarse recounting his misadventures. Now he slumped dejectedly against the kang table.

"All the others have laid down their arms for amnesty.... This band at Dushan was our last hope.... In one night it too was gone. How will I regain the throne? It's all over...." He fell across the kang table knocking over several wine cups. A small silver cup rolled onto the ground, making a clear tinkling sound.

"Ah ... wine!" Zhu Cizhao rolled over grimacing. "Wine!" He reached for the jug, poured and tossed it off as though it was water. He was quickly drunk.

"Nothing is as pleasant ... as a cup of wine..." he muttered incoherently. 'For how often is the fullmoon overhead?' Thus wrote my uncle Hongguang. How very apt! He at least enjoyed the luxury of being emperor for two years! What about me?"

Menggu blanched and tried to slip from the room, for she knew the Emperor Hongguang's poem always triggered the sadistic streak in her husband.

"Don't move!" Zhu Cizhao roared, fixing her with his bloodshot eyes that glowed with the ferocity of a wild beast. Menggu shrank into a corner. "So you want to run away too ... and beg amnesty? I'll never let you go...."

He closed in on her. A swift kick in the leg sent her tumbling to her knees. He grabbed her by the hair and with his free hand slapped her hard across the face until Menggu's cheeks swelled. Zhu Cizhao tilted his head to one side and leered at his handiwork.

"It's only when you're plump like you are now, that you're not ugly."

In his drunken state Zhu Cizhao had the strength of ten. He lifted Menggu off her feet and hurled her on the kang. Then he leaped upon her like a wild animal. Menggu shrivelled in pain. The blood seemed to congeal. She did not weep for there were no tears. Nor did she cry out. She longed only for death to end her torment.

He took her viciously. Though he was spent fear and despair would not leave him. Had the woman cried out, or begged for mercy, he would have had a momentary rush of being the strong man, the conqueror. That would have given him some emotional relief and restored a little of his pride. But this woman, whose beauty made him drool, was a block of ice. No matter what he inflicted upon her, she never made a sound. She did not respond. Perhaps she did not even think of him as a man.... But he was Zhu Cizhao ... son of generations of emperors ... a prince who should have been on the throne except for a nasty trick of Fate.... He glared at Menggu sprawled on the kang, and as usual rage exploded within him. He leaped upon her again with his fists, striking and pinching and kicking. "Why don't you die, woman of ice..." he muttered over and over.

Menggu shut her eyes and let him beat her. She had only one wish. Let him kill me quickly ... then it will all be over....

"Sister! Sister!" Ronggu's childish voice was full of excitement, "You'll never guess who's here!" Zhu Cizhao turned his attention to the girl outside, and a sardonic grin crossed his face as he slid off the kang. Summoning all her strength, Menggu seized his leg. "You can't..." she hissed through clenched teeth. "She's only a child!" Zhu Cizhao leered at her. "I see, you're finally responding!" He kicked her aside and called out, "Little Sister, come in!" Menggu started to cry out, to warn the girl, but a blow to the face stopped her.

The curtain in the doorway was lifted and as the girl skipped into the room, Zhu Cizhao leaped from his hiding place beside the door, seized her by the waist and hurled her onto the kang. Next moment he was tearing off her clothes. The girl screamed and lashed out with hands and feet at her assailant. Menggu also leaped into the fray, but Zhu Cizhao was like a mad man completely out of control. "My uncle Hongguang killed two young girls in one night!" he cried as he tore at the girl. "I can do it too!" Suddenly he let out a howl of pain, for Ronggu had sunk her teeth into his hand.

"Stop!" The voice seemed to fill the room. Next instant a large hand closed upon Zhu Cizhao's neck and hurled him into a nearby chair.

Ronggu rushed into her brother's arms. Qiao Bainian's rage was fearful to behold. It was the chasm separating monarch and commoner that saved Zhu Cizhao, for Qiao Bainian would not raise his hand against his lord. Instead, bowing low he said, "Sire, Qiao Bainian has returned."

Zhu Cizhao quickly recovered himself and, assuming the airs

of a great prince, sprawled in his chair.

"Ah! So it's you. Why, we haven't seen you in a long while...." Though anger still flashed in Qiao Bainian's eyes he spoke calmly. "Sire, your actions must not be excessive...." Zhu Cizhao cocked his eyebrow at him and replied, "There is nothing excessive about two sisters serving the same lord. It's a tradition...." Qiao Bainian's face suffused with blood.

"She is only a child of twelve!" he protested. Zhu Cizhao threw back his head and laughed.

"It's our custom to take them young."

Qiao Bainian was filled with rage. He longed to wipe the shameless grin off Zhu Cizhao's face, for hadn't an empire been lost through the folly of decadent men? Instead he dragged Ronggu from the room.

When Qiao Bainian left Huanxiu Nunnery the moon was already risen.

He had come to the nunnery to seek out the White-robed Monk to lodge his complaint. Zhu Cizhao was nothing but a bully, and it was up to the "Imperial Teacher" to correct him, or Qiao Bainian would abandon his title as an imperial in-law and seek advancement elsewhere. Besides, he had just returned from the south and there were urgent matters he wished to discuss. However, the White-robed Monk was gone. Abbess Yuan agitatedly recounted everything that occurred earlier.

The White-robed Monk and his disciple had returned from Dushan that afternoon without a word about their journey. The White-robed Monk began to drink. At first he insisted the Abbess drink with him. However, the nun did not have a head for liquor, so he ordered his servant to keep him company. The servant got drunk very quickly. Next the crippled gatekeeper was called in as a boon companion. He proved less than satisfactory as well. In high dudgeon, the White-robed Monk took a jug of wine and a cup and left the nunnery. The Abbess, concerned for his safety, followed at a distance. The White-robed Monk accosted strangers on the road and invited them to drink with him. It was disgraceful. When the Abbess tried to remonstrate with him, he heaped her with insults. And so she left him to wander on his own.

Something must have gone seriously wrong at Dushan. Qiao Bainian had made a tremendous effort to establish the contact with Dushan. They were his lifeline and he was greatly disturbed by their loss. But where had the White-robed Monk gone? The moonlight reflected off the snow lit the fields. There was no sign of a living soul for miles around.

From a knoll in the distance came a wild scream followed by a burst of song. In the clear stillness of the night the sound travelled. Qiao Bainian followed it and found the White-robed Monk drunk and dishevelled, seated unsteadily on a large rock, guzzling wine from a jug.

"Don't drink anymore, Sir." Qiao Bainian tried to take the jug away. The White-robed Monk shoved him aside with amazing strength and continued pouring wine down his throat. He did not recognize Qiao Bainian. Indeed he did not seem to be aware that he was no longer alone. He gulped down a few more mouthfuls, wiped his mouth and began to laugh and then to sing. The song became a wail, which in turn became the shrill barking of a dog. The White robed Monk mimicked a dog's bark, his voice rising higher and higher till it cracked. Suddenly he stopped and burst into drunken tears.

Qiao Bainian approached him again.

"Master ... I'm Qiao Bainian ... just back from the south."

The White-robed Monk smiled through his tears. "I'm not drunk," he insisted. "As a matter of fact I recognized you at once. Come. Drink with me!"

"If you're not drunk, why were you imitating a dog?" demanded Qiao Bainian.

The White-robed Monk replied, "No matter how drunk I get,

my mind stays clear. The barking always happens when I've had a drop or two. But I've never told a soul the reason. It's too tragic.... But with things the way they are ... I must get it off my chest ... or I will burst...." He grabbed Qiao Bainian by the collar and essayed a smile so grotesque that it sent a shaft of pain through him.

"You know the sort of man I am," Qiao Bainian blurted out. "You can tell me anything."

The White-robed Monk shook his head sadly. He gazed up at the sky with his lack-lustre eyes and was silent for such a long while that Qiao Bainian had to prod him.

"What was on your mind?"

"Yes, I will tell you..." he muttered. In that instant he seemed to age. His back bent and his shoulders drooped as he recalled the past.

At the time when the Tartars came south, he had been the governor of a small town. When the town was sacked, he and his household prepared to kill themselves. They had made their abeisance to the Emperor in the north and their peace with the gods. The entire household hanged themselves. His wife was pregnant at the time, and when she hanged herself the fetus dropped out. A dog they kept fended off wild dogs that swarmed around to attack the fetus. The dog fought valiantly, killing four others before it finally succumbed. The White-robed Monk tried to hang himself. But the rope snapped and he alone out of a household of twenty-six survived. Imitating a dog barking when he was drunk was his way of mourning his dead.

"My heaven, I must defeat the Manchu barbarians and restore the dynasty. Else how would I face those twenty-six souls who have gone before me?..." he sobbed.

Qiao Bainian rubbed his chest and massaged his back.

"Master, don't distress yourself." He hissed through gritted teeth, "The barbarians have destroyed our society, killed our people, taken our land and dishonoured our women. It is our duty to overthrow them."

The White-robed Monk lifted his head to the sky and sighed. "Our time has passed! There is no hope now. Rather than live in shame, it is better to die and rejoin those twenty-six courageous souls...." He covered his face and wept anew.

Qiao Bainian's heart lurched within him.

"What about the men at Dushan?"

The White-robed Monk shook his head and recounted how the men of the Dushan, Linshan and Yangcheng Mountains had thrown down their arms and gone over to the Qing all because of a promise of tax-free land and amnesty.

A cold band of steel seemed to wrap itself around Qiao Bainian's heart, turning him to ice. He struck the rock with his fist and cried, "I refuse to believe it!"

The White-robed Monk shook his head sadly.

"Believe what you will," he said dully. He recalled a time when the military governors of Datong and Jiangxi could rally men of all walks in life with a call to arms. Princes and generals, common folk, runaway slaves and outlaws answered the call. Those were heady times. Opportunity missed ... is lost forever....

The White-robed Monk lay on the rock like a fish out of water, gasping its last. He was quite sober now, calm but in despair. His arrogant, self-confident air, his cunning, his almost sinister strength had all dissipated. In spite of himself, Qiao Bainian pressed, "What will you do, Master?"

The White-robed Monk seemed not to hear the question, but continued in his flat voice:

"It is said in unity there is the seeds of dissent; and out of chaos comes new order. Such is the progression of history. After ten years of turmoil, the people long for order. The Tartars were quick to recognize the mood of the people. Dissidents were brought to heel both with force of arms and promises of amnesty. The old taxation laws of the Ming have been abolished. Land appropriation is forbidden. Runaway slaves are forgiven. Cultivation of wilderness is rewarded. Officials of the old regime are entrusted with important posts, and corruption has been eradicated from the imperial examinations.... All this was done to woo the people, and it has succeeded. What hope is there for you and I?"

But Qiao Bainian was not easily discouraged.

"Master, do not give up. The Yongli Reign has plenty of able men...." He recounted how he had gone south after failing the imperial examinations and had been in contact with members of the Yongli Reign in Nanjing. A decree had gone out to all the generals in the field, including Zheng Chenggong to stage an uprising when the Qing invaded Yunnan and Guizhou.

"... If we act together there is still hope..." he concluded.

"Stop dreaming," said the White-robed Monk. The defection of Dushan, Linshan and Yangshan convinced him that Yongli Reign did not have the forces they boasted of. Otherwise why had they called upon men such as Zheng Chenggong for help?

"To be honest I have never trusted Zheng Chenggong. Who can say he does not crave the crown himself? As for us ... we are too weak to make a difference...."

From inside his tunic Qiao Bainian took a roll of paper bearing various military titles and the red seal of the Yongli Reign. He also had in his possession a number of seals made of wood, copper and silver, together with a large yellow banner.

"Look, Master," he said triumphantly, "these have just been issued by the court, to be used to gather men of courage...."

The White-robed Monk took the silver seal and bounced it in his hand. "This is at least worth a few ounces of silver, the rest is rubbish." And with a sweep of his hand he scattered the paraphernalia on the ground.

Qiao Bainian could not be sure whether the White-robed Monk was drunk or sober. He seemed to have his wits about him when he spoke about the empire and his personal tragedy. But his actions seemed quite the opposite. As he bent down to retrieve the scattered seals and papers, the White-robed Monk said something that gave him pause.

"Where there is a heavy reward there will be brave men. Without silver who would put his life in jeopardy?"

The silence between them lengthened. Qiao Bainian snatched up the wine jug and took a few swigs, then wiping off his whiskers he asked, "Has His Highness no treasure?"

The White-robed Monk took his time answering.

"If he decides to wash his hands of the whole thing, he has a few things he could sell and live off the proceeds. Otherwise nothing...."

Qiao Bainian could not believe his ears.

"You mean to say there is something dishonourable about this Third Prince?"

The White-robed Monk chuckled mirthlessly. "What difference does it make whether he is honourable? It's the title that counts."

"In that case," Qiao Bainian retorted hotly, "the man's a coward and unfit for kingship." The White-robed Monk countered, "All of the sons of the house of Zhu are decadent and useless, otherwise we would not be in this predicament." Qiao Bainian's eyes snapped wide.

"We have come this far, I might as well tell you the rest," continued the White-robed Monk. "I was a Metropolitan Graduate and survived the courts of Chongzhen, Hongguang, Longwu and Yongli. Each was as decadent and corrupt as the other. They are beyond the pale...."

"Then you have no confidence in the restoration?" Qiao Bainian pressed.

"What can I say? I too am a Zhu, but not of the royal family. As they say Emperors must take their turn on the throne. So, why shouldn't there be a turn for me? If Zheng Chenggong can proclaim himself so can I. But that was a notion I had a long time ago. Now it's water under the bridge. I shall end my life in obscurity, amid poetry and strong drink...."

The White-robed Monk drunkenly clapped an arm around

Qiao Bainian's shoulders. His last pronouncement hit Qiao Bainian like a bolt of lightning. Suddenly everything became crystal clear, sweeping away all his doubts. A strange light blazed in his eyes when he in turn clapped the White-robed Monk across the shoulders.

"Master, I shall be equally honest with you. We are in the same boat. As long as we stick together, we might succeed."

"Have you a plan?" The White-robed Monk squinted at Qiao Bainian with blood-shot eyes.

"When I made contact with the men at Dushan, I also contacted several smaller bands. My idea was to attack a small town in the New Year. We would go in swiftly and leave, seizing valuables and stock-piles of grain. Once we have food and money, we will also have men."

The White-robed Monk's eyes flashed like a bird of prey. Nimbly he leaped off the rock on which he was perched and gathered up the scattered seals and documents.

Watching him, Qiao Bainian asked meaningfully, "Is this rubbish going to help us?"

The White-robed Monk laughed, cold sober now. All the despair and madness was gone. Qiao Bainian sighed to himself, thinking this man is like a bottomless tarn, a mystery ... not to be trusted ... but he also realized he needed the man and therefore they must stick together.

"There is a favour I would ask the Master...."

"By all means...."

"I want Menggu's marriage annulled."

"Ah ... that .... Let's wait till after the uprising...."

"Then it's agreed...."

A few days later a caravan arrived at Malan Village. The horsemen were followed by many mules carrying large sacks. All the men were armed with bow and arrows and wore swords. Some said they were rich merchants who had come to the village to visit Qiao Bainian. Others claimed they were a hunting party from the capital who were breaking their journey at Qiao

Bainian's large house. Still others averred they were bandits who had come to rob the village. However, nobody dared breathe a word of what they thought, for Qiao Bainian was rich and arrogant, and the White-robed Monk possessed certain uncanny powers, and no one dared offend them.

2

After nightfall and the city gates were shut, the streets of the capital emptied, except in the southern quarter, which was just coming to life. For this was the notorious demimonde of teahouses, restaurants, theatres, houses of ill fame, and the salons of fashionable actors of the opera who vied with the courtesans for the favour of the rich and powerful. Although Liu Tongchun had vowed never to set foot on the stage again three years ago, it was to this area he had come. His errand was to find Tongqiu, the current toast of the Peking opera, with whom he had shared a teacher. Though the popularity of the opera had dwindled in the early years of Shunzhi, it had made a remarkable recovery. Its revival had also brought back the practice of hiring popular actors to grace the tables of the rich and powerful. At the age of eighteen, and at the peak of his powers, Tongqiu was in great demand both off stage and on. His salon, one of the most elegant, was more like a scholar's than a wealthy actor's. Tongqiu was a female impersonator on stage. Through long years of practice the line between reality and fantasy had blurred, so that he was more like a delicate young girl than a man. Tongqiu was both delighted and surprised that Tongchun had come to seek him out. He was even more startled when he learned Tongchun's errand. He wanted Tongqiu's help to get back on the stage. No, he did not regret leaving the theatre. However, things had been hard since Li Zhenye was executed and Zhang Han went to prison. A man had to eat. It was a reason that Tongqiu could relate to. He was already beginning to feel the pinch as time sped on.

The real reason for Tongchun's desire to return to the stage was more complex. The fact is he had never forgotten Menggu. Through all his vicissitudes he had steadfastly clung to the jade bracelet and the embroidered purse she had given him long ago, mementos of simpler days when love was pure and unconditional. All that was gone. Though Menggu was married and lost to him, while he was in the employ of Li Zhenye and Zhang Han he still nourished a vague hope of finding someone like her and marrying. Now even that hope was gone.

He had been eking out a living, doing odd jobs in the market place when he encountered the old Manchu soldier Soordong and his grandson, Feiyose. It was from the boy that he learned of Menggu's plight, and fierce anger flared within him. He told himself he must return to Malan Village somehow and rescue her. It was that determination that brought him to Tongqiu's salon on a snowy night in the middle of the last month of the year.

The first day of the New Year was especially festive that year at Hongqiao Township in Yongping Prefecture. Aside from the usual folk dances, stilt walkers and lion dances, an opera troupe had come to perform. This was not an itinerant troupe, nor even one from the county seat, but one that was formed in the capital especially for the festive season. When the word got out, people from within a hundred miles poured into the town to see the show. They came early to secure the best places. Soon a huge crowd gathered before the stage. The sound of exploding firecrackers, the crash of drum and cymbal, horses neighing, carts rumbling, parents calling for their offspring blended into a merry cacophony that swept everything before it right to the footlights.

As the first curtain fell a troop of Manchu cavalry arrived and surrounded the makeshift theatre. Police armed with clubs, knives and ropes rushed through the crowd and onto the stage shouting, "Catch the bandits! Catch the bandits!" Anyone wearing a white cap was seized. Panic swept the crowd. A number of people were injured by the police, and others were trampled by the panicked throng rushing for exits. Nobody knew what was going on.

Tongchun and Tongqiu quickly discarded their costumes, wiped off their make-up as best they could and tried to escape. But the police had already found their way backstage. They were seized and clasped in irons. Tongqiu trembled with fear. Tongchun still had his wits about him and loudly proclaimed their innocence.

"Innocent," sneered the policeman who proceeded to drag them away. The rest of the troupe rushed forward and threw themselves on their knees.

"They are innocent," they cried. "Please release them. We are from the capital and we can't go back without them."

"Don't give me that nonsense about the capital!" the policeman retorted. "We're dealing with treason, one of the ten major crimes not covered by the amnesty."

Tongqiu swooned at the mention of treason. Tongchun was ready to argue the case but the troupe master intervened.

"My Lord," said he, "these are two famous actors we engaged from the capital. They are well-known among the gentry and would never be involved with treason. I beg you...." He surreptitiously slipped the policeman a red packet of money.

"Master, let me tell you, there's been a treasonous conspiracy here. Those involved carry Ming-dynasty coins, wear white caps or keep their hair long as a sign of recognition. These two were seen wearing white caps yesterday. And this one has long hair. Someone reported them. Now, let's go."

The troupe master had a ready-made explanation.

"There's been a misunderstanding. Tongqiu who plays female roles has the court's permission to wear his hair long. And yes, they did wear white caps yesterday as a mark of respect for their dead teacher. But they are not wearing them today!"

"Never mind. It'll all be settled in front of a judge." And so Tongchun and Tongqiu were locked up in the town gaol.

So many people were arrested that the gaol quickly filled. Tongchun and Tongqiu were confined in an office that opened onto the main hall, together with thirty odd other prisoners, waiting to be transported to the county seat that afternoon.

Tongchun was sorry for Tongqiu who was unused to hardship. "I'm sorry I got you into this..." he apologized.

Tongqiu's head drooped.

"What can I say? I wanted to come..." he said in a pathetic voice, close to tears. Tongchun quickly shucked off his jacket and rolled it up to serve as a cushion, then he helped Tongqiu sit down against the wall. Tongqiu began to weep.

Tongchun went over to the window to peep through a tear in the paper. Suddenly he caught sight of the familiar face of an old Manchu soldier.

"Mafa!" he shouted, "Mafa Soordong!" He shouted as loud as he could, hammering the window frames with his fists.

Tongchun had glimpsed the local prosecutor welcoming Soordong as he arrived. The commotion caused Soordong to glance in his direction. He said something to the prosecutor who, with a great show of deference, ordered Tongchun to be brought forth.

Soordong was surprised to see Tongchun and demanded to know what had happened. Tongchun related how he and Tongqiu had joined a touring troupe to perform in the town, and also to visit the grave of their teacher in Malan Village, and how they had been arrested without cause. The prosecutor, who acted as interpreter, watched Soordong's reaction as he listened. He was aware that the Manchu understood some Chinese though he could not speak it, and thus was scrupulous in his interpreting.

Soordong glowered at the prosecutor from under his bushy grey brows. "These two dolls of the theatre are not traitors. I know them as well as their teacher. Let them go."

"Of course ... of course ..." the prosecutor agreed. But Soordong was anxious to see his orders carried out. Tongqiu was brought out of his temporary cell and the two were released.

Before they left, Soordong who was familiar with conditions at Malan village warned Tongchun that trouble was brewing there.

"Trouble?" whispered Tongqiu querulously. Soordong's brows knit ominously.

"A white-robed monk together with the Abbess Yuan and the Qiao family have been plotting treason," he said in halting Chinese. "Stay away from Malan Village."

Tongchun was thunderstruck. Instinctively he knew it was not the time to ask questions.

Tongchun and Tongqiu were let out of the county gaol by a chatty guard who had seen them perform. Being a lover of the theatre, he was pleasantly disposed towards the actors.

"What a stroke of luck you know the old Manchu," he crowed. "It was he who discovered the plot. That is why the prosecutor bowed to his wishes. Otherwise he'd never let you go. Each prisoner earns him a merit point."

"Were many people involved? Did they all get caught?" asked Tongqiu.

"Of course! They've all been sent to the capital before the festive season. A cache of treasure, seals and letters of appointment from the Yongli Reign was also seized. It was quite something! Only one got away ... a fellow called Qiao Bainian. But a universal warrant will be issued any day now. He won't remain at large for long...."

They've all been sent to the capital! But there was no mention of Menggu and Ronggu? Have they also been swallowed up by these terrible events? A heavy weight had been lowered upon Tongchun's heart.

Three days later, Tongchun sent Tongqiu whom the ordeal had made ill back to the capital while he went alone to Malan Village.

The old apricot tree still stood alone on the knoll he remembered so well, its gnarled branches like out-stretched arms welcoming the return of the wanderer. It woke a flood of bittersweet memories. He climbed onto the tree and gazed north. From his vantage, Huanxiu Nunnery at the edge of the village and the house of the Qiao family not far beyond were clearly visible. The ancient gate of the nunnery was locked and sealed with crossed strips of paper. The same seals had been affixed to the redlacquered gate of the Qiao family's home. Not a soul stirred abroad. Tongchun quickly understood the reason, for the red tassel on the tops of soldiers' caps could be seen passing to and fro in the alley. A trap had been laid....

His last thread of hope snapped. The Qiao family, mother and daughters, had disappeared.... Tongchun did not have the strength to go on to the village. He sat down on the hard, old roots that protruded from the ground at the foot of the tree. The plains, mountains, streams and village were the same as he remembered them, but a pall covered them, draining them of colour until everything was as barren as his heart.

3

From a word here, a casual remark there Tongchun laboriously pieced together what had happened at Malan Village.

The White-robed Monk and his disciple had been plotting rebellion a long time, and the Qiao family had been drawn into it. In the waning part of the previous year the caravan that came to the village armed to the teeth were undoubtedly their accomplices. It was the busybody Wang Yongxiu who was in the habit of eavesdropping first got wind that something was afoot. Afraid of what Qiao Bainian might do to him, he took his story to the old tartar Soordong. Soordong was an amiable soul who minded his own business and was not a bully. But the mere mention of treason sent him into rage. He notified the banner at once, and they in turn took it to the county seat. Acting in unison, the White-robed Monk, his disciple and their followers were quickly rounded up.

Everything at Huanxiu Nunnery and in the house of the

Qiaos was confiscated. It was only then that it was revealed the young acolyte had also acquired a number of concubines. The Abbess Yuan was also caught in the net. Afterwards many of the rebels gave themselves up. Some produced documents. Others confessed to the planned attack on the county granary and treasury on New Year's day. With that information, the authorities quickly arrested all those with white caps or had long hair as possible suspects. There was also another point worth noting. A rhyme had been used as password.

"The red flower withers when the black flower blooms.
The black flower awaits the white flower."

This was doubtlessly a reference to the red topknots worn by Manchu soldiers ... and how the red flower would wither under the onslaught of winter which was symbolized by the white caps they wore.

As to the whereabouts of Menggu nobody knew. Being a woman she was not likely to be executed. However, being sold or given to some aristocratic household as a slave was a fate that all women in her circumstances faced. Tongchun had seen this happen before.

As the unattainable becomes all the more desirable, Tongchun found untapped strength within in adversity. He vowed he would find Menggu somehow.

When Prince Jidu arrived at his sumptuous home which rivalled the Imperial Palace, his servants were waiting at the gate to greet him. Though tired, he was too excited to rest, for on that day Duke Duoni whom the Emperor had appointed supreme commander for the pacification of the south had set out with his army.

As he sank into a soft divan with a piping hot cup of milk tea and a tempting plate of butter cakes, he relived the events of the day. Every fibre of his being tingled with excitement....

A host of flags and banners snapped in the breeze. Brilliantly coloured sunshades and robes flashed amid a myriad glittering battle axes, spears, staves and other weapons. They were flanked by ceremonial elephants and chariots gathered outside the Forbidden City. A guard of honour carrying great clubs marked the white marble pathway from Meridian Gate to the Hall of Supreme Harmony. Led by the Master of Protocol, the supreme commander and his generals marched in measured steps between the guard of honour and assembled nobles and courtiers toward that most august edifice where they knelt to receive their great seals of office from the Emperor's hand.

Afterwards the supreme commander followed the Emperor into the chapel for the consecration of his standard. In that moment, all the hopes of their ancestors and the destiny of the Manchu passed into the supreme commander's hands.

It was a glorious moment!

Outside the left Changan Gate a yellow tent had been set up for the Emperor. Here His Majesty offered a toast to the departing army. The supreme commander drained his goblet and took his leave. A large assembly of civic and military officials accompanied the supreme commander out of the city to bid him farewell. There the Minister of Rites and the Minister of War personally served tea. This was the last ritual. The supreme commander, facing the direction leading to his Emperor thanked His Majesty, and then all present; and the march to secure peace all under Heaven in the Emperor's name began....

The focus of that day's solemnities was Duke Duoni. However, to Prince Jidu it was a repeat of the ceremonies that took place three years earlier when he set out as supreme commander to conquer Zheng Chenggong. These ceremonies expressing the warlike spirit of the Manchu had been handed down by their ancestors. In Jidu's veins the blood of the ambitious Nurhachi mingled with that of the loyal and gallant Jirgalang. It was this combination that produced the notion of winning and ruling an empire by force of arms.

The same excitement compelled him to accompany Duke Duoni out of the city, though protocol did not require a prince to do so. He had also taken several other princes and dukes with him. At the moment of parting he had clasped hands with Duoni whom he fixed with his fiery gaze and said, "Make our banners proud!"

Still in a state of excitement, he had invited the younger princes and dukes who had accompanied him to an archery tournament that afternoon.

Milk tea soothed him. As he contemplated sending for his wife to chat with him a while, his guests were announced. Jidu was delighted and went out to greet them. They were Prince Changahdai, Prince Fushou, and his younger brother Duke Menger, Duke Jieshu, and Duke Lerjin. After formal pleasantries were exchanged and familial protocol had been observed, Jidu led his guests to his archery field.

The archery field was situated to the east of the estate, surrounded by a high wall and a row of Chinese scholar trees. The flat field could be used for racing horses, archery or practising martial arts. In the shade of the trees was a row of low buildings, beyond which were the flower and kitchen gardens. Servants who were responsible for the care of gardens and weapons were housed in the low buildings. A tower had been erected at one end of the field. Built in the traditional style of a princely residence, its painted beams, its roof of glazed green tiles with seven mythical beasts straddling the upturned corners of the eaves, matched the status of a prince. The tower was used by the prince and his guests to watch tournaments and to rest. Food and drink had already been prepared, and hassocks laid out for Jidu and his guests in the main room of the lower floor.

Among the princes of the imperial family there were only three who were of the same generation as the Emperor. Of the three, Duke Duoni had departed that day for battle. The other two were Prince Yuele and himself. He and Yuele had never been close, nor was the latter his equal in power or renown.

Those assembled on this occasion were all of a younger generation, mostly nephews. Jidu gazed at the assemblage with satisfaction. The cream of the court was all present and accounted for. He smiled benignly as an elder, an attitude strangely at odds with his fierce, warlike reputation.

"What were your impressions of today's solemnities?" he enquired.

Obviously the princes all had their own thoughts. However, Changahdai, whose forthright personality matched his rough-hewn exterior, was the first to respond in a loud voice. "It was most exhiliarating and gratifying. It swept away all the cobwebs and showed that it is still up to us bannermen to conquer all under Heaven and bring the rebels to heel."

Prince Fushou, son of Prince Haoge and therefore the Emperor's nephew, continued the conversation. He not only inherited his father's warrior's bearing, but also his candour. "Imperial Uncle, we bannermen have fought since the first day. The honour is our due." Jidu listening to their discourse was gratified, for they reflected his own sentiments exactly.

"This has indeed been a glorious day for the eight banners," he said happily. "It is especially gratifying to find such ambition among my kin. I am certain one day each of you will receive the same honours you witnessed today. Then your aged uncle can die in peace.... Our ancestors took the Empire by force of arms. Therefore, horsemenship and archery must be our first concern. I have therefore invited my dear nephews here, on this glorious day, for a small archery tournament. I have also provided a few paltry prizes.... "He ordered the prizes to be brought in.

The prizes were duly displayed on a table set in the centre of the room. They consisted of a vase carved out of the purest white jade, a pair of gold goblets encrusted with precious gems, and three silver bowls set with jade and white and red agates. All the prizes were extravagant.

Jidu pointed at the three frames set at the far end of the field and explained,

"Dear nephews, before you are three targets. To the right is the first called the Birds...." The targets were indeed intriguing. The birds consisted of four parts. The bird at the lowest part was as big as a swan. The one above it was the size of a pigeon in flight, and above that was one no bigger than a sparrow. The fourth was a tiny bird the size of a goat's eye.

"To win, your arrow must hit the goat's eye. In the centre is the second target, the Flower Basket...."

This was another ingenious construction of interlocking iron hoops made in the shape of a gourd. At its narrowest point was a small red hoop just wide enough for an arrow to pass through.

"...An arrow passing through it causes the gourd to unfurl into a flower basket. The last is a silk scarf which your arrow must penetrate...."

Each contestant would fire nine arrows, three at each target.

"He who fires nine arrows and scores a bull's eye each time wins the jade vase. He who hits the mark six times out of nine wins the gold goblets, and he who hits the mark three times out of nine wins the silver bowls. What do you say?"

The princes were all anxious to begin. Menger spoke wryly, "Princely Uncle, what if all of us have perfect score? There is only one jade vase...."

Jidu stroked his short bristly beard and answered with a twinkle, "In that case I will be pleased to supply four more. The question is do you all have the same skill?"

The five princes were the third and fourth generation descendents of the founders of the dynasty. Though not as warlike as their forebears, they were well schooled in the martial arts. Now they were anxious to show off their prowess. They rose and went over to the racks of armament to select their weapons. Lerjin hung back. He was the youngest and somewhat effete and the least accomplished.

To hit a target at a distance of more than a hundred paces requires a three-foot long arrow with a five-inch tip known as the

Armour Piercing Drill. A hard bow is the only weapon to make it fly. Lerjin gloomily selected a bow and nine shafts. As he returned to the main room he looked out at the targets.

"Lerjin, have you ever tried shooting at targets with arrows like these?" Jidu asked.

"No.... No.... My mother thinks I'm too young..." he stammered.

"Too young!" sneered Changahdai who was closest to him in relationship. "I started archery lessons at the age of eight, and at thirteen I was using the hard bow. How old are you anyway?"

Lerjin did not reply. Jidu took an arrow from his quiver and, stroking it lovingly between his fingers from tip to fletching, said, "This indeed is an Armour Piercing Drill. It penetrates whatever it hits. It can take down two men at a time. When your father attacked Nanjing as supreme commander for the pacification of the south, he shot such an arrow into the city gate and it penetrated up to its fletching. That feat so terrified the Hongguang Court that they immediately sued for peace. Thus our eight banners became masters of the world...."

"Yes, Sir, I shall do my best ..." Lerjin murmured with head bowed.

Changahdai glanced at him distastefully.

"Why can't you be a man? Take Ahlima for example, even in death he didn't let the Manchu down...."

Menger softly asked, "Wasn't Ahlima the brave general under old Prince Shuncheng, who lifted a stone lion with his bare hands? How did he die?"

"That's him!" Changahdai supplemented. "He was so used to having his own way that eventually he offended the Emperor. He was ordered to die and even that order he ignored. Only when he was tied to a tumbrel and on his way to the execution grounds did he finally realize the seriousness of his situation. As the tumbrel was going through Xuanwu Gate, his legs suddenly shot out and he anchored his feet in the crevices of the city wall. The tumbrel was brought to a standstill. In a loud voice he cried out that he was a Manchu and did not deserve to die under the derisive gaze of the Han. He wanted to be killed within the gate. His wish was brought to the Emperor, who allowed him to die as he wished."

"An uncommon man indeed," sighed Menger and Fushou. The older princes eyed Lerjin who blushed and hung his head. Jidu clapped him across the shoulders. "We Manchu must not be the laughingstock of the Han." He reached into Lerjin's quiver, took three of the Armour Piercing Drills and substituted them with arrows with smaller tips.

"You need a more slender arrow to hit the red ring," he explained. "Let us commence!" He seated himself in an armchair covered with a tiger pelt and watched the five princes compete through slitted eyes.

It the first item, shooting the Birds, all the competitors hit the mark, except Lerjin whose bow was too soft to propel the arrow far enough to reach the target. Changahdai and Fushou laughed in his face. Lerjin was afraid to rebut them in the presence of an elder, but was close to tears with embarrassment. Jidu commanded him to aim at the sparrow-sized bird using a lighter arrow. To his credit all three shafts hit the target and one made the bull's eye. For the moment his face was saved.

The next item was shooting the Flower Basket. Lerjin, knowing that he was not equal to the challenge, laid down his bow to watch the others. In this round Changahdai and Fushou each scored a direct hit twice. However, Changahdai's cousin Jieshu, and Fushou's brother Menger both scored three hits. Watching six gourds slowly open into six beautiful flower baskets, Jidu shouted his praise and ordered wine. Those who scored two hits were rewarded two cups, and those who scored thrice were rewarded with three.

The square silk scarf was the most difficult target because it was soft and hanging in the air, the angle of the shot must be exact or the arrow would bounce off harmlessly. Changahdai and Fushou shot off their shafts with great force. Though the arrows whistled through the air, they bounced off. Changahdai slapped his forehead in disgust. Menger was more careful. He took his time taking aim, still only one out of three shafts found its mark.

Jieshu, a man of few words, calmly raised his bow, bent it until it was like the curve of the moon and let fly his shaft. The first arrow penetrated the target. Swish ... swish ... two more arrows followed close behind and two more targets were penetrated.

Jidu rose from his seat laughing and applauding the competitors. "Ah, the jade vase has an owner!" he cried. "We have heard Duke Jieshu is a man of hidden depths. Now we know." And with that he presented the delicately carved camphor wood box containing the jade vase to Jieshu. The redwood box containing the goblets went to Menger who had scored seven out of nine. To Changahdai and Fushou who each scored five out of nine went the gold bowls. But what about Lerjin? True to his princely station, Jidu presented him with a jade finger guard. Originally designed as protection for the finger in archery, they were later also worn as jewellery. The prince made the gift with two things in mind: as a memento of the occasion and also as a reminder to practise archery.

"Princely Uncle, I would have scored one bolt only if I had known I would get a jade finger guard!" Changahdai teased. Lerjin was too embarrassed to rebut him.

The second month of the year had just begun. The days were still shorter than the nights. As dusk gathered a huge fire was lit to one side of the tower, over which a pot measuring five feet across was suspended. In it two whole pigs, weighing seventy to eighty jin were boiled. The mouth-watering aroma of cooking meat drifted across the archery field. Inside the main room, mats were laid on the floor over which a red carpet was spread. On top of the carpet six marten fur covered cushions were arranged in a circle. In front of each was set a silver platter measuring a foot across and a silver bowl half its width. Everyone knew this would be a typical Manchu meat feast which was only held on festive or religious occasions. The assembled princes were deeply moved that Jidu was honouring them with such a feast.

Jidu was discussing the skills his guests had just displayed.

"My dear nephews, you each have strong points," he declared. "'Changahdai's is strength, but Jieshu is the more rounded archer; as for cleverness, I still have hopes for Lerjin...."

Fushou chuckled.

"Our Princely Uncle is renowned for his skill with bow and arrow. It is a pity that it is already dark, or else we would beg a demonstration."

Jidu pondered the remark and, smiling, ordered his servants to set up targets more than one hundred and twenty paces away. He selected a hard bow and three Armour Piercing Drills with whistles attached. He strode up to the starting line, stood with feet apart and waited like a bronze statue, heroic, unconquerable. The fire light enveloped him in a red glow.

From across the field a loud cry signalled the target was in place. The assemblage strained to see what it was, and presently they discerned three tiny pinpoints of light, the lit ends of incense suspended in the air.

Jidu calmly raised his bow, fixed his arrow and let fly three arrows in quick succession. The arrows whined through the air, each at a higher pitch than the one before. In an instant the three pinpoints of light were extinguished one after the other.

The princes were overcome by this feat of precision, swiftness and strength. When they recovered themselves they let out a cheer of praise and astonishment.

Chefs brought in a silver platter measuring two feet across, on which was placed a slab of meat weighing ten jin or more. This was accompanied by a huge silver bowl containing rich meat juice, and a silver ladle. Next a rough pottery bowl was presented to Jidu on a gold platter. The server filled the bowl with strong aromatic sorghum wine. When all his guests were seated cross-legged on their cushions, Jidu lifted the wine bowl and addressed his guests:

"Dear nephews, this bowl has been passed down to us from our ancestors. It was used by Nurhachi and his brethren for feasting when they were carving out an empire. It is a reminder of their legacy maintained by our present monarch. It is also a reminder that the creation of an empire is not an easy undertaking, and that we must be worthy of our inheritance."

He lifted the bowl, drank deeply and passed it to his guests in order of their ages. First Changahdai drank and passed the bowl to Fushou and so on, until it returned once more to Jidu. From his waistband, Jidu drew a small knife with a razor-sharp blade. With one deft movement he sliced off a thin sliver of meat with layers of fat and skin and lifted it to his mouth. As he chewed he gestured for his guests to eat.

The guests drew their knives and set to heartily. The meat was served without salt or any other condiments except meat juice. But it had been cooked to a turn, and the men were ravenous after the long day's activities. Changahdai and Fushou were especially hearty eaters. The huge chunk of meat was quickly demolished. Changahdai raised his voice and shouted, "More meat! More meat!"

Their host laughed happily, thanking his guests, for according to Manchu custom the more the guests consumed, the more honour was accrued to the host. Manchu nobles had prodigious appetites. It was not uncommon for Changahdai to consume ten jin of meat in one sitting. Platter after platter of meat was brought on. Sorghum wine flowed. As host and guests became sated, the conversation became as heated as the fire under the pot.

A steward now approached and having offered his obeisance announced that ten slaves which were given to honoured nobles for meritorious service had arrived.

"So they've arrived!" Jidu exclaimed with joy. For a gift of slaves was like a gift of money, and it was also a mark of the

Emperor's regard.

"They are already in their quarters. Will My Lord inspect them?"

"That won't be necessary. Inform the Mistress, and she will dispose of them. But don't forget the household rule for new arrivals. By the way, where are they from?"

"It is said they are connected with the treason plotted at Yongping Prefecture. Quite a number were involved. Each of the princes were sent a few, but these were the first."

"That will be all. See that the supervisor is well treated." When the steward had withdrawn, Jidu turned to the princes and remarked, "No doubt your households will also receive some slaves. Treason cases usually involve many people."

Fushou giggled. "A pity they're northerners. If the treason had been in the south there might be a few pretty women among them." Everyone laughed. Changahdai, full of wine, asked Fushou, "Haven't you got enough slaves already? Are they still running away?" Fushou frowned, "They still do it." Changahdai turned to Jieshu and asked, "What about your household?"

Jieshu spoke in a gentle voice. "Since His Majesty's decree, we have been more lenient with our slaves. Strange as it may seem, by feeding and clothing them better, they have been less troublesome."

Changahdai brushed that remark aside with a rough hand. "Rubbish! I don't believe it. Fact is these wretches will take a yard if you give an inch. Also, think of the expense, feeding and clothing! Brother, I have a better way."

Lerjin quickly interposed, "What is my Princely Uncle's way?"

Changahdai laughed. "I'll teach you a trick. Make them sleep on a bench at night. Tie them down as tight as you can so they can't get away. Next morning untie them and send them to work."

Jidu shook his head at Changahdai. "You are disobeying the

Emperor's command. I have found that slaves must be tamed like horses. That is why I set up a rule for new arrivals. All new slaves are flogged, and the flogging must be severe. The more they cry out the more you beat them, until finally not even a whimper comes out of them. When the whip lash produces no more reaction than from a stone or a block of wood, the spirit is broken. That slave is tamed. Mind you, the whip must never be used again, unless it's for a serious transgression."

"I don't understand," Changahdai objected speaking with the Dutch courage that too much wine had given him. "I am thinking our ancestors conquered this land. Cities, pastureland, cattle, slaves were given us by the gods, yet after we have all under Heaven, we are told we can't do this and can't do that? We Manchus own all under Heaven, yet the Emperor prefers the southern barbarians and their strange ways!"

"That is so," Fushou chimed in. "He has passed over his own kind to advance the fortunes of barbarian scholars.... The Emperor is turning away from our ancestors' traditions and adopting those of the Han."

Menger whispered excitedly, "I heard the Emperor chided Lords Aobai and Sukesaha for their handling of the corruption at the imperial examinations. They were reprimanded for the depths of their investigations."

"Huh! And that Precious Concubine!" sneered Lerjin whose tongue was loosened by drink. "She's half barbarian but the Emperor favours her above anyone else. If the Fourth Imperial Son is proclaimed crown prince, then this Empire...."

Jieshu chipped in with concern: "It looks as if the Emperor is deposing the Empress. Well, really...."

Jidu cut him short with a gesture, "You're all talking nonsense. The Emperor has his difficulties...."

Everyone was the worse for drink, and drunken grumblings were unavoidable, especially as these noblemen had not yet acquired the Han intellectual's ability to disguise their thoughts behind clever rhetoric. However, Jidu was still relatively sober. He ordered the wine removed and ushered his guests back to the reception room where tea was served.

No sooner had these red-faced noblemen seated themselves when Jidu's wife burst into the room wailing at the top of her lungs. The nobles got to their feet uncertainly, startled by the lady's unseemly display of emotion.

"Aya! Something terrible has happened!" she shrieked, slapping her thighs. "The Fourth Imperial Son is dead!" Everyone was shocked. Jidu spoke first,

"What are you saying? Have you taken leave of your senses?"

"Aya! Chief Steward Li has just come from the palace with the news. The Third Imperial Son has survived the smallpox, but this morning the luckless Fourth Imperial Son...."

"Stop your cackling!" shouted Jidu and the lady fell silent.

Everyone was shocked by the news. Lerjin deliberately showed his satisfaction, but when he glanced at Changahdai's grim look, he controlled himself.

After a long while, Jidu joined his hands and lifted his eyes to heaven, murmuring, "It's a punishment of the gods.... The gods have spoken.... Now we shall see if His Majesty listens...."

4

A spring breeze gently ruffled the surface of Taiye Pool, splintering the reflections of the White Dagoba and the bridge which strung out like a ribbon of jade. To the southeast, the green trees stood in sharp contrast to the imposing structures of the Forbidden City and the serene beauty of Coal Hill. Closer, on Qionghua Island, pavilions and towers half hidden by dark pines rose in a jagged line on the slopes. A long covered corridor snaked along the shore. The infinite blue of the sky was reflected in the clear pool water, in which the new green branches of willows dipped their tender tips.

The view from Five Dragon Pavilions was breathtaking. The Empress Dowager's chair had been placed in the centre pavilion, but she was not seated. Instead she was leaning against the white marble balustrade watching the red gold fish swim to and fro.

The death of the Fourth Imperial Son in the first month of the year had been a heavy blow to everyone in the palace. Though the death affected people in different ways, two months later those who mourned and those who rejoiced had all regained their equilibrium. In order to dispel some of her lingering sorrow the Empress Dowager had taken the Empress and the imperial concubines on an excursion to Beihai. At Five Dragon Pavilions she dismissed the ladies to amuse themselves. They were happy to comply. Now, many a silk robe of red, green, pink, purple and blue flitted among the flowering shrubs, the tender green of grass and trees, adding dashes of colour to the beauty of the place.

The Empress Dowager strolled slowly eastward along the flat bridge following a large gold fish she had been observing until it darted out of sight. She turned her gaze toward the shore where she saw two of the ladies deep in conversation in a grove of lilacs.

One was dressed in an elaborately embroidered green satin robe, with matching thick-soled shoes. Her hair was done in the Manchurian way and she wore a pale green silk flower in it. The colour of her costume complimented the mild spring day. Her companion was dressed in a Han-style jacket with wide sleeves over a pleated skirt. Her pink costume was set off by a peony and several gold pins in her hair. This was, of course, one of the ladies of Yongshou Palace, known as Lady Ke. She was the only one who affected the Han style of dress. The green and the pink were a perfect match, like water lilies and their leaves. From that distance she could not recognize the one in green, and so she sent for them.

It never occurred to the Empress Dowager that it could be her own niece, Lady Jing. Since she was deposed, Lady Jing lost interest in her appearance. She became dowdy and morose, so that even the serving wenches avoided her. What was the matter now?

The Empress Dowager smilingly remarked, "I must be getting old for I didn't recognize you. Child, are you well?"

"I thank the Imperial Mother, I am well," Lady Jing replied with a bow. Her daintily embroidered shoes caught the Empress Dowager' eye, and she enquired, "Judging by the daintiness of the embroidery on your shoes I would venture a guess. They are the handiwork of the Precious Concubine."

"The Imperial Mother is correct," Lady Jing replied. The Empress Dowager's heart leaped in her breast. She looked at Lady Ke again and fancied she had also seen the gold hairpin in the shape of a phoenix before.

"My hairpin was also a gift from the Precious Concubine. Originally there was a pair. The other had been given to Lady Jing...." Lady Ke bowed again.

The Empress Dowager chuckled. "I am glad to see you two on such friendly terms...."

Lady Jing bowed her head and bit her lip. "Perhaps the Imperial Mother does not know that last month I caught a chill. I did not want to make a fuss..." However, the Precious Concubine learned of her illness, and personally supervised the preparation of her meals and medicines. She remained at Lady Jing's bedside until she had recovered.

As for Lady Ke, though she was the principal lady of Yongshou Palace, being a Han, the other ladies shunned her. Thus Lady Jing and Lady Ke, both out of favour for very different reasons, turned to each other for comfort.

"I never thought the Precious Concubine would take such a sincere interest in me!" Lady Jing bowed her head.

"She is truly kind..." Lady Ke added timidly and ducking her head retreated a few steps. Lady Jing spoke again, "I was in despair, but the Precious Concubine often comforted me, reminding me of His Majesty's high ambitions and the Empress Dowager's compassion, and how it is everyone's duty to play a part in helping the Emperor achieve his goals. And so I overcame my despair." The Empress Dowager was pleased.

"No wonder your spirits have improved. The Precious Concubine is absolutely correct. I am surprised at such wisdom in one so young."

"She approaches, Imperial Mother," Lady Jing said under her breath as she gazed westward. Indeed Lady Dongeh was coming towards them, moving slowly through the drooping branches of the willows along the shore, her pale blue robes billowing in the breeze. A young serving maid, pretty in a childish way, with a thick braid hanging down her back, followed a few paces behind.

"Is that Rongniu accompanying her? She seems smaller somehow," the Empress Dowager remarked, squinting. The two ladies giggled.

"That isn't Rongniu," explained Lady Jing. "Rongniu was twenty-three last year and the Precious Concubine thought it high time she was married. So a husband was found for her outside the palace. This girl has just been given her."

"You two run along. Don't forget the midday meal will be served at Xianbi Tower." The two ladies, aware that the Empress Dowager wanted a private conversation with Lady Dongeh, bowed to the waist and withdrew.

"Didn't I tell all of you to amuse yourselves? Why are you here?" Though she was pleased that Lady Dongeh had come of her own accord without being summoned, the Empress Dowager purposely pulled a long face.

Ignoring the look Lady Dongeh approached with a mischievous grin.

"With all of us gone, Imperial Mother would be alone. So I decided to come and see if there is anything I can do for you."

"A sweet mouth," scoffed the Empress Dowager, smiling in spite of herself. "No wonder even the ill-tempered Lady Jing has been tamed. You didn't mention looking after her...."

"Imperial Mother should not be bothered with trifles," Lady Dongeh replied, her head tilted at a coquettish angle. But she quickly composed herself and continued in a more serious tone:

"Lady Jing is most unhappy.... Mother, it's been four years. ... She is your niece ... and His Majesty's cousin...." The Empress Dowager sighed. Lady Dongeh came closer and whispered, "I've spoken to the Emperor several times, and he seems to be coming round...." "What did you say to him?" The Empress Dowager frowned. The Precious Concubine lowered her voice still further.

"At least make her the principal lady of a palace. Do you agree, Mother?" The Empress Dowager looked deep into Black Pearl's eyes. She was amazed and moved by this young woman who was becoming more and more the image of herself at the same age. Impulsively she clasped Black Pearl's tiny hand in hers and sighed, "My child, I am touched by your thoughtfulness. With you at my son's side, I know I can die in peace.. "

"Mother, don't talk about dying! I know I will go before you!" Lady Dongeh smiled.

"...When the Fourth Imperial Son left us ... a part of me was torn away..." murmured the Empress Dowager. "Even the Emperor became gaunt.... But you ... were busy from dawn to dusk looking after our comfort. I was afraid the loss of your son would be too much for you ... would make you ill. But you carried on as though nothing had happened. Don't you miss him?"

A fierce gleam flashed deep in Black Pearl's eyes, contorting her features the merest second. She quickly regained her composure and responded in a calm voice, "I am neither wood nor stone, Mother. However, you and His Majesty are the pillars of the nation. Since I am not fit to shoulder some of the burden for you, I must not add to them with my grief. Ever since the Fourth Imperial Son was born, I was afraid he might die and cause grief to Your Majesties. As he grew in your affections that fear became stronger. Now that he has left us I am glad Your Majesties have not been so overcome by grief as to do injury to your health or let it interfere with the affairs of state."

The Empress Dowager was deeply moved by this speech.

"My son had intended to proclaim him Crown Prince after his third birthday. Who could have imagined...."

"Mother, let it pass. So long as the throne is occupied by the Emperor's flesh and blood, the bloodline of Aisin Gioro is secure. Whether he is the first born, or chosen for some inherent quality, makes no difference...."

"Ah, my son has often mentioned how understanding and selfless you are. I doubted him.... Now I know.... You are indeed my daughter!" Black Pearl giggled at the Empress Dowager's last remark.

"Has Your Majesty forgotten that she adopted me?"

"Fate brought you to my side."

The Empress Dowager's bantering tone relieved some of her pent-up emotions. "Would you go to Xianbi Tower and supervise the midday meal? Sumalagu has taken the children to play, and I'm afraid there is no one else to look after things."

Lady Dongeh was surprised that the Empress Dowager was suddenly anxious to be rid of her. However when she had reached the white marble steps leading up to Jingying Pavilion she caught a glimpse of the Empress, Lady Shuhui, Lady Kang and Lady Jin going towards Five Dragon Pavilions. Perhaps the Empress Dowager had seen them first and had deliberately got her out of the way to avoid unpleasantness.

However, she was not intimidated by those ladies. She knew how to deal with them: to overcome hardness with pliancy. But it was also extremely tiresome. Perhaps it was just as well to avoid them. But how long must this go on? After today, there was tomorrow, and tomorrow's tomorrow. Still their enmity was diminishing. Lady Duan and Lady Gong were cowards without a mind of their own. Lady Ke had always been civil, and she had finally won over Lady Jing. Perhaps better times were ahead.

"Third Imperial Son, you've just recovered and you're not supposed to be reading!" Sumalagu's scolding came from the other side of the garden wall. "Your Imperial Grandmother sent you here to play! Now behave!"

Lady Dongeh rounded the corner just in time to see Sumalagu holding a book high above her head, and the Third Imperial Son jumping up and down trying to snatch it back.

Catching sight of Black Pearl, Sumalagu sank to her knees, but Black Pearl quickly stopped her.

"Sumalagu, you're the Empress Dowager's confidante. One of a younger generation such as I cannot accept such a salutation. Besides there is no need for ceremony between us." Sumalagu smiled, "Would that not make me impolite?" She bade the child greet his Imperial Mother. The Third Imperial Son, who was always fond of this pretty and gentle Imperial Mother, immediately dropped to one knee and piped, "The Heavens bless the Imperial Mother!" Black Pearl gathered him quickly in her arms. "You've been so ill. Let me look at you."

The child's round face had become pointed; the eyes more deep set; the complexion had lost its rosiness. The most noticeable change were the pockmarks scattered across his nose, forehead and cheeks but not numerous enough to mar the boy's handsome face. The pallor after a long illness could not suppress the boy's buoyant spirit that flashed in the intelligent eyes. He exuded a spring-like vivacity.

"I'm all better, Imperial Mother," he said with a smile. "But the Imperial Grandmother won't let me go back to school, and Sumalagu won't let me do anything I want." Then lowering his voice he whispered in her ear, "But I'll read anyway." Black Pearl whispered back, "What are you reading?" The whispered exchange continued.

"My teacher wants me to memorize *The Thousand Poems*. Please get it back for me."

"She won't give it to me. But I'll give you another copy."

"Good! I'll fetch it tomorrow!"

"All right."

Sumalagu, watching the two, smiled to herself.

"Third Imperial Son, don't be a nuisance. Let's go see the Imperial Grandmother and ask for a boat to go rowing. Wouldn't that be fun?"

"Yes! Yes!" the boy shouted, "lets go boating!" Then turning to Black Pearl he added, "Imperial Mother, can little Fourth Brother come too? I haven't seen him for such a long time and I miss him!"

The child's words struck Black Pearl like a blow. She wavered and blanched.

"Third Imperial Son, stop your nonsense," Sumalagu quickly interrupted.

"I'm not!" the boy protested. "You wouldn't let me see little Fourth Brother because I was ill. But I'm all better now!"

Black Pearl fought to control her trembling. Her throat was so constricted she could barely breathe. Sumalagu took the child by the hand and hurried away, saying the boat would leave without them. The Third Imperial Son, shouted over his shoulder, "Imperial Mother, please let little Fourth Brother come! When he's older I'll teach him poems ... and archery too...."

The child's voice faded in the distance. Finally she was alone. Black Pearl plunged into the maze made from the porous rocks from Lake Tai. At the end of the maze was a crabapple tree in full bloom. Black Pearl threw herself on the ground and pent-up tears flowed at last.

The loss of a child is the most devastating pain in all the world for a mother. Black Pearl's sorrow ran deeper, was harder to bear, because no one must know.

When the Fourth Imperial Son's death was announced, Black Pearl hid herself under a quilt and wept. Her pain was so great she thought she would die. Her life had become meaningless. Then she thought of Fulin and she found strength to go on.

For his sake and the sake of his ambitions she had to go on living. Henceforth she would gird herself in armour so that the sorrow within would not seep out. Nor would she allow herself to be touched by sympathy or the sorrow of others. With serenity she would comfort the Empress Dowager and the Emperor. With selflessness she would deflect the maliciousness and envy that surrounded her. This was the only way she could aid Fulin and protect herself. The price for loving Fulin was unspeakable anguish.

Seeing the Third Imperial Son today reminded her of her own dead child. The boy's innocent remarks shattered all her defences. All the banked-up emotions burst forth. She wept till the breath caught painfully in her breast.

A breeze rustling the crabapple tree showered her with petals that fell like teardrops; or were they drops of blood?

A strange echo came to her from the other side of the rockery. Someone else was weeping as bitterly as she.

That sound reminded Black Pearl of who she was, her position and her duties. She quickly dried her tears and, having tidied her hair and straightened her robes, called in a calm voice, "Who is there?"

Her personal maid, a girl of thirteen or fourteen, who had been sent to her early in the year, answered. Quite by coincidence the girl was also called Rongniu like her predecessor. Black Pearl liked this Rongniu's innocence and cleverness and kept her constantly at her side. Why was she crying?

Rongniu knelt and drying her eyes pressed her forehead against the ground begging forgiveness.

"I heard My Lady crying and I couldn't help crying too," she gulped, tears starting once more. Black Pearl was silent for a moment.

"Dry your tears, child," said she finally. "As long as you are good, you will not be mistreated. You must never tell a soul that your Mistress was weeping today. Do you understand?"

"I understand. But why shouldn't My Lady weep for her

child ... the way I sometimes grieve for my mother?'' Black Pearl fought back her tears and sighed. ''There are many things you don't understand ... and shouldn't ask.... Let us go.''

When Sumalagu and the Third Imperial Son arrived at Five Dragon Pavilions the Empress and Lady Shuhui had just left. Lady Kang and Lady Jin were conversing with the Empress Dowager.

''Imperial Grandmother!'' the boy shouted and ran to throw his arms around her neck. ''Oh! I've seen so many flowers,'' he crowed. Then realizing where he was, he quickly slipped onto his knees and said quite solemnly, ''The Third Imperial Son pays his respects to the Imperial Grandmother.''

The Empress Dowager chuckled.

''Since you've been ill, you've grown up.... Have you greeted your Imperial Mother?'' The Third Imperial Son turned to Lady Kang, and addressing her as ''Imperial Mother'', respectfully knelt again. Lady Kang quickly raised him, examining his countenance carefully. ''He is much better...'' she breathed. The Empress Dowager spoke to Lady Kang saying, ''In a few days it will be the Third Imperial Son's birthday. The gold lock around his neck should be changed for the occasion. I have already prepared a new one. Send the old one to Kunning Palace tomorrow.''

According to Manchu custom the shrine of the ancestors must be situated near the residence of the Empress. Hence it was in the western corner of Kunning Palace. It was also the custom of the imperial family that gold locks worn around the necks of princes and princesses during childhood must be renewed annually. The old ones were then deposited in the sack of descendents which hung in the western chamber of Kunning Palace as a token of thanks to the gods for their protection.

Lady Kang said she would do so. As she turned to examine the Third Imperial Son's gold lock, she noticed the boy staring at Lady Jin as though he were trying to remember something.

Lady Jin was disconcerted by the child's scrutiny but forced herself to be calm.

Sumalagu had temporarily captured the Empress Dowager's attention grumbling how the Third Imperial Son was unmanagable and always reading. Lady Kang turned the Third Imperial Son round to face her.

"Don't stare," she admonished. "Let me look at your lock...." At the same time, Lady Jin, complaining that she was dressed too warmly, begged to be excused that she might change. The Empress Dowager, constantly aware of the rivalry between the ladies, thought lady Kang and her son had somehow offended Lady Jin causing her to withdraw.

"You haven't greeted Lady Jin yet," the Empress Dowager reminded the boy.

Lady Kang's palms were moist with apprehension as the Third Imperial Son turned towards Lady Jin. Lady Jin blanched. She would have taken to her heels but for the Empress Dowager. She forced herself to be still, reminding herself that the boy had been running a high fever and was semiconscious. It was doubtful how clearly he could recall people or events of that time.

The Third Imperial Son bent a knee. As Lady Jin lifted him up, their heads came so close together that the child's face almost touched the lady's eyes and the down on her upper lip.

"Ah, I remember you!" the young prince cried. "Did you give my toys to the Fourth Little Brother, and did he like my stomacher?"

Lady Kang chided the child in despair, "What are you talking about, Third Imperial Son?"

Third Imperial Son turned to the Empress Dowager for sympathy.

"They're always saying I talk nonsense. But I'm not!" He tugged at the Empress Dowager with one hand, and with the other pointed at Lady Jin. "She was wearing a blue cloth jacket and her hair was done in a braid. She wasn't as pretty." The

Empress Dowager's smile vanished. Her eyes were now sharp and cold as daggers. Lady Kang and Lady Jin bowed their heads under her scrutiny. Lady Jin's purple satin robe threw off quivering beams of light for she was trembling. In a voice heavy with grief the Empress Dowager asked, "Third Imperial Son, when was this?"

The boy realized something was wrong. The sudden change in the atmoshpere frightened him.

"It was when I had smallpox..." he mumbled burrowing into Sumalagu's ample bosom.

In the silence that followed, a bee wandered from one of the flower beds, buzzed fretfully between the speechless people and disappeared. Then there was only the gentle lapping of the pool against the pilings of Five Dragon Pavilions.

The Empress Dowager's expression was severe when she ordered Sumalagu to take the Third Imperial Son back to the palace. In the same breath she dismissed Lady Kang.

"Lady Jin, you will follow me," she said as she strode out of the pavilion. Lady Jin's head came up at a haughty angle, as she followed the older woman with quick, sure steps. Lady Kang almost cried out, but she bit her lip in time to stop herself. In a moment Five Dragon Pavilions was deserted except for the hapless Lady Kang.

Yunqin Studio was a quietly elegant room. When the Empress Dowager had seated herself, she ordered the doors and windows shut, and all her attendants to withdraw. Left alone, she fixed an unrelenting gaze upon Lady Jin.

"Now tell me everything!" she commanded.

All her fears vanished. Kneeling ramrod straight before her aunt, Lady Jin recounted the incident from the beginning.

During the time when the Third Imperial Son was ill with the smallpox, Lady Jin had taken advantage of Lady Kang's visit to her son and, disguising herself as a servant, went along. Having gained the sickroom, she took some of the sick child's toys and one of his stomachers. Then she bribed one of the wet nurses to place the toys next to the Fourth Imperial Son's pillow, and to dress him with the stomacher. As a result the Fourth Imperial Son was infected....

"You..." the Empress Dowager uttered the single word through clenched teeth, pointing at Lady Jin with her finger. For a while she was too overcome to speak. Then sighing and shaking her head she asked, "How could you do it?"

"Aunt, I couldn't bear to see the Empire we fought for given away to that barbarian. I couldn't bear the thought that the purity of the Mongol and the Manchu race was being contaminated by the wretched blood of barbarians. I had to rid ourselves of that little barbarian. Imperial Mother, I did it for the ancestors. My loyalty is unquestionable!" Lady Jin spoke calmly without the slightest hint of histrionics. It was clear she was prepared for this eventuality.

"Have you forgotten who the Fourth Imperial Son's father is? Or who his grandfather is? He is an Aisin Gioro! You have killed the Emperor's son. It is an unforgivable crime!"

"I know But I have no regrets." The Empress Dowager paced the floor with a mannish gait, her brows furrowed in thought. Now and then she glanced at Lady Jin who remained stiffly on her knees, fearlessly waiting for the axe to fall.

When she stopped beside Lady Jin, the Empress Dowager spoke sternly but clearly, her eyes averted:

"Listen carefully, Ahqi," she had address Lady Jin with her familiar name used only by her family. "I am Empress Dowager of Great Qing. I cannot offend the memories of Nurhachi and Abahai or our reigning monarch. To ignore your crime would surely reap the vengeance of the gods. However, you are my niece, and a daughter of the Boerjijite clan. I cannot allow the name of our clan to be sullied in any way. Do I make myself clear?"

Lady Jin shuddered and replied dully, "I understand."

"Does Lady Kang know about this?" demanded the Empress Dowager.

"No! I told her I missed the Third Imperial Son and wanted to visit him. That is all." The Empress Dowager had her suspicions, but she nodded. There was another silence. The Empress Dowager suddenly wheeled on Lady Jin, fixing her eyes on the tiny flower made of pearls that she wore in her hair, and said, "Your aunt accepts your motive. Be assured, for your loyalty, you will be rewarded after you are gone." Lady Jin bowed her head to the ground. "I thank the Imperial Mother." The Empress Dowager turned away and with a gesture of the hand and in a raspy voice said, "You may go!" Lady Jin rose to her feet, her heart bursting with heroic feelings. She crossed the room in a few quick strides. At the door she paused and turning said, "Aunt ... I leave you now...." Her voice, with a slight quiver, hung in the silence of the room. Her aunt stood with her back to her. Though her shoulders shook ever so slightly, she did not turn, or speak. She only lifted one hand to her headdress and let it fall. Lady Jin felt a rush of emotion as she slipped from the room.

The Empress Dowager did not move until Lady Jin's footsteps faded into the distance. Her eyes were fixed upon the delicate decoration of the ceiling, but she saw nothing. Everything seemed enveloped in a white mist. Finally, she mumbled through grief-stricken lips, "Ahqi ... my headstrong ... child...." She shut her eyes and two heavy tears trickled past her high cheekbones and down her fleshy jaws.

The Empress Dowager remained alone for a long while. When she appeared at the midday meal in Xianbi Tower, she was her affable self, chatting easily. No one knew anything untoward had happened. True, when it was announced that Lady Jin, pleading indisposition, had retired to her palace, a look of determination not untinged by discomposure flashed briefly in her eyes. But it was gone in an instant. No one noticed except the guilt-ridden Lady Kang and the clever Precious Concubine.

It had been an exhausting day for Shunzhi, for it was the day of the great debate. In many ways it was more taxing than the daily audiences. For on this day, academicians, ministers and vice-ministers were required to present their thesis on the writings of ancient sages and history. The Emperor was also required to present a thesis of his own, as well as comment on those that were presented by his courtiers. This occasion involved many ceremonies and protocols. Eight Han officials and eight Manchus were selected to participate. After the debate, the participants were invited into the great hall where they were seated and served tea in recognition of their efforts. Fulin enjoyed the debates, for he gained many insights into the art of government from them.

Tired but exhiliarated, Fulin left the hall and went straight to visit his mother. On being told that the Empress Dowager had retired after an excursion to Beihai, he went directly to her bed chamber.

The Empress Dowager was propped up with cushions on the kang, dozing while a serving woman massaged her legs. The other servants stood solemnly beside the door and before the kang. When the Emperor entered, she roused herself and, smiling, greeted him.

"I recognized your footsteps! You must be tired."

"It's nothing. It is you who are tired after a day at Beihai."

"Not at all. I'm not so old that I can't move," the Empress Dowager gave her head a toss that brought an admiring gleam to her son's eyes. "What was your thesis?" the mother asked.

"My topic was *The Virtues of the Bow and the Pen*. I spoke for over an hour on the art of governing with an iron fist but a compassionate heart. My Lords were quite enthralled." Fulin couldn't help a note of self congratulation. The Empress Dowager nodded her approval, though it was not clear whether it was agreement with the sages or satisfaction with her son. "That was a worthy topic. However, if the bow is stretched too far might it not snap?''

"My Imperial Mother would surely be a formidable opponent in a debate,'' Fulin teased. The Empress Dowager became solemn as she asked, "My Imperial Son, has your bow been stretched too far?'' Fulin noticed the change in his mother's tone and quickly got to his feet.

"Imperial Mother, I await your instruction.''

"My Imperial Son, I applaud your zeal in completing the great task of your forebears and in uniting all under Heaven. However, are you too impatient? It is said he who makes haste stumbles. At present the Empire faces crises both within and without. This can lead to serious problems.''

"Will the Imperial Mother speak freely?'' The Empress Dowager's words made him uneasy. The Empress Dowager sighed.

"The facts are before you. Have you not noticed? Beyond these walls there is the clique of six princes, while within these walls the death of the Fourth Imperial Son....''

"Imperial Mother, what are you trying to say?'' Fulin grasped his mother's hand impulsively.

"Come. I will tell it to you plainly....''

Mother and son went into a small closet at the east end of the palace where they could not be overheard. Still Fulin's gruff voice raised in anger did penetrate once or twice accompanied by the sound of falling furniture and shattering porcelain and followed by silence. Just when their attendants were wondering whether something untoward might have happened Fulin was heard crying out at the top of his lungs, "It is not the will of Heaven! I don't believe this is the punishment of Heaven!'' The Empress Dowager had also raised her voice and she could be clearly heard saying, "Imperial Son, you are no longer a child! Think carefully!''

When the Emperor left Cining Palace, his attitude was strange and frightening. His movements were wooden, and his expression was as stiff and cold as though he wore a mask of wood or perhaps, ice. Only when one caught his glance did one notice the flame of rage and despair burning in their depths. And the Empress Dowager, departing from her usual custom, did not see him to the door.

The next day the rumour spread that the Emperor had lost his temper and gave several of his eunuchs a thorough flogging and also threatened to have them beheaded. That same evening, Lady Jin's death from a sudden illness was announced at Jingren Palace.

The Precious Concubine dressed the corpse.

"Sister, you came into the palace in your youth," she thought. "You are in your prime, why could you not serve the Emperor a while longer, instead of leaving? What a pity!"

The Empress and all the ladies were gathered around the corpse, dabbing at their eyes. Lady Kang, standing opposite the Precious Concubine, also dabbed at hers, though there were no tears. Never had she hated the woman opposite her as she did at that moment. Wasn't she the cause of all this? Lady Kang was consumed by rage and jealousy but dared not show her true feelings. She could only bow her head and bite her lips till she tasted salty blood and felt the pain.

A few of the princesses of the inner palace also came. Bound by duty and protocol they also dabbed at their eyes, though the death was nothing to them.

The Emperor's edict was delivered at that moment.

"Lady Jin of the Boerjijite clan, known for her virtue and her strength of character, has passed on after a sudden illness. In appreciation of her many fine qualities she is henceforth to be known as Lady Dao...." That is to say that in death Lady Jin had been elevated from a lower rank concubine to that of a full concubine, a principal lady of her palace, and would be buried with all the pomp and circumstance of her new station. The other ladies were gratified at this turn of events, and the dead too could now rest in peace.

As the other ladies withdrew, Kong Sizhen approached Lady Dongeh and softly called her, "Sister...." Lady Dongeh reached for the other's hand which she clasped without a word, her smiling eyes aglow. Kong Sizhen blushed and whispered, "Sister, you have eloquent eyes...." Lady Dongeh leaned closer and whispered in her ear, "I've heard the news from the Empress Dowager. When are you going to be installed in the palace...."

"Sister, I swear I'll scratch your eyes out!" Lady Dongeh's smile vanished. She held onto Kong Sizhen's slim hand and whispered urgently, "My good little sister, come soon! I need your help! You have no idea how hard it is for me!"

"I do know and I'm afraid," Kong Sizhen whispered back. "I've seen what happened to Lady Jin, and I'm terrified! This is a trap one can never escape from!"

"Then you won't come?" Lady Dongeh's beseeching eyes made her waver, but she steeled herself. "I can't.... I'm not as clever as you ... I will drown.... Sister, don't hate me. Take care of yourself.... I have already given the Empress Dowager my refusal...."

Lady Dongeh smiled wistfully. As she moved away she faltered and Rongniu quickly went to assist her. She seemed so fragile and worn-out that Kong Sizhen was almost moved to tears.

A few days later another case of corruption surfaced. Because it originated within the palace and the offence was exposed to no lesser a personage than the Empress Dowager, the Emperor was moved to a towering rage. The principal culprit, the chief eunuch Wu Liangfu, was immediately beheaded. The Han grand academician Chen Zhilin who was directly involved was dismissed and banished. Once again many people were implicated. All were either dismissed, demoted, or had their incomes confiscated. Again the nation was in an uproar. The Han officials who thought they were safe were once more thrown into a welter of uncertainty as rumours to their detriment spread. Those who had not yet been sentenced for their involvement in the corruption in the imperial examinations had their hopes of clemency dashed. Others uncovered since in the south, Henan, Shandong, and Shanxi could expect to be dealt with even more severely.

However, the Emperor, acting upon the wishes of his mother, restored the Empress' right to indulgences, and to everyone's gratification named Lady Jing, the former empress, principal lady of Changchun Palace. On the twenty-seventh day of the third month, the Fourth Imperial Son was given the posthumous title of Prince Shuorong. Finally everyone was able to breathe a sigh of relief. The bow that had been stretched too far relaxed.

5

Pomegranates bloomed in the fifth month of the year. Prince An was especially fond of these luscious, flaming red flowers, and at this time of year his garden was ablaze with them. However, in the last few days even the gaudy floral display faded against the varicoloured bunting, lanterns and other decorations that festooned the mansion in preparation for the prince's birthday. Indeed the hutong leading to the mansion was clogged with traffic from dawn, several days before, as gifts were carried or hauled in an unbroken stream to the mansion, sumptuously wrapped in red and green, silver and gold. It was as festive an occasion as the New Year!

On Yuele's birthday, visitors who came to offer their felicitations were all people of consequence. Not only the servants were awe-struck, but even the horses that pulled their carriages seemed quieter than usual.

In the eastern quarter of the mansion was a large garden, in the corner of which was a smaller one called the Courtyard of Pear Blossoms. Yuele had arranged a feast in these elegant surroundings for the princes and nobles who were related to him.

In the centre of the courtyard, a small stage had been constructed, jutting out from the rooms on the southern side. Under the stage small individual tables had been arranged, on which food and wine had been placed. Prince Changahdai, Prince

Fushou, Duke Jieshu, Duke Menger, Duke Lerjin, Prince Chikshin and Duke Nisiha and others were all present. Yuele's sons Yunduan and Marhun helped entertain the guests. To the right and left of where the men were seated, were two covered corridors hidden behind screens with openings that were round or square, six-cornered or in the shaped of flower vases. Here the ladies accompanied by Yuele's wife and concubines were seated. Facing the stage was an alcove in which two places had been set. These were reserved for the host, resplendant in his festive robes, and Prince Jidu.

Generationally, the men were equals. Socially, Yuele had only recently acquired the title of prince, and was therefore an inferior to Jidu. As the two men had their political differences, they seldom associated with one another. However, a semblance of harmony within the imperial family must be maintained. Also, Yuele was the elder. Therefore, Jidu dressed in formal robes and accompanied by his wife and two concubines arrived early to offer their birthday greetings.

It was an informal family gathering. The weather already quite hot, some of the ladies and gentlemen had changed into cooler attire. Now they sat fanning themselves as they ate and drank and chatted while an opera was performed for their entertainment.

The performance ended with a lively round of applause. The ladies were particularly taken with the two male leads. A moment later, the manager of the troupe appeared with the two actors and went straight to the alcove to present them to Prince An and Prince Jian and to receive their rewards.

Yuele looked at Tongchun and asked, "Are you not the actor Yunguan?" Tongchun bowed respectfully and replied that he was.

"Your singing, acting and recitative are better than I remembered. I thought you had left the theatre?"

"I had," Tongchun answered noncommittally. Whereupon the manager of the troupe added on his behalf, "My Lord, he only makes guest appearances from time to time. He does not entertain guests or have a master. He does not belong to a troupe."

"Ah, yes, once in the profession it is hard to made a living any other way. However, you can always look forward to teaching your art in your old age...."

"Yes, My Lord," Tongchun answered, and the three were dismissed to collect their rewards.

"Princely Brother, you have seen this actor before?"

"Yes. This man is a fine actor and quite unusual in theatrical circles. He doesn't trade on his good looks nor does he have the annoying affectations of the trade. He carries himself more like an intellectual. He is someone rare in the theatrical circles."

Jidu smiled disapprovingly.

"Aside from intellectuals, my Princely Brother even hobnobs with actors. What are intellectuals but ineffectual weaklings. We won all under Heaven by the force of arms. Arms mean strength!"

Yuele responded with a chuckle. "They are two sides of the same coin. One cannot exist without the other. An empire may be won on horseback, but can it be governed in the same manner?"

"Why not? Nurhachi and Abahai did it," Jidu retorted. Yuele did not comment directly on the military prowess of his ancestors. Instead he took a different tack.

"In history, each dynasty that lasted developed a code of laws. It was necessary. Our Great Qing is a new dynasty. Therefore it behoves us to study history and formulate laws if we are to govern this huge land and to have the Manchus, the Mongols and the Hans live in peace and harmony."

Jidu wrinkled his nose with distaste. "The Ming Dynasty had laws, yet it fell through the treachery of Li Zicheng and lost its empire to us."

"The situation was not that simple. His Majesty has pointed out that the laws of Emperor Taizhu of Ming were good and effective, deserving of being remembered through history. But they became corrupted in time, and the Empire decayed. By the last years of Wanli the dynasty was on the verge of collapse. It was the law that allowed it to stumble on a few decades longer. These are facts which we cannot ignore...."

Jidu's impatience was becoming obvious, but he forced himself to be pleasant. "Princely Brother, I cannot rebut your learned argument. Nor do I wish to. We of the Aisin Gioro clan are descendants of a goddess, born aristocrats, heroes favoured by the gods. Since the gods gave us all under Heaven, they will also help us keep it."

Yuele spoke with patience and a hint of irony:

"I have delved into the history of the Manchu race and discovered that, traced backward, we are a branch of Huang Di's line like the other Chinese races."

Instantly Jidu's brows arched with rage. How dare you link the Aisin Gioro with the bloodline of the barbarian he thought! Though his face was black with rage, Jidu reminded himself this was a birthday feast, and only a few incoherent words slipped through his lips.

"Are you all right, Princely Brother?" Yuele enquired. One could not tell whether he was being facetious or really concerned. He was about to summon a servant when the gatekeeper appeared with a eunuch from the imperial palace. The eunuch knelt and announced in a loud voice, "His Majesty commands Your Highness' presence immediately."

Both Yuele and Jidu were surprised but protocol forbade them to question the messenger.

Yuele quickly took leave of Jidu, promising to return the visit and make his formal apologies within a few days. Jidu, glad of the opportunity, also decided to take his leave.

The guests in the Courtyard of Pear Blossoms, entertained by Yunduan and Marhun, were enjoying themselves. The ladies who seldom saw one another were merrily exchanging choice morsels of gossip. After informing his ladies that he was leaving, Jidu departed with part of his retinue. Yunduan and his brother accompanied him to the gate. Jidu was deeply troubled on the way home, wondering what urgent business the Emperor had for summoning Yuele in such a precipitate fashion.

In the southwest corner of the Courtyard of Pear Blossoms was a low building which was set aside on this occasion as a dressing room for actors. Seated by the window, Tongchun caught a glimpse of Jidu leaving and asked the young eunuch who kept him company, "Isn't that Prince Jian leaving? Why doesn't he stay for the next show?" The young eunuch glanced out the window and replied, "It is he. Prince Jian only likes opera with action."

"Does Prince Jian often have actors perform for him?"

"He has his own troupe, but, as I said, he likes a lot of action...."

Tongchun mulled that over and asked again, "Please, were men like you given to His Highness by the Emperor or were you bought?..."

"Both ways. Most of us were bought."

"Are some assigned by the Ministry of Justice as slaves?"

"There are a lot of those ... but none are eunuchs. They mostly work on the farms. The women work in the laundry, in the kitchens, or serve in the house."

With a wildly beating heart, Tongchun pressed further, "Did you get new slaves lately?"

The young eunuch thought for a moment. "Not since the Mid-autumn Festival last year. Eat something. Why the hors d'oeuvres in Prince An's house are the talk of the town! I believe you still have another performance. There's bound to be a nice purse for you at the end. The ladies all have private incomes and they adore the theatre...."

Tongchun was disappointed at the young eunuch's information, but he forced himself to be amiable.

All the women involved in the treason at Yongping Prefecture had been arrested and assigned as slaves to noble households. In order to gain access to these houses, to discover Menggu's whereabouts and to earn a living, there was only one thing Tongchun could do: return to the stage. Without a moment's hesitation, Tongchun joined a famous troupe in the capital. He never refused an engagement in a noble house and always gave his best. However, months had gone by and there was not a trace of Menggu. Today was another disappointment. He felt he could not go on. Tongchun started taking off his make-up.

Watching from the other side of the room, the manager of the troupe enquired in a loud voice, "Yunguan, what is the matter! You have another show!" Tongchun replied, "I'm not well. Excuse me please. You'll have to get someone else."

"Oh! You'll be the death of me!" wailed the manager, bowing and scraping. "My dear Yunguan, people have come expressly to see you. If you don't appear, and My Lord is offended we may never leave this house in one piece! Perhaps the room is too stuffy. Get a breath of air outside...."

The room was indeed hot and stuffy, but actors were not allowed outside. Even the young eunuch who admired Tongchun dared not permit it. It happened that the steward in charge of the Courtyard of the Pear Blossoms was fond of opera. When he heard Yunguan was indisposed and unable to go on, he immediately gave permission for him to go into a small garden to the side for some air. However, it was understood that he would be accompanied by the young eunuch and they would not wander far.

The small garden was an oasis of tall trees and low shrubs, creating an atmosphere of light and cool shadows in which the air was clean and fresh. Near and far, pomegranate flowers glowed in the half light. Tongchun filled his lungs with sweet cool air. Tension drained out of his body as he followed the young eunuch along a path through the artful arrangements of rocks and water. For a while he was in such a euphoric mood that the young eunuch's running comments went almost unheard.

One comment struck a chord.

"...If you catch the ladies' fancy, you could live comfortably for a year on your tips...."

The ladies of all the great houses ... that was important. Tongchun's heart leaped within him. If he made an impression on the lords and ladies present today, this could be his entry into all their houses. That's right! He had to give the performance of his life; one they would never forget!

"Let's go back," he said. "I have a performance to give!"

"Are you feeling better?" the young eunuch enquired.

"The stroll did me good!" Tongchun tossed back at him cheerfully and strode down the path that wound through the rockery. The young eunuch hurried after him, muttering, "This isn't the right way ... you can't get back this way...."

The path suddenly ended. Before them was a corridor, roofed in green tiles supported by red lacquered pillars, elaborately decorated with finely carved railings also lacquered in red. Under the eaves were delicately painted panels of birds and flowers. The far end of the corridor was obscured by trees and shrubs. A screen of tall bamboos screened the corridor on one side. Through the clumps of bamboo, one caught a glimpse of a rose garden in full bloom, its heavy scent wafting on the breeze. Tongchun stopped as the young eunuch caught up with him.

"Come back!" He seized Tongchun and pulled him backward. "It's the wrong way!"

Tongchun was taken aback by the other's obvious fright.

"What's the matter?" he started to ask. Before the young eunuch could answer there came the sound of female voices and laughter from beyond the bamboos. The young eunuch dragged him by the sleeve down the path they had come as fast as his feet would carry him. Nor did he stop or let go of Tongchun till they had regained the Courtyard of the Pear Blossoms.

"You gave me an awful turn," the young eunuch gasped, clutching his heart with one hand for effect. "...that corridor ... leads to the garden for the ladies. Male servants are forbidden to enter unless they are summoned.... Intruders won't live to regret it...."

At that moment the very person whom Tongchun had been seeking emerged from behind the screen of bamboos. Her tall, slender frame was dressed in a pale yellow blouse over a white silk skirt. Over the top she wore a long vest of plain cloth. A blue sash was fastened around her waist. She took her place beside the path, eyes downcast, hands by her sides, waiting for her mistress, Prince Jian's concubine. Qiao Menggu had been given to the household as a slave because of her involvement in the treason at Malan Village.

Although she was numbed to everything that had befallen her, the events of that calamitous day and the days that followed were deeply etched in her memory.

That day the White-robed Monk and his disciple were closeted in their chamber deep in conversation. The women were as usual throwing coins and merrily telling each other's fortune, trying to forecast who would bear the first male child. Menggu stayed apart, her mind a blank, when her mother and Ronggu burst into the room in great agitation. Someone had warned Ronggu that Soordong and Wang Yongxiu were heading this way with the police to arrest the White-robed Monk, his disciple, and Qiao Bainian. They had to get away at once.

Hearing this, the White-robed Monk ordered his servant to guard the gate, while he and his disciple escaped through a back door. The women, wailing in fear, followed them up the mountain. By the time they caught up with the two men, Manchu soldiers had surrounded the foot of the mountain. The White-robed Monk quickly took the situation in hand. He ordered everyone to disband and try to make their way to the camp of the outlaw Li Qiushuang on Qinglong Mountain a hundred miles away. There they would regroup. Everything afterwards became a blur. Menggu got separated from her mother and sister, but remained in the clutches of the Third Prince of the house of Zhu. Together with a young nun, she was forced into a cave and threatened to be silent with a dagger.

Soon Manchu soldiers swarmed like locusts over the mountain. They were everywhere. It was clear they would not remain undetected for long. The Third Prince of the house of Zhu, half mad with terror, tossed his dagger at the women and commanded them to kill themselves. Menggu had witnessed these tantrums before, yet she was still terrified. Shakily she reached for the dagger, but she could not do away with herself. Suddenly the young nun who had been pushed to the limit cried out, "You want us to die, what about you?"

"I will vanish into the mountains and end my days as a monk," the Third Prince of the house of Zhu replied dully. The young nun's anger flared.

"You become a monk ... while we die!" she yelled. "We'll see about that!" She kicked the dagger aside. "I'm not dying without you!"

"Don't try my patience!" the Prince snarled. "I am a son of the Emperor Chongzhen! My women cannot fall into the hands of the enemy! You must die for me! Now!"

"At this moment, being a prince won't help!" the young nun retorted. "I refuse to die!" Menggu was dumbstruck by the angry exchange.

"Wretch! How dare you defy an imperial command! You will die!" He leaped upon the dagger, though he trembled like a leaf, and lunged at the young nun. Menggu shook off her lethargy and tried to stop him. The enraged prince wheeled on her and lunged again. Menggu was able to sidestep the blow. Nevertheless the blade caught her sleeve and grazed her arm.

"Help! Help! The Third Prince is killing us!" shrieked the nun.

Before he could strike again Manchu soldiers filled the cave. The other fugitives were also quickly rounded up. None got away.

They were brought back down the mountain walking single file. The White-robed Monk and his disciple were tied to one another, with a guard in front and another behind. The women were roped together and followed a troop of soldiers a short distance away. As they rounded a bend where the path clung to the edge of a precipice, the White-robed Monk somehow worked his hands free. Seizing the Third Prince of the house of Zhu, he dove into the chasm. The soldiers were thrown into confusion. The women screamed and wailed. When order was restored, soldiers ranged along the cliff edge shot arrows into the void. Afterwards a man was lowered into the ravine by a rope to report on the result. In the meantime the women were taken to Hongqiao Town and lodged in the gaol. They were never told the results of the search.... However, the following day, the head of the White-robed Monk was displayed on a pole.

Only when she had been given to the great house as slave and realized she would never again see her mother or sister did Menggu weep. And she wept bitterly, as though the tears would wash away all the humiliation and pain, love and hate. After the tears she became as remote as an ice statue. She did not smile before. Now she displayed no emotions at all. She was as placid as a tarn in autumn, or as insubstantial as a wisp of smoke. At the household of Prince Jian, she endured the first flogging without a murmur when grown men yelled for mercy. The chief steward was so impressed that he asked for her to serve as a housemaid. It was also this stillness that caught the eye of the concubine, who dismissed her talkative personal maid and took Menggu instead. That day she had accompanied her mistress to Prince An's house to attend the concubine's daughter.

Two luxuriously gowned young girls of about twelve or thirteen emerged from the rustling bamboos. The one in a red robe shot through with silver thread was the third daughter of Prince Jian. The other, dressed in a pale blue silk, was the third daughter of Prince An. The girls had been close friends since childhood but in recent years they seldom saw one another. Hence, whenever they met there was always a great deal to talk about.

" Is your step-mother good to you?" asked Prince Jian's daughter. She was slightly older and treated herself as an older sister. Prince An's original wife had died four years earlier. The young Lady Nahla was his second wife.

"She's all right. Only my father dotes on her little daughter."

"It's always the case. They always dote on the youngest, never the oldest. I heard my mother say, your step-mother almost died giving birth."

"It's true! They even sealed the courtyard she lived in, and nobody was allowed in. But she recovered. Then they said my little sister was born under an evil star, and had to be taken out of the house. She wasn't brought back until more than ten months later."

"Do you like your little sister?"

"I love her! She's adorable, with a sweet little mouth. She's just over two, but she speaks very well."

"I don't have a little sister. Can I see her?"

"What a wonderful idea!" Prince's An daughter clapped her hands in delight and immediately told her maid to go and ask permission. Prince Jian's daughter turned to Menggu and said, "Ahchou, you go too, and help bring the girl."

Ahchou, the name Menggu was given when she came into Prince Jian's household, bent a knee and followed.

Prince An's wife, Lady Nahla, held the little girl on her knee as she watched the opera. The child sat quietly on her mother's knee until she heard that her sister wanted her to go and play in the garden. Then she stretched out her plump little arms to the maid and demanded to be taken at once. On stage, Yunguan was in the midst of a tender scene in which the hero was declaring his profoundest feelings for his beloved. The ladies in the audience were deeply moved. Lady Nahla was glad to be relieved of the child.

Prince Jian's concubine, seated beside her, noticed that Ahchou stood with head bowed, without even a sidelong glance at the stage. She decided to have a little fun at her expense.

"Ahchou," she said, "you ought to feast your eyes on that lovely young man." Menggu peeped through the vase-shaped opening in the screen and quickly lowered her eyes again. Nothing interested her. She took a backward step and quickly followed the other servant carrying the little girl. Her mistress' voice followed her. "I chose Ahchou personally. None of this luxury interests her...."

Menggu followed the other in silence. As the servant shifted the weight of the child from one arm to the other, Menggu found herself gazing straight into the child's face. A sharp pain, like a steel claw raking her heart, shot through her. My Heaven, isn't that her child? Pray this is not a dream ... pray this is not madness....

The little girl's eyes were fastened on her. Those wide, shining eyes, fringed with long lashes, seemed to reach into the deepest recesses of her heart; eyes that she had kissed as she fed her babe; the daughter that was her only comfort....

Panic gripped Menggu. A white mist gathered about her. She faltered but the little girl was reaching for her, calling out in Manchu, "Momo, carry me!"

Those words in clear, concise Manchu sent a shiver down Menggu's spine. The mist before her eyes cleared and she was steady again. This was a little girl wrapped in silks and satins, destined for a life of luxury. How could she be the babe that had probably filled a hungry wolf's belly?

Menggu stretched out her arms and the child came to her, wrapping her tiny arms about her neck. This warm, tender contact roused in her a rush of maternal feelings, both joyous and painful, that she melted within.

The young lady in pale blue took the child. Then her companion snatched her away, loudly exclaiming, "What a beautiful little doll!" The two girls fought to carry her. They hugged and kissed her until the child cried out for Momo. The two young girls made garlands of flowers to hang upon the child. But the child clung to Menggu, only content to play when she was close. They frolicked in the garden till the sun began to sink in the west. Finally, the child crawled into Menggu's arms and fell soundly asleep.

The nurse came for the child. As Menggu handed her over, her trembling hands woke the child who looked around first at the nurse and then, catching sight of Menggu, lunged at her crying, "I want Momo!"

In spite of herself, Menggu took the child in her arms once more. The child clung to her and nothing would pry her loose. The child's wailing threw everyone in a confusion. The commotion brought Prince An's wife and Prince Jian's concubine, but no one could persuade the child to let go of Menggu. In the hubbub that followed, the child wailed, the adults scolded the servants, Ahchou and the wilful child. Nobody could understand a word of what anybody else was saying.

"Stop the commotion!" It was the stern, impatient voice of Prince An who had just returned from his audience with the Emperor. The servants fell to their knees, while his wife hurried to him to complain. Yuele arched his brows at what he heard. Approaching Menggu, he said to the child, "Bingyue, my darling, look at me." The child turned to Prince An, still with her arms locked around Menggu's neck and, smiling through her tears, called, "Father...."

"Come inside with Father. It's time for supper."

"No!" sobbed the little child, clinging to Prince Jian's house slave. Yuele spoke softly:

"I brought you a pair of little rabbits. Do you want to see them?" The child turned that over in her mind ... lovely little rabbits ... it would be nice to be carried by Father who was big and tall....

"Come, Bingyue." Yuele held out his arms to the child, strong, noble arms that had never before held a child. The child pressed her cheek to Menggu's and pleaded, "After I see the rabbits, I'll look for you.... Don't go away...." Prince Jian's concubine quickly ordered Ahchou to promise.

The child let go of her and slid into Prince An's arms. However, arms that accustomed to wielding weapons in battle were unused to carrying a child, and he almost dropped her. Ahchou leaped forward to catch the child, and in that instant Prince An noticed the silent slave woman for the first time. The skin on the thin, pointed face was stretched taut across the high cheekbones. The eyes were sunken. No wonder she was called Ahchou, the "ugly one".

Yuele turned to Prince Jian's concubine and said, "Sister, I apologize for the trouble this child has caused you. Forgive me if I don't accompany you, but I must take her in."

The lady smilingly accepted the apology. "We are family, Princely Brother. Think nothing of it, I have your good wife to keep me company."

By the time Lady Nahla returned to her luxuriously appointed bed chamber, Yuele had already changed into a light silk chemise and was pacing the floor with a cup of tea in his hand. His agitation showed on his clouded face. The child could be heard wailing in the distance.

Lady Nahla remarked in a teasing tone, "Listen to that little wench! I suppose that's fate...." Yuele frowned but did not speak.

"Just now Prince Jian's concubine promised to make me a gift of Ahchou. She said the girl is so ugly that she won't be a distraction. Isn't that an interesting observation! I should make her a gift too. Would a bolt of silk be appropriate?" Yuele remained silent. Lady Nahla who was young enough to be his daughter was getting impatient. Her eyes snapped wide with anger.

"Why don't you speak to me?" she demanded.

"All right. Don't shout," Yuele spoke at last. "There's no need to fuss. The child has to be sent to the palace soon."

"You must be mad," exclaimed Lady Nahla in fright. Yuele's face was grim.

"Since the Precious Concubine lost her son, she wishes to adopt a few little girls from noble households to dull her grief and to give purpose to her life. It's also the Emperor's wish." Lady Nahla burst into tears.

"She takes my child to dull her grief. Who will dull mine?"

Yuele sighed. "This is a mark of special favour from His Majesty, something most people pray for but never receive. Besides, she is not your flesh and blood."

"But I raised her! I won't let her go.... Why did he insist on a girl from our house...."

"There are two from Prince Jian's house, one each from Duke Shuncheng and us. Being adopted by the Precious Concubine means Bingyue will one day be given the title of princess and all the benefits accruing to that title. With her in the palace you would have easy access to the Empress Dowager and the Precious Concubine, two extraordinary Manchu ladies from whose vast learning and experience you can benefit...."

Her husband's reasoning alleviated Lady Nahla's anger somewhat. It was while she was mourning the death of her son at birth that this adorable child was brought to her. All the grief and frustrated love was transferred to this precious little girl. Her husband had made clear the importance of the situation, and she knew she had to bow to the unalterable. She glanced at her husband's gloomy face and sighed. "You must stop worrying too. Did the Emperor summon you on your birthday just for this?"

Yuele avoided his wife's eyes. He folded and unfolded his fan absent-mindedly, fanned himself a little, then as though he had made up his mind about something said, "I will go to the study for a while. Don't let anyone disturb me." With his hands folded behind his back he strode from the room.

Yuele was worried about something far more important.

Was the Emperor being childish? Or was it another of his sudden bursts of enthusiasm? It seemed more likely that he had already given the matter considerable thought, and summoned

Yuele because he was more likely to be receptive to the idea.

As the light left the western sky, a million stars appeared in the firmament. Yuele fixed his eyes on a large star that was exceptionally brilliant, shining with a bluish centre, so high in the sky that it made his heart quiver. He had seen a similar gleam in the Emperor's eyes when he was expounding his new ideas of government. A gleam that made him tremble within.

The Emperor had brushed aside the stacks of history books and books on the laws of Ming and announced with excitement, "Honoured Brother, we have decided to consult history, selecting the best and discarding the rest; abandoning the old to make way for the new. We shall promulgate a new system of government." He paused for effect and continued: "More importantly we are determined to disband the Council of the Nobles, replacing it with a Grand Secretariat which will be under our direct control...."

"But ... isn't this the same system as the Ming?" Yuele stammered, his breath coming in harsh rasps.

"If it works, where is the harm imitating it?" the Emperor parried the objection almost flippantly. "The members of the council have grown old serving the crown, and they do not have the ability or the foresight to govern. Their ideas cannot keep pace with the times. I will retire them with honours and generous endowments to allow them a life of leisure. Henceforth those in government must have ability and vision for the future. Otherwise, to govern well is not easy...."

The Emperor enthused over other plans. He would stamp out corruption; reward pioneers, and surround himself with men of ability. He would collect all literature scattered among the people, provide a livelihood for the survivors of the Imperial House of Ming, and honour their dead. He would engage a tutor whose duty it would be to guide him daily in the study of history, law and the writings of sages and so on. But all this flew over Yuele's head. The sweeping changes the Emperor proposed shook him to the core. He could imagine the effect it would have on the Manchu princes and the aristocracy when it were announced. The fierce opposition it would rouse could lead to disaster! Oh, young Emperor! In the first month of the year when the Fourth Imperial Son died, everyone said it was retribution for moving closer to Han ways and abandoning those of the ancients. Was that not warning enough! Five months later, when grief was still fresh, he was again defying Heaven by destroying the institution passed down from the ancestors. It would not do!

Among the Manchu nobles Yuele was considered a progressive. Only today he had been expounding the need to learn from history in order to create new systems, never dreaming the Emperor had already gone a few steps further.

It dawned upon him the real reason why the Precious Concubine was anxious to adopt four little girls from noble households was political. It was a way of honouring and appeasing the nobles. Jidu would be the strongest opponent to the new system. Therefore two of his children were chosen. The lady was a truly remarkable helpmate.

He understood the Emperor's position. He was young, anxious to govern this vast land in peace. But his power was diluted by the council which often put obstacles in his way. This was insupportable for someone as impetuous and strong-willed as Shunzhi. From Yuele's own point of view, as a member of the Council of Nobles, a life of luxury and ease in exchange for loss of power was unacceptable....

The light in the study burnt throughout the night. Prince Yuele passed the night uneasily contemplating his future.

6

Jidu brought his huge fist down hard on the little table, knocking over teacup, saucer and cup lid which smashed on the floor, splattering pale brown milk tea on everything including himself. He was oblivious of all that in his rage. His tigerish eyes flashed fire and the thick veins in his neck and forehead stood out as he roared, "Abolish the Council of Nobles! What nonsense!"

He paced the main hall of his house, hands clasped behind his back, like a caged animal, his breath coming in loud rasps. His already dark-complexioned face had turned a purplish hue. He suddenly stopped and roared again, "So he would change the ancestors' system! He's bewitched by that barbarian...."

Aobai stood to one side, looking solemn, wordless as usual. To the other side stood Sukesaha who was his usual amiable self.

"My Lord, there is no need for agitation," Sukesaha tried to comfort. "The Emperor only has these ideas which he casually let slip. He has no intention of taking immediate action...."

"No!" Jidu gestured with his large hand. "I know the Emperor. Once he gets an idea in his head, wild horses won't make him change his mind.... Disbanding the Council of Nobles and setting up a Grand Secretariat indeed! Isn't that betraying our ancestral system? You two are members of the council too. If the council is dissolved, how will he dispose of us?"

Sukesaha chose his words carefully when he spoke.

"I believe the Emperor intends to honour the princes with hereditary titles and rich pensions. Some of the lords will be absorbed into the Grand Secretariat and would still retain their position at court...."

"It's the Han way!" Jidu roared till the rafters rang. "The eight banners of the Manchu conquered all under Heaven and made slaves of the barbarians. Now ... this! I won't wait for him to dissolve the council. Tomorrow I will submit my resignation. I refuse to be emasculated."

Sukesaha chuckled and added in a low voice, "My Lord, if there are many resignations, the Emperor might change his mind...."

"What did you say?" Jidu was taken aback.

"I was merely thinking that before all under Heaven is subdued, how can we be without the support of the invincible eight banners...."

Jidu smacked himself on the forehead. "Ah, I see your point! Sukesaha you are indeed the fox of the Manchu! I did not think the Emperor could be so enamoured of Han ways as to ignore the bonds of blood with his own kind...."

Aobai who had been silent till now spoke solemnly:

"My Lord, this is not surprising. If the Regent Dorgon had not been the autocrat and nearly usurped the throne, His Majesty would not be so distrustful. As for concern for the family, His Majesty has decided to adopt several girls from noble families who will be given the status and honours of princesses. My Lord and his son have served the country well, so His Majesty has chosen two of your daughters for this honour." As he expected, Jidu was slightly mollified by the news. After a moment of silence he responded saying, "Thank you for telling me. I know what I must do," and dismissed the two men. As he departed Sukesaha advised, "My Lord, resigning from the council is a serious matter. If His Majesty accepts then you would find yourself on the back of a tiger and unable to get off. However, a judicious word dropped here or there is bound to reach the Emperor's ear. That should be sufficient." Jidu responded with a curious half smile: "No wonder they say you can plot the direction of the prevailing winds!"

Sukesaha's face reddened and he tried to laugh it off. Aobai shot a disapproving glance at him. A man as straightforward as Jidu usually despised a schemer such as Sukesaha. However he had to admire Sukesaha's ability to analyse the situation. Moreover, his bland remark expressed Jidu's confused emotions.

After he had seen the two men out the door, Jidu, still deeply troubled, turned toward the inner courtyard. The sound of voices and laughter issued from his wife's chamber.

"Sister, their steamed duck is simply delicious! I wonder how it was prepared!" It was the concubine speaking to the wife.

"The roast duck was excellent too. It was so tender that even with these miserable teeth, I enjoyed myself,'' countered the wife. Another of the ladies added enthusiastically, ''All the dishes had fancy names that I've never heard of. It's the work of a cook they brought from the south.... Sister, why don't we buy a few barbarian cooks? Roast mutton and boiled meat is so tiresome....''

Feasts at Prince An's house were renowned for being different. Even Jidu had to admit that he thoroughly enjoyed them, not to mention the ladies of his household.

''And did you notice the fans they use? The round silk ones and the little camphor wood ones. Such a fragrance! You hold it under your chin thus, and you flutter it ... thus, and smile thus ... that jade bauble hanging from the tassel starts dancing....'' By the laughter her remarks evoked, it was clear the speaker was striking an attitude. ''You mustn't laugh! I haven't perfected it yet! I swear even an ugly woman could capture a man's heart.''

The voice of a young girl, the Third Daughter, cut through the chatter and the laughter.

''Mother, their clothes are light and airy not like ours. They're not embroidered, but there are patterns woven in so that when you walk and the breeze catches the skirt, it billows. Ours are as stiff as boards.''

''Young Lady, speak to your father about it,'' encouraged one of the other ladies. ''Their fabrics were brought in from Suzhou and Hangzhou in the south. If your father gives the nod, it would be quite simple to send someone south to buy us some.''

''Mother, you speak to Father,'' the Third Daughter begged her mother, who laughingly said she would.

''My dear sisters,'' the lady who had been demonstrating the use of the fan caught everyone's attention. ''This is how Prince An's concubine taught me to apply rouge and powder.... This is called the Peach Blossom.... A little more rouge and it's the tipsy look.... Now if you add just a touch of powder ...

it becomes the misty look...." The ladies squealed their delight. One of them remarked that the barbarians with their long history had such poetic names for ladies' toilettes.

"That's not all. They even know how to deck themselves out when they're under the weather.... They put medicinal plaster on the backs of tiny bits of red silk cut in a diamond shape and stick them to the temples and on the bridge of the nose.... Now, isn't that a pretty effect? Isn't that sweet? It makes one irresistably fragile...."

"Oh, those barbarian women...." The exclamation did not have the usual disdain and derision. Rather there was a note of wistful envy.

When Jidu came into the room, his wife was reclining on a couch watching and listening to the others. At the moment the concubine was standing in the centre of the room with her personal maid demonstrating the use of cosmetics. The table was littered with powders and rouges, and the floor covered with bits of red silk. The maid on whom she was demonstrating was done up in the misty look. With the fingernail-sized pieces of red silk stuck to her temples and forehead, even Jidu caught himself glancing at her more than once, for she had been transformed.

The women immediately offered their greeting. The maid hurriedly prostrated herself and withdrew. Noticing the grim look on their lord's face, the ladies fell silent. It was the wife who cheerfully invited her lord to sit and talk with her.

Jidu stood on the threshold, his piercing eyes went from one face to the next. Desperately controlling his anger, he said in a mocking tone, "What were you so happy about just now?" The ladies bowed their heads. Unable to control himself any longer, Jidu roared at them, "You've all been bewitched! Out of my sight, all of you!" The concubine and the daughter hastily bent a knee and scrambled from the room.

"If I catch you learning barbarian ways again, I'll have your hide!" Jidu shouted after them.

The clatter of wooden-soled shoes followed the retreating ladies. The daughter fell in her haste. Her companion helped her up, and together they disappeared around the corner of the corridor.

Jidu's anger was not appeased. Now he turned to his wife and scolded, "See how you've spoilt them! Now the devilish ways of the barbarian have even invaded my house. Instead of reprimanding them you're encouraging them!"

The wife replied softly, "My Lord, why get so upset over trifles like food and dress. Women like to make themselves beautiful for your pleasure. Is that worth flying into a rage for?"

"We must preserve our own ancient customs. The ways of the Han must not be permitted within these walls. They are signs of decay, do you understand?"

The wife did not dare show her displeasure. An awkward silence descended between them, which the wife broke with a gentle remark.

"I merely said their food was delicious. You yourself said it was superior to boiled meat." Seeing that Jidu could not deny that, she added, "If we were to follow our ancestors' ancient customs we would have to go back to living in the wilderness and roasting a joint of mutton over an open fire instead of living in all this luxury."

Her words left Jidu speechless with anger. Pointing a finger at her he hissed, "You and your mealy-mouthed nonsense! Tradition is important. Can you understand that?" He took a small oil paper-wrapped object from his pocket and threw it at her.

"Perhaps you have forgotten. Read it!"

The wife bit her lip as she unfolded the packet that was warm from Jidu's body. In it was a piece of white silk covered in Manchu writing. Kneeling on a cushion she began to read, carefully forming the words.

On the square of white silk was copied Jidu's father Jirgalang's last petition to the Emperor, written on his deathbed. Copies of that last petition was everywhere in the house. It was carved on the camphor wood screen in the main hall, displayed in the main room of the tower in the archery field, in the reception room and the prince's bed chamber, and even carried on his person. Jirgalang could rest in peace knowing his last words were thus revered.

Everyone in the house knew Jirgalang's last petition by heart, including his wife.

"...At the beginning of our Empire Nurhachi held daily conferences with the lords in which the gains and losses in governance were discussed, as were the concerns of the people. Nothing was overlooked. Thus opponents were vanquished and great enterprise achieved....

"After he ascended the throne Abahai continued to hold conference with his vassal lords, rewarding the loyal and pardoning mistakes. Decrees were issued to win the hearts of the people. Concerned that the warlike arts would decay in peace, he frequently held tournaments. The habit of the lords in holding feasts and entertainments angered the monarch, who said, 'Our Empire was founded by force of arms. Our soldiers are our flesh and blood, who would lay down their lives for our cause, and who are invincible in battle. It is our fear that in generations hence these virtues may be abandoned in favour of the decadance of the Han. If such is the case, the glory of the empire will be in jeopardy.' The Lord Suoni was made to repeat these sentiments time and again.

"This day Your Majesty has commanded your vassals to speak their minds, your slave believes to rule all under Heaven in peace there must first be trust. The reconstruction of Qianqing Palace without consultation was a break with tradition. I beg Your Majesty to follow the examples of Nurhachi. Consult with your vassal lords on all matters of state before proceeding, and thus gain the blessing of the great ones who have gone before...."

The wife finished reading, folded the piece of silk and returned it to Jidu with both hands. Jidu accepted it and said, "Keep that in mind."

The wife replied, "I shall, My Lord."

"You may rise," Jidu said without looking at her. He solemnly returned the square of silk to his inner pocket. Seeing that he was calmer, the wife began tentatively, "There is a matter that I wish to consult My Lord."

"What is it?"

"Lady Tage has intimated that Prince An's wife wishes to have her maid Ahchou..." the wife began carefully. "When relatives request a few slaves I have never been ungenerous.... However, with the house of Yuele I am unsure...."

"Yuele..." Jidu muttered to himself, his brows knit in a terrible frown. The wife knew the two men were not on the best of terms. More than once she had overheard Jidu complain that Yuele was a traitor to his ancestors. She expected an instant refusal, and that would be the end of the issue. His hesitancy puzzled her.

Jidu paced up and down before the casement. Suddenly he wheeled round and with hands on his hips said in a loud voice, "We can't send one! It must be at least ten of the best, and don't be stingy. Add ten jin of ginseng, ten boxes of deer placenta extract and a string of eastern pearls of the best quality. These are all precious gifts of our homelands!" He waved his hands excitedly as he spoke. "They will be a fitting birthday gift. The slaves are only a minor consideration. That should be honour enough."

The wife gazed at him in puzzlement. "Only a while ago you were enraged because we had forgotten the precepts of our forebears ... and now...."

Jidu threw his head back and laughed. "Women only see what is in front of their noses! Deeper things are involved. Prince An is not only a relative, but also a member of the council. Is that clear?"

At dawn the Hall of Mental Cultivation was a beehive of activity. In the dim light of lanterns, shadows darted to and fro helping with the Emperor's toilette. The Emperor had not summoned any of his ladies, hence the morning preparations should have been simpler. Besides this was not a formal audience. Though the Emperor was meeting with his lords informally in Qianqing Palace he insisted upon wearing his full regalia. Since the death of his fourth son the Emperor had been irascible. Nearly every day a eunuch was flogged which meant that everybody was on edge.

A young eunuch brought a cup of tea. Fulin who had just finished dressing took it, drank and in one quick motion hurled the cup at the young eunuch, drenching him in hot liquid, and smashing cup, saucer and cup lid.

"Imbecile!" Fulin screamed at the hapless young eunuch. "Are you trying to scald us!" The young eunuch prostrated himself, trembling so hard he could hardly speak. "The more I'm in a hurry the more you idiots get in the way! Why do I keep you!"

The chief eunuch prostrated himself and begged the Emperor's forgiveness on the youngster's behalf. "Your Majesty ... he is new to the palace.... Please forgive his clumsiness...."

"Get out!"

The chief eucnuch, banging his head on the ground, motioned the young eunuch to withdraw.

"My beads! Where are my beads!" Fulin shouted impatiently. The eunuchs looked at one another in alarm for the fellow in charge of the beads was not in the room. Fulin ground his teeth with impatience, glaring at the chief eunuch.

"Your Majesty, I have the beads," a voice called from the antechamber. Next moment the eunuch dashed in like a mindless insect, threw himself on his knees with the beads held high over his head. Fulin snatched them from him and kicked the eunuch aside. The man quickly righted himself and crouched before the Emperor, too frightened to move.

"The lot of you seem to be determined to delay

me," shouted Fulin. "I shall have you all flogged!"

The eunuch in charge of the beads spoke in a quavering tone: "Forgive me Your Majesty. I couldn't find the beads in the bed chamber, so I looked for them in the ante-chamber. Finally I found them in the side-chamber. Please forgive the delay. Your slave deserves to die!" And with that he began slapping himself across the face.

Fulin remembered a few days ago he had left them in the west side-chamber where he had gone to practise calligraphy after audience. The strand of amber beads which he regarded as a good-luck charm was placed in his treasure cabinet and forgotten. He said no more, but glared meaningfully at the eunuch as he was escorted to Qianqing Palace.

When he was gone, the other eunuchs stopped the one in charge of the beads. "Enough now. It must hurt."

"Of course it does," the fellow retorted. "But it's better than the lash." Rubbing his red and smarting cheek he added, "If the Precious Concubine had spent the night here, this wouldn't have happened."

"That is true," sighed the others shaking their heads.

The eunuchs could not fathom all that churned in Fulin's mind and heart. His irascible behaviour was brought on by the fact that he regarded this as an especially important day; the day in which he would either be the victor or the loser.

The death of his fourth son had been a terrible blow. However, he chose to ignore the dire comments of the nobles that it was a warning and a punishment from heaven. Later when the Empress Dowager revealed the truth of the matter to him and invited him to examine his conscience and to ponder whether Lady Jin had been the instrument by which the gods wreaked their vengeance, he became frightened. The intervention of Heaven demonstrated to him the hatred of Manchu and Mongols alike for all he tried to achieve. Who knows how deep that hatred ran, and what terrible consequences it might lead to?

Fulin had only one aim in mind: to be remembered as a wise

and just ruler. Years of study convinced him that the traditional approach to governing would not be appropriate for the vast Empire that was Great Qing. New ways had to be found. The most convenient and practical was the system created by Taizhu of Ming. If the civilized but weak Han could acquire some of the strength and spirit of the Manchu and the savagery of the Mongol, and if the Manchu could be softened by Han culture, then the Empire that contained them all would be more glorious than anything before.

Fulin was full of ambition, dreaming of unifying all under Heaven and ruling in peace. Yet every innovation he tried to implement met with obstruction. He was discovering that the highest of the high in Great Qing was not as high as he thought. He could not do as he pleased. For he was confronted by a mountain of traditions. Would he dare change it?

Fulin had planned this a long time. His first supporter was naturally Lady Dongeh. Originally he had planned to name the Crown Prince then abolish the Council of Nobles. When his fourth son died, he was plunged into despair. The death seemed to dash all hopes for the future.

The victory of his armies campaigning in the south revived some of his ambition. He found a second supporter in the person of one of Abahai's great commanders, Grand Academician Fan Wencheng. Fan Wencheng urged Fulin to concentrate power in the hands of the Emperor and thus control all under Heaven. When Fulin brought up the subject of abolishing the Council of Nobles and creating a Grand Secretariat, this loyal old courtier was all in favour. However, he reminded the Emperor that the task would not be easily accomplished, for it not only ran contrary to ancestral precepts, it could turn the Manchu against him. He, therefore, counselled caution and to proceed slowly.

But Fulin was not a patient man. Once the idea took root, he wanted to put it into action without delay. Therefore he immediately looked for a third supporter, the Empress Dowager. The

Empress Dowager was not immediately receptive. She considered the matter for some time before she gave her consent. Though she did not disapprove the idea she advised against taking hasty, irreversable action. Everything must be done so as not to disturb the people or disrupt society.

Summoning Prince An and announcing his intentions was to use him as sounding board, and possibly a fourth ally. The usually unflappable Yuele was shocked by the Emperor's intentions. Finally he was able to say with a great deal of misgivings, "Thus far Your Majesty has ruled by honouring the ancestors. If the Council of Nobles is abolished, it may cause unrest among the people. At present the Empire has not yet been secured, and the eight banners are still at war, would it not be better to wait? I can see no harm in amalgamating the three palace academics into a Grand Secretariat and support it completely."

Fulin also deliberately let slip his intentions to some of his courtiers, as a means of testing the reactions of the nobles. The results were largely disappointing.

Fulin had spent a sleepless night, but his mind was made up. He would gamble everything he stood for on this morning's activities. He would receive the nobles one by one in Qianqing Palace, confront them with his intentions and force them to yield. It would be a desperate battle of wills.

With the honour and the power of the Emperor on his side, Fulin felt he had a reasonable chance of succeeding. However, he was going against tradition; something that both Nurhachi and Abahai had clearly forbidden by decree. Therefore, he could not proceed without a certain trepidation. Not only was he secretly afraid of the people's objections, but in the secret recesses of his soul there was a nagging guilt of having betrayed his ancestors. His irascibility and his cruelty masked his fear.

The first to be received in the east chamber of Qianqing Palace was Duke Lerjin, who was not a member of the council and belonged to a younger generation. Fulin chose him before all the others in order to strike the weakest link first. However, as soon as he spoke, Fulin's heart sank. Lerjin had never before exhibited such a sure grasp of events, or spoken with such eloquence. "May it please Your Majesty, in your slave's humble opinion the abolition of the council and the establishment of the Grand Secretariat should not take place...." He continued by quoting one of Abahai's decrees issued in the fourth month of the second year of Chengde, in which he lauded the virtues of military prowess and warned against decadence. Furthermore His Majesty had urged the nobles to remind one another of his dictum. "...These precepts are unalterable," the young nobleman reminded his Emperor with conviction.

"Sons and grandsons may neither forget nor change the commands of the sacred ancestors..." **Lerjin** concluded, knocking his forehead against the floor repeatedly.

Listening to his discourse spoken in a monotone as though he had committed the entire speech to memory, Fulin was angry, yet he also saw the comic side of the situation. He assumed the stern demeanor of one from an older generation and frowning deeply enquired, "How is your horsemanship and your skill with the bow? Can we have a demonstration at Coal Hill tomorrow?"

Lerjin prostrated himself without another word.

"I am surprised to hear you mouthing the precepts of our ancestors," Fulin remarked dryly. "Who put you up to it?" Lerjin, trembling all over, replied, "Actually all members of the Imperial Family ... are concerned about the abolition of the council.... Everybody agreed ... to petition against it.... They said ... Your Majesty would be persuaded.... I too prepared ... before coming ... here...."

"Don't you know that the situation is different from before the conquest? If the system is not changed, how can we win the hearts of the people and rule in peace?" Fulin saw only fear and stupidity in Lerjin's eyes.

"Have you understood a single thing we said?" he roared.

Lerjin broke into a sweat and, knocking his head against the ground, repeated that the ancient precepts must not be changed.

At the end of his patience, Fulin dismissed him with a wave of the hand, and Lerjin scrambled from the room.

Prince An came into the Presence in his usual inobstrusive manner. However, a spark of pity deep in those serene eyes annoyed Fulin.

After he had prostrated himself Yuele spoke in earnest tones:

"We had no fixed system of government when the conquest began. However, conditions change, and we must change also to be in tune with the land and its people. Otherwise it would be like a man trying to wear the clothes of his childhood. Either the man suffers or the garment is destroyed. Therefore the abolition of the council and the establishment of a Grand Secretariat are innovations Abahai himself would have made if he was able to come to the central plains."

"That is true!" Fulin enthused, forgetting for the moment a monarch's detachment which was expected when a vassal spoke. "Great Qing is now a giant and I intend to dress him in the clothes of a giant...."

Yuele sighed. "It is a good thing, Your Majesty, but it is too soon."

"Why?" Fulin could not keep the anxiety out of his voice. Prince An added carefully, "If it pleases Your Majesty, in Yuele's humble opinion when the Southern Ming is finally vanquished, and Yunnan and Guizhou are subdued, it would be a more appropriate time for changes."

The second person in whom Fulin had high hopes was Prince Jieshu, who resembled Yuele in many ways, except he was an exceedingly cautious man. He was a son of Prince Daishan, but not by his first wife. He was young, relatively inexperienced in affairs of state, neither as learned as Yuele nor as brave a man at arms as Jidu. Among the nobles he stood out as a humble gentleman who was well liked. Also he had been careful not to seem to favour any particular clique. Coming into the Presence today, he tripped on his robe in his nervousness and almost fell.

His eyes shifting from side to side betrayed his agitation.

He spoke thus, "To change the system of our ancestors may distress the Manchu. The great examples of Nurhachi and Abahai who founded the Empire are known to all. And honouring the ancestors is the cornerstone of Manchu civilization. I humbly beg Your Majesty to reconsider."

Fulin asked unhappily, "Does that mean you disapprove?"

"Not really. But I do not want to be exceptional. I'll agree if most of the lords do." He thought for a moment and added: "I hope Your Majesty would consider the indignation of the lords in case that they should resist with concerted efforts...."

Fulin was shocked. He demanded: "You mean they are banding together to resist us?"

"No! My lords are all loyal subjects. But if all of them should have the same sentiments...."

Jieshu had already left the room when a thought occurred to him and, in contradiction to protocol, he turned back. After prostrating himself, he spoke softly to Fulin, "Your Majesty ... is it possible to abandon the first matter and proceed with the second? I pray Your Majesty reconsider...."

Fulin understood Jieshu's meaning. Of course it would be simpler to establish a Grand Secretariat than to abolish the council. But to him the latter was the more important.

After three disappointments, Fulin's mood darkened. He was also fatigued, but he carried on speaking first to lords of the council, and then the six Manchu ministers. Everyone reaffirmed his loyalty to the Emperor and his ancestors. All praised the Emperor's wisdom. And all were unanimous in their belief in the Manchu's superiority and the sacred decrees that eschewed the traditions of the Han. A few even quoted Shunzhi's own decree, when he first ascended the throne, expressing similar sentiments. The nobles were also united in opposing the dissolution of the council, though their reasons varied. However, Fulin was able to detect a thread of commonality which he traced to Jidu.

Fulin paced the room for some time lost in thought. Finally

he ordered milk tea and pastries. The food revived his flagging spirits. He was now prepared to concentrate all his efforts on the last round when he would face Prince Jidu, knowing it would be a long, bitter struggle, regardless of the outcome. He could not know that the actual circumstances were quite different from his expectations.

The man whom Fulin had always considered uncultured and ineloquent presented himself and, when the ceremonies of greeting had been disposed of and he had taken his seat, the prince drew the square of silk on which his father's last petition had been copied and read aloud in a sonorous voice. At its conclusion he brought up the reign of the Regent Dorgon:

"Your Majesty will recall that the Regent Dorgon tried to bypass the Council of the Nobles and seize power. He also attempted to deprive the nobles of their authority over the six ministries, bringing them directly under his control. In wantonly changing the ancestral system Dorgon drew the wrath of the Manchu. The result was ignominy after death. Such is the vengeance of Heaven."

Fulin's face darkened. Though on the surface Jidu was talking about Dorgon, he was actually reproaching him. But he controlled his temper, for he meant to win this last round. In fact he was not given an excuse to vent his spleen. Jidu became more impassioned as he spoke:

"We Manchu straddle all under Heaven because of our ancient traditions. The system passed from one generation to the next has won a vast Empire for us. They are the heirlooms of the Manchu. Abandon them and we lose all we have gained, and the Empire will be wrested from our grasp. Our enemies have no need for bow or sword. Their culture and traditions are such that they will subvert us — the chosen of Heaven — and spell our doom...."

Fulin could control himself no longer. Slamming his palm on the table he shouted, "Nonsense!"

Without blinking an eyelash, Jidu fell to his knees.

"Forgive me, Your Majesty," he began. "Jidu speaks with sincerity. Your Majesty can put me to the sword, and my soul will appear before the ancestors without reproach. Since Your Majesty is displeased with Jidu, he will resign from the council, and never again take part in affairs of state. The other lords of the council are equally prepared to relinquish their posts according to Your Majesty's command. However, a consultative council must not be abandoned."

Where would a man find the courage to speak to the Emperor in this manner? Jidu had the courage of his convictions. If he was dealt with severely, it would appear that he had offended the Emperor by offering unpalatable advice. It would only enhance his reputation as a man of honour. Also, Jidu honestly felt he had the support of all the others. Therefore he had nothing to fear.

And what of the Emperor? Jidu's words had touched a tender spot. In spite of himself Fulin was plagued by a nagging guilt. At the same time he instinctively felt that his stature had somehow diminished. Jidu's cleverly disguised threats were not to be easily dismissed, for if he should resign, all the others would follow suit. That would not only disgrace Fulin but had the power to destroy his goal of securing all under Heaven. The consequences were shattering. Fulin quaked inwardly. He had no stomach to press for the abolition of the Council of Nobles. Nevertheless, rage boiled within him; against Jidu and the entire council of nobles; but especially against his own inability to change things.

With a slight quiver in his voice he asked, "How does My Lord view replacing the three palace academies with a Grand Secretariat?"

"If it pleases Your Majesty, the Ming Dynasty collapsed because civil officials had too much power. It is a system of defeat that must not be imitated."

"Is that not an exaggeration?" Fulin asked curtly, his nostrils quivering and his eyes narrowed to a squint. "Did Abahai not establish the three academies according to the Ming system?

Did they not exist during the reign of Nurhachi?'' The words rushed out unbidden.

Abahai had indeed established the three academies and the six ministries according to the Ming form of government. That was common knowledge. That he also pronounced continuing the Ming system was a wise policy was also common knowledge. Jidu was effectively muzzled on those grounds. However, he stubbornly held to his point. ''If it pleases Your Majesty, the Council of Nobles established by Nurhachi was not abolished by Abahai....''

Fulin forced a smile. ''Imperial Cousin, in your opinion if we do not abolish the council but only the ministries, would you agree?''

Jidu was startled by the Emperor's changed tones. It seemed His Majesty was giving way.

''That would be a matter ... to put to the council for deliberation,'' he replied non-commitally.

Fulin smiled. ''Our intention of abolishing the Council was because My Lords have given the best years of their lives to the service of the crown. Now in their old age, they deserve to retire with honour to a well-earned life of ease. Also, this would facilitate our governing the Empire. Since my Imperial Cousin and the others have opined that the council is a sacred institution that cannot be tampered with, we will bow to your judgement. Replacing the three academies with a Grand Secretariat will also facilitate our ability to govern. Moreover, we intend to create a Grand Secretariat of a size that would be appropriate to the needs of the state.''

Jidu, who had remained on his knees all this while, bowed his head in thought, then he responded earnestly:

''May it please Your Majesty, the projected Grand Secretariat will be at least double the present size of the three academies, employing Han scholars of various degrees. While I concede they are better educated than we and are probably able men, if they gain too much power it may prove detrimental to Great

Qing...."

Fulin gritted his teeth and asked, "And what does my Imperial Cousin propose?"

"In Jidu's opinion they should not be given an official rank higher than the sixth degree...."

"What?" Fulin could not hide his indignation. "At present academicians of the lowest rank in the three academies are at least of the second degree!"

Jidu continued without batting an eyelash. "Members of the Grand Secretariat will have direct access to the Emperor. With too much power they might hamper Your Majesty's ability to govern...."

According to the system of the Ming, the Grand Secretary of the Grand Secretariat was considered the inferior of one and the superior of a million. The title was bestowed on a person invited by the Emperor to be his First Minister, to manage the affairs of state in his name. Yet Jidu had proposed the post to be not higher than the sixth degree, which effectively reduced it to the stature of a minor official of a provincial or county level. It was a ridiculous suggestion. Fulin threw back his head and laughed out loud.

Jidu was taken aback by the Emperor's mirth.

"Your Majesty, what is the matter?" Fulin was seized by such a fit of laughter that he could barely speak. Jidu was dismissed from the Presence amidst this unnatural laughter. Jidu rose to his feet uncertainly.

"Go!" gasped Fulin. "I've not gone mad!"

Fulin continued laughing even after Jidu was gone. He was thoroughly defeated. What he wanted abolished he could not touch. What he wanted to change had been nipped in the bud. Those he wanted to raise were trampled. He had been completely routed.

Just as suddenly as it had burst forth, the laughter stopped. The rage that roared in Fulin's breast quickly became an uncontrollable conflagration that consumed him. He let out a terrible cry and seizing the low kang table flung it, together with the cups and papers on it, across the room. The table landed with a resounding crash. Everything on it was shattered. Shards and splinters were everywhere. The servants and eunuchs stood perfectly still, heads bowed, hearts beating wildly, fearful that the Emperor's wrath might fall upon their heads.

Fulin crossed the room in a few quick strides and left Qianqing Palace. His attendants followed as best they could, not daring to come too close. Fulin did not slacken his pace until he reached Yuehua Gate. Stopping, he spoke without turning:

"From this day forward we will receive no one! All petitions will be directed to the palace academies. Inform Her Majesty the Empress Dowager that we are in Xiyuan (West Gardens). Send immediately for Tang Jo-Wang and bring him to me in Xubai Chamber." His orders were given slowly word by word. When he was done he walked away with head held high.

The Xubai Chamber was situated in the northwest corner of the West Gardens. Being on low ground and surrounded by rockery from Lake Tai and shaded by evergreens, it was a retreat, as cut off from the world as though it was in some remote place. For two whole days Fulin remained closeted there with Tang Jo-Wang. No one was permitted near except a few eunuchs, and then only when they were summoned.

Bottles, jars, beakers, burners and scales were arranged on a long table. On a square table were the eye-catching volumes of *Compendium of Materia Medica* and a few books in German bound in leather. Fulin wanted to know how that most precious of oils, the amber oil, was extracted. He was determined to be a chemist.

Fulin and Tang Jo-Wang consulted books, conducted experiments, while eunuchs performed the menial tasks. Fulin tried to dissolve amber in a curious liquid. A whole day passed but he did not succeed in extracting oil from amber. Then he seized upon the idea of making pearl powder. Once again they consulted books and performed experiments. Pearl powder proved easier to make. On the third day, sitting in front of the scales, Fulin carefully wrapped three hundred packets of pearl powder. For the first time in a long while he broke into the child-like grin that Tang Jo-Wang knew so well.

"Mafa, I figure each packet of pearl powder is worth about ten ounces of silver."

"Your Majesty, if one takes into account the fact that it was made personally by the Emperor, its value would surely exceed one hundred ounces of silver per packet," Tang Jo-Wang said, stroking his long, curly beard.

"Is that so?" Fulin seemed happy. "I will send half to my Imperial Mother and fifty packets to the Precious Concubine. The rest I give you to be used for curing the sick among the poor."

"I thank Your Majesty. God will reward your charity." Tang Jo-Wang shook his head and sighed. "Your Majesty has grown haggard."

"I suppose I have..." sighed Fulin.

"The Fourth Imperial Son has been called by God and resides in heaven."

Fulin disagreed with the Catholic idea that death was a joyous event. The comfort of the supernatural could not dull the ache in his heart. He turned the conversation in another direction.

"Amber oil and pearl powder helped distract me. Tell me, Mafa, why can't a man move a mountain?" The question was strange and unexpected, but Tang Jo-Wang answered without hesitation, "Because one man alone is not strong enough."

"Also, the mountain is too big, too heavy," Fulin supplied angrily. There was a silent pause before he continued, "I dreamed I was pushing a rock up a hill. The hill was covered with trees and shrouded with mist. The longer I pushed the harder it became. The rock grew bigger and heavier until I couldn't budge it at all. Not only was I unable to move it, I was afraid to let go for fear of it falling upon me and crushing me.... Mafa ... what does the dream mean?'' Tang Jo-Wang shook his head.

"Your Majesty, I don't believe in dreams. There is an old Chinese saying, 'What you ponder by day, you dream by night....'"

Fulin stared at Tang Jo-Wang.

"Mafa, you must understand..." he said in a low voice. The pain of defeat had not left him. With his brows tightly knit he recounted his painful defeat three days ago and waited earnestly for his wise Mafa and teacher to comfort and guide him.

Tang Jo-Wang crossed himself and murmured a prayer, "Oh Lord, forgive these sinners." He turned to his former pupil and spoke to him like a wise, kindly elder,

"The Chinese are especially conscious of saving face. More than anything they must preserve a semblance of righteousness. As for their actual conduct, as long as their wrong-doing is hidden it is all right. This is an unfortunate trait. It is self-deception. People claim they are not afraid of death, but they have all sorts of excuses why they must stay alive. In the same way the lords of the council are greedy for power, but they use a pious excuse that ancestral precepts cannot be changed as a means of obstructing Your Majesty's attempts at change.... That is pitiful! Your Majesty, if you fail to muzzle your courtiers, there will be more problems in the future. All manner of dishonesty will become rampant. It is an ugly situation...."

One thing Tang Jo-Wang dared not utter. It was clear the Emperor wanted to concentrate more power in himself, yet perversely he also found an excuse for his intention. Fulin found the Mafa's moral judgement and his preaching tiresome. He was discovering that the Mafa's pure god was too far removed from himself. In a power struggle, the one who insists on truth will fail. Mafa did not understand China nor did his foreign god.

However Mafa's preaching did make certain things clear for Fulin. At this moment he could see that both Nurhachi and Abahai had given considerable thought to consolidating their power. While they advocated the advisory capacity of the council, they also set up the three palace academies, thus diluting the powers of princes, nobles and banner chiefs. Mafa would label that dishonest as well. But hadn't his predecessors done worse things than that? If Dorgon had not curbed the ambitions of the nobles, would he be Emperor today? It was not a question of righteousness or truth; it was one of courage and strategy.

Fulin suddenly shot to his feet as though a thought had suddenly come to him out of the blue.

"I know what I shall do. Since they want the academicians to be demoted to the sixth degree, I will appoint each official to several posts according to ancient custom. Thus they will retain their present rank. See what they'll have to say!"

Tang Jo-Wang was shocked by this outburst. He gazed at the young Emperor with eyes full of pity and regret as though he were gravely ill and about to die.

Fulin understood the value and the correctness of Tang Jo-Wang's moral teachings. He was embarrassed by the way the old priest looked at him. He sank into his chair, swamped by dismay.

7

Time fled. Once again it was mid-autumn.

Accompanied by Academicians Wang Xi, and Feng Pu, Shunzhi was receiving two famous monks in Wanshan Hall at Xiyuan. One was Hanpu Xingcong, Abbot of Haihui Monastery, whom the Emperor met by chance last winter in the southern suburbs. The other monk present on this occasion was Yulin Tongxiu who had come from the south. Since their chance meeting Hanpu Xingcong had been invited to instruct the Emperor and to meditate with him. For his efforts, the Emperor bestowed upon him the honorary designation of Master Mingjue.

The death of his fourth son plunged the Emperor into deep melancholy. As an act of expiation he purchased many statues of the Buddha and, at the urging of his eunuchs who were devout, invited famous monks of great learning from the south to preach in the capital. To this end Hanpu Xingcong had recommended one of his own masters, Yulin Tongxiu.

Fulin experienced an extraordinary sense of well-being in the company of these monks. Yulin Tongxiu sat cross-legged. His bushy brows and sparse beard, his long ascetic face, exuded serenity like a cooling balm. Fulin's disquietude disappeared and in its place was a wonderful lightness of spirit.

Fulin spoke deferentially, "Since time immemorable all rulers have been occupied by affairs of state from dawn to dusk. Yet we are devout. Whence comes this interest in Buddhism?"

Yulin Tongxiu replied, "In his letter Xingcong praised Your Majesty as being devout and endowed with a great capacity for wisdom and that Your Majesty had been studying Buddhism although occupied by affairs of state. Having been honoured with Your Majesty's company, I have found he was completely correct in his observations. In this old monk's view, Your Majesty is the reincarnation of the Prince of the Golden Wheel, who had great wit and benevolence. Thus, you are devoted to the Buddha, kind and wise by nature, worthy of being the almighty ruler."

The monk's flattering speech pleased Fulin.

"We must have been a monk in another life. For whenever I visit a monastery, I am captivated by its simplicity and hate to leave."

"Your Majesty has retained memories of a previous life," Yulin Tongxiu agreed. Fulin was encouraged to further reveal himself.

"We can no longer sleep with another person. In fact we order everyone from the room when we retire. If there is so much as a human breath in the room, sleep eludes us."

"That too is a memory. It is said of sleep, first repose the heart, then the eyes."

"That is indeed profound," Fulin exclaimed. "When one has perfected meditation, will one be freed from all joy, anger, sadness and laughter?"

"One is joyful when all things proceed as one wishes, and angered when they do not."

"But that is nature. Wherefore the difficulty in meditation?" persisted Fulin.

"It is neither easy nor difficult. One eats when one is hungry, and sleeps when one is weary." Meditation is discovered within the heart where there is neither love nor hate. Once that is achieved one learns that past endeavours were as nothing." Fulin fervently agreed and put a further question to the monk.

"We have heard great things of the monks Shouchang Wuming and Yunmen Zhanran. Are they indeed the wise teachers they are reputed to be? There is also one Xueqiao who is said to be a forthright man and one who brooks no nonsense. Does the Master know him?"

"Indeed. He was the brother monk of my own master. On the nineteenth day of the eighth month in the year of Dinghai he was slightly indisposed. He wrote a note intimating that he wandered on the path of life and death and would achieve nirvana one night after a cup of tea. He was wafted to heaven exactly as he predicted days later."

Fulin was completely enthralled by the pure, mysterious but poetic events that the old monk related. They were the balm his soul craved for the wounds inflicted by being tossed about in the ocean of worldly lust. His spirit was refreshed by this exchange. Fulin could not resist probing further:

"We greatly admire the calligraphy of the Monk Xueqiao. How does it compare with the great master, your teacher?"

Yulin Tongxiu, smiling, replied, "My Master was learned but lacked talent, while Master Xue had talent in abundance but lacked learning. Thus Master Xue's brush-strokes lack structure, while my Master's lacks vivacity. What his work does show is courage."

Fulin smiled.

"Courage makes his brush-work unique! Without courage, the result lacks fluidity. Your own brush-work is very fine. There is individuality in every stroke, instead of slavish imitation of current fashions. Whose example does the Master favour in the regular script?"

"Tongxiu began with Huang Ting, but lacking success, then looked for models in scriptures and on tablets in the Temple of Confucius. Because of a lack of devotion to any one form, I cannot consider my calligraphy worthy of notice." Fulin responded, "I too have used the same examples, but cannot compare to the old Master's artistry."

"Your Majesty is blessed by Heaven and knows without having to learn. However, Tongxiu has not had the honour of seeing Your Majesty's handiwork."

Fulin immediately ordered ink to be ground and brushes and paper laid out on the desk. When all was ready, he selected a thick brush, dipped it in ink and wrote the character "*jing*" meaning to respect. In a burst of enthusiasm, he went over to the big square table and did a few big ones. The monks and the academicians crowded round to watch. Fulin selected the last to show Yulin Tongxiu.

"Do you like it?" he asked, pleased with himself.

Yulin Tongxiu answered,

"This is the finest. May I beg Your Majesty for it?" Fulin laughingly refused, saying, "It's not worthy." But the monk had gently took it from his fingers and thanked him profusely. Still laughing, Fulin remarked, "Our poor efforts are nothing compared to the work of the Emperor Chongzhen." He ordered the young eunuchs to bring the scrolls of Chongzhen and the books which he often read. When they were laid before him, Fulin unrolled the scrolls for the monk.

Yulin Tongxiu examined each carefully, nodding his appreciation but not uttering a word. This was one of his particular traits: that he would not offer comments unless the Emperor asked. He avoided commenting on the rights and wrongs of government policy, now or bygone. Nor would he comment on the virtues or faults of any person, thus showing a true follower of Buddha was above such common considerations. Fulin greatly admired him for this.

Fulin also pointed out the books that the eunuchs had laid out.

"I have read all these. Would the Master care to examine them?"

Tongxiu examined the volumes of history, philosophy and poetry. Indeed all the great works of literature were represented from Qin, through the two Hans, to Tang, Song, Yuan and Ming. The monk was impressed. Joining his palms he said, "Your Majesty is indeed well read and the possessor of great wisdom!"

Fulin sighed. "We were unfortunate. At the age of five His late Majesty Abahai died. I was the Empress Dowager's only son and terribly spoilt. Thus the opportunity for study was lost. When we were thirteen the regent died and we took the reins of government. However, we were too ignorant to understand the various petitions placed before us. Hence, aside from affairs of state, we studied each day from morn till dusk. However, we were also frivolous and found it difficult to commit everything to memory. Often passages had to be repeated over and over before it was fixed in the mind. We studied till we spat blood. However, since the Master Hanpu has come to us, we no longer study the same way. Now we merely scan."

Yulin Tongxiu was deeply affected by this revelation. At first he was intrigued by this barbarian Emperor who spoke fluent Chinese and had such a firm grounding in its culture. Now he was impressed.

"It is rare to find the Son of Heaven pursuing learning with such earnestness. This proves that Your Majesty should find no difficulty in mastering the principles of religion as well."

A heady fragrance floated into the hall on a breeze. The Emperor drew a deep breath.

"It seems to be the scent of the orange osmanthus," he commented. "What thinks the Master?" Tongxiu answered wordlessly with a smile. It was Wang Xi who reminded Fulin it was the Mid-Autumn Festival.

"Why, of course," Fulin exclaimed. "We almost forgot. This afternoon I must pay my respects to the Empress Dowager and, therefore, cannot tarry. We shall meet another day to seek the Master's guidance." Tongxiu, murmuring that he was not worthy of such honour, accompanied him out of the hall.

Wanshan Hall stood in a pine grove, in which were also a few osmanthus trees laden with blossoms, filling the air with fragrance. Fulin in a happy mood quoted a few lines of a poem in praise of the osmanthus tree.

"Does it not describe the old Master's surroundings?" he remarked. "I cannot say," countered the monk. "Everything Your Majesty touches turns into poetry."

The surroundings inspired Fulin to linger and to discuss the separate virtues of the poetry of the past. Personally, he favoured the work of the Song-dynasty poet Su Shi and asked the monk's opinion of his two poems on the battle at Chibi Mountain. The monk thought that the first one complemented the second one. "...Therefore it is impossible to decide which is superior...."

Fulin clapped his hands, delighted with the monk's reply which duplicated his own feelings. He began to recite Su Shi's epic on the Battle of Chibi, his voice rising and falling with grace and assurance, his eyes fixed upon the sky beyond the tops of the pines that shaded them. He was transported by the poet's words to another time and another place.

Wang Xi, Feng Pu and Xingcong were enthralled. Yulin Tongxiu stroked his sparse beard, lost in thought. And Fulin, feeling that he had finally found a friend after his own heart, lost some of his aching loneliness. A smile lit his face for the first time in a long while.

The view was lovely along the banks of Taiye Pool south of Wanshan Hall. Green lily pads and pink flowers mirrored in the still waters became thicker as one moved southward until they became a mass of green as far as the eye can see. Fulin strolled beneath the trailing branches of willow trees, content and at peace with himself.

A gentle breeze wafted the subtle perfume of water lilies to him, mingled with the distant sound of music. Fulin felt every muscle in his body relaxing. He felt such a wonderful lightness that he seemed to glide along effortlessly. The music became louder. Did it emit from the sky, or float upon the water, or was it the breath of the water lilies? For the moment Fulin had drifted into an enchanted world. His footsteps slowed as he listened.

The beaded curtains were half rolled on Lily Blossom Pavilion. Lady Dongeh was seated on a chaise longue, with sheets of music spread on a small table beside her. A group of serving maids all about thirteen years of age were playing flute, pipes, fife, drums and stringed instruments accompanying another group who sang. They had been practising for some time. At Fulin's approach the musicians stopped and fell to their knees. Lady Dongeh hurried to greet him.

"I knew it was you," Fulin exclaimed on seeing her.

"We are practising for tonight's family feast," Lady Dongeh smiled. Fulin gestured for everyone to rise.

"Please continue. We shall listen."

The two went into the pavilion talking companionably together. Inside, beside the maid Rongniu, there was a nurse carrying a small child. The chubby little girl's adorable rose-bud mouth pouted, as her eyes travelled solemnly around the room. When Fulin had been seated, Lady Dongeh sat down beside him and took the child from its nurse. The child gazed fixedly at Fulin, evoking a delighted laugh. He reached for a small tender hand

and asked gently, "How old are you? And what is your name?"

"Three years old! I'm called Bingyue!" the child piped in a chirpy voice like a lark.

"Bingyue.... What a pretty name! Where are the other three from Jidu and Lerjin?"

"They're with their nurses. But this one is older and so adorable that I try to keep her by my side."

"In looks and personality she is more like a daughter than a niece of yours. She will be a Manchu beauty one day!" Fulin teased. Lady Dongeh brushed a stray lock of hair off the child's forehead. "It's strange, but this one took to me from the beginning.... You look well ... and happy today...."

"They say, a thousand cups of wine is nothing among friends. Though I haven't touched a drop today, I am slightly tipsy...." Then he told her about the morning spent in the company of the monks, and the feeling of lightness and peace he derived from it.

"You should learn to meditate as well. To conquer all desires and shuck off the troubles of the world are such a release. The last two years have been fraught with troubles for you too...." Lady Dongeh's head drooped. There was a long silence before she lifted her face to Fulin. "I will be Your Majesty's pupil if you will have me."

Fulin laughed. Suddenly he waved at the musicians outside and commanded them to stop. He went out and told them a certain passage required a little more breadth. Taking up the clapboard, he rehearsed them personally. The mistake was quickly corrected. Satisfied, Fulin went back inside.

After the rehearsal, Lady Dongeh rewarded the musicians with a platter of pastries, promising there would be another reward if they performed well later.

When the musicians had gone, Lady Dongeh suggested they too should leave.

"I'm not ready to leave," teased Fulin. "They get a platter

of food for their efforts, but I don't even get a cup of tea."

Lady Dongeh was happy to see him in such good spirits. Her nerves which had been stretched to their limits eased. She suggested sending for some pastries and plain tea, cautioning, "You mustn't eat too much, because the Empress Dowager's family dinner promises to be sumptuous indeed!"

"In that case," Fulin responded cheerily, "we'll just have something light. And you will have some tea with me."

Lady Dongeh sent Rongniu for food, but Bingyue stretched out her arms wanting to go with her. Instructing Rongniu to put Bingyue straight to bed, "or she will be sleepy at the banquet later", Lady Dongeh dismissed the servants except two serving wenches.

Rongniu's clear bell-like voice when she answered drew Fulin out of the pavilion.

Lily Blossom Pavilion is built on the water, surrounded by lily-pods and blossoms. The water-lilies have grown so lush that they completely obscured the courseway leading to the land. Rongniu, the nurse and little Bingyue soon disappeared among the foliage. Only the pale blue of the servants' costumes and the goose-down yellow of the child's robes could be glimpsed flashing among the luxuriant growth from time to time until they faded into the distance.

From the pavilion, the three lakes of Xiyuan were spread before him. High the White Dagoba loomed over the trees on Qionghua Islet. Below, the white marble bridge spanned the waters of Taiye Pool like a rainbow. In the distance, beyond the Palace walls, rose clusters of imposing roofs and turrets. Looking back, the elegant buildings of Sea Terrace Island rose shimmering like a mirage above tree tops and lake.

Fulin was content sitting on the red rails of the corridor with one arm around Black Pearl's waist drinking in the view.

"Taiye Pool is indeed beautiful in autumn," he breathed. "It makes one happy. Though it isn't West Lake it is beautiful in its own way. Next year when the nation is at peace, we shall journey south, and we shall discover how the soil of Suzhou and Hangzhou produced so beautiful and wise a person as our beloved lady."

"Your Majesty is teasing," Black Pearl smiled. Fulin looked out at the water lilies in full bloom and back again at the woman beside him and blurted out, "The romantic, elegant water lily should be named after you."

"Your Majesty is too kind," Lady Dongeh blushed.

"You and I are fortunate to be together at this place on this festival day. After the banquet you shall come to me in the Hall of Mental Cultivation and we will make a vow to be man and wife for eternity." Fulin, bursting with passion, was a boy again.

Lady Dongeh was silent a while. When she spoke it was in a dull voice:

"Your Majesty is blessed by Heaven with many years before you. This poor weak creature is unworthy of your favour, but will forever be grateful to have served you. However, such a miserable person might not have the luck to enjoy Your Majesty's love and remain at his side for long...."

Fulin could not understand what had prompted these gloomy thoughts. He tried to comfort her saying, "Perhaps, the damp autumn air has made you melancholy. Let us leave." Lady Dongeh put on a brave smile and said brightly, "But we can't leave before the food arrives." Then quickly kneeling she added, "I have two requests to beg of Your Majesty."

"Tell me."

"I beg Your Majesty to give his attention evenly to the principal ladies of the six palaces, so that there should be no discontent. Your Majesty lacks sons, and the Empire cannot be without heirs. This concerns the safety of the Empire. I beg Your Majesty not to allow personal feelings to interfere with the larger scheme of things...."

Fulin tried to brush her remarks aside with a flippant reply: "But, my dear, you can provide us with another prince."

Black Pearl's eyes brimmed. "I fear your slave does not have that blessing. Besides, who can tell if the death of your fourth son was not brought on by discontent within the six palaces! A discontent so deep that the gods were moved to intercede...."

Fulin blanched at the mention of discontent. For he knew the truth of the matter. Discontent had indeed caused the death of his fourth son, but he did not speak.

"Your slave hoped to recommend Sichen, the Empress Dowager's other adopted daughter, to be brought into the palace, that we might both serve Your Majesty. However, she refused as she was betrothed before her father died. Thus your slave's hopes came to nought. However, your slave has a cousin who, at sixteen years of age, bears a striking resemblence to your slave. She is not as well versed in literature, but carries herself with dignity. As the day for the selection of beauties draws near, your slave would be eternally grateful if Your Majesty would drop a hint to the Empress Dowager in her favour." Black Pearl refused to rise until Fulin had granted her requests. As the servants were coming in with the food, Fulin was forced to consent in spite of himself.

While they ate, Lady Dongeh once more became animated, talking happily about things that interested Fulin, enquiring after the learned monk he had been studying with, and so on. Fulin brightened under her gentle prodding. They whiled away the afternoon with cheerful conversation and laughter.

Fulin once more reminded himself how fortunate he was in having so beautiful, clever and learned a lady by his side. He was convinced that, in all of history, there was not another to equal her.

Lady Dongeh forced herself to avoid the love and passion that burned in his eyes, for it would only add to the pain deep in her soul. Shortly after her child's death, she began to feel a nameless weakness which grew inexorably. She was short of breath and often plagued by bouts of blackness. When she started coughing up specks of blood, she feared she had contracted some dreaded disease...."

But she told no one. Not even Fulin.

Part 7

At the beginning of the sixteenth year of Shunzhi, news of victories in the south blew across the capital like a January blizzard. In the first month of that year, Duoni, Wu Sangui, and Zhou Butai's armies swept everything before them. Soon Yunnan and Guizhou were subdued. The pockets of resistance put up by the adherents of Southern Ming were quickly destroyed. In the third month, Zheng Chenggong made a desperate invasion of Taiping in the Province of Zhejiang, in a vain attempt to divert Manchu forces from Yunnan and Guizhou. But he failed and fled across the seas to the island. With Wu Sangui firmly entrenched in Yunnan, Shang Kexi and Geng Jimao holding Guangdong and Sichuan the great task of unification was completed. This was an occasion of great joy for the entire court, especially for the Manchu who had achieved much more than their ancestors dared dream.

The ill-will caused by the aborted dissolution of the Council of Nobles was swept aside in the euphoria of victory. Though he failed to dissolve the Council of Nobles, Shunzhi did succeed in establishing a Grand Secretariat in place of the three academies. Also the Imperial Hanlin Academy was set up. Shunzhi was satisfied for the time being and began planning the great tasks that still lay ahead: recalling the armies; reducing the cost of their maintenance; tax reforms; pacifying remnant rebels; and promoting and rewarding pioneers of remote areas.

In Fulin's personal life there was peacc within the imperial household. The Empress Dowager was in good health. Since the Emperor had been distributing his favours, there was less jealousy and resentment among the principal ladies of the six palaces. They lived in harmony with one another, and Shunzhi's children were all in good health.

Lady Dongeh's cousin was brought into the palace. Though she was given the title of Lady Zhen, an imperial concubine of a lesser degree, she was also favoured by the Emperor. In his leisure, Shunzhi occupied himself with his ladies, holding feasts, attending performances of the opera, or pursuing his interest in literature and poetry with the members of the Grand Secretariat and the Hanlin Academy. Or he would be in the company of the high monks at Wanshan Hall, discussing scripture and practising meditation under the tutelage of Yulin and Muchen. Life was pleasant.

On the seventh day of the seventh month, the festival of young maidens, four or five bowls of water were placed in the sun on the terrace. On this day young girls would drop needles into the bowls. If the needle sank, it indicated the girl was clumsy. If it floated then it showed the girl was good at needlework. But that was not all. The shadow of the needle had to be considered as well. A blurred shadow showed that the girl's needlework was only ordinary. However, if the shadow was as thin as thread and sharp as a needle, she was peerless. This little ritual was known as "testing the skills". In the evening, when the moon was risen, the girls would make offerings to the Weaving Maid in the Milky Way, with fruit, nuts and cakes together with samples of needlework, asking her blessing for the skills they lacked.

Sunlight danced upon the water. The young girls clustered round the bowls, laughed or sighed or pouted. Rongniu was the last to drop her needle into a bowl. It floated as though it was glued to the surface, light as down, casting a shadow as fine as thread.

"Ah! Rongniu is the best of us!" The young girls clapped their hands and cheered.

Their laughter brought Lady Dongeh onto the terrace. The young girls quickly quietened and stood with heads bowed. Lady

Dongeh noticed the bowls of water and remarked, "So you've been testing your skills. Well, who is the best?" The Empress' maid fell to her knees and replied, "If it pleases the Precious Concubine, it was Your Ladyship's own Rongniu."

"Rise. There is no need for ceremony," Lady Dongeh responded. "I had no idea Rongniu was so fortunate. Will you pray to the Weaving Maid tonight?" All the young girls nodded their heads.

"That's good. However, the Empress is recovering from illness. Try not to disturb her," Lady Dongeh requested in a kindly fashion. The girls could not refuse. Watching her go indoors, looking so frail that she could almost be blown away in a gust of wind, they could not refrain from discussing her.

"No matter which of the ladies is ill, the Precious Concubine is always the one to nurse her. She is really thoughtful."

"Huh! If anyone still says she's ambitious and wants to be empress..." one of the youngest serving maids of the Empress began. The others quickly covered her mouth and cautioned, "That is not for you to say!"

Rongniu listened but did not join in. Actually she knew more than any of the others. She knew that the Precious Concubine's head had not touched a pillow since the Empress took ill. When it was thought she might not live, Lady Dongeh set up an altar and offered prayers. She was deeply distressed, for the Emperor had asked her to care for the Empress. What would she do if Her Majesty died? After five sleepless nights, the Precious Concubine was more wan and haggard than before. She had also been coughing blood more often. However, her mistress had also sworn Rongniu to silence, threatening to dismiss her from the palace if she breathed so much as a word.

Rongniu did not want to leave the palace. Until she came here she had not been attached to anyone. She was a carefree child when she lived in Malan Village. Though she had deep feelings for mother, sister and brother, she did not respect her mother, she pitied her sister, while she feared her brother. Her devotion to the Precious Concubine was something she had never experienced before. To her, Lady Dongeh was a celestial being come to earth. When Rongniu and her family were arrested she was quickly given as slave to one of the princely households in the capital. Being young and unsuited for heavy work nobody wanted to keep her. Finally she was given to the family of an imperial bondservant. Though a slave himself, the bondservant was exceedingly cruel to his own slaves. Within weeks, the girl's body was covered with bruises, and her hair had been pulled out by the handful. In a short time the vivacious young girl had turned into a pitiful wraith.

Quite unexpectedly her master's attitude suddenly changed. They were kind to her. A few Manchu-styled robes were made for her. A clean, comfortable room was provided her, and she was fed good, nourishing meals. Rongniu did not give much thought to what was happening. She did not hold grudges. Nor was she inclined toward introspection. Soon she was her cheery self again, until the mistress of the house spilled beans that she was being groomed to take the place of the master's daughter in the selection of palace maids.

Palace maids were selected by the officials of the thirteen yamen or government departments. The selection took place once a year, with candidates drawn from the households of imperial bondservants between the ages of thirteen and eighteen. These maids served the principal ladies of the six inner palaces. When they turned twenty-five they would be dismissed from service, and it would be the responsibility of their families to find them husbands.

Rongniu's master had made all the necessary arrangements in that year's selection. The only hurdle was the need to keep Rongniu from telling the truth. Hence Rongniu was warned that if she ever revealed the truth he would have her mother and sister killed.

So Rongniu entered the imperial service in this curious fashion. At first she was sent to Chengqian Palace as a drudge. But her prettiness and cleverness attracted Lady Dongeh's attention. When her personal maid was married off, she chose Rongniu to take her place.

Rongniu was devoted to her mistress. The Precious Concubine was also fond of her. But she showed this fondness in subtle ways so that the other maids and eunuchs would not become jealous. In spite of how highly the Precious Concubine was regarded, or how amiable she appeared, Rongniu knew her mistress had many sorrows and often wept without anyone knowing. At such times Rongniu wanted to throw herself at her mistress' feet and weep for her. Or at least offer some words of comfort. But she didn't dare.

"Rongniu," The Empress' maid startled her out of her reverie. "The Precious Concubine is telling a story! Let's go and listen."

Indeed, laughter was coming through the open windows of the chamber. Now that the Empress was recovering, the Precious Concubine was saddled with the extra duty of reading to the convalescent from history and scriptures. Lady Dongeh frequently lightened this dull material with stories. However, when she should be ill and alone, who would come to amuse Lady Dongeh? Rongniu shook her head. She had no enthusiasm for stories just then.

Meanwhile, in the east chamber, Lady Dongeh struggling against weariness was telling a story:

"Once upon a time there was a Metropolitan Graduate by the name of Xing. Xing was so short that he was known as Little Xing. One day on the banks of Poyang Lake he encountered a pirate. The pirate not only relieved Xing of all his goods, but threatened to cut off his head to prevent him from reporting the robbery. As the pirate raised his broad sword, Xing quipped, 'They already call me Little Xing. If you cut my head off, I will become even smaller.' The remark made the pirate laugh, and so he set Xing free."

The Empress laughed, saying, "That Xing was a brave

man."

"That is true. One has to accept things as they come. Even death. Then everything will turn out right," Lady Dongeh countered cheerfully.

The Empress reclined on a chaise while Lady Dongeh sat in a chair placed close beside her. The strong rays of sunlight, passing through the fine green silk screens fixed to the window, was softened, lightly tinted. In this light, Lady Dongeh seemed more wan, the dark circles around her eyes blacker. The Empress felt a pang of pity seeing her thus.

"I am recovered. Now you need rest.... Don't come to keep me company everyday."

"My Lady is too kind. A concubine's duty is to look upon the Emperor as a father and the Empress as mother. My Lady must speak out if I fail in my duties...."

The Empress, gazing at the other's pretty face, felt a rush of warmth. She was deeply moved but did not know what to say. Finally she sighed and taking Lady Dongeh's hand in hers spoke with tears in her eyes.

"You are a kind ... good person.... And you have always been so.... But I thought you were intent on currying favour, trying to take my place ... or at least becoming Empress Dowager in due time.... When I fell ill, I thought how happy you must be.... Perhaps you were praying for my early demise.... But it was not like that.... Instead you cared for me.... I have been such a fool...."

Lady Dongeh reached over to stroke the Empress' plump hand.

"His Majesty carries the burden of the Empire on his shoulders, and Your Majesty has the responsibility of the six palaces on yours. Now that all under Heaven is united these burdens will become even heavier. If I can relieve that burden in some small way, it will be my duty and a joy to do so."

The Empress replied, "I am truly recovered. Tomorrow I shall go to Cining Palace to pay my respects to the Empress Dowager who has showered me with kindness, much to my shame.... Sister ... let us go together."

That new, unfamiliar form of address — the word "sister" — made Lady Dongeh's throat constrict with emotion. She nodded her consent, quite overcome.

When Lady Dongeh took her leave she was at the end of her endurance. With a superhuman effort she pushed herself out of her chair. Instantly there was a fierce buzzing in her ears and stars danced before her eyes. She wavered and almost fell, but the Empress cried out and the serving maids rushed in to hold her up. The colour drained from Lady Dongeh's face and lips. Frightened now, the Empress wanted to send for the imperial physician.

Lady Dongeh stopped her. Forcing a smile she assured the Empress, "I will be all right ... I need to rest ... and I'll be better...." Rongniu and another maid supported Lady Dongeh on either side. When she left the room she reminded the Empress, "My Lady, tomorrow we will go to Cining Palace ... together...."

Early next morning the ladies of the inner palace went as usual in twos and threes to pay their respects to the Empress Dowager. After the Empress' week-long absence, the others were happy to see her and the Precious Concubine, and they clustered around them to wish them well. The Empress noticed how popular the Precious Concubine had become. She would have felt a rush of resentment before, but no longer. Now she was genuinely pleased, for she understood that if she were amiable and kind like Lady Dongeh, she too would win hearts.

Lady Shuhui and Lady Zhen were chatting with the Empress Dowager when the Empress and the Precious Concubine arrived. The Empress Dowager was delighted as the two made their obeisance together. As they rose, the Empress fearing the Precious Concubine might have difficulties reached out to help her. It was a natural gesture but the Precious Concubine was deeply moved. However, some of the others were shocked, for in their eyes the Empress had demeaned herself. Lady Shuhui frowned and glared at her sister with undisguised disapproval. Lady Zhen who was young and guileless smiled at her cousin, blushing prettily. The Empress Dowager was pleased and, having invited the two ladies to sit, enquired after the Empress' illness.

The Empress spoke with gratitude for the Precious Concubine's care. The Empress Dowager listened to her recitation with frequent nods, her eyes fixed upon the Precious Concubine. When the tale was told, Lady Dongeh rose to her feet and, blushing with embarrassment, said in a low voice, "My Lady is too kind ... I have only done my duty...." Seeing her so frail and drawn the Empress Dowager's heart went out to her. Impulsively she reached for Lady Dongeh's hand. "My child ... it's been a hardship for you..." she murmured lovingly.

The Empress Dowager searched Lady Dongeh's face, and with her other hand reached for the Empress'.

"In ancient times," she said, "the great Emperor Shun achieved many things with the help of two women, the ladies Ehhuang and her sister Nuying. They were the wisest women of all times. You two in harmony with each other will be our Emperor's great help...."

The two ladies thanked Her Majesty for her compliment. However, Lady Dongeh was also reminded of the tragic conclusion of these ladies who took their own lives after their Emperor died. The Empress Dowager's comparison sounded like an ill omen that filled her with fear.

The Empress Dowager adopted an enquiring tone when she said, "Now that it is autumn I have been thinking of spending a few days at the hot springs. Seeing that you are just recovered, it would do you good. And Black Pearl should come too." Lady Dongeh hesitated a moment before replying, "Your child has been feeling a weakness of the body. Perhaps she should not go...." The Empress added, "Your Majesty, yesterday the Precious Concubine nearly fainted. She is exhausted...." The Empress Dowager countered, "We are aware that you have weathered many troubles, and are in a weakened state. We have, therefore, ordered certain medicines and tonics for the ailments that plague womankind especially for you. Also Lady Zhen will come as your companion. Your cousin will look after you...." Hearing these words, Black Pearl felt truly loved. Lady Zhen who was present quickly interjected, "I'd love to go! It would be such fun being with my dear cousin!" The Empress Dowager shot Lady Zhen an angry look.

"You're coming along to take care of your cousin!" Judging her tone of voice it was clear the Empress Dowager was fond of the childlike Lady Zhen. When the Empress Dowager was not looking, Lady Zhen winked mischievously at Lady Dongeh, who pretended not to see.

"Your child shall keep Your Majesty's kindness locked in her heart. However, since the Empress has been ill there are many trifling matters within the palace that have been neglected. I should like to attend to them...."

The Empress Dowager sighed. "At this rate even a piece of jade will be worn down, not to mention flesh and blood. You are cleverer than most, and you are understanding. These are good traits. But from year end to year end, there are so many things that need attention in the inner palace, and you can not possibly take them all on your shoulders. You are over-worked. I command you to come to the hot springs. I have neither seen nor spoken to you in days and days. Can you not come to please an old woman?"

Lady Dongeh fell to her knees.

"The Imperial Mother is too kind. Your child will do as she is told. When shall we depart?"

"Oh! I have already given orders to start out immediately after the morning meal. You two should make preparations right away. Lady Shuhui will take charge of things for a few days. I have already notified His Majesty and requested that important matters be communicated to us by messenger at the hot springs." Lady Shuhui received her orders on her knees. The ladies left Cining Palace and headed for their respective residences. As they parted at Yuehua Gate, Lady Dongeh paused and, bowing to Lady Shuhui, said, "Sister, I leave everything in your capable hands...." Lady Shuhui smiled back, "It's my duty...." When the other had turned away, her smile quickly disappeared, and she muttered angrily to herself, "The vixen! How pleased she is with herself...."

The Empress frowned. "What are you muttering about?"

In the two years she had been in the palace, Lady Shuhui had lost some of her childishness, but her jealousy had grown deeper.

"I can't stand her posturing! Did you see how she had the Empress Dowager wrapped round her finger!"

"There was nothing wrong with what the Empress Dowager said."

"Oh, my poor sister! You've fallen under her spell too. Can't you see you are never going to be this dynasty's Lady Ehhuang and Lady Nuying with that one!"

"Why not?"

"Just as there aren't two suns in the sky, so the inner palace cannot have two empresses. That vixen has bewitched the Empress Dowager and His Majesty. Everybody says she's so good, so much better than you that one day you'll have to yield your position to her!" The Empress frowned darkly. "If she wants to be empress why didn't she let me die?"

"...I suppose she was winning hearts..." Lady Shuhui blurted out a remark that rang false even in her own ears. The Empress sighed. "Sister, one has to live by one's conscience. She saved my life. How can I be suspicious of her after that?"

"Sister, don't you understand? You two will always be fire and water...." The Empress shook her head. "Whether it's fire and water or wood and stone, I cannot ignore the fact that when I was dangerously ill she never left my bedside, day or night. You, my sister, came briefly during the day. That was all...." Lady Shuhui bit her lip, unable to rebut her.

"Sister, I suggest you think about how you will manage things, instead of wasting energy on the Precious Concubine ...." The Empress left Lady Shuhui who was still grumbling: "You'll be sorry ... but it'll be too late...."

Lady Shuhui could not overcome her hatred for Lady Dongeh. She was no longer naive. She knew that from the point of view of tradition and advantage to Great Qing, the Empress had to be a daughter of either the Horqin Mongol or the Boerjijite clan. Therefore she would be the ideal successor to the Empress should anything untoward befall her. However, the advent of Lady Dongeh not only dashed her hopes for the future, but also jeopardized her sister's. If Lady Dongeh had come from one of the other powerful tribes, she could at least bow to the inevitable. But she was the daughter of a southern barbarian. Lady Shuhui would never bow to the likes of her.

When Lady Jin was alive, she had a sympathetic ear in which to pour all her vitriol. But Lady Jin was dead. Lady Shuhui thought of another ally. However, from another perspective Lady Kang was a powerful adversary because she had borne the Emperor a son, while Lady Shuhui and her sister hadn't produced any offspring. Lady Kang could also be a successor to the Empress. However she did not have the same clout as Lady Dongeh. Despite all that Lady Shuhui decided to make an ally of Lady Kang.

Lady Shuhui went through Yuehua Gate and headed for Jingren Palace. The principal lady of this palace tended to be taciturn. However, Lady Shuhui was keenly aware her pronouncements were usually worth heeding.

After the Empress Dowager, the Empress, the Precious Concubine and their entourage of princes and princesses had left for the hot springs, the inner palace grew silent. Fulin did not have his daily visits to his mother to occupy him, or Lady Dongeh and her cousin to amuse him in his leisure. Though he read, practised calligraphy, played his flute with a band of musicians, and summoned Lady Shuhui, or Lady Duan, or Lady Kang to spend the night in the Hall of Mental Cultivation, it was not the same. He was unaccustomed to being alone. Though he missed the passion he shared with Lady Dongeh, time passed placidly. A few more days, and those who had gone to the hot springs would return. Fulin longed to see them.

After the evening meal Fulin strolled upon the terrace outside the Hall of Mental Cultivation. The tubs of crabapple bushes were laden with various shades of red flowers. Under the shrubs were a number of delicately made porcelain jars in which the eunuchs kept crickets which filled the air with their merry chirping. As a child, and even into his twelfth and thirteenth year, Shunzhi had been fond of fighting crickets. He delighted in staging fights with the young eunuchs, and betting on the winner. Of course he never lost. Actually, at that time he was afraid the regent might have him assassinated, and he deliberately cultivated the image of a frivolous child to distract him. Naturally the eunuchs, who were none the wiser, thought he liked crickets and were careful to keep the jars filled. Nor did Fulin object to the joyous noise they made.

Fulin took a date from a plate on a small table set inside the doorway and, breaking it into tiny pieces, fed it to the proud chirping fighter.

"The Lady Shuhui is approaching!" announced the young eunuch at his side.

Fulin raised his head and glanced toward the gate. His brow shot up in astonishment. The eyes of his attendants also bulged with surprise.

Lady Shuhui had been summoned, and as usual she had come on a small, open sedan chair. This type of light conveyance was usually carried on the shoulders of four stout men. However, on this occasion it was carried by braided palace maids dressed in blue cloth robes. The number had been increased from four to eight. Though Lady Shuhui was not heavy, the girls were not used to heavy work and the hard wood sedan chair seemed like a load of bricks. By the time they arrived they were gasping for air with sweat pouring down their backs.

Lady Shuhui relished the sensation her arrival caused. "I want you to come for me in the morning, and nobody else," she commanded as she alighted. The maids staggered away bearing the empty sedan chair which did not seem lighter.

Once they were in the bed chamber, Fulin could contain himself no longer.

"What made you force the maids to carry the sedan chair?"

"That is why I used eight of them. Wasn't that clever of me?"

"Why didn't you use young eunuchs?" It was the question she had been hoping for. Lady Shuhui smiled mysteriously.

"Huh! Young eunuchs are so wild and unmannerly that I'd sooner walk."

"Oh. Is that so?"

"I...." Lady Shuhui seemed younger today. She winked mysteriously and lowered her voice. "I've never heard of such a thing before. Sister Kang made the discovery. Your Majesty should send for her...." Fulin was annoyed now.

"Since you brought it up, you might as well make a clean breast of it. No need to involve anyone else." Afraid that Fulin might lose his temper, Lady Shuhui stammered: "I'll speak. It's a curiosity. Lady Kang didn't mention it because she was afraid Your Majesty might be angry...." Fulin was impatient now.

"What is this about?" Though Lady Shuhui was nervous, she forced a smile and, lifting a cup of cold tea from a small table which had probably been left by the Emperor, downed it in one gulp. The tea calmed her and she said almost ingenuously, "Your Majesty is familiar with history. No doubt you know about the scandal of Wet Nurse Ke of the Ming Dynasty...." She then recounted the relation of the wet nurse and two eunuchs. The affair was eventually brought to the attention of the Emperor, who not only condoned it but asked the lady which of the men she preferred. He then pronounced them man and wife.

"...These relations were known as 'Dui Shi' or 'eating opposite one another'. Has Your Majesty heard of that?" Fulin had to admit he hadn't. Lady Shuhui giggled.

"It was quite common in the palace during the Ming Dynasty. Palace maids often form relations with eunuchs. Our palace maids still cling to these old practices, but they don't call themselves husband and wife anymore. Instead they take eunuchs as brothers or even uncles ... in spirit."

"It's for the sake of looking after one another. What is so strange?"

"That may be on the surface, but underneath it's probably the same old thing." Fulin laughed.

"Even if they used the term husband and wife, it can only be in name. Where's the harm?"

Lady Shuhui bit her lip and blushed. "I thought it was in name too ... but it isn't...."

"What?" Fulin was astonished. "Are you saying there are false eunuchs?"

"No.... The eunuchs are real enough...."

"Speak or hold your tongue!" A cold gleam had come into Fulin's eyes. Blushing to the roots of her hair, but still forcing a smile, Lady Shuhui leaned close and whispered in Fulin's ear. Fulin's brows arched. In hushed tones he asked, "Did you see it?"

"No. Of course not ... but the maids gossip.... There are some ... in Chengqian Palace...." Lady Shuhui covered her mouth and giggled as though she was telling a naughty story. Fulin thrust her aside in a rage. Lady Shuhui stumbled backwards and fell to her knees, trembling. Fulin, with flaming eyes, grabbed the front of her robe.

"You lie!" he thundered. Lady Shuhui's eyes were wide with fright. She knew he would be angry, but she did not expect such rage or that it would erupt so swiftly. For a moment her breath caught, then like a dam bursting tears flooded her cheeks. She banged her forehead on the ground again and again.

"Your Majesty, your slave would not dare lie," she wailed. "I repeated the story to amuse ... not to distress Your Majesty.... Actually, Sister Kang's eunuch Wu Lu has made an alliance with the Precious Concubine's personal maid Rongniu. Lady Kang overheard Wu Lu boasting to the other young eunuchs. Concerned it might affect the Precious Concubine's reputation, she dismissed him. I was revolted by the story. That's why I use maids to carry my sedan chair. These are the wicked ways of the Ming that the servants still cling to. It has absolutely nothing to do with the Precious Concubine. I was indiscreet ... please don't ask anymore...."

"Chengqian Palace..." Fulin muttered. There was a peculiar look in his eyes.

"Your Majesty! Your Majesty!" Lady Shuhui crawled frantically toward Fulin on hands and knees. "None of this involves the Precious Concubine! It's the fault of those wretched servants. Your Majesty has shown the Precious Concubine special favour. Surely she would not do anything unworthy of your love. For pity's sake don't let this spread. Above all, don't blame the Precious Concubine ... and don't search for that thing ... in Chengqian Palace."

Lady Shuhui's words struck him like a whiplash, from which his heart recoiled in indescribable pain. The pain caused a rush of blood to his head, so that his thoughts became a muddle.

"Why search Chengqian Palace?" he yelled.

"No! No!" cried Lady Shuhui, "you mustn't search it! You mustn't! Your Majesty, I beg you, treat this as the prattling of a foolish woman ... or pretend I never uttered a word...."

Fulin's head throbbed. Thick veins stuck out from his temples. He seemed to have taken leave of his reason, completely obsessed now with discovering the truth. He loomed menacingly over Lady Shuhui.

"Why don't you want me to search Chengqian Palace? Where will I find the thing? With Wu Lu or Rongniu?" Lady Shuhui shrank from Fulin, unable to speak. Fulin grunted, his eyes darting daggers, full of hatred and death. Lady Shuhui shrivelled into a quivering ball. "...According to Wu Lu ... it's in Rongniu's keeping...."

Fulin ground his teeth. He summoned the chief eunuch of the Hall of Mental Cultivation and ordered him to take a search party at once to Chengqian Palace and search Rongniu's quarters. As the eunuch Li Guozhu was about to depart, another thought came to him. He called the eunuch back and added, "Take men you can trust. If a word of this gets out, I'll have your head."

Within the hour Li Guozhu returned with a small wooden box which he presented to the Emperor. The box had been found among some clothes kept in a trunk under Rongniu's bed, in a room to the east of the Precious Concubine's bed chamber. Fulin's hands shook as he lifted the lid. The box contained several small objects wrapped in silk. He unwrapped one, glanced at it and slammed the lid shut. He left the room, fighting waves of nausea that assailed him. It was as though the tranquility of a garden on a spring night had been rudely shattered by the raucous mating of cats.

The remnants of the evening meal had not yet been removed from the table set in the main room. He lifted the jar of strong new wine to his lips and drank as though it was water. When he had drained the last drop, he heaved the jar through the open door. The sound of the smashing jar echoed throughout the hall.

"Shameless!" he shrieked like a mad man.

Though he was dead drunk, he could not forget the little wooden box or its hideous contents. With his own hand he wrote the seal and affixed it. The rest was oblivion. He was not aware of the eunuchs undressing him and putting him to bed, or

Li Guozhu carefully putting the offending box away. Nor did he see Lady Shuhui's mysterious smile when she stole into the chamber.

The next day the Empress Dowager and the ladies returned. When Fulin went to visit his mother he found the ladies rested and refreshed. The youthful Lady Zhen was especially appealing, like a rose-bud about to unfold.

Fulin glanced casually at Lady Dongeh, who responded with a look of such tenderness that only a lover would recognize; a look that made Fulin quiver so that he could barely breathe.

"She isn't that sort," he told himself. "She's as pure as an angel."

That night Fulin summoned Lady Dongeh to the Hall of Mental Cultivation, but not to the bed chamber. They met in the west chamber which was his study. Lady Dongeh was surprised but did not show it. When she came into the Presence she was her usual warm, gracious self. Her gaze was full of love as she gently enquired, "Is Your Majesty well?"

Fulin did not reply but fixed her with an angry gaze. "If she's innocent she will not turn a hair.... If she's uneasy...."

Lady Dongeh had never been treated with such coldness. Though taken aback, she forced a smile and enquired, "Your Majesty, is something wrong?"

Huh, look at her, he thought. Look at how she forces that smile! A cold clammy hand gripped his heart as he faced Black Pearl. All his plans flew out the window. The traps he would set, the interrogation carried out step by relentless step were abandoned in confusion. In spite of himself he slammed the little wooden box on the table and ordered her to open it.

If she was puzzled by the box; if she had never seen its revolting contents that would prove she had no knowledge of the shameful events that had taken place. Fulin's face was grim as he fixed his unblinking eyes upon Lady Dongeh, his heart beating wildly.

The box was opened and its contents unwrapped. Lady

Dongeh averted her face and bowed her head. She knew! Every fibre of his being shrieked, but he controlled himself.

"You ... know what it is?"

"...I suppose ... I do...." Ah! She's embarrassed.... She pretends ... but ... maybe not.... Fulin suddenly tossed the most damaging information at her. If she was startled then it was clear she was innocent.

"That was found in a trunk belonging to your personal maid Rongniu."

Fulin watched Lady Dongeh intently. If only she would cry out, or exhibit some evidence of shock and dismay. But all she showed was more embarrassment than surprise, and all she said was a soft, non-committal "Oh!"

Fulin's heart turned to ice. She knew! She knew all along! She's been protecting Rongniu, keeping me in the dark.... But why? Why? Does she love that half-crazy maid so much? Is she a part of their filthy activities? Once that thought flashed in his mind, it quickly took root. In his mind's eye were vivid visions of Rongniu using those unspeakable objects.... Of Rongniu and the eunuch Wu Lu in an embrace.... The image of Rongniu melted into Black Pearl ... and it was she in the eunuch's embrace.... Black Pearl and the unspeakable eunuch.... Fulin's mind was in a whirl. He brought his fist down heavily on the table.

"Do you know what you have done?"

The table leaped under his fist. The expression on Fulin's face was so terrible that Lady Dongeh cried out, "Your Majesty, what is the matter!"

Fulin struck her across the face with the flat of his hand. His face was crimson with rage, and his eyes blazed like hot coals. Black Pearl was pale with fear, not knowing what to do.

"Do you dare deny!" roared Fulin. Black Pearl fell to her knees, head bowed, too fearful to speak.

Fulin turned his back on her, gazing sightlessly out the window. When he had regained his composure somewhat, he spoke in a voice that almost equaled the dignity of his position.

"Withdraw and examine your conscience." He did not wait for her to take her leave, but strode from the room. Everything went black before Lady Dongeh's eyes, and she collapsed in a faint.

From that day on Lady Dongeh never left Chengqian Palace. The Empress and the other ladies were mystified. Their entreaties to the Emperor fell on deaf ears. Nor could they get any information from Lady Dongeh when they visited her. Though Lady Shuhui and Lady Kang knew what had happened their lips were sealed.

For ten days the Emperor did not summon the Precious Concubine. The whispers within the inner palace finally reached the ears of the Empress Dowager and she summoned the Emperor to wait upon her at Cining Palace.

2

Fulin was dominated by his filial feelings for his mother. He visited her daily except when he was away from the Forbidden City and his decrees concerning the inner palace were invariably issued according to the wishes of Her Majesty the Empress Dowager. Hence, whenever he was summoned, he went without delay both out of affection and the dictates of protocol.

Mother and son had been in conversation for some time.

"Imperial Son," the Empress Dowager began almost teasingly, "how did we conquer Southern Ming and unite all under Heaven?" Fulin had been giving this some serious thought of late and replied without hesitation, "From above we had the blessings of Heaven and the Ancestors. And on earth we had brave warriors and able commanders. Furthermore, our own governing was, if not brilliant, adequate, never wanton."

"Imperial Son, what do you consider your greatest forte?" Fulin mulled the question over before replying. "In these times when Han and Manchu are like fire and water, compassion and understanding are needed." The Empress Dowager nodded in approval.

"Correct. How is it that you can be wise in handling affairs of state and so utterly foolish when it comes to affairs of the family?" Fulin reddened. He was sure the Empress Dowager had discovered the guilty secret of Chengqian Palace. Such sordidness could not be discussed even between mother and son who were as close as they.

The Empress Dowager pretended not to notice his uneasiness and, gazing casually at the water lilies standing so pure and straight in a pair of vases on a small table, quoted from the wisdom of the ancients: "'The relation between man and woman is a natural phenomenon. There is peace when these desires are fulfilled.' Recognizing this, the present dynasty had made it a rule that palace maids must be married off when they reach the age of twenty-four. On the contrary, the Ming kept thousands of palace maids, but despite stringent rules 'Dui Shi' was a common practice.

"Things that happen within our walls," the Empress Dowager continued, "are contained with discretion. One opens one eye and shuts the other. In this regard my Imperial Son has shown less wisdom and forebearance than the Precious Concubine."

"She..." Fulin stammered, his cheeks blazing.

"She has been aware of it for some time and discussed it with me. She was quite right in treating it with understanding and compassion. Why, our ancestors adopted the same attitude before the conquest...."

Fulin sputtered angrily, "But could she herself...."

The Empress Dowager shook her head grimly at him. "You should not think such a thing! Among all your ladies only she would willingly cut out her heart for you!" Fulin bowed his head in shame and mumbled, "The Ladies Shuhui and Kang treat this as something shameful and ... comical...."

"Naturally it's a stain. But if you searched Jingren Palace, or Chuxiu Palace, you would find the same thing." Fulin bit his lip in chagrin.

That night when Li Guozhu returned with a search party from the two palaces he reported that the same incriminating evidence had been found. Fulin's rage flared. He ordered the boxes to be sent to the principal ladies of each palace, with strict orders to deal with the matter themselves. He further decreed that the matter was to be treated with utmost secrecy and never mentioned again, on pain of death.

This discovery lifted a great weight from Fulin's heart, although what had been unearthed was something far from creditable. However, there was still the problem of resolving the rift between himself and the Precious Concubine. He thought of summoning her, but quickly abandoned that notion. It would be tantamount to an admission that he had been wrong. That was too humiliating. Instead he would wait for her to come to him to beg forgiveness. Since the Empress Dowager had spoken on her behalf, she must know how matters stood.

He waited from dusk to moonrise; from the first appearance of the evening star to the fading of the Milky Way. Fulin restlessly prowled the terrace, idly counting the fireflies; or painted, crumpling each picture immediately afterward. He read Tang-dynasty poems aloud, but his voice faltered, falling silent before the stanza was completed. He drifted into brooding thought. No matter how he tried to occupy himself, his ears were trained to the slightest noise, his nerves were on edge. The eunuchs watching this laughed to themselves though their faces were kept as blank as those of doll's, not betraying the least emotion.

Fulin spent a sleepless night, for Black Pearl did not come to him. Worry and impatience fuelled his passion until it was as hot as it had been when they first met. He had not seen her for twelve days. Though he tried desperately to hide his emotions and even to find release in other directions, he could not deny his longing. By day food lost its savour and the long, sleepless nights wore him down. In those twelve days, he was irascible.

He flew into rages, smashing things, beating the eunuchs and kicking the maids. A young eunuch was given twenty lashes and made to kneel for half the day for not placing a marker in a book the way the Precious Concubine might have done. His fiery outbursts in the presence of the ladies he summoned might have resulted in the intervention of the Empress Dowager who must have learned about the incident from the ladies' complaints.

His longing for Black Pearl was especially intense in the Hall of Mental Cultivation, for it was too full of memories. There were traces of her everywhere. In the study were the ink-stone and brushes she had used, and examples of her calligraphy. On the dressing table were a pair of pearl earrings which she had forgotten. The east bed chamber was theirs exclusively. Even the Empress was not permitted to spend the night with him in that room. Though the bed had been empty now for twelve nights, her warmth and fragrance clung to it still. The tiny satchel of sweet-smelling herbs she had made for him still hung from his belt.... If he went from the bed chamber into the main hall the flood of memories was even stronger.... For it was here on a day when the peonies were in bloom that they had first consummated their love....

At daybreak Fulin was still wandering on the terrace outside the Hall of Mental Cultivation. He was in a turmoil, racked with impatience and ennui not unmixed with memories of unbearable sweetness. He longed for Black Pearl with all his heart and soul, yet the dignity and honour of the Emperor stood in his way. He had to find some way to bring Black Pearl back to him. He fingered the small satchel of sweet herbs hanging from his waist, lost in thought.

"If it pleases Your Majesty, Grand Academician Fu Yijian of Wuying Hall, and Ministers of War Yitu and Liang Qingbiao beg an audience," announced the eunuch in charge of messages tentatively. Fulin glanced his way absent-mindedly as though he had neither seen nor heard him. The eunuch did not dare move without any indication from the Emperor, nor did he dare look up. So he raised his voice and repeated the message.

"Admit them," Fulin barked with a wave of the hand and strode into the main hall.

Led by a eunuch the three courtiers hurried into the room. Liang Qingbiao was clearly troubled. Yitu also wore a grim expression. Only Fu Yijian seemed his usual calm and collected self, the epitome of an experienced prime minister. Nothing but the slight tremour of his hands betrayed his agitation.

After they had prostrated themselves, the three courtiers lifted their heads to their monarch. The Emperor was dressed in a pale blue silk robe woven in a pattern of dragons. Round his waist he wore a yellow sash in which was tucked a small dagger encrusted with precious stones. There were a few other small ornaments that added colour to his costume. But he was bareheaded and did not wear his court beads. Under a thatch of jet-black hair, his face was the colour of burnished ivory with a touch of red upon the cheeks. Thick black brows arched over eyes that gleamed like the morning star. He was fanning himself impatiently with a fan painted with orchid in ink.

"What urgent matter has brought My Lords before the morning audience?" Fulin enquired.

Yitu spoke quickly: "Your Majesty, Zheng Chenggong's army has reached the walls of Jinling City!"

The blood drained from Fulin's face. To hide his confusion, he slammed his hand down hard upon the table beside him. The fan broke. He rose and in a harsh voice demanded, "Where is Hetehe's army?"

In the sixth month when Zheng Chenggong attacked the Yangtze River delta, the court had sent Hetehe with an army to halt him. Despatches reporting victory had only been received days before. What had gone wrong? Yitu stammered, "Hetehe died in battle ... at Zhenjiang ... and his army ... was ... destroyed...."

"What! Zhenjiang!..." The words burst from Fulin almost as a shriek. The strategic town of Zhenjiang so crucial to safeguarding the Yangtze River and the Grand Canal was lost! Forcing himself to be calm, Fu Yijian reported the disastrous news in his usual unflappable manner.

"Your Majesty, Zheng Chenggong had been preparing for a major assault since the sixth month..." he began. Naming himself the Great General of Recovery and, with Zhang Huangyan as second in command, Zheng Chenggong had gathered a force of one hundred seventy thousand men to launch an attack by land and water. The army, divided into eighty-three battalions, took the field. Under Zheng Chenggong's personal leadership they landed on Chongming Island, then attacked Jiaoshan, sacked Guazhou, and took Zhenjiang. Now they laid seige to Jinling. Meanwhile, Zhang Huangyan sailed up the river with his army, quickly taking Wuhu and turning on Huizhou, Ningguo, Taiping and Chizhou. Some thirty county towns fell. At present the governor of Jinling, Lang Tingzuo, with three thousand men under his command, was dangerously outnumbered by Zheng Chenggong. "...He cannot hold out much longer. Rebellion is breaking out across the south. Your Majesty must make a quick decision...."

Fulin was silent a while before he spoke in a choked voice, "We shall call upon the eight banners to lift the seige at Jinling."

Liang Qingbiao spoke in a tone that matched his troubled heart: "Your Majesty, the armies now deployed in Yunnan and Guizhou are too far to be of assistance. And the capital can not be left unguarded. Also the army of the eight banners now stationed at the provinces must not be moved at such a time. It seems the only forces that can be deployed are those of the Green Banner, however...." He allowed his words to trail off. His meaning was quite clear. The forces of the Green Banner were all Han. Under the present circumstances they might not be trustworthy.

Fu Yijian spoke as calmly as he could:

"Your Majesty must send help to reassure the people. At present Shandong separates Jiangsu and the capital. If the war is not contained the capital could be endangered...." He added the news would spread quickly. The people would be confused and frightened. Subversives would take advantage of the situation to widen the turmoil.... "In my humble opinion the troops of the eight banners as well as the Green Banner in Shandong and Anhui which are within striking distance be deployed to lift the seige of Jinling. That would stop Zheng Chenggong's northward march."

After the three courtiers left, Fulin could no longer control his anxiety. Fear and confusion assailed him in waves, flooding his mind with horrible images.

The south! The south! The treasure house of the Empire. Half of all taxes collected came from the south. To hold Yunnan and Guizhou, the south must be subdued, so that food and money could flow in an unbroken stream into the imperial coffers. If it should fall to Zheng Chenggong, then the dynasty itself was threatened.

Zheng Chenggong whose father and siblings I have killed will fight to the end. Surrender is out of the question.... Who is this man? He fights in the name of Ming and the Hans with the least spark of patriotism would follow.... Didn't Fu Yijian say he had already taken some thirty county towns and everywhere people were preparing to rise to his aid? Even the Han officials at court would quickly change sides.... Though Jinling had a garrison of three thousand men, only five hundred were Manchu. Could the Han troops under Lang Tingzuo's command be trusted?

The fall of Jinling was only a matter of time. Once it was lost half of the south would be in Zheng Chenggong's hands. Then Anhui and Shandong would stage an uprising that would light the prairie fire which would quickly engulf Shanxi, and Zhili, and finally the capital. All the Hans under heaven would take up arms against their Manchu overlords, drowning them in a torrent of hatred. Against such a flood the armies of the eight banners would be powerless. This would be the end of the Manchu, and the destruction of the Aisin Gioro clan....

The more he thought the more frightened he became. Great beads of sweat popped out on his brow. Reason and calm were shattered. Even the dignity of his position vanished. Panic seized him. With a loud cry, he ran blindly toward Cining Palace and his mother as though persued by all the devils in hell.

Fulin rushed headlong into the Empress Dowager's bed chamber. The mad gleam in his eyes, his hands clutching at the air, and his convulsive movements frightened her. Before she could respond to him, Fulin had thrown himself on his knees and cried out, "Imperial Mother, let us withdraw beyond Shanhaiguan! Let us go back to the grassland of our forefathers ... where we belong...." The Empress Dowager arched her brows.

"My Imperial Son must have taken leave of his senses!"

"No! No!" Fulin scrambled to his feet, shaking with panic. "The south is lost! Zheng Chenggong will take Jinling.... Anhui and Shandong will rebel.... The Capital will soon fall.... There are millions of Hans out there crying for our blood. Imperial Mother, let us go quickly!"

"Be silent!" the Empress Dowager cried through gritted teeth, her cheek muscles quivering with agitation. But Fulin was out of control. His eyes rolled horribly as he continued to babble:

"We must flee ... before it's too late...."

In a rage the Empress Dowager seized Fulin by the nape of his neck. Fulin had never seen such rage in her face before. He tried to duck as she raised her free hand, cringing at the blow that was sure to fall. Instead she reached for a cup of ice water and poured it over his head. The shock brought him to his senses and he crumbled heavily onto his knees.

The Empress Dowager loomed over him, with an angry finger pointed at him. Her words struck him like heavy stones.

"You wastrel! Useless piece of baggage! The rabbits on the grassland are better than you. The Empire your father and grandfather fought for, you would abandon without a fight to save your own skin! How would you dare call yourself the heir of Aisin Gioro! Where is the blood of heroes in your veins, miserable weakling! I should have fed you to the eagles when you were born!''

Never before had the Empress Dowager who was always so warm, loving and wise been in such a rage. Had she not been suddenly reminded of the Emperor's dignity she would have struck the highest of the high.

Drenched in cold water, Fulin was dumbstruck. As the colour crept back into his face, the veins in his temples stuck out, and shivering violently he leaped up with a roar like a mad man. "I will fix that Zheng Chenggong!'' he cried.

He drew his dagger from its sheath and raising it toward heaven cried out, "The Emperor will lead the army himself, and we shall return victorious or die in battle!'' The Empress Dowager reached out for him, but he eluded her and raced from Cining Palace.

The Empress Dowager was shaken by this hundred and eighty degree change in her son. She could not bear him being a coward, or a ruler of no consequence. However, personally leading the army into battle affected the stability of the sixteen-year-old Empire, and even its continued existence. If he was defeated or killed in battle, then all hope would be lost.

The Empress Dowager pressed a cup of ice water to her burning temples. With the nation's future at stake, she had to regain her equilibrium quickly. She pondered the matter a moment and immediately headed for the Hall of Mental Cultivation. But she was too late. The chief eunuch reported that His Majesty had returned in a fury. Without taking his breakfast, he had hurriedly dressed, knocking down several young eunuchs who attended his toilette, and went to Qianqing Hall for the morning audience.

In the solemn atmosphere of Qianqing Hall Fulin, as white as a sheet, announced in a piercing voice, "...We have determined to lead the army ourself...."

The Court had already been thrown into confusion by the news of Zheng Chenggong's successes. This announcement was like a peal of thunder over their heads. The courtiers were familiar with the Emperor's impetuous personality, and were even more aware of the inherent dangers of his proposal. Grim-faced they approached the throne en masse to beg him to reconsider. The sight of so many men kneeling before him only enraged Fulin. He raised his sword and hacked at his throne until it lay in shambles. Throwing the sword on the ground he bellowed, "Whoever dares oppose us shall end up like this throne! Fu Yijian and Hu Shian will immediately issue our decree that our intentions be made known to all the people under Heaven!"

Fulin's voice rang through the vast hall, waking echoes that bounced from wall to wall. No one dared oppose him.

The inner palace was thrown into confusion the next few days. The news that the Emperor was going to war caused great agitation. It was rumoured that the Empress Dowager had tried to dissuade him with wise and gentle counsel. But it fell on deaf ears and did nothing to appease his violent temper. The Emperor would not change his mind. Next, the Empress Dowager sent Fulin's old nurse to speak to him, for he revered the old woman as much as his own mother. However, before the old woman could screw up enough courage to speak, Fulin cut her off.

"Hold your tongue lest you be chopped into little pieces!" he cried. The old woman fled as from a mad man.

Confusion spread like a plague through the capital. Rumours of the fall of Jinling panicked the populace who feared the fragile peace in all under Heaven was about to be torn asunder once more. The decree announcing the Emperor's intention of personally leading the army was posted on all the city gates. It confirmed the people's fears that disaster loomed. The city was turned into a disturbed hornet's nest as businesses shut down, and those who were able to prepared to flee. In the homes of the bannermen preparations were being made for war. Gloom descended upon the city.

Fearing to enrage the Emperor, yet unwilling to let matters stand, the court and the aristocracy went to the Empress Dowager to beg her intervention with His Majesty. Perhaps it was at her suggestion that they finally turned to Tang Jo-Wang for help.

The street leading to the Catholic church was clogged with horses and carriages. When servants who knew one another met, instead of the usual greetings, the words exchanged were invariably, "Did the Lord Tang agree?" The response was a dismal shake of the head as though the person had just come from a wake.

Princes and noblemen, ministers and courtiers came. Tang Jo-Wang grew impatient with this constant stream of visitors, but his answer to their entreaties was always a firm refusal. The matter was quite simple. The Emperor was a man of his word. Also, he had made up his mind in the heat of anger. Therefore, it was clear, whoever tried to persuade him to change his mind was most likely going to be "chopped into little pieces" as he had threatened.

After nightfall, when the last visitor had gone, Tang Jo-Wang stretched out on his chaise, exhausted by the day's futile activities. There was a deep hurt within, which he could not put into words. In the last two years his pupil had become more and more absorbed in Buddhism and avoided the Mafa whom he once revered. This neglect hurt him deeply. Perhaps his refusal to intervene was not untouched by personal feelings. His new assistant, a young man with brown curly hair and brown eyes, whom the people called Father Nan Huairen, poured him a glass of white Rhine wine which he had brought from Europe.

"Johann, you are over tired..." he said with deep concern.

"Thank you," Tang Jo-Wang accepted the wine and sighed.

Father Schaunard faced him with a sigh. "These courtiers are despicable cowards. They wouldn't risk their necks to dissuade the Emperor but think nothing of involving a helpless old man."

The priest known as Bai Naixin, a tall thin man with deep-set blue eyes, shrugged. "It's not surprising. The Chinese Emperor has more power than our European monarchs. Also, this one has an unpredictable temper and is totally unreasonable."

Tang Jo-Wang wagged a finger at him. "No! No! This young man is not unreasonable. Anyone can do foolish things in a moment of rage."

Bai Naixin disagreed. "I cannot understand why you stick up for him? He is drifting away from you. Such an important matter as leading his army personally, and you had no inkling of it!"

Tang Jo-Wang's lips moved but no sounds issued. However, his face reddened. The others noticed the old man's hurt.

"Oh, the poor boy..." sighed the old man.

The silence was broken by Father Schaunard. "I suppose the Emperor will go to war...."

"I have just come in and the city is already in an uproar," said Bai Naixin. "If the Emperor leaves with all his imperial guard the situation will be worse. If the Emperor is defeated, then an upheaval will be inevitable...." Though he tried to sound flippant, the serious undertones of his words were not lost on the usually taciturn Father Nai Huairen.

"If there is turmoil, what would be its effect on the church? If the Manchu and the Emperor are destroyed would it be a blessing or a curse to our endeavours?" Everyone present felt the weight of Nai Huairen's remark. A foreboding silence settled on the simply furnished room. Although his gaze was fixed upon the painting of the Virgin Mary behind Bai Naixin's shoulder, and he spoke as if to himself, what he said touched a chord in Tang Jo-Wang. Martyrdom is not a matter of age or qualification. The other men in the room were both younger than Tang Jo-Wang. The old man looked sharply at Nai Huairen as he put down his glass.

Tang Jo-Wang pushed himself out of the chair. A look of blessed resignation flooded his features.

"Very well, I will go," he said, stroking the crucifix hanging from his neck. "For the sake of the people, the glory of our order, our future, and that unfortunate boy. If I have to gamble with my life, it will be worth it. May God have mercy upon me."

The next morning the three priests celebrated a special mass for Tang Jo-Wang, beseeching God's grace and protection. When they thought of the Emperor's unpredictable temper and the Manchu's blood-thirsty nature, the four friends were close to tears when they took leave of one another. Nevertheless, Tang Jo-Wang managed a smile. "Friends, let us not turn this into a wake. God will bless a righteous deed."

In the morning mist, the gate tower of Xuanwu Gate loomed menacingly large, indistinct and mysterious. Father Schaunard watched the old man disappear in the fog, wondering whether they would ever see him again.

As the Forbidden City came into view Tang Jo-Wang shrugged off his melancholy. With it came peace. It was true that the Emperor had become distant. This was largely because he was surrounded by Buddhist monks who hated Christians. It could become a serious disadvantage for the church. However, the Emperor was no longer the youth Tang Jo-Wang used to know. He was a young man, and in his present mood he was dangerous. Nevertheless, Tang Jo-Wang felt he understood Fulin. He was clever, had good judgement and foresight. He also understood Fulin's almost pathological sense of self importance. Surely he would comprehend the situation that even a foreigner such as Father Bai Naixin could grasp. Maybe his arrogance and his dignity as Emperor had put him in a situation from which he felt he could not retreat.

Two whole days had passed but no one had dared counsel the Emperor. The courtiers gathered in the antechamber surrounded Tang Jo-Wang as though he was a saviour, jabbering their solicitude, their gratitude, their admiration not unmixed with impatience. Tang Jo-Wang despised the lot of them, but he listened patiently. When the eunuch came to conduct him into the Presence, he bowed to the assembled lords and said, "My Lords, I deeply admire your love of the Emperor and the country. Adieu." With head held high he followed the eunuch out of the room, unmindful of the curious glances that followed him.

The eunuch was acquainted with Tang Jo-Wang and quickly filled the priest in on all that had happened in the previous days. Finally he added, "His Majesty is calmer today, no ranting and raging as he has been doing the last two days."

Tang Jo-Wang was relieved. Perhaps the Emperor had come to his senses. However, he would never change his mind about leading the army voluntarily. Someone had to provide the step for him to get off his high horse. Perhaps that someone was he. Tang Jo-Wang could not help being glad. For this might change the Emperor's attitude toward himself and benefit his missionary work as well.

Fulin received him in his study in Qianqing Palace. He looked stern; his brows tightly knit, and his lips set in a thin straight line. He exuded an air of stubborn arrogance that chilled Tang Jo-Wang. Then he noticed the Emperor was holding a folding fan with peonies painted upon it, and in his other hand was a book of poetry. He felt a rush of warmth for the young monarch. These were the conditions he had prayed for.

Tang Jo-Wang approached the Emperor, fell to his knees and presented his petition with both hands, which he had spent the better part of the night composing. Now he prostrated himself, not looking up. He could hear the rustle of paper as Fulin read the document. Tang Jo-Wang did not wait for the Emperor to speak before he spoke in an earnest tones:

"To anger Your Majesty is to die. But Jo-Wang cannot betray Your Majesty's trust and his duty by keeping silent for fear of death. Your Majesty is the pillar of the nation and the hope of his people. In the name of several decades of service to the crown, your old slave begs Your Majesty not to lead the army personally, and thus imperil the nation's future...."

The silence lengthened. Then he heard a gentle voice speak.

"Mafa, please rise."

Tang Jo-Wang lifted his head, not sure he had heard correctly. Fulin's attitude had changed. Though he seemed remote, there was a gleam in the eyes that the old man recognized with relief.

"We are moved by the sincerity of Mafa's petition. With a thorough grasp of history, Mafa has analysed the situation brilliantly. Though we would hesitate to be numbered among the wise monarchs of history, we are cognizant of the wisdom of bowing to good advice...."

Fulin may have made some other remarks, but they were lost on Tang Jo-Wang in his excitement. He was so relieved when the Emperor praised him for his analyses of the situation that he had difficulty getting to his feet. When he had recovered himself, he suggested to the Emperor:

"Even if Zheng Chenggong takes Jinling the situation will not be completely hopeless. Large rewards would quickly raise a willing army to cut off the roads to the north. Then the armies already in Yunnan and Guizhou can be deployed. Zheng Chenggong will not gain a toe hold in the south...."

The courtiers who had been summoned to draft the Emperor's new decree were full of gratitude for what Tang Jo-Wang had done. The news spread quickly through the Forbidden City. When Tang Jo-Wang emerged from his audience he was greeted by guards standing at attention. The nobles and courtiers were profuse in their congratulations, bowing to the waist. The guards at the gates through which he passed cried out, "Yili!" as a mark of respect. Tang Jo-Wang was deeply affected by their honest joy. He walked proud and tall, nodding and smiling. This deed had greatly enhanced his reputation. Indeed he felt he had saved the nation from disaster. In spite of himself he muttered in his mother tongue, "If the church gains from this ... it will be worth it...."

Fulin's nerves which had been stretched to breaking point relaxed. Secretly he breathed a sigh of relief. The previous day, upon receiving Lady Dongeh's petition wishing him well and begging forgiveness, he realized his folly and the rage that filled him passed. In her petition, Lady Dongeh had not only begged forgiveness but also, in a gentle, inobstrusive way on behalf of the nation, pleaded that he did not place himself in danger. She pointed out the importance of the capital to a young dynasty. If the Emperor was as immovable as Mount Tai, Zheng Chenggong could not hope to succeed though he held the southeast. Her sincerity made him see his error. But the decree had already been pasted in public places. Furthermore, the throne had been destroyed. How would he undo all that?

In counselling the Emperor Tang Jo-Wang had acted in the nick of time. The Mafa was the Empress Dowager's spiritual father, and also the Imperial Minister of Astronomy, a learned man known among the people as a saint. Therefore, bowing to his counsel would be entirely appropriate. It would also show Fulin as a monarch able to accept good advice.

The courtiers quickly dispersed to attend to various tasks involved in retracting an imperial decree. Fulin was content. He accepted a cup of tea from a young eunuch, but as he sipped it, his brow knitted once more. There was still the unresolved matter of Zheng Chenggong.... What was to be done? Duoni and Luo Keduo were still in Yunnan and Guizhou. Nor could he dispense with Yuele. That left Jidu. In the eleventh year of Shunzhi, Jidu had been supreme commander with orders to vanquish Zheng Chenggong. That Zheng had survived all these years and was able to regroup was largely due to Jidu's failure. Therefore, to call upon him in this exigency would be appropriate. However, Fulin was aware that Jidu was displeased with him. Could he be trusted on a critical campaign such as this?

Fulin's long sensitive fingers stroked the armrest of his chair absently as he pondered his dilemma. His thoughts suddenly turned to Lady Kang who was Jidu's niece. He recalled that only a few days earlier Jidu's wife and Lady Kang's mother had visited her in her residence at Jingren Palace. Perhaps he could get an inkling of Jidu's state of mind through Lady Kang and the extent of the prince's discontent before he made a decision.

Fulin had almost decided on spending the night at Jingren Palace and was about to give the orders when he hesitated. He took Lady Dongeh's petition from its redwood case and re-read it for the umpteenth time. The rows of neat, elegant script was a reflection of the writer, the mere sight of which suffused him with warmth. He thought of summoning Black Pearl to the Hall of Mental Cultivation but quickly rejected that idea. Resolutely he returned the petition to its case and thought, Black Pearl would have to wait....

At that moment Black Pearl was chatting with the Empress in Kunning Palace. Both were relieved the crisis was over, but the Precious Concubine was preoccupied.

"...Zheng Chenggong still has to be dealt with," Lady Dongeh was saying.

"There are all the lords and officials of the court to assist His Majesty," countered the Empress who darted a worried glance at Lady Dongeh. "You fret too much. What you need is a good rest."

Lady Dongeh smiled. "My dear Sister is too kind. I am one of those unfortunate who take everything to heart, and I worry needlessly. It's an unfortunate trait. I don't have a happy nature."

The Empress shook her head. "Tell your clumsy but well-meaning sister why His Majesty is so upset with you." Lady Dongeh bowed her head, and in a small voice said, "I ... angered him.... Now he's avoiding me...." The Empress sighed. "Without you he can't eat, he can't sleep. He has a vile temper. He smashes things and he beats the servants. If you were with him, he wouldn't be so stubborn this time...." One of the young eunuchs rushed in stammering that His Majesty had arrived.

The two women were aghast. It was past the second watch. What would cause the Emperor to visit Kunning Palace at such an hour? Was there another disaster? The Empress quickly gathered her wits about her.

"Sister, you will greet His Majesty with me."

Lady Dongeh hastily replied, "Sister, until I am forgiven I can not be present. Go quickly!"

Fulin strode into the room aflame with impatience. He brushed past the Empress who hastily fell to her knees and went into the inner chamber. The Empress followed. Fulin stood in the centre of the room, hands on his hips, breathing noisily. He was grinding his teeth, white with rage. In a loud voice he shouted for the eunuch Li Guozhu. He drew his sword and threw it down before the eunuch who was grovelling on hands and knees, trembling like a cornered rat.

In a voice that reverberated through the hall Fulin commanded: "Take that to the guard of Qianqing Palace and bring me the head of Lady Kang!"

Cries of dismay echoed from various corners of the room. The Empress threw herself at the Emperor's feet, crying fearfully, "Your Majesty! Your Majesty! What is happening?..." Fulin kicked her aside, ignoring her cry of pain.

"Li Guozhu, I will have your head first if you delay!" he roared. Li Guozhu ran from the room. Lady Dongeh rushed out of the bed chamber and threw herself at the Emperor's feet. Wrapping her arms around his legs, she begged, "Your Majesty! Don't...." Fulin never dreamed that Lady Dongeh would appear at this moment. Surprised but also pained, he raised her gently to her feet.

"Your Majesty, Lady Kang is the mother of your son. She has contributed greatly to the royal house, therefore, the death penalty must not be visited upon her. Your slave has offended you and not been pardoned. Let me be punished in her place!"

Lady Dongeh banged her forehead on the ground and then ran from the room. Fulin tried to stop her, but she eluded him and slipped into the night, the tapping of her wooden-soled shoes fading quickly into the distance. Fulin was shaken. The Empress picked herself up, gingerly rubbing her thigh where the Emperor had kicked her. Once more she tearfully begged, "Your Majesty, for our sake, forgive Lady Kang...."

Fulin realised "our" referred to the Empress and the Precious Concubine. He noticed her rubbing her thigh and felt a pang of remorse. The maids and eunuchs were also on their knees, begging with their mistress. The atmosphere was so tense that one could hardly breathe. The only sound was the relentless ticking of the European clock. Anger began to drain from Fulin's features.

Li Guozhu hurried in and falling on his knees held high the Emperor's sword.

"Your Majesty, when your slave and the guard arrived at Jingren Palace, the Precious Concubine was there. She threw her arms around Lady Kang saying that if Lady Kang was harmed she too had to be beheaded. Your slaves did not know what to do...."

"Where is the woman?" Fulin demanded angrily.

"Lady Kang admitted her fault and ordered your slave to bring word, saying her death is as nothing, however, she has only one request ... that she be killed by Your Majesty's hand ... and she would die in peace...."

There was a long silence in which no one dared lift their head.

"Why did the Precious Concubine not return?" Fulin's question caught everyone by surprise.

Li Guozhu quickly rallied, "Your slave left the two ladies weeping together...."

Fulin slumped into the throne set in the centre of the room, mired in a welter of emotions: sweetness and bitterness, love and hate.

3

As soon as the new decree receding the Emperor's intention to personally lead his army was posted, the city calmed down. Dasu was named commander for the pacification of the south. With Suohong and Laita as second in command, the army marched south. Before long conditions in the capital returned to normal. The streets were thronged once more with happy, prosperous people.

Two men approached from a distance. The one in front was dressed in a robe that obviously did not belong to him, for it was so large, it threatened to drown him. Though he strutted along, chest and belly arrogantly protruding he could not hide the pallor of his cheeks or the dark-circled sunken eyes or the air of poverty that clung to him. A servant, somewhat shorter than he, staggered behind under a sack of rice.

The servant let the sack slip off his shoulder onto the pavement and stood gasping for breath.

"Stopping again!" the master cried, stamping his foot with irritation.

"Please allow this humble one to catch his breath!" the servant panted.

"At this rate it will take forever to get home!" The master's loud voice roused the curiosity of passers-by who stopped to gawk. Out of the crowd came a tall man in a grey silk robe. "What is going on?" he asked.

The servant who was thin as a rail stammered apologetically, "It's my fault ... delaying the master ... I haven't the strength...."

"If you haven't the strength then you shouldn't have taken the job!" The master glared balefully at him.

When he saw the man in grey he was struck by the man's fiery gaze and the high, arrogant bridge of his nose. He surmised this was an unusual man, perhaps even one who might interfere in other people's business. Adopting an obsequious tone he explained, "Master, I hired this fellow to carry a sack of rice. But he has to rest every few steps. In the time it takes to serve a meal, we have barely gone half a mile. Meanwhile, the family is waiting to eat. Can you blame me for being impatient?"

The tigerish eyes under the heavy brows swept round onto the servant.

"What sort of man are you that you have such difficulty with a little matter of sixty or seventy jin?"

The servant glanced at the stranger then at the crowd clustered around and sighed, "I am not suited to this kind of work.... My grandfather was Grand Secretary Liu in the court of the former Ming...." He squatted down and hugged his head with both arms.

A curious buzz swept through the crowd. Even the man in grey stepped back to get a better look at this nobleman down on his luck. To everyone's surprise the master cried out, "Then you must be cousin Erbao.... We are related!" The servant shot to his feet, eyes wide with surprise.

"I am the grandson of Zhang Songjiang, which makes us seccond cousins," the master said, glad and sad all at once. An old fellow in the crowd shouted with a smile, "Since you're both gentry and related to boot, why don't you give him half the rice!"

The master blushed. "I can't do that.... There's been no food in the house for two days.... I had to beg these five measures of rice and two hundred coppers from an old retainer...." He gritted his teeth and turning to the servant said, "Cousin, come home with me for a meal." The master rolled up his sleeves and tried to lift the sack himself, but he was even more useless than the other. He couldn't budge it. Derisive laughter and rude remarks swept through the crowd, typical of the disdain of the strong for the weak. It was particularly gratifying for the lowly to see their betters humbled. Finally the two hapless offsprings of noble forebears embraced each other and burst into exasperated tears.

The man in grey crossed the road, broke off a young sapling that grew by the wayside and, tearing off the branches, thrust the rude pole at the two.

"Carry the sack between you," said he.

The two man fastened their load to the pole and staggered away. The crowd gradually dispersed. The man in grey stopped the old man who had spoken earlier and asked, "Who are Grand Secretary Liu and Zhang Songjiang?"

The old man gathered his wandering thoughts and answered absently, "They were ministers at the court of the Ming Emperor Chongzhen.... Who would have thought their descendants could fall this low...." He wandered off muttering to himself about two young noblemen ... five measures of rice ... and the uselessness of education ... and the expectations of ancestors....

The man in grey stood where he was as fierce and immovable as a bronze lion, deep in thought. Only when servants approached him leading a horse did he rouse himself and rode away.

The man was Prince Jian, Jidu, who was in the habit of dressing as a commoner to roam the streets for amusement. The scene that he had just witnessed was an extra weight added to his already burdened heart.

Ever since he had openly opposed Fulin's intention to abolish the Council of Nobles and forced him to back down, his reputation had risen among the Manchu nobility. At the same time, he felt the Emperor's distrust had also increased. Although the crisis of the council had blown over, what was in store for him in the future? Jidu's loyalty to the eight banners was unswerving, even superseding imperial decrees. Would the Emperor really back down? What would he do to one whose loyalty to the Manchu came first?

The Emperor had appointed Dasu as supreme commander to fight Zheng Chenggong when he, Jidu, should have been the first choice. Hadn't he driven Zheng Chenggong onto the island three years ago? That feat alone should have ensured him the supreme commander's seal. Instead the Emperor had passed him over. It was clear that he was not trusted. Jidu considered the Emperor's reaction to Zheng Chenggong's seige of Jinling, and the crisis he plunged the capital into the actions of a spoilt child. The Emperor's panic on hearing of Zheng Chenggong's victories made him doubt Shunzhi's ability to rule.

The two descendants of Ming officials he encountered that day troubled him greatly. He wondered if one day the descendants of the eight banners, including his own sons and grandsons, might fall that low.... As for the young Emperor who was so enamoured of the Ming system of government, the wisdom of the sages, the traditions of the Han, was he not leading the descendants of the Manchu down the path to certain ruin? When he thought of his descendants in rags, becoming humble useless weaklings begging for a living and dying in abject poverty, he shuddered. He urged his horse into a gallop back to his residence.

As soon as he arrived home, he summoned his six sons to the main hall. Seated on the throne, with his sons lined up before him, he commanded them to recite their grandfather Prince Jirgalang's last petition. His sons understood their father's peculiar habits. The same scene had been enacted many times before. Nevertheless they feared him. They recited loudly in unison.

Jidu's sons had been rigorously trained in horsemanship and archery since childhood. Now they stood before him as sturdy as a row of young pines. Their grandfather's words had also been drilled into them since they were small. Now those words could be summoned to their lips at will. Listening to the strong young voices tinged with a note of hoarseness, Jidu's breast swelled with paternal pride. For the moment the dark thoughts that plagued him were cast aside.

At the end of the recitation it was Jidu's custom to lecture his sons. This day's discourse had more substance and was less dull than usual. Though he was not good with words, Jidu related his encounter in the street that day in great detail. At the end of his story, his face darkened.

"We are the chosen of Heaven," he said heavily. "The clans of the eight banners must not be tainted with the decadence of the Han, or the Empire and our own noble house will fall. We have swept the world with our prowess on horseback and our skill with bow and sword. I hurried home with one intention: to test your skills in the archery garden."

"Yes, Princely Father," his sons chorused.

"Second Brother! Second Brother!" A woman's voice echoed down the corridor outside. In a moment, a woman dressed in a plain blue silk robe, her hair done in the Manchurian style, stumbled into the room on the arms of two serving maids, weeping hysterically. Jidu rose, frowning, and strode across the hall to meet her. His sons quickly stepped aside to let him pass. Everyone knew their father's cousin Madam Tong.

Madam Tong's mother was a cousin of Jidu's father, thus she was not closely related. Normally the wife of a commander-in-chief who was a Han would have little communication with this noble house. However, Madam Tong's daughter was Lady Kang, principal concubine at Jingren Palace and mother of the Emperor's third son. That shed a different light on the woman.

Madam Tong was unable to control her emotions. Wailing hysterically, she begged the Prince to save his luckless niece. Jidu and his sons were dumbfounded by this outburst. The youngsters pressed forward to pay their respects, but they were brusquely waved aside.

"Cousin, what troubles you? Is your daughter gravely ill?"

"Ay-ya-ya!" the woman cried. "How is it that you haven't heard! My poor misguided daughter!" Jidu was about to question her further, but seeing his sons' curiosity, he frowned and commanded them to withdraw.

"Where is the mistress?" Jidu asked one of the servants.

"Prince An's wife and daughter are visiting. The Mistress has taken them into the gardens to enjoy the flowers."

"Ask the other ladies to entertain Prince An's wife. Let the Mistress wait for me in the waterside pavilion."

Surrounded by water with only an arched bridge connecting it to the gardens, the waterside pavilion was a perfect place for private conversations. After the servants were dismissed, Madam Tong related what had happened at Jingren Palace two nights earlier to Jidu and his wife:

That evening, the Emperor who was now at peace and having issued his new decree had gone to Jingren Palace for the first time since Lady Dongeh came into the palace. It was an honour that the other ladies would have given their eye for. Yet, the accumulated disappointments of years must have overwhelmed Lady Kang that night. She was exceedingly cold. Though the Emperor made an effort to be amusing, she responded with sarcasm.

The Emperor reported that the Third Imperial Son was well cared for in the Empress Dowager's Palace. He had learned the works of the sages and the poetry of the Tang by heart, and his calligraphy was improving. Lady Kang responded by thanking the Empress Dowager and the Emperor for their interest in the Third Imperial Son, adding, "It is hoped his skill in horsemanship and archery will improve as well, and that he will grow into a very powerful man." The Emperor steered the conversation in another direction.

"The siege of Jinling is critical. We have been considering appointing a supreme commander for a southward push. However, none of the princes seem equal to the task." Lady Kang answered, "Zheng Chenggong had once been thoroughly defeated by Prince Jian." The Emperor nodded. "If he had been thoroughly defeated as you say, would he be back today?" Then he added with a dry smile, "Are you speaking for your kinsman?" Lady Kang did not dare press the matter further and taking another tack remarked gently, "Your Majesty has always shown a special fondness for the south. Now that Zheng Chenggong has returned even the Han officials you appointed have turned on you. It is clear these southern barbarians have no sense of loyalty...." Perhaps he had caught the irony in her words, or he might have been pricked by innuendo. Fulin cut her off saying, "The rebellion in the south is mainly due to corruption in government. Thus far we have not been able to win people's hearts completely. As master of all races, we must love Han and Manchu equally." Lady Kang who was not talkative suddenly found her tongue. Falling upon her knees she beseeched the Emperor, "In recent years Your Majesty has adopted Han ways and grown closer to them at the expense of the Manchu. The ways of our ancestors are being eroded and gradually abandoned. Your slave fears this may cause the people to turn against the Emperor...." Though Fulin's attitude remained cool, fire flickered in his eyes.

"Who put those words in your mouth? Has your kinsman been coaching you?"

"Nobody's been coaching me," Lady Kang's voice rose with excitement. "Your Majesty must not offend the ancestors. Heaven will not allow it and the people will turn against you. If a disaster occurs, it may not even be possible to retreat to Liaodong." Suddenly all the blood rushed to Fulin's head He flew into a rage.

"How dare you threaten me!" he cried and kicking the hapless Lady Kang aside he rushed from Jingren Palace.

The Emperor had gone straight to Kunning Palace and ordered Lady Kang beheaded at once. Lady Kang had dared point out his weaknesses! In his present mood neither the Empress Dowager, nor the Empress could save her life. Had it not been for the presence of the Precious Concubine and her protection, Lady Kang would have been executed. Now she waited to be judged in Jingren Palace.

"Second Brother, help her." Madam Tong covered her face and wept. All through Madam Tong's narration, Jidu had hammered his knee with his fist, barely containing his agitation. However, when the tale was told he became calm, almost cold. His eyes turned inward, something terrifying gleamed in their depths as he pondered all he had heard. The two women seeing him thus fell silent; none dared open their mouths again.

Indeed, the thoughts that flashed through Jidu's mind were terrible and fraught with danger. For danger seemed all around him. Hadn't the Emperor's words contained a note of suspicion, and therefore, seeds of doom? Otherwise would he have ordered Lady Kang beheaded without a moment's hesitation? It was clear the unpredictable weakling was capable of anything.

Jidu's mind was made up. He fixed his eyes on the two women and squeezed out two words between clenched teeth.

"Abolish him!" Those words, spoken so softly that were barely audible, struck the ladies like a peal of thunder. They huddled together, pale and trembling, watching Jidu unblinkingly.

Jidu drew a noisy breath and repeated "Abolish him!" with an air of resignation. "Or I will not be able to face the heroic souls of my ancestors."

After Prince Jian's wife had been called away, the three concubines remained. Being closer in age to their guest, the conversation became more informal and animated. Seated in the pavilion beside the lily pond where fruit, lotus roots and melons were served in abundance, the ladies were enveloped by the heady scent of the gardens.

Little Bingyue was the centre of attention, as she was passed from the lap of one lady to the arms of another. Her wide expressive eyes and tiny mouth won the hearts of all who saw her. At the age of three she spoke quite fluently.

"Sister," the lady who was dandling Bingyue said to Prince An's wife, "your little daughter — I mean little princess — will one day grow into a stunning beauty."

Little Bingyue tossed her head and in a voice as clear as a lark retorted, "My Imperial Mother says when I grow up I'll be more beautiful than she." The Imperial Mother she referred to was, of course, Lady Dongeh who had adopted her. In fact she spoke of her more naturally than her natural mother. Though it chagrined Prince An's wife, she dared not show it.

"Does your Imperial Father also say that?" asked one of the other concubines. The little girl's head drooped.

"My Imperial Father says my Imperial Mother is the most beautiful person in the whole world..." she mumbled. The ladies exchanged amused glances. They all knew that Lady Dongeh was in disfavour, awaiting the Emperor's pleasure. For a while that news filled them with glee. That was the real reason the child was taken back to Prince An's house for a "family reunion". The babes of Prince Jian who were younger had not been granted the same privilege. The lady who held the child leaned closer and, masking her curiosity in a teasing tone asked, "Is that true?" The child was annoyed.

"I'm not lying. That day my Imperial Mother was holding me and talking to my Imperial Father at the same time. They were laughing. Then my Imperial Father pulled us onto his lap and hugged us so tight that I could hardly breathe! That's when he said it." The ladies blushed in confusion, desperately suppressing their giggles, wanting to speak yet not daring, for the child's Imperial Father was none other than the reigning Emperor. Sensing things had gone far enough, Prince An's wife chided Bingyue, "Stop talking nonsense, child!"

The child tilted her head at an obstinate angle. "I'm not talking nonsense. My Imperial Father also said if I don't study hard later on, I won't even amount to a little finger of my Imperial Mother." Prince An's wife found she could do nothing with the child.

"Enough, my precious babe! Ahchou, take her to play with the other girls in the garden." It was words the child had been waiting for. She immediately launched herself into Ahchou's arms. Nestled contentedly against the servant's shoulder, she allowed herself to be carried away.

There was silence in the pavilion after the child had gone. "Sister, this Ahchou seems to have a special affinity to the little princess." The remark, not untinged with flattery, came from Ahchou's former mistress.

Prince An's wife quickly responded. "We have to thank your generosity in sending her to us. For some strange reason Bingyue will have no one else. When we sent for her in the palace to bring her home, she threw such tantrums, refusing to come. But when we sent Ahchou for her, she came quite happily." The lady neglected to mention that the child had even rejected her.

"In that case, you mustn't let Ahchou escort her back to the palace."

"I fear that will not happen within the foreseeable future," one of the concubines remarked maliciously.

"Sister, we should think of a new name for Ahchou," another of the ladies changed the subject. "She seems less ugly, but as silent as ever."

Prince An's wife was grateful for the diversion and quickly took up the new topic.

"One would think she's mute. But someone heard her muttering to Bingyue when she thought no one was around...."

Meanwhile, in the depths of the garden, in a grove of trees where some porcelain seats had been set around a small stone table, Ahchou cuddled little Bingyue, murmuring softly to her just as Prince An's wife described.

Menggu had been a slave for a year and a half. She was as cold as ice and silent as a stagnant pool. However, in the fifth month of that year when she first saw Bingyue, the captivating child enchanted her, awakening dormant maternal instincts. She was enthralled by the child. Half a month later the child was taken into the palace and something went out of her. Menggu became dangerously ill. When she recovered, she was once again a woman of ice.

The child had returned, unchanged, still attached to her. Though she was comforted by that love, she knew her happiness would not last. Anticipating the pain of loss to come, she forced herself to be sensible, to curb her emotions and not let them run away with her.

Something else diverted her attention from Bingyue.

The day she went to Chengqian Palace to bring the child home, she encountered several palace maids outside the second gate. As she stood aside to let them pass she noticed at once that one of them was held under guard. As she passed the girl lifted her face, and Menggu's heart missed a beat. For she was sure the innocent, childish face turned to her for an instant was that of her younger sister, Ronggu. At that moment the child clinging to her sqirmed around in her arms and shouted in her clear piping voice, "Rongniu!"

The girl under guard flashed a tentative smile at the child and was gone. Menggu's heart hammered wildly. She longed to run after them, to see for herself whether it really was her sister, but she didn't dare. For this was the Forbidden City, and one step out of place would mean certain death. Since the girl was under guard she must have done something wrong. Could one speak to her? Thinking about it more coolly, if the girl was indeed her sister, then she must have gained access to the palace by false pretenses. She should not, and dared not approach her, lest the secrets of her past be discovered, for it would mean death. Menggu held the child more tightly as her legs turned to jelly.

That chance encounter struck a tiny spark in her frozen heart. It awakened in her the love of family and siblings ... memories of happier times. A small patch of warmth grew and spread imperceptibly within her....

"Who is Rongniu?" she asked Bingyue for the umpteenth time in a low voice.

"When did she go into the palace?"

"Momo!" The child snuggled against Menggu, playing with the lobe of her ear. "I've already told you, she's my Imperial

Mother's personal maid for a year. She likes me and I like her. Only she got locked up in her room. I asked for her lots of times ... but my Imperial Mother took no notice.... Let's not talk about her anymore ... I want a story....''

Menggu realized she could not get anything more out of the child. She nuzzled Bingyue's soft cheek and, in a voice as gentle as a babbling brook, launched into an ancient folk tale.

"Once upon a time ... there was a boy who looked after some cattle.... His father and mother were dead ... and people called him the Cowherd....''

The story came to an end, but the child wanted another. She reached up a small hand and touched Menggu's face.

"Momo, you're crying,'' exclaimed the child. "Never mind, I'll ask my Imperial Father to send an army and build a huge bridge across that awful river which separates the Cowherd from his Weaving Maid. Then they can be together whenever they like! Won't that be nice?''

The tears had come unbidden. Perhaps the glimpse of Ronggu had unlocked a secret place in her heart, and memories came gushing forth. Whereas the Cowherd and the Weaving Maid in the story could meet once a year, the love of her youth was lost forever.

"Bingyue! Bingyue!'' called the daughters of Prince An and Prince Jian as they came across the gardens. Menggu stopped speaking, dashed away her tears and stood. The child clung to the servant and protested vehemently when the two young girls tried awkwardly to take her in their arms. Prince Jian's daughter whispered enticingly, "Would you like to watch an opera with me?'' She imitated the sound of drums.

"Yes!'' cried the child, but she would not let go of Menggu. "Momo can come too!'' Prince Jian's daughter shot a sidelong glance at Menggu. "She can come. But don't you tell anyone. If we get a scolding, Ahchou will be whipped.'' Prince An's daughter chimed in enthusiastically now that mischief was afoot. "She won't dare talk. She can't.''

The two young girls skipped along, leading the way while Menggu followed with the child. They went deeper into the gardens past a small green knoll. The sound of music floated toward them on the breeze. They quickened their pace.

"Oh! It's my mother!" Prince Jian's daughter exclaimed as they rounded a corner. They quickly stepped back into the shadows of an arbour of climbing roses set beside a rockery. The daughter of Prince Jian signalled the others not to make a sound, wondering if her mother had already spotted them.

Obviously she had not. She was completely alone. As she came closer, the girl noticed how deeply troubled her mother looked. Her eyes blinked rapidly. With each sigh she seemed to age before the girl's eyes. Finally she stopped and leaned against a rock as though she could not go on.

Prince An's daughter was about to go to her, but her companion held her back. After all, the woman was only a step-mother.

Prince Jian's wife caught her breath and turned toward the arbour. Those huddled in it shrank deeper into the shadows. Little Bingyue, thinking it was an amusing game, peered curiously at the agitated lady.

The lady sat down heavily on a stone seat. With soft groans and deep sighs the others heard her pray, "Buddha and our ancestors protect us ... guide us to victory.... Vouchsafe our success ... that we will not lose our lives on the headsman's block...." Then she gathered her wits about her. When she left the arbour she was once more a great lady, calm and dignified. The two young girls soon forgot what they saw.

The sound of the music coming from the stage distracted the young girls. Prince Jian's daughter had a great deal to show off to her companion for her house boasted the best opera troupe in the capital. Indeed, the best performances of the more acrobatic plays were given here. "We are not as good with the romantic plays," said Prince Jian's daughter. "But that's going to change. My father insists ours must be the best all-round troupe, so we've engaged a young actor who specializes in female roles to teach our actors. You won't believe how handsome he is! He's like a new year's picture come to life!"

"Really!" squealed the daughter of Prince An. Young girls of her age often confused the actor with the roles they play, worshiping both.

Finally they stopped in a corridor some distance from the stage. To their dismay the rehearsal had just ended. The eunuchs were getting out of their costumes and the musicians were packing their instruments. The instructor hired from outside stood out like a crane among chickens in that motley crew.

The actors on the stage noticed the presence of the young ladies and the eunuch in charge hurried forward to pay his respects and to report their progress. The others stood with their arms by their sides, obsequious smiles glued to their lips. The instructor arched his eyebrows at his young disciple and asked, "Who are they?"

"The third daughter of our master, and the third daughter of Prince An. A pair of angels."

"I meant the woman holding the child." Menggu had put the child down to straighten her robes. She did not have time to look at the stage.

"Oh, that's Ahchou. She used to be the maid of one of the concubines. But she was given to Prince An's wife, and is the nurse to their littlest daughter. As ugly as a monkey, she is."

The instructor shook his head as though to rid himself of some troubling thought and headed back stage. At that moment, Menggu lifted her head. Her hand flew to her lips. She blanched. Her body became as insubstantial as paper, shivering in the wind. A half-crazed gleam rose from the fathomless depths of her eyes and fastened upon the instructor's retreating back. Every fibre in Menggu's body, stretched to breaking point, suddenly loosened. She sank heavily against the balustrade of the corridor.

It's he!

"Brother Tongchun...." Menggu's lips soundlessly formed the name. All the banked-up tears within her welled up. If they were allowed to flow freely, they would never stop....

"Momo, what's the matter?" The childish voice reminded her of where and who she was. She had no right to weep, or to seek out Tongchun. She was a prince's slave. Worse than that she was too ashamed to face the man she had abandoned.

Prince An's wife and third daughter were playing with Bingyue when Prince An entered the boudoir. Earlier in the evening his wife had been at an entertainment. Bingyue ran to her father as soon as he came into the room. Yuele reached down to caress the child's soft curls, and taking a gold necklace from his pocket fastened it around her neck. Then he ordered the child to be taken away. Ahchou led the happy child from the room.

"Bingyue returns to the palace tomorrow," Yuele announced blandly.

"So soon?"

"She's been home twelve days as a special dispensation from His Majesty."

His wife was crestfallen. "Can't she stay a few days longer?"

"She has to leave sooner or later. Why drag it out?"

"It would have been better if she hadn't returned at all! And the Precious Concubine..."

"His Majesty has pardoned her. All is well." Yuele sighed with relief. Just when Jinling was besieged, the scandal surrounding the Precious Concubine set the palace on its ears, seriously compromising the Emperor's dignity.

"How was your entertainment?"

"Boring," the wife replied without enthusiasm. Yuele caught a note of displeasure.

"Our families have not been close in the past. There's bound to be a few negligences which one must overlook," he said.

"I...." The wife turned to her husband blushing and stammered, "Although I'm young and a second wife, I am still a prince's spouse. But it is always their concubines who entertain me...."

"Did the Mistress not appear?"

"She was present at first and seemed quite amiable. Then the prince sent for her, and she disappeared for an hour. When she returned she seemed preoccupied as though she wanted me to leave...."

"Don't take it to heart. Maybe something happened," Yuele tried to comfort.

"She didn't pull the wool over my eyes!" the wife retorted hotly. "I noticed she was preoccupied and asked her straight whether there were other guests and I should withdraw. She became quite agitated and assured me that no one else had been invited because she was aware I'm not fond of crowds. However, when I left I recognized the retainers of Changahdai and Chikshin waiting at the gate. I also passed Nisiha on the way home."

An uneasy thought crossed Yuele's mind. Aside from Changahdai, Prince Nisiha was another who vehemently opposed abolishing the Council of Nobles. Although Prince Chikshin was his own nephew, they did not share the same political views. On the contrary he was a frequent guest of Prince Jian. Why was a gathering of friends treated with such secrecy?

"I wonder if something is going on..." he mused. His third daughter quickly chimed in with what she had seen in the garden. "Something must be going on or else why would Prince Jian's wife be in such a pickle, praying to the gods and our ancestors...." However, try as she might, she could not recall her exact words.... Yuele was excited now.

"Who else could have overheard?"

"There was Prince Jian's third daughter ... and ... Ahchou was carrying Bingyue!"

"Send for Ahchou!"

Ahchou knelt before the prince and his wife. Though she was

small and frail-looking she did not appear to be afraid. She was icy cold. The strange events of that day had affected her deeply. In her despair, life and death were meaningless to her.

The mistress questioned her about the events that took place in the garden. Ahchou answered in her usual dull, mechanical manner, repeating the prayer she overheard Prince Jian's wife utter.

"That's exactly what she said!" crowed the third daughter.

"You may go," Yuele dismissed Ahchou heavily.

What does it all mean? What is Jidu planning? Yuele knitted his brows, a coldness ran through him. Only treason can put a prince on the executioner's block. Is Jidu following the footsteps of Dorgon? Yuele broke into a cold sweat at the thought.

"My Lord, I remember now. Madam Tong was at the house too!" said the wife.

"Which Madam Tong?" Yuele asked absently.

"The mother of Lady Kang and Prince Jian's cousin. I'm sure Prince Jian's wife was called away on account of her. It was the servants that let the cat out of the bag...."

That night Yuele hardly slept. He tried desperately to make some sense of all the loose strands. Instinctively, he felt some terrible plot was being hatched. But there was no proof. He tossed and turned for hours, finally deciding to consult Fan Wencheng and Tang Jo-Wang. That decision eased his mind. As he drifted off, the image of Ahchou flashed through his mind. So cold, so still and calm, the shadows of her long lashes making tiny crescents on her face. Dimly he wondered why she was called Ahchou — the ugly one — for he found her not ugly at all.

4

Another autumn.

Early in the eighth month, news of victory swept the capital. The siege of Jinling had been lifted. Zheng Chenggong and the remnants of his army were driven beyond the Yangtze delta. In the south of Anhui Province, Zhang Huangyan was also in retreat. In no time the thirty county towns were re-taken. Joy swept the nation; from the inner palace to princely mansions; from ministries to official households, and into homes of the common folk. The people brought out bunting and lanterns as though it was a holiday. Feasts were held to thank the gods, the Emperor and the ancestors for their blessing. Festivities lasted several days. People filled with euphoria, meeting strangers in the street, would greet each other with hands folded, saying, "Congratulations! Peace reigns all under Heaven!" Twenty years of war were finally at an end and the peace that the people longed for had arrived. The vast Empire of Ming now belonged to Great Qing.

In this euphoric state, strange stories circulated among the people. It was claimed that the spirit of Lord Guan, the revered warrior of the Three Kingdoms, had come to the aid of beleaguered Jinling. Others swore that monsters appeared within the ranks of Zheng Chenggong's army, causing panic and its subsequent collapse. Zheng's final defeat was the will of the gods. How else could an army of tens of thousands be routed by a mere three thousand?

The fact was when the siege of Jinling began and the nearby county towns surrendered, Zheng Chenggong became complacent. He believed the fall of Jinling was only a matter of time. Discipline became lax. The governor of Jinling, Lang Tingzuo, knowing he was out-numbered, procrastinated by prolonging negotiations of the terms of surrender, while waiting for reinforcement to arrive. Meanwhile the invaders spent their days and nights carousing. The besieged Qing generals Susong and Liang Huafeng watched from their vantage point on the city walls. When their enemy was least prepared, they launched a surprise attack. Supported by canon fire and a rain of rocky projectiles from the city walls above, they destroyed the enemy camp swiftly. In the pitched battle that followed one of Zheng Chenggong's principal generals, Gan Hui, was killed. The army lost heart and was routed. Before long they were driven out of the Yangtze delta and back to Xiamen. The collapse of the army to the north left Zhang Huangyan isolated in the south, and he was quickly defeated too.

It seemed the heavens favoured Great Qing, turning defeat into victory in mysterious and wonderful ways. However, these events could be logically explained. Aside from considerations of strategy, determination, the right and wrong in decision-making, the turn of events mirrored basic changes in the people. After two decades of war and sixteen years of relatively wise rule under the Qing, the people longed for peace. This longing surpassed any racial desire to oust the Manchu.

With the conquest of Yunnan and Guizhou and the final defeat of Zheng Chenggong, the unification of the country was complete. This had a tremendous effect upon the intelligentsia, who regarded these events as "the will of Heaven". Xiong Cilu also subscribed to that view. Like many of his caste, ambition that lay dormant received the impetus it had been waiting for. He was once more determined to make something of his life.

A few days earlier he had mentioned to the steward that he intended to resign his teaching post. The steward had put him off, saying that he was not in the position to take any action in that regard. Xiong Cilu would have to wait until the master's next visit to broach the subject himself. As he had been well treated, Xiong Cilu could not leave on a moment's notice, so he resigned himself to waiting.

In the afternoon, his two pupils arrived as usual. After the customary pleasantries had been exchanged, the younger of the two boys, Ahjin asked without preamble, "Master, are you leaving?"

"Who told you?" countered Xiong Cilu.

"The steward mentioned it yesterday. Don't leave us, Master. Our father will increase your salary," said the older boy Ahyu. The boys were about a year apart in age and bore a strong resemblance to one another. Both had high-bridged noses and long, narrow eyes, with heavy black brows. Whereas the older boy was stocky the other was slight and quick-witted. The older boy also tended to blurt out whatever was on his mind.

"Master, you mustn't leave. Our fifth brother is growing up and soon he will come to school also," said Ahjin earnestly. Xiong Cilu felt a pang of regret.

"Though I am not the most learned of men, I do have some useful knowledge. Now is the time for men like me to seek a place in officialdom that I may contribute to society." The older boy remarked, "That's simple. We'll ask our father to give the Master a post." Ahjin made a face at his older brother, who stuck out his tongue and shrugged. Unfortunately, Xiong Cilu, engrossed in his own thoughts, did not notice this little by-play.

"The notions of children are so simple! Do you think official positions can be given away?"

"Master," Ahyu quickly changed the subject. "Yesterday when you were out, a gentleman came to see you. But the steward sent him away...."

"Oh. What was his name?"

"...I don't know..." the boys chorused.

Xiong Cilu was annoyed. Since he came to teach he had been treated well except he had no freedom. At first he was not permitted to leave the grounds at all. He rebelled and threatened to leave. As a result, each month he was given one day off when he was allowed out. However, he was sworn to secrecy about everything related to the place where he lived, and he could not have visitors. At first he chaffed at these restrictions, but he soon lost interest in society and seldom went out. It was during those heady days when victory in the south was first announced in the capital that he encountered some friends in the street. They had just heard the Emperor was holding a special imperial examination to celebrate the victory. All his peers were anxious to take part. Xiong Cilu was also persuaded to participate. Since he had made up his mind to leave his post, he did not feel constrained to give his address to his friends. Had they submitted his name as a candidate and come expressly to inform him?

"What a nuisance, you don't know the man's name!" Their master seldom scolded. Now the boys hung their heads in embarrassment. It was Ahjin who broke the silence.

"Master, we peeped through the window and had a good look at the man..." he said. Reaching for brush and paper he began to draw, mumbling all the while to himself.

"He didn't have a hat.... His hair was very black ... with a wide forehead ... eyes round yet long ... like this.... His nose was like this.... He didn't have a beard ... but there was a black mole on his cheek.... He wore a long robe with a silk sash round the waist...." A picture appeared on the paper as he spoke. Though the proportions of the figure were not quite correct, the man's features were recognizable. Especially the mole at the corner of the mouth.

"Why, it's Xu Yuanwen of Kunshan!" chortled Xiong Cilu. The older boy clapped his hands with glee.

Xiong Cilu was delighted with his pupils. The younger boy was exceedingly gifted. He loved to read, and whatever he read was almost immediately committed to memory. As his employer insisted, the boys were taught according to their natural bent. So the six-year-old younger boy progressed much more rapidly. Whereas the older was still struggling through *The Analects of Confucius*, the younger boy had already ploughed through *The Four Books* and *The Five Classics* except for *The Book of Changes* which was both difficult to comprehend and to explain. Ahjin's extraordinary brilliance had made Xiong Cilu think that if he was doomed to a life of obscurity, he would be content to bask in the reflected glory of having tutored this prodigy. Indeed, the boy was especially blessed by the gods, for even the dreaded smallpox which took so many young lives only left a few pockmarks on the sides of the nose and a cluster between the eyebrows like a three-petalled flower. Far from marring the beauty of the young face, they added a certain piquancy to it.

"I shall look up Xu Yuanwen," Xiong Cilu shook out his

sleeve, indicating the subject was closed. "Now repeat yesterday's lesson."

Ahjin recited a passage from *The Book of Changes* and explained it without difficulty. He was assigned another passage to read, which the master would explain after he had heard Ahyu. The older boy stumbled through his recitation and explanation.

According to his instructions, the Master was not permitted to punish or reprimand his pupils. All Xiong Cilu could do was repeat the lesson all over again, keeping an eye on Ahjin out of the corner of his eye. Ahjin sat ramrod straight, absorbed in his book. But why did he prop himself up with both arms on the table?

When Ahyu had finished, Xiong Cilu couldn't help chiding his pupil:

"Though the two of you began school together, your progress has not been as good as your younger brother because you are not as studious. You have to make an effort and act like the older brother."

Ahyu pouted. Xiong Cilu quaffed a few mouthfuls of tea and summoned Ahjin to listen to his explanation. Ahjin quickly shut his book, giving the Master his full attention.

"Have you read the passage?"

"I have."

"Did you understand it?"

"I did."

"Ah. Can you tell it to me?"

Ahjin immediately recited the designated passage and explained the gist of its meaning. Xiong Cilu knotted his brows in astonishment.

"How did you come to understand the passage so well?"

"I read the annotated version of the thirteen classics yesterday, and they 'lifted the veil from my mind'." The boy shook his head sagely, delighted at the use of the metaphor.

"Where did you get the book?" Xiong Cilu was surprised that such a book existed in the noble house.

"He stole it!" Ahyu chimed in from across the room. "Our Momo locked up the books because she says he reads from morning to night. So he stole a copy."

Ahjin silenced his older brother with a meaningful look.

"Then you were reading ahead in *The Book of Changes* just now?" Xiong Cilu reached for the book. There were actually two volumes laid one on top of the other. The one on top was *The Book of Changes*, however, the one beneath was Sima Guang's *Mirror of Governance*. It was clear the boy was not absorbed in *The Book of Changes*! Xiong Cilu held up Sima Guang's book and asked, "Do you understand it?" Ahjin nodded. Xiong Cilu glanced at the cover of the volume: Chapter two hundred and five.

"How long have you been reading this?" As the Master did not appear to be angry, the boy replied truthfully,

"Since the summer...." He rubbed the back of his head in embarrassment. Xiong Cilu was delighted and remarked that he would speak to the boy's uncle so that such a keen mind did not go to waste.

He was in such a happy frame of mind that when his employer came to visit that evening he left the matter of his resignation to the last. He was extravagant in his praise of Ahjin's brilliance, begging his employer to find a better teacher, for the boy had great potential.

Master Luo smilingly listened without disrupting Xiong Cilu's discourse until he had finished.

"Find a better teacher? Why there can be none better than yourself. As jade is worthless unless carved by the hand of genius, so is a mind unburnished by a great teacher. Therefore, there is no need for the Master to relinquish his post...."

"To tell the truth, I wish to resign in order to take the imperial examination."

"I thought such matters did not interest you," Master Luo was surprised.

"Circumstances have changed. Zheng Chenggong has been defeated and the country is unified. It is clear Great Qing has the mandate of Heaven. Furthermore, the severity with which the corruption at previous examinations have been dealt with indicates the court's intentions of gathering men of learning to itself. Men such as I, therefore, must respond to the will of Heaven as well."

Gladness sparkled in Master Luo's eyes and bubbled forth in a burst of laughter. Xiong Cilu was taken aback by his employer's response. The employer put Xiong Cilu's request aside for the moment and posed a completely unrelated question.

"Master, I have long admired your wisdom. To what do you attribute the success of Great Qing?"

Xiong Cilu pondered the question and replied, "Cilu knows nothing about the battles that won Yunnan and Guizhou, and lifted the sieige of Jinling. However, I would venture that the weariness of the people was one cause. The people long for peace after years of turmoil. The court was able to win their hearts by overthrowing the harsh government of the Ming, by correcting the evils of land appropriation, the laws against runaway slaves, and official corruption. All these things gave the people pause and won their trust. With peace, agriculture and industry will expand. The nation will prosper. Cilu attributes these things to Great Qing's success." The employer joined his hands happily and said, "Most apt! Most apt indeed! Surely a brilliant career awaits the Master at any time. Therefore, why not teach my nephews two more years?"

"I beg your understanding. With peace, the work of reconstruction is at hand, Cilu cannot wait."

The employer was visibly moved. "I can see the Master has great ambitions. Nevertheless, would he consider staying one more year?"

Although he was growing anxious, Xiong Cilu maintained his outward serenity. "Master, I am deeply indebted to your kindness, but friends have already made arrangements on my behalf to take the special imperial examination this year."

"Friends?" The employer was vexed. "Did your friends come to this house?" Xiong Cilu was embarrassed now, for the employer had repeated time and again that no one might visit.

"Because Cilu was determined to resign," he said, "I asked friends to make arrangements on my behalf. Yesterday, one of them came here, but I was out...." The employer mulled this over. It was clear the unwanted visit helped make up his mind.

"Perhaps my nephews have reached the age when they can study on their own," he said finally. "I will not detain you ... against your will...."

A great weight was lifted from Xiong Cilu's breast, and he wanted to leave at once.

"But not so fast," exclaimed his employer. "The Master must wait a few days so that we might properly show our appreciation before he leaves us."

Yuele left the secret courtyard at the rear of his residence in a happy frame of mind. It was already dark. A guard in front and behind him, carrying lanterns, led the way. He was happy because although Xiong Cilu's remarks had been brief they reflected the mood of the people and their aspirations. He was confident that Great Qing would stabilize; though the Emperor had alienated the nobility, he had won the hearts of the people. Yuele was not fond of ostentation or jockeying for position at court. He was a solid, inobstrusive man, one of the few wise men sincerely concerned about the future of the Empire.

Yuele came to the moon-shaped gate leading to the garden, and the scent of a multitude of night-blooming flowers enveloped him. He took a deep breath, absorbing the tranquil beauty that lay before him. He lifted his head to the sky, where a fragment of pale gold moon floated in the deep azure of the infinite sky. Its silvery sheen washed over trees, rockery, arbours, pavilions and ponds making the garden he knew so well magical. He gestured his attendants to put out their lamps and went in with light, measured steps, enjoying the peace of the moonlit night. A brook murmured under a bridge. Moonlight sparkled in the water, while the greenish glow of fireflies darted hither and yon. Crickets chirped merrily in the grass. However his quiet joy was not untinged by a nameless melancholy.

Another fragrance invaded his nostrils. Who could be burning incense in this garden? The Manchus were not in the habit of using incense in their worship, and making offerings to the sacred rabbit in the moon did not take place till the middle of the eighth month. He followed the scent, passed the rockery and went around the flower beds to a clump of palm trees next to the wistaria arbour. He recognized the slave Ahchou immediately.

Ahchou touched her forehead to the ground thrice and stuck another bunch of lighted joss sticks into a mound of earth. With hands folded before her breast, she lifted her face to the moon, her lips moving in silent prayer. In the moonlight that covered her like a benediction, her face glowed smooth as ivory against which the brows tilted slightly at the ends were black as night. The eyes gleaming with unspilled tears clutched at the beholder's heart.

Ahchou shut her eyes. Her hands dropped wearily to her side. Her body sagged until she sat upon her heels. As her head drooped onto her breast, the moonlight outlined the beautiful curve of her neck. Tears gathered at the ends of her long lashes, trickled down her cheek, passed her chin and onto her breast. She was as motionless as a statue carved out of ivory. Only the teardrops moved one after the other; a lonely, sad young woman, heartbroken and with nobody to turn to.

Many years ago Yuele had been a strong, savage youth who delighted in hunting. He derived a strange pleasure from the death throes of animals. The sight of blood excited him. Once, he brought down sixteen heads of deer in one day. In his elation he literally danced with joy. A root tripped him and sent him crashing into a thicket. There, hidden by tall grass he found a newborn deer, no bigger than a cat, shivering with fear, bleating plaintively for its mother. Suddenly a tear fell from the animal's big, gentle eyes. For the first time in his life Yuele felt a rush of unfamiliar warmth within. He recalled a doe had been among the animals he killed that day. He gathered the fawn in his arms, took it home and raised it. When it was full grown, the deer was released in the same forest. That experience seemed to have taken something from him, but he also gained something. Perhaps it taught him compassion and understanding that made Yuele the man more accepting of the conquered Han.

Now he saw the fawn's sad, frightened eyes again in the slave woman. A string deep in his heart had been plucked, that reverberated through his being. He longed to gather her in his arms as he had the fawn so many years ago and shield her from the buffeting of life, from evil, from cruelty.

The leaves of the arbour rustled in the silence of the night. A firefly, darting past, touched Yuele's face and shattered his revery. As he waved it aside, one of his attendants approached on tiptoe, wanting to say something. Yuele motioned him to be still. He paused a moment longer, then coughed gently

Ahchou shot to her feet, covering her mouth with her sleeve, trembling with fear. Yuele slowly emerged from his hiding place. Seeing her shiver like a frightened animal, he spoke genlty:

"Aren't you called Ahchou?"

Ahchou quickly knelt, head bowed, shaking uncontrollably.

"What are you doing in the garden at this late hour?" No reply.

"Why do you burn incense, pray and weep?" Ahchou lifted her head slowly, but no words came.

Yuele was a veteran of many battles and was instrumental in the conquest. However, he was also a cultured man. Among the Manchu nobility he was something of a rarity, being both a man of action and of learning. However when it came to women he was out of his depth. Yuele sighed and waving a hand said, "You may go!"

Ahchou glanced at him and, seeing that he was not angry, went away with a feeling of relief. Yuele watched her recede into the distance, bathed in moonlight like an angel gliding into the night.

Yuele was troubled. He had always thought of himself as a warrior who placed duty to his monarch above all things. Yet this cold, wordless, melancholy slave touched his heart.

The crickets went on chirping. Everything was as it should be on an autumn night. His attendants had waited for some time, but Yuele seemed reluctant to leave. Nor did they dare hurry him.

The sound of quick footsteps approached from the direction of the house.

"Stop! Who goes there!" demanded the guard in a loud voice. The person approaching shouted back, addressing the guard by name.

"Saiban, is that you? I'm Yakulah. Where is My Lord?"

"What is the matter?" Yuele answered. Moonlight highlighted the planes and angles of his face, bringing out an air of confusion and melancholy.

"Prince Jieshu has arrived."

Yuele was surprised. "What hour is it?"

The guard replied, "It is approaching nine o'clock."

Instantly, all the strange, disturbing thoughts that plagued him were swept from his mind. He was once more his cool-headed, sharp-witted self. A host of questions rushed through his mind as he went to greet his visitor.

Jieshu was a steadfast, thoughtful young man. Like his cousin Changahdai, Jieshu was devoted to Prince Jian, Jidu. Last year Yuele had been deeply troubled by the tournament of the six princes. Jieshu had been present on that ocassion.

About ten days ago there had been a secret meeting at Jidu's house. He was almost sure that Prince Jian had called the meeting because Lady Kang had fallen from favour. Yuele had been shocked at the time and had sent his spies to make enquiries. But all they had to report was that it was a gathering of friends to drink and talk together. Though he could not discover what they talked about, Jidu's wife's alleged behaviour was puzzling. Why fabricate lies to hide a gathering of friends and relatives? Though he tried, Yuele could not find out what really happened. Then the news of victory sent the court and the entire nation into a paroxysm of joy. The Emperor had taken that opportunity to pardon the Precious Concubine, Lady Kang, all the palace maids and the eunuchs for their wrong-doings large or small. Everyone ought to be happy. There was peace on earth.

But things are never that simple. Yuele believed that some important matter, possibly related to the secret meeting had brought Jieshu to him. A prince did not pay visits late at night to discuss trifles.

Yuele's face clouded. The three straight lines between his brows deepened.

"Show the prince to the study," he ordered and, as an after thought, added, "Post guards outside. No one is allowed near."

After her mother had gone, Lady Kang went into her bed chamber and sat in her favourite redwood armchair. She took no notice of the maid who came in with tea and small cakes. The servants had grown accustomed to seeing her sitting staring into space, sometimes for hours at a time. They tiptoed in and, having laid out food and drink, left as quietly as they came, leaving Lady Kang alone, wrapped in her heavy, unending loneliness.

Had the maids and eunuchs of Jingren Palace been more observant they would have noticed the change in their mistress. For her eyes had lost the glow of life and became lifeless glass orbs. Her brain turned as ponderously as a millstone.

What did Mother say? In order to save me and to save Great Qing, they would abolish the Emperor! He had disobeyed the commandments of the ancestors, gone against the will of Heaven, given way step by step to the southern barbarians, until he had offended both the gods and man. The time was ripe to take matters into their own hands, before Great Qing was destroyed....

Abolish him. Make him a commoner. Or if one had to be kind, give him a title and let him live in leisure. Then who would be emperor? Of course it would have to be the son of Lady Kang. Then I will be Empress Dowager, she thought. And what would become of the present Dowager? Why she would be the Grand Empress Dowager, a title she would relish.

And what about the Empress, Lady Dongeh and her cousin? Since the Emperor is abolished, they will be driven out of the Forbidden City with him. Only by abolishing this faithless man can you be sure of saving your life. Although he has pardoned you, it was merely another impulsive act that means nothing.... You mustn't be foolish....

What we need you to do is very simple. All you have to do is watch his movements and let us know. Utmost secrecy is important, for the consequences would affect us all.

Lady Kang hated Fulin.

She became an imperial concubine when she was little more than a child. The first time she gave herself to him, her joy was indescribable. She fell passionately in love. He was her god. She would give everything of herself for his sake, even her life. She worshipped the ground he stood on. And he loved her. When duty forced him to share his bed with another, she would take any bit of his clothing she could find to hers, or she would not sleep. If he was away on a royal progress, she would be as restless as an ant on a hot stove until he returned. She was always the first to be summoned to the Hall of Mental Cultivation, and their first meeting after a separation was always as sweet and passionate as the first time they lay together.

She became pregnant, and that brought new dreams. He deposed the Empress. Was it because of her, she used to wonder. She was loved and she was carrying his child. It would be natural for her to succeed the Empress. She had no doubts about it at all. And hadn't he hinted as much? She loved him more than ever, her lord and master, her god, the father of the child she carried. He was so young, so handsome, and master of all under Heaven.

She never dreamed that he would destroy her dreams and quench the flame in her heart with ice water.

The selection of a new empress chilled her. The arrival of Lady Dongeh drove her to despair. She hated him for turning his back on their love. She hated him for allowing himself to be bewitched by a barbarian woman. Their happiness drove a red-hot poker through her heart. A passionate young woman, abandoned by the man she loved, was driven to despair. She had the empty title of concubine, for she lived alone, year after year. That loneliness could drive her mad. But she did not go mad. Instead love curdled into relentless hate. If the belief that the Emperor was higher than any other living being hadn't been drilled into her, and if she had not been bound by implacable protocol, who knows what she might have done.

She became cold and taciturn. The few times Fulin summoned her to the Hall of Mental Cultivation had not been happy occasions. As a result he became even more distant.

Did she give up? She did not. Secretly she sought to win him back. But she failed badly. That was the recent incident at Jingren Palace.

That day, Fulin's unannounced visit threw her off balance. She had spoken the way she did partly to get things off her chest, but deep inside it was prompted by a misplaced hope of changing Fulin's opinion of herself. She wanted to be seen as a woman of wisdom, with courage to speak her mind. It had taken her a long time and considerable effort before she realized she could only win him back by surpassing Lady Dongeh in some way. Unfortunately, she had followed the traditional morality of the Manchu in her thinking. Also she failed to understand Fulin and chose the wrong time. Fulin's fragile self-esteem was at its lowest ebb, and picking the scabs of his wounded pride sent him into a rage, causing him to demand her head.

Her defeat robbed her of the will to live. Even the Emperor's pardon failed to dispel any of the gloom. On the other hand, Lady Dongeh who had been pardoned at the same time became a frequent visitor. She hated Lady Dongeh; yet when all seemed lost, she tried to save her. For that she could not be ungrateful. Lady Dongeh did her best for Lady Kang. Whenever the Empress Dowager or the Empress sent her gifts of food, clothing or ornaments, Lady Dongeh never failed to share them with her. These little kindnesses began to wear away Lady Kang's hatred, and her mother's shocking revelations left her in a turmoil. In this state of confusion, Lady Dongeh's voice sounded in her mind:

"...He is monarch as well as husband and father. You and I are bound to him by destiny. We share in his glory and in his failures. We share his life and, afterwards, his tomb. With such a bond what is there that cannot be forgiven?"

Lady Kang was completely motionless while a storm raged within. Her placid world had been tossed on its ears. Nothing was as it seemed. Trying to sort it out made her head spin. She was dizzy from thinking. The noonday sun shining in her eyes made it hard to keep them open. She would rest a while, she thought. Just lean back and rest a while.

Suddenly, two eunuchs from the Hall of Mental Cultivation stood before her. The Emperor had sent for her. Shaking with her guilty secret she followed. Had he somehow discovered the plot. Mounted on horseback, Fulin was waiting outside the inner left gate. His face darkened when he saw her. "What took you so long?" he demanded. "What were you up to?"

Her heart was in her throat. She dared not speak, much less look at him. Suddenly he burst into peals of laughter.

"I was only joking! Come, we will ride out to Nanyuan." She lifted her head then, and her heart leaped. His gaze was full of sweet passion, his smile would melt any woman. She felt such a rush of warmth that tears filled her eyes.

They rode, side by side, on the grassland that stretched as far as the eye could see. She was drunk with happinness, basking in his smile.

"Why do you look at me like that?" she grumbled. In answer he threw his arm around her waist and drew her roughly to him, so close that she could feel his hot breath on her neck and ears. "Let me go," she protested half shyly. "They're looking at us ... and laughing."

Fulin laughed. "Who would dare!" He whipped the horses, urging them to a faster gallop. Tightening his grip on her with one arm, they sped on together. Her breath came in short, sharp gasps. She could hardly breathe as pride and joy surged through her.

The horses suddenly reared up, whinnying with fear. The men that surrounded them seemed to have risen out of the earth. As they closed in brandishing swords, clubs, bows and arrows she thought they resembled her uncles and cousins. Yet they did not. Who were these men? What were they yelling?

"Unjust Monarch!"

"Betrayer of ancestors! Sinner!"

"Depose him! Depose him!"

She heard the swish of an arrow and watched with horror as Fulin tumbled off his horse. The arrow had gone right through him. Lady Kang threw herself upon him. Fulin tugged feebly at the shaft that pierced him.

"I'm dying ... dying ..." he gasped. Frantically she cried out, "You can't die! You mustn't! What will become of me?" She wailed until her throat was dry.

Lady Kang shook herself. She was still seated in her favourite redwood armchair. Everything around her was silent except the wild beating of her heart. The dream image of Fulin's death clutched at her innards. She realized with a pang that she hated Fulin because she loved him. Loved him deeply.

What would become of her if he died? What would become of her if he was deposed? It would be the same. Would her son really be proclaimed? Would she really become the Empress

Dowager? What were the chances of the son succeeding to the throne of a deposed father?

What was it that Lady Dongeh said about sharing his glory and his failure? That was food for thought.

As long as Fulin lived she would be an imperial concubine, the mother of the Third Imperial Son. In time she could become Empress Dowager, or at least the mother of a prince. If Fulin was deposed or died she would be nothing more than a fallen monarch's widow, and, like his Empress and all his harem, would be driven from the palace. It would end badly for her ... that much was certain. Her uncle had lied to her, and probably also to her mother.

In the peace after the storm, Lady Kang knew exactly what she must do. She quietly re-arranged her coiffure, changed into a long robe of moonlight silver, and ordered a sedan chair to carry her to Cining Palace.

The Empress Dowager was calm; but intelligence, kindliness and trust gleamed in her eyes as she listened to Yuele's report, just as she did earlier, listening to Lady Kang.

After she had finished telling all she knew, Lady Kang begged forgiveness for her mother and herself. The Empress Dowager had been so moved that she left her chair, raised the kneeling Lady Kang to her feet and clasped her to her ample bosom.

"My child, how can a mother thank you enough for what you have done? You have risen above pettiness and done a great deed for which our ancestors in the nether world will also be grateful.... My son always had a wicked temper, and that day you struck a nerve. He was furious at the time, but regretted it afterwards...." As Lady Kang, almost desolving in tears, took her leave, the Empress Dowager reminded her, "Keep this a secret. Report any movement at once."

Of course she could not behave as impulsiyely with Yuele. She listened carefully to what he had to say, her thin black eyebrows knotted in concentration.

"Why do you suppose Jieshu betrayed them?"

"Jieshu was never really one of them. Now that all under Heaven has been subdued, he knows his loyalty belongs to the Emperor."

The Empress Dowager nodded. "In your opinion what should we do?"

Yuele quickly put forth his proposal. Arrest Jidu and his clique immediately, thus putting an end to future threats.

The Empress Dowager did not reply at once, but paced the room in swift sure mannish steps, her robes making a soft swishing sound with every step. Watching her reminded Yuele of his uncle, the late Emperor Abahai. Once he had gone to him with a battle plan. He had paced the floor in the very same manner. This aunt was so much like her dead husband that even the way she stood with one hand on the elbow of the other hand which absent-mindedly rubbed her chin resembled him.

She turned and went back to her chair. Leaning back she breathed a long sigh. Her brows had come unknotted. She wore the expression of a great commander with a brilliant plan of action.

"We will take our time. Tell Jieshu to gain their confidance and report any changes to you immediately. I shall also have Sumalagu and others contact you daily. They are waiting for an opportunity to strike, and we must be ready to catch them redhanded."

"Yes, Your Majesty!" Yuele agreed, full of admiration for the Empress Dowager's sagacity.

"Furthermore, this involves the Imperial Family. Jidu has a formidable reputation, and the scandal will be damaging to both the Imperial Family and Great Qing. Therefore, you must proceed with utmost secrecy. The fewer people that know the better. Under no circumstances should any of this leak out to the Han officials or the people."

"Yes, Your Majesty," Yuele replied. It was as though the Empress Dowager had read his mind, for she had laid to rest all the problems that plagued him.

"Another thing, the Emperor is young and hot-headed. He must not know about this. On the other hand he must be protected by men we can trust. Suoni and Aobai's loyalty is unquestionable. Aobai is also an excellent swordsman. There is no harm telling them the truth and have them be on their guard night and day. However, the Emperor must be kept in the dark."

The Empress Dowager was unruffled in a crisis. Her thoughts were clear, her plans well rounded. She cut a heroic figure among her sex. Though she appeared to be a kindly, compromising, peaceful grandmother, intent upon enjoying a life of leisure and peace, she could be a determined commander when the future of the crown was at stake. She would be the force that could turn defeat into victory in a struggle. Yuele was in agreement with all her plans except for a slight change in the choice of bodyguards for the Emperor.

"If it pleases Your Majesty," he began, "recently Aobai and Sukesaha have become relatives through marriage of their children. The two men have no secrets between them. Since Suoni is advanced in years, would it not be appropriate to replace him with Sukesaha?"

"Sukesaha..." the Empress Dowager hesitated a moment, "is a wily man. But Suoni can still be a useful ally. Work with them."

The rest of the details were left to Yuele. As he left the palace, Yuele thought to himself: the Emperor is a fortunate man. In Chengqian Palace he has a good helpmate, and in Cining Palace a formidable mother who watches over his interests.

Left alone, the Empress Dowager was thinking, my son, my son, all things can not be as you wish. Changes made too quickly cause enmity. Though joy reigns after a great victory, and for the moment at least petty hatreds are forgotten, there is tomorrow, and tomorrow's tomorrow to contend with. It is time to pull back, my son, lest you ride for a fall.

5

"Imperial Mother, today I acquired a superb Zhuangyuan*!" Fulin's expression was full of pride and an almost ingenuous joy. The Empress Dowager smiled indulgently at her son. His bright eyes and rosy cheeks brought to mind another Fulin, a child who ran and played on the grasslands, standing on tiptoe to increase his height, eager to show off the butterfly he caught after many a tumble.

Fulin was four years old and the Empire had not yet begun. In the blink of an eye seventeen years went by. Now he was the young ruler of a vast empire. The Empress Dowager's heart swelled with mixed emotions, contemplating those stormy years. She weathered them all. Her smile was serene when she spoke:

"Where is this excellent Zhuangyuan who has given my Imperial Son such joy?"

"Ah, Imperial Mother, this time, we set the questions ourselves, conducted the examination and read the papers ourselves as well. Therefore, this batch of Zhuangyuan and Jinshi are ours personally. The Zhuangyuan is not only learned, his calligraphy is superb and he is handsome to boot!"

"And what about his character?" asked the Empress Dowager.

"I have examined him in person. I asked him to write a poem on cranes. He recited: 'It crows loudest to the moon on high. It dances beautifully, but not to attract attention.' These two lines show his noble character." The Empress Dowager nodded her agreement.

---

*The examinations of the Qing Dynasty could be devided into three main stages: the prefectural examination; the provincial examination; and the highest examination comprising the metropolitan examination, the test examination and the palace examination, as well as a final test at the imperial court. The scholars who passed the final test became palace graduates (*Jinshi*). There were three men in the first grade, the highest being called the Number One Scholar (*Zhuangyuan*).

"This paragon is Xu Yuanwen, from Kunshan in Jiangsu, a learned man of the south. I have summoned six scholars of the top three grades to an informal audience at Longzong Gate. The other southern scholar is among them. Didn't my Imperial Mother wish to see him?" Mother and son exchanged a knowing smile.

Meanwhile at Longzong Gate, the eunuch in charge of ceremonies had summoned the six new scholars who entered in single file. Among them was Xiong Cilu walking slowly as if in a daze.

The evening before the steward had come to him and escorted him to a closed carriage. He was driven through streets he did not recognize. It was so dark that soon he had lost track of where he was or the direction he was being driven. Once or twice the carriage had been stopped. But each time the steward spoke a few words to whoever it was and they were allowed to resume their journey. At length they came to a tall building with a long corridor in the front. He was ushered into a room that opened onto it, and told to wait there, but not to speak to anyone. On the morrow the Master would come to express his gratitude. Before he left the steward left him a parcel of clothes, with instructions that he should put them on the next morning.

Several other men in the room were already sound asleep. The room was clean and neat, and did not seem to be a disreputable place. In one corner stood a bookcase. He selected a volume and sat down by the lamp to read, thus whiling away the autumn night.

At daybreak a loud voice outside summoned all the new officials to fall in line. The other inhabitants of the room scrambled outside. He was all at sea when a man came in and enquired, "Aren't you Xiong Cilu of Huguang? Oh but you aren't dressed!" Without further ado, the man quickly helped him into ceremonial robe, boots and cap and hustled him outside where two long lines of men had already formed. He was inserted into the tenth place in the right-hand line. Still dazed, Xiong Cilu looked about him. There must have been at least a hundred or more men waiting in line. In the early morning gloom he could only make out the features of the few nearest him, the others faded into the half light. But he could tell they were all nervous, their bodies and movements stiff with tension. No one spoke. Xiong Cilu looked about apprehensively. As the sky lightened, a white fog covered the earth like a thick curtain. Was it joy or disaster that lurked behind it, he wondered. He had to pinch himself to convince himself this was not a dream.

Xiong Cilu gritted his teeth. He had lived his life according to his conscience. He had no regrets, nothing to reproach himself with, come what may.

The double file began to move. Only the scraping sound of the men's boots on the flagstones broke the silence. The path was so broad and smooth, the fog so thick that they seemed cut off from the rest of the world.

The ponderous, resonant ringing of a bell pierced the fog, ending in a buzzing echo that shook the ground. Xiong Cilu started, for the bell sounded like the bell atop Meridian Gate that was struck on the mornings of the Grand Audience.

They followed the sound of the bell, passed through several gates set in stout walls, and crossed an arched white marble bridge. By now it was daylight. Xiong Cilu glanced at himself for the first time that morning and discovered to his astonishment that he was in the same ceremonial garb as the men around him. A burst of music came from somewhere in front. Xiong Cilu looked around him and through the swirling fog made out the imposing outlines of the Hall of Supreme Harmony. It dawned upon him that this was the presentation of new Jinshi. How did he get here? He had not taken the general examination or the special examination. Was he impersonating someone, or had there been some mistake? Xiong Cilu broke into a cold sweat, for the crime of deceiving the Emperor hovered over his head.

The music swelled to a climax. An officer announced the top three grades of Jinshi selected from the special examination held in the ninth month of the sixteenth year of Shunzhi. The top honour of the first grade went to Xu Yuanwen of Kunshan, however, the second place of the second grade went to Xiong Cilu. In a daze, Xiong Cilu was guided out of the line and told to kneel to the left of the imperial pathway behind four other men. My heavens! What is happening!

Xiong Cilu went through the long, involved rituals that followed like a marionette manipulated by a sardonic puppet master. Still in a daze he heard his name announced once again and discovered he had been appointed to the Hanlin Academy. He had no idea how or why this honour had been accorded him. Had the post been bought for him by Master Luo?

Contrary to tradition, the Emperor chose to receive the top ten scholars at Qianqing Gate. Once again Xiong Cilu heard his name called out. In the Hall of Supreme Harmony he would not be permitted near the throne, but here he found himself within ten paces of His Majesty. He lifted his head to gaze upon the Emperor, just as Fulin turned toward him. Their eyes met. In that split second Xiong Cilu thought he detected a hint of amusement in the Emperor's expression. He let his gaze drop, but his mind was once more in a whirl, for there was something familiar about those eyes, those brows, those delicately chiselled lips. It seemed that he had seen them once contracted into an expression of rage.... That's it! It was the young bannerman! Two years ago they had met at a teahouse to the south of the city. Later they met again at the crude shack of the old peasant.... It was him.... It had to be! With that realization Xiong Cilu breathed more freely. His title of Jinshi must have been a gift of the Emperor himself.

Nevertheless, Xiong Cilu was uneasy about a royal gift which he had not earned. The whole incident was shrouded in too much mystery for comfort. He was so deep in thought that he almost stepped on the heel of the man in front of him.

Finally they were led into Cining Palace and presented to the Empress Dowager. Xiong Cilu, racked with doubts, felt the

Empress Dowager sizing him up, and detected a glint of amusement in her expression as well. He bowed his head, not daring to look up.

The Empress Dowager was delighted with these bright and cultivated young Jinshi. She made a short speech of encouragement and dismissed them each with a gift of a purse, a gold flower and a nugget. The Zhuangyuan received double gifts. The whole assemblage left the Presence amazed at their good fortune.

Not until they had passed through Tiananmen Gate and reached East Changan Street did the new Zhuangyuan Xu Yuanwen politely tug at Xiong Cilu's sleeve.

"Oh, Brother Cilu, what uncommon good fortune that we should take the examination and be selected at the same time! How did I manage to miss seeing you earlier? Where have you been hiding yourself?"

In a matter of days the fearlessly outspoken Xu Yuanwen had become a carefully decorous courtier.

Xiong Cilu mumbled some inane reply. Now he was indeed uncomfortable, for several layers of clothing were soaked through with sweat.

At Cining Palace, mother and son were in rapt conversation.

"Imperial Mother, did I make a good choice?" Fulin demanded proudly.

"Very good indeed. I can see that the repeated examinations at Shuntian and in the south have not been futile."

"If we hadn't taken drastic steps to stamp out corruption we would never find men of this calibre. Although the Han officials continue to whine about our harshness, we are convinced we were right. We have no regrets."

The Empress Dowager glanced at her son.

"Let us not dwell upon the Shuntian incident. Most of the culprits were let off. However, too many were executed in the south...."

Actually in the Shuntian case only the seven principal offenders including Li Zhenye and Zhang Wopu had been beheaded. All the rest had been pardoned because the Emperor was afraid of too wide an involvement. However, when the case in the south was exposed soon afterwards, the chief examiner and the adjudicators, numbering fourteen persons, were all executed. Not one escaped.

Shunzhi spoke as though he were arguing a case:

"Since Nurhachi's reign we Manchu have relied on marriage as a means of winning our Mongolian allies. Now that all under Heaven is united, how are we to bind the Hans to us? I feel the imperial examination is the strongest tool we have. A great many learned men live to the south of the Yangtze River. In the future they will be the pillars of the nation. Therefore, killing the few to win the hearts of many was worthwhile."

The Empress Dowager was about to rebut him with the siege of Jinling and how the local officials had surrendered in droves at the first hint that the tide might have turned on Great Qing. Could that have been an expression of resentment against his harshness in dealing with the corruption at the examinations of the south? Then she remembered her son's thin skin and held her tongue. The siege of Jinling must never be mentioned again, she told herself. She deftly changed the subject of conversation. "Now that the examinations are over, isn't it time to relax a little?"

Indeed, in his effort to stamp out corruption, he had re-examined all those who qualified at Shuntian, personally winnowing out the unworthy. This time in the special imperial examination he had also undertaken a major portion of the work himself. He had a right to be fatigued.

Fulin laughed.

"All these scholastic matters are behind us. Now is the time for horse and bow. These brisk autumn days are perfect for hunting."

The Empress Dowager's heart skipped a beat. A hunt was just the occasion for something untoward to happen. Forcing herself to remain calm, she asked, "Does it have to be soon?"

"I need to stretch myself," Fulin chuckled. "The Second and the Third Imperial Sons are old enough to see a little of the world. Also my Imperial brothers, nephews and their children should be brought together for a tournament to show off the courage and skill of the Aisin Gioro clan. We should properly celebrate the uniting of all under Heaven. Besides, I am anxious to try the new falcons that have been brought as tribute...."

The Emperor became more and more animated as he spoke, and the Empress Dowager became more worried listening. Good Heavens, he was thinking of inviting the imperial clan to the hunt! It was tantamount to serving himself up as the sacrificial lamb.

"Imperial Son," the Empress Dowager began hesitantly, "why make such an occasion out of an entertainment? It will only cause criticism...."

"Imperial Mother," Fulin chuckled, "I agree the hunt is unimportant but we have bigger fish to fry."

"What do you mean?"

"Has the Imperial Mother forgotten?" Fulin teased. "We had decided long ago to go to Changping County to pay our respects to the tomb of Emperor Chongzhen. It will be killing two birds with one stone."

The Empress Dowager pondered his words. She agreed visiting the tomb of the last Ming Emperor was something her son indeed must do. The more she thought of it the more she felt it was probably a good thing for her son to experience a little danger so long as suitable precautions were taken. And she was confidant of both her foresight and the arrangements she would make. Finally she softly quoted an old saying in Mongolian: "The wings of an eagle grow strong with the buffeting of storms." However, Fulin's Mongolian was not very fluent.

"Imperial Mother, what eagle are you speaking of?" he asked.

The Empress Dowager smiled and steered the conversation onto other things.

Upon their arrival at the town of Gonghua, the imperial party immediately repaired to the royal lodge at Shahe. That afternoon a tournament would take place in an open field in front of the main hall. All the male children of the imperial family under the age of fifteen, including the imperial nephews, sons and grandsons, were commanded to attend.

The Emperor was seated on a dias set high in front of the main hall, flanked on either side by Prince An and the trusted old Suoni. The lords Aobai and Sukesaha stood on either side of him, but slightly behind. Like the Emperor they were all clad in full armour. The grand academicians Jin Zhijun and Fu Yijian, and Minister of Rites Wang Xi and other civic officials were also in attendance. The gold and silver of the imperial guards with their colourful trappings made a brilliant display.

The archery tournament of the imperial children began. Those participants over the age of ten shot five times, while those under ten shot thrice. The targets were arranged more than thirty feet away. Competitors appeared in pairs according to their age. Some strutted full of confidence. Others were nervous and fumbling. The results were no more than ordinary. No one was outstanding. On the other hand neither did anyone disgrace themselves. The fathers and elder brothers of the participants in the audience were dismayed by the Emperor's obvious boredom.

The youngest participants were the Emperor's two sons. The Second Imperial Son was a full six years old. The Third Imperial Son was not quite six. As the ten year olds were about to finish, Prince An leaned close to the Emperor and politely whispered, "Your Majesty, the two Imperial Sons are still young. Perhaps they should be excused." Suoni glanced quickly at his companion from under his bushy grey brows and concurred, saying, "Majesty, they are young and their limbs are brittle. Her Majesty the Empress Dowager might be concerned for their safety."

All the courtiers agreed. In the hubbub that followed, a few words caught the Emperor's attention.

"...The targets are too far ... the children are small ... and may not be strong enough...." Fulin's face clouded immediately. He shot out of his chair, but he managed to control his temper. Nevertheless he spat out one short sentence:

"No one will be exempt!"

The Second Imperial Son's first arrow fell short of the target. The assemblage held its breath. Fulin's face was grim. His lips tightly pursed. A vein throbbed faintly in his temple.

The second arrow struck the bull's eye, and so did the last.

Everyone breathed a sigh of relief. The assembled princes and lords were quick to offer their congratulations, praising the Second Imperial Son's marksmanship and averring that he would one day grow to be a heroic protector of the Empire. Amid all this praise, Fulin allowed himself a faint smile of satisfaction.

It was now the Third Imperial Son's turn to shoot. But where was he?

Once again Prince An and Suoni suggested that the Third Imperial Son was too young and, as he wasn't present, he should be excused. Fulin was indifferent toward this third son, born of the Lady Kang. It was ironic that both he and the Fourth Imperial Son had the smallpox, yet he lived. Had he stolen the life of his beloved fourth son? When he thought of the apple of his eye lying in his grave, he found himself loathing this third son. Whether he participated in today's festivities really didn't matter, but being absent at the moment he was expected to appear was unforgivable. Fulin's face darkened again. "Find him! He will shoot!"

The Third Imperial Son had not gone far. His attention had been attracted by a young boy tending a falcon, who was standing among the other falcon handlers ranged around the edges of the archery field. He had stretched out a hand to pat the falcon, but the boy quickly moved it out of reach.

"Take care, My Lord!" he said in fright. "He attacks strangers. He's a mean one."

"No wonder in books they are described as having talons of

jade, eyes of gold and wings of iron!"

The youth was delighted that the bird he loved was so well appreciated. "He can fly really high," he said in spite of himself. "When he's circling up there he can spot a grasshopper on the ground. When he's sitting in a tree he can see a sparrow up among the clouds. He darts into the sky like a streak of light. No bird can out fly him...."

"Third Lord! It's your turn to shoot! His Majesty will be angry!" A guard rudely interrupted the two boys, and taking the Third Imperial Son by the arm hustled him away.

The Third Imperial Son stood alone in the huge archery field, like a young sprout freshly thrust out of the earth, or a mushroom with a red cap, or a tiny sparrow surrounded by birds of prey. But he was not afraid or nervous. Nor was he really aware of his surroundings. He was intent upon shooting. He raised his small bow, stretched it to the fullest, squinted at the target and let fly. The arrow whistled through the air and struck the bull's eye.

"Good shot!" someone in the crowd shouted. The assemblage laughed.

The second arrow also found its mark.

Laughter mingled with cheers. The atmosphere of the archery field relaxed. A guard below the dias announced in a loud voice,

"His Majesty has ordered a reward of a yellow waistcoat for hitting the bull's eye a third time!" That announcement cut through the tumult.

The Third Imperial Son took aim and hit the bull's eye a third time.

A cheer went up all around. The Third Imperial Son, the youngest, had won. Even the grim-faced Emperor permitted himself a faint smile. The Third Imperial Son quietly put away his bow and, mimicking his elders, walked in measured steps toward the dias where he fell on his knees before the Emperor.

Fulin pretended not to understand. "What do you want?" he asked.

The Third Imperial Son did not reply but gazed up at Fulin smiling. Fulin burst into laughter. "All right! All right! Bring the yellow waistcoat." Suoni quickly interposed, "This is so sudden. Where would we find such a small waistcoat?"

The guards brought a full-sized yellow waistcoat. Prince An held it up against the boy and it reached down to his feet. He quickly wrapped the boy in it and picked him up in his arms.

"The Third Imperial Son is a brilliant shot. What great things will you do when you grow up?" The Third Imperial Son smiled at his father but did not reply. Fulin was in a happy mood. He beckoned the Third Imperial Son to him and said, "We should like to know ambitions of you and your brother." The Second Imperial Son thought for a moment and said, "I shall be a great warrior and go into battle. Everyone will know me as the fiercest general in all the world." Yuele laughingly remarked, "You shall grow to be a worthy prince. What about the Third Imperial Son?" The Third Imperial Son levelled a gaze full of love and admiration at his father.

"I shall be like my Imperial Father and work hard so that my people can live in peace and prosperity," he said in a clear childish voice.

Fulin was shocked and moved by the child, not unmixed with a bitter regret. The princes and courtiers gathered around were also surprised by this child of six. A peculiar feeling of awe rushed through Yuele. From this day forward he would no longer regard this child as a nephew whom he could carry in his arms.

Amid laughter and congratulations, Fulin rose and, taking his two sons by the hand, one on each side, headed for the inner hall. As they went he bent down to speak to them. Yuele, Suoni, Aobai and Sukesaha followed close behind. Whereas Yuele and Suoni were calm, the other two barely held the tension they felt in check. However, Fulin was none the wiser.

The next morning Fulin was up at dawn. With the help of eunuchs he donned plain clothes and, having ordered his sedan chair, sat down to breakfast. It was then that Prince An and Suoni presented themselves to pay their respects. There was an air of tension about the two men as they entered the room which chilled the room as though they had brought in the sharp air of autumn. Yuele quickly presented a yellow silk envelope with both hands. Fulin opened it and scanned the simple message written in a familiar Manchu hand.

"Imperial Son must do exactly as Prince An and Suoni have arranged. Mother."

Fulin sensed something was afoot. He cocked his eyebrows and asked, "What is going on?"

"If it pleases Your Majesty, act according to the arrangements your slaves have made by order of the Empress Dowager," Yuele hastily replied in a low voice. "Your Majesty will please go into the inner chamber and not make a sound." Without further ado, the two men hustled Fulin into a tiny inner chamber which was quite dark. He pointed out a small hole in the wall and bade Fulin observe the happenings in the other room.

Fulin pressed his eye close to the hole in the wall just as the beaded curtain of the other room was lifted and Li Guozhu entered. At first sight of the man who followed him in Fulin gasped in surprise. For the other man resembled himself down to the last detail of dress and mannerisms.

The impostor sat where he had been sitting, ate and drank as though nothing untoward was happening. Only a slight tremour of the hand betrayed his agitation.

Outside the eunuch announced the sedan chair was waiting for His Majesty.

The impostor motioned that he was ready. His attendants rushed out of the room. The "Emperor" slowly crossed to the door with Li Guozhu close at his heels. At the door he turned and, finding himself alone with Li Guozhu, he faced Fulin's hiding place, knelt and touched his forehead to the floor quickly three times. He rose, straightened his robes and, imitating

Fulin's posture, one hand fingering his court beads and the other folded behind his back, left the hall with Li Guozhu.

Fulin finally recognized the man. It was one of the young eunuchs who usually swept the terraces and courtyards of the Hall of Mental Cultivation. The youth bore a vague resemblance to himself, but in that costume and his carefully studied mannerisms, no one could tell the difference. But what was the meaning of the final obeisance? Fulin was about to ask what the masquerade meant, but Yuele and Suoni signalled him not to make a sound. In a moment the usual cries that accompanied a royal departure was heard: "His Majesty is leaving...."

Flags and ribbons snapped in the breeze. Battle axe, sword and spear jangled; chariots rumbled; horses neighed. The great cavalcade left the imperial lodge, and following a northwesterly direction headed for the Ming Tombs in solemn procession.

All was silent now in the imperial lodge. Yuele and Suoni accompanied Fulin out of his hiding place. Yuele quickly reported, saying, "Certain persons have planned to assassinate Your Majesty during the solemnities at the tombs. We went along with their plan to see how they will proceed. The young eunuch Li Zhong was willing to impersonate Your Majesty in this exigency." Now Fulin remembered the name of the young eunuch whom he barely noticed before. But there was no time for regrets.

"Who is plotting against us?"

Yuele and Suoni exchanged a look. Finally it was Yuele who spoke. "At present there is insufficient proof against anyone. If Your Majesty will change into plain clothes, we can ride south and double back into the hills and the woods which will afford us enough cover to observe their movements."

Fulin half guessed the truth. "Prince Jian, Prince Xun, Duke Kang and a few others have all gone ahead to prepare for the ceremonies...."

Yuele's eyes met Fulin's and a spark of understanding swiftly passed from the one to the other.

"Just so," said Yuele. "They will greet Your Majesty at the

entrance to the tomb."

Suoni added, "They would then be caught red-handed and can not escape."

Fulin grasped the hands of his two loyal courtiers. "Imperial Brother and Suoni, you two are the backbone of the Empire and the loyal servants of Great Qing. You have acted with precision and secrecy...."

Yuele hastened to add, "We are merely carrying out orders from Her Majesty the Empress Dowager who planned this action together with the Precious Concubine."

"Ah! The Imperial Mother!" Fulin was deeply moved.

Half an hour later a small troop of cavalry of about thirty men wearing the outfit of the guards of Qianqing Gate galloped out of the imperial lodge and headed west along the road, kicking up a cloud of dust that spread across the plain, obliterating them from view.

A great procession almost two miles long, with a myriad banners flying in the brisk, clear autumn air, moved at a stately pace northwestward toward the mountains. A vanguard of all colours of ceremonial banners, fans and umbrellas led the way, followed by troops carrying glittering ceremonial weapons. After them were mounted guards in yellow waistcoats. The imperial chariot followed, drawn by eight matching horses with dazzling gold headdresses. Ten of the palace ministers surrounded the chariot at a leisurely pace. Behind were palace guards and eunuchs carrying various utensils which the Emperor might require during the journey. Last of all came the imperial guards armed with spears and bows and arrows. The accompanying princes, courtiers, imperial sons and nephews followed. Five hundred crack cavalry men brought up the rear.

Nothing unusual happened along the way. At regular intervals the eunuchs presented tea and refreshments to the Emperor. As the sun rose and the temperature rose with it, cooling teas and potions were also served.

Two hours later the column reached the gates leading to Chongzhen's tomb. The tomb was surrounded on three sides by mountains, while a stretch of level land lay to the south. Completed in recent years, its yellow tiles and crimson walls still looked new. Compared to the other Ming Tombs in the area it was imposing enough, except the young pines and cedars planted along the road seemed stunted and forlorn. The lords Ebilong and Feiyanggu sighed at the drabness of the bare yellow earth that covered the remains of Chongzhen as compared to the green-clad mounds of the other tombs nearby.

The sound of the beating wings of a bird in flight cut across Ebilong's thoughts. He looked up in time to see a white dove which one of the guards walking beside the imperial chariot let loose took to the sky. Ebilong urged his mount forward and apprehended the culprit.

"Careless fool!" he hissed at the man. Before he could continue another white dove flew up. This time it was released by a courtier beside Feiyanggu. Feiyanggu's usually smiling face darkened, and turning he scolded his colleague loudly:

"Have you gone mad? Startling His Majesty could cost you your head!"

Many of the guards and courtiers craned their necks at the commotion. The two men responsible seemed quite unconcerned. The offending courtier turned nonchalantly away declaring everything would be made clear in due course. Though everyone was curious, protocol forbade any further discussion. In the meantime the vanguard had halted. The imperial chariot moved forward a short distance, passed the pavilion in which the stone tablet was kept and stopped by Lengen Gate.

The princes and courtiers who had arrived ahead were already kneeling before the gate. The others who had accompanied the Emperor now joined their ranks. At the front of this assembly was Prince Jian, Jidu.

A while ago when he saw the two white doves, Jidu knew success was his, and he quietly thanked Heaven for its protection.

The Empire of Great Qing was safe, and his worries were over. Earlier the commander of the garrison guarding the tomb had reported the arrival of the imperial guards at the southwestern gate with an urgent message for the Emperor from the Empress Dowager. What could be so urgent, he wondered? Had the plot been discovered? He decided that was impossible. As the Emperor had not yet arrived, the commander was ordered to keep the imperial guard outside the grounds. Now that success was his, the doting Empress Dowager, who allowed her spoilt and wilful son to do whatever he pleased, would be completely helpless. In his elation he failed to notice two important men, Prince An and Suoni, were missing from the Emperor's entourage.

Jidu led the assembled princes and lords in a loud cry.

"Greetings to His Majesty!" Though the sound was somewhat ragged, rising here, falling there, echoing from one peak to the other, it was not lacking in enthusiasm. However, the curtains of the imperial chariot did not part. The assemblage exchanged looks of consternation.

"Greetings to His Majesty!" The cry went up a second time, more loudly than before. Still there was no movement from within the imperial chariot. Prince Jian was becoming impatient. Being the most highly placed and respected among the princes, all eyes turned upon him. It was up to him to move, and he made up his mind quickly. Inviting Prince Xun and several courtiers to accompany him, he approached the chariot bowing low. Jidu lifted the curtain of the chariot and saw the Emperor sitting inside. For a moment everything went black before his eyes. Jidu forced himself to be calm and peered closely into the gloom. The Emperor sat motionless, head bowed, his body twisted to one side and his right arm twisted awkwardly behind his back in an un-natural attitude. Prince Xun, stretching out a hand to try and find a breath or a pulse, turned ashen.

"The Emperor is dead!" he cried in a loud voice.

The assembled princes and courtiers were thunderstruck. A moment of ominous silence erupted into panic as they broke ranks and rushed toward the imperial chariot, stirring up a huge cloud of dust.

In the midst of confusion Prince Jian remained unruffled. Grim-faced, he shouted commands, ordering the imperial guards to form three protective rings around the imperial chariot so that the body of the dead Emperor was not disturbed. With one bound he mounted the steps in front of Lengen Gate.

His raspy voice cut through the turmoil like the sound of a muffled gong. The throng, seeing Prince Jian was about to speak, felt the situation was in control and quickly calmed down. They turned to Jidu, hoping for a decisive solution to this crisis.

Jidu immediately gathered together the courtiers, guards and eunuchs who had followed the Emperor's chariot that morning and questioned them closely,

"Was His Majesty in good health when he left the hunting lodge?" All the men agreed the Emperor was in good health but seemed listless. Jidu's tone turned severe, "His Majesty must have been assassinated en route," he pronounced heavily. Ebilong's mind suddenly cleared. He stepped forward and pointing at the guard who had released a white dove started to say, "My Lord, he...." But the courtier who had also released a dove cut him off,

"My Lord, Ebilong and Feiyanggu released two doves on the way!" This unexpected counter-attack took Ebilong and Feiyanggu by surprise. They stammered, unable to rebut. Prince Jian, frowning, shot them a sidelong glance and, in an equable tone, enquired, "Doves, you say? What doves?" The guard seized the opening and cut in,

"My Lord, they released doves! It must have been some kind of signal. I saw them, that's why they're blaming me!"

Though Ebilong and Feiyanggu were honest men, usually diffident in the presence of their betters, both defended themselves vociferously. Prince Jian shouted for quietness. "Among the four of you, two must be lying and have something to do with the Emperor's death. Guards! Take them away."

The four men were quickly taken into custody and spirited away in spite of their protests of innocence.

Jidu stood like a bronze lion on the steps above the throng. His grim eyes surveyed the princes and courtiers gathered before him, and he spoke in a tone that was both severe and sorrowful.

"His Majesty's untimely demise has come as a shock to us and is a tragic loss to Great Qing. At this time two things must be accomplished. An imperial funeral must be arranged and a new Emperor proclaimed. His Majesty has gone to his ancestors, leaving young sons. The Empress Dowager is in her dotage and unable to govern. Therefore the question of succession must be settled at once. Fortunately, all the princes and nobles are gathered here today. Therefore, I propose the Council of Nobles be convened immediately to deliberate this question. We will then present our decision to Her Majesty the Empress Dowager upon our return to the capital...."

He spoke on, full of confidence, buoyed up by the expressions of consent that surrounded him. They are a flock of sheep, he thought. He made a few more remarks touching on the succession, emphasizing the virtues of obeying Heaven and honouring ancestors. As he spoke he noticed a strange expression on those who stood closest to him. Several of his audience registered looks of consternation and even fear. He cut short his speech, concluding lamely, "...Today's commemorative ceremonies will have to be abandoned. My Lords, kindly wait in the side halls while the Council of Nobles...."

"Why should the ceremonies be stopped?" The voice that sounded to the left and behind him was pitched low, but clear and familiar. It sent a shiver down Jidu's spine. He was almost afraid to turn around, but he could not do otherwise.

Fulin stood smiling beside him and continued, "We have come here today expressly to honour the memory of the Emperor Chongzhen."

The Emperor was dressed in a plain robe and matching cap,

and a sword hung from his jade encrusted belt. Behind him were Prince Yuele, the palace ministers Suoni, Sukesaha and Aobai. All had changed into fresh garments. The dust on their hair and boots was the only evidence that they had arrived after a hard ride. As usual those who accompanied the Emperor were armed with swords.

The princes and lords, dazed by this swift succession of events, fell to their knees, shouting, "Long live the Emperor!" Their shouts were more ardent and rang in the air longer than ever before. Jidu fell on his knees with the others.

Fulin's expression was almost friendly when he spoke again. "We decided to play a prank. Therefore, someone else took our place in the chariot, while we and our guards travelled on horseback, intending to meet my lords here. However, these unexpected events occurred. Nevertheless, we are gratified that Prince Jian quickly took matters in hand. It is good to know we have such an able man about us. If, by chance, we should die unexpectedly, we will rest in peace knowing the affairs of state will be in Prince Jian's capable hands." He burst into laughter that seemed both unnatural and inappropriate to the occasion. His listeners were filled with suspicion and fear not knowing whether the Emperor was speaking the truth, or dealing in riddles.

The Emperor was clearly anxious to end the masquerade.

"We commend Prince Jian for his decisive actions. The persons responsible for this death must be among the guards and courtiers attending us. Let them all be apprehended for questioning. Prince Jian will personally investigate Ebilong and the three others. My Lords Sukesaha and Aobai will assist him. Leave us."

Sukesaha and Aobai approached the prince and bowed, inviting him to precede them. Prince Jian prostrated himself before the Emperor and, rising, left with his head held high. Meanwhile the courtiers and guards who had escorted the imperial chariot were quickly disarmed by the guards of Qianqing Gate and taken into custody.

Fulin turned his gaze upon Prince Xun, who blanched and trembled in spite of himself. Ignoring him, Fulin concluded in the same equable tones, "My Lords, you may withdraw until three quarters after the noon hour when the memorial services shall begin."

The ceremonies were conducted with great pomp and circumstance. The Emperor Shunzhi of Great Qing personally poured the ceremonial wine and made offerings to Chongzhen, the last Emperor of Ming. Meanwhile, twelve academicians were ordered to perform similar ceremonies before all the other twelve tombs of Ming Emperors. Furthermore, the Emperor commanded the number of tomb keepers to be increased, that repairs be undertaken and the cutting of trees in the vicinity forbidden.

It was only in the evening when he had returned to his bed chamber in the hunting lodge that Fulin was overcome with fatigue. A fatigue so deep that he had to prop himself against the doorjamb to prevent himself from falling. He slumped into a nearby chair, his limbs so heavy that he could barely move. More than the physical fatigue, he felt as though some part of him had been torn out. He sank into deep depression, and all he wished was to weep.

The facts of the matter were soon made known. The culprits were the guard and the courtier who had released the doves, acting in concert with certain bandits in the mountains nearby. Both men were executed. However, no confessions were presented to the Ministry of Justice. Thus the two went to their deaths without a word to offer a clue.

The eunuch Li Zhong who had been killed in the Emperor's place was buried with honours and his parents given a title. An only brother was also granted an education. Ebilong and Feiyanggu were also honoured.

It seemed that all is well that ends well.

Soon afterwards, for their misdeeds ten years earlier, the late Prince Xun (named Mandahai) and Prince Duanzhong (Bole) were stripped of all their titles. Their sons Changahdai and Chikshin were also deprived of titles they had inherited and reduced to mere lords. However, Prince Xun was a descendant of Prince Li (Daishan), and thus held a title in perpetuity. Therefore, by special decree, his title was bestowed upon Jieshu, who would henceforth be styled Prince Kang.

Prince Jian (Jidu) resigned his position at court a month afterwards claiming ill health and retired. Shortly afterwards he died. Rumours circulated that he had taken his own life but there was no proof. However, his funeral was not one befitting a prince. Also the Emperor's decision regarding the inheritance of his title was unduly delayed and eventually forgotten altogether.

Part 8

The cobblestones in front of Qianqing Gate sizzled under the blazing sun of the seventh month. There was not a breath of air. The duty room for members of the Imperial Hanlin Academy — the College of Literature — built against the towering walls of the palace, was stifling.

These quarters, situated to the left of Qianqing Gate, had only been completed a month ago. Henceforth, members of the Academy, with the highest literary degree of Hanlin, took turns being on duty, ready to consult with the Emperor at a moment's notice. This was a singular honour as princes and noblemen who came to the Hall of Supreme Harmony hoping for an audience were also made to cool their heels in similar surroundings on the other side of the gate. That the Hanlins were permitted to mingle with the aristocracy was an innovation.

Out of the three Hanlins present today, it was Xiong Cilu's first tour of duty while the other two Xu Yuanwen and Ye Fangai had taken their turns several times before. Since the beginning of summer, the Emperor seldom called upon them. At the moment Xu Yuanwen was seated at a small square table painting. Ye Fangai watched with interest, while Xiong Cilu sat on the kang reading and sipping tea. Xu Yuanwen rose and stretched. Muttering about the heat, he dofted his cap and laid it on the table. Though it was contrary to court protocol, Ye Fangai smirked but did not comment. Xiong Cilu did not notice it and the tranquillity of the room was not disturbed.

The door opened and in came Yuele, Prince An, who had just left an audience. The Hanlins quickly rose to their feet. Prince An seeing Xu Yuanwen with brush in hand bade him continue.

"Actually I have come to collect a debt," he said with a twinkle. Xu Yuanwen resumed his seat without prompting. He had even forgotten to put on his ceremonial cap.

"Actually, this unworthy scholar was making a painting expressly for My Lord," he replied in the same bantering tone.

"Ah, in that case, I shall just have a peek and leave you in peace," the prince stood behind the painter and peered over his shoulder. As he straightened his eyes met those of Xiong Cilu, and joining his hands asked, "And who might this be?"

"Examining editor of the Hanlin Academy, Xiong Cilu," Ye Fangai hurriedly made the introduction.

"Delighted! And of which examination?" From the moment he entered the room, Xiong Cilu found him familiar. Now he was certain. The man was none other than his erstwhile employer. The wealthy merchant Master Luo was actually a royal prince. Yet, why would a royal prince go to such lengths instead of employing a teacher openly? On the other hand Yuele was giving the impression that they had never met before. In the smile that was not a smile, and the hidden menace in his eyes, it was clear Yuele meant him to forget the year he had spent in his residence. That part of Xiong Cilu's history must never be mentioned. Before he could phrase an answer, Ye Fangai had already spoken for him, "My Lord, we are from the same year. Brother Cilu is a famous scholar of Daoism from Huguang." Yuele chuckled stroking his beard.

"The court needs wise men. Gentlemen, your futures are full of promise. See to it that you do not take the Emperor's interest in you for granted."

When Prince An had departed, Xu Yuanwen continued painting, while Ye Fangai, in an expansive mood, prattled about the Emperor's love of learning, averring that he was indeed a great monarch of the era.

Xu Yuanwen sighed. "Though the Emperor is wise and the prince is loyal and we are employed for the good of the state, yet there are those who privately grumble against us. The Emperor is constantly accused of favouring the Han and surrounding himself with southerners. Even building this room became a major undertaking. As for the rest you can imagine...."

Ye Fangai exclaimed, "How can that be?"

"The Emperor ordered this room to be built a long time ago. But the Council of Nobles raised objections. First it was said that scholars should not be given so much attention. Then it was said that permitting their presence within the inner sanctum of the palace posed many problems. The Emperor ordered the building three times and thrice it was blocked. Finally the Emperor lost his temper, and the council knuckled under." Xu Yuanwen who was frequently in consultation with the Emperor knew the details.

"You mean to say, they can block the Emperor's wishes?" Ye Fangai was incredulous.

"Ah, the council is a tradition that dates before the conquest. No one can touch it. I heard that the Emperor tried to abolish it a few years ago, but was forced to back down."

"What strange and wonderful things!" exclaimed Ye Fangai. He and Xu Yuanwen were both from Kunshan in Jiangsu, had both passed the imperial examinations in the same year, though they did not hold equal rank. However, Ye had been in the north a relatively short while and still found some of the Manchu traditions and codes hard to fathom.

"That's not all. Lately, Prince Kong's daughter has been given a title, actually made to check the forces in Guangxi; and Princess Heshuo was married to the son of Prince Pingnan in Guangdong. Although the match is of tremendous political importance, intended to keep Prince Pingxi (Wu Sangui) in line, the council delayed its approval until recently." Although Xu Yuanwen had lowered his voice, he did not intend to exclude Xiong Cilu from the conversation.

"You mean to say the princes and nobles are so ignorant and narrow-minded?" exclaimed Ye Fangai. He turned to Xiong Cilu and asked, "What do you think?" Xiong Cilu laid down his book and replied with a straight face, "We who study Daoism follow the teachings of great men. However, to be blind to one's faults is to block the path to true wisdom. To find fault in others, on the other hand, is to destroy the harmony between heaven and earth." Ye shot a helpless glance at Xu Yuanwen who responded with, "I told you to leave him in peace. You got what you deserved."

Ye chuckled. "We have a young pedant among us!" However both men understood Xiong Cilu's meaning and turned to other topics of conversation.

"His Majesty summons Xu Yuanwen, Ye Fangai, and Xiong Cilu!" The eunuch's call from outside startled the three men. They quickly straightened robes and caps and, led by the eunuch, passed over a white marble bridge, through Qianqing Gate and headed for the Qianqing Palace. Before long they were soaked with sweat, not only because of the summer heat but because of nervousness.

Since the memorial service for the Emperor Chongzhen the previous autumn the Emperor had become exceedingly quick tempered. There were constant wrangles with the Council of Nobles. The most recent quarrel had occurred the day before. For some unknown reason the Emperor had flown into a rage, and dismissed the minister of personnel Kerkun and the two Manchu vice ministers. However, the Han minister and two vice ministers were allowed to keep their posts. This was unheard of. For the Ministry of Personnel, which dealt with the appointment and removal of all the civil officials of the country, was the most critical of the six ministries and the Emperor's action had virtually turned it over to the Hans. The Manchu nobles and officials were in an uproar. Placed in an untenable position the Han ministers petitioned that Manchu officials be quickly appointed to the ministry.

The Emperor refused and ordered the minister to "perform his duty as usual". In this dispute, the Grand Secretariat and the Hanlin Academy, newly created by the Emperor, naturally sided with him. The Council of Nobles and the Manchu officials who controlled the other five ministries were not about to let sleeping dogs lie. Did the Emperor's summons today have anything to do with these matters? The Hanlins who were new at court found themselves caught between the opposing sides. What should they do? In their mind's eye they already saw the un-natural red glow of ill-suppressed rage on Fulin's over sensitive face....

As they approached the great sweep of steps leading up to the terrace before Qianqing Palace, with its massive upward sweeping eaves, the three Hanlins trembled in their boots. Guards armed with broad swords lined the path, twenty paces apart all the way from the gate.

The three men held their breath as they entered the main hall where the throne stood. They kept their eyes on the floor not knowing whether the Emperor was present. Instead they were quickly led into the west chamber. The eunuch lifted the curtain that hung in the doorway, and fragrance of many flowers enveloped them. The three men stepped over the threshold and the heat of summer was left behind. Lifting their heads slightly they caught a glimpse of a dashing young scholar seated upon the kang. Could this be the Emperor? It had to be. They sank to their knees and in a loud voice cried in unison, "Your Majesty's servants, Xu Yuanwen, Ye Fangai and Xiong Cilu offer their greetings." They rose, moved closer to the kang and knelt again on the red carpet, waiting for the Emperor to speak.

The Emperor was bare-headed. Instead of the dragon robes, he wore a light summer tunic over a pale-coloured cassock. On his bare feet were a pair of straw sandals made in the style popular in the south. His jet black hair, eyebrows and moist eyes contrasted with the palour of his face. In his hand he held a folding fan painted with landscapes. To the three learned men, he was the epitome of the wealthy southern gentleman of learning. The Emperor smiled. "Rise, gentlemen. We have summoned you because you share our love of books. In our leisure, we have summoned you to view our library and to recommend what we miss."

Fulin slid off the kang and gestured the others to follow him. He led the way to the main hall and pointed out the bookcases that lined three walls. Xu Yuanwen and his companions examined their contents avidly. Not only were therc the writings of the sages, scriptures and histories, but also poetry, mythology and novels. Between the bookcases stood display cases in which were kept a dazzling array of antiques; artifacts of all sorts; seals carved from semi-precious stones of every hue, size and shape. The feet of the bookcases and display cases were garlanded with orchids of white, pale pink, yellow and green, mixed with jasmine whose delicate perfume filled the room. The three Hanlins were awed by everything they saw.

Fulin beamed at their expressions of surprise and pleasure. He led them back to the west chamber and having offered them tea and seats said, "At the collapse of Ming and the beginning of the present dynasty there were many years of turmoil. During that time a great many books were scattered among the people. It would be a great pity if they were lost. Though we have decreed scholars of all provinces to help locate these treasures, and there have been some notable finds, we fear a great many are still unaccounted for. Therefore it is our wish that you jot down titles that are missing from our library, that we may make a special effort at finding them."

Xu Yuanwen and his companions quickly complied and, using the little tea tables which were close at hand, each wrote down a number of titles for the Emperor. The Emperor scanned the lists with interest and asked specific questions about unfamiliar works and their authors. Though they were monarch and vassal, with the establishment of a common interest the barrier of caste disappeared and the conversation became unrestrained.

The Hanlins concluded that this was a man intent on ruling with culture instead of force. They were greatly encouraged. After a while they felt it was appropriate to end, when the Emperor asked quite casually, "They say the eyes of an outsider are often more observant than those who are closely involved. You gentlemen are all new at court. In your view which of the courtiers is the most able and which are unworthy of their positions? And are our policies suitable to the times?"

The Hanlins exchanged looks of dismay. None were willing to speak; not from lack of opinion, but from lack of confidence. For a careless word could cost someone his future and earn the speaker undying hatred. Ye Fangai, being quick witted, spoke for the rest: "We thank Your Majesty for his trust regarding such weighty matters. However, your servants are new to court and lack knowledge."

Smiling, Fulin turned to another topic.

"Of late we hear many intellectual associations have been formed. Is this true?" Xu Yuanwen replied, "These associations are a legacy of the Ming Dynasty." Xiong Cilu added, "They have existed since long before the year of Tianqi."

"We believe the Shenjiao and Tongsheng Associations are the most popular. Do you gentlemen belong to such an association?"

All three replied in the negative. Fulin had no further questions. Still smiling cordially, he dismissed them.

The three Hanlins prostrated themselves, rose one after the other and backed their way out the door.

In accordance with court protocol they traversed the corridor in a southerly direction at a stately gait. As they reached Qianqing Gate they were halted by a eunuch hurrying up from behind.

"Xu Yuanwen is summoned!" he cried. Xu Yuanwen exchanged a look with his two colleagues, turned and followed the eunuch back. The other two looked at each other in puzzlement, but the questions that rose in their minds could not be spoken. They continued back to the duty room.

When Xu Yuanwen re-entered the Presence another official was seated with the Emperor. He was Wang Xi, Vice Minister of

Rites and also an academician in charge of the Hanlin Academy. As such he was Xu Yuanwen's immediate superior. Fulin said, smiling, "We are in the mood for conversation. We are about to visit Wanshan Hall to discuss scriptures with the great monk Yulin. You gentlemen shall accompany us."

Thus, the Emperor borne in a sedan chair and followed on foot by the two scholars and a swarm of eunuchs carrying books and scrolls went out in the summer sun. Meanwhile at the West Gardens, the monk Yulin Tongxiu and his disciple Maoxi Sheng waited on their knees outside the hall.

After the usual pleasantries had been exchanged, Yulin and the Emperor took their seats. Wang Xi and Xu Yuanwen stood on either side of the Emperor while Maoxi stood behind his master. The monk's study was a deep, cool room with tall beams, simply furnished but immaculate. It was a room filled with the shadows of pine and the scent of tea — a place for contemplation where worldly desires melt away. On a long table beside Yulin were piled the books and scrolls that the eunuchs had brought.

"Previously we showed you the books that we read in our youth. The present collection is what has been occupying us of late," said Fulin.

Yulin glanced at the books casually and selected a volume comprising two hundred essays written by candidates who sat the imperial examinations during the Ming era.

"What is the value of reading this, Your Majesty?" he asked. Fulin chuckled.

"The old monk perhaps is not aware that we have personally conducted examinations in which we also personally read the treatises. We have already personally selected three Zhuangyuans. This is the new Zhuangyuan, Xu Yuanwen."

Xu Yuanwen stepped forward and bowed deeply to the aged monk. Yulin quickly rose to return the salutation, then joining his hands scrutinized the scholar. Turning to the Emperor he said, "Your Majesty is to be congratulated for his choice." Fulin sighed, "Too many brilliant minds are buried in obscurity while unworthy ones find fame. Such is the mischance of fate." Yulin said, "Me thinks the Monarch can manipulate destiny. Since the Emperor recognizes a man of brilliance why not use him to advantage?"

Fulin's face clouded. Even a simple thing like building a duty room for the Hanlin required a superhuman effort. The storm of protest that raising every man of learning to a position of responsibility would be unimaginable. Nevertheless he forced himself to agree with the aged monk.

The conversation turned to history, literature and drama. Xu Yuanwen listened with interest. He was surprised how widely read the Emperor was, despite the isolation in which he lived.

The conversation shifted to the old monk's imminent departure for his monastery. The Emperor was visibly dismayed, though he forced a smile and tried to sound cheerful saying, "Old monk, you've promised to return on our thirtieth birthday. That is not too far away. However, Monk Baoen has promised to come to my fortieth birthday. I don't think I can wait that long." Yulin comforted him saying, "Your Majesty will live a thousand years. Wherefore such gloomy thoughts?" Fulin pinched his own cheek and replied, "This flesh seems firm enough, yet the body is as withered as old wood. Such a body cannot last long."

"Your Majesty is overworked. Rest is essential. We beg Your Majesty to take care of himself for the sake of his people," the old monk said earnestly. The monk's words seemed to rouse more gloomy thoughts. After a pause Fulin said in a low voice, "The love of wealth and women are the two desires of mankind hardest to shake off. We are not concerned with the acquisition of wealth, and even the love of women has diminished to nothingness." He bit his lip before adding, "If it were not for the Empress Dowager, we would gladly follow the old monk to the monastery."

Those present were shocked. Wang Xi and Xu Yuanwen were

at a loss for comment. However, Yulin Tongxiu was quick to respond.

"If an ordinary mortal abandons all for the monastic life it is no more than an accident of fate. However, the Buddha moves in mysterious ways. He assumes many forms, now as a ruler of the heavens, now as a monarch on earth. In this incarnation, in order to fulfil his duty as protector of the land and its people, he must also accept the troubles that plague mankind. If such a being were to abandon all in pursuit of tranquillity, his act of selfishness will gain him nothing. Nirvana will be denied him. Thus, if the Emperor does not fulfil his duty, who is there to perform it on his behalf? Therefore it is hoped that Your Majesty would abandon such unworthy notions."

Since Shunzhi had taken it up, Buddhism made great strides within the capital. With the financial support of the imperial family, temples and other places of worship began to proliferate. The influence of Buddhism spread. Many famous monks such as Yulin were drawn into the Emperor's inner circle. These learned men, who were widely read, shared many of Shunzhi's interests. Since Shunzhi was also fond of Han culture he was easily influenced. Tang Jo-Wang's admonition that monks were not to be trusted was quickly forgotten.

There was another reason for Fulin's faith. Had he been content to be an ordinary ruler, wallowing in decadence, he would have led an untroubled life. However, he was clever and ambitious, intent on making something of his life, but hemmed in by the special historical conditions that prevailed at the beginning of a dynasty. The pain and despair he experienced made the monastic life attractive.

As a monk of renown, Yulin Tongxiu would be committing a grave misdeed if he encouraged the Emperor to abandon the crown. Therefore he had counselled against it as befitting his title of Imperial Teacher. Shunzhi nodded his agreement, but would not let the matter drop.

"If we do not enter the monastic life, would the old monk accept us as disciple instead?''

"How would that be appropriate?'' Yulin was unprepared for such a proposal.

"It is hoped the old monk will disregard our station and treat us as he would his disciple Maoxi.''

"In that case ... this old monk must bow to Your Majesty's wishes.'' Yulin agreed reluctantly, afraid that the headstrong young Emperor might propose something more difficult to deal with. Besides, having an emperor as disciple would be a glorious achievement for Buddhism.

"Then, the Master must give us a name.'' Yulin tried to put that request aside, but Fulin would not let him off. Finally when the old monk took up his brush and was about to write a name, Fulin sighed from the depths of his soul and said sadly, "The name that the Master choses for us must be the ugliest....'' Wang Xi and Xu Yuanwen, watching the shifting lights in their monarch's eyes and wondering what was expected of two scholarly companions, were afraid to interfere in any way.

Yulin wrote a dozen characters which he handed to Fulin for approval. He chose the character "*chi*'' meaning "foolish'' to be preceded by the character "*xing*''. Thus his Buddhist name would be Xingchi, meaning an act of foolishness.

Fulin next insisted upon performing the usual obeisance between master and disciple. The old monk would not agree. This was an opportunity for the two courtiers to intercede, for such an act would be against all the rules of protocol. Fulin was forced to back down, however, he said to Maoxi, "Hence forth I shall call you my Buddhist brother.''

When Fulin claimed he had lost interest in women, he did not include Lady Dongeh in that statement.

Lady Dongeh had been bed-ridden ever since she took ill in the spring of that year. Though the imperial physician prescribed all sorts of drafts and potions there was no sign of recovery. Fulin visited her daily at Chengqian Palace. The sight of Black

Pearl wasting away pained him. The imperial physician had hinted that it was only a question of time, but Fulin could not accept the fact that she would one day leave him. Perhaps it was the thought of losing Black Pearl that also inspired the idea of entering a monastery.

After leaving the monk, he went straight to Chengqian Palace to visit Black Pearl. Although he had been happy in the company of his scholars and monks, their discussions had also left him with a vague melancholy. If Black Pearl was not ill she would comfort him and give him peace.

The last rays of twilight brushed the palace with a red glow that was invigorating yet not untinged with foreboding. Fulin stopped the servants from announcing him as he crossed the threshold of Chengqian Gate. He rounded the carved screen wall, crossed the terrace, and as he approached the front hall, he was greeted by the sound of a zither mingled with the scent of blooming tuberoses. He stopped, his pulse racing. For it could only be Black Pearl. No one else played the zither. She was better!

Fulin quickened his steps. The sound of the zither became clearer, leading him on, gently drawing him into another realm ... a realm of moonlight ... shooting stars ... summer dew ... and autumn frost. As he approached the bed chamber the music wrapped him in a gossamer of sound. He stopped and gave himself up to its gentle blandishments.

Suddenly the music changed. A series of angry, crashing chords sounded like thunder and lightning before a storm. Fulin was surprised that the dainty fingers of his Black Pearl could produce such violent sounds. With a loud twang as though something heavy had struck the strings the music ended. In its place was the sound of weeping, heart-rending in its despair. Fulin rushed into the room.

A long horizontal scroll hung on the north wall. Under it was an altar on which offerings of seasonal fruits and nuts had been placed. Before the altar was a long, low black lacquered table on which lay Black Pearl's favourite zither which she called Spring Breeze. Black Pearl was slumped across its strings, tears trickling silently down her cheeks. The sound of weeping Fulin heard came from the serving maid Rongniu kneeling beside her mistress. The bowl of medicine had slid from her hands and smashed on the ground.

Fulin rushed to Black Pearl in a state of near panic and gathered her up in his arms. She turned to him. This time she did not try to kneel though he had forbidden that ceremony, nor did she essay the smile that smote the hearts of all who saw it. Instead she clung to him and wept hysterically. Fulin had never seen her like this before. He held her close, stroking her glistening black tresses, murmuring comforting words in a halting whisper. The light, brittle bundle of bones he held in his arms sent a stab of pain through him. He lowered his head and pressed his cheek against her tear-streaked face. Black Pearl suddenly looked up at him and asked, "What is the matter with you?"

Fulin forced a smile.

"I should ask that question...."

"I..." Black Pearl bit her lip, and her gaunt face dimpled. "I am sad.... I can't bear to be without you...." Fulin had never heard her express her feelings so boldly. The rush of warmth they evoked caused his eyes to mist.

"Is it because someone told you we entertained the notion of entering a monastery?" he asked huskily.

"Enter a monastery?" Black Pearl's eyes went wide. She dashed the tears from her face with one hand while the other tightened its grip on Fulin's arm.

"...Why?" she gasped through trembling lips.

"There's nothing to worry about," Fulin comforted. "I've only taken a teacher and received a religious name. That's all."

"You're ... tired of us?" Black Pearl sighed and the tears fell afresh.

"Don't you know how bitter and miserable I am?" Fulin whispered, head bowed. "Perhaps only a monastery will give me peace." Black Pearl gazed at him dully. Rongniu quietly picked up the shards of the broken bowl and withdrew.

Fulin rose to his feet with a long sigh. Slowly he lifted his face, forcing back tears that were on the verge of falling. Or perhaps his gaze pierced the painted ceiling to touch the infinite arch of the sky beyond. There was an unusual melancholy in his voice when he spoke, so that one was not sure whether he was quoting poetry or speaking from the heart. "The heavens overshadow us, and the earth gives us life. We have ambition. We try to be just. We dare not compare ourselves to our august ancestors, but we aspire to being at least an equal of the founders of Tang and Ming. But our hopes are constantly dashed. Every step we take is fraught with difficulty. Still we go on, pushing a huge rock uphill. The hill keeps getting higher ... and steeper.... I am weary ... I can't push any more.... It's too heavy ... too heavy...."

Black Pearl stood shivering like a sapling in a storm after the tears. Fulin clutched her impulsively to him.

"Why do you have to be ill?" he cried. "I need you. Only you can help me push that rock up the mountain. Without you, I'm lost ... Black Pearl...."

Black Pearl's tiny hand traced the outline of Fulin's trembling lips and his burning eyes.

"Don't ... Your Majesty," she whispered. "There is always Her Majesty the Empress Dowager to support you...."

"But...." Fulin released Black Pearl as abruptly as he had embraced her. His voice rose to almost a scream. "In her heart she will always despise me.... I remember the things she said last summer ... her tone of voice ... the look in her eyes.... Oh, to think I could be so cowardly ... so weak! It was shameful! Something I would never be able to atone. How would I have the gall to discuss affairs of state with the Imperial Mother now!" He clutched his head between two large hands and slumped onto the low divan. His whole body shrivelled with pain.

Instantly Black Pearl shook off her own misery. She gently gathered Fulin into her arms, caressing his head, shoulders and back, murmuring softly in his ear less like a lover than a mother comforting an ailing child.

"Lately I've been thinking about my childhood. When I was six years of age my parents took me to the south. My mother visited her family in Suzhou with me. I was delighted at the prospect of meeting my cousins. However they greeted me with disdain, calling me a half-bred and a vixen. Then they got together and beat me. I complained to my mother, and she was more upset than I, for my grandparents had disowned her for having married a Manchu, saying she had dishonoured the family name and demanded her death.... When we returned to the capital my father introduced me to his family, and again my Manchu cousins insulted me and I got another beating...." Black Pearl's voice broke. Evidently the memory of these childhood hurts remained fresh in her mind. She paused until she was calm again before she continued. "...I was furious. My father was a hero in the wars. My mother was an accomplished woman who wrote poetry, painted and played the zither. They were a perfect match, and I was the jewel in their crown. I vowed then, that I would become an extraordinary woman and win the respect of my father's Manchu relatives as well as my mother's Han family.

"When I was grown, I came to understand the need to combine the courage and warlike nature of my father's ancestry with the learned, cultured ways of my mother's race. I became convinced that the merging of military feats with a civilized rule would produce the sword that will bring prosperity to Great Qing and lasting peace and prosperity to all under Heaven."

Fulin listened intently, hanging upon her every word. Black Pearl had never mentioned the unhappy experiences of her childhood before. He was at a loss to find a reason for these revelations now. He liked Black Pearl's ideas which were quite above the ordinary. Black Pearl seemed to sense his thoughts. Her bony fingers glided ever so lightly across his face, and her voice dropped even lower.

"I would not dare say I have the same ambitions as Your Majesty, but at least I understand all that Your Majesty hopes to accomplish. And I believe Your Majesty has read the situation of the world correctly, and your deeds are not contrary to the will of heaven and earth. If I can contribute a little to your endeavours, I'll die content...."

Watching her, Fulin's despondency slowly vanished. Deep in his fathomless orbs was a glint of hope. "...We will not let you leave us..." he said. Black Pearl was moved to quote a line of poetry, and seeing its effect upon Fulin quickly explained, "Though we remain together a hundred years, there will come a day when we must part. Your Majesty must accept the inevitable or else what comfort would the study of scriptures bring?" Fulin pondered that a moment and replied, "You and I will be husband and wife in life, after life, for all eternity." Black Pearl responded with a wistful smile. Turning to the scroll on the wall, Fulin remarked, "Isn't this called *Summoning the Gods*? Is it hanging there as decoration or is it for worship?"

The painting was a masterpiece of elegant simplicity. In the lower right-hand corner a lady in court dress is seen leaning against a finely carved balustrade. Her upward tilted face is suffused with hope and longing. The middle of the painting is blank, without a single brush-stroke or the least hint of colour, signifying the vastness of the universe. Finally, a crescent moon is seen through clouds in the upper left-hand corner. There is a feeling of space and loneliness about the picture.

Black Pearl replied, "A little of each."

"Is the Lady of the Palace summoning the Lady of the Moon, or is it the vice versa?"

"I suppose there is a little of both as well," Black Pearl responded uncertainly. Fulin did not catch the note of hesitation, and still gazing at the picture remarked, "The lady in the picture resembles you."

"Do you think so?" Black Pearl tried to sound casual, but ducked her head nevertheless.

"Are you better today? I heard you playing when I arrived."

"In the afternoon I did feel better, and had them hang up the scroll and played a tune called *Lament of the Moon*."

"That's not quite true. It was *Lament of the Moon* to begin with, but what happened afterwards? Those stormy chords certainly did not belong...."

"That is called *Ode to a Storm*," Black Pearl supplied. "My teacher taught it to me a long time ago."

"Why did you burst into tears before you finished?" Fulin pressed.

Black Pearl did not have the heart to tell him the truth. In the afternoon she had felt better and wanted to play the zither to pass the time and to test her own stamina. However, she had no sooner begun the *Ode to a Storm* when she was overcome with weakness. Her head spun, she broke into a sweat, and blackness threatened to engulf her. She almost swooned. She knew instinctively that there was little hope for her. In despair she had pushed aside the bowl of medicine Rongniu had brought her and burst into tears.

No. She would not tell him. She had glimpsed the wounds of his heart and soul, and she was determined not to add to his agony. However, there were so many things she wanted to tell him; so much she wanted to leave with him. He was the only man she loved. They had shared so much, weathered so many storms. When they first met they were like a pair of phoenixes flying wing to wing in the sun. They had such dreams. Then came the storms that battered them. Now she was on the brink of death. Would he have the courage to fly alone?

Black Pearl cupped Fulin's face tenderly between her hands, and her tearful eyes traced every line of his face. With all her flagging will she summoned up a smile and breathed a line from a poem, "To die before a warrior wins his battle, always drenches the hero with tears of grief...." Fulin's throat constricted as he clasped his lover, friend and the only wife in his heart, unable to force words out his trembling lips. Black Pearl's icy fingers twined themselves round his. In a barely audible voice she whispered, "If breath fails, where should the body lie?"

Fulin held her in his arms like a child, his cheek pressed tight against hers. A sob rose in his throat but he held it down with all his strength. When he first began studying the Buddhist scriptures and encouraged Black Pearl to do likewise she often questioned him with that quotation. At first he used to brush it aside with a smile. Later when she became ill he avoided it. Now he was too filled with misery to answer.

2

Shunzhi issued a decree calling upon physicians from across the land to come to the capital to heal the Precious Concubine. The Emperor also ordered sacrifices to the gods for the Precious Concubine's recovery. To this end, an amnesty was granted to all prisoners except those convicted of the ten most grievous crimes. But it was all in vain. The Precious Concubine remained gravely ill.

In desperation, Fulin made a pilgrimage to the Temple of the Azure Clouds in the Western Hills to pray for her recovery. It was the first time he had done this since the Empress Dowager's illness.

The Temple of the Azure Clouds, floating like a mirage above the dark green of pine and cedar, was an oasis of peace. The sweet scent of osmanthus filled the mid-autumn air.

Fulin prayed in the main hall. The abbot respectfully handed him a bundle of joss sticks, which he held to the eternal flame that burned day and night before the altar. The sticks caught in tiny puff of smoke. Clutching them, Fulin lifted his eyes devoutly to the kindly face of the Buddha looming over him.

Suddenly, the joss sticks sputtered brightly and went out. At that moment a eunuch rushed in and throwing himself on his knees gasped, "Your Majesty, the Precious Concubine is dying."

Fulin went pale. He thrust the joss sticks into the nearest incense burner and without a word strode quickly out of the hall and went half leaping, half running down the long, interminable flight of steps. His attendants scurried after him as best they could. He shunned the chariot, but grabbed the reins from one of his startled guards and leaped into the saddle. With a flick of the rein he urged the jet black steed into a gallop before his attendants realized what was happening.

The chief eunuch, flapping his arms in a panic, shouted, "What are you idiots gawking at! Follow him!"

For a eunuch to speak so rudely at the imperial guards was a serious breach of decorum. However, no one was concerned with those niceties now. The guards leaped into their saddles and followed. A black stallion streaked down the road leading from the Western Hills, followed by a group of horsemen who kicked up a cloud of dust that could be seen for miles, scattering people and animals in their path, trampling others. It was only when the heavily armed cavalry, travelling slower than the rest passed, that the people realized it was the Emperor, and quickly sank to their knees along the way.

The guards finally caught up with Fulin at Xizhi Gate where the gate keeper, not recognizing Fulin, would not allow him to pass without paying the toll. Fulin lashed out with his whip, preparing to charge through when his guards drew up, shouting, "Make way for His Majesty the Emperor!"

The gate keeper fell to his knees in confusion, but he had already been forgotten. Fulin was intent on rushing into the city. The guards had taken charge of the situation in the meantime, and went thundering down the street crying, "Make way for the Emperor," clearing the path for him.

Fulin was oblivious of all this. Only one notion stuck in his mind. Quick.... Quick.... He must see her again ... even if it was to be for the last time....

The city gate and archways flew by unnoticed. Both stallion and rider were soaked with sweat. The Emperor rode like a mad man, pressing his mount relentlessly, dashing the sweat from his brows when his vision blurred.

Finally he reached the entrance to the Forbidden City where everyone must dismount. The guards had stopped, preparing to dismount when, with a crack of the whip, the Emperor galloped past, his body pressed tight against the back of his horse.

Fulin had lost his ability to react to his surroundings. Instinct guided horse and rider through the maze of lanes and gardens. For over two centuries since the Emperor Yongle of Ming began building this massive group of palaces, no one dared bring a horse within the precincts of its yellow-tiled roofs and crimson walls.

Fulin was only conscious of the wind, the hoof beats and his own inner voice shrieking faster! Faster! Faster!

Chengqian Gate flew past. The startled faces of eunuchs and serving maids blurred. Fulin leaped from the saddle. As the quivering legs of his mount buckled. Fulin dashed inside.

Ah, there she lay, waiting for him as she promised. Hadn't she bade him not to be late? He rushed to her, but someone blocked his way. Who would dare!

Through a haze he recognized his mother, but her features were indistinct. He had the impression that her face was white as chalk, with two curious red patches on it. He had no time to think about those things now. He wanted to speak to Black Pearl. Again the Empress Dowager barred his way.

In a hoarse whisper she said, "Imperial Son, you are too late...."

Fulin could not grasp what she said. His eyes widened first at his mother, then at her. He pushed past the ladies that crowded around him, taking one step at a time like a sleepwalker ... until suddenly he threw himself upon her. He reached out a hand to cover her nose and mouth and let out a wail for there was no breath. Then another shriek tore out of him, like the agonized cry of a wounded beast. Blood spurted from his mouth, and he fell backwards, unconscious.

The ladies who had come to Chengqian Palace to weep for the Precious Concubine swarmed around the Emperor, rubbing his temples and chest. Only the Empress Dowager remained calm. Drying her eyes, she ordered the ladies to withdraw and the eunuchs to carry the unconscious Emperor to a chaise. The imperial physician was summoned and she composed herself to wait by her son's side.

The same physician who had attended the Precious Concubine when she breathed her last quickly returned. Meanwhile the other ladies had congregated in an adjoining chamber straining to hear what was said. The physician's face turned the colour of parchment when he saw the Emperor. He wobbled forward on his knees and, desperately controlling his breathing that was all out of rhythm, pressed three finger-tips on Fulin's wrist searching for a pulse. A moment later, with head bowed he reported to the Empress Dowager, "Your Majesty, the Emperor has suffered a severe shock. I will prescribe a cooling draught which will help His Majesty. Your Majesty need have no fears."

The Empress Dowager was relieved. As though the physician's departure was a signal, the ladies gathered in the adjoining room again burst out wailing. The Empress came into the room and, seeing the Emperor still unconscious, asked the Empress Dowager whether he should be moved to the Hall of Mental Cultivation.

The Empress Dowager's distracted gaze slid past the Empress as she shook her head.

"But there is so much confusion here.... And Sister Dongeh's ... still here.... It might not be proper...." The Empress bowed her head unable to finish.

"You ... don't understand ..." sighed the Empress Dowager. She turned away. No one understood her son better than she. She knew the moment he came to, he would want to see his Black Pearl. Even if he were taken from the room, he would insist on returning, and woe betide whoever tried to stop him. She knew that he would not hesitate to put whoever got in his way to death. She knew his passionate nature needed release, or his deep love for Black Pearl and his loss would drive him mad.

The Empress Dowager called Sumalagu to her and ordered her to find four stout serving maids and four strong eunuchs to watch the Emperor's every move. If anything untoward transpired she would have their heads.

The Empress watched the Empress Dowager making these arrangements without any understanding.

"Imperial Mother, what are you...?"

"Don't ask," the Empress Dowager sniffled. She covered her nose and mouth with her handkerchief to stifle her sobs. "You will know in due course."

The Empress Dowager expected a wild exhibition of emotion from Fulin, but she did not foresee its violence.

He woke quietly, as though he had been in a deep sleep. The room was bathed in the reddish glow of twilight, in which his mother's face floated, warm and loving.

"Imperial Mother, what are we doing here?" He tried to push himself up but his mother held him down. He fell back, too tired to move.

"Am I sick?" he asked. "I am sore all over and so weak.... Imperial Mother, I had a terrifying dream.... I was trying to get back from somewhere ... but when I finally reached Chengqian Palace ... Black Pearl had already gone...."

The Empress Dowager turned away and pretended to pick something up from the floor.

"Imperial Mother, they say everything in dreams is turned around. So if I dreamed she was dead, then it means she lives.... She will get better...." The Empress Dowager's shoulders quivered. Though her back was turned, it was clear she was weeping.

"Imperial Mother, what is the matter? Let's go together to Chengqian Palace. Black Pearl will cheer you up."

The Empress Dowager could contain herself no longer and quickly left. Soft sounds of weeping filled the room. The Empress, who had been standing at the head of the chaise where the Emperor lay, went round to the other end. She gazed down at Fulin through tear-reddened eyes.

"Has Your Majesty forgotten? This is Chengqian Palace...."

Fulin pushed himself up to a sitting position.

"What are you saying? This is the Hall of Mental Cultivation...." The Empress hid her face and moved away. Fulin suspiciously examined the chaise he lay on, and then looked around him. His brain was like a slow grinding mill-stone. He looked at the ladies gathered silently in the room. Finally his gaze fastened on the painting on the wall. He remembered it was a masterpiece of the Ming Dynasty called *Summoning the Gods*.

Suddenly his befogged mind cleared. He shivered violently as everything came back to him. His face became deadly pale and strange lights flickered in the depths of his eyes. He got to his feet and walked with unfaltering steps toward the bed chamber, not at all like a sick man.

Everyone watched him fearfully, but no one tried to stop him. The eight serving maids and eunuchs followed close on his heels. No one dared to speak, for the murderous expression on his face precluded any attempt at solicitude. Black Pearl looked as though she were alive, only more quiet, more peaceful. There was even the faintest wisp of a smile lingering at the corners of her mouth as though she was pleased to find release at last. She had become an exquisitely carved statue of white jade, so pure and breath-takingly lovely that it brought one to one's knees. Fulin stood over her for a long while. Finally he knelt and taking her two tiny hands folded on her breast pressed them to his face and bathed them with tears. He folded them on her breast and whispered, "Black Pearl ... my black Pearl ... wait for me...."

He calmly drew the jewel-encrusted dagger from his scabbard, held it up as though to show his Black Pearl his determination to die, and aimed its point at his throat.

The throng gathered in the doorway let out a terrified scream. The Empress Dowager and the Empress rushed toward him. However, it was one of the eunuchs who reached him in the nick of time. Perhaps, Fulin's movements were too deliberate. The blade was quickly wrestled from his grasp. Two of the hefty serving maids wrapped their arms around him and held him fast.

"Imperial Son, you must not act foolishly..." gasped the Empress Dowager.

"Your Majesty ... you mustn't ..." the Empress shouted at the same time.

However none of their words penetrated. Fulin's aborted attempt at suicide turned to rage. A wild burst of strength surged through him. He threw off the serving maids who held him and aimed a swift kick at the eunuch closest to him.

"I will kill whoever tries to stop me on the spot!" he roared. "I do not wish to live...." He ducked his head and ran for the wall. The eunuchs and serving maids threw themselves upon him once more.

The room was a bedlam of cries and lamentations. Fulin struggled free of his captors and made another attempt. This time the Empress Dowager threw herself in his path.

"Fulin," she cried, "kill me first!"

Fulin was stopped in his tracks. Ever since he could remember, no one ever addressed him by name. Now his grief-stricken mother standing before him, speaking to him thus, shocked him into awareness. Reason sparked in the depths of his eyes.

"Shall I pour ice water over your head again?" the Empress Dowager demanded angrily. A shiver ran up Fulin's spine, and he crumpled to his knees.

The Empress Dowager slumped into a chair, breathing hard.

When she had regained her composure, she forced herself to speak in her usually placid voice though with a noticeable tremour.

"Even at the end Black Pearl thought of you. Her last wish was that you should accept her going as the will of Heaven; that you should curb your grief for the sake of the nation and the great work of the ancestors you have inherited. You, however, have placed private feelings above all else. How can you face her!"

The Empress came forward and, kneeling beside the Emperor, whispered, "At the end, our Sister Dongeh insisted she did not regret being called away as much as it did not allow her time to repay the munificence of the Emperor and the Empress Dowager. She was troubled that grief might do injury to Her Majesty's health even at the last moment.... Your Majesty too must bear that in mind...." The other ladies also gathered around the Emperor and the Empress Dowager, entreating His Majesty to restrain himself from any rash acts for the sake of his mother and the memory of the departed Precious Concubine. Fulin wavered on his knees in a semi-conscious state and finally crumpled in a swoon.

That night, lights burned all night in the Forbidden City. As Fulin refused to leave Chengqian Palace, the Empress Dowager and the Empress also remained there, while the other ladies returned to their own palaces to light joss sticks and pray for the Emperor's safety.

During the next two days and nights twenty-four stout serving maids and eunuchs took turns guarding the Emperor to prevent any further attempts at suicide. Anything that might be used to harm himself, and even ornaments such as vases and clocks, were removed. Nothing was left to chance. Perhaps it was due to the Empress Dowager's gentle reminders, or the effect of increasingly potent doses of tranquilizing drugs the imperial physician administered, that on the third day Fulin fell into a deep sleep. The Empress Dowager, Empress and the other ladies were then given a respite to rest also.

The Empress Dowager was too exhausted to sleep. The events of the previous days awoke memories of her husband, Fulin's father. Abahai loved her older sister, the imperial concubine Lady Chen. When Lady Chen died he was beside himself with grief. Six months later he would still burst into tears whenever he passed the place where Lady Chen had lived. He became despondent and pined away. A year later he was dead. Now the son reminded her of the father. Both were men of vision, but both were also romantics. It was this flaw that led to the father's doom.

The Empress Dowager was genuinely fond of both her older sister, Lady Chen, and Black Pearl whom she had adopted as a spiritual daughter. Yet she could not help also resenting them. For the former had alienated the affections of her husband, and the latter captured the heart of her son. However, the Empress Dowager was capable of putting personal feelings in the right perspective. Therefore when she returned to Chengqian Palace, she knew exactly what she must do.

Fulin had moved into the main hall of Chengqian Palace. According to custom, the main hall of the palace was a reception room, not intended as living quarters. However, that was overlooked to comply with the Emperor's wishes. Fulin, in a weakened state, reclined on his couch. The Empress, and the ladies Shuhui, Kang, and Ke who kept him company reminiscenced about Lady Dongeh's goodness. At least one or two dabbed at crocodile tears.

The Emperor and the ladies rose as the Empress Dowager entered the room. She seated herself in a square-backed chair beside the couch. Fulin quickly went down on his knees before his mother.

"Imperial Mother, forgive your worthless son's foolish behaviour. However, I have one wish which I hope the Imperial Mother will not deny."

Seeing that he was more himself, the Empress Dowager replied gently, "So long as the wish is reasonable and not contrary to protocol it shall be granted."

"Your son wishes to bury Black Pearl with the full honours of an empress," Fulin blurted.

The room sank into shocked silence. The ladies bowed their heads, unable to look at the Empress. The Empress would have fled the room if she dared. The Empress Dowager frowned, wondering whether the Emperor knew what he demanded. Finally she shook her head. "Imperial Son, there has never been such a precedent," she said sternly. "The Empress is alive and well. In life Black Pearl was the Precious Concubine, how can she be accorded the honours of the Empress in death? The nation and the family will not permit it. Why stir up another hornets' nest?" Fulin replied dully, "I haven't the strength to go on. If the Imperial Mother will not grant this wish, I shall shave my head and become a monk, and never again interfere with the affairs of mankind...."

The Empress Dowager was filled with grief and rage; bursting with words she had to suppress. At that moment she wished Black Pearl had never existed. She cursed the day these two met. That day was the blight of Great Qing. If she had the power to control the next generation she would see to it that the Emperor would not have a favourite concubine. Nay, he would not be permitted to love.

To everyone's surprise it was the Empress, kneeling beside the emperor, who broke the silence.

"Imperial Mother, Sister Dongeh served His Majesty for five years. In truth she was the wife I failed to be. It was my intention to abdicate in her favour, had she lived. Therefore it would not be inappropriate to bury her with the rites reserved for the Empress. And if my humble wishes are conveyed to the nobles, none could object. Nor could later generations look upon this as the Emperor's misdeed...."

Fulin shot her a look of astonishment not unmixed with gratitude. The Empress accepted that fleeting glance with resignation.

Though the others dared not comment at the moment, they exchanged looks full of hidden meanings.

The Empress Dowager was relieved and spoke in even tones.

"Since the Empress is agreeable then I shall not stand in your way." Turning to Fulin she added, "Your Majesty will convey the Empress' wishes to the Council of Nobles. However, the mandate will be written in my name."

Fulin gratefully touched his forehead to the ground, and the Empress also prostrated herself.

The next day, the Emperor issued a decree in the name of the Empress Dowager announcing the death of the Precious Concubine Lady Dongeh; and in recognition of her many virtues it was decided that she be proclaimed empress posthumously. The Ministry of Rites was ordered to arrange the necessary ceremonies accordingly.

The Ministry of Rites acted immediately. Four days after Lady Dongeh's death the solemn ceremonies bestowing the posthumous title of Empress Dong on her were performed at Chengqian Palace where she lay in state.

On the day of Lady Dongeh's death the Empress Dowager, acting for herself as well as for the Emperor, decreed that audiences be cancelled for the next five days; and that all persons under the rank of prince, all Han and Manchu officials above the fourth grade, and all princesses and ladies of the harem were to observe official mourning. Now that Lady Dongeh was officially empress, Fulin could make arrangements for her funeral suitable to her rank.

The high monks of Mount Wutai and those in the south were summoned to conduct religious rituals for the repose of the soul of the departed.

The best craftsmen of the land were engaged to construct her tomb.

The Accademicians Wang Xi and Hu Zhaolong were commanded to compile the sayings of the Lady Dongeh, and the grand academician Jin Zhijun was commanded to write her biography.

The Grand Secretariat was commanded to use blue ink on all documents from the eighth to the twelfth month as a sign of mourning. Red ink would not be used until the New Year.

National mourning was declared from the date of the decree. All officials were required to wear mourning robes for a period of one month, and common folk for three days.

In the seventeen years since the conquest there had never been such a grand funeral. Spirit shrines and white funerary banners appeared from east to west, north to south across the vast Empire. Never before had a death received such widespread attention.

Fulin locked himself away in the east chamber of the Hall of Mental Cultivation permitting no one to enter. There, surrounded by memories and objects she had touched, he began to write about the six years he spent with his beloved Black Pearl, spilling his passion onto paper in a mingling of ink and tears.

After the seventh day, the Empress Dong's coffin would have to be moved to Shouchun Hall on Coal Hill.

Fulin had to finish his elegy and burn it before her coffin the evening before. All day he wrote. Though his brush-strokes flew, they could not keep up with his racing thoughts. Finally when he laid down his brush, a great weight seemed to have been lifted from his breast. Even the sadness seemed to have dulled. He went onto the terrace where some young eunuchs were copying what he had written, with many sighs and suppressed sobs. Seeing him they quickly fell to their knees.

Fulin scanned their handiwork and asked, "Why the tears?" A young eunuch replied, "Your slaves were moved by Your Majesty's sentiments." Fulin turned and quickly retraced his footsteps.

It was the twenty-sixth day of the eighth month. After the hour of the second drum, Fulin changed into plain clothes and, lit by a young eunuch with a lantern, he went with a few attendants to Chengqian Palace for a final tryst with Black Pearl. The autumn night was moonless and still. The stars reminded him of

Black Pearl's eloquent eyes. Even the wind had died down.

As they drew near to Chengqian Palace they heard the sound of weeping. What was happening? Since the third day of the Empress Dong's death, the monk Maoxi Sheng had been commanded to set up an altar and to pray for the repose of her soul. Was he still there at this late hour? Actually it was the Empress Dowager and the other ladies who had come to bid a last farewell to Empress Dong.

After the proprieties had been observed, Fulin took a seat to the left of the Empress Dowager and begged her to curb her sorrow and retire.

As the moment of the Empress Dong's departure from the Forbidden City drew near, the Empress Dowager's sense of loss became more acute. "She was indeed the perfect match for Your Majesty," she cried. "I had hoped you would spend your lives together, and gladden my declining years. But she is gone! Who would look after me now? Who is there that knows my mind and heart? Who can I talk to? Who can I plan with?" She was seized with such a paroxysm of weeping that she could not continue. Fulin bowed his head without a word. The other ladies sobbed in sympathy.

"Control yourselves!" The Empress Dowager suddenly turned upon the ladies. For once they did not heed her. Their tears were not entirely for the dead. To a large measure they wept for themselves. For the Empress Dowager's words had wounded them deeply, awakening feelings of bitterness and hurt pride. The Empress Dowager took a deep breath and said through her tears, "You are such a collection of dolts. She would have known how to comfort me.... Go!... Leave us.... You only increase our misery...."

Fulin also made a gesture of impatience. After the ladies had withdrawn, Fulin once more urged his mother to leave this sad place. The Empress Dowager searched his face doubtfully.

"Imperial Mother," Fulin said sadly, "trust me."

After the Empress Dowager was gone, Fulin was left alone

with the coffin. A young eunuch set a gold incense burner in front of it, and Fulin proceeded to read the elegy he had written out loud. At first his voice rang with fervour. However, he was gradually overcome by grief. He faltered, his voice becoming tear-choked so that it took a superhuman effort to finish. At the end the eunuch lit a fire in the burner, and Fulin burnt the elegy page by page.

Fulin sat beside the coffin overwhelmed with grief. He thought of shutting his eyes and resting. Even that was impossible. With Black Pearl gone, something of him was gone also. All that was left was an empty shell.

At dawn, a hundred officials of the second and third grade from the eight banners gathered before Chengqian Palace. The monk Maoxi Sheng would conduct the last rites before the coffin of Empress Dong was moved. After he had offered his obeisance to the Emperor, the monk lit incense and softly intoned the prayer of departure, conducting the soul of the dead upon its journey to the next world.

The thirty-two pall-bearers made up of officials of the second degree from the eight banners, dressed in mourning robes and with white topknots on their caps, ranged themselves on either side of the coffin. The monk intoned a final prayer and raising his staff cried, "Rise!"

The massive coffin slowly rose off the ground on the shoulders of the pall-bearers and with great solemnity moved out of the main hall of Chengqian Palace festooned in white banners.

As the coffin moved out the way was barred by eunuchs and servants of Chengqian Gate. Weeping and wailing they would not let the coffin pass. Nor could the official in charge convince them to stand back. With the Emperor present no one dared to clear the way by force.

Fulin was astonished by this display of emotion.

"Why do you block the way?" he asked dully.

"We can't bear losing Lady Dongeh," sobbed one of the eunuchs. Fulin smiled. "Now that she is gone you will have new mistresses. Will that not please you?"

"No!" protested the eunuch. The servants were uncomfortably aware of the crocodile tears that had been spilled by the other ladies whose resentment of Lady Dongeh would then be visited upon those who served her. One of the maids cried, "I'd sooner go with her...."

"Poor girl. We too wanted to go with her, but could not.... Clear the way. We have things to say...." The servants and the eunuchs stood aside, and the coffin was allowed to proceed.

Fulin searched the faces of the sorrowful servants around him and said slowly, "Our wish could not be accomplished, but we can grant yours. All of you shall follow her. Serve her well for our sake." The weeping increased in intensity. Many swooned. Fulin glanced about at this display of grief with satisfaction, and was about to follow the coffin. The monk Maoxi hurried after him, finally catching up at the gate.

"Your Majesty," he began with a deep bow, "your feelings are indeed sincere. However, the ever merciful Buddha loves life. Therefore, it is hoped Your Majesty will revoke the order that so many should die...." Fulin's face clouded.

"This is our tradition, otherwise who would serve the Empress Dong in the next world? I myself was prevented from following her. However, we shall not prevent these servants whose loyalty prompts them to do so...."

Maoxi was about to protest but the Emperor had already turned away. There was indeed a tradition of live burials among the Manchus, and there was nothing more the compassionate monk could do.

3

On the tenth day of the ninth month, which was the twenty-first day after the Empress Dong's death, she would be cremated.

As the Emperor, the Empress Dowager and the Empress were still too overcome by grief they would not attend this ceremony.

In their place Prince An would officiate. Accordingly, a round apricot-hued umbrella with a throne underneath it was placed in front of Shouchun Hall for his use.

The ladies of the harem, princesses and ladies of the nobility waited in the main hall. The Manchu aristocracy and the Han officials waited in the side halls to the east and west.

The monk Maoxi who was to light the funeral pyre was not yet there.

To while away the time, Yuele strolled toward the east hall in which a hubbub of voices could be heard. However, as he crossed the threshold the conversations stopped. In the sudden silence, one phrase stood out. "...It was extremely heavy. Must have been stuffed with treasure...." A nudge in the ribs silenced the speaker, who averted his face, swallowing the rest.

Almost a hundred people gathered in the hall, including the Princes Jieshu, Fushou, Dukes Douni, Lerjin, some minor lords, and the commanders-general and commanders-in-chief of the eight banners. Those close to the imperial family were seated while the rest stood in the presence of their betters. A moment ago they had been sipping tea, smoking and chatting in low voices. Now there was an uneasy silence, the breathless calm before a storm.

The princes rose to greet Yuele, who was now the highest in rank and generation among them. Yuele invited them to resume their seats. Many avoided his probing glance and once more raised tea cups or pipes to their lips. Yuele however was determined to shatter their silence. "My Lords," he said casually, "you were just discussing something that was exceedingly heavy.... "

One of the commanders-in-chief standing by the window bowed.

"I was just saying, the Empress' coffin was very heavy."

"It seemed much heavier than Abahai's," another chimed in.

"Nor was the Emperor Abahai's funeral as lavish," another voice came from somewhere in the crowd. There followed a long, pregnant silence. The princes seated nearby pretended not to hear. In was clear they were simply not giving vent to their chagrin. A few days earlier an official had been dismissed and imprisoned and a nobleman's title was revoked for failing to observe the strict code of national mourning. Furthermore, during the first days of mourning, the Emperor decided certain officials and their wives lacked sincerity in their expressions of grief, and ordered the Ministry of Rites to device suitable punishment. It was only due to the Empress Dowager's intervention that the order was withdrawn. The majority of the Manchu aristocracy had objected to the Emperor's attachment to Lady Dongeh who was half a barbarian and a so-called reformist to boot. They could hardly be expected to condone the present extravagance.

The silence was finally broken by someone saying softly, "...It's overdone." Yuele stopped himself from looking round for the speaker. Nevertheless as he raised his head, his eyes met those of Prince Jieshu who shook his head almost imperceptibly.

Yuele left the east hall and went on to the west hall which was noisy by comparison. Everybody was talking at once, the conversation bordering on boastfulness. As Prince An entered everyone fell to their knees. The prince bade them rise. Beckoning to the grand academician Fu Yijian he led the way to a quiet side chamber.

"I believe My Lord has gone through a lot of hardwork to device a suitable title for this late Empress," he remarked. A look of doubt spread across Fu Yijian's face. He was usually scrupulous and steady. He bowed as he replied saying that several attempts were made before the Emperor would accept a title for her expressing all her virtues and accomplishments in life. After a pause, Yuele asked, "Is His Majesty satisfied?" Fu Yijian shook his head.

"Not entirely. His Majesty was dissatisfied because the title lacked the characters 'heaven' and 'sacred'. However, according to protocol the former can only be used for a principal wife, and the latter only when there is a child who will succeed to the throne. Neither of these conditions exist." Another silence ensued. The sound of voices penetrated to the small antechamber.

"That rascal Zhang Chen was quick to snatch opportunity. He's been promoted to be an assistant in an official office."

"Now that's news! Tell us!"

"The Emperor commanded eulogies to be written in honour of the Empress Dong. All those who made submissions were generously rewarded. However, few pleased His Majesty. Zhang Chen submitted his which contained four lines of poetry that moved the Emperor to tears and he was promoted." It was impossible to decide whether the exclamation that followed was one of pleasure or dismay.

"There's more," a third voice persisted. "The other day, those who failed to weep convincingly before the coffin were punished. On the other hand, those who put on a good show were rewarded with precious gems. It is said the princesses and the ladies of rank were outdoing one another...."

"Ah, what a romantic monarch...." That remark might have been either praise or condemnation. Fu Yijian stole a glance at the prince and said, "In My Lord's opinion has the Emperor gone beyond the bounds of good taste?" Yuele frowned.

"The censors and the supervising secretaries are the people to speak out," Yuele said. "Yet no one has petitioned in this regard." Fu Yijian replied, "Ordinarily, His Majesty is open to advice, but in this instance he is immovable...."

Yuele shook his head helplessly. He knew the Emperor's temper better than any Han official. If the Empress Dowager whom he revered above all others could not change his mind, no one else could. The Manchus' displeasure was a foregone conclusion, but the doubts of the Han officials and their violent reaction came as a surprise. The rift at court between Han and Manchu, and between both factions and the Emperor could very well deepen. What did these divisions bode for the future?

Would the action of Jidu recur? He began to doubt whether Fulin was capable of being a wise and just ruler....

Yuele left Fu Yijian with a heavy heart. Why had the ceremonies not begun he wondered? The delay was making him impatient. He crossed the forecourt of the main hall. The open space beyond had been swept clean. Sentries armed with broad swords guarded two glittering structures that were the Empress Dong's spiritual dwelling place. One was a scaled replica of the main hall of Chengqian Palace, the other represented the bed chamber. Both were framed in camphor wood, with gilded roofs and windows framed in silver. The walls were made of the finest silks and satins from the south and decorated with pearls and precious stones. Replicas of Empress Dong's furniture, utensils and ornaments were placed exactly as they had been in Chengqian Palace. Every article had been copied. The Empress' coffin had already been moved into the main hall of the spirit palace. Around it knelt monks beating wooden fish and chanting prayers. The old monk Maoxi Sheng, who had supervised the ceremony at the Coal Hill, was seated in their midst upon a round rush mat.

Since Maoxi had arrived what was delaying the ceremony? Yuele frowned. When he noticed the back door to the bed chamber of the spirit palace was open he realized the cause for the delay.

"Stop! Stop!" a guard shouted behind him. Yuele turned just in time to see a woman run out of Shouchun Hall and stumble toward the iron railings surrounding the spirit palace. There was a clash of metal as lances and swords crossed to bar her way. The woman fell to the ground, but she did not cry out. Perhaps she was mute.

Yuele's pulse quickened. In a few strides he was beside the prostrate woman. The guards lowered their weapons and knelt at his approach. Yuele did not wait for the guards to report the incident but spoke angrily to the woman.

"Get back at once!"

It was Ahchou who should have been attending his wife inside

Shouchun Hall. At Yuele's voice, Ahchou cowered like a frightened animal. What was the meaning of this recklessness, thought Yuele. Before anyone could seize her, Ahchou made another attempt to reach the iron barrier. This time the prince caught her by the arms and held her fast.

"How dare you disgrace me!" he hissed. "Get back at once." Ahchou, who seldom spoke in his presence before, mumbled, "My Lord, I beg you! They're coming...." Who were coming? Yuele followed Ahchou's horrified gaze.

A procession of ten eunuchs and twenty palace maids was slowly trudging up Coal Hill. All were dressed in new robes and caps. Even the jewels and headdresses of the heavily made-up palace maids were new. They stumbled along, heads lolling from side to side, shoulders hunched, feet dragging, making a desperate effort to reach the two spirit palaces where they would be cremated with their mistress. All had been drugged. Only by dying within the spirit palaces would their families receive the handsome reward of silver that had been promised.

Ahchou pressed her cheeks tightly against the iron rails. Only the anxious eyes that searched the throng of those about to die betrayed any signs of life. Yuele was embarrassed. A slave had dared to flaunt the commands of a prince! He seized her by the arm fiercely enough to break it, but she did not utter a sound. Angrily he threw her down. She struck her head on the ground as she fell. He raised his fist ready to strike. Dimly he thought if she begged or wept he might let her off. But she remained silent.

Ahchou shot him a glance full of madness, rebellion, loathing, and hate, but not a shred of fear or entreaty. Blood oozing from the cut on her forehead added to the balefulness in her eyes. But she quickly turned away, absorbed in the stumbling procession, completely ignoring the prince. Yuele was at a loss; for mingled with embarrassment and awkwardness was something else he could not name.

Suddenly a young palace maid of fifteen or sixteen broke ranks and, tearing her hair, ran in the direction whence she had come, screaming for her mother. Her cries, "I don't want to die! I don't want to die!" echoed all over Coal Hill.

The escorting guards felled her with a club and carried her unconscious into the spirit palace. The back door was then secured.

Ahchou muttered, "Where is she? Where is she?" She swooned. Yuele realized that perhaps some relative was among those who were about to be sacrificed. He ordered Ahchou to be handed over to his steward. He would get to the bottom of this later and he would not be lenient with the wilful slave.

The funeral pyre was lit. The imperial concubines, princesses, princes, noblemen, their ladies, and courtiers gathered round on their knees. Several hundred monks chanted prayers as flames shot high in the air, its roar drowning out their voices. Tiny explosions sounded as the precious ornaments within the spirit palace disintegrated. The peculiar scent of burning camphor wood drifted across the Forbidden City and the capital.

The assemblage prostrated themselves as the spirit of the departed rose to heaven. Though no one could see the expression on anyone else's face, in his mind's eye Prince An visualized looks of anger, derision and indifference. Out of these would come the most fearful betrayal. Yuele hoped this huge bonfire would wipe out the past, that the people would quickly forget this funeral. Perhaps the Emperor would finally come to his senses and never again commit such excess.

However, the Emperor's excesses did not cease. More shocking deeds were to follow.

The eighth day of the tenth month was the final day of the funerary rites conducted by the monk Maoxi on Coal Hill. During the last forty-nine days, the clamour of bells and gongs split the skies. At dusk paper money was burnt and food was distributed to the poor. At night great bonfires burned. It was a tumultuous time during which countless monks, courtiers and slaves were kept busy. Every seventh day the Emperor took part in the rituals, and his obvious grief even moved the usually impassive monks.

With the rites for the passage of the soul into the nether world completed, the monks departed. The Empress' ashes was kept in an urn before which fresh flowers were placed. The court and indeed the populace breathed a sigh of relief.

After his exertions of forty-nine days the monk Maoxi Sheng longed for rest. But even this was denied him, for no sooner had he stretched out on his cot than the Emperor's messenger arrived announcing His Majesty's imminent arrival at Wanshan Hall. The monk hastily prepared to receive his monarch. What further rites did the Emperor have in mind for the departed Empress, he wondered. Was there no end to the grieving of this romantic young Emperor?

Maoxi Sheng waited for the Emperor under the ancient pines outside Wanshan Hall. The Emperor's appearance came as a surprise. For a calm resignation not unmixed with a certain coldness had replaced intense grief. Seated upon a round rush mat in the main hall, Fulin smiled like a benevolent donor. The weariness left Maoxi, and he attended his monarch with care.

"We thank the monk for conducting the rites on Coal Hill so that the spirit of our Empress may safely reach the nether world. For that blessing we are eternally grateful." Fulin spoke serenely. "Only thus could we repay her for her love. That wish at least has been fulfilled." Maoxi quietly responded, "The daughter of the dragon has joined the Buddha. Your Majesty must now take care of yourself."

Fulin also spoke in a quiet voice. "Our heart is dead. Nothing matters any more. We have come to the monk that he might shave our head so that we too may be a monk."

Maoxi was shocked.

"Your Majesty must not harbour such thoughts," he cried, red-faced with agitation. "The monarch is the pillar of the nation...."

Fulin interrupted dully, "Is it not said that to reach nirvana one must avoid all violent emotions?" Maoxi nodded in confusion. Fulin continued, "Brother Monk, the chamber adjoining this one shall be the place where we shall study and meditate. Henceforth we shall not return to Chengqian Palace or the Hall of Mental Cultivation. Would not great merit accrue to my Brother Monk for bringing an emperor into his fold?" Maoxi was silent for a long while, and finally murmured, "Your Majesty must not do this. Must not do this."

"Perhaps my Brother Monk does not believe our sincerity." Fulin inclined his head, reached behind with one hand for the thick braid of hair hanging down his back, and unsheathing his dagger with the other cut it off at the roots with one swift stroke. The attendants rushed forward with a terrified cry, but they were too late. Up to that moment the Emperor's behaviour had been completely in keeping with his station. They had been lulled into complacency. The act of cutting off his queue happened so fast that they were left breathless, not knowing what to do. The braid was thrown writhing onto the floor as though it had a life of its own.

Fulin burst into peals of laughter. He threw down his cap and shook out his shorn hair which fell unevenly at the back of his head. His laughter, a mixture of exhilaration and sadness ricochetted off the gloomy walls of the hall. Fulin laughed until he cried.

"How easily one is rid of the thousand strands of troubles that plague one's life. From now on I have nothing.... Brother Monk, will you shave my head?" He burst into another peal of wild laughter.

Perhaps it was fear, or that he was deeply moved, or arrogance that prompted Maoxi to order his disciples to set up an altar and lay out the shaving knife. There in Wanshan Hall, with trembling hands, the monk Maoxi shaved the head of the Emperor of Great Qing. A short time later the Emperor, with his freshly shaven head and dressed in a scarlet cassock, became a monk.

The news that the Emperor had become a monk shocked the court. That an emperor of Great Qing could commit such folly was unthinkable. The Council of Nobles met in an emergency session at once. Their first decision was that the news must not be leaked out on pain of death. Their second decision was that the entire court would take turns in persuading the Emperor to return to the world and take up the reins of government. There was even greater confusion in the inner palace. The Empress and all the ladies of the harem were now in the precarious position of being abandoned. Consequently there was much weeping and lamentation.

In spite of the strict orders of silence the news spread like wildfire through the capital. The people murmured against the great extravagance of Empress Dong's funeral and gossiped about the romantic Emperor's unseemly behaviour. The Han officials who had some knowledge of the case, embellished it into a scandal. Devout buddhists hailed this as a shining example of a man abandoning a life of luxury and ease for his beliefs. Still others saw it as a golden opportunity to ferment unrest. The possibilities of civic disturbances were quickly reported to the Council of Nobles, who immediately ordered the garrison to increase their patrols of the capital day and night, and to be on the alert for trouble.

Princes, nobles, and courtiers of all grades streamed to Wanshan Hall to persuade the Emperor to return to the world, while the ladies of the inner palace, the princesses and the ladies of rank flocked to Cining Palace to comfort the Empress Dowager. In all these comings and goings two people remained serenely unconcerned. Fulin shut himself away to meditate, refusing all visitors. Occasionally an academician might be admitted. Their discussions invariably centred around literature or art. There was never a breath of politics. The other was the Empress Dowager who neither went to Wanshan Hall nor seemed particularly perturbed. She received all visitors, graciously accepting the solicitude they offered.

It was the second time Prince An's wife had been to the Forbidden City since the Emperor became a monk. The first visit was to comfort the Empress Dowager who, to her astonishment, was not in need of comfort. When she returned she broached the question of bringing home the child Bingyue with her husband. Since the Empress Dong was dead, and the Emperor had become a monk, the child in the palace might just as well be orphaned. Prince An agreed. So that day husband and wife set out together, the one to visit the Empress Dowager, and the other to attempt to see the Emperor, no doubt to be turned away as he had been before.

They parted at Donghua Gate. Yuele continued to Xiyuan while the Lady Nala accompanied by Ahchou went on to Jingyun Gate. No one but Ahchou could fetch Bingyue home. However, without permission a slave could not enter Jingyun Gate. Therefore, when she alighted from her sedan chair, Lady Nala bid Ahchou wait in the waiting rooms for servants and slaves, while she went in alone.

Lady Nala was puzzled by Ahchou. Of late she seemed to have grown prettier though the strange vacant look in her eyes had also deepened. After the Empress' cremation, her husband had told her of Ahchou's strange behaviours and ordered her to question the girl. She had made a huge effort at eliciting something from the girl but to no avail. Finally, in exasperation, she had gone against the rule of compassion for which her household was renowned, and had the girl flogged. Still the girl would not speak. It was as though she were mute. When her husband chided her for using force, she retorted angrily, "Question her yourself. Personally, I don't think that lump of stone has any worries in her mind."

The things Menggu had witnessed and experienced these last years taught her the only way to survive was to be mute. She had been worried about Ronggu ever since she discovered her in Chengqian Palace. But she had no means of getting any news of her. That day, waiting like a frightened mouse in the waiting room for servants on Coal Hill, she overheard the other servant girls gossipping. A word here and a word there and she pieced together the shocking fact that all the maids and eunuchs of Chengqian Palace were to be burnt alive. Menggu was sure her luckless little sister would be among them. All the carefully suppressed emotions of love, rage, and despair boiled to the surface. Something within her snapped. She flew to the place where the cremation would take place. Surely she would have been put to death had her master Prince An not been there and saved her out of some unexplained curiosity. She watched while the sumptuous replicas of hall and palace, jewels and ornaments, and the Empress' great coffin, together with thirty living souls, went up in flames. But Ronggu had not been among those who had died. What had become of her? If only she could leap over these hated palace walls she would go to Chengqian Palace and see for herself.

A whistle, sounding now near, now far, came from a grove of trees nearby. Men in palace uniforms were exercising falcons there. With their feet bound together the birds that were used to flying free over plain and mountain could go no more than ten or so yards.

A familiar figure flashed before Menggu's eyes. Her heart missed a beat, for that figure roused deep memories. Beautiful memories of hills covered with bluish grass; an old apricot tree in bloom. Memories of her mother, Ronggu her sister, Brother Tongchun and Tongqiu, and the young Tartar Feiyose.... Yes, she was sure it was he ... the same young tartar who had come to warn Ronggu of impending disaster that fateful day two years ago. Only he was taller now. Menggu shivered with apprehension. It was the first time she had seen a familiar face in two years. Her eyes misted. What if she was mistaken? And if not, would he speak to a lowly slave?

Menggu gritted her teeth. A desperate plan was hatched. She went out of the waiting room slowly, eyes fixed to the ground as if she was looking for something she lost. The guard, noticing her moving toward the trees, glanced her way lazily and turned back to the eunuch with whom he was chatting.

Menggu slowly approached the man, with her heart in her throat. She forced herself to be calm and, lifting her head, blurted out in a voice that sounded strange even to her own ears, "Young Master, have you seen an embroidered silk handkerchief?" The youth casually answered, "No, I haven't ...." Then his eyes went wide.

"Why ... you're Sister Menggu...."

"Feiyose..." Menggu managed to force out. Her throat was so constricted she could not utter another word. Heedless of consequence, Feiyose quickly asked, "Where have you been? How did you get here?"

"I ... am a slave ... in the household of Prince An.... I accompanied the mistress...."

"Have you seen Sister Ronggu?"

"Where is she? Tell me, is she alive?" Menggu clutched Feiyose's arm anxiously.

"Be patient," replied Feiyose, "and I will tell you everything I know...."

The day before the cremation, Feiyose had been ordered to escort the Empress' favourite falcon to Coal Hill, together with two white cats, a cage of canaries and a cage of love birds. All these were to be cremated with her. He was led to a cottage situated half way up Coal Hill whose windows had been boarded up. Though nothing of its interior could be seen, it was known to be the place where the servants who were about to die were kept. The birds and animals that would share the same fate would also be kept there.

As he was about to leave, the chief eunuch suddenly appeared and exchanged a few hasty words with the sentry. They went inside and presently emerged half carrying and half dragging a palace maid who seemed more dead than alive. He was shocked when he recognized the girl was Ronggu.

Feiyose had watched for her at the cremation, and was sure she wasn't among those who had been sacrificed. He made discrete enquiries but to no avail. Finally, he learned the truth by overhearing a conversation between his superiors. It seemed the Empress Dowager's confidante Sumalagu complained to Her Majesty that Ronggu had committed fault and was unworthy of being sacrificed. Furthermore she raised doubts about her ancestry, saying that Rongu was not the daughter of bannermen. That would make her even less worthy of following the Empress into the next world. The Empress Dowager ordered an immediate investigation. It was discovered that Ronggu was an imposter. The Emperor flew into a rage and ordered her original owners beheaded at once. As Ronggu was unfit for service in the Forbidden City, she was driven out.

"...What became of her, I don't know." Feiyose looked around nervously and added, "Someone's coming.... If you hear anything, let me know...."

"Feiyose!" A rough-looking man who appeared to be in charge ran over and collared the youth. "Haven't you been warned not to speak to slaves? Where is the falcon? How shall I face the master?" He lashed out at Feiyose with his whip. Feiyose covered his head with his arms, and the whip lashes fell on his back. Hopping up and down, he yelled at the top of his lungs: "She was asking whether I saw a handkerchief she lost! Is it my fault? So what if the falcon's lost! The Third Imperial Son ordered me to train it without fetters. Why pick on me? Everyone knows I'm the youngest falcon trainer of the imperial menagerie...." He had deliberately yelled out where he could be found for Menggu's benefit, winking all the while as he dodged the whip lashes.

The mention of the Third Imperial Son gave the other pause. However he had to have the last word.

"Stop the howling! You lost a valuable bird. And I shall be punished with you!"

Feiyose tilted his head to one side and sneered before he

turned and whistled loudly. The iron grey falcon, sitting proudly high in the branches of a tall pine, spread its wings and swooped down to perch on the youth's shoulder.

"Hey! That's quite a trick," crowed the little bureaucrat. "I'm sorry I hit you. Come, I'll buy you a drink, and maybe you can show me how you did that trick." The man clapped a heavy arm around the youth's shoulders and the two strolled away.

Menggu watched Feiyose out of sight then slowly returned to the waiting room. She was wild with joy. Her sister had escaped the pitiless flames and lived. She wanted to run, to skip, to shout her joy to the heavens. Instead she slunk into a dark corner and pressed her palms then her flaming cheek to the cold, hard wall. A sliver of hope pierced the inky blackness of her soul.

At that moment her mistress' hopes were being shattered for the Empress Dowager refused to relinquish her child Bingyue. In fact it was impossible to object to the Empress Dowager's kindly smiles and gentle words.

"...I'm old. And one of the few pleasures of old age is having grandchildren around me. Little Bingyue is a darling child. Recently I took a chill, and all the windows were kept shut against drafts. The child snuggled against me and asked if I was afraid of the cold. I said I was. Then the child said, quite seriously, 'The wind is also afraid of the cold.' When I asked her why, she replied, 'It must be afraid of the cold or it wouldn't hide against people.' How can a grandmother bear to be separated from such a dear little thing?"

Prince An's wife could only smile in agreement, though there was bitter disappointment in her heart. The Empress Dowager seemed to read her mind.

"There is one more consideration. Bingyue has been made a princess, and a title once bestowed cannot be retracted..." Lady Nala nodded in spite of herself. Just then Prince An was announced.

"Ah, he has come," remarked the Empress Dowager. "Let him enter." Yuele's face clouded when he saw his wife. After making his obeisance to the Empress Dowager he bade his wife to withdraw. The wife had intended to grumble at her husband to try and bring Bingyue home for a short visit. However, Yuele's expression made it clear he did not wish to speak to her at that moment.

"I have confidential matters to discuss with Her Majesty. You had better leave." The wife did as she was told. The Empress Dowager watched this by-play between husband and wife without comment. Nor did she object when Lady Nala begged permission to withdraw.

As soon as she left the room, Yuele spoke:

"Your Majesty, the Emperor refused to see me. However, he sent word by a young monk, commanding me to see Your Majesty and to remind you of the matter he has entrusted you."

The Empress Dowager did not reply. Instead she waved a hand at Sumalagu who quickly went into an inner chamber. Moments later she returned with a jade box decorated with a pattern of dragon and phoenix wrought in gold thread. The Empress Dowager lifted the lid and took out a folded sheet of paper which she handed wordlessly to Yuele.

Yuele immediately recognized the Emperor's strong, sweeping brush-strokes. The note read:

"From the Monk Xingchi to the blessed Empress Dowager." Yuele's face went deathly pale after the first few lines, and he sank to his knees before the Empress Dowager.

"Your Majesty, if Yuele harboured such thoughts, may the heavens strike him dead," he cried with agitation.

In his letter the monk Xingchi had begged forgiveness for his unfilial actions, but reiterated his determination to embrace the monastic life. But the gist of the letter was that he wished Yuele to conduct the affairs of state in his stead, and with the Empress Dowager's consent, he proposed to abdicate in Yuele's favour.

The Empress Dowager bade him rise. "Had I suspected

you I would not have shown you the letter." Yuele dabbed the sweat that popped out on the back of his neck.

"What shall we do? The Emperor will neither receive anyone nor listen to advice." The Empress Dowager pondered a moment.

"Before the right moment arrives, there is no use worrying. Last year during the siege of Jinling it was the same. The more one tried to reason with him the less receptive he became. However, he is not stupid. In due course he will come round." But that was cold comfort to Yuele.

"This is different," he insisted. "Grief over the death of Empress Dong has unhinged his mind...." The Empress Dowager sighed.

"Even you do not understand that all this is not because of Black Pearl alone...." Yuele started. Suddenly everything became crystal clear and he was overcome with sadness. After a silence in which the Empress Dowager strove to regain her composure she said, "If the choice is between an empire and a beautiful woman — a dead beautiful woman — it would be simple. Even if he does not come to his senses immediately the affairs of state will not grind to a halt. There is still the Grand Secretariat, the six ministries, and the Council of Nobles. However, it is as the saying goes, the bell must be removed by the hands that hung it."

"And Your Majesty means...."

The Empress Dowager chuckled. "The monk Xingchi's teacher Yulin Tongxiu is on his way back to the capital. Send an important courtier to greet him."

Exactly as the Empress Dowager had predicted, the imperial teacher Yulin Tongxiu arrived in the capital a few days later on the fifteenth day of the tenth month, and went straight to Wanshan Hall. The following day the Emperor returned to the palace. On the third day he appeared at audience and took up the affairs of state with quiet confidence as though nothing untoward had happened. However, he never doffted his cap. Though the courtiers knew he did not wear a queue, no one dared to take a curious look.

Another crisis had blown over.

Later the eunuchs reported to the Empress Dowager that the imperial teacher Yulin had resolved the problem swiftly, with no more than a few well chosen words.

As soon as he arrived at Wanshan Hall, the imperial teacher Yulin ordered his disciples to apprehend Maoxi Sheng. For daring to shave the head of the reigning monarch, he was tied to a pillar. Firewood was piled at his feet ready to be put to the torch. Then Yulin went in search of the monk Xingchi as the Emperor chose to be called, whom he found in meditation. Thus the bald-headed monk faced the bald-headed Emperor. Though Yulin was deeply troubled, he could not ignore the ridiculousness of their predicament.

Fulin quickly declared himself to his teacher:

"In ancient times, Sakyamuni and Bodhidharma abandoned princely titles to seek perfection. I wish to do the same.... Does my teacher approve?"

Yulin shook his head vehemently. "From a worldly point of view, Your Majesty must stay at your throne to comfort your mother, and to bring peace and prosperity to your people. From another point of view, it would be better for you to always be the monarch in order to uphold the truths of the Buddha." Fulin pondered all that the monk had said. Meanwhile outside, the pile of firewood had been lit, and above the hubbub of voices, the voice of Maoxi Sheng could be heard praying. Fulin rushed to the window and, when he saw what was happening, cried out, "Master, have pity! I forced him to shave my head!"

"It is not a question of pity. Unless Your Majesty returns to the world, Maoxi must die." Billowing flames and smoke obscured Maoxi Sheng from view.

"Forgive him! I will do anything the imperial teacher demands!" Thus, in exchange for Maoxi Sheng's life, Fulin returned to the world.

Those who believed the crisis was over were in for a rude awakening. The Emperor returned to the world a changed man. He was no longer interested in affairs of state, or the welfare of his people. Petitions were allowed to accumulate unread. He would not receive courtiers who requested audiences. He spent his days reading or studying scriptures, or he would be away on hunts and imperial progresses. In the palace, he was diffident to the Empress Dowager but aloof to all his ladies except Lady Dongeh's cousin whom he summoned constantly, causing much jealousy. At court, he seemd to heap all the rage and despair of Jidu's treachery and the Empress Dong's early death on the heads of the Manchu aristocracy, from whom he was estranged and towards whom he showed a marked hostility. As a result there was a constant feeling of uneasiness among the Manchu, wondering what mischief the Emperor would perpetrate next.

He never mentioned the Empress Dong. Perhaps time was wearing away the past. However, at the beginning of the twelfth month, when Yulin Tongxiu was about to return to his monastery, Fulin made him a gift of a poem of the Tang Dynasty which he had written in his own fluently elegant hand.

It was the same love poem that he had once given his beloved Black Pearl.

4

According to custom all ministries closed their offices on the twenty-third day of the last month of the year. This signalled the beginning of a holiday period lasting until the Lantern Festival about twenty days later. During this period the capital took on a festive air, especially the few days preceeding New Year's day and after it. Firecrackers exploded day and night. Jostling crowds jammed the streets. Official sedan chairs and carriages vied for right of way as officials at court and common folk alike rushed about exchanging visits with family and friends, honouring the souls of ancestors and begging the blessings of the gods. The southern quarter of the city from Liulichang to Qianmen became a gigantic market filled with all manner of goods. A merry throng gathered there amid streets festooned with lanterns, coloured bunting, spring couplets written on bright red strips of paper, and colourful pictures of household gods. The people, decked out in festive garb, exchanged greetings. The sound of laughter, pedlars hawking goods, the thud and clang of drum and gong accompanying folk dances blended into a joyful din.

From the first year of Shunzhi onwards the price of staples such as rice, wheat, oil, cloth and pork had gradually dropped and stabilized. With a stable economy, the people's lives became easier. The capital prospered. It was indeed a festive season for noblemen and commoners alike.

After the third day of the New Year, the number of visitors to the home of the grand academician Fu Yijian began to drop off. On the fourth day, husband and wife had intended to rest and not receive callers. However, two special visitors put an end to that plan. The first was the wife of Gong Dingzi, the lady Gu Meisheng, whom Suyun entertained for an hour in her boudoir. The other was the director of the Hanlin Academy, and Minister of Rites, Wang Xi. Wang Xi and Fu Yijian had not been close friends until the fifteenth years of Shunzhi, after the Grand Secretariat and the Hanlin Academy were established. Both men's careers were advanced by changes in the structure of government. Furthermore as both were trusted by the Emperor, they came into contact with one another more frequently. In fact they often consulted each other on important matters. Thus a friendship developed between the two men, which lately included some discussion of marriage between their children.

After Wang Xi had gone it was almost noon. Fu Yijian retired to his living quarters where he found his wife in the sitting room, casually leafing through some picture scrolls and art folios spread on a long table set under the window where it was light. Suyun turned to him with a smile.

"What were you discussing for such a long time? You should have kept him for the midday meal."

"How could I! What can you prepare for him?"

"For a dish of West Lake fish cooked in vinegar and a goose roasted in the southern style prepared by me in person, he would never leave!" Suyun chuckled.

"Better let me enjoy those delicious food!" Fu Yijian countered with a bantering laugh. Suyun had not seen him so happy for a long time, and she was glad. She poured him a cup of hot tea and brought it to him.

"You seem happy," she remarked. "What good news did Wang Xi bring?"

"I can't keep anything from you," chuckled Fu Yijian.

He recalled that Wang Xi had been summoned by the Emperor the day before and was closeted with him a whole hour.

"Wang Xi was excited by the Emperor's trust in a Han official and said that he would serve His Majesty with unswerving loyalty for the rest of his life."

"But what did they talk about?"

"That of course he could not tell me. But there was a hint that the Emperor has great plans."

"Ah, and that got you all excited!"

"It's time the Emperor took an interest in government. It's been a whole year...."

"What's a year! Why, the emperors of Ming hid themselves away in the inner palace from one generation to the next. They didn't care about government.... In fact they didn't even know their courtiers...."

"His Majesty is a wise ruler, who must not be compared with the decadent men who occupied the throne in the past. By forbidding cliques at court and the ladies of the inner palace from meddling in matters of state he showed he was a man with a mind of his own. The Emperor is a hard worker. Nothing passes unnoticed. However, in recent years there have been problems ... and that was unavoidable.... However, he has weathered them.... Now he has plans and he will see them to fruition....''

Suyun resumed her seat before the table, leafing through the books.

"How would the Emperor's plans affect you?'' she remarked. ''I suppose you will go on reading documents and doing what you are told. A mindless task that any servant can do as well. Your talents are wasted unless the six ministries are put under the control of the Grand Secretariat. Only then can you be a real prince minister....'' Fu Yijian chuckled. "Wang Xi touched upon that just now. He hinted the gist of his conversation with the Emperor which centred on that very subject.'' Suyun turned her attention to her husband.

"But will the Council of Nobles and the Manchu officials of the six ministries agree? These days the Manchu aristocracy are not bothering to hide their dissatisfaction. Did you know that Prince An is being snubbed by them?''

The smile congealed on Fu Yijian's face. He was painfully aware of the Manchu nobles' dissatisfaction with the Emperor, whom they censured for dishonouring the ancestors by adopting Han traditions. Now, favouring a concubine and devotion to the Buddha were added to the list of his other sins. This referred, of course, to Empress Dong's lavish funeral and the Emperor's aborted attempt to become a monk. To the Manchus, the Emperor was beyond the pale. However, it was on Prince An whom they vented their ire. Prince An was cold-shouldered at the ceremonies honouring the ancestors on the first day of the New Year. And to add to his embarrassment, he had few well-wishers....

A servant announced the arrival of a messenger from the Grand Secretariat. Fu Yijian hurried out to receive him. The messenger fell on his knees and reported that word had been received via the imperial guard that the Emperor was taken ill last night, and his condition quickly worsened. "Therefore the grand academicians and officials are ordered to gather before

Houzuo Gate at dawn to pay their respects."

Fu Yijian was shocked by the news, but steadying himself, he asked in an almost casual tone, "What is His Majesty's illness?"

"He has a high fever and is very agitated. There hasn't been a proper diagnosis."

"You may go." Having dismissed the messenger, Fu Yijian went back to his wife and told her the news. Both husband and wife spent a sleepless night. At dawn the princes, nobles, courtiers, officials of the various departments, members of the Grand Secretariat and the Academy were all gathered before Houzuo Gate to pay their respects to the Emperor. Though it was the festive season, the images of the guardian gods had been removed from the palace gates. The lanterns, bunting, and spring couplets written on red paper had all been taken down. It was a sure sign that the Emperor was gravely ill. The chief eunuch emerged from the palace and engaged the lords of the council in a whispered conversation. For the onlookers, their agitated expressions boded no good. Kneeling among his colleagues of the Grand Secretariat, Fu Yijian shivered as though with the ague, but his face burned as if with a fever. Confused thoughts raced through his mind. Through it all he was vaguely aware of a movement nearby. Looking up he recognized the imperial astronomer, Tang Jo-Wang, trembling violently on his knees. Though a mane of white hair and his beard half obliterated his face, Fu Yijian could tell the old man was grief-stricken.

Fu Yijian, representing the assemblage, read their greetings out loud, begging the Emperor to rest and praying for a speedy recovery for the good of the nation; also assuring His Majesty that the Grand Secretariat would be faithful to its mandate to serve him in all things.

To which the kneeling court added in one voice, "May His Majesty have a speedy recovery!"

The imperial guard bid the assembled court wait while he reported to the Emperor. As he was about to enter the Hall of

Mental Cultivation, Tang Jo-Wang cried out, "Wait!" Then with tears in his eyes he asked the guardsman to beg the Emperor's permission for his old servant to visit him.

A short while later the imperial guard emerged with the Emperor's verbal message. His Majesty acknowledged the greetings of the court, saying that he had caught a chill and would be well within a few days. Meanwhile, petitions from all ministries were to be channeled to the Grand Secretariat.

Turning to Tang Jo-Wang, the guard delivered the Emperor's personal reply. Once again the Emperor acknowledged the loyalty of his Mafa and promised to summon Tang Jo-Wang as soon as he had recovered.

A murmur rippled through the throng. The Chief Eunuch of Cining Palace appeared and read a decree from the Empress Dowager, saying that there would be a general amnesty. Prisoners would be released, or have their sentences reduced. Those condemned to death would have their sentences commuted. Furthermore an order was to go out to the populace forbidding the frying of beans, lighting lamps, or spilling water. At last the court understood the Emperor had smallpox.

Smallpox! The dreaded disease was almost always fatal to adults! The court was thrown into panic. No one spoke. The cold wind seemed to penetrate their very innards. The small elegant courtyard at Houzuo Gate was filled with officials in all their finery, yet it was as silent as though it was deserted.

Finally it was Prince An who spoke.

"Let us leave. There is nothing we can do." The courtyard quickly emptied. Not another word was spoken.

Tang Jo-Wang, however, lingered a while longer. Collaring one of the eunuchs he begged him take a small picture book to the Emperor, and also to pass on a verbal petition:

"The welfare of Your Majesty's immortal soul is in danger. For this your servant is greatly troubled. I hope Your Majesty would glance through this book, for it depicts the life after death, and the eternal bliss of heaven."

The eunuch who had always revered the old missionary agreed to carry the message. A half hour later, the eunuch returned to say that the Emperor had looked at the book and was deeply moved. He also carried back a verbal message in which the Emperor acknowledged the Mafa's concern. "...However we have committed so many grievous sins that we are unfit to face your God. Nevertheless, if we recover we might consider adopting the Mafa's religion. However, as we are now stricken with smallpox, we cannot make that commitment...." Tang Jo-Wang prayed in his own language for God's forgiveness. However, the Emperor had further instructions for his Mafa: "The Mafa must straight away go to the Empress Dowager who has important matters to discuss...." Neither sorrow nor old age would prevent the missionary from following the eunuch to Cining Palace at once.

The Empress Dowager, red-eyed with weariness, slumped in her chair, her head propped up with one hand. Her sorrow and fear could be heard in her deep sighs. Sumalagu quietly dabbed her eyes as she spread a dark blue cape lined with martan fur across the Empress Dowager's shoulders. Although several braziers had been lit, the vastness of the main hall made it much colder than the bed chamber.

A eunuch announced Tang Jo-Wang. The Empress Dowager quickly sat up, ramrod straight, hands folded upon her lap; the air of majesty erased the lines etched upon her face by sorrow. She was her usual self: reserved, dignified, only the smile was missing. She offered Tang Jo-Wang a seat and ordered milk tea to be served.

The Empress Dowager did not wait for the niceties dictated by protocol to be observed before coming to the point.

"Mafa, the Emperor is seriously ill, but a successor has not yet been named," she began. "I have pressed this matter, and His Majesty nominated a cousin. I have discussed this with the lords, who agree that the father should be succeeded by his son according to natural law. The Emperor wants the Mafa's opinion on the matter."

A warm rush of emotion suffused Tang Jo-Wang's being. That Fulin would turn to him for advice on such a weighty matter proved that he had not turned his back on the friendship of his youth. In that instant all disappointments and misunderstandings vanished. Without hesitation Tang Jo-Wang replied:

"That a father should be succeeded by a son has always been the rule in China. It is also thus in Western lands. Nay, in every corner of the world. Therefore, Your Majesty, a successor must be found among the Emperor's sons."

The Empress Dowager nodded agreement.

"The Emperor's sixth son is three years old; his seventh, two years old, the eighth is only thirteen days old, and quite out of the question. The Emperor's fifth son is now six years old, his second son is eight years old, while the third is seven. The fifth son and the second son were both born to ladies of low rank. However, the third son was born of the principal lady of Jingren Palace, the Lady Kang. The child is exceedingly clever, fond of study, but is also a fine horseman and archer for his age...." The Empress Dowager paused, thinking she had already said too much. "Mafa, whom do you think is most suitable?"

Tang Jo-Wang was conscious of the direction the Empress Dowager's thoughts led. If what she said was true and unbiased, the Third Imperial Son would be the logical choice. However, he did not wish to appear too eager to concur and thus lower the value of his advice. He pondered the choices for a few moments longer before he replied,

"As far as I am aware, the Third Imperial Son has already survived the smallpox. If, as Your Majesty has described, he is also clever and fond of learning, your old servant would venture to say that his succession to the throne would be advantageous to the stability of Great Qing."

Under the prevailing circumstances, it was a choice that would muzzle all dissension. Tang Jo-Wang had thus cemented the decision. However, at that moment neither he nor the Empress Dowager could know that the child they chose as the next emperor would grow to be one of the most illustrious in Chinese history. During his reign of sixty years, China would become the largest and strongest empire in the East. With his reign would begin a century of peace and unprecedented prosperity for his people.

The Empress Dowager was satisfied. She rose to her feet signalling the end of their interview. She ordered her eunuchs to help the old man out the hall, and to carry him from the Forbidden City in a light sedan chair. Thus, the German missionary was again accorded the highest possible honour.

One troubling matter was settled. But there were others that the Empress Dowager had to deal with one at a time. Though she was not emperor, her policy and her deeds at the moment were more onerous than that of the monarch. It was to her advantage that her early years were spent on the grasslands which gave her strength and resilience. Otherwise she would not have withstood the buffeting of crises upon crises.

Sumalagu quickly brought her mistress a fresh cup of milk tea, some cream and small pastries, and also an elegant hand warmer studded with jade and agate. The Empress Dowager tucked the hand warmer under her tunic while she partook of the food. All the while she was deep in thought. Sumalagu waited till she had finished before asking in the Manchu vernacular, ''Shall I summon the Empress?'' The Empress Dowager shook her head.

"Send for Lady Dongeh." Since her death, the Empress Dong's cousin who bore a striking resemblance to her had assumed the dead woman's title. Sumalagu kept her eyes averted as she went to transmit the Empress Dowager's order.

Lady Dongeh arrived. She had become more and more like her dead cousin. Even her expression and her movements were hers. However, she did not have the same clever, vivacious eyes, or the poise and grace that was so greatly admired in her cousin. She was barely eighteen years of age, and only recently became an imperial concubine. Having made her obeisance, she stood to one side, head bowed nervously. It was the first time that the Empress Dowager had formally summoned her.

"Have you been to pay your respects at the Hall of Mental Cultivation?" the Empress Dowager enquired in a matter-of-fact tone.

"I have."

"Do you think the Emperor will recover?" Choking back tears Lady Dongeh replied, "I wish I could be ill in His Majesty's place...." For a moment a fierce gleam shone in the Empress Dowager's eyes. Controlling herself she said, "Really?"

"I would give my life for His Majesty...."

The Empress Dowager mulled that over, then suddenly shot back, "What would you do if His Majesty dies?"

Lady Dongeh's eyes went wide, her heart beating wildly in her breast.

"Aren't you his favourite concubine?"

"I...." Lady Dongeh's head drooped in confusion.

"Hasn't that caused bitterness and jealousy among all the other ladies? How could you live hereafter, or protect yourself?" Lady Dongeh's legs turned to water, and she fell to her knees, trembling.

"What is the matter?" the Empress Dowager could barely contain her irritation. Cocking an eyebrow at the hapless young woman she added, "Are you pregnant?" Lady Dongeh shook her head and lifted her now tear-streaked face, as pretty as a pear blossom in a storm. "Your Majesty, till I die I shall never understand.... Everyone says His Majesty dotes on me because I am summoned every day to the Hall of Mental Cultivation. But I am there to serve tea when he is reading. I grind the ink when he practises calligraphy or paints. When he prays and meditates I stand behind him, as he says, like an angel behind the Buddha. He seldom speaks, and almost never smiles, and certainly never...." She blushed to the roots of her hair.

"What?" the Empress Dowager was shocked. "Did you

not sleep with him?" Lady Dongeh's head drooped even lower. Her cheeks flamed and her voice was almost inaudible.

"We share a bed every night.... But he is like a block of ice ... that nothing can melt.... He takes no notice of me ... and sleeps till dawn...."

"How long has it been like that?" the Empress Dowager demanded.

"Ever since my cousin died...."

The Empress Dowager was shaken by what she heard. How could this romantic son of hers be so cruel? He should not have been born a prince, whose life was destined for troubles and anguish. The Empress Dowager raised a weary hand. "You may go...."

Lady Dongeh prostrated herself and, covering her face to hide her shame, withdrew. The Empress Dowager understood her son. She believed what she had been told. But who else would? Would the other concubines? Would the Empress?

At dusk news arrived from the Hall of Mental Cultivation that the Emperor was better. The fever had broken. Gladness swept the palace. Led by the Empress Dowager the ladies of the harem went to see him at once.

Fulin was propped up on his bed bundled in quilts. He seemed weakened, thinner, his pale skin almost translucent. However the tiny cold sparks in the depth of his eyes were unwavering. He greeted the Empress Dowager with a quivering smile.

"Imperial Mother, your unfilial son has caused you much grief...." The Empress Dowager seated herself beside the bed and forcing a smile replied, "These have been troublesome times. It is natural to be fatigued. However, there is no need for ceremony between mother and son...." Fulin also smiled.

"I regret I shall be unable to repay the Imperial Mother for all her love and care these twenty-four years in this life. I pray that in the next we shall again be mother and son. Then we shall have other fish to fry...." The Empress Dowager fought back her tears and comforted him, saying, "You seem better already. Why speak of such gloomy things?"

"That is correct. I will soon be much better...." Fulin's eyes wandered to the foot of the bed where the Empress and Lady Kang stood. Quickly, the ladies fell to their knees and in unison piped, "We wish Your Majesty well...." Fulin spoke to them quietly:

"In days to come it will be your duty to comfort the Empress Dowager and to aid the young Emperor. It is hoped you will acquit yourselves well...."

Suddenly Lady Kang grasped Fulin's hands and pressed it tightly against her breast. In that movement all her practised reserve, her icy shell with which she had encased herself cracked. Emotions which she hardly understood burst through layers of restraint. She cried out between wild sobs, "Take me with you! I don't want to be without you! Neglect me ... hate me ... beat me ... kill me ... I don't mind ... I'd rather die!" Everyone in the room was moved by this unexpected outburst. Faced with this passionate, almost unrecognizable woman, Fulin was speechless. Finally he spoke in an even voice, "You must stay. The Third Imperial Son will soon succeed to the throne...." All those present drew a breath of consternation at the Emperor's announcement.

The Empress Dowager was relieved. The Empress expected nothing less. The other ladies were satisfied. Only Lady Kang, roiling with surprise, joy, pain and regret, wept all the more bitterly, until she could barely catch her breath.

Fulin carefully freed his right hand from Lady Kang's grip and reached for the Empress.

"You mustn't cry..." he said to the two ladies. "We never meant to harm you. It was just that we were too weak to fight the flaws in our nature.... I pray in the next life you will not reincarnate into a noble house, and that you will have the joy of experiencing love as all humans should.... Little Pearl.... Where is Little Pearl?"

Since her cousin's death no one had called Lady Dongeh by that name. Now she hurried forward from the fringes of the crowd. Fulin tried again to free his hand but Lady Kang pressed it to her face and would not relinquish it. So he released the Empress' and took Lady Dongeh's tiny hand.

"These six months have been hard on you," he said gently. "You have been forced to live under false pretences but you never complained. The fact is you are too much like your cousin. Even your character is similar. In times to come, there will be no place for you in the palace, or even in the world. Instead of bearing the slings and arrows of life, come with me. We will go to her together...." Lady Dongeh fixed her eyes unblinkingly upon Fulin and slowly nodded.

Fulin's gaze travelled past the lavishly gowned ladies clustered around his bed to the table on which were spread books and scrolls, and sighed in a wondering voice, "We shall soon be gone.... I wonder whether in the nether world there will be time to read ... or if there is ... to absorb what one reads...." At that moment the icy coldness in his eyes seemed to melt. He quickly wiped away the moisture, and in the same composed tone continued, "Imperial Mother, we have chosen a name for the Third Imperial Son. He shall be called Xuanye."

On the next day, the sixth of the first month, Wang Xi was hastily summoned to the Hall of Mental Cultivation shortly after the third drum. Fulin was burning with fever. Though his face was suffused with blood, his mind was clear. Reclining on a chaise, he spoke to Wang Xi in a whisper:

"We have the pox and will not recover. You shall write down our last words as I speak." Wang Xi was so overcome with grief that he could not respond. Fulin sighed. "We have worked well together. However, we have come to the point where destiny forces us to part. Therefore there is no need for sorrow. We have no time to waste...." Wang Xi forced himself to be calm and to take down the Emperor's words at the bedside. In this way the first part of Fulin's last will and testament was written down. Seeing how difficult it was for him to speak, Wang Xi proposed that the Emperor should tell him his intentions, which he would note down, then compose the document for the Emperor's approval.

Fulin nodded his consent and painfully told the courtier the gist of his will. Armed with his notes, Wang Xi retired to an antechamber in Qianqing Palace and began composing the rest of the Emperor's last will and testament. As each section was completed the manuscript was sent to the Hall of Mental Cultivation for Fulin's approval. In this way the document was completed in three sections. As the sun sank in the west, the imperial guard came to inform Wang Xi that the Emperor had approved the will. The academicians Ma Jile and Jia Bujia were commanded to present the document to the Empress Dowager who would then present it to the Council of Nobles and the court at large.

Wang Xi stumbled out of the Forbidden City. In the waning light the inner palace was a gloomy, forbidding place from which not a sound issued. Wang Xi was filled with foreboding. The gusts of northwest wind cut to the very marrow of his bones.

The Emperor's last will and testament which Wang Xi had composed was already lying on the Empress Dowager's desk. She had already read it several times. Could it be proclaimed as it was, she asked herself? No! It was impossible. Fulin's obstinacy was reflected throughout the document. The notion of a union between Manchu and Han could not be put in the will. Furthermore, what would be the result of placing the six ministries under the control of the Grand Secretariat, and the abolition of the Council of Nobles? What rebellions might arise out of those ideas? The Empress Dowager paced the floor, her brows in a tight knot. She was not perturbed. In fact she was quite calm. What she had to do was not only to distinguish between right and wrong, but also to weigh their consequences.

In the deepest recesses of her heart, the Empress Dowager

stood with her son. His attempt to concentrate his power, his interest in Chinese culture and his employment of Hans were done for the sake of consolidating the Empire and securing the dynasty. However, he was acting like one obsessed, paying no heed to consequences. He had gone too far in assimilating Han ways. Why had the former Ming Dynasty collapsed? Also he had acted with such force and suddenness that it would bound to rouse the resentment of the Manchus.

At this moment, when the Han were newly subdued, and the rule of the Manchu not yet firmly established, the monarch had more reason to fear the latter than the former. How could he dare risk going against the tide? As for appointing Prince An as regent, that was clearly unacceptable. The pain inflicted by the regency of Dorgon and Jirgalang were still fresh in the memory. No! The last will and testament could not be proclaimed as it was. Nevertheless those were the last wishes of her only son! The Empress Dowager threw herself down on her couch and covered her face with both hands. Memories of Fulin's childhood, the countless vicissitudes of his painfully short life flashed before her eyes. His joys, his sorrows, his cruelty, his ambition were all an extention of herself, linked inexorably to her heart. As a mother how could she not do her utmost to fulfil his last wishes? There is a terrible sadness when the old bury the young. Tears streamed through the cracks between her fingers.

However, she could also visualize the result of proclaiming this will. The Empress Dowager vividly recalled the days before Fulin ascended the throne, and how the eight banners nearly went to war against each other in the struggle for power. In her mind was also the image of the proud and obstinate Prince Jidu, the rage and suspicion of countless nobles and generals of the eight banners. At this time when the Empire had just been stabilized and the dust of battle was gradually settling on the frontiers, danger lurked all around. In the south there were the aboriginal tribes, the forces of Wu Sangui, Shang Kexi and Geng Jimao that seemed to grow stronger day by day. Then there was Zheng

Chenggong exiled to the island but still a menace. The only forces that could keep them at bay were the Manchus of the eight banners....

The Empress Dowager was reminded of her husband's ambition and her own responsibility. She would not allow personal feelings between mother and son to cloud her judgement of the larger scheme of things, or jeopardize the safety of the realm. She rose from her couch, her mind made up. She carefully washed her face in cold water and changed into a fresh robe of dark blue satin, then she seated herself calmly at the desk.

She brushed aside the last will and testament that Wang Xi had carefully composed according to the Emperor's wishes, and resolutely began to write.

On the eighth day of the first month, government offices resumed work earlier than usual. At dawn all officials were supposed to present themselves at their offices in full regalia. However those with reliable sources of information quickly heard that the gate at Tiananmen had opened briefly and closed again. Only the grand academicians, officials of the ministries and that of the Ministry of Rites were admitted, and the topknots of their caps had been removed as soon as they crossed the threshold. All other officials were told to go home.

It was the present dynasty's custom that the topknot on official caps are removed when an imperial death occurred. Though the Emperor was gravely ill, he was young. Would it come to that? Low-ranking officials who did not know the details went abroad to seek information from whomever they met. Though rumours were flying no one actually knew anything for certain. However, the city gates were tightly shut and the soldiers of the eight banners were patrolling everywhere, enforcing a curfew. There were few people in the streets and they too hurried home to await further developments.

When the westering sun dipped toward the horizon, a decree was issued from the inner palace requiring all officials to proceed to the palace in their full regalia. They were to report first to the Ministry of Personnel where they would be issued a white mourning sash, then they were to gather in the courtyard before the west chamber of the Hall of Supreme Harmony and await further orders. By this time news of the Emperor's death had spread like wildfire. However, it was also rumoured that the Third Imperial Son would be proclaimed his successor. With a new monarch on the throne the court breathed easier.

On the stroke of the second watch, the Empress Dowager, escorted by the princes, nobles and officials at court arrived at the Hall of Supreme Harmony. In accordance with the rules of the grand audience, the court knelt according to rank for the reading of the Emperor's last will and testament. It was a bitterly cold and dismal day. Many people shed tears as the readers stationed on the terrace and below read in loud clear voices that carried to every corner of the vast space.

"We inherited the throne at a tender age and have kept it these eighteen years..." Fulin's last will began. He went on to accuse himself of misgoverning, offending the spirits of the ancestors. "...This is our first sin." He lauded the Empress Dowager for her guidance and accused himself for failing in his filial duty. "...This is our second sin."

The Emperor's will continued in the same ponderous vein. In all he accused himself of thirteen faults beside the first which shocked the assemblage. The others were:

"We accuse ourselves for alienating our noble lords and failing in our duties of friendship. We accuse ourselves of distrusting our Manchu courtiers and favouring the Han. We accuse ourselves of excesses committed in the name of grief at the death of our Empress, and not being able to assuage grief with reason. We accuse ourselves for delegating to eunuchs with official titles and thus encouraging corruption."

At the end of these self-accusations, the readers were already going hoarse. They paused to catch their breath and continued onto the final section of the document.

The last part of the will concerned the succession. The Emperor's third son named Xuanye was proclaimed Crown Prince, who according to tradition, would ascend the throne twenty-seven days later. The document also named the Lords Suoni, Sukesaha, Erbilong and Aobai as joint regents. The document ended with praises for the great deeds of the four lords in the service of their Monarch.

After the reading was concluded, the readers announced that the Emperor's will would now be distributed to the people of all under Heaven.

During the reading of the will the courtyard was dead silent. Afterwards those assembled there burst into loud wails. The vast space before the Hall of Supreme Harmony resounded with the weeping and wailing from the courtyard and from the inner palace. However, the motives for this public display of grief varied markedly. Some wept because they were expected to. Others wept for the death of a friend. Still others wept for themselves, perturbed about the future. There were also those who wept out of relief. As for the Manchu nobles, princes and bannermen, they wept out of satisfaction.

Wang Xi's garments were soaked with cold sweat. The Emperor's will that had just been proclaimed was not the document he had written according to His Majesty's wishes. Of his carefully chosen words, only a few remained. Did it mean that once the Emperor was gone the direction of government would change? According to the tone of the will, from now on the regents would lean heavily on the princes and nobles, and would act in favour of the eight banners. What would happen to the government and the people? Furthermore, what would happen to Wang Xi who had seen the original document? Would he be able to save his head? Thus Wang Xi wept mainly for himself.

Suoni, Sukesaha, Erbilong, and Aobai, the four lords named as regents, now slowly mounted the steps of the terrace and knelt.

"In his will His Majesty named us joint regents. However,

matters of state have always been in the hands of the imperial family. As we are not related we propose the council should act as regent too."

The assembled lords refused the proposal. Prince Jieshu responded on behalf of all those present:

"Our departed Emperor was keenly aware of the four Lords' merits and therefore left this great task to you. His will must not be interfered with in any way. Therefore, accept this honour without reservation. Express your acceptance to Her Majesty the Empress Dowager and take your vows according to tradition before the Emperor's shrine." The four lords humbly accepted their orders and went straightaway to report to the Empress Dowager. A short while later the Empress Dowager decreed that the Empire must not be without a ruler, and that the court must await the immediate proclamation of the new Emperor.

The court retired to the offices and duty rooms within Tiananmen Gate. Those didn't belong sat on the ground in front of Meridian Gate waiting for dawn. The four regents wrote out their oaths of allegiance which they burned in front of the Emperor's coffin and again upon the altar of the god of Heaven....

The ninth day of the first month dawned brisk and clear. At dawn nobles and courtiers waited in full regalia. At the fifth drum, thousands of ceremonial guards were lined up from the Hall of Supreme Harmony all the way to Tiananmen. Large musical instruments such as bells, gongs and cymbals were placed at strategic points. Congratulatory notes written by officials in Beijing were taken into the hall by an official. At dawn, the courtiers streamed into the great open space before the Hall of Supreme Harmony through four portals according to their rank. After the court was assembled two officials from the Ministry of Rites went to Qianqing Palace to escort the new emperor to audience. Bell and drum sounded from atop Meridian Gate, announcing that a new emperor was being proclaimed.

As it was in a period of national mourning, the musicians did not play. Surrounded by officials of rites, ten ministers and a glittering array of imperial guards, the young Emperor moved with measured steps toward the Hall of Supreme Harmony. He sat on his throne, straight and solemn, his feet dangling above the ground, but he did not seem like a child.

Once more bell and drum pealed out from Meridian Gate, and the audience began.

The Third Imperial Son, Xuanye was proclaimed emperor; known to history as the Emperor Kangxi.

5

The four joint regents and all the courtiers assembled before the Emperor's catafalque in Qianqing Hall, for the reading of the joint regents' oath of office.

"...Our late Emperor has deigned to honour Suoni, Sukesaha, Ebilong and Aobai with the task of guiding and protecting our new monarch. We do solemnly swear to devote our lives to that endeavour. As joint regents we shall refrain from being influenced by familial ties; refrain from acts of vengeance; refrain from heeding the inducement of those close to us; refrain from accepting unearned wealth; refrain from personal contacts with noble houses and thus protect ourselves against extravagant gifts; refrain from forming cliques; refrain from accepting bribes; but to strive with loyalty and honour to justify the late Emperor's trust. Should we fail in our labours may the gods visit their wrath upon us, and may we be dealt with to the letter of the law."

The entire court clad in white mourning robes knelt both inside and outside as the voices of the readers, rising and falling in cadence, echoed through the white-draped hall, filling it with an air of mysterious solemnity.

"We the court, in accordance with the wishes of the late Emperor, do solemnly swear to uphold the new Emperor. From this day forward we shall refrain from forming cliques; refrain from giving precedence to personal concerns; refrain from disputes; refrain from intrigues to the injury of the innocent; refrain from obstinately holding personal views to the detriment of the state...."

This oath also echoed across the capital. It was read aloud not only by members of the Grand Secretariat gathered for the ceremony at Wuying Hall but also by members of the Imperial Hanlin Academy, the staff of the six ministries, the Chief Surveillance Office and Court of Judicial Review, as well as the commanders and troops of the eight banners at their yamen or drilling grounds. The oath together with the late Emperor's death announcement were quickly distributed throughout the provinces. Three copies of each document were made. One was burnt before the Emperor's catafalque, another before the shrine of the god of Heaven, and the last copy was kept in archives.

This was donc in accordance with the Empress Dowager's instruction upon receiving the oath of office from the four joint regents.

As soon as the announcement of the death of the Emperor had been published, all officials were required to keep vigil at their respective offices for a period of twenty-seven days. During that time they were forbidden to return to their homes. For nine days they were required to mourn, with tears both at dawn and dusk.

A period of national mourning was declared lasting one hundred days. During this period it was forbidden to hang red decorations, or hold banquets or any other form of celebration. Offenders would be severely dealt with. The silver tide of funerary rites, swelling in the capital, swamped the vast land.

On the twenty-first day of the first month, the Emperor's coffin would be moved to Shouhuang Hall on Coal Hill. A day before honour guards were posted along the route leading from Donghua Gate to Coal Hill. Most people, who could find some acquaintances who lived along the way, took advantage of it to get a glimpse of this lavish display. However, the inner city was mainly inhabited by bannermen and few Hans had access to their homes.

However, Liu Tongchun had such an advantage.

In the hundred days of national mourning that followed the death of Empress Dong, Tongchun and his fellow actors became unemployed. Then came the last month of the year, and the festive season around the New Year was always a busy time for actors. The manager of the troupe had great hopes of recouping his losses at the Lantern Festival. However, another royal death intervened. Tongchun, as a famous actor, had some savings which would not only tide him over another hundred days of unemployment for national mourning, but also allow him to assist a few of his less fortunate colleagues. Third and fourth rate actors would have to seek temporary employment wherever they could.

A certain young Manchu nobleman who was fond of *kunqu* opera wanted to employ Tongchun for his private troupe. Although he had been approached several times, Tongchun always found some excuse to refuse. Recently, the young nobleman sent his steward with a request that Tongchun undertake the task of editing his collection of opera scores. He would be well compensated.

As he was unemployed and anxious to earn some extra cash to help his friends, Tongchun accepted.

The young nobleman's home was situated outside Donghua Gate, on a street known as Beichizi. The room assigned to Tongchun was on the upper floor of a small two-storied building fronting the street, affording an excellent view of Beichizi. On the day before the funeral, the steward had warned Tongchun that under no circumstances was he to open any window overlooking the street on pain of death. He also quietly told him a small pane of glass set in the corner of his window afforded a view of the street below. However, Tongchun must keep his door firmly shut so that no one would know he had been peeping. In all truth Tongchun had no interest in imperial funerals other than that they had thrown him out of work. Otherwise the affairs of royalty were too far removed to be of interest to an actor. Nevertheless, he was curious about the spectacle.

Three sharp cracks with long trailing reverberations like the sound of firecrackers woke Tongchun from a sound sleep. For a moment he was not sure where he was. The first light of day dappled the four white walls of the room. Through a gap in the curtain hanging in the doorway, he could see the brazier burning in the outer room, and a desk set under the window piled high with manuscripts. He came awake at once. That was not the sound of firecrackers but the sound of whips clearing the streets. He leaped into his clothes and glued himself to the small pane of glass in the window. It was a dismal day, with a sprinkling of snow which covered the roofs and streets in a thin sheet of white. Outside, the street had been swept clean. Not a soul was out of doors except courtiers in plain robes and a white topknot on their caps, lining either side of the street. There they stood shivering in the cold blast of north wind, like a white serpent whose head to the south and tail to the north were both obscured from view. These courtiers had been wakened earlier than he to await the imperial funeral procession. A courtier's life is not a bed of roses, Tongchun mused. Three more cracks of the whip heralded the arrival of the vanguard of the procession.

Commandants appeared in pairs, wielding way-clearing red clubs decorated in black lacquer and gold, dressed in bluish grey robes but with the red topknots cut off their caps. About ten pairs passed. Then came more men armed with shorter clubs. As they disappeard from view the steward came into the room. While Tongchun hastily finished dressing the other set a small table before the window for the food and hot tea he brought. Then the two men sat down to share a meal and to enjoy the spectacle below.

After the club bearers came the ceremonial guards carrying various types of spears and lances, all with red-lacquered shafts and gold tips. Then followed a dazzling array of battle axes and curiously shaped weapons whose names no one knew. The two secret spectators were so excited by the passing cavalcade, they forgot their food.

Another pair of club bearers preceded an eruption of colour provided by a myriad flags, banners, bunting and streamers in yellow, red, blue, white and black. There were also many decorative umbrellas, round, square, fan-shaped, funnel-shaped.... Some were decorated with the dragon pattern, others with lotus blossoms or bunches of flowers. At the rear of the group was a pair of yellow silk umbrellas with a twisted shaft.

Following close behind were eighty horses with reins but no saddles. Behind them were another twenty horses whose reins, saddles and stirrups were all studded with gold and pearls. The saddles were decorated with dragons in whose mouth was a pearl the size of a man's thumb. On the back of the saddles was a pattern of flowers made of three smaller pearls. Each saddle carried a cushion on which was embroidered a gold dragon with a pearl in its mouth.

The two secret observers marvelled at the pomp and splendour passing before them.

"Why, those saddles are priceless," exclaimed Tongchun.

"True," echoed the steward. "What a waste. They're going to 'The Great Tearing of Paper!'"

"What on earth is that?"

"Why, cremation of course!"

Tongchun's eyes widened with disbelief, but the steward forestalled any further questions.

"Look! The camels are coming!" Dozens of heavily caparisoned dromedaries lumbered into view, laden with tapestries, silks, awnings and other articles of daily use. Next a troop of cavalry armed with bow and arrow appeared. Behind them were guards carrying bows and arrows belonging to the Emperor. The arrows were fledged with raven feathers dipped in gold. The quivers were of yellow silk whose seams were hidden by pearls. Who knows how many people a single quiver would feed! After they passed came the trainers of hunting dogs and horses together with their charges.

There was more to come. The utensils and furniture of gold rendered Tongchun and his companion speechless with wonder.

"All these things that the Emperor had used will go to the 'Great Tearing of Paper'," whispered the steward.

"Such a waste," sighed Tongchun.

"That's the way it has to be," enthused the steward. "The other day the young master went with his father to mourn and witnessed 'The Little Tearing of Paper'...."

"There is also a 'Little Tearing of Paper'" Tongchun was aghast.

"After the first seven days, all the Emperor's clothes and belongings had to be burned. Two huge tents were erected outside the gate of Qianqing Palace. On the east side for the Buddhist and the west for the Daoist. A pole flying the flag of each denomination was erected before the tents. The Little Tearing of Paper took place in the open space between them. In this way, the gods of both sects would be made aware of the Emperor's passing and would protect him on his journey to the netherworld. The young lord said the Empress Dowager was present too, dressed in a black satin robe, and was almost overcome with grief. All the ladies and eunuchs wept, and so did the assembled courtiers. In the distance the ladies of the harem could be heard wailing. A great bonfire was lit, whose many coloured flames shot high into the air and made a crackling sound like frying peas. Pearls made small explosions as they ignited. And there were tens of thousands of these tiny explosions. That was the 'Small Tearing of Paper'! You can imagine what this will be like."

"Here they come!" Tongchun cut the steward off.

The street below had filled with a silvery grey torrent. The sound of weeping and lamentation split the air. Amidst this white-clad throng the Emperor's spirit chariot fitted with yellow screens and curtains of cloth of gold and coverlets of martan fur moved forward slowly, followed by the gigantic catafalque. Covered with a red satin quilt it appeared like a huge red building that moved. Leading the catafalque was a group of about twenty to thirty young boys dressed in black, weeping. Following the catafalque were mounted princes, Manchu nobility, and the Han courtiers carrying banners and dressed in white mourning garb, also weeping. A smaller spirit chariot and coffin covered with purple brocade also came in the wake of the catafalque.

"Who is in the other coffin?" asked Tongchun.

"It's the one they call Little Lady Dongeh who died with the Emperor. They have bestowed the name of Lady Zhen upon her posthumously. She was the Empress Dong's cousin...."

"Are the boys in black to die as well?"

"I'm not sure. By their dress I would say they are probably the sons of noblemen brought up in the Empress Dowager's household. But look! There is the Empress Dowager!"

Eunuchs carrying a plain white-curtained sedan chair appeared surrounded by serving maids in white robes and kerchiefs. In the midst of all this white, the Empress Dowager in a black satin mourning robe stood out. Her chalky, expressionless face, and her stillness made her appear as remote and lonely as a statue. Five more white carriages and six or seven others draped with black curtains followed. These contained the Empress, the imperial concubines and imperial sons.

Now the princesses and ladies of the nobility appeared in their carriages. With their appearance the sounds of lamentation coming from the street grew thrill. The courtiers lining the street continued to kneel with heads bowed. In truth the two secret observers had a better view of the proceedings than they. The steward, who had been in the nobleman's employ for some time and was familiar with the aristocracy, pointed out this one and that one, babbling merrily about their connections with one another and the imperial household.

"...And there passing beneath us is Prince An's wife," he

was saying when suddenly Tongchun lunged for the window. With one swift blow, the steward knocked him to the ground before he could get it open.

"Do you want to lose your head?" he hissed. "I want to keep mine!" Tongchun brushed him aside and glued his eyes to the pane of glass. Now he was sure. The serving maid clad in white following the carriage the steward had pointed out was Menggu.

After all his vicissitudes, after all the searching, he had finally caught a glimpse of her. He wanted to call out to her, to open the window, but that was not allowed. Would she disappear again into that sea of humanity? With a heaving heart he madc a dash for the door, and again the steward stopped him.

"They'll behead you on the spot if you go out there!"

Tongchun ground his teeth with chagrin.

In a more conciliatory tone the steward enquired, "What did you see that made you so reckless?" Tongchun had a ready made answer.

"I just caught a glimpse of my sister who got lost five or six years ago. She was beside that fancy carriage...."

"Then she must be one of Prince An's servants. All you have to do is go and ask."

"No. I have to get a good look at her. What if I was mistaken?"

"In that case, wait till the Great Tearing of Paper is over. Prince An's entourage is bound to pass this way again. And you'll be watching out for her." Tongchun looked out at the street. The carriages of the noble ladies had all disappeared. The courtiers were getting on their feet and making ready to follow the procession to Coal Hill. For the moment there was nothing more he could do. Tongchun nodded.

The morning passed. At noon a shred of sunlight peeped through the dense clouds. The Forbidden City was still shrouded in silence. An hour later the mournful baying of long horns sounded from Coal Hill was accompanied by a distant thudding that might have been either drums or thunder. Another hour passed. Suddenly Beichizi Street filled with traffic. Liu Tongchun who had been waiting for quite a while already had to brace himself against the wall of the building to avoid being swept away. Eagerly he searched the swirling crowd that rushed by. People screaming and cursing, the distressed neighing of horses, the rumbling of carriages blended into an ear-splitting cacophony. Menggu had become a needle in a haystack.

I'll go to the residence of Prince An, to the home of that elegant carriage. Menggu, wait for me. I'm coming for you.

The grand academician Fu Yijian returned from Coal Hill with a heavy heart. Seated in his sedan chair he tried to nap, but sleep deserted him. The four joint regents had already taken the reins of government. Between the ceremonies surrounding the imperial funeral, the regents had issued their first decree to the princes and nobles as well as all officials in the name of the new Emperor. The gist of it was that there would be a detailed review of the policies of Nurhachi and Abahai. Using as an excuse the late Emperor's self-criticism in his will — that he had not followed the code laid down by his ancestors and thus offended them — this would be the first step towards returning to old traditions, in keeping with the late Emperor's wishes.

Like many of the Han officials, Fu Yijian was a reed caught in an autumn breeze, feeling the approach of winter. There would be changes at court. He had quickly communicated his unease to his wife. Suyun was silent a while before she asked, "Do you think there will be significant changes?"

Fu Yijian shook his head. "If they attempt serious changes so soon, wouldn't they risk the anger of the people?"

Suyun gave him a lopsided smile. "Not necessarily. The people have been down-trodden too long. I would suggest you think of sweeping changes that will happen swiftly."

Suyun was correct. The regents soon issued a second decree abolishing the Imperial Hanlin Academy, the Grand Secretariat and other offices. In short all the government structures adapted from the Ming were abandoned and replaced by traditional institutions sanctioned by the ancestors.

Fu Xijian was deeply distressed by these changes. Suyun said, "The Council of Nobles should be happy now!"

Fu Yijian forced himself to rebut his wife.

"It's not that simple. For example the abolition of the thirteen yamens and the dismissal of the eunuch officials from the inner palace might not be a bad thing. The corruption that existed among them during the Ming was scandalous. With them out of the way, its like nipping the bud that might become a problem. I heard some four thousand eunuchs were dismissed." Suyun smiled sourly, "It might look like a good thing, but the thirteen yamens were conceived after the Ming model.... And what plans do you Han officials have for the future?..."

Fu Yijian responded with some hesitation, "I was one of the late Emperor's trusted courtiers. Surely they would not dismiss me." Suyun did not say more immediately, but the look she gave him left no doubt what was in her mind. She was thinking that is why your future is looking dim. Instead she reached out and rubbed his shoulders, saying, "You coughed blood last autumn, but you carried on without rest. It's time you looked after yourself." Fu Yijian did not grasp why she had digressed in this manner and smiled at her uncertainly.

The day before the Grand Secretariat received a third decree which concerned two matters that shocked the grand academicians. The first was that Prince Jidu's heir Desai would inherit his title. The second was the reinstatement of the law governing runaway slaves. Once more those who harboured runaways would be condemned to death, and their immediate neighbours and even village heads of the fugitives in the countryside would be persecuted.

Allowing Desai to assume his father's title was a clear victory for the line that linked Jirgalang to Prince Jidu. However it was the reinstatement of the law on runaway slaves that caused the most concern. For it was feared that this would bring about new rebellions.

Fu Yijian told Suyun about this. Though her face clouded she did not offer a single word of comfort. And now at Coal Hill, facing the Emperor's catafalque, Fu Yijian's sorrow was real. For in the half month since his death, everything the Emperor had fought for was blowing away like chaf in the wind.

The sedan chair came to a stop. The curtain was lifted and Fu Yijian alighted. He went into the house unhurriedly, passing through the front gate, the inner gate, the corridor and into the parlour. He was astonished that his wife was not there to greet him. Nevertheless he lingered in the parlour to sip a cup of tea as he always did. Suddenly a new painting hanging on the north wall caught his eye. It was a picture of Zhang Guolao, the mythical figure known for riding a donkey backwards. To one side was written a poem:

How many in the world resemble this old man?
Unless one rides backwards, one has to look behind.

Fu Yijian stared at the picture for a long while, carefully mulling over the last line of the poem. What would he see if he looked backwards? He would see that the late Emperor had trusted him because he was capable and careful in the execution of his duties. However, he was a Han in a position of importance which was bound to rouse the suspicion of the Manchu nobles. Fu Yijian's pulse quickened at that thought. Suyun must have hung that picture deliberately as a means of persuading him to relinquish his post while he could. However, it was not easy to turn his back on the honours he had come to enjoy. He would have to speak to Suyun at once.

He left the parlour and following a wide corridor came to a small study which led into the boudoir. This was the room where he relaxed and read. On a small square table he used for painting, a fresh sheet of white paper was spread out on which a few lines of limerick was written in a seal-cutting script.

Others ride a horse, while I ride a donkey.
They are better off, I mused.
Looking back I find
Others walking.

Fu Yijian looked at the limerick with admiration. She is a remarkable woman with a broad mind, he thought. Are things really as bad as this? It can't be! With a hand pressed to his pounding heart, he went into the bed chamber expecting to see Suyun there. Instead there were only two maids in the antechamber.

"Where is your mistress?" Fu Yijian asked.

"The mistress is preparing the evening meal."

Fu Yijain seated himself in a gaudily carved ebony chair to wait. As he looked up, he saw another new scroll hanging on the wall. This was a pastoral scene of mountains, streams and ponds with here and there shepherds herding cattle or playing the flute perched on an animal's back. Every detail was true to life. On the upper right-hand corner was a poem:

Shepherd riding the buffalo flies,
That the rain might not wet his straw cape;
Laughingly pointing beyond the grove of peach trees
At those that tarry too long and have not returned.

Fu Yijian stroked his beard with appreciation, thinking to himself what a wise and clever woman Suyun was indeed. He called for ink and paper.

The two maids quickly laid out paper and ground ink. Fu Yijian approached the table and as he raised his brush, Suyun's voice sounded behind him.

"So you have finally decided to write."

"My Lady, you have made me see the light," Fu Yijian

smiled. "I am just now writing my letter of resignation."

"I think you are still a little hesitant. What will be your reason?"

"I was just mulling it over...."

Suyun chuckled. "You've forgotten you spat blood...."

Fu Yijian laughed out loud. "That is it!"

All was silent in Cining Palace. The dismal atmosphere was partly attributed to the period of mourning being observed, but also because the Empress Dowager had fallen ill. If anything happened to her at this time there would be turmoil in the country. Thus the maids and eunuchs crept about softly in an effort not to disturb Her Majesty.

In the bed chamber the Empress Dowager was sleeping. Sumalagu sat beside the bed sewing, while under the south window, seated beside the kang table Xuanye was absorbed in a book. The only sound in the room was the ticking of the clock and the rustle of paper as Xuanye turned the pages of his book.

A pair of tiny feet stole across the threshold of the room. A pair of plump little hands lifted the curtain, revealing the round apple cheeks and bright eyes of little Bingyue. The child tiptoed to her imperial grandmother's bedside. Sumalagu quickly signalled her not to wake the Empress Dowager and picked her up in her arms. Planting a kiss on the child's plump cheek, Sumalagu carried her to the kang and deposited her beside Xuanye.

"Play quietly," she whispered.

Xuanye, acting the big brother, signalled with hands, face and eyes for the child not to disturb their imperial grandmother. The child responded by making faces at him. The two giggled merrily together. Since the death of Empress Dong, Bingyue had been living in Cining Palace with the Empress Dowager, where she quickly became the favourite of her older brothers and sisters. However, her third older brother was the fondest of her, and the one she liked to play with.

Bingyue took one of Xuanye's brushes and began to write on the paper laid out on the kang table. Here no one chided her for being forward. Though he was Emperor, Xuanye was still patient with the child. Bingyue had trouble forming the character for wind. Xuanye took the brush from her and wrote the character three times for her to copy. Bingyue pouted with annoyance until he took her hand and guided it. And she smiled again.

The Empress Dowager turned over and asked, "Sumalagu, have there been any urgent petitions?" Little Bingyue threw down her brush and ran to embrace her grandmother.

"Imperial Grandmother, are you better? No matter what you get, you always get better!"

The Empress Dowager felt a rush of joy. She kissed the child's cheek.

"Bingyue, you love your Imperial Grandmother, don't you?"

From the other side of the room, Xuanye chimed in with a bit of annoyance. "Imperial Grandmother, what about me?"

The Empress Dowager chuckled. "Of course there's you too. If I hadn't grown up on the grasslands, I wouldn't live through all this. Now let me get up." Bingyue shook her head and frowned. "Imperial Grandmother mustn't die. Otherwise there won't be anyone to look after Bingyue."

"Imperial Grandmother won't die," the Empress Dowager reassured the child. Bingyue finally let go of her. Sumalagu helped the Empress Dowager into a fur robe and, having seated her on the bed, proceeded to comb her hair.

"The regents' decrees have been sent out in the Emperor's name," she reported. The Empress Dowager did not comment. Those decrees had to be made. Faced with the current situation, the regents had acted in the only way they could to defuse the enmity caused by Fulin's deeds over the last few years. Lady Zhen's death also smoothed over the rage and envy that existed in the Inner Palace. That the death of the Emperor did not cause great disturbances in the land pleased the Empress Dowager.

The child Bingyue prattled at her, attempting to be amusing, but it was Xuanye who occupied the Empress Dowager's attention.

Finally she asked, "You've been proclaimed for twenty days now. What kind of emperor shall you be?" Xuanye became solemn at his grandmother's question.

"Your grandson has only one wish," he said respectfully, "that there be peace and prosperity throughout the land." The Empress Dowager was gratified to hear words that were not those of a child. She drew him into her arms, and her eyes were moist.

"You have inherited a heavy load. You must learn, be ambitious, think of the welfare of the masses; otherwise the Empire of Great Qing...."

Her voice faltered and she could not continue. She shut her eyes and it seemed she was flying upward, higher and higher. Looking down everything was shrouded in mist. When it parted she saw altars, fluttering banners, smoke curling upward, and lamentation that rose wave upon wave. This great land that is China! How much misery and tragedy are buried in its earth! How much turmoil lies hidden under its surface. The eyes of the people are on the capital. The eyes of the capital are trained upon the Forbidden City. While within its impenetrable walls a lonely old woman clad in black held a child of seven in white mourning robes, silently shedding tears.

图书在版编目(CIP)数据

少年天子：英文/ 凌力著. — 北京：中国文学出版社，1995. 3
ISBN 7－5071－0288－2/I.254（外）

I.少 ... II.凌 ... III.①长篇小说－中国－当代－英文 ②历史小说－中国－当代－英文 IV.I247.5

少年天子
凌力

熊猫丛书
*
中国文学出版社出版
(中国北京百万庄路 24 号)
中国国际图书贸易总公司发行
(中国北京车公庄西路 35 号)
北京邮政信箱第 399 号　　邮政编码 100044
1995年 第 1 版（英）
ISBN 7－5071－0288－2/I.254
03460
10－E－2983P

June 9, 1996

Gift, from C.K. Harper

Beijing, China